THE LOBBYING MANUAL

A COMPLETE GUIDE TO FEDERAL LOBBYING LAW AND PRACTICE

EDITORS

Rebecca H. Gordon

Thomas M. Susman

FOREWORD BY

Robert F. Bauer

FIFTH EDITION

Cover design by Perkins Coie LLP.

The materials contained herein represent the opinions of the authors and/or the editors, and should not be construed to be the views or opinions of the law firms or companies with whom such persons are in partnership with, associated with, or employed by, nor of the American Bar Association or the Administrative Law Section, unless adopted pursuant to the bylaws of the Association.

Nothing contained in this book is to be considered as the rendering of legal advice for specific cases, and readers are responsible for obtaining such advice from their own legal counsel. This book is intended for educational and informational purposes only.

Printed in the United States of America.

20 19 18 17 16   5 4 3 2 1

Library of Congress Cataloging-in-Publication Data

Names: Gordon, Rebecca H., editor. | Susman, Thomas M., 1943- editor.
Title: The lobbying manual : a complete guide to federal lobbying law and practice / Edited by Rebecca H. Gordon and Thomas M. Susman.
Description: Sixth edition. | Chicago : American Bar Association, 2016.
Identifiers: LCCN 2016021778 | ISBN 9781634254540
Subjects: LCSH: Lobbying—Law and legislation—United States.
Classification: LCC KF4948 .L62 2016 | DDC 342.73/05—dc23
LC record available at https://lccn.loc.gov/2016021778

Discounts are available for books ordered in bulk. Special consideration is given to state bars, CLE programs, and other bar-related organizations. Inquire at Book Publishing, ABA Publishing, American Bar Association, 321 N. Clark Street, Chicago, Illinois 60654-7598.

www.ShopABA.org

Preface to the Fifth Edition

The legal environment for lobbyists changed rapidly and significantly in the two years preceding the 2009 publication of the Fourth Edition of *The Lobbying Manual*. The intervening years have been a period of adjustment and, eventually, stabilization. Lobbyists and the organizations that employ them have adjusted to the provisions of the Honest Leadership and Open Government Act (HLOGA) that increased the scope and frequency of Lobbying Disclosure Act reporting and added liability for compliance with congressional gift rules. Political appointees entering government have accepted the limitations the president placed on their service in his 2009 Executive Order on Ethics Commitments. Government employees leaving to take private employment with lobbying firms have digested the additional limitations they face in their new positions.

As we noted in the preface to the Fourth Edition, many of the 2008 reforms resulted from a recognition that three distinct areas of law—lobbying disclosure, congressional gift rules, and federal campaign finance law—often intersect when private entities interact with the government. No industry must handle this intersection more often, and with more care, than government relations professionals. And in the intervening time since the last edition of *The Lobbying Manual*, lobbying disclosure and gift laws have seen little change at the federal level, although the Department of Justice is now tracking closely, and reporting publicly, its LDA enforcement efforts. Campaign finance law in particular has been in a nearly constant state of flux. The Supreme Court began loosening restrictions on corporate political activity in its 2010 *Citizens United* decision, and that deregulatory trend has continued through another Supreme Court decision that invalidated certain contribution limits and, most recently, federal legislation that has increased significantly the monetary limits on contributions to national party committees.

One of our principal objectives when embarking on the production of this Fifth Edition was to add a more comprehensive discussion of that third leg of the stool: campaign finance law. This is an acknowledgment of the political reality, which is that almost every private organization that interacts with government, whether corporate or not, whether for-profit or nonprofit, will eventually bump up against the laws around private support of candidates. Knowing the laws that may constrain that activity is crucial to maintaining corporate goodwill and a reputation for winning on the merits.

Consistent with this goal, this Fifth Edition features several chapters with a focus on campaign finance. Chapter 23 provides the reader the basics of corporate involvement in federal electoral activity. Chapter 24 dives deeper into the sorts of advertising that are now permitted after the Supreme Court's 2010 *Citizens United* opinion. And Chapter 25 focuses on one of the fastest-growing areas of campaign finance regulation: pay-to-play laws.

For those private entities that may be looking to hire individuals with government experience (and for those individuals themselves), we have also added two chapters that address the revolving-door restrictions that President Obama implemented in his Executive Order on Ethics Commitments. These restrictions were implemented too late for fulsome inclusion in the Fourth Edition, but as the administration comes to a close, many may find them useful.

Substantively, of course, *The Lobbying Manual* continues to focus on the basics of lobbying law. We have updated our chapter on the basics of the federal Lobbying Disclosure Act. We have added a chapter that addresses the semiannual LD-203 requirement of the federal LDA and another on the GAO's audit process. We included a new chapter that addresses the peculiar ethical restrictions that are unique to lawyers who lobby, and we added a new chapter to address the law of political intelligence. We conclude with a chapter—for those who might be looking for practical advice—on the fundamentals of building a government relations compliance program.

Some chapters of the Fourth Edition have been omitted from the Fifth, not because they are no longer relevant or useful but because, in the interest of constraining the size of the new edition, we decided to focus on the core legal issues of primary concern to lobbyists at the federal level in Washington. Those chapters that have been omitted from this volume will continue to be available to the public online, along with an online resource and updating service, at http:// ambar.org/lobbyingmanual.

As with previous editions, the Fifth Edition would not have been possible without substantial time commitments by all of the authors of the chapters included in this volume. As the editors, we extend our sincere appreciation for their efforts to make this book the comprehensive, readable, and practical treatment of the law that was our goal at the outset. Rebecca Gordon thanks in particular her colleagues at Perkins Coie, including the lawyers and others in the Political Law Group, and Julie Pambianco and Michael Kupka for their assistance.

Rebecca H. Gordon
Thomas M. Susman

Foreword to the Fifth Edition

This Fifth Edition of *The Lobbying Manual* is usefully compared with its predecessors. Most striking are the various directions over time the law has taken in governing the conduct of lobbying activity—"lobbying" understood to refer to the different means of influencing the shape of public policy. The practitioner must, of course, ground her advice in lobbying law that goes by that name, such as the Lobbying Disclosure Act, but also—to cite a handful of other sources—in campaign finance law, tax law, the ethics rules of the legislative and executive branches; enactments directed at specialized concerns, like the STOCK Act (the uses of political intelligence) and the Byrd Amendment (lobbying with appropriated funds); and the evolving theories of public corruption by which abuses present the risk of criminal exposure.

In short, we are a long way from the legal regime in place for most of American history, one characterized by no rules, or by rules enacted with self-defeating gaps and followed by indifferent enforcement.

This account may seem odd to the passing contemporary observer who has listened to the public debates about the state of the law and the need for reform. The most prominent line of argument and analysis holds that the law in this field is weak in design and/or, for want of competent administration or enforcement, in near collapse. Certainly the changes in political practice in the last several decades have taxed the capacity of the law to catch up with them. Today, any discussion of campaign finance will turn quickly to the Roberts court and its limiting jurisprudence on campaign finance, and to the aftermath of cases like *Citizens United* in which super PACs have grown in visibility and, arguably, impact.

But in the background of these large and important issues remains a complex of legal requirements and challenging legal issues that have transformed the lawyer's role in guiding lobbying and public policy advocacy. It is decidedly not a world in which "anything goes." The business of "influence"—influencing electorates, legislatures, the executive, and the public—has been systematically regulated. Some may believe that it is insufficiently regulated and others that it is regulated too much, but there is no doubt that it is regulated.

These chapters also demonstrate the ways that the relevant laws and rules intersect, which must be a fundamental concern for practitioners and clients alike. The ethics rules in the legislature and executive branch impose restrictions on gift giving, and the issues presented under these rules overlap with those under the illegal gratuity statute and in "honest services" public corruption investigations and prosecutions. A campaign contribution, which enjoys significant constitutional protection, is not a bribe, except in the circumstances where it might begin to resemble one—or at least figure in a thorough and competent assessment of legal liability. Lawyers who work in this field appreciate the risks of viewing any one law or rule governing political activity in isolation from the others. They will find in this manual considerable assistance in maintaining this focus—in keeping the "dots connected."

This is good enough reason for a unique resource allowing practitioners to understand the legal lay of the land and to see how those dots connect. *The Lobbying Manual* has met this need now for several editions. In the pages of this Fifth Edition, as in the previous editions, are found lucid, expert presentations on a host of statutory and regulatory requirements for conducting lawful activities to influence government policy and decision making.

A strength of this treatment is the inclusion of rich context and sound practical advice. Together with the identification of specific laws and regulations are discussions of the sensitive constitutional environment in which this lawmaking takes place. There is also a vitally important emphasis on the course of interpretation and enforcement, which enables readers to appreciate how the Government Accountability Office has audited compliance with federal lobbying disclosure law, how the Department of Justice has investigated compliance with the Foreign Agents Registration Act, and how trends have developed in the criminal and civil exposure faced by the individual lobbyist. The manual closes with expert counsel on the elements of an effective federal compliance program.

The American Bar Association has been fortunate over the years to have recruited leading practitioners to direct the project and to contribute to the volume. This year, my colleague Rebecca Gordon and the ABA's Thomas Susman, two well-known experts in this field, have collaborated in a splendid compendium of pieces that will stock the shelves of anyone who works on these kinds of issues. It is a genuine achievement, a true service to the Bar.

Robert F. Bauer

About the Editors

Rebecca H. Gordon is a partner in the Political Law Group at Perkins Coie LLP. She counsels companies, trade associations, and other nonprofit organizations on how to interact lawfully with public officials. She focuses her practice on compliance with the federal Lobbying Disclosure Act, the Federal Election Campaign Act, state campaign finance laws, federal and state pay-to-play laws, and federal and state laws governing the conveyance of gifts to public officials. She works with her clients' legal and government relations teams to help them create and administer PACs, construct compliance programs, and handle the day-to-day legal questions that face government relations professionals. She also assists clients with the construction of political advertising programs, and helps vendors who serve the political space lawfully develop candidate-facing products.

Ms. Gordon's clients include Fortune 100 corporations, nationwide trade associations and nonprofits, and prominent lobbying firms. She has represented clients before the Federal Election Commission and federal courts on campaign finance issues, and before the U.S. House and Senate Ethics Committees on ethics issues.

Ms. Gordon serves on the faculty of the Practising Law Institute's Corporate Political Activities course and was a member of the ABA Task Force on Federal Lobbying Laws. Before focusing her practice on corporate clients, she served as Deputy General Counsel to Obama for America during the 2008 presidential campaign and as Deputy General Counsel to the Democratic National Committee during the 2010 election cycle.

Thomas M. Susman is Director of the Governmental Affairs Office of the American Bar Association, which serves as the focal point for the Association's advocacy efforts before Congress, the Executive Branch, and other governmental entities on diverse issues of importance to the legal profession. Before joining the ABA in 2008, he was a partner in the Washington Office of Ropes & Gray LLP for over 27 years, where his work included counseling, litigation, and lobbying on a wide range of issues. Before joining Ropes & Gray, Mr. Susman spent 12 years in various capacities in the U.S. Senate, including Chief Counsel to the Antitrust Subcommittee, General Counsel to the Judiciary Committee, and Legislative Director for Senator Edward M. Kennedy. He has served as an advisor on lobbying regulation to the chairman of the Senate Ethics and Transparency Committee in Chile and has advised OECD and the Parliamentary leadership in the Czech Republic on lobbying disclosure regulation. He has also trained lobbyists with state and foreign bar associations.

Mr. Susman was editor of the first edition of the ABA *Lobbying Manual*; taught Lobbying and the Legislative Process as an adjunct professor at The American University's Washington College of Law; and chaired the Ethics Committee of the American League of Lobbyists (now the Association of Government Relations Professionals) for over a decade. He was counsel to the ABA Task Force on Federal Lobbying Laws; and is an Advisor to the American Law Institute's Project on

Government Ethics. He received a B.A. from Yale University and a J.D. from the University of Texas Law School, where he was Editor-in-chief of the *Texas Law Review*. After law school he was law clerk to Judge John Minor Wisdom on the U.S. Fifth Circuit Court of Appeals, followed by service in the Office of Legal Counsel of the U.S. Department of Justice.

About the Authors

Robert F. Bauer is a partner at the law firm Perkins Cole LLP. He has over 30 years of practice and has provided counseling and representation on matters involving regulation of political activity before the courts and administrative agencies of national party committees, candidates, political committees, individuals, federal officeholders, corporations and trade associations, and tax-exempt groups. Bob served as White House Counsel to President Obama and returned to private practice in June 2011. In 2013, the President named Bob to be Co-Chair of the Presidential Commission on Election Administration.

Bob is the author of several books: *United States Federal Election Law* (1982, 1984), *Soft Money Hard Law: A Guide to the New Campaign Finance Law* (2002), and *More Soft Money Hard Law: The Second Edition of the Guide to the New Campaign Finance Law* (2004), as well as numerous articles. He also serves on the National Advisory Board of Journal of Law and Politics. In 2000, he received the "Burton Award for Legal Achievement" for his legal writing.

Kathleen Clark practices law in Washington, D.C., and is an expert on legal and government ethics standards and the law of whistleblowing. She is Associate Reporter for the American Law Institute's Principles of Government Ethics and is on the D.C. Bar Rules of Professional Conduct Review Committee and the board of the Association of Professional Responsibility Lawyers. Clark is a law professor at Washington University in St. Louis, and her extensive academic work has been cited in hundreds of articles and books. Her report on applying government ethics standards to contractor personnel became the basis of a recommendation by the Administrative Conference of the United States and a resolution by the ABA House of Delegates. She served as counsel to the U.S. Senate Judiciary Committee, working on issues of white-collar crime, and as Special Counsel to the Attorney General of the District of Columbia, writing an ethics manual for the District's 32,000 employees.

James B. Christian Jr. At Squire Patton Boggs, Mr. Christian engaged in legislative and policymaking projects encompassing a wide range of domestic and international issues. In conjunction with this representation, he advised clients with respect to compliance with Federal Election Law, Lobbying Disclosure Act, and Foreign Agents Registration Act matters, including training for both clients and firm colleagues. Mr. Christian administered the Squire Patton Boggs' lobbying compliance program and is a previous contributor to the ABA *Lobbying Manual*. Mr. Christian recently retired from private practice.

Barak Cohen is a partner in Perkins Coie's White Collar & Investigations practice. He was formerly a federal prosecutor in in the U.S. Department of Justice's Public Integrity Section, which specializes in prosecuting election and campaign-finance offenses and public corruption on a national basis. In this role, he investigated and tried white-collar criminal matters throughout the United States in cases relating to public figures such as legislators, lobbyists, political consultants, judges, and senior Department of Defense officials. Currently, Barak represents companies and individuals in criminal and government enforcement matters before federal and state law enforcement authorities, in addition to regulatory agencies. He also conducts internal investigations and provides compliance advice. His most recent work has focused on the Foreign Corrupt Practices Act (FCPA), the False Claims Act, the health care and defense industries, and public corruption offenses. National news media regularly call on Barak to provide commentary and insight regarding current legal issues.

Jamie Conrad founded Conrad Law & Policy Counsel in 2007. He provides legislative and regulatory representation to businesses, associations, and coalitions in the areas of environment, occupational health and safety, homeland security, and administrative procedure, focusing often on the use of science for regulatory purposes. He worked previously at the American Chemistry Council and two major national law firms. Mr. Conrad is a former Chair of the ABA's Section of Administrative Law & Regulatory Practice. He developed and edits the *Environmental Science Deskbook* (http://legalsolutions.thomsonreuters.com/law-products/Treatises/Environmental-Science-Deskbook-Environmental-Law-Series/p/100029493). He has testified before Congress and the U.S. Sentencing Commission and is a frequent speaker. His writing has appeared in numerous law reviews and trade journals, as well as *The New Republic* and the *Washington Post*. J.D. with high honors, GW Law School; B.A. and Department Prize in Philosophy, Haverford College.

Cheryl Embree follows the federal employee gift rules with extra enthusiasm as a Deputy Ethics Official and General Attorney at the Federal Trade Commission. Previously, she served at the Department of Housing and Urban Development in a similar role as an ethics and administrative appeals attorney. Please know that the views expressed in this chapter do not necessarily represent the views of the Commission or the United States. This is her second ethics publication. She also coauthored a chapter called "Faux Transparency: Ethics, Privacy and the Demise of the STOCK Act's Massive Online Disclosure of Employees' Finances" with Kathleen Clark and hopes you will find time to read that, too.

Taryn Frideres holds degrees in political science and business administration from Drake University and a law degree from the University of Iowa College of Law. After law school, she joined the firm of Patton Boggs LLP (now Squire Patton Boggs LLP) as an associate in the firm's International Policy and Trade groups. In 2013, she cofounded a nonprofit organization—Pretrial Rights International—to advocate for Americans detained abroad, and in 2014, she was selected to participate in the Foreign Policy Initiative's Future Leaders Program. In 2015, she took a job in the U.S. Senate.

Tyler Hagenbuch, an associate with the Perkins Coie Political Law Group, focuses his practice on advising clients who are engaged in activities across the political spectrum. He helps clients understand, navigate, and meet their compliance obligations and political objectives in areas such as federal, state, and local campaign finance; lobbying disclosure; government ethics; and pay-to-play laws. Tyler also has significant experience counseling clients on election administration activities such as voting rights, voter registration, and get-out-the-vote campaigns.

Tyler has successfully sought Federal Election Commission advisory opinions for corporations and political campaign committees and has successfully defended clients in front of both federal and state regulators. He advises Fortune 500 companies, corporate PACs, and trade associations on how to engage in the political process and construct effective compliance programs, especially when clients' political activities subject them to regulation under both federal and state laws. He also helps clients understand the Internal Revenue Service rules for engaging in political activity.

Craig Holman is currently Government Affairs Lobbyist for Public Citizen. He serves as the organization's lobbyist on campaign finance and governmental ethics. Previously, Holman was Senior Policy Analyst at the Brennan Center for Justice, New York University School of Law.

Holman worked closely with reform organizations and the leadership of the 110th Congress in drafting and promoting the "Honest Leadership and Open Government Act," the federal lobbying and ethics reform legislation signed into law on September 14, 2007. Dr. Holman has continued to work at improving lobbying disclosure and ethics regulations, both in the United States and in Europe, by providing advice and consultations in promulgating transparency and ethics rules and regulations.

Virginia E. Davis Horton is an associate at Gray Plant Mooty, where she focuses her practice on franchise litigation. Ms. Horton represents franchisors in a variety of commercial disputes, and prides herself on helping her clients achieve positive results consistent with their business goals. She advises some of the nation's largest franchisors and regularly defends and prosecutes cases on their behalf in matters involving breaches of franchise agreements, the enforcement of covenants not to compete, vicarious liability, fraud, and trademark infringement, among others. Ms. Horton also practices in the area of government investigations and white-collar criminal defense. She received her law degree from the University of Virginia and her bachelor's degree from Rhodes College. Before attending law school, Ms. Horton worked for a Fortune Global 500 consumer products company in sales analysis and account-specific marketing.

Kate Sawyer Keane is a partner in the Political Law Group at Perkins Coie LLP. She focuses her practice on political law including federal and state campaign finance law, Congressional and Executive Branch ethics regulation, and lobbying registration and disclosure. In her practice, she counsels federal and state elected officials, candidates, political parties, trade associations, corporations, PACs, and other political organizations on campaign finance issues as well as lobbying disclosure, foreign agents' registration and reporting requirements, pay-to-play restrictions, and governmental ethics statutes and rules at the federal, state, and local level. Kate received her J.D. from New York University School of Law in 2003 and her B.A. from Yale University in 1999.

William McGinley represents a broad range of clients as to lobbying disclosure, congressional and executive branch ethics, and federal and state campaign finance compliance issues. He advises corporations and trade associations regarding the design and implementation of lobbying compliance programs and the establishment and administration of political action committees. He also represents Members of Congress, candidates, and corporations in investigations before the Office of Congressional Ethics and the House and Senate Ethics Committees; enforcement matters before the Federal Election Commission and state agencies; and in grand jury proceedings. Mr. McGinley also advises several national organizations regarding the establishment and operation of their independent expenditure units and grassroots lobbying programs. Mr. McGinley received his J. D., with honors, from The George Washington University Law School, M.A. in History from California State University at Long Beach, and B.A. in History from the University of California at Los Angeles.

Ronald Meltzer is a member of WilmerHale's Regulatory and Government Affairs Department in Washington, DC. Mr. Meltzer's practice focuses on compliance and enforcement matters relating to U.S. economic sanctions and export controls. He has been recognized for many years as a leading practitioner in this area of law by Chambers Global, Chambers USA, and The Best Lawyers in America.

Mary C. (Molly) Moynihan has practiced securities law for nearly thirty years, with a focus on investment management clients including registered open-end investment companies, registered investment advisers, private funds, and independent directors of fund complexes. She also specializes in advising political policy and political intelligence firms regarding compliance with federal and state securities laws.

Daniel Nudelman is an associate in the Political Law Group at Perkins Coie LLP. He counsels political, corporate, and nonprofit clients on a wide range of campaign finance, lobbying, and ethics laws at the federal, state, and local level. He assists clients with the formation and operation of federal and state PACs, advocacy groups, and other nonprofit organizations and advises corporate clients on the implementation and operation of campaign finance, lobbying, and FARA compliance programs. Daniel has represented clients before the Federal Election Commission, the Internal Revenue Service, and state ethics and campaign finance regulators. He received his undergraduate degree from McGill University and his law degree from New York University School of Law.

Trevor Potter is a member in Caplin & Drysdale's Washington, D.C., office, where he leads the firm's Political Law Group. He is one of the nation's best-known and experienced campaign and election lawyers. Mr. Potter was the former Commissioner and Chairman of the Federal Election Commission, and counsel to several presidential campaigns. Mr. Potter counsels political candidates, for-profit entities, and nonprofit organizations on a variety of political law issues. He is a leading authority on lobbying regulation, government ethics, and campaign finance issues and is known nationally for his experience in compliance programs, campaign finance investigations, and questions concerning lobbying registration and disclosure, as well as federal and state ethics rules.

Ezra W. Reese is a partner in the Political Law Group of Perkins Coie LLP. Ezra focuses his practice on nonprofit tax law and on political law. He specializes in nonprofit organizations that wish to engage in lobbying or electoral activity. His clients include charities, issue organizations, trade associations, and political committees. He counsels with respect to Internal Revenue Service restrictions, in particular those regarding lobbying and political activities; and on issues relating to federal, state, and local campaign finance and lobbying restrictions and filings. He also counsels organizations on media law regarding political and issue advertisements. He has represented clients before the IRS, the Federal Election Commission, and in federal and state court on campaign finance, election, and nonprofit tax issues.

Linda Rockwell is the Lobbying Compliance Manager in the Political Law Group at Perkins Coie LLP, where she manages the preparation, submission, and maintenance of federal and non-federal lobbying registrations and reports for lobbying firms, corporations, trade groups, and charities. Ms. Rockwell assists clients in identifying the activities and expenditures that may trigger registration or reporting obligations and also provides guidance in creating internal information tracking systems and processes that are responsive to a variety of complex jurisdictional disclosure requirements.

Thomas S. Ross is a successful entrepreneur and former member of the Republican National Committee who specializes in government affairs and project finance. Ross is currently the cofounder of McCarter & English LLP's government relations affiliate, McCarter Government Solutions, LLC. Ross, who twice was unanimously elected Republican State Chairman in Delaware, was managing director at Lexden Capital, where he focused on project finance and used his network to coordinate debt and equity financing for major developments. A serial entrepreneur, Ross launched several successful small businesses whose operations focused on finance and commercial real estate and also has broad-based experience in banking and mergers and acquisitions. He was appointed to the RNC's ethics committee by Michael Steele, then RNC chairman, and later was instrumental in the successful campaign of current chairman Reince Priebus.

Matthew T. Sanderson served as General Counsel of Senator Rand Paul's 2016 presidential campaign, Outside Counsel for Governor Rick Perry's 2012 presidential campaign, Legal Counsel to Governor Mitt Romney's Commonwealth PACs, Campaign Finance Counsel for Senator John McCain's 2008 presidential campaign, and General Counsel for a government reform commission created by Utah Governor Jon Huntsman, Jr. Mr. Sanderson is also a founder of PlayoffPAC, which was nominated in 2011 for *Sports Illustrated*'s Sportsman of the Year award for its work in bringing down college football's unpopular former post-season system, the Bowl Championship Series. Mr. Sanderson is an Adjunct Faculty Member at the University of Virginia School of Law, where he teaches an advanced course on campaign finance regulation. He is frequently quoted on political matters in national media outlets, such as the *New York Times, Wall Street Journal, USA Today,* and *Associated Press.* He is also a trustee for the American Council of Young Political Leaders, a nonprofit that connects rising political leaders in the United States and around the world.

Mr. Sanderson is a graduate of the University of Utah and of Vanderbilt University Law School, where he was a Chancellor's Scholar and member of the *Vanderbilt Journal of Transnational Law.*

Joseph Sandler is a member of the firm Sandler, Reiff & Young P.C., in Washington, D.C., where his concentration is corporate, commercial, and tax issues affecting political and advocacy activities, campaign finance, election law, nonprofit organizations, government ethics, and regulation of lobbying. Joe has represented progressive groups, ballot committees, and vendors throughout the country on issues and in litigation related to initiatives and referenda. Joe has been named in the 2010 through 2015 editions of *The Best Lawyers in America*; in Washington, D.C.'s "SuperLawyers" for Political Law for the years 2007–2015; and as one of the nation's leading lawyers in political law by Chambers USA for 2008–2015. He served as general counsel of the Democratic National Committee from 1993 through 2008. He is former cochair of the Election Law Committee of the Section of Administrative Law and Regulatory Practice of the American Bar Association and served as cochair of the ABA's Task Force on Lobbying Regulation. Joe is the coauthor of *Bipartisan Campaign Reform Act of 2002: Law and Explanation* (CCH 2002), and he wrote the chapter on election law aspects of the 2007 ethics and lobbying reform law for *The Lobbying Manual* (4th ed., 2009) and chapters on congressional ethics and the Foreign Agents Registration Act for *The Lobbying Manual* (1st ed., 1993), published by the ABA Administrative Law Section. Joe graduated from Harvard College in 1975 and from Harvard Law School in 1978.

Brian G. Svoboda is a partner in the Political Law Group at Perkins Coie LLP. He is one of the nation's leading practitioners in the field of political law. He counsels companies, trade associations, political parties, candidates, nonprofit organizations, and individuals on all aspects of ethics and campaign finance laws, and he has appeared often before agencies and courts across the country on campaign finance issues. He has also successfully represented several members of Congress in ethics investigations before the U.S. House Committee on Ethics, Office of Congressional Ethics, and U.S. Senate Select Committee on Ethics. Before joining Perkins Coie, he was a legislative assistant to U.S. Senator Bob Kerrey. Brian is a graduate of the University of Virginia School of Law and the University of Nebraska.

Robert G. Vaughn is Professor of Law Emeritus and A. Allen King Scholar at American University Washington College of Law. He is the author of books and articles on public information law, whistleblower laws, and public employment law, including books on conflict of interest regulation in the federal government and on principles of civil service law. His articles on public employment law include pieces on ethics in government, the British regulation of public service ethics, and on restrictions regarding the political activities of federal employees. He served as the vice chairman of the Ethics Committee of the ABA's model procurement code project and as a consultant to the Treasury and Civil Service Committee of the House of Commons on post-employment restrictions placed on Crown servants.

Robert L. Walker is Of Counsel in the Election Law and Government Ethics Practice Group at Wiley Rein LLP in Washington, D.C. Mr. Walker is a former Chief Counsel and Staff Director of the Senate and House ethics committees and a former federal prosecutor with the Public Integrity Section of the Department of Justice and with the U.S. Attorney's Office for the District of Columbia. He counsels a wide range of clients on congressional and other government ethics rules; federal, state, and local lobbying rules and compliance; congressional investigations; and white-collar defense matters. Mr. Walker regularly represents corporations, associations, and individuals—including congressional officials, other government officials, and candidates—in federal and state ethics advisory and investigative matters (including in connection with financial disclosure obligations), in internal investigations, and in prosecutions arising under campaign finance, fraud, public corruption, and other criminal laws. Mr. Walker testified in both the House and the Senate during consideration by Congress of the Stop Trading on Congressional Knowledge (STOCK) Act; he is quoted frequently in the national media on government ethics, financial disclosure, and public corruption issues. Mr. Walker serves as Chair of an Ad Hoc Hearing Committee of the D.C. Board on Professional Responsibility.

Kip Wainscott is an attorney experienced in the areas of political law and elections, litigation, and public policy. Mr. Wainscott currently is an appointee in the Obama administration, where he has held positions at the White House and the Department of Justice. Before entering government, he was an attorney in the Political Law Group at Perkins Coie LLP, where he counseled elected officials, candidates, and politically active organizations on legal issues including election law, congressional and executive branch ethics, and investigations and litigation. He also was counsel to the DNC Rules and Bylaws Committee, a role in which he advised on issues related to the presidential primary process and the Democratic Party's delegate selection rules. For the 2012 election cycle, Mr. Wainscott served as counsel and national delegate director for the Obama–Biden reelection campaign, overseeing procedures for President Obama's ballot access, party nomination, and other legal issues. Mr. Wainscott serves on the Board of Governors for the Washington Foreign Law Society and is a member of the Board of Advisors for the New Leaders Council. He received his undergraduate and law degrees from the George Washington University.

Andrew Werbrock is a partner at Remcho Johansen & Purcell, LLP. He counsels corporations, candidates, PACs, and ballot measure committees on federal and state campaign finance and election law, as well as ethics regulations and lobbying registration and disclosure. Andrew represents clients in administrative matters in front of the Federal Election Commission, the California Fair Political Practices Commission, and other state regulatory authorities, and has successfully represented clients in civil litigation against the FEC. Since 2012, Andrew has coedited the Bloomberg BNA Corporate Practice Series Guide to the Regulation of Corporate Political Activity. He graduated cum laude from Harvard Law School in 2007, and magna cum laude from Williams College in 2000.

Contents

CHAPTER 23
The Use of Corporate Resources in Connection with Federal Elections 401
Andrew Werbrock

CHAPTER 29

**Restrictions on Service by Former Lobbyists in the Obama Administration
and on Service by Lobbyists on Federal Advisory Committees** **529**

Robert L. Walker

CHAPTER 30
Building an Effective Lobbying Disclosure Act Compliance Program   553
Rebecca H. Gordon

Part I
Lobbying Regulation and Disclosure

Introduction to Part I

From the early years of our nation, lobbying has been constitutionally protected activity that is crucial to the process of making and interpreting our laws. As its practice has become more sophisticated, so too has the regulation of government relations work expanded. This Part I of The Lobbying Manual begins with a brief discussion of the constitutional protections of lobbying. Following that, we have included a summary of how laws are made in Congress and how agencies make rules. These discussions set forth the processes that lobbyists must try to impact. The rest of this Part focuses on the Lobbying Disclosure Act and related laws and rules, which are the backbone of lobbying regulation at the federal level.

CHAPTER 1

Constitutional and Legal Protections of Lobbying

BY WILLIAM MCGINLEY*

1-1 Introduction

Lobbying has been a tradition in the United States government from the beginning of the Republic. The tradition was so valued that it became entrenched in the fabric of American society as part of the First Amendment's protection. Despite this hallowed position, the public has almost as traditionally been skeptical of those "special interests" that petition the government—especially when money plays a role—and a number of scandals over the years have understandably contributed to that skepticism.

Those with experience in government or lobbying, however, understand that lobbying and lobbyists play a vital role in our government, representing and advancing the interests of millions of individuals and providing valuable information and perspective to legislators and executive branch officials concerning those who will be affected by legislation or regulation. As Senator Robert Byrd put it in his essay commemorating the bicentennial of the U.S. Senate:

> Although we often hear a hue and cry about "special interests," every-one, in a sense, belongs to a multitude of these interests: we are defined by our gender, race, age, ethnicity, religion, economic status, educational background, and ideological bent. Some groups are better funded or bet-ter organized than others: corporate interests, organized labor, New Right

*The author wishes to acknowledge the assistance of Stephen A. Vaden and Ann M. Donaldson, associates in Jones Day's political law group, whose research and writing assistance made this chapter possible.

political action committees. Some groups, especially the very young, the very old, the very poor, are the least organized and the least able to make their needs heard. Nevertheless, they all have a "special interest" in congressional actions. Members of Congress, of course, attempt to represent all of the various interests within their constituencies, but they must establish some priorities. Lobbyists attempt to shape those priorities by reminding them of the needs of specific groups.[1]

Today's lobbyists operate in an increasingly high-stakes, highly competitive, and highly scrutinized environment—one that requires in-depth policy knowledge, hard work, and no small amount of savvy. The industry is now populated by tens of thousands of lobbying professionals, attorneys, policy analysts and experts, and countless others who operate in a strictly regulated environment. Lobbying professionals, and those attorneys and compliance officers who advise them, must have a sophisticated understanding of the myriad local, state, and federal laws that govern their activity, as well as the ethics rules that govern the governmental entities with which they interact.

The following chapters present a brief history of lobbying regulation, an explication of the legislative and rulemaking process, and in-depth information and insight regarding various regulations of lobbying activities. But first, this chapter examines the importance of lobbying, as well as the constitutional and legal protections it enjoys, by first discussing the origins and constitutional basis for lobbying, early lobbying practices, and landmark cases that have shaped the bounds of its constitutional protections. This chapter concludes by discussing the important role lobbying and lobbyists continue to play in the government today.

1-2 Lobbying: The Constitutional Framework

Lobbying may have "surely been around as long as there has been government itself,"[2] but its place in the constitutional firmament is of slightly more recent vintage. In his famous *Federalist No. 10*, James Madison considered the dangers and potential benefits of "factions."[3] Balancing the good with the bad, the constitutional system Madison established allowed those factions to compete in the political marketplace for ideas while being simultaneously checked by each other and the three branches of both the federal and state governments. The Supreme Court has similarly sought to strike a balance between the rights of competing factions and the desire on the part of the public at large for honest and open government. Five key cases—all from the 20th century—trace the Supreme Court's modern acceptance of lobbying as a protected and beneficial activity under the First Amendment.

---

1. 2 Senator Robert C. Byrd, *Lobbyists, in* The Senate, 1789–1989: Addresses on the History of the United States Senate, S. Doc. No. 100-20 (Mary Sharon Hall ed., 1989), *available at* http://www.senate.gov/legislative/common/briefing/Byrd_History_Lobbying.htm#2.

2. Nicholas W. Allard, *Lobbying Is An Honorable Profession: The Right to Petition and the Competition to Be Right*, 19 Stanford L. & Pol'y Rev. 23, 36 (2008) (quoting Thomas M. Susman, *Lobbying in the 21st Century—Reciprocity and the Need for Reform*, 58 Admin. L. Rev. 737, 738 (2006)).

3. *See* The Federalist No. 10 (James Madison) (Mentor Book ed. 1962).

1-2.1 Constitutional Foundations

Perhaps more than any other Founding Father, Madison understood that it was imperative for the Framers "to design a form of republican government that would provide a positive role for, but also a system of balances against, the work of organized interests."[4] Madison sought to establish "an extraordinary theory of effective governance in which the principal legislative task of government is to regulate competing interests by involving the spirit of those interests in the ordinary operations of government."[5] The separation of powers between the three branches of government—executive, legislative, and judicial—combined with the further separation of power between the federal government and competing state governments would provide multiple opportunities for factions to influence the work of government while also having their "ambition . . . to counteract ambition."[6]

Here is one of the main indictments of King George III found in the Declaration of Independence:

> In every stage of these Oppressions, We have Petitioned for Redress in the most humble terms: Our repeated Petitions have been answered only by repeated injury. A Prince, whose character is thus marked by every act which may define a Tyrant, is unfit to be the ruler of a free people.[7]

The colonists' complaint gave birth to the Bill of Rights in 1791, whose First Amendment provided, "Congress shall make no law . . . abridging the freedom of speech, or of the press; or the right of the people peaceably to assemble, and *to petition the Government for a redress of grievances.*"[8]

1-2.2 Modern Jurisprudence

In the modern era of constitutional jurisprudence, the Supreme Court has seemingly walked a similar tightrope, seeking to balance the needs of citizens and their chosen advocates to communicate their interests to Congress while also protecting the rights of the public and members of Congress to "self-protection"[9] in the form of greater information about who is engaged in such advocacy. Finally forced to confront the issue directly, the Justices acknowledged the First Amendment concerns at stake.

United States v. Rumely presented the Supreme Court with a challenge to a congressional subpoena to the Committee for Constitutional Government (CCG) issued by the House Select Committee on Lobbying Activities.[10] The committee was investigating whether the Federal Regulation of Lobbying Act of 1946, the first comprehensive codification of lobbying regulations in American history, was

---

4. Allard, *supra* note 2 at 37.
5. THE FEDERALIST No. 10 (James Madison), *supra* note 3.
6. *Id.; see also* Allard, *supra* note 2 at 37.
7. THE DECLARATION OF INDEPENDENCE para. 30 (U.S. 1776).
8. U.S. CONST. amend. I (emphasis added).
9. *See United States v. Harriss*, 347 U.S. 612, 625 (1954).
10. 345 U.S. 41, 42 (1953).

doing its intended job of promoting greater disclosure of "lobbying activities."[11] Its subpoena required the CCG to turn over to Congress the names of all those who had bought its publications in bulk—presumably to use for advocacy purposes. CCG refused to comply with the subpoena, and its secretary was convicted criminally for failing to turn over the list of purchasers.[12]

Although the Court dodged the direct question of whether lobbying was a protected activity under the First Amendment, the Justices chose to apply the doctrine of constitutional avoidance to read the resolution authorizing the congressional committee's subpoena power narrowly.[13] Doing so, the Court held that the congressional resolution authorizing the committee did not empower it to inquire into efforts to shape the opinion of the public at large. It only allowed for the committee to examine "representations made directly to the Congress, its members, or its committees."[14] Of course, the doctrine of constitutional avoidance only applies where it is necessary to "avoid serious doubt of [a provision's] constitutionality."[15] *Rumely* therefore serves as an implicit acknowledgment by the Court that the regulation of lobbying implicates the protections of the First Amendment.[16] Indeed, the two concurring Justices would have expressly reached the First Amendment issue and held the subpoena to be unconstitutional.[17]

Just one year later, the Court found the question of the constitutionality of regulating lobbying more squarely presented in *United States v. Harriss*.[18] There, by a six-to-three vote, the Justices upheld the defendants' convictions for violating the Federal Regulation of Lobbying Act by failing to report contributions made to and expenditures made by the National Farm Committee to influence "the passage or defeat of any legislation by Congress."[19] Using a narrow construction of the statute to save it, the majority found the Act to apply only to those who (1) solicited or expended money, (2) to gain passage or defeat of legislation, (3) through direct communication with Congress.[20] So narrowed, the Court held the Act did not impinge on any of "the freedoms guaranteed by the First Amendment" because it did not seek to prevent the "pressures" lobbyists could bring to bear on Congress.[21] It only sought a "modicum of information" about those who hire lobbyists to provide "self-protection" for Congress.[22] "Otherwise, the voice of the people may all too easily be drowned out by the voice of special interest groups seeking favored treatment while masquerading as proponents of the public weal."[23] The views of

---

11. *Id.* at 45; *see also* Allard, *supra* note 2 at 38 (discussing the origins and role of congressional regulation of lobbying).

12. 345 U.S. at 42.

13. *Id.* at 45–47.

14. *Id.* at 47 (quoting *Rumely v. United States*, 197 F.2d 166, 175 (D.C. Cir. 1952)).

15. *Id.* at 45 (quoting *Richmond Screw Anchor Co. v. United States*, 275 U.S. 331, 346 (1928)).

16. *See id.* at 46 (taking note of the D.C. Circuit's view that the subpoena and accompanying regulations "raise[] doubts of constitutionality in view of the prohibition of the First Amendment").

17. *Id.* at 58 (Douglas and Black, JJ., concurring).

18. 347 U.S. at 614.

19. *Id.* at 614–15.

20. *Id.* at 623.

21. *Id.* at 625.

22. *Id.*

23. *Id.*

the dissenters that "our constitutional system is to allow the greatest freedom of access to Congress" did not carry the day.[24]

Those concerns had more weight in the cases of *Eastern Railroad Presidents Conference v. Noerr Motor Freight, Inc.*[25] and *United Mine Workers v. Pennington* in the 1960s.[26] Both cases involved efforts to use the federal antitrust laws to prohibit working in concert to gain passage of legislation or regulations that would harm one's business competitors.[27] In *Eastern Railroad*, the Court held that the Sherman Act did not prohibit "associating together" to influence the passage of legislation.[28] Such a construction would violate the First Amendment's protection of "the right of petition."[29] Indeed, "the whole concept of representation depends upon the ability of the people to make their wishes known to their representatives," and the motive to make a profit results in the dissemination of most of the information Congress receives.[30] Rather than seeing this profit motive as problematic, the Court viewed it as vitally deserving of First Amendment protection as it may be the motive "of the most importance to [citizens]."[31] *Pennington* extended this same legal reasoning and result to "joint efforts to influence public officials" found in federal agencies—protecting the right of citizens to petition those executive branch officials whose regulatory authority affects their business and personal decisions.[32]

By the time of *Regan v. Taxation with Representation of Washington* in 1983, the three concurring Justices were ready to openly declare that "lobbying is protected by the First Amendment."[33] Justices Blackman, Brennan, and Marshall went so far as to declare that, in their view, the only reason the Internal Revenue Service's strict prohibition on lobbying by section 501(c)(3) charitable organizations is constitutional is because a charity may establish a separate arm under section 501(c)(4) that can lobby.[34] Later Courts have taken up this theme to find that the Federal Election Commission cannot constitutionally regulate "grassroots lobbying" efforts[35] and to find that the government may not prohibit independent political advocacy by corporations and unions.[36] This trend of greater First Amendment protection for the right to petition one's government likely will only continue.[37] In short, Madison's design for "ambition . . . to counteract ambition" will only grow more robust.[38]

---

24. *Id.* at 635 (Jackson, J., dissenting).

25. 365 U.S. 127 (1961).

26. 381 U.S. 657 (1965).

27. *Eastern R.R.*, 365 U.S. at 129–34; *Pennington*, 381 U.S. at 659–61.

28. 365 U.S. at 136.

29. *Id.* at 138.

30. *Id.* at 137, 139.

31. *Id.* at 139.

32. *Pennington*, 381 U.S. at 670.

33. 461 U.S. 540, 552 (1983) (Blackman, Brennan, and Marshall, JJ., concurring).

34. *See id.* ("The constitutional defect that would inhere in § 501(c)(3) alone is avoided by § 501(c)(4)"). Considering the current politics surrounding donations to (c)(4) organizations, the fact that the Court's historic "liberal wing" viewed the political abilities of (c)(4) organizations as necessary to save the tax-exempt organization statutes from unconstitutionality may surprise many readers.

35. *See FEC v. Wis. Right to Life, Inc.*, 551 U.S. 449, 457–58 (2007) (plurality opinion); *see also* 551 U.S. at 504 (opinion of Scalia, Thomas, and Alito, JJ., concurring in the judgment).

36. *See Citizens United v. FEC*, 558 U.S. 310, 342 (2010).

37. *E.g.*, *McCutcheon v. FEC*, 134 S. Ct. 1434 (2014) (invalidating the biennial aggregate limit on donations to federal candidates and political committees).

38. THE FEDERALIST No. 10 (James Madison), *supra* note 3.

1-3 Lobbying: An Evolving but Ever-Present Force

In a way, the fundamentals of lobbying have changed little over the years. Lobbyists have always represented interests to decision makers, gathered and relayed facts, and sought to create coalitions behind their intended result. On the other hand, some of the specific tactics and practices that held sway in the 19th and early 20th century would be shocking by today's standards.[39] Technology has long been a driver of progress in the field: Senator Byrd reported that the telephone, telegraph, and radio "intensified the development of grassroots lobbying" in the 1920s—much as television, the Internet, and social networking would do later.

Though lobbying's roots in the United States go back as far as the formation of our Republic,[40] and the Supreme Court has consistently interpreted the First Amendment to protect the institution, many have viewed the practice with suspicion, and it has been the target of increasing regulation over the years. Attempts—both failed and successful—to regulate lobbying date back at least to the mid-1800s. At present, lobbying the federal government is regulated by federal law and U.S. House, Senate, and executive branch ethics rules that form an elaborate tangle of do's, don'ts, and musts that would be entirely foreign to earlier practitioners, and that have fundamentally transformed what was once an art largely governed only by the outer bounds of propriety to a heavily regulated industry. And that does not include the additional web of statutes, regulations, ordinances, and other rules governing activity on the local and state level across the country.

Much regulation of lobbying over the years has come as a result of discovered abuses and scandals perpetrated both by advocates and lawmakers. The lobbying industry has not been devoid of such troubles—the Abramoff scandal and fallout is one of the most recent and notable instances—though the professional lobbyists themselves are often not the sole wrongdoers when something goes awry. One of the earliest "lobbying" scandals, the Crédit Mobilier scandal of 1872, involved not a hired advocate but rather Congressman Oakes Ames, who distributed shares of stock of a railroad construction company he helmed to other members of the House and Senate in return for support of legislation concerning railroad construction. So it comes as no surprise that attempts to curb abuses and questionable practices target not only the lobbyists, but also the lawmakers and government officials themselves.

As such, lobbyists must take care to comply with the rules targeting them while also being mindful of government ethics laws and House, Senate, and executive branch rules governing the targets of their efforts. After all, lobbyists' reputations are the key to their success, and an easy way to ruin their reputation is to conduct events or engage in practices that may jeopardize the official's own compliant

---

39. Senator Byrd's essay provides some especially colorful anecdotes on this topic. *See* BYRD, *Lobbyists*, *supra* note 1.

40. Senator Byrd's account of the first forays into lobbying, which is included in essay form in the U.S. Senate's 1989 bicentennial commemoration, is especially enlightening. *Id.*

status. "In an environment of fundamental honesty and dynamic competition to prevail, quick fixes and cutting corners are paths to failure."[41]

Our history suggests that as the size and complexity of the government grows— as well as the size and complexity of the problems the government attempts to address—it seems, inevitably, so too does the lobbying profession. The so-called Gilded Age of lobbying began during Reconstruction when lobbying began to become more professionalized—and attempts to regulate it began.[42] Lobbyists then provided information, insight, and perspective to congressmen who typically had little to no staff support, and independent research was arduous at best. Though the staff ranks have grown considerably since Reconstruction, in modern times, "despite the increase in the scale and complexity of governance, the number of staffers in congressional offices has remained nearly the same over the past twenty years" and "experience is spread thin."[43] As such, the constraints on Congress are the same or similar to those that legislators have faced from the beginning of the Republic, and, officials and staff continue to rely on lobbyists to provide information and perspective.[44] In times of rapid government expansion, the lobbyists' ranks grow almost geometrically, a trend that continues today.

Despite the ever-present suspicions of lobbying on the part of the public and press, increasingly tough lobbying and ethics regulations, and the words of numerous public officials—including the current administration—the constitutional protections of lobbying and simple necessity of it to the system mean that the lobbying industry will continue to play a vital role in law and policymaking for some time to come.

---

41. Allard, *supra* note 2 at 34.

42. In 1876, the House of Representatives required the registration of all lobbyists with the Clerk of the House. BYRD, *Lobbyists, supra* note 1. By the first half of the twentieth century, attempts at passing lobbying rules, registration of lobbyists, and House and Senate ethical rules related to lobbying were increasing, and lobbying practices were increasingly coming under scrutiny.

43. Allard, *supra* note 2 at 43.

44. *Id.* at 44.

CHAPTER 2

The Structure and Organization of Congress and the Practice of Lobbying

BY CRAIG HOLMAN AND JAMIE CONRAD*

2-1 Introduction

The First Amendment to the United States Constitution guarantees "the right of the people … to petition government for a redress of grievances."[1] Scholars and lawyers interpret this right to petition government as constitutional protection for the modern profession of lobbying, whereby contracted or in-house professionals receive compensation to represent interests before Congress and the executive branch. Constituent efforts and the congressional public liaison offices for each member of Congress, and similar liaison offices in federal agencies, have institutionalized the constitutional right to petition. As a result, the right of citizens and organizations to petition government for legislative and executive action is firmly entrenched in the structure and organization of the federal government.

---

*This chapter was written with great help from Victoria Hall-Palerm, legal research associate, and Anthony Szewczyk, research assistant, Public Citizen.

   1. U.S. CONST. amend. I.

But the Founding Fathers could not have envisioned professional lobbying to the extent we see it today; consequently, how the government ought to deal with lobbyists is *not* written into its structure and organization. Instead, the working relationship between government and lobbyists has evolved over the decades, from an informal (and sometimes unspoken) relationship into a patchwork of sometimes confusing statutory and regulatory schemes.

The history of the office in charge of the disclosure requirements of the Lobbying Disclosure Act of 1995 (LDA)—or, more accurately, the multiple offices in charge of the disclosure requirements—is a useful example of this patchwork evolution of lobbying regulation. During the congressional debates that led to passage of the LDA, Congress was considering enhancing its system of regular public disclosure filings of lobbyists' financial activity. But Congress met a dilemma: who should administer this disclosure system? The Office of Government Ethics (OGE) did not want the responsibility for lobbying disclosure. Stephen Potts, former Director of OGE, testified that the lobbying disclosure requirements would "ask us to begin working with an entirely new constituency: the law firms, public relations firms, and membership organizations which represent client interests to members of Congress and members of the executive branch."[2] The Department of Justice (DOJ) did not want the responsibility. DOJ viewed itself as an enforcement agency whose proceedings are confidential, not as a public disclosure agency. As such, it wanted no part in policing a system of public disclosure.

The Federal Election Commission (FEC), on the other hand, was willing and able to take on the new lobbying disclosure responsibilities. Scott Thomas, then chairman of the FEC, testified that the agency was already developing computerized technology to make campaign finance reports readily available to the public. Expanding the program to include lobbyist financial activity reports would not take much additional effort.[3] The FEC's willingness to assume the disclosure responsibilities alarmed some members of Congress, however, who were uncomfortable with the idea of posting lobbying activity on the Internet for everyone to see in a searchable, sortable, and downloadable format.

Thus, rather than agree to the FEC's suggestion, Congress gave the burden to two resource-challenged congressional offices: the Clerk of the House and the Secretary of the Senate. Both offices had previously served as administrators of lobbying registration and reporting under the 1946 Federal Regulation of Lobbying Act. Initially, the House Clerk and Senate Secretary proceeded to develop slightly different lobbyist disclosure forms. This meant that lobbyists had to fill out two separate financial activity reports, one with each office, disclosing essentially (but not exactly) the same information. Those who lobbied the executive branch rather than Congress would likewise have to file two separate reports with the two congressional offices.

Today, the Clerk of the House and Secretary of the Senate remain the institutions in charge of lobbyist registration and disclosure of lobbying activity under the LDA, despite the addition of new laws that attempt to further regulate the

---

2. Testimony of Stephen D. Potts, Director, Office of Government Ethics, before the Subcommittee on Oversight of Government Management, U.S. Senate, 8 (Mar. 26, 1992).

3. Testimony of Scott E. Thomas, Chairman of the Federal Election Commission, before the House Judiciary Subcommittee on Administrative Law and Governmental Relations, U.S. House of Representatives, 276–77 (Mar. 23, 1993).

process.[4] Helpfully, the offices have adopted a more cooperative approach to the filing process. For example, they have developed an electronic filing program that allows simultaneous filing via the same software in both offices.[5]

This chapter summarizes the processes by which Congress makes laws and agencies make rules. These are the government structures that lobbyists must attempt to influence. With this chapter, we hope to illustrate for the reader the points of entry in the process for a lobbyist and the places that their work can be most fruitful. We first address the legislative process and then turn to the rulemaking process.

2-2 Overview of the Legislative Process

While lobbyists generally advocate a single interest or perspective on a given issue, Congress is designed to serve as an institution that mediates competing interests. Progressing from an expression of interest to passing actual legislation (or, alternatively, defeating legislation) is a long and complicated process. Legislation normally has to wind its way through multiple stages: seeking a congressional sponsor, markups, and hearings before various subcommittees and committees, the assignment of rules of consideration and debate, and, finally, floor votes. Then it moves to the second chamber to repeat these same steps. Finally, differences in bills between the chambers are ironed out in conference proceedings—if congressional leadership allows the conference proceedings to go forward—and then the reconciled package is resubmitted for floor consideration in both chambers. Even if consensus is reached, the legislation still must obtain the president's signature or risk being killed by a presidential veto.[6] Congress may override a presidential veto by a two-thirds majority vote in both chambers (Figure 2.1).

Throughout this complex path, an effective lobbyist must be attuned to the structure and workings of Congress that affect the prospects for a piece of

---

4. Efforts to develop a system of disclosure of lobbyist financial activity began in earnest during World War II. The first attempt at comprehensive lobbying reform at the federal level was the Foreign Agents Registration Act (FARA) of 1938. FARA's primary purpose was to limit the influence of foreign agents and propaganda on American public policy. FARA arose in response to a perceived propaganda drive by Adolph Hitler to fan the Nazi movement in the United States, and therefore originally focused on the Nazi movement. In fact, the lobbying material identified as "foreign propaganda" and subject to disclosure read "Nazi propaganda" in early versions of the legislation. But FARA was later expanded to include concerns about pro-communist propaganda as well. *See* Michael Spak, *America for Sale: When Well-Connected Former Federal Officials Peddle Their Influence to the Highest Bidder*, 78 Ky. L.J. 237, 242–43 (1990).

FARA was followed shortly thereafter by the Federal Regulation of Lobbying Act of 1946 (FRLA), which required domestic lobbyists to register with the Secretary of the Senate and Clerk of the House of Representatives. FRLA did not provide clear, concise definitions of "lobbyist" or reportable lobbying activity. Accordingly, it was widely ignored by the lobbying community. Testimony of Craig Holman, Public Citizen, before the Committee on Constitutional Affairs, European Parliament, Brussels (Oct. 8, 2007).

5. See Chapter 4 for an overview of the LDA's filing obligations.

6. And this is only half the battle. Once it is approved by Congress and signed by the president, the law then must be interpreted and implemented by administrative agencies, monitored for compliance and enforced, and survive potential court challenge. An effective lobbyist should be prepared to participate in, or at least track, each of these subsequent steps to turn an interest into lasting public policy.

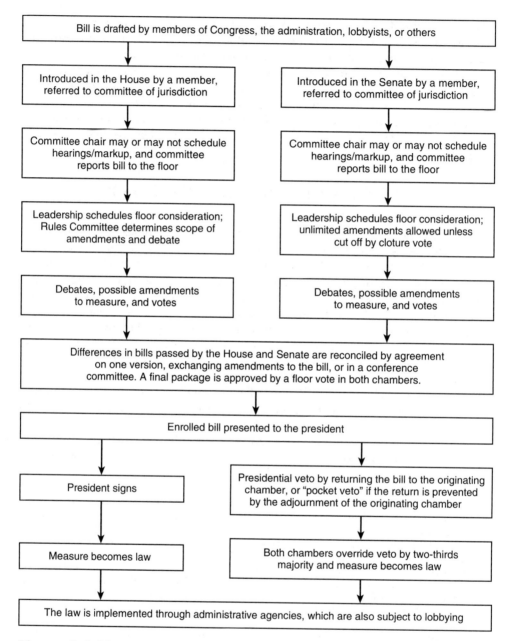

Figure 2.1 How a Bill Becomes Law

legislation, including the parliamentary procedures of the House and Senate, the committees of jurisdiction and their members and staff, the participation of congressional leadership and their staff, the rules of engagement, and even security measures that can prevent timely delivery of lobbying materials.

The maze of obstacles a lobbyist must navigate to achieve consensus in Congress and turn an idea into a law explains why it is sometimes far easier for the lobbyist to defeat legislation than to attain enactment. It also explains why a final law almost never ends up in the same form as it began.[7]

The first step a lobbyist generally takes in advancing a legislative proposal is to find one or more congressional sponsors. Bills must be "put into the hopper" by a member of Congress, and amendments and even stealth or hidden "riders" (i.e., provisions discreetly inserted into unrelated legislation) must be sponsored by a member.[8] Next, when a bill is introduced, it is referred to the standing committee(s) that have jurisdiction over the subject matter of that bill.[9]

This is as far as most bills go, unless the committee chairman chooses to support it or congressional leaders, fellow members, or even the public apply pressure to the committee, urging further consideration of the bill. The legislation leading to the ultimate enactment of the Honest Leadership and Open Government Act of 2007 (HLOGA) suffered precisely this fate, finding itself buried by committee chairmen without a hearing. Only when the Jack Abramoff scandal erupted in January 2006, accompanied by public outrage, did the House take up further consideration of the HLOGA reform measures.[10]

If the committee chairman deems further consideration of a bill appropriate, the chairman usually assigns the bill to a subcommittee for a public hearing to collect information. In some cases, the full committee itself may conduct such a hearing. The measure is then scheduled for a markup before the full committee, at which time the bill is subject to amendments, rewriting, and approval or rejection by a vote of the committee. If a majority of the full committee approves the bill, the congressional leadership then chooses whether to schedule it for floor consideration. At this point in the process, a measure in the House is sent to the

---

7. For example, persuading a single committee chairman or congressional leader to refuse to place an item on the congressional calendar will doom legislation, as would a simple "hold" by a single senator on an otherwise popular legislative proposal. A relevant example of the power of the "hold" by an individual senator has been the failure in the Senate to require electronic filing of campaign finance reports for senatorial candidates, even though all other federal candidates must file their campaign finance reports electronically. While senators have nearly unanimously approved the legislative proposal for electronic filing in public statements, such legislation has been repeatedly defeated by a secret "hold" from a single senator. Beginning with the 110th Congress, "holds" are still allowed but no longer secret due to new lobbying and ethics legislation. Under the new rules, the identity of the senator and reason for a hold must be disclosed within six session days, unless the "hold" is passed from senator to senator every six days. Senators also avoid disclosure of holds by making a mere threat of a hold to prevent a lawmaker from advancing the legislation. This circumstance is quite common.

8. The phrase of putting a bill "in the hopper" comes from reference to an actual wooden box at the rostrum of the House chamber in which representatives drop their bills before further consideration. Legislative ideas, and even legislative text, may come from any number of sources including citizens, lobbyists, state legislatures, members of Congress, or the president; but the actual bill must be sponsored by a member of Congress.

9. The rules of the House and Senate provide for more than 200 different classifications of the subject matters of bills that determine which committees are assigned jurisdiction. If a bill has multiple overlapping subject matters, it may be assigned to multiple committees. This option can either advance or stop the legislation in its tracks depending on the assigned committee's (and chairman's) receptiveness to the legislation. *See* Charles Johnson, Parliamentarian of the House of Representatives, How Our Laws Are Made, 10 (2003).

10. Much of the final Honest Leadership and Open Government Act (S.1) approved by the 110th Congress and signed into law by the president on September 14, 2007, originally had been proposed before to high-profile ethics controversies implicating both political parties, only to be ignored and not even given a hearing.

Rules Committee.[11] The House Rules Committee receives any amendments to the measure that any member offers, and determines which amendments, if any, will be considered on the floor. These decisions tend to be heavily influenced by the position of the Speaker of the House. An "open rule" by the Rules Committee allows all amendments to be considered, a "closed rule" bans consideration of all amendments, and a modified or restricted rule limits which amendments may be considered.[12] The House then considers the measure under the rules dictated by the Rules Committee.[13]

No similar Rules Committee process exists in the Senate. In the Senate, the measure is sent directly to the floor for a vote as scheduled by the Senate Majority Leader. Any amendments may be offered on the Senate floor, and debate is cut off only by a cloture vote of at least sixty senators.

Any differences in the bills passed by the House and the Senate are then reconciled in conference committee, and the final package is approved by a floor vote in each chamber.

2-3 Earmarks

"Earmarks," as they are commonly known, are a special category of legislation that deserves highlighting. Though there is no agreed-upon definition, an earmark is, in the broadest sense, an appropriation for a specific project, a specific recipient, or a specific location that is inserted in a spending bill. Under ordinary circumstances, Congress appropriates a lump sum to an executive branch agency to spend at the agency's discretion. When Congress deviates from this standard procedure and specifies how the agency must spend an appropriation, that action is known as a congressional earmark. Under the Constitution, the executive branch is charged with allocating specific appropriations and contracts within the overall congressional budgetary framework.[14] However, given that implementation of legislative priorities and the budget is seen as falling within the rightful constitutional role of the executive branch, most (though not all) of the controversies and reform proposals regarding earmarks focus on the growing practice of congressional earmarks.

The first recorded congressional earmark came from Rep. John Calhoun almost two centuries ago. Calhoun introduced the Bonus Bill of 1817, which would have diverted the earnings from the Second Bank of the United States to a road system linking the eastern United States with the western frontier. President James Madison

---

11. Bills not reported out of committee may still be brought to the floor for a vote of the entire chamber. This is done through a discharge petition in the House, signed by 218 Representatives. Similar procedures exist in the Senate to bypass the failure of a committee to report out a popular bill.

12. Between 1995 and 2005, the percentage of bills debated on the House floor under open rules steadily declined, from 45 percent to fewer than 22 percent in 2004–2005. LOUISE SLAUGHTER, BROKEN PROMISES: THE DEATH OF DELIBERATIVE DEMOCRACY, REPORT OF THE MINORITY OFFICE OF THE HOUSE RULES COMMITTEE 14 (2006).

13. Through a process known as "suspension of the rules," a bill may bypass the Rules Committee and go straight to the floor if the majority and minority party leadership agrees. Suspension requires a two-thirds majority of the full House (290 votes) for passage and is designed to expedite consideration of noncontroversial matters.

14. Which, technically, could be referred to as executive branch earmarks.

vetoed the bill as an unconstitutional overreach of congressional authority.[15] However, until the most recent few decades, congressional earmarks were uncommon.

Congressional earmarks began to surge in frequency and value in the late 1970s when a prominent lobbying firm began securing earmarks for clients as a business practice. The firm represented several universities, and lobbyists at the firm realized that they could create value for their clients by identifying their clients' strengths and matching those strengths with budgetary appropriations under consideration in Congress. The lobbyists would then approach the local member of Congress and convince him or her to insert a specific appropriation in the budget that would play to their clients' strengths. The specific appropriation also diverted federal money into the congressional district, which provided the incentive for the congressman to agree.[16]

The firm soon expanded this earmarking model to other corporate clients and began earning substantial fees. Creating earmarks for clients became such a successful business model that other lobbying firms entered the market. At the same time, the practice of congressional earmarking grew rapidly. Citizens Against Government Waste (CAGW) identified 546 earmarks in the 1991 federal budget, worth a total of approximately $3.1 million. Those figures jumped to 4,326 earmarks—worth $17.7 billion in 2000—and then to a record high of 9,963 earmarks, worth $29 billion in 2006.[17]

Even at their high point, earmarks constituted a small portion of the federal budget—they amounted to less than 1.5 percent of appropriations in fiscal year 2010.[18] Nevertheless, many earmarks drew scrutiny from the public and lawmakers as being particularly wasteful of taxpayer dollars. The classic example is the infamous "bridge to nowhere" earmark, in which Alaskan representatives targeted $315 million to build a bridge as long as the Golden Gate Bridge and taller than the Brooklyn Bridge to Gavina Island (population: fifty).[19]

Also of particular public concern was the growing evidence that many earmarks were being awarded to major campaign contributors. The head of one major lobbying firm, PMA Group, pled guilty to charges that he solicited and made campaign contributions to congressional appropriators in return for obtaining earmarks and government contracts for his clients from those same congressional appropriators.[20] A congressional ethics investigation into whether seven congressional appropriators were in fact awarding earmarks based on these contributions failed to find evidence of quid pro quo corruption and dismissed the case.

---

15. Jason Iuliano, *Eliminating Earmarks*, 112 West Virginia Law Review 948, 952 (2010), *available at* https://dash.harvard.edu/bitstream/handle/1/3428428/Jason%20Iuliano%20-%20The%20Congressional%20Line%20Item%20Vote.pdf?sequence=4.

16. Robert Kaiser, *So Damn Much Money* 160–61 (2009); *see also* John M. de Figueiredo & Brian S. Silverman, *Academic Earmarks and the Returns to Lobbying* 7 (June 2002), http://www.law.harvard.edu/programs/olin_center/papers/pdf/370.pdf.

17. Citizens Against Government Waste, *Pork Trends*, 1991–2010, http://cagw.org/reporting/pig-book.

18. Carol Hardy Vincent & Jim Monke, *Earmarks Disclosed by Congress: FY 2008–FY 2010 Regular Appropriations Bills*, CRS Report to Congress, April 16, 2010.

19. Nick Jans, *Alaska Thanks You*, USA Today (May 17, 2005), *available at* http://usatoday30.usatoday.com/news/opinion/editorials/2005-05-17-alaska-edit_x.htm.

20. Paul Blumenthal, *PMA Group Investigation*, Sunlight Foundation Blog (Feb. 11, 2009), http://sunlightfoundation.com/blog/2009/02/11/pma-group-investigation; *see also* John Bresnahan, *Paul Magliocchetti Pleads Guilty*, Politico (Sep. 24, 2010), *available at* http://www.politico.com/news/stories/0910/42690.html.

Nevertheless, the process of earmarking became tainted by the scandal. Suddenly, earmarking was more than wasteful "pork"; it was a potential source of corruption through which some lawmakers appeared to be doling out appropriations projects in exchange for gifts and campaign contributions.

Despite these issues, the earmarking process does have its defenders. One argument in support of the practice is that banning congressional earmarks would prohibit Congress from participating in decisions on how to allocate appropriations, leaving these decisions exclusively in the hands of the executive branch. Furthermore, executive agencies tend to allocate spending projects disproportionately to urban areas and large corporations based on cost efficiency. Congressional earmarks can help spread federal funds to rural areas and smaller companies.[21] Another argument sometimes offered in defense of earmarks is that the process provides members of Congress with leverage to negotiate compromises—essentially, if you allow an allocation for a bridge in my district, I'll support an allocation for a road in your district. Ending earmarks, it is suggested, may be a contributing cause to congressional gridlock.

Congress approved significant reforms to the earmarking process in 2007 as part of HLOGA. The 2007 reforms focused almost entirely on disclosure, requiring that each earmark be attributed to a congressional sponsor and that it be listed in the *Congressional Record* in the House or posted on the Internet in the Senate before a floor vote. In the House, the earmark disclosure rule cannot be waived, and any representative may raise a point of order to end consideration of a bill that fails to disclose its earmarks. Furthermore, those who sponsor earmarks in the House must certify that they and their spouses have no personal financial interest in the earmarks. In the Senate, the earmark rule can only be waived by a vote of three-fifths of the members of the Senate, and any senator may raise a point of order objection against earmarks "air dropped" into conference bills without committee consideration. (An "airdropped" earmark is essentially one that was not included in the version of the bill introduced to the chamber, but it is nonetheless later included in the conference committee reports.[22]) As in the House, Senate sponsors of earmarks must also certify that neither the senator nor any immediate family has any financial interest at stake in the earmark.

The HLOGA earmark disclosure rules have largely failed to allay criticisms of the process. Though there was a dramatic initial reduction in earmarks following the implementation of disclosure rules, the number and value of earmarks climbed once again in 2009 and 2010, reaching roughly half their previous highest point. Lacking a uniform definition of earmarks, the rules allowed many earmarks to go undisclosed, and allegations of awarding earmarks in exchange for gifts and campaign contributions continued.

The 2010 congressional elections saw a resurgence of Republican victories, with the party taking control of the House and building a cloture-proof minority in the Senate. The overarching political issue in the campaign was excessive

---

21. *See* The Ferguson Group, *The Alternative to Earmarks* 4 (Feb. 10, 2011), http://www.thefergusongroup.com/sites/default/files/alternative_to_earmarks_2011_0.pdf.

22. LegiStorm, *Airdropped Earmarks*, http://www.legistorm.com/earmarks/features/airdropped/page/1/sort/amount/type/desc.html (last visited June 10, 2014).

government spending and the federal deficit, which prompted a commitment in the new Congress to address the earmarking. Several legislative proposals were introduced in the House and Senate to ban congressional earmarks altogether. A more narrowly focused proposal by an unusual coalition of nonprofit groups and professional lobbyists, whose goal was to allow congressional earmarks but prohibit earmarks to campaign contributors, gained some measure of bipartisan support in Congress.[23]

In the end, however, the new Congress imposed a two-year moratorium on earmarks, with an eye toward revisiting the issue at a later date. The original moratorium applied to fiscal years 2011 and 2012, but the 112th Congress decided in 2013 to renew the ban for the duration of 2013 and 2014.[24] The moratorium was first approved by the Republican majority in the House and later adopted with bipartisan support in the Senate.

The moratorium has been fairly successful in reducing the number and cost of earmarks, although it has by no means totally eliminated them. A Congressional Research Service report showed that the short-term spending bills for FY 2011 left half of earmark spending untouched.[25] In 2012, the Citizens Against Government Waste claimed the total number of earmarks in FY 2012 dropped by 98.3 percent when compared to FY 2010—from 9,129 to 152. The total cost of earmark spending also dropped about 80 percent to $3.3 billion, the lowest sum since 1992.[26]

On the other hand, the moratorium has had a negative effect on earmark disclosure and transparency. Given that there are to be no earmarks at all under the moratorium, legislators have declined to attach their names to the ones that do exist. There are also no comprehensive lists of earmarks in any appropriations bills or reports. Lawmakers also added language to the moratorium to the effect that the earmarks are only advisory and have "no legal effect." Finally, executive agencies tend to comply with earmark requests out of concern for alienating Congress: in both the House and Senate, the practice of lawmakers sending letters or e-mails to executive agencies requesting special earmarks has increased since the moratorium.[27] Accordingly, the moratorium thus far appears to have reduced the level of earmarks, at least temporarily, but it has also resulted in the earmarks that do exist no longer being publicly disclosed.

---

23. The coalition of nonprofit groups and professional lobbyists consisted of Citizens for Responsibility and Ethics in Washington; Citizens Against Government Waste; Public Citizen; Taxpayers for Common Sense; Former Congressman James Walsh (R-NY), *K&L Gates*; Rich Gold, *Holland & Knight*; Manny Rouvelas, *K&L Gates*; and Dave Wenhold, *Miller/Wenhold*. Press Release, Public Citizen, *Bipartisan Coalition of Lobbyists and Advocates Announces Commonsense Earmark Reform Principles* (Sept. 28, 2010), http://www.citizen.org/pressroom/pressroomredirect.cfm?ID=3195. Draft language for their proposal is available at http://www.citizen.org/documents/Earmark-Reform-Proposal.pdf.

24. Louis Jacobson, *GOP Approved Earmark Ban for 112th Congress and Re-Upped for 113th*, Tampa Bay Times (Jan. 8, 2013), *available at* http://www.politifact.com/truth-o-meter/promises/gop-pledge-o-meter/promise/685/refuse-to-consider-house-legislation-that-includes/.

25. Congressional Research Service, *Earmark Accounts Reduced (and Not Reduced) in Three-Week CR*, CRS Report to Sen. Tom Coburn, March 17, 2011.

26. Citizens Against Government Waste, *2012 Congressional Pig Book Summary*, http://cagw.org/sites/default/files/pdf/2012-pig-book.pdf.

27. Marc Heller, *Both Parties Pushing Highway Bill*, Wash. Times, April 10, 2011.

2-4 Concentration of Power in Congressional Leadership

The House and the Senate often have very different institutional structures and internal power relationships. Due to the sheer size of the House (435 members), individual members generally have less power to promote or block legislation and must rely on strong coalitions and majority power to move a bill through the legislative process. House rules are such that a simple majority often is able to impose its will on the chamber. The smaller size of the Senate chamber (100 members) provides each member with greater relative authority to affect legislation and encourages greater cordiality. Also, unlike House rules, Senate rules allow individual members and minority coalitions to "hold" or block legislation and prevent further consideration of bills.

Nevertheless, both chambers go through periods of varying concentration of power among committee chairmen and congressional leaders. The 109th Congress, under the leadership of House Speaker Dennis Hastert (R-IL) and Senate Majority Leader Bill Frist (R-TN), displayed an unusually strong concentration of power in the hands of congressional leaders. The Republican leaders of that Congress built upon the foundation established in previous years when Democrats held the reins of power in both chambers and in the White House.

This concentration of power sometimes is viewed as undermining the deliberative and democratic process that is supposed to be the function of Congress.[28] Under direct order of the House leadership, for example, closed rules that stifle floor debate—which can be issued under direct order of House leadership as dictated by the Speaker—became the norm rather than the exception for significant legislation. In the 103rd Congress (1993–1994) there were 49 open rules and 18 closed rules, while in the 109th Congress (2005–2006) there were 22 open rules and 49 closed rules.[29] Even the unsuccessful lobbying and ethics reform legislation in the 109th Congress was subject to closed and restricted rules of debate, prompting criticism from members regarding their inability to affect the legislation.

Another way to measure of the concentration of power in the House leadership is the use of suspension of rules, which is another procedural mechanism that stifles floor debate on measures. Traditionally, suspension of the rules was used only for noncontroversial legislation. Recently, however, it has been used to disempower the minority on significant legislation as well, growing in use from about 400 occurrences in the 104th Congress (1995–1996) to more than 900 in the 109th Congress.[30] The 109th Congress even provided 146 bills and resolutions with "blanket waivers" of all rules of the House.[31]

Majority party control over setting the rules of consideration for bills provides the leadership with disproportionate authority to make or break legislation. Often, the result is legislation that is developed outside the usual, public

---

28. Thomas Mann and Norman Ornstein, THE BROKEN BRANCH (New York: Oxford University Press, 2006).

29. H.R. REP. No. 109-743, at 22 (2007) (Conf. Rep.).

30. *See* James Thurber, *Lobbying, Ethics and Procedural Reforms: The Do-Nothing 109th Congress Does Nothing About Reforming Itself*, EXTENSIONS (Fall 2006).

31. *See* Steven Smith, Jason Roberts and Ryan Vander, *The American Congress* (Cambridge: Cambridge University Press, 2007).

congressional process, and most of the substantive work is done by committee chairmen, party leaders, and any lobbyists who may be privy to those proceedings.

For example, congressional leaders sometimes arrange for closed meetings of conference committees, inviting only those conferees supportive of the leadership and excluding others from the deliberations. With regard to the 2004 Medicare bill, for instance, Senate leadership excluded liberal Democratic Senate conferees Tom Daschle (D-SD) and Jay Rockefeller (D-WV), while John Breaux (D-LA) and Max Baucus (D-MT), who were more agreeable to the leadership's views, were invited to the meetings. All four Democratic House conferees were excluded.[32] With representation so favorable to leadership, the conferees crafted a major proposal out of two different bills and sent it to each chamber for a final vote.

This same 681-page conference measure—written substantially outside of the public process and not submitted to members and the public for timely consideration before a floor vote—was then ratified by the House only after an extended voting period so that congressional leaders could persuade other members to vote their way. According to House rules, floor votes should typically occur within fifteen minutes after being called. The floor vote on the Medicare prescription drug bill was held open for nearly three hours (doubling the previous record for an extended vote) and concluded shortly before 6:00 a.m. In the course of these three hours, allegations of attempted bribery and threats emerged, as did complaints from C-SPAN that leadership censored its news coverage of the proceedings. The resulting legislation was viewed by some as highly favorable to the pharmaceutical industry: it prohibited the federal government from using its buying power to leverage lower prices from the drug industry and also banned the importation of less expensive drugs from Canada and Mexico. The legislation was criticized by conservative Republicans and liberal Democrats alike on the basis of its limited deliberation, faulty assumptions, and questionable cost estimates.[33]

The subsequent Democratic-controlled 110th Congress pledged to bring "democracy back to Congress." The House and Senate separately adopted various measures in an effort to guard against the abuses that can sometimes accompany excessive concentrations of power in the hands of congressional leaders. The House adopted a resolution to prohibit keeping floor votes open for the "sole purpose of reversing the outcome of such vote."[34] The House also added a "pay-go" rule under which new spending projects were supposed to avoid increasing the budget deficit within a five-year or ten-year time frame.[35]

Both the House and the Senate also amended their respective rules governing conference proceedings, requiring that all conferees be notified of the time and place of each meeting and be allowed to participate in the proceedings.[36] Both chambers also adopted greater disclosure requirements with regard to "earmarks" (i.e., allocation of money for specific pet projects; see Section 2-3), requiring that

---

32. *See* Robert Kuttner, *America as a One-Party State,* American Prospect, Feb. 1, 2004, *available at* http://prospect.org/article/america-one-party-state.

33. Mann and Ornstein, *supra* note 28 at 6.

34. House Rule XX(2)(a) (110th Cong.).

35. House Rule XXI(10) (110th Cong.).

36. H.R. Res. 6, 110th Cong. (2007); S.1, 110th Cong. §§ 511, 515 (2007).

every earmark be identified with a sponsor and made a matter of public record in the Congressional Record (House) or on the Internet (Senate). A list of earmarks and their sponsors was also required to be printed in conference reports, or else the full report (in the House) or particular earmark (in the Senate) could be removed by a simple point of order raised by any member on the floor.[37]

Nevertheless, these reforms did not totally alleviate the issues that can accompany the concentration of power in leadership. As of May 1, 2008, House Democrats had employed more closed rules (fifty-one) on legislation during the 110th Congress than invoked by their Republican counterparts in the 109th. This trend continued in the 112th Congress with fifty-three instances of closed rules.[38] Nor does either party appear to be shy about suspending the rules to push their legislative agenda. The Republican caucus strenuously objected when House Speaker Nancy Pelosi (D-CA) extended the voting period by an additional sixteen minutes to secure passage of a significant revamping of the House Committee on Ethics.[39]

Then, during the 110th Congress, the lobbying and ethics reform legislation passed by the House and the Senate almost perished because Sen. Jim DeMint (R-SC) placed a "hold" on the appointment of Senate conferees. But, in a rare parliamentary procedure, Senate Majority Leader Harry Reid (D-NV) and House Speaker Nancy Pelosi (D-CA) narrowly averted Senator DeMint's effort to defeat the legislation by rewriting the House and Senate versions of the bill: if the Senate and the House could pass identical bills, there was no need for conference proceedings.

Rewriting of the legislation—which occurred outside of any public process—caused considerable anxiety for all parties involved. Leader Reid and Speaker Pelosi held the rewriting negotiations as closed sessions, including to outside advocates of the reform legislation. Organizations supporting the reform legislation expressed concern that the legislation might be rewritten in a way that damaged its effectiveness during this process. Congressional Republicans similarly voiced concern that whatever new legislation would emerge might ignore Republican proposals, such as earmark reform. However, to the surprise of all, the new lobbying and ethics reform package that leadership unveiled contained nearly all the sweeping reforms of the original package, including much of Sen. DeMint's earmark disclosure provision.

The new lobbying and ethics reform bills produced by Leader Reid and Speaker Pelosi were identical and were resubmitted to their respective chambers. Unwilling to vote no on ethics reforms, the House overwhelmingly approved the legislation by a vote of 411 to eight. The Senate followed suit two days later by a vote of eighty-three to fourteen. Since the bills were identical, no conference proceedings were necessary, and Senator DeMint's efforts to defeat the legislation fell

---

37. House Rule XXIII (110th Cong.); Senate Rule XLIV (110th Cong.).

38. U.S. House of Representatives Committee on Rules, *Survey of Activities of the House Committee on Rules for the 112th Congress* (Jan. 3. 2013), *available at* http://www.gpo.gov/fdsys/pkg/CRPT-112hrpt751/pdf/CRPT-112hrpt751.pdf.

39. Susan Crabtree, *Still Seething Over Prolonged Ethics Vote, Boehner Mulls Stonewalling Appointments*, The Hill, Mar. 12, 2008, *available at* https://thehill.com/homenews/news/14536-still-seething-over-prolonged-ethics-vote-boehner-mulls-stonewalling-appointments.

short. Despite a chorus of Republican congressional objections that they had been locked out of participation in drafting the final legislation, President George Bush signed HLOGA into law on September 14, 2007.[40]

All of this history suggests that congressional leaders and committee chairmen will continue to be essential players in promoting or defeating legislation. Congressional leaders and chairmen determine which bills move on the agenda and which do not. Moreover, committee chairmen often have disproportionate control over the language of bills that flow through their committees, making it a priority among lobbyists to get the "chairman's mark" (the committee chairman's version of a bill), knowing this version will be closer to the final version than the original bill. Congressional leaders also determine the rules of debate and provide the whip for mustering votes. Conference proceedings provide leadership another avenue to significantly affect legislation.[41] The lobbying and ethics reform bills approved by the House and Senate in the 109th Congress, for example, perished in conference simply because former Speaker Dennis Hastert (R-IL) declined to appoint House conferees. Thus effective lobbyists must, in attempting to move or quash significant legislation, focus their attention on influencing the leadership.

2-5 The Role of Lobbyists in the Drafting Process

While all bills must be sponsored by a member of Congress, the original draft of the legislation may be written by anyone (with or without expertise in the subject). Lobbyists are often accused of drafting legislation on behalf of special interests, and that practice does occur. The text of the original bill heavily influences the tone and scope of the legislative debate that follows. Therefore, an extremely effective position for any advocate of an issue is to start with drafting the text of the proposed legislation.

In some cases, lawmakers simply sponsor bills or amendments exactly as written by lobbyists. One such case involved a special tort liability exemption for the Eli Lilly pharmaceutical company from several pending lawsuits, when an amendment was anonymously inserted into a 475-page homeland security bill. The amendment was not publicly discovered until after passage of the bill, prompting the website TomPaine.com to offer a $10,000 reward for the identity of

---

40. Wary that President Bush might use a pocket veto to kill an overhaul of ethics and lobbying rules, congressional leaders delayed sending the measure to the White House until after the August recess. Normally, bills not signed by the president within ten days of their presentment become law by default. However, if Congress adjourns or goes into recess during that ten-day period, bills not signed by the president may not become law since, if the president objects to them, he cannot "return" them to the originating house as the Constitution requires. This is known as a pocket veto. The legal permissibility of the pocket veto remains in dispute in the courts. *See* Louis Fisher, *The Pocket Veto: Its Current Status*, CRS REPORT FOR CONGRESS, Mar. 30, 2001, *available at* http://www.senate.gov/reference/resources/pdf/RL30909.pdf.

41. Conference proceedings used to be the most likely venue for "air dropping" earmarks into appropriations and spending bills. Conferees had traditionally written allocations for personal spending projects in conference reports, outside the scrutiny of committee hearings and other public deliberations. The 2007 lobbying and ethics legislation and rules, however, required all earmarks to be identified with their sponsors and published. See Section 2-3.

the lawmaker or lobbyist responsible for the Eli Lilly exemption. Though outgoing Rep. Dick Armey (R-TX) claimed responsibility on the basis that he had committee jurisdiction over the final legislation, no legislator or lobbyist claimed specific credit for writing the provision.[42] The Eli Lilly exemption was subsequently repealed in follow-up legislation.

Cases like this one are the exception rather than the rule. Far more frequently, lobbyists will suggest legislative text for original bills and amendments, which is then subject to extensive scrutiny and rewriting by congressional staff, other concerned interest groups with the ear of the member, and, finally, by the Office of Legislative Counsel. Nevertheless, the drafting stage is one of the most critical steps by which a lobbyist can influence legislation. Providing a lawmaker with suggested text helps frame the legislative debate. It also provides the lobbyist with the opportunity to ensure that various fine points get included in the debate that might otherwise be overlooked.

In drafting particularly sweeping or sensitive legislation, a lawmaker will often convene meetings of lobbyists and representatives of several organizations to negotiate a consensus on bill language before it is introduced. A prominent, but eventually unsuccessful, example of this drafting strategy involved the "grassroots lobbying disclosure" provision of S. 1 as originally introduced in the 110th Congress; S. 1, with amendments, was ultimately enacted as the HLOGA.

Disclosure of grassroots lobbying activity—generally defined as advertising campaigns intended to encourage public participation for or against pending legislation—was deleted in 1995 from the LDA because of intense opposition from the nonprofit community.[43] When Congress decided to revisit this issue in the 109th and 110th Congresses, the Senate Democratic Policy Committee hosted a series of meetings with the nonprofit community, as well as with advocates of a grassroots disclosure provision. The two sides came to an amicable agreement, drafting legislative text that required disclosure of the financial interests behind grassroots lobbying campaigns and also protected the privacy rights of those pursuing issue advocacy. The key compromise narrowed the application of the disclosure provision to corporations and large organizations that spent substantial sums on direct mail and television and radio campaigns designed to encourage the general public (rather than a group's members) to contact government officials, urging support of, or opposition to, specific legislation.

Included as section 220 of S. 1 in the 110th Congress, this provision illustrated a "best practices" in legislative drafting. A policy proposal that may have been viewed as overreaching was scaled back, but it still achieved its primary objective while accommodating concerns of other lobbying organizations. In the end,

---

42. In December 2002, TomPaine.com offered a reward for the identity of the person responsible for the Eli Lilly exemption, whom TomPaine.com referred to as the "Eli Lilly bandit." A spokesman for Eli Lilly claimed the company knew nothing about the exemption. Alex Chadwick, *Web Site Seeks ID for "Lilly Bandit,"* NPR Morning Edition (NPR radio broadcast Dec. 19, 2002), *available at* http://www.npr.org/templates/story/story.php?storyId=884660.

43. Opposition to a grassroots lobbying disclosure provision in 1995 was so intense that final approval of the landmark Lobbying Disclosure Act of 1995 was held up until the grassroots lobbying provision was removed from the bill. After the provision was deleted, the LDA was then approved in both chambers of Congress.

however, even this grassroots lobbying disclosure provision failed to survive an opposition campaign that itself included grassroots lobbying.[44]

The fine points in legislative text can make all the difference for the actual effect of the legislation. For example, two provisions in the HLOGA that govern disclosure of future employment negotiations by members of the House and Senate—section 301 governing representatives and section 532 governing senators—establish very different disclosure requirements because of differences in wording that may have been overlooked during the drafting process.

The original intent of both provisions was to require members to publicly disclose when and with whom they were negotiating future private sector job offers. Instead, section 301 requires that members notify the House Ethics Committee, rather than the Clerk of the House, of job negotiations within three days after commencement of such negotiations.[45] Section 532 requires senators to notify the Secretary of the Senate, rather than the Senate Ethics Committee, of employment negotiations within three days after commencement of negotiations.[46] The congressional ethics committees are offices that are not required to conduct most of their business through an open public process. The House Clerk and Senate Secretary are considered public disclosure offices. So when section 301 mandated notification to the House Ethics Committee, the information the Ethics Committee received would not then become public. During the 110th Congress, several members planned their departures from the House and negotiated private employment without any of their job negotiations becoming public information until after private employment was accepted. For example, the public became aware that Rep. Al Wynn (D-MD) was negotiating private sector employment only after he had accepted a job with a Capitol Hill lobbying firm and announced his early resignation from Congress. On the other hand, since section 532 requires senators to notify the Secretary of the Senate of future employment negotiations, this means that any such notice would be immediately disclosed to the public.

Interpretation of legislative text is another issue that must be considered in drafting legislation. For instance, implementation of the same private sector employment disclosure provisions relies on how the phrase "commencement of negotiations" is interpreted.[47] To date, neither the House nor Senate Ethics Committee has provided a fulsome definition of when job negotiations commence. In its guidance, the Senate Ethics Committee simply states: "Negotiation in this context is the discussion of terms and conditions of employment after an offer has been made and the Member or Senate staffer is considering accepting."[48] On the other hand, the OGE, which interprets 18 U.S.C. § 208 for executive branch personnel, has followed the existing judicial precedent and issued clear guidance as

---

44. Opposition to the grassroots lobbying disclosure provision of S.1 was spearheaded by the Free Speech Coalition, Inc., consisting of James Bopp (James Madison Center), Paul Weyrich (Free Congress Foundation), Richard Viguerie (CONSERVATIVEHQ.COM), Rev. Louis Sheldon (Traditional Values Coalition), Edward Nelson (U.S. Border Patrol), and others.

45. Pub. L. No. 110–81, § 301, 121 Stat. 735, 751 (2007).

46. *Id.* § 532, 121 Stat. 735, 765 (2007).

47. For further discussion of these provisions, see Chapters 27 and 28.

48. Senate Select Comm. on Ethics, *Senior Staff: Employment Negotiations and Arrangements* (Feb. 4, 2008), http://ethics.senate.gov/downloads/pdffiles/senior%20staff_employment%20negotiations. pdf.

to when job negotiations commence. According to ethics rules promulgated by the OGE, an executive branch official has begun seeking private sector employment when that official becomes involved in a two-way communication with a prospective employer wherein both parties express an active interest in employment.[49]

The House Ethics Committee has signaled its intent to defer to this interpretation regarding the requirement for filing confidential notices of future employment with the ethics committee.[50] However, the House Ethics Committee does not require public notices of future employment negotiations by members unless the members themselves determine there is a potential conflict of interest that would make recusal from official actions appropriate.[51] As a result, despite the retirement or reelection defeat of 236 members of the House of Representatives between 2008 and 2014, only nine public disclosures of employment negotiations were filed during that time by House members.[52]

In short, in drafting legislation, lobbyists must be particularly attuned to the fine points of legislative text to ensure that the intent of the legislation is expressed in the language and to minimize unfavorable interpretations of the text that run counter to the intent.

A final note on the drafting process: bills are always submitted by a lawmaker to the office of Legislative Counsel for final drafting and formatting before being dropped in the hopper. Lobbyists should carefully review the final legislative text that comes from the Legislative Counsel. Though this office is usually precise in its drafting, it is possible that even the Legislative Counsel could overlook or misunderstand finer points in the legislative text.

2-6 Opportunities and Pitfalls of Selected Procedural Maneuvers

After legislation is drafted and introduced, most lobbying activity focuses on finding cosponsors and building support for the measure from members and congressional staff, especially among the committees of jurisdiction and congressional leadership. The normal legislative process for the lobbyist at this point may involve influencing the legislation by testifying at congressional hearings, meeting with members and staff to flag concerns and explain issues, providing technical assistance while the legislation is modified in committee markup, and encouraging constructive amendments during committee and floor considerations of the bill.

However, the structure and workings of Congress provide other opportunities (and pitfalls) for influencing legislation through various procedural maneuvers.

When a lobbyist seeks to affect a very narrow aspect of public policy, especially if the policy objective may not supported by a majority of members, encouraging a member to attach a discreet "rider" to a popular bill can sometimes produce the desired outcome. A rider is an additional provision affixed to a bill that has only

---

49. 5 C.F.R. § 2635.603(b) (2015).

50. COMMITTEE ON STANDARDS OF OFFICIAL CONDUCT, U.S. HOUSE OF REPRESENTATIVES, HOUSE ETHICS MANUAL (2008) (hereinafter HOUSE ETHICS MANUAL), at 209.

51. HOUSE ETHICS MANUAL, 211.

52. These data were the results of an analysis undertaken by Craig Holman of the publicly available records held at the Legislative Resource Center of the Office of the Clerk of the U.S. House of Representatives on October 5, 2015.

peripheral, if any, relation to the subject matter of the bill itself. Riders are usually employed as a tactic to pass what may be seen as a controversial provision that would not likely be approved as a stand-alone bill but can slip by, often unnoticed, if affixed to a bill that has wider support. On the other hand, members may also attach a rider that is seen as outrageous or extremely unpopular as a tool to kill the underlying legislation.

The rider tactic, for example, was once used in an attempt to save a New Jersey state law—known as a "pay-to-play" law—prohibiting campaign contributions from potential government contractors.[53] Following adoption of the controversial law for state contractors in New Jersey, the Federal Highway Administration (FHWA) decided to intervene, even though similar pay-to-play laws were on the books in other states. The Division Administrator of FHWA decided to withhold federal highway transportation funds for New Jersey under the theory that the state's pay-to-play law stifled federal contract competition rules.

The 109th Congress was seen as unlikely to consider and pass stand-alone legislation overruling FHWA's action, so advocates of New Jersey's pay-to-play law attempted to insert a rider into the massive federal highway transportation bill. The one-sentence rider simply recognized the right of states to impose pay-to-play restrictions on government contractors. Drawing little congressional or public attention, the rider passed largely unnoticed through the House and was then added to the Senate version of the bill. While the transportation bill was pending Senate approval, the U.S. Chamber of Commerce caught wind of the rider and successfully launched a concerted lobbying effort to strike it from the legislation.[54]

Much of the legislative business of Congress, particularly in the Senate, depends on filibuster and full debate to bring a bill to a final floor vote. In the Senate when unanimous consent is not forthcoming, perhaps the most critical vote determining the fortune of a bill is the cloture vote. (In the House, the counterpart is the suspension of rules.) Legislation on the Senate floor can be amended or talked to death in a filibuster, unless floor consideration is called to a halt by a cloture vote of sixty or more senators.

At times when a highly charged, partisan atmosphere exists in Congress, most significant legislation faces a filibuster threat on the Senate floor. From 2001 through 2012, there have been 592 cloture votes.[55] The trend for more cloture votes is continuing. The subsequent 113th Congress alone held 218 votes on cloture.[56] For comparison, in the decade after cloture was first used in 1917, the Senate held fewer than ten cloture votes.

Cloture votes are the subject of intense lobbying activity, since it is far harder to win a cloture vote than to win a vote on the bill under consideration. (Numerically, only a majority is needed to win a vote on the bill, but a sixty-vote majority

---

53. See Chapter 25 of this manual for a discussion on pay-to-play laws generally.

54. Had the rider remained under the congressional radar, it would have become law during a Congress that was otherwise hostile to campaign finance reforms. New Jersey modified its pay-to-play law to exempt highway construction contracts. The amended law was sufficient to appease the Federal Highway Administration, and it resumed sending New Jersey its $160 million in federal highway construction funds.

55. United States Senate, Secretary of the Senate, *Senate Action on Cloture Votes by Year*, http://www.senate.gov/pagelayout/reference/cloture_motions/clotureCounts.htm.

56. *Id.*

is required to end a filibuster.) If the cloture vote is not won, the bill often perishes. A cloture vote is difficult to win, not only because it requires a supermajority but also because a cloture vote is not technically a vote for or against the bill under consideration. Thus a senator who may not want to go on the public record against a popular measure will find it much easier to justify (from a public relations standpoint) a vote against the cloture motion. This vote still has the indirect effect of killing the bill, but without the bad publicity that might accompany actually voting against the bill itself.

As a result, a lobbying campaign always focuses on promoting or defeating the cloture vote as part of legislative strategy. Any significant or controversial measure has to muster sixty votes in the Senate, so when it comes to floor consideration of a bill, lobbyists focus their attention on finding those sixty votes, or ensuring they are not forthcoming.

2-7 The Administrative Rulemaking Process

2-7.1 Introduction

The specific requirements of most laws are not all, or even mostly, produced by Congress. While Congress enacts statutes, those statutes are commonly not self-implementing. Rather, statutes typically establish a basic legal framework and then authorize federal agencies to implement that framework. A statute may specifically instruct the administering agency to issue rules fleshing out a particular statutory mandate. In other cases, a statute may simply give the agency "housekeeping" authority to issue rules as necessary to accomplish its functions under that law. In any case, an agency also has some ability to issue rules or decisions interpreting a statute, even in the absence of any express authorization to do so.

The work lobbyists do in front of Congress often attracts the most attention from the press and the public. But lobbyists must often work directly with agencies to shape the rules that interpret the laws. Administrative rules often help the law work more efficiently. They facilitate adaptation to new technological developments, fill in gaps that court decisions expose, and respond to needs for clarity that emerge as a law is implemented.

The procedural rules for what agencies can do, and how, are sometimes spelled out in the authorizing legislation referred to above. More commonly, though, the authorizing law does not specify any procedure. To the extent this is the case, the default rules for agency behavior are set out in the Administrative Procedure Act (APA), a 1946 enactment that has been amended very infrequently. To a surprising degree, the statute does not actually spell out much of what the process requires; rather, the latter is a gloss produced by the accumulation of decades of court decisions interpreting the APA.

Under the APA, all agency action falls into two bins: adjudication and rulemaking.[57] As the word suggests, adjudication is where the agency functions somewhat like a judge: the proceeding generally involves the agency acting "versus" or "in the matter of" one or more named parties, and the resulting final agency action is legally binding, but only on that party or parties. Enforcement actions are

---

57. *See* 5 U.S.C. § 551(5) and (7).

the paradigmatic examples of agency adjudication. This section does not discuss adjudicatory processes any further, however, since its main focus is rulemaking, discussed immediately below.

Because the APA is basically about procedural due process, it establishes a presumption that adjudications and rules are reviewable in court.[58] Again, the authorizing statute can provide additional or different detail on the topic, such as which courts have jurisdiction. Also again, courts have made up much of the law that is attributed to the APA. The topic of judicial review is discussed after rulemaking.

2-7.2 Rulemaking

2-7.2.1 *Types of Rules*

Unlike an adjudication, a rule by definition applies to everyone who falls within its scope. The APA's definition of "rule" sweeps more broadly than common parlance does, and it encompasses four sorts of general agency pronouncements:[59]

1. Legislative rules, or regulations. These kinds of rules are issued pursuant to a grant of rulemaking power given to an agency by a statute, and they have the force and effect of law. That is, they bind both the issuing agency and the persons to whom they apply. They are required to be proposed in the *Federal Register* for public comment before they can go final, unless an exception applies. Once they are finalized, these rules are then codified in the Code of Federal Regulations (or CFR). Legislative rules will be the principal focus of this section.

2. Interpretive rules. These differ from legislative rules in that they purport merely to explain what a law or existing rule means, rather than to create new law based on a statutory authorization. Interpretive rules do not have independent binding effect. They do not require notice and comment before being issued.

3. Statements of policy. Often referred to as "guidance documents," these are nonbinding statements of an agency's current intentions or views. They also do not require prior public notice and comment. Under Office of Management and Budget (OMB) policy, they are supposed to be phrased in terms of "may," rather than "shall."[60] A common problem in administrative law is whether a given policy statement is really a de facto rule, either on its face or as applied, and should have undergone notice and comment before being issued.

4. Procedural rules. These determine agency organization, procedure or practice, and are only binding on the agency. They also do not require notice and comment.

Only legislative rules, therefore, must be noticed for public comment before they can go final. That process is discussed next.

---

58. *Id.* § 702.
59. *Id.* § 553(b)(3)(B).
60. 72 Fed. Reg. 3432 (Jan. 25, 2007), § II.2.h.

2-7.2.2 *Notice and Comment Rulemaking*

Notice and comment rulemaking was an invention of the APA. It was intended to bring a greater degree of fairness and openness to the process by which administrative agencies sought to bind classes of people, and the process burgeoned with the New Deal. The legal expert Kenneth Culp Davis called notice and comment rulemaking "one of the greatest inventions of modern government,"[61] and it has come to define the way that federal agencies interact with organized sectors of the U.S. economy. It is also a prime example of where courts have inferred requirements that are not nominally part of the APA.

The APA requires an agency seeking to issue a legislative rule to publish in the *Federal Register* a notice of proposed rulemaking (NPRM) containing:

(1) a statement of the time, place, and nature of public rule making proceedings;
(2) reference to the legal authority under which the rule is proposed; and
(3) "either the terms or substance of the proposed rule or a description of the subjects and issues involved."[62]

While the APA thus does not require an NPRM to include the CFR text that the agency proposes to issue, virtually all agencies now do this. The bulk of an NPRM, however, consists of a fairly detailed "preamble" that explains why the agency intends to take the proposed action. These preambles commonly seek comments on specific questions or issues. Neither the APA nor the related Federal Register Act specifies a minimum comment period. Most are 45 to 60 days, but 30- to 90-day comment periods are also common.

Neither statute says anything about a "docket," but agency practice and relevant court decisions have come to make a docket mandatory. In particular, the *Portland Cement* decision and its progeny require an agency to make publicly available any information on which it ultimately relies, so that interested persons can comment on it.[63] As a result, agencies establish a docket at the time a rule is proposed, and all comments or other material submitted by members of the public during (or after) the comment period are customarily placed there. Agencies also place (or should place) all the significant analytical documents underlying the rule (often referred to as "background documents" or "technical support documents") in the docket. While agencies are not prohibited from meeting with interested persons during or after a comment period, they are well advised to document the fact and subject matter of those conversations in the docket as well.

Rulemaking dockets historically were physical files, usually in unpleasantly hot basement rooms. Today, however, all electronically available elements of these dockets are available at the www.regulations.gov website.

---

61. Kenneth Culp Davis, Administrative Law Treatise § 6.15, at 283 (Supp. 1970).
62. 5 U.S.C. § 553(b)(3) (2015).
63. Portland Cement Ass'n v. Ruckleshaus, 486 F.2d 375, 393–94 (D.C. Cir. 1973).

Agencies do not have to propose a legislative rule if they have "good cause" not to do so; that is, because[64]

- The rule is so noncontroversial, technical or transient in effect that notice and comment are "unnecessary";
- A congressional deadline or other exigency makes it "impracticable" for the agency to turn around an NPRM; or
- A proposed rule would be "contrary to the public interest," for example, where advance notice to persons engaged in a bad practice would give them an opportunity to try to circumvent the rule.

These exceptions are frequently litigated.

2-7.2.3 Role of OMB

The Office of Management and Budget, located within the Executive Office of the President, has had some involvement with agency rulemakings since the 1970s. The process has been formalized by executive order since the Reagan administration and is currently governed by Exec. Order No. 12866, issued early in the Clinton administration.[65] Two features of OMB's role are most significant:

1. Agencies are required to prepare cost-benefit analyses of "economically significant" rules; that is, those that are likely to impose annual costs on the economy of $100 million. A draft analysis must accompany a proposed rule.[66]
2. OMB gets to review all proposed and final "significant rules" (mainly economically significant rules plus those raising "novel legal or policy issues" or generating significant interest from other agencies). OMB gets ninety to 120 days for this review,[67] but in practice has often held rules for longer periods of time.

Exec. Order No. 12866 only applies to cabinet departments and single-head agencies; independent regulatory boards and commissions are exempt.

Because they are purely a matter of how the executive branch will govern itself, Executive orders like Exec. Order No. 12866 do not create rights that private entities can enforce. OMB will meet with interested persons while it is reviewing a rule, however, and such meetings can often be a useful means of drawing OMB's attention to effects of a rule that it might otherwise not have fully appreciated.

2-7.2.4 The Final Rule

Notice of a final rule is published in the *Federal Register*. These notices contain both the CFR text of the rule and a preamble that explains the changes from the proposal and the reasons for them. The notice typically also responds to comments filed on

---

64. *See generally* 5 U.S.C. §§ 551(4), 553(b)(3)(B).
65. Exec. Order No. 12866, 58 F.R. 51735 (Sept. 30, 1993).
66. *Id.* § 6(a)(3)(C).
67. *Id.* §§ 6(a)(3)(B), 6(b).

the NPRM, although for major rulemakings many of the responses are contained in a "response to comments" document that is placed in the docket. The APA requires a thirty-day period from the date of publication before the rule can become effective, unless an exception applies.[68]

2-7.3 Judicial Review

As with the process for making rules, the APA also supplies the process (and standards) for challenging rules, unless the authorizing statute prescribes a different process or prohibits review outright. Because rules by definition apply to classes of individuals or entities, and many are controversial, lawsuits are common—and in some fields, more the rule than the exception. Indeed, many rulemakings are themselves the outgrowth of lawsuits challenging prior rules, and the schedule and scope of the rulemaking may have been specified in a consent decree or settlement agreement involving the earlier rule.

Under the APA, a challenge to rule must be brought in a federal district court.[69] This allows for a fair amount of forum shopping and potential divergence in judicial opinions, as there are ninety-four federal judicial districts. Many statutes, particularly in the environmental area, are very specific about where challenges can be brought. Some of these challenges require review to be in the courts of appeals and often restrict review to the D.C. Circuit, the federal court with the most expertise (and precedent) in administrative law.

The APA does not contain a statute of limitations, and so a challenge to a rule would be subject at the outside to the general six-year statute of limitations applicable to suits against the United States,[70] subject to potential arguments for a shorter deadline based on the doctrine of laches. Again, an authorizing statute may set a shorter deadline, as little as sixty days. These deadlines are often construed to be jurisdictional; miss one and you may have waived your right to challenge the rule.[71] Absent such a deadline—

- It is permissible to wait until a rule is enforced against you to challenge it.
- It is also permissible to challenge a rule before it is enforced against you if your challenge is "fit for judicial resolution" and not allowing the challenge would create a hardship.[72]

Most agency rules are defended by the Justice Department, which can be expected to throw up a host of objections asserting lack of standing or ripeness. These issues, particularly the former, are highly complex and beyond the scope of this chapter—but vital to any would-be challenger.

Review of rules is based on the "administrative record," a legal construct that typically is assembled from docket materials by the agency after a challenge is filed. Most important, however, the concept of record review means that opportunities for discovery are severely limited in rulemaking challenges. Motions to

---

68. 5 U.S.C. § 553(d) (2015).
69. 5 U.S.C.. § 703, 28 U.S.C. § 1331 (2015).
70. 28 U.S.C. § 2401(a) (2015).
71. *See, e.g.*, Hallstrom v. Tillamook County, 493 U.S. 1037 (1989).
72. *See* Abbott Laboratories v. Gardner, 387 U.S. 136, 153 (1967).

supplement the record (e.g., to include a document that assertedly was before the agency during the rulemaking but was excluded from the record) are more common.

Again due to the range of persons or entities potentially affected by rules, challenges to many rules become highly complex, involving dozens of trade associations or other entities seeking to challenge the rule or intervene in support of it. (Sometimes a litigant may find itself on both sides of a lawsuit, challenging aspects of a rule that it dislikes but intervening to defend aspects that it likes against challenges by others.)

The APA establishes several standards of review for rules. Some are fairly simple, such as:

- Is the rule constitutional; does it violate regulated entities' constitutional rights?[73]
- Was the rule promulgated "without observance of procedure required by law"?[74] For example:
  - Did the agency have "good cause" to skip proposing a rule? Is the "policy statement" being challenged really a legislative rule?
  - A final rule can differ from what the agency proposed without triggering another round of notice and comment, so long as the final rule is a "logical outgrowth" of the proposal.[75]

Several other standards are more complex:

- Was the rule in fact authorized by the statute?[76] Some statutes authorize agencies to issue rules on some subjects but not others. For example, the Clean Air Act authorizes—indeed, requires—the Environmental Protection Agency (EPA) to issue standards for emissions of hazardous air pollutants, but it does not authorize EPA to establish "affirmative defenses" to violations of those rules caused by equipment malfunctions.[77]
- Did the agency follow the statute?[78] Or did the agency stretch the words beyond Congress's intent?

These questions of statutory interpretation are governed by the *Chevron* standard, which asks:

- First, whether Congress has spoken clearly to the question. If it has, then the agency either wins or loses. Courts assess this issue essentially de novo.
- Second, if the statute is ambiguous, was the agency's interpretation a reasonable one? It need not be the most reasonable or the one the court may have formulated if left to its own devices. This step embodies the interpre-

---

73. 5 U.S.C. § 706(2)(B) (2015).
74. *Id.* § 706(2)(D).
75. *See* Long Island Care at Home, Ltd. v. Coke, 551 U.S. 158, 174 (2007).
76. 5 U.S.C. § 706(2)(C).
77. NRDC v. EPA, 749 F.3d 1055 (D.C. Cir. April 18, 2014).
78. 5 U.S.C. § 706(2)(A) (2015) ("otherwise not in accordance with law").

tive deference that federal courts give to agencies charged by Congress with implementing statutes through binding action.[79]
- Third, was the rule otherwise arbitrary and capricious?[80] This standard encompasses several related questions, which ask whether the agency:
  — Provided an adequate factual basis for the rule;
  — Provided a rational explanation for how it got from those facts to its conclusion;
  — Responded rationally to significant comments; or
  — Failed to consider a statutorily relevant factor, or considered a statutorily impermissible factor.[81]

If an agency loses on one of these grounds, the question then becomes what remedy is appropriate. If the rule is simply not legally sustainable, a court must vacate it. More often, the failing is something that could be rectified by further rulemaking, and so the court will remand the rule to the agency. Where a court is concerned about risks that might be presented while the rule is on remand, however, the court may not vacate it and instead leave it in effect, sometimes for years—a source of understandable consternation among the "victorious" litigants.

---

79. Chevron USA Inc. v. NRDC, 467 U.S. 837 (1984). Interpretive rules and statements of policy (to the extent they are reviewable) receive a lesser degree of deference, generally referred to as *Skidmore* deference, and defined as its "power to persuade." *See* Christensen v. Harris County, 529 U.S. 576, 587 (2000) (quoting Skidmore v. Swift & Co., 323 U.S. 134 (1944)).

80. 5 U.S.C. § 706(2)(A) (2015).

81. *See generally* JEFFREY S. LUBBERS, A GUIDE TO FEDERAL AGENCY RULEMAKING 425–45 (5th ed. 2012).

CHAPTER 3

Brief History of Federal Lobbying Regulation

BY THOMAS M. SUSMAN*

3-1 Introduction and Background on Federal Regulation of Lobbying

Few problems are as intractable in our representative democracy as the regulation of "lobbying," that is, the efforts of groups and individuals to secure the enactment or defeat of legislation by their elected representatives. The lobbying problem is difficult because it brings into focus the tension between two images of government, both of which are important to our democracy.

On the one hand, we have traditionally believed that our elected representatives should be responsive to the desires of their constituents; thus our system of politics assumes a vigorous contest among competing interests for the attention, and the votes, of legislators. This model of government suggests that individuals and groups should be permitted—in fact, encouraged—to make their views known to their representatives. This is reflected in the First Amendment's guarantee that no law shall abridge the people's right to petition the government for redress of grievances.[1] One of the goals of the right to petition is to encourage and foster a

---

*William N. Eskridge, Jr. wrote the first two sections of this chapter in earlier editions of this manual.

1. "Congress shall make no law . . . abridging the freedom of speech, or of the press; or the right of the people peaceably to assemble, and to petition the Government for a redress of grievances." U.S. Const. amend. I.

"pressure" system of politics, in which interest groups are expected to influence representatives through a wide array of techniques, with very few out of bounds, in a continuing game of struggle and domination.

At the same time, few Americans would endorse an unrestrained pressure system, and a variety of lobbying techniques are widely considered deplorable, or at least unethical. To take a dramatic example, bribery is a form of lobbying that not only is unprotected by the right to petition, but is a criminal offense.[2] More generally, the public often discerns lobbyists as unsavory figures, "influence peddlers" who secure for their clients an unfair advantage in the deliberations of government. (The series of scandals commonly associated with lobbyist Jack Abramoff that came to light in 2005–2006[3] did nothing but reinforce this image in the popular mind.) The impulse to safeguard the integrity of government decision making is recurrently fueled by allegations (well founded or otherwise) that lobbyists have made secret deals with legislators to benefit special interests at the expense of the general welfare, or that intense pressures (in the form of bribes, threats, or coercion) have been brought to bear upon legislators, or that some groups have been well represented in the lobbying process while others have been substantially or completely unrepresented.

Lobbying Congress and the executive branch, by fair means or foul, has been an important and accepted part of national politics since the foundation of the Republic. Complaints about the excessive influence of lobbyists have been equally persistent. As early as 1852, the House of Representatives passed a lobbying-regulation statute prohibiting a newspaperman "who shall be employed as an agent to prosecute any claim pending before Congress" from being on the floor of the House.[4] In 1854, the House adopted a resolution establishing a select committee to examine "whether money has been offered to members, or other illegal or improper means used, either directly or indirectly, to secure the passage or defeat of any bill before Congress."[5]

At the state level, some legislatures concluded that lobbying as commonly understood during the 19th century should simply be banned; the Constitution of Georgia made lobbying a crime, and efforts were made by courts and legislatures to distinguish between "good" lobbying, which involved presentation of facts and appeal to reason, and "bad" lobbying, involving efforts to wield personal influence.[6]

---

2. *See, e.g.*, 18 U.S.C. § 201(b) (2015) (deeming it a federal crime to give or receive a bribe); *Id.* § 201(c) (deeming it a federal crime to give or receive an unlawful gratuity). *See generally* WILLIAM N. ESKRIDGE, PHILIP P. FRICKEY, & ELIZABETH GARRETT, CASES AND MATERIALS ON LEGISLATION: STATUTES & THE CREATION OF PUBLIC POLICY 301-10 (4th ed. 2007); Daniel H. Lowenstein, *Political Bribery & the Intermediate Theory of Politics*, 32 UCLA L. REV. 784 (1985). *See also* Chapter 22.

3. *See generally, e.g.*, PETER H. STONE, CASINO JACK AND THE UNITED STATES OF MONEY: SUPERLOBBYIST JACK ABRAMOFF AND THE BUYING OF WASHINGTON (2006).

4. CONG. GLOBE, 32d Cong., 2d Sess. 52 (1852). The prohibition was expanded in 1867 to exclude from the House floor former members of Congress who were interested in any claim before Congress. On the history of federal lobbying regulation, *see* CONG. RESEARCH SERVICE, REPORT TO SUBCOMM. ON INTERGOVERNMENTAL RELATIONS, SENATE COMM. ON GOVERNMENTAL AFFAIRS, 99th CONG., CONGRESS AND PRESSURE GROUPS: LOBBYING IN A MODERN DEMOCRACY 8–10, 34–39 (1986).

5. H.R. REP. No. 33-353, at 1 (1854).

6. Richard Briffault, *The Anxiety of Influence: The Evolving Regulation of Lobbying*, 13 ELECTION L.J. 160, 166–170 (2014).

The history of lobbying regulation in the United States thus reflects the dynamic effort to accommodate both norms—to give the citizenry a voice in the system by which they are governed and to regulate or prevent the worst abuses of lobbying. On the national level, this effort was a notable failure—at least until 1995.

3-2 Federal Regulation of Lobbying Act (1946)

After decades of occasionally intense but frustrating effort, Congress enacted comprehensive federal lobbying regulation almost by accident in 1946. The Federal Regulation of Lobbying Act[7] (Lobbying Act) addressed only lobbying of Congress and not lobbying of the executive branch. The critical portions of the Lobbying Act specified who had to register and the conditions under which a registrant's receipts and expenditures for lobbying had to be reported.[8] Individuals and groups had to register if they "engage[d] [themselves] for pay or for any consideration for the purpose of attempting to influence the passage or defeat of any legislation. . . . "[9] A registration statement had to specify the person by whom the lobbyist was employed, the interest the lobbyist represented, compensation, and expenses.[10] Each registered lobbyist had to make quarterly reports of all money received and expended for lobbying activities and had to specify in the reports the proposed legislation that the lobbyist was paid to support or oppose.[11] More generally, the sum of all contributions and expenditures whose purpose was the passage or defeat of any legislation or whose purpose was to influence the passage or defeat of any legislation had to be reported.[12]

The statute required more than a general sense of how much money was being spent and for what purposes. Registrants had to disclose names and addresses of contributors to the lobbyists making contributions aggregating $500 or more.[13] They also had to report names and addresses of persons to whom they made expenditures aggregating $10 or more.[14] The Lobbying Act contained a number of exceptions: individuals who merely appeared before congressional committees,

---

7. 2 U.S.C. §§ 261–270 (1994) (repealed 1995). This law was the focus of the first edition of this manual: THE LOBBYING MANUAL: A COMPLIANCE GUIDE FOR LAWYERS AND LOBBYISTS pt. I (Thomas M. Susman ed., 1993).

8. Section 305 of the Lobbying Act directed persons covered by certain provisions of section 307 to file statements with the Clerk of the House; section 307 specified that the Lobbying Act applied to any person who received anything of value principally for the purpose of influencing the passage or defeat of legislation in Congress; and section 308 further delineated who had to register under the Lobbying Act (that is, any person who engaged herself for any consideration for the purpose of influencing the passage or defeat of legislation by Congress), what she had to do in registering, and certain activities that were not covered by the act. The scope of the Lobbying Act's applicability was rendered somewhat unclear by the ambiguous and arguably contradictory description in these sections of the persons to whom the Lobbying Act applied.

9. Federal Regulation of Lobbying Act, ch. 753, § 308(a), 60 Stat. 839, 841–42 (1946).

10. *Id.*

11. *Id.*

12. *Id.* §§ 305, 307, 60 Stat. 840–41.

13. *Id.* § 305(a)(1), 60 Stat. 840.

14. *Id.* § 305(a)(4), 60 Stat. 841.

public officials acting in their official capacity, and newspapers (as long as the newspaper did not engage in any other influencing of legislation outside of its pages). Those required to register had to file reports every quarter and keep receipts for two years.[15]

3-2.1 The Lobbying Act and Early Experience Under It

The passage of comprehensive lobbying regulation was a significant victory for reformers. Unfortunately, the birth of the statute was attended by a number of complications. The time pressure during the drafting stage, the use of a previous compromise, and the inherent problems of regulating political speech combined to result in the enactment of a weak statute. While all three factors caused problems, the inherent difficulty of regulating political speech was doubtless responsible for many of the Lobbying Act's flaws.

The most serious practical problem with the 1946 Lobbying Act was the lack of a workable enforcement mechanism. The act required a host of filings with the Clerk of the House and Secretary of the Senate,[16] but nowhere did it authorize the Clerk of the House or the Secretary of the Senate to penalize lobbyists who did not comply or even to investigate to determine compliance. The sanctions provided for in the Lobbying Act were criminal penalties,[17] which seemed rather harsh for most violations of the statute. Though the responsibility is never made explicit, it appeared that the Department of Justice was charged with enforcement because the only sanctions were criminal ones.[18] There was no provision for coordination between the Clerk of the House and the Secretary of the Senate (each charged with receiving registration statements and reports), or between them and the Department of Justice (responsible for enforcing the requirements). Since the normal channels of bureaucratic paper flow did not exist between Congress's administrators and the Department of Justice, this omission created a framework conducive to non-enforcement of the statute.

A second major problem was a central conflict on the face of the statute. Congress appears to have constructed the Lobbying Act to bring under public scrutiny two different practices. The first was the employment of lobbyists and the expenditure of funds for and by these paid lobbyists. The Lobbying Act addressed this concern in section 308 by requiring registration by these lobbyists and the filing of quarterly financial reports. The second was the collection of "contributions"—principally by trade associations and special interest groups—to be used to influence legislation by means of hiring lobbyists or otherwise. Because of threshold prerequisites to coverage found elsewhere in the Lobbying Act and potential constitutional imperatives, as well as practical considerations, the distinction between

---

15. *Id.* §§ 305, 306, 308, 60 Stat. 840–42.

16. *Id.* §§ 305(a), 308, 60 Stat. 840–42.

17. *Id.* § 310(a), 60 Stat. 842 (stating that "any person who violates any of the provisions of this title, shall, upon conviction, be guilty of a misdemeanor, and shall be punished by a fine of not more than $5,000 or imprisonment for not more than twelve months, or by both such fine and imprisonment"); *Id.* § 310(b), 60 Stat. 842 (stating that a person convicted of a violation loses the right to lobby for three years).

18. For a short time the Department of Justice set up an enforcement division, but no specific division concentrated on enforcement of the Lobbying Act after the early fifties. *See* John F. Kennedy, *Congressional Lobbies: A Chronic Problem Re-examined*, 45 Geo. L.J. 535, 542 (1957).

these two practices ultimately lost its meaning. Yet Congress's attempt to meld together treatment of the two resulted in a statute of remarkable opaqueness.

3-2.2 Difficulties of Early Implementation (1946–1954)

The problems evident on the face of the statute made it difficult to implement. From the time of its enactment to the mid-1950s, compliance with the registration and disclosure requirements was very uneven. For example, between 1946 and 1950, only 3,494 quarterly reports were filed under the Lobbying Act,[19] representing, surely, a small fraction of the active lobbyists during that period.

Notwithstanding these small numbers, few people were investigated for failing to file.[20] Moreover, through 1954 there were only three reported prosecutions.[21] None of the defendants was convicted in any of these prosecutions. In a fourth case, *National Association of Manufacturers v. McGrath*,[22] Judge Alexander Holtzoff (for a three-judge district court) ruled that the Lobbying Act was unconstitutional in two respects. First, he held that various provisions violated the due process clause because they were "manifestly too indefinite and vague to constitute an ascertainable standard of guilt."[23] Second, he held that the provision of section 310(b) prohibiting violators from further lobbying for three years was inconsistent with the First Amendment.[24] The statute was off to a bad start.

Judge Holtzoff was also the judge to whom the government's prosecution in *United States v. Harriss*[25] was assigned. The information named the following parties as defendants: Robert Harriss, a commodities broker; Tom Linder, Commissioner of Agriculture for the State of Georgia; James McDonald, Commissioner of Agriculture for the State of Texas; Ralph Moore, a trader of commodities futures; and the National Farm Committee.[26] The information alleged that Linder, McDonald, and Moore, as directors of the National Farm Committee, used the organization (ostensibly organized to further the interests of farmers) to influence Congress and advance their private interests in commodities futures trading. In addition, Moore received money during this time from Harriss to influence Congress so commodities futures prices would rise.[27] Moore would pay for dinners and other gifts for members of Congress, held in the name of

---

19. H.R. Rep. No. 81-3239, at 45 (1951).

20. Between 1947 and 1954, approximately fifty investigations were initiated. *Oversight of the 1946 Federal Regulation of Lobbying Act: Hearings Before the S. Comm. on Governmental Affairs*, 98th Cong. 192 (1983) (statement of Mark Richard, Deputy Assistant Attorney General, Criminal Division).

21. United States v. United States Sav. & Loan League, 9 F.R.D. 450 (D.D.C. 1949) (dismissed); United States v. Slaughter, 89 F. Supp. 876 (D.D.C. 1950) (ending in acquittal); United States v. Harriss, 347 U.S. 612 (1954). There was one successful but unreported prosecution of violations of the Lobbying Act where defendants pleaded guilty. *See* United States v. Neff, No. 768-86 (D.D.C. Dec. 14, 1956).

22. 103 F. Supp. 510 (D.D.C.), *vacated as moot*, 344 U.S. 804 (1952).

23. 103 F. Supp. at 514. Judge Holtzoff found the phrase "to influence, directly or indirectly, the passage or defeat of any legislation" infinitely elastic and the "principal purpose" test quite ambiguous.

24. *Id.*

25. 109 F. Supp. 641 (D.D.C. 1953).

26. Information filed Aug. 31, 1949, United States v. Harriss, *reprinted in* Record at 1 ff., *United States v. Harriss*, 347 U.S. 612 (1954) (No. 1212-49).

27. In the last three months of 1946 alone, Harriss paid Moore $50,000. Brief for Appellant at 46, United States v. Harriss, 347 U.S. 612 (1954) (No. 1212-49).

groups such as the Farm Commissioners Council, Southern Commissioners of Agriculture, and the North Central States Association of Commissioners. The real purpose of these organizations was never revealed, since no statements were filed under the Lobbying Act.[28]

The case never reached a jury. Judge Holtzoff granted a motion to dismiss in 1953 based upon his earlier decision in *McGrath* that the judge considered "at least *stare decisis*, if not *res judicata*."[29] The government took a direct appeal to the United States Supreme Court.

3-2.3 Supreme Court's Decision in *United States v. Harriss* (1954)

By 1953, the last-minute, awkwardly drafted lobbying statute was on the verge of extinction. Three judges had found it unconstitutional,[30] and the results of the two other reported cases were equally inauspicious—one acquittal[31] and one dismissal.[32] Defending Judge Holtzoff's opinion in the *Harriss* appeal, defendants asserted the unconstitutionality of the Lobbying Act on three grounds. First, sections 305, 307, and 308 (registration and reporting) were too vague to satisfy due process. Second, they violated the First Amendment's guarantee of freedom of speech, freedom of the press, and right to petition. Third, section 310(b) (the three-year ban on lobbying by those who violated the Lobbying Act) was inconsistent with the right to petition.[33]

By a five-to-three vote, the Supreme Court rejected these attacks in *United States v. Harriss*. To avoid the constitutional doubts, it construed the statute so as to essentially rewrite it. Chief Justice Warren's decision for the Court began with the issue of vagueness. A statute violates the due process clause if it "fails to give a person of ordinary intelligence fair notice that his contemplated conduct is forbidden by the statute."[34] But, the Chief Justice continued, if there is a reasonable construction that leaves the statute constitutionally definite, the Court ought to give the statute that construction.[35]

To cure the perceived vagueness, the Court found section 307 to be the controlling provision of the Lobbying Act. Thus, to be covered by the Lobbying Act, one had to be within section 307, which the Court found established three prerequisites for the application of the statute:

(1) the "person" must have solicited, collected, or received contributions;

28. A further aspect of this scheme involved payments by Moore and Harriss to Commissioners Linder and McDonald via accounts at Harriss's brokerage firm. Similar payments were made to other individuals, though those individuals were not charged in this information. Not surprisingly, this activity was not reported as required by the Lobbying Act.

29. *Harriss*, 109 F. Supp. at 642.

30. Namely, the three-judge court in *McGrath*, 103 F. Supp. 510 (D.D.C. 1952), whose decision was followed by the author of the *McGrath* opinion, Judge Holtzoff, in *Harriss*.

31. In United States v. Slaughter, 89 F. Supp. 876 (D.D.C. 1950), the defendant waived his right to a jury trial and was found not guilty—again by Judge Holtzoff.

32. The court dismissed the indictment in United States v. United States Savings & Loan League, 9 F.R.D. 450 (1949), because one of the counts was too vague and the other two counts failed to charge an offense under the Lobbying Act.

33. *Harriss*, 347 U.S. at 617.

34. *Id.*

35. *Id.* at 618.

(2) one of the main purposes of such "person," or one of the main purposes of such contributions, must have been to influence the passage
or defeat of legislation by Congress; and

(3) the intended method of accomplishing this purpose must have been
through direct communication with members of Congress.[36]

The Court thus rejected the government's view that section 305 required reports by
any person making expenditures to influence legislation, even though that person
did not solicit, collect, or receive contributions.

In spite of—or perhaps because of—the narrowing of persons covered by the
Lobbying Act to those who solicited, collected, or received contributions, the Court
defined the limiting word of section 307 (that money be received or expended
"principally" for the purpose of influencing legislation) broadly to mean that influencing legislation had to be "one of the main" purposes of that receipt or expenditure. The Court then spun another 180 degrees, returning to a narrow construction
by adding a new limitation to the Lobbying Act—the requirement of "direct communication" with Congress.[37]

After both narrowing and expanding the Lobbying Act to deflect the due process
challenge, the Court proceeded to the First Amendment argument. Chief Justice Warren pointed to the danger of unregulated lobbying: "[T]he voice of the people may
all too easily be drowned out by the voice of special interest groups seeking favored
treatment while masquerading as proponents of the public weal."[38] The Court then
balanced the prevention of this evil against the possible chilling effect of minimal
disclosure required by the Lobbying Act and found the Lobbying Act constitutional.[39]

Justice Douglas, joined by Justice Black,[40] dissented on the ground that "the
formula adopted to save this Lobbying Act is too dangerous for use. It can easily
ensnare people who have done no more than exercise their constitutional rights of
speech, assembly, and press."[41] Justice Douglas began his analysis by stating that,
in determining whether a statute is constitutionally definite, the Court must judge
the statute on its face. Phrases such as "any other matter which may be the subject

---

36. *Id.* at 623.

37. *Id.* at 620. It appears that Chief Justice Warren considered an "artificially stimulated letter
campaign" to be "direct" communication. *Id.*

38. *Harriss*, 347 U.S. at 625.

39. "The hazard of [self-censorship] is too remote to require striking down a statute which on
its face is otherwise plainly within the area of congressional power and is designed to safeguard a
vital national interest." *Id.* at 626. The last claim of the defendants was that section 310(b) violated the
First Amendment's right-to-petition clause. The Court dismissed the claim: the appellees had yet to be
found guilty, so the question of the constitutionality of the penalty provision was not yet ripe. *Id.* at
627. The Court added that the section could be severed under the separability clause of the Legislative
Reorganization Act, so the constitutionality of the statute as a whole was not in danger. *Id.*

40. Justice Black's dissenting position is ironic. Part of the language of the Lobbying Act held
constitutional by the majority was taken from S. 2512, 74th Cong. (1935), a bill he had introduced while
a Senator from Alabama. Indeed, he had stated in 1935 that "[t]here is no constitutional right to lobby.
There is no right on the part of greedy and predatory interests to use money taken from the pockets
of the citizen to mislead him." William A. Gregory & Rennard Strickland, *Hugo Black's Congressional
Investigations of Lobbying and the Public Utilities Holding Company Act: A Historical View of the Power Trust,
New Deal Politics, and Regulatory Propaganda*, 29 OKLA. L. REV. 534, 551 (1976) (quoting *Hearings Before a
Special Comm. to Investigate Lobbying Activities*, 74th Cong. (1935)).

41. *Harriss*, 347 U.S. at 628 (Douglas, J., dissenting).

of action" by Congress, "principally to aid," and "retained for the purpose of influencing" used throughout the statute prevented the Lobbying Act from being precise enough to satisfy due process, according to Justice Douglas.[42]

Justice Douglas strongly objected to the Court's having significantly rewritten the statute to render it constitutional.[43] For example, nothing on the face of the statute suggested (as the Court did) that it covered only "direct communication" with Congress, and there was clear legislative history to the contrary.[44] Justice Douglas was not entirely opposed to reading a statute "with the gloss a court has placed on it,"[45] but objected to such a drastic salvage operation where the First Amendment was involved. The vagueness of the statute that confronted the people prosecuted, and others who worried about prosecution, could not be undone by the Court. As the Lobbying Act collided directly with First Amendment activities, the statute's vagueness had "some of the evils of a continuous and effective restraint," a chilling effect on protected activity.[46]

Justice Jackson dissented separately. He shared Justice Douglas's concern about the statute's vagueness, its infringement of First Amendment rights, and the Court's wholesale rewriting of it.[47] Justice Jackson's dislike for the rewriting of the Lobbying Act stemmed in part from his fear that a narrowly construed statute might at some later point again be expanded, leaving individuals at the mercy of the Court's interpretation, after the potential violation of the Lobbying Act had occurred.[48]

On the First Amendment issue, Justice Jackson went further than Justice Douglas. Justice Douglas was concerned with the impact of a vague statute on the right to free speech, implying that the Lobbying Act might have been constitutional had it been written more clearly. Justice Jackson, however, found the Lobbying Act to endanger the right to petition. Justice Jackson's approach was anchored in a decidedly pluralistic image of the American polity: "[O]ur constitutional system is to allow the greatest freedom of access to Congress, so that the people may press for their selfish interests, with Congress acting as arbiter of their demands and conflicts."[49]

3-2.4 Subsequent (Post-*Harriss*) Developments and Enforcement

Harriss all but ended any effort by the Department of Justice to prosecute violations under the Lobbying Act. On November 2, 1955, the government dropped the charges against the last defendant in *Harriss*, Ralph Moore.[50] After 1955, only a few indictments were returned under the act. As the Department of Justice told Congress in 1979, "the law has been reduced to virtually a nonentity by interpretation."[51]

---

42. *Id.* at 628–30.

43. *Id.* at 629.

44. *Id.* at 631.

45. *Id.* at 632.

46. *Id.* at 633.

47. Justice Jackson characterized the majority's handiwork this way: "The clearest feature of the Court's decision is that it leaves the country under an Act which is not much like any Act passed by Congress." *Id.* at 633 (Jackson, J., dissenting).

48. *Id.* at 633–35. "Judicial construction, constitutional or statutory, always is subject to hazards of judicial reconstruction." *Id.* at 635.

49. *Id.*

50. *See supra* note 18, Kennedy, at 552 note 102.

51. *Public Disclosure of Lobbying Activity: Hearings Before the Subcomm. on Administrative Law and Governmental Relations of the House Judiciary Comm.*, 96th Cong. 56 (1979) (statement of Assistant Attorney General Patricia Wald).

Of course, the Clerk of the House and the Secretary of the Senate still accepted registration statements and reports and encouraged compliance, but without effective monitoring and enforcement, there was incomplete compliance with the requirements of the Lobbying Act. Although an exact figure is impossible to calculate, partially due to the vagueness of the Lobbying Act itself, one estimate was that only 20 to 40 percent of those required to register actually did so.[52] According to the General Accounting Office, of the reports filed, 48 percent were incomplete[53] and 61 percent were late.[54] No one dared to guess how many were inaccurate or misleading.

These and other weaknesses attracted the attention of lawmakers and reformers, who, almost from its enactment, made a variety of proposals to strengthen the Lobbying Act, especially after Watergate.

3-3 Reform of Lobbying Disclosure Law: The LDA (1995) and HLOGA (2007)

The inherent problems with the Federal Regulation of Lobbying Act of 1946, combined with the narrowing construction in *United States v. Harriss*, seriously undercut efforts to regulate lobbying. Yet Washington continued to swarm with lobbyists—and with proposals to reform the Lobbying Act.

The reform proposals generally targeted five perceived weaknesses of the Lobbying Act:

1. An imprecise, under-inclusive definition of the activities constituting "lobbying";
2. the inapplicability to grassroots lobbying;
3. the failure to require lobbyists to disclose the identities of all contributors;[55]
4. the failure to cover lobbying of congressional staff and members of the executive branch;[56] and
5. inadequate enforcement provisions.[57]

Unfortunately, while there was general recognition of the problems with the Lobbying Act, there was no consensus about appropriate solutions given the substantial practical and constitutional issues presented.

---

52. Barbara Bado, Comment, *Federal Lobbying Disclosure Legislation*, 26 Am. U. L. Rev. 972, 986 n.64 (1977) (citing Staff of the Senate Comm. on Gov't Operations, 94th Cong., Report on Lobbying Disclosure Act of 1976, 6–7 (Comm. Print 1976)). *See also The Federal Lobbying Disclosure Laws: Hearings Before the Subcomm. on Oversight of Government Operations of the Senate Governmental Affairs Comm.*, 102d Cong. 388 (1991) (statement of Ann McBride, Senior Vice President, Common Cause).

53. General Accounting Office, The Federal Regulation of Lobbying Act—Difficulties in Enforcement and Administration (1975) (1975 GAO Report). *See also The Federal Lobbying Disclosure Laws: Hearings Before the Subcomm. on Oversight of Government Operations of the Senate Governmental Affairs Comm.*, 102d Cong. (1991) (statement of Milton J. Socolar, Special Assistant to the Comptroller General, GAO).

54. 1975 GAO Report, at 9.

55. Mary Kathryn Vanderbeck, Note, *First Amendment Constraints on Reform of the Federal Regulation of Lobbying Act*, 57 Tex. L. Rev. 1219, 1247 (1979).

56. Barbara Bado, Comment, *Federal Lobbying Disclosure Legislation*, 26 Am. U. L. Rev. 972, 996 (1977).

57. Guy Paul Land, Note, *Federal Lobbying Disclosure Reform Legislation*, 17 Harv. J. on Legis. 295, 300–01 (1980). *See generally* The Lobbying Manual, A Compliance Guide for Lawyers and Lobbyists chs. 2–5 (Thomas Susman ed., 1993) (containing a detailed examination of the operation and uncertainties of the 1946 Lobbying Act).

In this regard, a fundamental challenge was crafting disclosure requirements that appropriately furthered the public's knowledge of efforts made to influence governmental action without imposing too significant a burden on the rights protected by the First Amendment.[58] Grassroots solicitation of public support presented (and continues to present) an issue of particular concern:[59] while such solicitation often provides organizations with a very effective means to influence governmental officials, it also falls within the scope of the First Amendment, whether it is considered petitioning the government for redress of grievances or pure political speech.

From the 1950s on, both the House and the Senate saw repeated attempts to set threshold requirements for coverage under a revised lobbying law that appropriately balanced these competing interests. Such requirements were proposed for both expenditure levels[60] and for particular levels of activity (usually measured by numbers of contacts with Congress).[61] In proposed legislation, House members concentrated almost exclusively on setting threshold spending limits, while Senators tried an approach combining spending limits and activity levels.[62] All of these threshold standards were, of necessity, arbitrary, since there are no clear constitutional touchstones for determining the legality of any specific level.[63] Thus, until 1995, House and Senate advocates of reform could not agree on any standard for triggering lobbying disclosure requirements.

However, the momentum for reform accelerated in the early 1990s. When, in the summer and fall of 1995, the long-awaited conjunction of the political factors necessary to create consensus took place, the Lobbying Disclosure Act of 1995 replaced the 1946 Lobbying Act, accompanied by the hope in many quarters that, finally, effective—if not complete—lobbying reform had been achieved. Various technical amendments to the Lobbying Act followed in 1998.

Then, more than a decade after the LDA's enactment and in reaction to a series of well-publicized scandals involving lobbyists and various congressional and executive branch officials, Congress expanded many of the disclosure obligations of the LDA. In the process, it focused specifically on the money nexus linking lobbyists and federal officials, imposing new disclosure mandates as well as substantive restrictions on lobbyists' behavior. These changes were embodied in the Honest Leadership and Open Government Act of 2007. The requirements of the LDA, as amended by HLOGA, are addressed in detail in the following chapters.

---

58. Land, at 309; Vanderbeck, *supra* note 55, at 1222, 1239.
59. *See* Land, at 329; Vanderbeck, *supra* note 55, at 1250.
60. Vanderbeck, *supra* note 55, at 1237.
61. *Id.*
62. Bado, *supra* note 56, at 993.
63. *See, e.g.*, S. REP. No. 99-161, at 49 (1986).

CHAPTER 4

Lobbying Disclosure Act Registration and Reporting Requirements

BY REBECCA H. GORDON, KATE SAWYER KEANE, AND LINDA ROCKWELL

4-1 Overview

Almost everyone who interacts with government believes he or she knows what it means to lobby. (And any lawyer who works in this field comes across lots of people who are certain that, whatever it means, *they* don't do it.) Frustratingly, as anyone who peruses this volume surely finds out, "lobbying" is a term the law uses in many different places, and it means different things depending on which set of laws you're working with at any one time.

The Lobbying Disclosure Act of 1995 (LDA)[1] is the principal disclosure statute governing lobbying activity at the federal level of government. Its application depends on a particular definition of lobbying that is much broader than most people think it is. It applies to legislative work, agency/executive branch work, and work seeking government contracts, and may be triggered any time an organization has an employee who spends more than a minimal amount of time interacting with the Congress or executive branch on almost any issue. It applies to lobbying firms, self-employed lobbyists, and organizations with employees who lobby for them.

The LDA is foremost a disclosure statute. An organization triggers the responsibility to register and report by (1) employing an individual who meets the statutory definition of "lobbyist" and (2) reaching certain income or expenditure thresholds. Once an organization triggers registration, the LDA requires it to file an initial registration form notifying the government and the public that it is performing lobbying work, and indicating the client whose interests it is representing. (If the organization is lobbying for itself, it discloses itself as the "client.")

The LDA also requires the filing of regular reports with the Clerk of the House of Representatives (Clerk) and the Secretary of the Senate (Secretary).[2] These two offices must receive each registration and each report. This is the case even if the work is focused only on one chamber of Congress. Indeed, the Clerk and Secretary receive the filings even if the work is focused exclusively on the executive branch.

The Clerk and Secretary are initially responsible as well for enforcing the LDA. Registrants who fail to file required reports timely, or whose reports are obviously defective in some material way, will receive a notice from one or both of these offices, and will have sixty days to cure the problem.[3] If the filer does not address the issue, the matter may be referred to the Department of Justice for further investigation.

A self-lobbying organization files one registration, while lobbying firms and self-employed lobbyists file a registration for each client. Because lobbying firms and self-employed lobbyists are treated virtually identically under the LDA, when we use the term "lobbying firm" in this chapter, we are referring to both.

Once registered, each registrant must file two separate series of reports on an ongoing basis. The first are quarterly reports on which the registrant discloses the substantive lobbying activities that it undertook during the reporting period. A lobbying firm must file a separate report each quarter for each client for whom it is registered. A self-lobbying organization files a single report each quarter.

The second set of reports are political and honorary activity reports, filed semiannually. Each registrant must file one of these twice each year, and each individual lobbyist must also file one twice each year on which he or she discloses the required information about his or her personal political and honorary activity.

As noted above, the LDA is principally a disclosure statute. It does contain some substantive limitations, however, which are discussed in more detail below.

This chapter begins with a discussion of the terminology and definitions that are most prominent in the LDA. It then covers the registration and reporting

---

1. 2 U.S.C. §§ 1601–1614 (2015).
2. 2 U.S.C. § 1604 (2015).
3. 2 U.S.C. § 1605 (2015).

requirements in more detail. We have included hypothetical examples to help illustrate particular points where helpful.

4-2 Key Definitions

4-2.1 Lobbyist

Under the LDA, a lobbyist is any natural person:

- who makes at least two federal "lobbying contacts" over the course of services provided for a particular client (or his or her employing organization), even if the second contact occurs in a different quarterly period from the first; and
- whose federal "lobbying activities" constitute at least 20 percent of his or her total time for the client (or employing organization) over any three-month period.[4]

The lobbyist definition is conjunctive; an individual will trigger registration as a lobbyist only if he or she makes more than one lobbying contact *and* meets the 20 percent lobbying activity threshold. If the lobbyist works for multiple clients, both inquiries must be done for each client. The same individual can qualify as a lobbyist for one client he services but not for another.

Example: *Mary and John joined Consulting Firm as new employees on January 1 and will provide various services to the firm's clients. The firm is registered to lobby for two of its clients, Alpha Co. and Bravo Co. During the first quarter, John engages solely in legislative lobbying work for Alpha Co. and makes multiple contacts. Mary assists Alpha and John in designing the lobbying strategy, but makes no lobbying contacts and there is no expectation that she ever will. John meets the definition of lobbyist for Alpha and should be identified as a new lobbyist on the firm's first quarter report for Alpha Co. Mary does not meet the definition of lobbyist for Alpha Co. and need not be listed.*

For Bravo Co., Mary makes multiple lobbying contacts in the executive branch. She spends 25 percent of her time engaged in executive branch lobbying, 25 percent in crisis counseling, and 50 percent in general public relations work. John is not assigned to the Bravo account, but at Mary's request makes two substantive calls to members of Congress on the company's behalf. There is no expectation that John will provide other services to Bravo. Mary and John both meet the definition of lobbyist for Bravo Co. and should be listed as such. Because John made two lobbying contacts for Bravo and spent 100 percent of his time on Bravo matters engaged in lobbying, he has triggered disclosure as a lobbyist for this client and should be listed as a new lobbyist on the firm's first quarter report for Bravo. If there is no reasonable expectation that John will provide other services to Bravo in the future, John's lobbyist status may also be terminated on the same report.

Note that direct contacts are required to trigger lobbyist status. For a further discussion on the tax implications of grassroots lobbying, see Chapter 13.

---

4. 2 U.S.C. § 1602(10) (2015).

4-2.2 Lobbying Contact

Lobbying contacts are those communications with government officials that are most central to LDA disclosure. They also comprise one of the elements that must be met for an individual to qualify as a lobbyist.

An individual makes a lobbying contact if he or she makes

- An oral or written communication (including an electronic communication)
- To a covered federal executive or legislative branch official
- On behalf of a particular client (or his or her employing organization) regarding
  - The formulation, modification, or adoption of federal legislation, federal rules, regulations, executive orders, or other government programs, policies, or positions;
  - The administration or execution of federal programs or policies (including the negotiation, award, or administration of federal contracts, loans, grants, permits or licenses); or
  - The nomination or confirmation of a person for a position subject to confirmation by the Senate.[5]

Note that the range of substantive topics that can be the subject of lobbying contacts is extraordinarily broad. It includes legislation, of course; but it also includes creating or amending federal rules, awarding government contracts or grants, and formulating or changing any federal policy at all. For LDA purposes, then, lobbying covers much more than just work on legislation.

It is at least possible for a single contact to range over more than one conversation; for example, if a telephone conversation is interrupted and then restarted again later in the same day. However, in most situations, every conversation with a covered official will count as a separate contact.

4-2.3 Covered Officials

A communication with a government employee is only a lobbying contact if the employee is "covered" under the statute.

In the Congress, this again is a very broad universe. Covered legislative branch officials are virtually anyone paid by the Congress:

- Senators and members of the House of Representatives;
- Elected officers of the House and Senate;
- Employees of senators, members, committees, leadership, working groups, and caucuses; and
- Legislative branch employees required to file public financial disclosure forms.[6]

Those officials covered under the LDA in the executive branch are a much smaller group relative to the whole. They are

---

5. 2 U.S.C. § 1602(8)(A) (2015).
6. 2 U.S.C. § 1602(4) (2015).

- The president;
- The vice president;
- Officers and employees (and those functioning in the capacity of an officer or employee) of the Executive Office of the President;
- Individuals serving in positions in Levels I through V of the Executive Schedule;
- Schedule C employees; and
- Any member of the uniformed services serving at grade O-7 or above.[7]

These are the officials in the government who most likely have responsibility for making policy decisions. Not all senior executive branch officers and employees are covered, nor are all political appointees covered. Determining whether a particular employee is covered often requires some legwork. Classifications are made job by job; there is no centralized database that features a list of covered employees. LDA registrants often engage counsel to help determine whether individual employees are covered. Alternatively, if asked, each government employee, or the office that employs him or her, is required to indicate whether the employee is covered.[8]

By definition, communications with federal government employees who are *not* covered officials are not lobbying contacts. This means, for example, that meetings and other contacts with many career employees in executive branch agencies are not lobbying contacts.

Example: *Susan, an in-house lobbyist for registrant Foxtrot Lending Co., contacts the deputy director of the Consumer Financial Protection Bureau (CFPB) regarding rule implementation issues. At the time, the director is the only covered official at the CFPB. Susan's communication with the deputy director is not a lobbying contact.*

Example: *John, a lobbyist for registrant Alpha Co., meets with an employee in the Office of Management and Budget to discuss issues related to repatriation policy at a time when there is no pending or proposed legislation regarding repatriation. Because all OMB employees fall within the definition of "covered executive branch official" and the substantive discussion involved matters of federal policy, John's meeting with the OMB employee constitutes a lobbying contact.*

4-2.4 Lobbying Activities

"Lobbying activities" includes the universe of preparatory and coordinating work that supports lobbying communications. It encompasses both lobbying contacts and all efforts in support of such contacts, including

- preparation and planning activities;
- research and other background work that is intended, at the time it is performed, for use in contacts; and
- coordination with the lobbying activities of others.[9]

---

7. 2 U.S.C. § 1602(3) (2015).
8. 2 U.S.C. § 1609(c) (2015).
9. 2 U.S.C. § 1602(7) (2015).

Lobbying firms and self-lobbying organizations typically deploy a significant amount of time and energy on lobbying activities. Activities may include monitoring legislation, preparing memoranda or other internal documents for review and use by those meeting directly with government officials, and working with other lobbyists interested in the same matters or working for the same clients. It also includes researching and compiling data for use in contacts, and drafting materials for presentation in lobbying meetings.

As noted above, communications with federal government employees who are *not* covered officials are not lobbying contacts. However, such contacts may be considered lobbying activities if they are intended to support planned, later communications with covered officials (that would be considered lobbying contacts).

Example: *Acme Inc.'s CEO makes semiannual visits to Washington, D.C., during which he meets with various members of Congress and senior executive branch officials to discuss items on Acme's federal lobbying agenda. Throughout the course of his employment with Acme, the CEO has made well over 100 lobbying contacts. However, the amount of time the CEO devotes to lobbying activities (i.e., participating in strategy talks for Acme's federal lobbying efforts, preparing for the D.C. trips, traveling to and from D.C., making lobbying contacts, following up on those contacts, briefing others regarding the contacts, etc.) has never approached 20 percent of his work time in any three-month period. Consequently, the CEO does not meet the definition of lobbyist.*

4-3 Excepted Communications

The LDA describes several types of communications that do *not* count as lobbying contacts. We have categorized these types of communications below to help ease the discussion.

4-3.1 Administrative Requests

Requests for appointments, status requests, or similar administrative communications made without attempting to influence a covered official are not considered lobbying contacts.[10] This exception is used often in practice. It is the one that allows secretarial or administrative staff to request meetings with government officials, request updates on status, or send e-mails requesting meetings without becoming lobbyists themselves. Note, though, that any communication made pursuant to this exception must not include an attempt to influence the recipient of the communication. So an e-mail requesting a meeting does not generally qualify for the exception if the e-mail has briefing materials attached.

4-3.2 Information Required or Requested by the Government

The LDA excepts from the definition of lobbying contact a variety of communications that originate with a government request or requirement. Here is a list of these communications, with a brief description where necessary or helpful:

10. 2 U.S.C. § 1602(8)(B)(v) (2015).

- Written information provided in response to a request by a covered official for specific information.[11] This is a little-known, underused exception that permits lobbyists to provide data or other specifically requested information to a covered official. Note that only provision *in writing* is excepted and only to the extent specifically requested.
- Communications required by subpoena, civil investigative demand, or otherwise compelled by statute, regulation, or other action of Congress or a federal agency, including communications compelled by a federal contract, grant, loan, permit, or license.[12] Practical considerations dictate the exception of most of these. Notably, among other things, this permits federal government contractors that must communicate with the government as part of their contract administration to do so without turning the government-facing employees into lobbyists. We include one note here with respect to subpoenas. Only the communications actually required by the subpoena, including the scheduling of meetings and delivery of documents, are excepted under this provision. Any communications with covered government officials to try to shape the terms of a subpoena, or to intervene before a subpoena is issued, would not be excepted.
- Communications made to agency officials with regard to judicial proceedings, criminal or civil law enforcement inquiries, investigations or proceedings, or filings or proceedings required by statute or regulation to be maintained or conducted on a confidential basis.[13]
- Communications made in compliance with written agency procedures regarding an adjudication conducted by the agency under the Administrative Procedure Act, or substantially similar provisions.[14]
- Formal petitions for agency action, made in writing and required to be a matter of public record pursuant to established agency procedures.[15]
- Communications made in the course of participation in an advisory committee subject to the Federal Advisory Committee Act.[16]
- Communications between officials of a self-regulatory organization that is registered with or established by the Securities and Exchange Commission (SEC) or a similar organization that is designated by or registered with the Commodity Futures Trading Commission (CFTC) and the SEC or CFTC, respectively, relating to the regulatory responsibilities of the self-regulatory organization.[17]

Example: *A staffer in Rep. Smith's office e-mails Acme Inc.'s policy team requesting information on the percentage of Acme employees working and/or residing in the member's district. An Acme employee providing that information, in writing, is not making a lobbying contact. However, if, in addition to the requested information on Acme's workforce, Acme's response includes the company's position on pension reform, the excep-*

---

11. 2 U.S.C. § 1602(8)(B)(viii) (2015).
12. 2 U.S.C. § 1602(8)(B)(ix) (2015).
13. 2 U.S.C. § 1602(8)(B)(xii) (2015).
14. 2 U.S.C. § 1602(8)(B)(xiii) (2015).
15. 2 U.S.C. § 1602(8)(B)(xv) (2015).
16. 2 U.S.C. § 1602(8)(B)(vi) (2015).
17. 2 U.S.C. § 1602(8)(B)(xix) (2015).

tion for written information would not apply.

Example: *Acme Inc. was awarded a consulting contract with the Department of Education. The contract requires Acme to provide weekly progress reports to individuals who qualify as covered officials. The progress reports are not lobbying contacts.*

4-3.3 Inherently Public Communications

The LDA also excepts certain categories of communications that are made on the public record. These include

- Testimony given before a committee, subcommittee, or task force of Congress, or submitted for inclusion in the public record of a congressional hearing.[18]
- Written comments filed in a public docket and other communications that are made on the record in a public proceeding.[19] The "public proceeding" aspect of this provision raises a number of questions about the kinds of communications that might be covered here other than those made through the normal notice-and-comment proceeding process.
- Communications in response to a notice in the *Federal Register, Commerce Business Daily,* or other similar publication soliciting public comment.[20]
- Communications made by a representative of a media organization to the extent that the purpose is to gather and disseminate news and information to the public.[21]
- Speeches, articles, publications, or other materials that are distributed and made available to the public, or through radio, television, or other medium of mass communication.[22] This exception is exceedingly useful to most organizations that have, or work with, communications shops that use the Internet or mass e-mail to communicate to the public about their issues.

Example: *In response to an agency's Notice of Proposed Rulemaking, Acme Inc.'s policy team prepares and submits written comments into the public record. The comments are not lobbying contacts, nor are the efforts expended in preparing the comments lobbying activities.*

Example: *Acme Inc. posts an open letter to the Secretary of the Interior on its website. The posting of the letter is not a lobbying contact.*

---

18. 2 U.S.C. § 1602(8)(B)(vii) (2015).
19. 2 U.S.C. § 1602(8)(B)(xiv) (2015).
20. 2 U.S.C. § 1602(8)(B)(x) (2015).
21. 2 U.S.C. § 1602(8)(B)(ii) (2015).
22. 2 U.S.C. § 1602(8)(B)(iii) (2015).

4-3.4 Inherently Private Communications

Also excepted are certain categories of private or confidential communications that are viewed as needing protection for public policy or other reasons:

- Disclosures protected under amendments made by the Whistleblower Protection Act of 1989, under the Inspector General Act of 1978, or another provision of law.[23]
- Any disclosure that could not be made without disclosing information that may not, by law, be disclosed.[24]
- Communications made on behalf of an individual with regard to such individual's benefits, employment, other personal matters involving only that individual (and not with respect to private legislation for relief).[25]
- Communications by a church or religious order that is exempt from filing federal income tax returns.[26]

4-3.5 Additional Excepted Communications

In addition, communications made by a public official acting in the public official's official capacity are not considered lobbying contacts.[27] The term "public official" is broadly defined to include any (1) elected official, appointed official, or employee of a federal, state, or local government in the United States (other than a college or university, a government-sponsored enterprise, a public utility, a guaranty agency, or a state agency functioning as a student loan secondary market); (2) government corporation; (3) organization of state or local elected or appointed officials; (4) Indian tribe; (5) national or state political party; or (6) national, regional, or local unit of any foreign government or group of governments acting together.[28]

Finally, communications made on behalf of a foreign government or foreign political party that are disclosed by foreign agents pursuant to the Foreign Agents Registration Act (FARA) also are not considered lobbying contacts.[29]

Although these excepted communications themselves do not count as lobbying contacts, they may be considered lobbying *activities* if they are efforts in support of other lobbying contacts. To the extent such activities are considered lobbying activities, the time spent engaging in the activities does count toward the 20 percent of time threshold used to identify individuals as lobbyists under the test described above.

---

23. 2 U.S.C. § 1602(8)(B)(xvii) (2015).
24. 2 U.S.C. § 1602(8)(B)(xi) (2015).
25. 2 U.S.C. § 1602(8)(B)(xvi) (2015).
26. 2 U.S.C. § 1602(8)(B)(xviii) (2015).
27. 2 U.S.C. § 1602(8)(B)(i) (2015).
28. 2 U.S.C. § 1602(15) (2015).
29. 2 U.S.C. § 1602(8)(B)(iv) (2015). See generally Chapter 19 for a discussion of the Foreign Agents Registration Act.

4-4 Registration

A lobbying firm or self-lobbying organization must file a registration when it both (1) has an employee who meets the definition of a lobbyist described above with respect to a client (or itself), and (2) meets the dollar thresholds on income or expenses described below.

If a self-lobbying organization employs an individual who meets the "two contacts/20 percent of time" definition of a lobbyist described above, *and* the organization spends more than $12,500 in a quarterly period on its federal lobbying, the organization must register with the Secretary and the Clerk.[30] The registration must be filed within 45 days after an employee of the organization makes the second contact (while meeting the 20 percent of time threshold), or the organization employs an individual to make the contacts (and meet the 20 percent of time threshold), whichever is earlier.[31]

Similarly, if a lobbying firm employee meets the two contacts/20 percent of time definition of a lobbyist described above with respect to a particular client, *and* the firm receives (or reasonably anticipates receiving) more than $3,000 in a quarterly period for its lobbying activity on behalf of the client, the firm must file a registration statement on behalf of the client within 45 days after the lobbyist makes the second contact (while meeting the 20 percent of time threshold), or the lobbyist is retained to make the contacts (and meet the 20 percent of time threshold), whichever is earlier.[32]

Example: *Acme Inc. does not have an internal government relations group or any employees who engage in federal lobbying activities. All federal lobbying efforts are conducted by consultant lobbyists, at a cost to Acme in excess of $12,500 per quarter. Although Acme's federal lobbying-related expenditures exceed the monetary threshold, it has no obligation to register if it does not have an employee who meets the definition of lobbyist.*

Example: *On May 1, Acme Inc. hires Mary Miller as an employee to be its internal federal lobbyist. It is anticipated that Mary will make multiple federal lobbying contacts and that 90 percent of her time will be spent on matters relating to Acme's federal lobbying efforts. Acme must file a registration with the House and Senate, and should list May 1 as the effective date. The registration must be filed by June 15 (i.e., forty-five days after Mary was hired as the company's federal lobbyist).*

Example: *Black Consulting Co. provides lobbying services to its clients. On January 15, Acme Inc. hires Black Consulting to engage in state-level lobbying on its behalf. In June, a discrete federal lobbying issue develops and a Black Consulting lobbyist makes several federal lobbying contacts on the issue. No further federal activity is anticipated. As long as the lobbyist's time spent on the federal issue did not consume 20 percent or more of the*

---

30. 2 U.S.C. § 1603(a)(3) (2015). The expenditure and income thresholds are indexed to inflation. These figures will be indexed again in 2017. *See id.*

31. 2 U.S.C. § 1603(a)(1) (2015); *see also* Sec'y of the Senate & Clerk of the House of Representatives, Lobbying Disclosure Act Guidance (revised Feb. 15, 2013) [hereinafter "Revised Guidance"], *available at* http://lobbyingdisclosure.house.gov/amended_lda_guide.html and text version attached as Appendix 4-A.

32. 2 U.S.C. § 1603(a)(1) (2015); *see also* Revised Guidance, Appendix 4-A.

lobbyist's entire time spent on Acme matters during a three-month period, Black Consulting need not file a federal registration for Acme as its client.

Example: *Global Inc. hires Black Consulting on January 1 for a small three-month federal lobbying project. Global will pay Black Consulting $900 per month for the work. A Black Consulting lobbyist makes multiple lobbying contacts and spends 100 percent of her time for Global engaged in federal lobbying activities on its behalf. She therefore meets the definition of lobbyist. However, because the $3,000 monetary threshold will not be met, Black Consulting does not have an obligation to file a registration for its work for Global. On April 1, Global and Black Consulting agree to extend their engagement, with an increase in fees to $1,200 per month. Black Consulting must file a registration with the House and Senate, identifying Global as its client and listing April 1 as the effective date. The registration must be filed by May 16.*

Organizations file the registration statement electronically on Form LD-1. Once filed, these forms are available for public viewing online. A sample version of what a filed, redacted registration form looks like to an online viewer is attached as Appendix 4-B.

To file the registration, the entity or individual will need a user ID and password. New filers may obtain a user ID and password request form online by visiting http://soprweb.senate.gov/. The completed request form must be signed and returned (via e-mail, fax, or mail) to the Senate Office of Public Records. The ID and password will generally be activated by the end of the business day following receipt of the request.

The registration statement must identify

- The organization or lobbying firm as the registrant;
- The client's name, address, and principal place of business (with respect to organizations employing in-house lobbyists, the client's name will be the name of the organization);
- The general federal issues expected to be lobbied and "to the extent practicable," specific issues already addressed or likely to be addressed;
- Each employee who has acted or is expected to act as a federal lobbyist on behalf of the client and any covered federal official position the employee has held during the past twenty years;
- Where applicable, any organization other than the client (like a parent or another organization) that contributes more than $5,000 during the quarterly period toward the client's federal lobbying activities, *and* "actively participates" in the planning, supervision, or control of such lobbying activities (an "affiliated organization");
- Any foreign entity[33] that:
  — holds at least 20 percent equitable ownership in the client or an affiliated organization;

---

33. The term "foreign entity" mirrors the definition of "foreign principal" under the Foreign Agents Registration Act, and includes (1) a government of a foreign country and a foreign political party; (2) a person outside of the United States, unless it is established that such person is an individual and a citizen of and domiciled within the United States, or that such person is not an individual and is organized under or created by the laws of the United States or of any state or other place subject to the jurisdiction of the United States and has its principal place of business within the United States; and (3) a partnership, association, corporation, organization, or other combination of persons organized under the laws of or having its principal place of business in a foreign country.

- directly or indirectly, in whole or in major part, plans, supervises, controls, directs, finances, or subsidizes the activities of the client or of an affiliated organization; or
- is an affiliate of the client or an affiliated organization, and has a direct interest in the outcome of the lobbying activity; and
• Where applicable, the amount of any contribution of more than $5,000 from the foreign entity (as described above) to the client for its lobbying activities and the percentage of equitable ownership in the client held by the foreign entity.[34]

The affiliated organization provision requiring identification of any organization, other than the client, that actively participates in the registrant's work for the client, while also helping to fund the work, is an anti-circumvention provision. It is intended to help ensure that the parties who are truly driving the lobbyist's work are disclosed. It most famously applies when a lobbyist's client is a coalition made up of more than one company. If the lobbyist is working on behalf of the coalition, the coalition should be listed on LDA forms as the client. But the registration should list as an affiliated entity each member of the coalition that meets the two reporting criteria—paying in more than $5,000 per quarter and "actively participating" in the work.

Affiliated organization disclosure also applies in a subcontracting relationship, in which a lobbying firm hires a consultant to help with a client's project and then pays the consultant from its proceeds from the client. In that case, the consultant identifies the lobbying firm as *its* client, but also discloses the ultimate client as an affiliated entity.

No disclosure of an affiliated organization is required if the affiliated organization that would be identified is listed on the registrant organization's publicly accessible Internet website as being a member or contributor to the registrant organization. This is true unless the affiliated organization in whole or in major part plans, supervises, or controls such lobbying activities. To use this exemption, the registrant organization must disclose the website containing the information on its registration.

Example: *Lobbying Firm is registered on behalf of its client, Alpha Co. When a unique issue of interest to Alpha develops, Lobbying Firm and Alpha agree that specialized experience is needed and that Consultant should assist in the effort. Lobbying Firm engages Consultant, paying $5,000 per month from the $15,000 per month it receives from Alpha. Consultant files a registration listing its client as "Lobbying Firm (on behalf of Alpha Co.)" and disclosing Alpha Co. as an affiliated organization.*

Determining when an organization has exceeded the $5,000 threshold is usually straightforward. By contrast, determining whether an organization actively participates in the planning, supervision, or control of the lobbyists' work can be time-consuming, requiring a full review of many different aspects of the relationship among the client, the lobbyist, and any organizations that fund the client's

---

34. 2 U.S.C. § 1603(b) (2015).

work. This is particularly true when the client has many donors, but a small number are perhaps more involved in the organization's day-to-day business than the others (e.g., a nonprofit organization).

The Clerk of the House and the Secretary of the Senate have provided some guidance on the kinds of activities that qualify as active participation. The definition includes, for example, (1) participating in decisions about which lobbyists to hire; (2) designing lobbying strategies; (3) if the client is a coalition, performing a leadership role in forming it; and (4) serving on a committee with responsibility over lobbying decisions. According to the Clerk and the Secretary, merely receiving information or reports on legislative matters, or occasionally responding to requests for technical expertise or other information in support of the lobbying activities, does not qualify as active participation. Mere occasional participation, such as commenting on lobbying strategy in the absence of any formal or regular supervision or direction of lobbying activities, does not generally constitute active participation.[35]

Example: *Association has 100 entity members. It has a broad mission and asserts that federal lobbying on issues of interest to its membership is a substantial part of that mission. Each member pays annual dues of $40,000; half of that annual dues payment ($20,000) is used to fund Association's lobbying efforts. A fifteen-member board is charged with general governance of Association, while oversight of federal lobbying matters has been delegated to a five-member lobbying committee. Representatives from various member organizations serve on the fifteen-member board, while representatives from Alpha Co., Bravo Co., and Charlie Co, respectively, serve on the five-member lobbying committee that is tasked with prioritizing lobbying initiatives, defining strategy, and selecting lobbying firms to engage on those initiatives when necessary. Association has an employee who meets the definition of lobbyist, and it, therefore, files a registration. Alpha Co., Bravo Co., and Charlie Co. should be listed as affiliated organizations.*

Example: *Same facts as above. Association also maintains a website that includes a "Who We Are" section listing all 100 of its members. Rather than listing each of the three member entities whose employees serve on the lobbying committee as affiliated organizations, Association may disclose the URL for the web page listing its members.*

Example: *Same facts as above, except that two Alpha Co. employees serve on the lobbying committee. By virtue of holding two of the five committee seats, Alpha Co.'s active participation in Association's lobbying activities rises to the level of planning, supervising, or controlling those activities "in whole or in major part." While Association may still disclose the URL for the web page listing its members in lieu of listing Bravo Co. and Charlie Co. by name as affiliated organizations, Alpha Co. must be disclosed by name.*

Example: *Alpha Co.'s and Bravo Co.'s vice presidents of government relations identify five other organizations with common interests on immigration reform issues. The seven organizations join to form Visa Coalition, with each agreeing to contribute $10,000 per*

---

35. See REVISED GUIDANCE, Appendix 4-A.

quarter to the coalition's budget. The Alpha Co. and Bravo Co. employees retain leadership roles with respect to the coalition's lobbying activities and select Lobbying Firm to engage in lobbying on the coalition's behalf. The five other member organizations receive regular updates on the coalition's activities and are solicited for comments on proposed strategy initiatives, but decision making and control rest with the Alpha and Bravo Co. representatives. Lobbying Firm files a registration, listing Visa Coalition as its client. Alpha Co. and Bravo Co. are listed as affiliated organizations. The other five coalition members, which met the contribution requirement but not the active participation requirement, are not disclosed.

Example: *Same facts as above, except Alpha Co. provides the initial funding for the coalition by contributing $60,000 while the other six members agree to contribute $4,000 per quarter. Lobbying Firm files a registration, listing Visa Coalition as its client. Only Alpha Co. is listed as an affiliated organization.*

4-5 Quarterly Reporting

The heart of the LDA disclosure regime is the quarterly activity reporting. These quarterly reports, filed electronically on Form LD-2, are due April 20, July 20, October 20, and January 20 (or the next business day) of each year.[36] Each quarterly report gives a summary of the work the registrant performed for a single client. Therefore, just as they must register separately for each client, lobbying firms must file separate quarterly reports for each client.[37] Note that if a particular registration's "effective date" is before the end of a quarterly reporting period, then the registrant must file a quarterly report for that initial period.[38]

A sample report is attached as Appendix 4-C for reference. On each quarterly report, the registrant must identify

- The client for which the report is being filed (which is the registrant's name if the registrant lobbies on its own behalf);
- Any updates to the information provided in the initial registration;
- The specific federal issues lobbied during the reporting period (including bill numbers and references to specific executive branch actions);
- The specific interest, if any, of any foreign entity in these specific issues, if the foreign entity meets the criteria described above;
- With which House(s) of Congress and federal agencies the registrant's lobbyists made lobbying contacts during the reporting period;
- All previously listed lobbyist-employees who engaged in any lobbying activities in the reporting period, plus any additional employees who met the definition of lobbyist during the reporting period;
- In the case of a self-lobbying organization, a good faith estimate of the total expenses during the quarterly period that the organization incurred for federal lobbying activities; and

---

36. 2 U.S.C. § 1604(a) (2015).
37. 2 U.S.C. § 1604(a) (2015).
38. See Revised Guidance, Appendix 4-A.

- In the case of a lobbying firm, a good faith estimate of the total income earned during the quarterly period from the client for federal lobbying activities.[39]

Estimates of lobbying expenses or lobbying income in excess of $5,000 must be rounded to the nearest $10,000.[40] Where lobbying expenses or lobbying income do not exceed $5,000 for the quarterly reporting period, the registrant must include a statement that income or expenses fell below $5,000.[41]

A lobbying firm must disclose a quarterly estimate of all of the federal lobbying income earned or accrued from that client for lobbying activities during the quarterly period.[42] Fees that have not yet been billed or received during the quarterly reporting period should still be included in the quarterly estimate of lobbying income if such fees were accrued for lobbying services provided during the period.[43]

With respect to self-lobbying organizations, the estimate of expenses (if not drawn from tax figures; see below and also Chapter 9 for further discussion) should include appropriate percentages of salaries and overhead, as well as other expenses incurred in support of the organization's lobbying activities. That includes expenses for the work of individuals who are not employees (such as consultants) and employees who are not lobbyists (such as support staff and researchers who may not make lobbying contacts but do develop background analyses that the organization's lobbyists use). It also should include travel expenses attributable to lobbying, and an allocable portion of dues payments to organizations that lobby on the registrant's behalf.[44] All expenses incurred in connection with federal lobbying activity should be included, even if such expenses were incurred by non-lobbyist employees. In general, expenses should be reported in the quarter in which they are incurred, even though payment may be made later.[45] However, organizations should include dues payments made to outside entities (such as trade associations) for federal lobbying activities in the estimate for the quarter in which they are actually paid.[46] Each organization will need to develop a reliable process for tracking and calculating its expenses consistently and accurately each quarter.

Example: *Acme Inc. has one employee lobbyist who spends 90 percent of her time on federal lobbying activities. For a particular quarter, her quarterly salary, including benefits, is $30,000. Airfare and lodging expenses for the lobbyist's federal lobbying-related travel during the quarter were $2,000. The lobbyist has an assistant who spends 10 percent of his time engaged in federal lobbying activities. The assistant's quarterly salary, including benefits, is $15,000. Acme estimates that overhead expenses allocable to the federal lobbying activities of the lobbyist and her assistant total $10,000 for the quarter. Fees for consultant*

---

39. 2 U.S.C. § 1604(b) (2015).
40. 2 U.S.C. § 1604(c)(1) (2015).
41. 2 U.S.C. § 1604(c)(2) (2015).
42. 2 U.S.C. § 1604(b)(3) (2015).
43. See Revised Guidance, Appendix 4-A.
44. 2 U.S.C. § 1604(b)(4) (2015).
45. See Revised Guidance, Appendix 4-A.
46. *Id.*

federal lobbyists are $30,000 per month. Acme belongs to several trade associations that engage in federal lobbying activities on its behalf. During the quarterly reporting period, Acme paid Big Trade Association $100,000 for its annual dues. The dues invoice stated that 60 percent of dues are allocated to federal lobbying.

Acme's estimate of federal lobbying related expenses for the quarter would be $190,500 and rounded to $190,000 for reporting purposes. Components of the expense estimate are as follows:

Lobbying Labor Costs	*$27,000*	*90% of lobbyist's salary and benefits*
	$ 1,500	*10% of assistant's salary and benefits*
Overhead	*$10,000*	*Overhead expenses allocable to federal lobbying activity*
Expenses	*$2,000*	*Federal lobbying-related travel expenses*
Consultants	*$90,000*	*Fees accrued in quarter, regardless of when invoiced or paid*
Dues	*$60,000*	*Portion of dues payment made in quarter allocable to federal lobbying*
TOTAL REPORTED	*$190,000*	*Rounded to nearest $10,000 for reporting purposes*

Example: *Black Consulting Co. was retained by Acme Inc. at a rate of $10,000 per month. The invoice for the last month of the quarterly reporting period has not been issued (or paid). Black Consulting's estimate of lobbying-related income from Acme will be $30,000, as income is reported as earned.*

4-6 Semiannual Reporting

In addition to the quarterly reports described above, the registrant and each employee who qualifies as a registered lobbyist under the above definitions must file semiannual political and honorary expenditure reports with the Secretary and the Clerk on July 30 and January 30 (or the next business day). The reports, filed electronically on Form LD-203, must include a certification that the filer has read and is familiar with the congressional gift rules and has not provided, requested, or directed a gift, including travel, to a member, officer, or employee of Congress with knowledge that the receipt of the gift would violate the congressional gift rules. The report also must disclose the filer's political contributions to federal candidates and certain other federal political committees, and certain honorary payments made in connection with covered officials. These reporting requirements are complex and wide-ranging, and we have devoted a later chapter to discussing them in more detail. See Chapter 5 for additional information about the LD-203 filing requirement.

4-7 Termination (Lobbyist and Registrant)

A registrant may generally terminate an individual as a lobbyist if the individual is no longer reasonably expected to meet either one of the two contacts/20 percent of time prongs of the definition of a lobbyist for the particular client. A registrant may terminate an employee as a lobbyist for a particular client if the employee did not spend 20 percent or more of his or her time for the client during the current quarter on federal lobbying activities, and is not expected to spend 20 percent of his or her time for that client on federal lobbying activities during the subsequent quarter.[47] Alternatively, an employee may be terminated if he or she does not reasonably expect to make additional lobbying contacts on behalf of the client.[48] In the case of a self-lobbying organization, the analysis is the same, but the organization itself is the client.

A registrant terminates an individual as a lobbyist by listing the name of the terminated lobbyist on Line 23 of the registrant's next-occurring quarterly LD-2 report.

Example: *Mary, John, and Susan are registered lobbyists for registrant Alpha Co. During the first quarter, Mary's federal lobbying activities occupied only 10 percent of her time as her responsibilities on state lobbying initiatives increased. Alpha anticipates that Mary will lead its state lobbying efforts going forward and will engage at the federal level only occasionally. John made no federal lobbying contacts in the first quarter and spent little time on federal lobbying activities, as the issues on which he focused were dormant. It is anticipated that those issues will be subject to renewed legislative interest in future quarters. Although Susan made frequent lobbying contacts during the quarter, Alpha determined that her talents were better suited to strategy and planning and that she would no longer make contacts on Alpha's behalf. Because Mary's time spent in lobbying activities in the quarter was less than 20 percent in the first quarter and there's no reasonable expectation that she will spend 20 percent or more of her time on federal lobbying activity in the second quarter, Alpha may terminate Mary's lobbyist status. In the absence of any reasonable expectation that she will make future lobbying contacts, Susan's lobbyist status should also be terminated. John should remain active.*

A lobbying firm may terminate its registration for a particular client when it is no longer employed or retained by the client to conduct federal lobbying activities and does not anticipate any additional lobbying activities for the client.[49] Similarly, a self-lobbying organization may terminate its registration when it no longer conducts lobbying activities and its lobbying activities are not expected to resume. To terminate a registrant's registration, the registrant must check the "Termination Report" box on its next quarterly LD-2 report and list on that report the date that the lobbying activity terminated. All lobbying activity and lobbying income or expenses must be disclosed through the date of termination.[50]

Example: *Due to changes in job responsibilities, one of Acme Inc.'s registered lobbyists, Mary Miller, spent only 10 percent of her time on federal lobbying activities during the quarterly reporting period. It is anticipated that Mary's federal lobbying activities will consume less than 10 percent of her time going forward. Mary's name should be listed on Line 23 ("Name of each previously reported individual who is no longer expected to act as a lobbyist for the client") of the quarterly report to formally terminate her status as a lobbyist.*

---

47. *Id.*
48. *Id.*
49. 2 U.SC. § 1603(d) (2015).
50. See Revised Guidance, Appendix 4-A.

Example: *Acme Inc. has notified Black Consulting Co. that it will not be renewing Black's consulting contract, which terminates on July 31. Black Consulting Co. will file its third quarter report for Acme as a Termination Report (checking the box on Line 10) and list the termination date of July 31.*

A registrant that terminates its registrations must still file a semiannual LD-203 report for the period during which termination occurred. The form may be filed early, before the statutory filing deadline, but it must include all required information through the date of termination. The same is true for an individual lobbyist whose active registrations are all terminated. The individual must file a semiannual LD-203 report for the period, complete through the final termination date. See Chapter 5 for further discussion on the LD-203 reporting requirement.

4-8 Tax Code Election

The LDA allows certain organizations the option of using a lobbying expense figure derived for federal tax purposes for LDA registration and reporting purposes. Under the option referred to as Method B, section 501(c)(3) organizations that have made an election under section 501(h) of the Internal Revenue Code have the option of using the amount reported to the Internal Revenue Service as lobbying expenditures both to determine whether the organization has exceeded the $12,500 LDA registration threshold and to determine the amount of its quarterly lobbying expenses for LD-2 reporting purposes.[51] Similarly, under the option referred to as Method C, taxable businesses and certain trade associations may use the amount of the organization's nondeductible lobbying expenditures under section 162(e) of the Internal Revenue Code both to determine whether the organization has met the LDA registration threshold and to determine the amount reported on its quarterly LD-2 reports.[52]

See Chapter 9 for additional information about the tax code election and alternative reporting methods.

4-9 Recordkeeping and Reporting Compliance

The LDA requires the Secretary and the Clerk to retain LDA registrations for at least six years after termination, and reports for at least six years after filing.[53] Accordingly, it is recommended that registrants also retain copies of their filings and supporting documentation for the same length of time (six years).

The Comptroller General, head of the Government Accountability Office (GAO), annually audits the level of compliance with the LDA by conducting random audits of the LDA reports filed by lobbyists and registrants.[54]

We provide herein a separate, detailed discussion of the audit process at Chapter 7. We provide guidance on building an effective LDA compliance program in Chapter 30.

---

51. 2 U.S.C. § 1610(a) (2015). See generally Chapter 9 for additional information about the tax code election.

52. 2 U.S.C. § 1610(b) (2015).

53. 2 U.S.C. § 1605(a)(5) (2015).

54. 2 U.S.C. § 1614(a) (2015).

APPENDIX 4-A

Lobbying Disclosure
Act Guidance

Guide to the Lobbying Disclosure Act

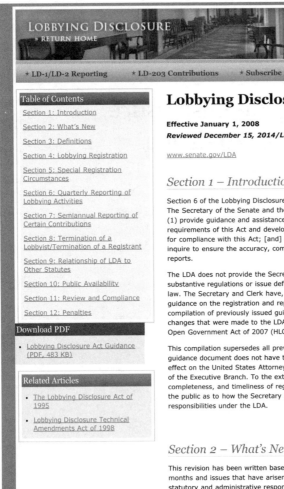

Lobbying Disclosure Act Guidance

Effective January 1, 2008
Reviewed December 15, 2014/Last Revised February 15, 2013[1]

www.senate.gov/LDA

Section 1 – Introduction

Section 6 of the Lobbying Disclosure Act (LDA), 2 U.S.C. § 1605, provides that: The Secretary of the Senate and the Clerk of the House of Representatives shall (1) provide guidance and assistance on the registration and reporting requirements of this Act and develop common standards, rules, and procedures for compliance with this Act; [and] (2) review, and, where necessary, verify and inquire to ensure the accuracy, completeness, and timeliness of registrations and reports.

The LDA does not provide the Secretary or the Clerk with the authority to write substantive regulations or issue definitive opinions on the interpretation of the law. The Secretary and Clerk have, from time to time, jointly issued written guidance on the registration and reporting requirements. This document is both a compilation of previously issued guidance documents and our interpretation of the changes that were made to the LDA as a result of the Honest Leadership and Open Government Act of 2007 (HLOGA).

This compilation supersedes all previous guidance documents. This combined guidance document does not have the force of law, nor does it have any binding effect on the United States Attorney for the District of Columbia or any other part of the Executive Branch. To the extent that the guidance relates to the accuracy, completeness, and timeliness of registrations and reports, it will serve to inform the public as to how the Secretary and Clerk intend to carry out their responsibilities under the LDA.

Section 2 – What's New

This revision has been written based upon comments received in the last six months and issues that have arisen as a result of the Secretary's and Clerk's statutory and administrative responsibilities. It also includes non-substantive grammatical changes throughout.

Updated Registration Threshold
As required by the LDA, the lobbying disclosure thresholds referenced throughout the Guidance have been updated to reflect changes in the Consumer Price Index (as determined by the Secretary of Labor) during the preceding 4-year period. After January 1, 2013, an organization employing in-house lobbyists is exempt from registration if its total expenses for lobbying activities does not exceed and is not expected to exceed $12,500 during a quarterly period. The $3,000 income

Table of Contents

Download PDF

- Lobbying Disclosure Act Guidance (PDF, 483 KB)

Related Articles

- The Lobbying Disclosure Act of 1995
- Lobbying Disclosure Technical Amendments Act of 1998

threshold for lobbying firms remains unchanged. See Guidance Section 4 on "Who Must Register and When" for additional information.

Section 3 – Definitions

Actively Participates:
An organization "actively participates" in the planning, supervision, or control of lobbying activities of a client or registrant when that organization (or an employee of the organization in his or her capacity as an employee) engages directly in planning, supervising, or controlling at least some of the lobbying activities of the client or registrant. Examples of activities constituting active participation would include participating in decisions about selecting or retaining lobbyists, formulating priorities among legislative issues, designing lobbying strategies, performing a leadership role in forming an ad hoc coalition, and other similarly substantive planning or managerial roles, such as serving on a committee with responsibility over lobbying decisions.

Organizations that, though members of or affiliated with a client, have only a passive role in the lobbying activities of the client (or of the registrant on behalf of the client), are not considered active participants in the planning, supervision, or control of such lobbying activities. Examples of activities constituting only a passive role would include merely donating or paying dues to the client or registrant, receiving information or reports on legislative matters, occasionally responding to requests for technical expertise or other information in support of the lobbying activities, attending a general meeting of the association or coalition client, or expressing a position with regard to legislative goals in a manner open to, and on a par with, that of all members of a coalition or association – such as through an annual meeting, a questionnaire, or similar vehicle. Mere occasional participation, such as offering an ad hoc informal comment regarding lobbying strategy to the client or registrant, in the absence of any formal or regular supervision or direction of lobbying activities, does not constitute active participation if neither the organization nor its employee has the authority to direct the client or the registrant on lobbying matters **and** the participation does not otherwise exceed a de minimis role.

Affiliated Organization:
An affiliated organization is any entity other than the client that contributes in excess of $5,000 toward the registrant's lobbying activities in a quarterly period, and actively participates in the planning, supervision, or control of such lobbying activities. The 2007 amendments to the LDA did not change the way in which LDA identified affiliates (i.e., those that in whole or in major part plan, supervise, or control such lobbying activities) are to be disclosed on Forms LD-1 and LD-2.

Client:
Any person or entity that employs or retains another person for financial or other compensation to conduct lobbying activities on behalf of that person or entity. An organization employing its own lobbyists is considered its own client for reporting purposes.

Contribution Reports:
Form LD-203 is required to be filed semiannually by July 30th and January 30th (or next business day should either of those days fall on a weekend or holiday) covering the first and second calendar halves of the year. Registrants and active lobbyists (who are not terminated for all clients) must file separate reports that detail FECA contributions, honorary contributions, presidential library contributions, and payments for event costs. (See discussion in Guidance Section 7 below.)

Covered Executive Branch Official:

The application of coverage of Section 3(3)(F) of the LDA (who is a covered Executive Branch official) was intended for Schedule C employees only. Senior Executive Service employees are not covered Executive Branch officials as defined in the Act unless they fall within one of the categories below. Covered Executive Branch officials are:

- The President

- The Vice President

- Officers and employees of the Executive Office of the President

- Any official serving in an Executive Level I through V position

- Any member of the uniformed services serving at grade O-7 or above

- Schedule C employees.

Covered Legislative Branch Official:
Covered Legislative Branch officials are:

- A Member of Congress

- An elected Officer of either the House or the Senate

- An employee, or any other individual functioning in the capacity of an employee, who works for a Member, committee, leadership staff of either the Senate or House, a joint committee of Congress, a working group or caucus organized to provide services to Members, and any other Legislative Branch employee serving in a position described under Section 109(13) of the Ethics in Government Act of 1978.

In whole or major part:
The term "in major part" means in substantial part. It is not necessary that an organization or foreign entity exercise majority control or supervision in order to fall within Sections 4(b)(3)(B) and 4(b)(4)(B). In general, 20 percent control or supervision should be considered "substantial" for purposes of these sections.

Lobbying Activities:
Lobbying contacts and any efforts in support of such contacts, including preparation or planning activities, research, and other background work that is intended, at the time of its preparation, for use in contacts, and coordination with the lobbying activities of others.

Lobbying Contact:
Any oral, written, or electronic communication to a covered official that is made on behalf of a client with regard to the enumerated subjects at Sections 3(8)(A) of the Act (2 U.S.C. § 1602(8)(A)). Note the exceptions to the definition at Section 3(8)(B) of the Act (2 U.S.C. § 1602(8)(B)). See Discussion at Guidance Section 4 below.

Lobbying Firm: A lobbying firm is a person or entity consisting of one or more individuals who meet the definition of a lobbyist with respect to a client other than that person or entity. The definition includes a self-employed lobbyist.

Lobbying Registration:
An initial registration on Form LD-1 filed pursuant to Section 4 of the Act (2 U.S.C. § 1603).

Lobbying Report:
A quarterly report on Form LD-2 filed pursuant to Section 5 of the Act (2 U.S.C. § 1604).

Lobbyist:
Any individual (1) who is either employed or retained by a client for financial or other compensation (2) whose services include more than one lobbying contact; and (3) whose lobbying activities constitute 20 percent or more of his or her

services' time on behalf of that client during any three-month period.

Person or Entity:
Any individual, corporation, company, foundation, association, labor organization, firm, partnership, society, joint stock company, group of organizations, or state or local government.

Public Official:
A public official includes an elected or appointed official, or an employee of a Federal, state, or local unit of government in the United States. There are five exceptions to this definition, including a college or university, a government-sponsored enterprise, a public utility, guaranty agency, or an agency of any state functioning as a student loan secondary market. The 1998 amendments to the LDA expanded the definition of a public official in Section 3(15)(F) to add a group of governments acting together as an international organization. Its purpose was to ensure those international organizations, such as the World Bank, would be treated in the same manner as the governments that comprise them.

Registrant:
A lobbying firm or an organization employing in-house lobbyists that files a registration pursuant to Section 4 of the Act.

Section 4 – Lobbying Registration

Who Must Register and When
Lobbying firms are required to file a separate registration for each client. A lobbying firm is exempt from registration for a particular client if its total income from that client for lobbying activities does not exceed and is not expected to exceed $3,000 during a quarterly period.

> Note: A lobbyist is not the registrant unless he/she is self-employed. In that case, the self-employed lobbyist is treated as a lobbying firm.

Organizations employing in-house lobbyists file a single registration. An organization is exempt from registration if its total expenses for lobbying activities do not exceed and are not expected to exceed $12,500 during a quarterly period.

The registration requirement of potential registrants is triggered either (1) on the date their employee/lobbyist is employed or retained to make more than one lobbying contact on behalf of a client (and meets the 20% of time threshold), or (2) on the date their employee/lobbyist (who meets the 20% of time threshold) in fact makes a second lobbying contact, whichever is earlier. In either case, registration is required within 45 days.

> Example 1: Lobbying firm "A" is retained on May 1, 2008 by Client "B" to make lobbying contacts and conduct lobbying activities. "A" files an LD-1 on behalf of "B" with an effective date of registration of May 1, 2008.

> Example 2: Corporation "C" does not employ an individual who meets the definition of "lobbyist." Employee "X" is told by her supervisor to contact the Congressman representing the district in which Corporation "C" is headquartered. "X" makes a lobbying contact on June 1, 2008. "X" does not anticipate making any further lobbying contacts, but spends 25% of her time on this legislative issue. No registration is required at this point. In August 2008, "X" is

instructed to follow up with the Congressman again. "C" registers and discloses August 5, 2008 as the effective date of registration (the date that "X" contacted the Congressman for the second time and thereby met the definition of a lobbyist).

Preparing to File a Registration – Threshold Requirements

In order to determine the applicability of the LDA, one must first look at the definition of "lobbyist" under Section 3(10) of the Act. Under this definition, an individual is a "lobbyist" with respect to a particular client if he or she makes more than one lobbying contact **and** his or her "lobbying activities" (as defined in Section 3(7)) constitute at least 20 percent of the individual's time in services for **that** client over any three-month period. Note that a registration would not be required for pro bono clients since the monetary thresholds of Section 4(a)(3)(A)(i) in the case of a lobbying firm, or of Section 4(a)(3)(A)(ii) in the case of an organization employing in-house lobbyists, would not be met. Keep in mind that the obligation to report under the LDA arises from active status as a registrant. Therefore if a registration has been filed for a pro bono client, LD-2 and LD-203 reports would be expected to be filed until the registration is validly terminated.

More than One Lobbying Contact

"More than one lobbying contact" means more than one communication to a covered official. Note that an individual falls within the definition of "lobbyist" by making more than one lobbying contact over the course of services provided for a particular client (even if the second contact occurs in a later quarterly period).

Example 1: Lobbyist "A" telephones Covered Official "B" in the morning to discuss proposed legislation. In the afternoon she telephones Covered Official "C" to discuss the same legislation. Lobbyist "A" has made more than one lobbying contact.

Example 2: Under some circumstances a series of discussions with a particular official might be considered a single communication, such as when a telephone call is interrupted and continued at a later time. Discussions taking place on more than one day with the same covered official, however, should be presumed to be more than one lobbying contact.

Clarification of an Exception to Lobbying Contact

Section 3(8)(B)(ix) excepts from the definition of "lobbying contact" communications "required by subpoena, civil investigative demand, or otherwise compelled by statute, regulation, or other action of the Congress or an agency." The 1998 amendments to the LDA clarified that communications that are compelled by the action of a Federal agency include communications that are required by a Federal agency contract, grant, loan, permit, or license.

Example: Contractor "A" has a contract to provide technical assistance to Agency "B" on an ongoing basis. Technical communications between Contractor "A's" personnel and covered officials at Agency "B" would be required by the contract and therefore would not constitute "lobbying contacts."

Note, however, that this exception would not encompass an attempt by "A" to influence covered officials regarding either matters of policy, or an award of a new contract, since such communications would not be required by the existing contract.

Do Lobbying Activities Constitute 20% Or More of an Individual's Time?

Lobbying activity is defined in Section 3(7) as "lobbying contacts and efforts in support of such contacts, including ... background work that is intended, at the time it is performed, for use in contacts, and coordination with the lobbying activities of others." If the intent of the work is to support ongoing and future lobbying, then it would fall within the definition of lobbying activities. Timing of the work performed, as well as the status of the issue, is also pivotal. Generally, if work such as reporting or monitoring occurs at a time when future lobbying contacts are contemplated, such reporting and monitoring should be considered as a part of planning or coordinating of lobbying contacts, and therefore included as "lobbying activity." If, on the other hand, a person reports back to the relevant committee or officer regarding the status of a completed effort, that activity would probably not be included as a lobbying activity, if reports are not being used to prepare a lobbying strategy the next time the issue is considered.

Communications excepted from the definition of "lobbying contact" under Section 3(8)(B) of the LDA may be considered "lobbying activities" under some circumstances. Communications excepted by Section 3(8)(B) will constitute "lobbying activities" if they are in support of other communications which constitute "lobbying contacts."

> Example: Under Section 3(8)(B)(v), the term "lobbying contact" does not include "a request for a meeting, a request for the status of an action, or any other similar administrative request, if the request does not include an attempt to influence a covered Executive Branch official or a covered Legislative Branch official." However, a status request would constitute "lobbying activity" if it were in support of a subsequent lobbying contact.

Please note that the 20% of time threshold applies to registration and not to the reporting section.

Is it Lobbying Contact/Lobbying Activity?

If a communication is limited to routine information gathering questions and there is not an attempt to influence a covered official, the exception of Section 3(8)(B)(v) for "any other similar administrative request" would normally apply. In determining whether there is an attempt to influence a covered official, the identity of the person asking the questions and her relationship to the covered official obviously will be important factors.

> Example 1: Lobbyist "A", a former chief of staff in a congressional office, is now a partner in the law firm retained to lobby for Client "B." After waiting one year to comply with post employment restrictions on lobbying, Lobbyist "A" telephones the Member on whose staff she served. She asks about the status of legislation affecting Client "B's" interests. Presumably "B" will expect the call to have been part of an effort to influence the Member, even though only routine matters were raised at that particular time.

> Example 2: Company "Z" offers temporary employment to recent

college graduates. The graduates are hired to conduct surveys of
congressional staff by reading prepared questions and recording the
answers. The questions seek only information. These communications
do not amount to lobbying contacts.

Lobbying Contacts and Activities Using Section 15 Election (Alternate Reporting Methods)

Section 15 of the LDA permits those organizations that are required to file and do file under Section 6033(b)(8) of the Internal Revenue Code (IRC) and organizations that are subject to Section 162(e) of the IRC to use the tax law definitions of lobbying in lieu of the LDA definitions for determining "contacts" and "lobbying activities" for Executive Branch lobbying. Registrants should note that the tax definition of lobbying is broader with respect to the type of activities reported, while it is narrower with respect to the universe of Executive Branch officials who qualify as covered Executive Branch employees.

Under the 1998 amendments to the LDA, registrants making a Section 15 election must use the Internal Revenue Code definition for Executive Branch lobbying, and the LDA definition for Legislative Branch lobbying. Because there are fewer Executive Branch officials under the IRC definitions than under the LDA definitions, this may result in fewer individuals being listed as lobbyists and fewer lobbying contacts reflected on the Form LD-2.

Also note that definitions under the tax code include "grass-roots" and "state" lobbying, while the LDA excludes those types of lobbying from the definition of "lobbying activities." The LDA does not permit modification of the tax code definition to exclude such expenditures when reporting lobbying expenses.

Relationship Between 20% of Time and Monetary Threshold

If the definition of "lobbyist" is satisfied with respect to at least one individual for a particular client, the potential registrant (either a lobbying firm or an organization employing the lobbyist, or a self-employed individual lobbyist) is **not** required to register if it does not meet the monetary thresholds of Section 4(a)(3)(A)(i), in the case of a "lobbying firm," or of Section 4(a)(3)(A)(ii), in the case of an organization employing in-house lobbyists. Note that the monetary exemption is computed based on the lobbying activities of the potential registrant as a whole for the particular client in question, not simply on the lobbying activities of those individuals who are "lobbyists."

Example 1: A law firm has two lawyers who perform services for a particular client. Lawyer "A" spends 15 percent of the time she works for that client on lobbying activities, including some lobbying contacts. Lawyer "B" spends 25 percent of the time he works for the client on lobbying activities, but makes no lobbying contacts. Neither lawyer falls within the definition of "lobbyist," and therefore the law firm is not required to register for that client, even if the income it receives for lobbying activities on behalf of the client exceeds $3,000.

Example 2: Employee "A" of a trade association is a "lobbyist" who spends 25 percent of his time on lobbying activities on behalf of the association. There are $6,500 of expenses related to Employee "A's" lobbying activities. Employee "B" is not a "lobbyist" but engages in lobbying activities in support of lobbying contacts made by Employee "A." There are $6,5 00 of additional expenses related to the lobbying activities of Employee "B." The trade association is required to register because it employs a "lobbyist" and its total expenses in connection with lobbying activities on its own behalf exceed $12,500.

> Example 3: Same as Example 2, except the expenses related to the lobbying activities of Employees "A" and "B" total only $9,000, but the trade association also pays $5,000 to an outside firm for lobbying activities. Registration is still required because payments to outside contractors (including lobbying firms that may be separately registered under the LDA) must be included in the total expenses of an organization employing lobbyists on its own behalf.

Timing

The registration requirement of a potential registrant is triggered either (1) on the date their employee/lobbyist is employed or retained to make more than one lobbying contact on behalf of the client (and meets the 20% of time threshold), or (2) on the date their employee/lobbyist (who meets the 20% of time threshold) in fact makes a second lobbying contact, whichever is earlier. In either case, registration is required within 45 days of that date.

> Example: Lobbying Firm "A" is retained to monitor an issue, but whether or not lobbying contacts will be made depends on future legislative developments. In another case, Corporation "B," which employs an in-house lobbyist, knows that its lobbyist will make contacts but reasonably expects its lobbying expenditures will not amount to $12,500 in a quarterly period. However, issues of interest to "B" turn out to be more controversial than expected, and the $12,500 threshold is in fact met a month later.
>
> Lobbying firm "A" has no registration requirement at the present time. The requirement to register is triggered if and when the firm makes contacts, or reasonably expects that it will make contacts. Corporation "B's" registration requirement arose as soon as it knew, or reasonably expected, that its lobbying expenditures will exceed $12,500. "B" needs to register immediately.

Listing of Foreign Entities

Each registration must contain the name, address, principal place of business, amount of any contribution greater than $5,000 to the lobbying activities of the registrant, and approximate percentage of ownership in the client of any foreign entity that: holds at least 20% equitable ownership in the client or any affiliate of the client required to be listed on line 13; **or** directly or indirectly, in whole or major part, plans, supervises, controls, directs, finances, or subsidizes the activities of the client or affiliate of the client required to be listed on line 13; **or** is an affiliate of either the client, or an organization affiliated with the client identified on Line 13 or 14 of Form LD-1 and has a direct interest in the outcome of the lobbying activity. The purpose of the disclosure is to identify the interests of the foreign entity that may be operating behind the registrant.

> Example: Lobbying Firm "A" is retained to lobby on behalf of Company "B," which is wholly owned by Foreign Company "C." "C" is wholly owned by Foreign Company "D," and "D" is wholly owned by Foreign Company "E." "C," "D," and "E" must be disclosed on Line 14.

Section 5 – Special Registration Circumstances

Elaboration on the Definition of Client

In some cases a registrant is retained as part of a larger lobbying effort that encompasses more than one lobbying firm on behalf of a third party. Generally, the entity that is paying the registrant is listed as the client on behalf of the third party. The third party, who is paying the intermediary (client), is listed also on Line 13 of Form LD-1 as an affiliate.

> Example: Client "P" retains lobbying firm "F" for general lobbying purposes, but has a new interest in obtaining an outcome in an area new to "P." "F" realizes that a boutique lobbying firm "L" has an excellent track record for obtaining the type of outcome "P" is seeking, and talks to "P" about subcontracting. "P" agrees with "F's" strategy. "F" contacts "L" to retain the latter to do the project. "F" is responsible for paying "L." Within 45 days, "L" registers disclosing "F on behalf of P" as the client, and listing "P" as the affiliate on Line 13 of Form LD-1.

Lobbying Firms Retained Under a Contingent Fee

Law other than the LDA governs whether a firm may be retained on a contingent-fee basis. There is, for example, a general prohibition on the payment of contingent fees in connection with the award of government contracts. Assuming, however, that the agreement is not contrary to law or public policy, an agreement to make lobbying contacts for a contingent fee, like other fee arrangements, triggers a registration requirement at inception. The fee is disclosed on Form LD 2 for the quarterly period that the registrant becomes entitled to it.

> Example 1: On January 1, 2008, Lobbying Firm "G" agrees to lobby for Client "H" for a fee contingent on a certain result, **and the agreement is permitted under other applicable law**. Lobbying activities begin. "G" is required to register by February 14, 2008. The result is not obtained and "G" is not entitled to any fee during the first quarterly period. "G" must report its lobbying activities for the first quarterly period; the income reported is "Less than $5,000." The desired result does occur in the second quarterly period of 2008. In the report for that period, "G" discloses its lobbying activities for that period and the total contingent fee.

> Example 2: Lobbying Firm "J" discusses an arrangement to accept stock options worth $4,500 from Client "M" in lieu of payment of a contingency fee. After determining that acceptance of a success fee is not a violation of another statute, "J" signs a contract with "M," and registers. Late in the first quarter of the lobbying activities, it appeared "J" achieved the result. "J's" initial quarterly lobbying report disclosed lobbying income of less than $5,000. "M's" stock value increased shortly thereafter to be valued at $6,000, so "J" exercised its options. "J" amended the previously filed quarterly report to reflect income of "$5,000 or more," and rounded the amount to $10,000.

Registration for Entities with Subsidiaries or State and Local Affiliates

Assuming a parent entity or national association and its subsidiary or subordinate are separate legal entities, the parent makes a determination whether it meets the registration threshold based upon its own activities, and does not include subordinate units= lobbying activities in its assessment. Each subordinate must make its own assessment as to whether any of its own employees meet the definition of a lobbyist, and then determine if it meets the registration threshold with respect to lobbying expenses.

> Example: Lobbyist "Z" is an employee of Company "A," which is a wholly owned subsidiary of Company "B." "Z's" lobbying activities advance the interests of both. Which company is responsible for registering and reporting under the LDA?
>
> The registration and reporting requirements apply to the organization of which Lobbyist "Z" is an employee. Therefore, Company "A" would register and file the quarterly reports.
>
> If Company "B" contributes $5,000 or more to "Z's" lobbying activities during a quarterly period and actively participates in the planning, supervision, or control of the lobbying activities, Company "B" must be listed on Company "A's" Form LD 1, Line 13. A contribution may take any form, and may be direct or indirect. For example, if Company "B" established Company "A" with an initial capital contribution of $1,000,000, which "A" draws upon for employee salaries, including "Z's," and to pay for office space used by "Z," a $5,000 contribution probably has been made.
>
> If Company "B" is a foreign entity, and the facts are otherwise the same as above, "B" would be listed on Line 14 of the Form LD 1 filed by Company "A." "B's" interests in specific lobbying issues would also be disclosed on Line 19 of Form LD 2.

The LDA does not make any express provision for combined or consolidated filings. A single filing by a parent corporation may be appropriate in some cases, especially when there are multiple subsidiaries and the lobbyists address the same issues for all and act under the close control of the parent. In this regard, note that the LDA does not contain any specific definition of "employee" (there is only the general definition of Section 3(5)), and the policy of the LDA is to promote disclosure of real parties in interest.

In circumstances in which multiple subsidiaries each have only a fraction of the lobbyist's time and little control over his work, the parent which in fact exercises actual control can be regarded as the "employer" for LDA purposes. In such cases, the parent may file a single registration, provided that Line 10 of Form LD 1 discloses that the listed lobbyists are employees of subsidiaries and the subsidiaries are identified as affiliated organizations on Line 13.

Effect of Mergers and Acquisitions on Registrations

The following examples serve to illustrate hypothetical situations regarding mergers and acquisitions:

> Example 1: Corporation "C" registered under the LDA during 2008. Effective upon close of business on December 31, 2008, "C" merged with Corporation "D." "D," the surviving corporation, had no lobbyist employees before the merger and is not registered. How and when

should this information be reported? Assuming that "D" retains at least one of "C's" lobbyist employees and will incur lobbying expenses of at least $12,500 during the January March quarterly period, Corporation "D" is required to register. The 45 day period in which its initial registration must be filed begins to run on December 31, 2008, the date "D" first had lobbyist employees, and the registration is due by February 14, 2009. On the other hand, if "D" will not be lobbying after the merger, it is not required to register. In pre merger discussions, Corporation "C" might have agreed to terminate its registration and file its final lobbying report before ceasing its corporate existence. If, however, "C" did not do so, Corporation "D" should terminate the registration and file the outstanding lobbying report in "C's" name. "D" may simply annotate the signature block on Form LD 2 to indicate that it is filing as successor in interest to "C."

Example 2: Lobbying Firm "O" is a registrant under the LDA. It merges with Lobbying Firm "P," which is also a registrant. The new entity will be known as Lobbying Firm "T." How and when should this information be reported? The answer depends on the particular facts. If Lobbying Firm "T" is a newly created legal entity, it should file a new registration within 45 days. The registrations of both "O" and "P" should be terminated by filing separate termination reports for each remaining registrant/client relationship. But if "T" is simply the new name adopted by "O" following the merger with "P," with "P" going out of existence, "O" should report its new name and other updated information (such as the names of lobbyist employees of "P" who are retained or hired by "T") on Form LD 2. "P's" registration should be terminated, and P should file termination reports for each remaining registrant/client relationship, but only after P ceases to exist.

Example 3: Corporation "J," a registrant, acquired Corporation "K," a non registrant. At the time of the acquisition, "J" changed its name to "J & K." How and when should this information be reported? For LDA purposes, this is simply a change in the name of the registrant. The change should be reported on Line 1 of the next LD-2 quarterly report.

Associations or Coalitions

The LDA provides that "[i]n the case of a coalition or association that employs or retains other persons to conduct lobbying activities, the client is the coalition or association and not its individual members" (Section 3(2)). A bona fide coalition that employs or retains lobbyists on behalf of the coalition may be the client for LDA purposes, even if the coalition is not a legal entity or has no formal name. A registrant lobbying for an unnamed informal coalition needs to adopt some type of identifier for Line 7 of Form LD 1, and indicate "(Informal Coalition)" or another applicable description. For all coalitions and associations, formal or informal, the LDA requires further disclosures, e.g., of organizations other than the client that contribute more than $5,000 toward the lobbying activities of the registrant in the quarterly period, **and** actively participate in the planning, supervision, or control of the lobbying activities (Section 4(b)(3)). Such organizations are identified on Line 13 of Form LD 1.

Example 1: Association "A" has 20 organizational members who each pay $20,000 as a portion of their annual dues to fund "A's" lobbying activities. "E" is an employee of Organization "O," which is a member of "A." "E" serves as a member of "A's" board, as a representative of "O." While "A" carries out various functions, a substantial part of its mission is lobbying on issues of interest to its member organizations. "E's" board membership constitutes active participation by "O" in the lobbying activities of "A," and thus "O" would need to be listed as an affiliated organization of "A."

Example 2: Another association "A" has 1000 organizational members who each pay $20,000 as a portion of their annual dues to fund "A's" lobbying activities. "E" is an employee of Organization "O," which is a member of "A." "E" serves as a member of "A's" board, as a representative of "O." "A" performs numerous functions, only a modest portion of which is lobbying. With regard to "A's" lobbying activities, "A's" board is only involved in approving an overall budget for such activities, but otherwise leaves supervision, direction, and control of such matters to a separate committee of member organizations. "E's" board membership in this case does not constitute active participation by "O" in the lobbying activities of "A."

Example 3: Another association "A" has 1000 organizational members who each pay $1,000 a month in annual dues to "A." "E" is an employee of Organization "O," which is a member of "A." "E" serves as a member of "A's" lobbying oversight group as a representative of "O." The lobbying oversight group plans and supervises lobbying strategy for "A." While "E's" activities in "A" would constitute active participation, because "O" does not contribute $5,000 in the reporting quarter to the lobbying activities of "A," "O" would not need to be listed as an affiliate of "A."

Example 4: Another association "A" has 100 organizational members who each pay $30,000 a month as a portion of their annual dues to fund "A's" lobbying activities. "E" is an employee of Organization "O," and attends "A's" annual meeting/conference, informally provides "O's" list of legislative priorities to "A," and also facilitates responses from "O" to occasional requests for information by "A's" lobbyists. These activities would not make "O" an active participant in the lobbying activities of "A."

Example 5: Organization "O" joins with a group of nine other organizations to form Coalition "C" to lobby on an issue of interest to it. Each contributes $50,000 to "C's" budget. "O's" vice president for government relations is part of the informal group that directs the lobbying strategy for "C." "O" would be considered an active participant in "C's" lobbying activities and would have to be disclosed.

Note that a coalition with a foreign entity as a member must identify the foreign entity on Line 14 of Form LD-1 if the foreign entity meets the test of either Section 4(b)(3) or 4(b)(4).

Churches, Integrated Auxiliaries, Conventions or Association of Churches and Religious Orders – Hiring of Outside Firms

Although the definition of a lobbying contact does not include a communication made by a church, its integrated auxiliary, a convention or association of churches and religious orders (Section 3(8)(B)(xviii)), if a church (its integrated auxiliary, a convention or association of churches, and religious orders) hires an outside firm that conducts lobbying activity on its behalf, the outside firm must register if registration is otherwise required.

Registration of Professional Associations of Elected Officials
The Section 3(15) definition of "public official" includes a professional association of elected officials who are exempt from registration. If the association retains an outside firm to lobby, the lobbying firm must register if otherwise required to do so, i.e., the firm employs a lobbyist as defined in Section 3(10) and lobbying income exceeds $3,000 in a quarterly period.

Section 6 – Quarterly Reporting of Lobbying Activities

When and Why a Report is Needed
Each registrant must file a quarterly report on Form LD-2 no later than 20 days (or on the first business day after such 20th day if the 20th day is not a business day) after the end of the quarterly period beginning on the first day of January, April, July, and October **of each year** in which a registrant is registered. Lobbying firms file separate reports for each client for each quarterly reporting period, while organizations employing in-house lobbyists file one report covering their in-house lobbying activities for each quarterly reporting period. All reports must be filed electronically (with exceptions as noted below). **The Secretary and Clerk do not have the authority under the LDA to grant extensions to registrants.**

The obligation to report under the LDA arises from active status as a registrant (i.e., a registration on file that has not been validly terminated). Section 5(a) of the LDA requires a registrant to file a report for the quarterly period **in which it incurred its registration requirement**, and for each quarterly period thereafter, through and including the reporting period encompassing the date of registration termination. A timely report using Form LD-2 is required even though the registration was in effect for only part of the reporting period. So long as a registration is on file and has not been terminated, a registrant must report its lobbying activities even if those activities during a particular quarterly period would not trigger a registration requirement in the first instance (e.g., a lobbying firm's income from a client amounted to less than $3,000 during a particular quarterly period). A registrant with no lobbying activity during a quarterly period checks the no activity box on Form LD-2.

> Example 1: "A" is the only lobbyist of Lobbying Firm "Z" listed in the registration filed for Client "Y" on February 14, 2008. During January – March 2008, "A" lobbied for "Y" nearly full time. During the April – June period in 2008, however, "A" made only one lobbying contact for "Y" in April, but lobbying fees for the quarter were $10,000. For the April – June quarterly period, even though "A" had minimal lobbying activities, Lobbying Firm "Z" must report "A's" lobbying activities (due to "A's" being listed as a lobbyist) and must report the $10,000 lobbying fees.

> Example 2: Lobbying Firm "Z" is retained by Client "X" on June 1,

2008 for thirty days to lobby on a particular issue that is on the legislative calendar and the issue is settled prior to the departure of House and Senate Members for the July 4th recess. Firm "Z" must file its registration by July 15, file its Q2 LD-2 Report by July 20, and, if it chooses to terminate, file its termination report by October 20.

Disclosing that a Client is a State or Local Government or Instrumentality

If the client is a state or local government or instrumentality, check the box on Line 7 of Form LD-2.

Mandatory Electronic Filing

Section 5 of the LDA was amended to require the mandatory electronic filing of all documents required by the LDA. The only exception to mandatory electronic filing is for the purpose of amending reports in the format previously filed, or for compliance with the Americans with Disabilities Act. Each electronic lobbying disclosure form provides usability for people with vision impairments who have the appropriate software and hardware. If you have questions regarding additional ADA accommodations, please contact the Senate Office of Public Records at 202-224-0758.

Preparing to File the Quarterly Report – Income or Expense Recording

The LDA does not contain any special record keeping provisions, but requires, in the case of an outside lobbying firm (including self-employed individuals), a good faith estimate of all income received from the client, other than payments for matters unrelated to lobbying activities. In the case of an organization employing in-house lobbyists, the LDA requires a good faith estimate of the total expenses of its lobbying activities. As long as the registrant has a reasonable system in place and complies in good faith with that system, the requirement of reporting expenses or income would be met. Since Section 6(a)(5) requires the Secretary and Clerk to "retain registrations for a period of at least 6 years after they are terminated and reports for a period of at least 6 years after they are filed," we recommend registrants retain copies of their filings and supporting documentation for the same length of time.

Lobbying Firm Income

Lobbying firms report income earned or accrued from lobbying activities during a quarterly period, even though the client may not be billed or make payment until a later time. For a lobbying firm, gross income from the client for lobbying activities is reportable, including reimbursable expenses, costs, or disbursements that are in addition to fees and separately invoiced. Line 12 of Form LD-2 provides boxes for a lobbying firm to report income of less than $5,000, or of $5,000 or more. If lobbying income is $5,000 or more, a lobbying firm must provide a good faith estimate of the actual dollar amount **rounded to the nearest $10,000**.

Organization Expenses Using LDA Expense Reporting Method

Organizations that employ in-house lobbyists may incur lobbying-related expenses in the form of employee compensation, office overhead, or payments to vendors, which may include lobbying firms. Organizations must report expenses as they are incurred, though payment may be made later. Line 13 of Form LD-2 provides for an organization to report lobbying expenses of less than $5,000, or $5,000 or more. If lobbying expenses are $5,000 or more, the organization must provide a good faith estimate of the actual dollar amount **rounded to the nearest $10,000**. Organizations using the LDA expense reporting method mark the

"Method A" box on Line 14 of Form LD-2.

To ensure complete reporting, the Secretary and Clerk have consistently interpreted Section 5(b)(4) to require such organizations to report all of their expenses incurred in connection with lobbying activities, including all payments to retained lobby firms or outside entities, without considering whether any particular payee has a separate obligation to register and report under the LDA. Logically, if an organization employing in-house lobbyists also retains a lobbying firm, the expense reported by the organization should be greater than the fees reported by the lobbying firm of which the organization is a client. An organization must contact any other organization to which it pays membership dues in order to learn what portion of the dues is used by the latter organization for lobbying activities. It is necessary for the former organization to include the portion of the dues that is designated for lobbying activities in the total of lobbying expenses reported by the former organization. A registrant cannot apportion the lobbying expense part of the dues to avoid disclosure. Dues payments for lobbying activities should be included in the estimate for the quarter in which they are paid.

All employee time spent in lobbying activities must be included in determining the organization's lobbying expenses, even if the employee does not meet the statutory definition of a "lobbyist."

> Example: The CEO of a registrant, "Defense Contractor," travels to Washington to meet with a covered DOD official regarding the renewal of a government contract. "Defense Contractor" has already determined that its CEO is not a "lobbyist," because he does not spend 20 percent of his time on "lobbying activities" during a quarterly period. Nonetheless, the expenses reasonably allocable to the CEO's lobbying activities (e.g., plane ticket to Washington, salary and benefit costs, etc.) will be reportable.

Similarly, all expenses of lobbying activities incurred during a quarterly period are reportable. The Section 3(7) definition of lobbying activities is not limited to lobbying contacts. Examples of lobbying expenses to be included are reflected below.

> Example 1: A research assistant in the Washington office of the registrant, "Defense Contractor" (described in the example above) researches and prepares the talking points for the CEO's lobbying contact with the covered DOD official. Likewise, the expenses reasonably allocable to the research assistant's lobbying activities will be included in "Defense Contractor's" expense estimate for the quarterly period.

> Example 2: Corporation "R" is a registrant that is interested in building a bypass around a city in state "S." "R's" governmental affairs team is comprised of lobbyists who are federally-focused, and lobbyists who are state-focused. The entire staff prepares a strategic lobbying plan to support the building of the bypass. This includes both federal and state lobbying. In this example, the time spent by the state level lobbyists preparing the materials would be included in "R's" good faith estimate of lobbying expenses for the quarter because, at the time the materials were prepared, they were to be used for federal lobbying.

> Example 3: Same circumstances as Example 2, but in this situation, the aforementioned strategic lobbying plan includes hiring one firm to help with the production of the plan, and another firm to place advertising in media in "S" to encourage citizens in "S" to contact their representatives about the importance of building the bypass. The total cost of producing the plan, but not the cost of the advertising media fees, must be included in "R's" good faith estimate of lobbying expenses for the quarter.

The examples below are intended to be illustrative of the possibilities of LDA expense reporting, and are not intended to require detailed accounting rules.

> Example 1: An organization employing in-house lobbyists might choose to estimate lobbying expenses by asking each professional staffer to track his/her percentages of time devoted to lobbying activities. These percentages could be averaged to compute the percentage of the organization's total effort (and budget) that is devoted to lobbying activities. Under this example the organization would include salary costs (including a percentage of support staff salaries), overhead, and expenses, including any third-party costs attributable to lobbying.

> Example 2: Another organization, which lobbies out of its Washington office, might avoid the need for detailed breakdowns by including the entire budget or expenses (whichever, the organization believes in good faith is closer to the actual amount) of its Washington office.

Organizations Reporting Expenses Under Section 15 (Optional IRC Reporting Methods)

Section 15(a) of the LDA allows entities that are required to report and do report lobbying expenditures under section 6033(b)(8) of the Internal Revenue Code to use IRC definitions for purposes of LDA Sections (4)(a)(3) and 5(b)(4). Charitable organizations, as described in IRC Section 501(c)(3), are required to report to the Internal Revenue Service their lobbying expenditures in conformity with Section 6033(b)(8) of the IRC. They may treat as LDA expenses the amounts they treat for "influencing legislation" under the IRC.

Section 15(b) of the LDA allows entities that are subject to section 162(e) of the IRC to use IRC definitions for purposes of LDA Sections (4)(a)(3) and 5(b)(4). The eligible entities include for-profit organizations (other than lobbying firms) and tax-exempt organizations such as trade associations that calculate their lobbying expenses for IRC purposes with reference to IRC Section 162(e) rules. We believe that this reporting option is available to include also a small number of trade association registrants not required by the IRC to report non-deductible lobbying expenses to their members (i.e., those whose members are tax-exempt).

If an eligible organization elects to report under Section 15, it must do so consistently for all reports covering a calendar year. The electing organization also must report **all expenses that fall within the applicable Internal Revenue Code definition**. The total that is ultimately reportable to the Internal Revenue Service is the figure that would be used for Line 13 reporting. Line 13 of Form LD-2 would require any organization to report if the amount of lobbying expenses was less than $5,000, or $5,000 or more. If the expense amount is $5,000 or more, it should be **rounded to the nearest $10,000**. Line 14 of Form

LD-2 requires the electing organization to mark as applicable, either the "Method B" box (IRC Section 6033(b)(8)) or the "Method C" box (IRC Section 162(e)). The Secretary and Clerk are aware that the IRC and LDA are not harmonized in terms of expense reporting. Registrants are advised that if they elect to report under Section 15, they may not subtract lobbying expenses for lobbying state and local officials and grassroots lobbying from the total expenses reported under the LDA. Doing so alters the IRS reportable total, and is not permitted.

Quarterly Reporting of Lobbying Activities – Contents of Report

The two core disclosures required by Section 5(h) and 5(c) of the LDA and incorporated into Form LD-2 are: (1) lobbying income or expenses; and (2) lobbying issues. Form LD-2 has been designed to allow registrants the greatest flexibility in terms of document length to correspond with the varying amounts of information relating to the core disclosures. The following examples illustrate how the nature of the core disclosures builds the form.

> Example 1: Registrant "A" represents Client "B" to monitor an issue of interest to B and make occasional lobbying contacts as necessary. During the Q1 2008 reporting period, "A" received $3,000 from "B," but had no lobbying activity because "B's" issue was dormant. "A" would complete Form LD-2, , mark the box on Line 11 labeled "No Lobbying Activity," mark Line 12 as "Less than $5,000," and file the report.

> Example 2: Same circumstances as above, except that "A" has two lobbyists who make lobbying contacts on a single lobbying issue with the Senate and the House. In this case, "A" will need to complete the Lobbying Activity section of Form LD-2 and file the report.

> Example 3: Same circumstances as example 2, but one of the lobbyists retires during the reporting period. In this case, an update page of Form LD-2 would be required, listing the lobbyist's name on Line 23, which has the effect of reflecting the removal of the lobbyist's name (his/her retirement) from "A's" registration and reports.

Section 5(b) of the LDA requires specific information on the nature of the lobbying activities. The Lobbying Activity Section of Form LD-2 requires the registrant to:

- Disclose the general lobbying issue area code (list 1 code per page).

- Identify the specific issues on which the lobbyist(s) engaged in lobbying activities.

- Identify the Houses of Congress and Federal Agencies contacted.

- Disclose the lobbyists who had any activity in the general issue area.

- Describe the interest of a foreign entity if applicable.

When reporting specific lobbying issues, some registrants have listed only House or Senate bill numbers on the issues page without further indication of their clients' specific lobbying issues. Such disclosures are not adequate, for several reasons. First, Section 5(b)(2)(A) of the LDA requires disclosure of "specific issues upon which a lobbyist employed by the registrant engaged in lobbying activities, including … bill numbers[.]" As we read the law, a bill number is a required disclosure when the lobbying activities concern a bill, but is not in itself a complete disclosure. Further, in many cases, a bill number standing alone does not inform the public of the client's specific issue. Many bills are lengthy and complex, or may contain various provisions that are not always directly related to the main subject or title. If a registrant's client is interested in only one or a few specific provisions of a much larger bill, a lobbying report containing a mere bill number will not disclose the specific lobbying issue. Even if a bill concerns only one specific subject, a lobbying report disclosing only a bill number is still inadequate, because a member of the public would need access to information outside of the filing to ascertain that subject. In our view, the LDA contemplates disclosures that are adequate to inform the public of the lobbying client's specific issues from a review of the Form LD 2, without independent familiarity with bill numbers or the client's interest in specific subject matters within larger bills. The disclosures on Line 16 must include bill numbers, where applicable, but must always contain information that is adequate, standing alone, to inform the public of the specific lobbying issues.

> Example: Client "A's" general lobbying issue area is "Environment." During the first quarter of 2008, lobbyists for "A" made contacts concerning the Department of Defense appropriations for environmental restoration. For fiscal 2009, the Department of Defense Appropriations Act was part of the Omnibus Consolidated Appropriations Act for 2009, H.R. 3610, a lengthy and complex bill that did not have numbered sections throughout. Title II contained separate but unnumbered provisions making appropriations for "Environmental Restoration, Army," "Environmental Restoration, Navy," "Environmental Restoration, Air Force," "Environmental Restoration, Defense Wide," and "Environmental Restoration, Formerly Used Defense Sites." Lobbying contacts for Client "A" addressed all environmental restoration funding within the Defense Department bill. An appropriate disclosure of the specific lobbying issue would read as follows: H.R. 3610, Department of Defense Appropriations Act for 2009, Title II, all provisions relating to environmental restoration.

The TAR code is used for tariff bills, including miscellaneous tariff bills. Filers must use this general issue area code to report lobbying activity related to tariff issues, including miscellaneous tariff issues. For any other trade-related issues, filers should use the TRD code.

> Example: Registrant "R" is retained by Client "B" to pursue a bill to provide a temporary tariff suspension for chemical X, and a separate bill to provide a temporary tariff reduction for chemical Y. During the first quarter of 2008, "R" made lobbying contacts concerning both matters on behalf of "B" and a separate bill was introduced for each matter (S.123 for chemical X and S.456 for chemical Y). "R" reports in its LD-2 filing for Q1 that the general issue area code for these bills is "TAR," and the specific issues lobbied upon were the substance of the bills, citing to the bill number, if a bill has been introduced (e.g., "temporary tariff suspension for chemical X (S.123) and temporary tariff reduction for chemical Y (S.456)"). In the Q3 reporting period, the two chemical tariff provisions are each rolled into an omnibus bill (e.g., S.789, the "Miscellaneous Tariff Bill"). If "R" had lobbying activities during the Q3 reporting period encompassing all three bills, then "R" reports that the general issue area code for these bills is "TAR" and the specific issues lobbied upon were the substance of the bills (e.g., "temporary tariff suspension for chemical X and temporary tariff reduction for chemical Y, included in the original bills (S.123 and S.456) and in the Miscellaneous Tariff Bill

(S.789)"). In Q4, "R" had lobbying activities focusing on the omnibus bill which "R" then discloses on its Q4 report, using TAR for the general issue area code as well as reporting the specific issues lobbied upon ("modification focused on tariff suspension for chemical X and tariff reduction for chemical Y, included in Miscellaneous Tariff Bill (S.789)").

The Houses of Congress and Federal agencies contacted **by lobbyists** during the reporting period must be disclosed on Line 17 of Form LD-2, picking from the list of government entities provided on the form. If the list does not display the government entity contacted, then select the department in which the entity is housed. **In the event that no lobbying contacts were made, the registrant must mark the "Check if None" box.**

Previously identified lobbyists and new lobbyists for this reporting period must be listed on Line 18 of Form LD-2 if they had any lobbying activities during the reporting period, whether or not they made lobbying contacts. The Lobbying Activity Section is only intended to reflect lobbying activity by lobbyists, and not activity of those who are not lobbyists. The registrant does not report the names of individuals who may perform some lobbying activities, but who do not and are not expected to meet the LDA definition of a lobbyist.

Example: Lobbying Firm "A" filed its initial registration for Client "B" on February 14, listing Lobbyists "X," "Y," and "Z." From January through March, Lobbyists "W" (hired in February) and "X" and "Y" made contacts for "B," while Lobbyist "Z" was assigned work for other clients. Lobbyist "Z" is expected, however, to be active on behalf of Client "B" after Spring Recess until adjournment. In its Q1 LD-2 report for Client "B," filed on or before April 20, Lobbying Firm "A" lists "W," "X," and "Y" on Line 18. "W" is also identified as "new," and Firm "A" would disclose if "W" occupied a covered position within the last twenty years. "Z" is not listed on the Form LD 2 filed for Client "B" for the January – March quarterly period, but because of the current expectation that he will lobby during the April – June quarterly period, his name is not deleted as a lobbyist for "B."

New lobbyists must be disclosed in the appropriate Lobbying Activity section for the reporting period in which the individual first meets the definition of lobbyist. Filers need to list a new lobbyist's previous covered executive or legislative branch positions held within twenty (20) years of first acting as a lobbyist for a client. Once a filer has met the previously described statutory requirement for listing a new lobbyist's previous covered position(s), then the filer does not have to list those positions again for subsequent reports concerning the same client. If a Registrant lists that lobbyist for the first time on a report/registration regarding a different client, then the Registrant must list that lobbyist's previous covered positions held within twenty (20) years of first acting as a lobbyist for the new client.

We are aware that there will be situations in which a registrant expects an individual to become a lobbyist and wishes to disclose the name of that individual as a matter of public record. Section 5 of the LDA, however, provides that updated registration information is contained in the registrant's next quarterly report. Therefore, there may be a period of time in which an individual is legitimately making lobbying contacts but is not identified on the public record until the next quarterly report is filed. In such cases, the registrant reports updated information as the LDA requires.

A foreign entity is reported on Line 19 of Form LD-2 if both of two circumstances apply: 1) the foreign entity must be an entity that is required to be identified on

Form LD 1 or on the registration information update page. That, in turn, depends on whether the entity meets one of the three conditions of Section 4(b)(4) of the LDA; and 2) the entity must have an interest in the specific lobbying issues listed on Line 16. If a foreign entity has an interest in the specific issues, Line 19 requires a description of that interest. For the sake of clarity the registrant should indicate whether the foreign entity(s) is/are the same as identified on the registration. The requirement to disclose a foreign interest on Line 19 on Form LD-2 is not contingent upon the entity making a contribution of $5,000 or more to the registrant during that particular reporting period.

> Example: "[Name of foreign entity], identified on Form LD-1, exports [type of product] to United States and would benefit from [specific desired outcome]."

Section 7 – Semiannual Reporting of Certain Contributions

When and Why a Report is Needed

Registrants and lobbyists must file a semiannual report on Form LD-203 by July 30 and January 30 (or on the next business day should either day occur on a weekend or holiday) for each semiannual period in which a registrant or lobbyist remains active (and regardless of whether they do or do not make reportable contributions). An "active" registrant is one that has not filed a valid termination report for all clients. An "active" lobbyist is an individual who has been listed on any registrant's Form LD-1 or LD-2 and who has not been terminated by the registrant on Line 23 of an LD-2. If a lobbyist is listed as active for all or any part of a semi-annual period, he or she must file an LD-203 report for that period (see Guidance Section 8). Section 5 of the LDA states that "each person or organization who is registered or is required to register…and each employee who is or is required to be listed as a lobbyist… shall file a report." Thus, the requirement to file an LD-203 report falls upon all lobbyists who were listed on an LD-1 or LD-2 report, regardless of whether they were required to be listed (as in the case in which a registrant listed an individual as a lobbyist in an abundance of caution). Any lobbyist who is reported on Line 10 of Form LD-1 or Line 18 of Form LD-2 must file an LD-203 report, unless that lobbyist has been listed on Line 23 of Form LD-2 as removed for all clients of the registrant prior to the beginning of the relevant LD-203 filing period. The Secretary and the Clerk view Lines 10 (LD-1), 18 and 23 (LD-2) as determinative for an individual lobbyist's obligation to file an LD-203 report, rather than the mechanics of the contributions electronic filing system, which is not relevant in the determination of a filer's legal obligations.

Sole proprietors and small lobbying firms are reminded that two contribution reports are required: one filed by the registrant and one filed by the listed lobbyist (even if the lobbyist is the registrant and vice versa).

Filers are expected to use reasonable care when filling out and submitting LD-1, LD-2, and LD-203 forms.

The coverage periods for the semiannual reports are January 1 through June 30, and July 1 through December 31. **The Secretary and the Clerk do not have the authority under the LDA to grant extensions for filing LDA documents.**

Mandatory Electronic Filing

Section 5 of the LDA was amended to require the mandatory electronic filing of all documents required by the LDA. The only exception to mandatory electronic filing is for the purpose of amending reports in the format previously filed, or for compliance with the Americans with Disabilities Act. Each electronic lobbying disclosure form provides usability for people with vision impairments who have the appropriate software and hardware. If you have questions regarding additional ADA accommodations, please contact the Senate Office of Public Records at 202-224-0758.

It is necessary for each active lobbyist to obtain his/her individual user identification number and password in order to file semiannual LD-203 reports electronically with the Secretary and Clerk. Each and every registrant and lobbyist is responsible for maintaining the confidentiality and use of the user password and for all filings made using their assigned user ID and password. Filers should notify the Secretary and Clerk immediately upon learning of any unauthorized use of a user ID and/or password, as it is presumed that filings are made by the filer.

Semiannual Reporting of Certain Contributions – Contents of Report

The core information required by Section 5(d) of the LDA and incorporated into Form LD-203 is: (1) certain contributions that are not disclosed in the LD-2 report; and (2) a certification that the filer has read and understands the gift and travel provisions in the Rules of both the House of Representatives and the Senate, and that the filer has not knowingly violated the aforementioned Rules.

The beginning part of Form LD-203 contains identifying information. Section 5(d) requires specific information regarding certain contributions and payments made by the filer (i.e., each active registrant and active lobbyist), as well as any political committee established or controlled by the filer. In determining contributions and/or payments to report, it is important to note that, in some cases, a leadership PAC (as defined by the Federal Election Campaign Act, FECA) or a former leadership PAC (for example, in the case of a lobbyist who was previously a covered official) may be a political committee established, financed, maintained, or controlled by a lobbyist. Also, a political committee that has changed from a principal campaign committee into a multicandidate committee (defined in the FECA) could be considered to have been established by a covered official or federal candidate. Finally, the FECA defines those organizations that may establish separate segregated funds (SSFs).

The middle part of Form LD-203 requires the filer to disclose for itself, and for any political committee the filer establishes or controls:

- The date, recipient, and amount of funds contributed (including in-kind contributions) to any Federal candidate or officeholder, leadership PAC, or political party committee (registered with the Federal Election Commission), if the aggregate during the period to that recipient equals or exceeds $200. Please note that contributions to state and/or local candidates and committees not required to be registered with the Federal Election Commission need not be disclosed.

- The date, the name of honoree and/or honorees, the payee(s) and amount of funds paid for an event to honor or recognize a covered Legislative Branch or covered Executive Branch official (except for information required to be disclosed by another entity under 2 U.S.C § 434).

- The date, the name of honoree and or honorees, the payee(s) and amount of funds paid to an entity or person that is named for a covered Legislative Branch official, or to an entity or person in recognition of such official (except for information required to be disclosed by another entity under 2 U.S.C § 434).

- The date, recipient, the name of the covered official, the payee(s) and amount of funds paid to an entity established, financed, maintained, or controlled by a covered Legislative or Executive Branch official or to an entity designated by such official (except for information required to be disclosed by another entity under 2 U.S.C § 434).

A non-voting board member (e.g. honorary or ex-officio) does not control an organization for these purposes. For purposes of the LDA, the term "designated," for instance, includes a covered legislative branch official's or covered executive branch official's directing a charitable contribution in lieu of an honoraria pursuant to House, Senate, or executive branch Ethics rules. It also includes a payment that is directed to an entity by a covered official who is also on the board of the entity. In contrast, a contribution following a mere statement of support or solicitation does not necessarily constitute a reportable event under Section 5(d) of the LDA without some further role by a covered official.

Please note that a charitable organization established by a person before that person became a covered official and where that covered official has no relationship to the organization after becoming a covered official, is not considered to be one established by a covered official.

Please also note that a covered official's de minimis contribution to a charity (in proportion to the charity's overall receipts of contributions) is not an indication of financing, maintaining, or controlling the charity (although supplemental facts might require reporting the contribution).

- The date, the name of honoree and/or honorees, the payee(s) and amount of funds paid for a meeting, retreat, conference, or other similar event held by, or in the name of, one or more covered Legislative Branch or covered Executive Branch officials (except for information required to be disclosed by another entity under 2 U.S.C § 434). Costs related to non-preferential sponsorship of a multi-candidate primary/general election debate for a particular office do not have to be disclosed on an LD-203 report.

- The date, the name of honoree, the payee(s) and amount of funds equal to or exceeding $200 paid to each Presidential library foundation and each Presidential inaugural committee. Please note that contributions to the official Presidential Transition Organization ("PTO") of the President-elect and Vice President-elect are reportable under the Presidential Transition Act.

In the case of items 2–6 above, if a lobbyist makes a reportable payment but is reimbursed by a registrant, the Registrant reports the payment as its own, rather than the lobbyist reporting the payment.

This section of the LDA has been written broadly, and, in light of other provisions in HLOGA (P.L. 110-81), it would be prudent to consult with the appropriate Ethics Committee, as well as the Office of Government Ethics, in order to determine if any event listed above is otherwise prohibited under law, Senate or House Rules, or Executive Branch regulations. For some events, it may be prudent to consult with the Federal Election Commission as well. Please note that HLOGA and the Federal Election Campaign Act are not harmonized to contributions of exactly $200.

> Example 1: In State "A," a group of constituents involved in widget manufacturing decide to honor Senator "Y" and Representative "T" with the "Widget Manufacturing Legislative Leaders of 2008" plaques. Registrant "B" is aware that "Y" has checked with the Senate Select Committee on Ethics regarding her ability to accept the award and attend the coffee, and "T" has checked with the House Committee on Ethics. "B" pays caterer "Z" $500 and Hotel "H" $200 to partially

fund the event. "B" would report that it paid $500 to "Z" and $200 to "H" on November 20, 2008 for the purpose of an event to honor or recognize "Y" and "T" with the plaques.

Example 2: After checking to discover if the activity is permissible, Lobbyist "C" contributes $300 on June 1, 2008 to Any State University toward the endowment of a chair named for Senator "Y." "C" would report the information above noting that the payment was made to Any State for the endowment of "Y's" chair.

Example 3: Senator "Y" has been asked to speak at a conference held in Washington, DC, sponsored by a professional association of which Registrant "B" is a member. "B" makes a donation of $100 to Charity "X" in lieu of the association paying a speaking fee (i.e., a contribution in lieu of honoraria). "B" would disclose a contribution of $100 on the date of the payment, with the notation that the payment was made as a contribution in lieu of honoraria to an entity designated by "Y."

Example 4: There is a large regional conference on "Saving Our River," sponsored by three 501(c)(3) organizations. Senator "Y" and Representative "T" are given "Champions of Our River" awards at a dinner event that is part of the conference. Registrant "B" contributes $3,000 specifically for the costs of the dinner event, paying one of the sponsors directly. At the time of the specific or restricted contribution, "B" was aware that "Y" and "T" would be honorees. Regardless of whether "B" is a sponsor under House or Senate gift rules and although B is not listed on the invitation as a sponsor (or the like) nor is publicly held out as a sponsor (or the like), since "B" partially paid for the cost of the event, "B" would disclose a payment of $3,000 on the relevant date payable to the sponsor with the notation that "Y" and "T" were honored.

Example 5: Registrant "B," an industry organization, hosts its annual gala dinner and gives a "Legislator of the Year" award to Representative "T." Revenues from the gala dinner help fund Registrant "B's" activities throughout the year. Registrant "B" must report: 1) the cost of the event (hotel, food, flowers, etc., but not indirect costs such as host staff salaries and host office overhead); 2), the payee(s) (as a convenience to filers, separate vendors may be aggregated by using the term "various vendors"); and 3) that the event honored Representative "T." Please note that "B" must still separately report the cost of any item that "B" gave "T." The fact that the event helped raise funds for the organization does not change the reporting requirement, though it could be noted in the filing.

Example 6: Registrant "B," an industry organization, has an annual two-day "Washington fly-in" for its members. Among the events for its members is an event on "The Importance of Industry G to the U.S. Economy." Senator "T" is listed on the invitation as a speaker at the event. Based on these facts alone, Registrant "B" would not need to report the event under this section. For a covered official to speak at such an event would not, in and of itself, form the basis for concluding that the official is to be honored or recognized. Supplemental facts might require reporting the cost of the event. For example, if Senator "T" were given a special award, recognition, or honor (which may not necessarily be through the receipt of a physical object) by the organization at the event, the cost of the event would have to be reported, even if the invitation did not indicate that such would be given. Simply designating a covered official as a "speaker" at an event at which the covered official receives a special award, recognition or honor, will not permit the filer to avoid or evade reporting the expenses of the event.

Example 7: Senator "Y" and Representative "T" are "honorary co-hosts" of an event sponsored by Registrant "R" to raise funds for a charity, which is not established, financed, maintained, or controlled by either legislator. "Y" and "T's" passive allowance of their names to be used as "co-hosts," in and of itself, is not sufficient to be considered "honored or recognized." The purpose of the event is to raise funds for Charity "V," not to honor or recognize "Y" or "T." Nor are these facts (i.e. being passive honorary co-hosts), in and of themselves, sufficient to treat the event as being held "by or in the name" of "Y" or "T." Supplemental facts might require reporting the cost of the event.

Example 8: Registrant "R" sponsors an event to promote "Widget Awareness." "The Honorable Cabinet Secretary Z" is listed on the invitation as an "attendee" or "special invitee" but will not receive an honor or award at the event. Based on these facts alone, "R" would not need to include the costs of this event on "R's" disclosure under this section. Mere listing of "Z's" anticipated attendance at an event the purpose of which is to promote Widget Awareness, in and of itself, is not sufficient to be considered "honored or recognized". Use of the phrase "The Honorable" in this context is consistent with widely accepted notions of protocol applicable to referencing certain very senior government officials. Supplemental facts might require reporting the cost of the event. For instance, if "Z" received a special, award, honor, or recognition by "R" at the event, "R" would have to report the costs of the event noting that "Z" was being honored or recognized.

Example 9: Registrant "B" buys a table at a dinner event sponsored by a 501(c) organization to honor Representative "T" but Registrant "B" is not considered a sponsor of the event under House and Senate gift rules. Lobbyist "C" pays the $150 individual ticket cost to attend the dinner, but is not considered a sponsor of the event under House and Senate gift rules. The purchase of a table or ticket to another entity's event, in and of itself, is not sufficient to be considered paying the "cost of an event." Supplemental facts might require reporting the cost of the event. For example, if (1) "B" or "C" undertake activities such that "B" or "C" becomes a sponsor of the event for House and/or Senate gift rule purposes; or (2) "B" or " C" purchase enough tickets/tables so that it would appear that they are paying the costs of the event and/or would not appear to be just ticket or table-buyers (regardless of whether "B" or "C" is a sponsor under House or Senate gift rules), then "B" or "C" would need to report the costs incurred by "B" or "C" (as the case may be) for the event, noting that Representative "T" was the honoree. In the case of filers purchasing multiple tickets and/or tables to an event, a case-by-case analysis will be needed to determine if the quantity is such that it would appear that the filer is paying the costs of the event.

Example 10: Lobbyists "C" and "D" serve on the board of a PAC as member and treasurer respectively. As board members, they are in positions that control direction of the PAC's contributions. Since both are controlling to whom the PAC's contributions are given, they must disclose applicable contributions of the PAC on their semi-annual LD-203 reports. If "C" and "D" serve on the board of a Separate Segregated Fund (SSF), they may report that they are board members of an SSF in lieu of reporting the SSF's applicable contributions as long as the SSF's contributions are reported in the connected organization's LD-203 report.

Example 11: Registrant "L" holds an annual fundraising event that honors one person from each of the 50 states whom "L" deems to have played a significant role for the cause "L" supports. In 2009, four of the honorees were covered legislative and executive officials. "L" must disclose the total amount that it paid for the event, disclosing in the payee section "various vendors," and disclosing the names of the four covered officials. Although not required, and thus at its option , "L" could note in the comments section that 4 of the 50 honorees were covered officials. Section 5(d) of the LDA does not contemplate a breakdown, delineation or separation of expenses

Example 12: Registrant "O" is a university. In June 2009, in conjunction with its commencement event, "O" conferred an honorary degree upon Senator "P." "O" would report all payments relating to the commencement event (chair rental, lunch for honorees, etc.) on its LD-203 report, listing "various vendors" as the payee, and Senator "P" as the honoree. Although not required, and thus at its option, "O" could comment that "P" received an honorary degree.

The final part of the LD-203 form is a certification that the filer has read and is familiar with those provisions of the Standing Rules of the Senate and the Rules of the House of Representatives relating to the provisions of gifts and travel and has not provided, requested or directed a gift, including travel, with knowledge that receipt of the gift would violate either Chamber's Rules. The form contains a check box for the certification, and the user ID and password process will verify the filer identity. Each and every registrant and lobbyist is responsible for maintaining the confidentiality and use of the user password and for all filings made using their assigned user ID and password. Filers should notify the Secretary and Clerk immediately upon learning of any unauthorized use of a user ID and/or password, as it is presumed that filings are made by the filer.

Please note that in the case of a registrant, a signatory is an individual who is responsible for the accuracy of the information contained in the filing. In all cases an individual lobbyist is responsible for all information contained in his or her report. Under section 6 of the LDA, the Secretary and Clerk refer the names of registrants and lobbyists who fail to provide an appropriate response within sixty (60) days to either officer's written communication rather than the name of the signatory. Both signatories and any third-party preparers should retain appropriate documentation to verify report contents. Third-party preparers should also retain appropriate documentation to demonstrate that they have authorization to make such filings on behalf of all filers (including lobbyist-employees of registrants) using their services.

Each registrant and active lobbyist, regardless of any contribution activity or any lack thereof, must file Form LD-203 semiannually due to the certification provision.

Section 8 – Termination of a Lobbyist/Termination of a Registrant

Termination of a Lobbyist

The LDA is not specific as to how far into the future the registrant should project an expectation that an individual will act as a lobbyist. It seems neither realistic nor necessary to expect registrants to make such projections beyond the next succeeding quarterly reporting period. Accordingly, if a registrant reasonably expects an individual to meet the definition of a lobbyist in either the current or next quarterly period, the lobbyist should remain in an "active" status. If a registrant does not believe this to be the case, the lobbyist can be removed from the list of lobbyists for the registrant. A registrant may remove a lobbyist only when (i) that individual's lobbying activities on behalf of that client did not constitute at the end of the current quarter, and are not reasonably expected in the upcoming quarter to constitute, 20 percent of the time that such employee is engaged in total activities for that client; or (ii) that individual does not reasonably expect to make further lobbying contacts. In order to properly terminate a lobbyist, the registrant must complete Line 23 of Form LD-2, which is used to remove names of employees who are no longer expected to act as lobbyists for the client due to changed job duties, assignments, or employment status. Amending the LD-1 or LD-2 reports to erase a lobbyist listed on lines 10 or 18, respectively, is not a proper termination.

> Example 1: Lobbying Firm "Y" registers for Client "Z" on March 15, 2008, listing employees "A," "B," "C," and "D" on Line 10 of Form LD 1. For the first quarterly reporting period in 2008, "Y" will list "A," "B," and "C" on Line 18 of Form LD 2. "D" has no lobbying activities for that quarterly period, so he would not be listed. During the second quarter of 2008, "D" leaves firm "Y" to start his own lobbying business. For the second quarterly period, "Y" will report that "D" no longer meets the definition of "lobbyist" for Client "Z" on Line 23 of Form LD-2.

> Example 2: Lobbying Firm "Y" registers for Client "Z" as above listing the aforementioned "A," "B," "C," and "D" as lobbyists on March 15, 2008. One month after registration, "C" and "D," who engaged in lobbying activities for "Z" as partners of "Y," decide to leave the partnership effective June 1, 2008. On the Q2 Report for 2008, "Y" would report any lobbying activity for "C" and "D" on Line 18 of Form LD-2. "Y" would also reflect "C" and "D's" departure by listing them on Line 23 of Form LD-2 in the same filing.

An individual who no longer meets the definition of lobbyist under Section 3(10) of the LDA can be relieved from having to file an LD-203 report for future semiannual periods by proper removal from the registrant's active lobbyists list. This is accomplished by the registrant listing such an individual on Line 23 of the LD-2 quarterly report for each client for which the individual was previously listed. The obligation to file an LD-203 report arises from being listed as a lobbyist and not being terminated by the registrant/employer. Thus, if a lobbyist has not been properly terminated by being listed on Line 23 of the Form LD-2 for every client for which the lobbyist was listed, the Secretary and Clerk will expect to receive a semi-annual report from him/her.

> Example: Registrant "A" employs Lobbyist "C" who has lobbying activity on behalf of Client "R" in January and February 2008. In March, Lobbyist "C" no longer expects to engage in lobbying activities for "R" or any other client in the firm, although "C" will continue to do non-lobbying consultation for numerous clients. "A" removes Lobbyist "C" as an active lobbyist by listing "C" on Line 23 of the LD-2 form for the Q1 reporting period, and "C" is not listed on subsequent quarterly LD-2 reports. However in July, Lobbyist "C" is required to file an LD-203 report due July 30 disclosing his activity from January 1 through the date of his termination.

Termination of a Registrant/Client Relationship

Under Section 4(d) of the LDA, a lobbying firm may terminate a registration for a particular client when it is no longer employed or retained by that client to conduct lobbying activities and anticipates no further lobbying activities for that client. An organization employing in-house lobbyists may terminate its registration when in-house lobbying activities have ceased and are not expected to resume. Similarly, in situations in which a registration is filed in anticipation of meeting the registration threshold that subsequently is not met, a registrant also has the option of termination. Just as we interpret that the obligation to report quarterly under the LDA arises from active status as a registrant, we believe that a report disclosing the final lobbying activity of a registrant is mandatory. In order to terminate the registration, the registrant must file Form LD 2 by the next quarterly filing date, checking the "Termination Report" box, and supplying the date that the lobbying activity terminated. A valid termination report discloses lobbying income or expenses **and** any lobbying activity by lobbyists during the period up to and including the termination date.

> Example 1: Lobbying Firm "A" accepted a contract with Client "B" on January 1, 2008, began lobbying activities, and timely registered on or before February 14. On March 31, the contract with "B" ended. Lobbying Firm "A" must file Form LD 2 by April 20, 2008, disclosing the lobbying income from and lobbying activity for Client "B" that took place during the period January 1 through March 31. The firm will check the "Q1" box on Line 8, the "Termination Report" box on Line 10, and fill in "3/31/2008" in the Termination Date space (also on Line 10).

> Example 2: Corporation "C" filed its registration on February 14, 2008, listing employee "E" as its only lobbyist. Through March 31, "E" spends less than 20 percent of her total time in lobbying activities. "C" would not have filed a registration if it had foreseen that its lobbying activities would be so limited, and there is no expectation that "E" or any other employee of "C" will meet the LDA Section 3(10) definition of "lobbyist" for the April – June quarterly period nor that lobbying expenses will exceed $12,500. While

Guide to the Lobbying Disclosure Act

Corporation "C" as a registrant must file a report for January March 2008, "C" will check the "Termination Report" box on Form LD 2, write in 3/31/08, disclose the amount of expenses for the reporting period, and "E's" lobbying activity for the reporting period.

Section 9 – Relationship of LDA to Other Statutes

LDA and FARA

The technical amendments to the LDA made in 1998 reflect a determination that the Foreign Agents Registration Act (FARA) standards are appropriate for lobbying on behalf of foreign governments and political parties, but that LDA disclosure standards should apply to other foreign lobbying. An agent of a foreign commercial entity is exempt under FARA if the agent has engaged in lobbying activities and registers under the LDA. An agent of a foreign commercial entity not required to register under the LDA (such as those not meeting the de minimis registration thresholds) may voluntarily register under the LDA. The amendments reaffirm the bright line distinction between governmental and non-governmental representations, and are not meant to shroud foreign government enterprises. Questions relating to the Foreign Agents Registration Act must be directed to the Department of Justice Foreign Agent Registration Unit at (202) 252–2537.

LDA and IRC

Restrictions on lobbying by tax-exempt organizations are governed by the definitions in the IRC, not those of the LDA. The LDA and the IRC intersect in three different ways.

First, Section 15 of the LDA defines which registrants are eligible for the "safe harbor." LDA Section 15 allows entities that are required to report and do report lobbying expenditures under Section 6033(b)(8) of the IRC to use IRC definitions for purposes of LDA Sections 4(a)(3) and 5(b)(4). Section 15(b) of the LDA allows entities that are subject to Section 162(e) of the IRC to use IRC definitions for purposes of LDA Sections 4(a)(3) and 5(b)(4).

Second, Section 15 of the LDA advises registrants regarding how they should use IRC definitions. Prior to the 1998 technical amendments, the statute was not clear as to the extent to which eligible organizations could use IRC definitions for other (i.e., non-expense) reporting and disclosure requirements of the LDA. As a result of the amendments, registrants who make the Section 15 expense election must use for other reporting the IRC definitions (including the IRC definition of a covered Executive Branch official) for Executive Branch lobbying, and the LDA definitions for Legislative Branch lobbying.

Third, Section 15 allows electing registrants to insert the amount that is ultimately reportable to the Internal Revenue Service for LDA quarterly reports.

LDA and False Statements Accountability Act of 1996

The False Statements Accountability Act of 1996, amending 18 U.S.C. § 1001, makes it a crime knowingly and willfully: (1) to falsify, conceal or cover up a material fact by trick, scheme or device; (2) to make any materially false, fictitious, or fraudulent statement or representation; or (3) to make or use any false writing or document knowing it to contain any materially false, fictitious, or fraudulent statement or entry; with respect to matters within the jurisdiction of the Legislative, Executive, or Judicial branch. The False Statements Accountability Act does not assign any responsibilities to the Clerk and Secretary.

LDA and Prohibitions on the Use of Federal Funds for Lobbying

The LDA does not itself regulate lobbying by federal grantees, or contractors, though other laws, as well as contractual prohibitions, may apply. Questions concerning lobbying activities of federal grantees or contractors should be directed to the appropriate agency or office administering the contract or grant.

Note, however, that Section 18 of the LDA prohibits 501(c)(4) organizations who engage in lobbying activities from receiving federal funds through an award, grant, or loan.

Section 10 – Public Availability

The Act requires the Secretary of the Senate and the Clerk of the House of Representatives to make all registrations and reports available for public inspection over the Internet as soon as technically practicable after the report is filed.

Section 11 – Review and Compliance

The Secretary of the Senate (Office of Public Records) and the Clerk of the House (Legislative Resource Center) must review, verify, and request corrections in writing to ensure the accuracy, completeness, and timeliness of registrations and reports filed under the LDA.

Section 12 – Penalties

Whoever knowingly fails: (1) to correct a defective filing within 60 days after notice of such a defect by the Secretary of the Senate or the Clerk of the House; or (2) to comply with any other provision of the Act, may be subject to a civil fine of not more than $200,000, and whoever knowingly and corruptly fails to comply with any provision of this Act may be imprisoned for not more than 5 years or fined under title 18, United States Code, or both.

For Further Information

Senate Office of Public Records
232 Hart Senate Office Building
Washington, DC 20510
(202) 224-0758
http://www.senate.gov/lobby

Legislative Resource Center
135 Cannon House Office Building
Washington, DC 20515
(202) 226-5200
http://lobbyingdisclosure.house.gov

[1]The Secretary and the Clerk review the Guidance semiannually. Any questions, comments and suggestions should be directed to the Senate Office of Public Records and the House Legislative Resource Center in sufficient time for evaluation before the next semiannual reporting cycle (by May 15, 2015).

Guide to the Lobbying Disclosure Act

* **Home** • **LD-1/LD-2 Reporting** • **LD-203 Contributions** • **Subscribe** • **Contact** • **FAQ**

Office of the Clerk
United States House of Representatives
U.S. Capitol, Room H-154
Washington D.C., 20515-6601
202-225-7000

APPENDIX 4-B

Lobbying Registration

Clerk of the House of Representatives   Secretary of the Senate
Legislative Resource Center   Office of Public Records
135 Cannon Building   232 Hart Building
Washington, DC 20515   Washington, DC 20510
http://lobbyingdisclosure.house.gov   http://www.senate.gov/lobby

LOBBYING REGISTRATION

Lobbying Disclosure Act of 1995 (Section 4)

Check One: ☐ New Registrant ☑ New Client for Existing Registrant ☐ Amendment

1. Effective Date of Registration _____

2. House Identification . _____   **Senate Identification** . _____

REGISTRANT ☑ Organization/Lobbying Firm ☐ Self Employed Individual

3. Registrant   Organization _____

Address _____   Address2 _____

City _____ State __ Zip _____ Country _____

4. Principal place of business (if different than line 3)

City _____ State __ Zip _____ Country _____

5. Contact name and telephone number   ☐ **International Number**

Contact _____ Telephone _____ E-mail _____

6. General description of registrant's business or activities
_____

CLIENT *A Lobbying Firm is required to file a separate registration for each client. Organizations employing in-house lobbyists should check the box labeled "Self" and proceed to line 10.* ☑ *Self*

7. Client name _____

Address _____

City _____ State ___ Zip _____ Country ___

8. Principal place of business (if different than line 7)

City _____ State ___ Zip _____ Country _____

9. General description of client's business or activities
_____

LOBBYISTS

10. Name of each individual who has acted or is expected to act as a lobbyist for the client identified on line 7. If any person listed in this section has served as a "covered executive branch official" or "covered legislative branch official" within twenty years of first acting as a lobbyist for the client, *state the executive and/or legislative position(s) in which the person served.*

Name			Covered Official Position (if applicable)
First	Last	Suffix	

LOBBYING ISSUES

11. General lobbying issue areas (Select all applicable codes).

12. Specific lobbying issues (current and anticipated)

AFFILIATED ORGANIZATIONS

13. Is there an entity other than the client that contributes more than $5,000 to the lobbying activities of the registrant in a quarterly period and either participates in and/or in whole or in major part supervises or controls the registrant's lobbying activities?

☐ No --> Go to line 14.   ☑ Yes --> Complete the rest of this section for each entity matching the criteria above, then proceed to line 14.

Internet Address:

Name	Address	Principal Place of Business
	Street	
	City State/Province Zip Code Country	

City _____

State _____   Country _____

FOREIGN ENTITIES

14. Is there any foreign entity

a) holds at least 20% equitable ownership in the client or any organization identified on line 13; or

b) directly or indirectly, in whole or in major part, plans, supervises, controls, directs, finances or subsidizes activities of the client or any organization identified on line 13; or

c) is an affiliate of the client or any organization identified on line 13 and has a direct interest in the outcome of the lobbying activity?

☐ No --> Sign and date the registration.   ☑ Yes --> Complete the rest of this section for each entity matching the criteria above, then sign the registration.

Name	Address Street	Principal place of business	Amount of contribution	Ownership
	City State/Province Country	(city and state or country)	for lobbying activities	

City _____

State _____   Country _____   _____ %

Signature | Digitally Signed By: | **Date** _____

ADDITIONAL LOBBYISTS

10. Supplemental. List any additional lobbyists for this client not listed on page 1, number 10.

First	Name Last	Suffix	Covered Official Position (if applicable)

ADDITIONAL LOBBYING ISSUES
11. Supplemental. General lobbying issue areas. Enter any additional codes for issues not listed on page 2, number 11.

_____ _____ _____ _____ _____ _____ _____ _____

ADDITIONAL AFFILIATED ORGANIZATIONS
13. Supplemental. List any other affiliated organization that meets the criteria specified and is not listed on page 2, number 13.

Name	Address	Principal Place of Business
	Street	
	City State/Province Zip Code Country	

		City _____
		State _____ Country _____
		City _____
		State _____ Country _____
		City _____
		State _____ Country _____

ADDITIONAL FOREIGN ENTITIES
14. Supplemental. List any other foreign entity that meets the criteria specified and is not listed on page 2, number 14.

Name	Address Street City State/Province Country	Principal place of business (city and state or country)	Amount of contribution for lobbying activities	Ownership
		City _____ State_____ Country _____		%
		City _____ State_____ Country _____		%
		City _____ State_____ Country _____		%

APPENDIX 4-C

Lobbying Report

Clerk of the House of Representatives	Secretary of the Senate
Legislative Resource Center	Office of Public Records
135 Cannon Building	232 Hart Building
Washington, DC 20515	Washington, DC 20510
http://lobbyingdisclosure.house.gov	http://www.senate.gov/lobby

LOBBYING REPORT

Lobbying Disclosure Act of 1995 (Section 5) - **All Filers Are Required to Complete This Page**

1. Registrant Name ☑ Organization/Lobbying Firm ☐ Self Employed Individual
_____

2. Address
Address1 _____ Address2 _____
City _____ State __ Zip Code _____ Country _

3. Principal place of business (if different than line 2)
City _____ State _____ Zip Code _____ Country _____

4a. Contact Name _____ **b. Telephone Number c. E-mail** _____ | **5. Senate ID#**

7. Client Name ☑ *Self* ☐ *Check if client is a state or local government or instrumentality* | **6. House ID#**

TYPE OF REPORT
8. Year _ Q1 (1/1 - 3/31) ☑ Q2 (4/1 - 6/30) ☐ Q3 (7/1 - 9/30) ☐ Q4 (10/1 - 12/31) ☐

9. Check if this filing amends a previously filed version of this report ☐
10. Check if this is a Termination Report ☐ Termination Date _____ 11. No Lobbying Issue Activity ☐

INCOME OR EXPENSES - YOU MUST complete either Line 12 or Line 13

12. Lobbying	**13. Organizations**
INCOME relating to lobbying activities for this reporting period was:	**EXPENSE** relating to lobbying activities for this reporting period were:
Less than $5,000 ☐	Less than $5,000 ☐
$5,000 or more ☑ $ _____	$5,000 or more ☐ $ _____
Provide a good faith estimate, rounded to the nearest $10,000, of all lobbying related income for the client (including all payments to the registrant by any other entity for lobbying activities on behalf of the client).	**14. REPORTING** Check box to indicate expense accounting method. See instructions for description of options.
	☐ **Method A.** Reporting amounts using LDA definitions only
	☐ **Method B.** Reporting amounts under section 6033(b)(8) of the Internal Revenue Code
	☐ **Method C.** Reporting amounts under section 162(e) of the Internal Revenue Code

Signature Digitally Signed By: _____ **Date** _____

LOBBYING ACTIVITY. Select as many codes as necessary to reflect the general issue areas in which the registrant engaged in lobbying on behalf of the client during the reporting period. Using a separate page for each code, provide information as requested. Add additional page(s) as needed.

15. General issue area code

16. Specific lobbying issues

17. House(s) of Congress and Federal agencies ☐ Check if None

18. Name of each individual who acted as a lobbyist in this issue area

First Name	Last Name	Suffix	Covered Official Position (if applicable)	New
				☐

19. Interest of each foreign entity in the specific issues listed on line 16 above ☑ Check if None

Information Update Page - Complete ONLY where registration information has changed.

20. Client new address

Address _____
    City _____ State _____ Zip Code _____ Country _____

21. Client new principal place of business (if different than line 20)

    City _____ State _____ Zip Code _____ Country _____

22. New General description of client's business or activities

LOBBYIST UPDATE

23. Name of each previously reported individual who is no longer expected to act as a lobbyist for the client

First Name	Last Name	Suffix	First Name	Last Name	Suffix

ISSUE UPDATE

24. General lobbying issue that no longer pertains

AFFILIATED ORGANIZATIONS

25. Add the following affiliated organization(s)

Internet Address:

Name	Address		Principal Place of Business (city and state or country)
	Street Address		
	City	State/Province Zip Country	

26. Name of each previously reported organization that is no longer affiliated with the registrant or client

FOREIGN ENTITIES

27. Add the following foreign entities:

Name	Address	Principal place of business (city and state or country)	Amount of contribution for lobbying activities	Ownership percentage in client
	Street Address			
	City State/Province Country			

28. Name of each previously reported foreign entity that no longer owns, or controls, or is affiliated with the registrant, client or affiliated organization

CHAPTER 5

Semiannual Reports on Contributions and Disbursements by Registrants and Lobbyists

BY DANIEL NUDELMAN

5-1 Introduction

To accomplish its titular aim of providing "greater transparency in the legislative process,"[1] the Honest Leadership and Open Government Act of 2007 (HLOGA) made several enhancements to the public disclosure and reporting requirements of the Lobbying Disclosure Act (LDA or the Act), including the creation of a new semiannual reporting obligation applicable to both lobbying registrants and individual lobbyists. Section 203 of HLOGA amended section 1604(d) of the LDA to require registrants and individuals listed as lobbyists in registrant filings to report certain political and honorary contributions or payments made by the filer and federal PACs the filer has established or controls, and to certify their understanding of and compliance with congressional gift and travel rules.[2] The Secretary of the Senate and the Clerk of the House of Representatives subsequently created the semiannual contribution form LD-203 to implement this new disclosure requirement, naming it after section 203 of HLOGA. This chapter reviews the key procedural and substantive requirements of the semiannual LD-203 report. It should be noted at the outset that section 1604(d) of the LDA, as amended by HLOGA, contains several provisions with broad or vaguely worded statutory language, and very little formal guidance exists to assist filers in parsing exactly what types of disclosures these provisions require. The principal official source of substantive guidance for semiannual reports is the Lobbying Disclosure Act Guidance (Revised Guidance) issued by the Secretary of the Senate and the Clerk of the House. Although the Secretary and the Clerk have periodically revised this guidance to issue interpretative clarifications or modify otherwise duplicative reporting requirements,[3] a number of ambiguities remain unresolved.

5-2 Who Must File?

Separate LD-203 reports must be filed by each lobbying registrant and any individual who was or should have been listed as a lobbyist on a registrant's registration form (LD-1) or quarterly report (LD-2) and was "active" for all or any part of the semiannual reporting period. A registrant lobbying on its own behalf is considered "active" until it has filed a termination report for itself, and a registrant registered to lobby on behalf of others is "active" until it has filed a termination report on behalf of every organization that it has listed as a client.[4] An "active" lobbyist is an individual who has been listed on any registrant's form LD-1 or LD-2 and who has not been terminated by that registrant on Line 23 of an LD-2.[5]

---

1. HONEST LEADERSHIP AND OPEN GOVERNMENT ACT OF 2007, Pub. L. No. 110–81, § 203, 121 Stat. 735 (codified as amended at 2 U.S.C.A. § 1603-5 (2012)) [hereinafter HLOGA].

2. 2 U.S.C. § 1604(d) (2015).

3. SEC'Y OF THE SENATE & CLERK OF THE HOUSE OF REPRESENTATIVES, LOBBYING DISCLOSURE ACT GUIDANCE (revised Feb. 15, 2013) [hereinafter REVISED GUIDANCE], available at http://lobbying disclosure.house.gov/amended_lda_guide.html and contained in Appendix 4-A. Substantive revisions to the section of the Revised Guidance addressing semiannual contribution reporting were made in 2008, 2009, and most recently in 2010. See OFFICE OF THE CLERK, U.S. HOUSE OF REPRESENTATIVES, Lobbying Disclosure, Notices and Announcements, available at http://lobbyingdisclosure.house.gov/.

4. REVISED GUIDANCE, supra note 3, Appendix 4-A.

5. Id.

If a lobbyist is active for all or any part of a semiannual reporting period, an LD-203 report must be filed for that period. The Revised Guidance provides the following illustration:

Example: *Registrant "A" employs Lobbyist "C" who has lobbying activity on behalf of Client "R" in January and February 2008. In March, Lobbyist "C" no longer expects to engage in lobbying activities for "R" or any other client in the firm, although "C" will continue to do non-lobbying consultation for numerous clients. "A" removes Lobbyist "C" as an active lobbyist by listing "C" on Line 23 of the LD-2 form for the Q1 reporting period, and "C" is not listed on subsequent quarterly LD-2 reports. However in July, Lobbyist "C" is required to file an LD-203 report due July 30 disclosing his activity from January 1 through the date of his termination.[6]*

The Revised Guidance only explicitly addresses a lobbyist's filing obligation after termination,[7] though the same filing obligation also attaches to a registrant that does not terminate its registration until partway through a semiannual reporting period.

The disclosures required on LD-203 reports are not client-specific, and, in most cases, a registrant or listed lobbyist will need to file only one LD-203 for each semiannual period no matter how many clients he or she represents.[8] The only exception is for an individual lobbyist who is self-employed and, therefore, is registered as a lobbying firm.[9] This individual must file two LD-203 reports each semiannual period: one as a registrant, and one as a listed lobbyist.[10]

An LD-203 must be filed even if there are no contributions or payments to be reported because the certificate of compliance with congressional ethics rules, discussed in Section 5-5 of this chapter, must be completed every reporting period.[11]

5-3 When Is the LD-203 Due?

The semiannual reporting periods run from January 1 through June 30, and July 1 through December 31. The LD-203 is due thirty days after the close of the reporting period, or the next business day when the thirtieth day falls on a weekend or holiday.[12]

---

6. *Id.*

7. *Id.*

8. *See* OFFICE OF THE CLERK, U.S. HOUSE OF REPRESENTATIVES, Lobbying Disclosure, Frequently Asked Questions—Contribution Reporting [hereinafter REPORTING FAQ], *available at* http://lobbying disclosure.house.gov/FAQ_CR.html.

9. See Section 3-4 of this manual.

10. REVISED GUIDANCE, *supra* note 3, Appendix 4-A. ("Sole proprietors and small lobbying firms are reminded that two contribution reports are required: one filed by the registrant and one filed by the listed lobbyist (even if the lobbyist is the registrant and vice versa)").

11. *Id.*

12. 2 U.S.C. § 1604 (d)(1) (2015).

5-4 What Is the Process for Filing?

Registrants and listed lobbyists must prepare and file LD-203 reports through the web-based Lobbying Disclosure Contribution Reporting System (CRS).[13] Technical instructions on using CRS are available online and include a printable "Lobbying Disclosure Electronic Filing Contribution Reporting System User Manual" (User Manual).[14]

Access to CRS is limited to registrants and to listed lobbyists for whom CRS accounts have been activated. Registrants can access the system with the ID and password previously assigned to them to file their LD-1 and LD-2 reports.[15] Listed lobbyists must have their accounts activated by a registrant and obtain their own user ID and password before they will be granted access to the CRS, and registrants are only able to initiate this process for individuals who have already been listed as a lobbyist on a filed LD-1 or LD-2.[16] Once signed in, registrants and lobbyists have the ability to create a new filing, open a saved contribution form and edit it, or retrieve a previously filed form and amend it.[17] The system saves the form for each filing period, and it can be retrieved and edited at any time. Registrants can populate data from a database using an import tool, and a printable version of the form can be generated at any time to facilitate review.[18] Lobbyist forms are digitally signed with the lobbyist's name. For registrant forms, the digital signature will be the name of the individual listed as the "Contact" in CRS, which should be the person in the organization who manages LDA registration and reporting filings.[19] The Revised Guidance cautions that registrants and lobbyists "are responsible for maintaining the confidentiality and use of the user password and for all filings made using their assigned user ID and password."[20] The signatory for a registrant's report "is an individual who is responsible for the accuracy of the information contained in the filing," whereas "in all cases an individual lobbyist is responsible for all information contained in his or her report."[21] While third-party preparers may submit filings on behalf of filers, they must keep documentation on file demonstrating that they have authorization to make filings on behalf of filers using their services, including lobbyist-employees of registrants.[22] Signatories and third-party preparers should also retain appropriate documentation to verify report contents.

---

13. U.S. CONGRESS, Lobbying Disclosure Act Contributions Reporting, https://lda.congress.gov/LC/. HLOGA amended the LDA to require the mandatory electronic filing of all documents required by the LDA. 2 U.S.C. § 1604(e).

14. U.S. CONGRESS, Lobbying Disclosure Electronic Filing Contribution Reporting System User Manual (July 2009) [hereinafter USER MANUAL], *available at* https://lda.congress.gov/lc/help/WordDocuments/LCUserManual.pdf. An electronic version of the manual is available on the Lobbying Disclosure website at https://lda.congress.gov/LC/help/default.htm?turl=WordDocuments%2Fintroduction.htm.

15. USER MANUAL, *supra* note 14, at 8–9.

16. *Id.* Detailed guidance for registrants and lobbyists on accessing CRS and managing CRS accounts is available in the USER MANUAL and on a "Frequently Asked Questions" page on the House Lobbying Disclosure website. *See* REPORTING FAQ, *supra* note 8.

17. *See* USER MANUAL, *supra* note 14, at 34.

18. *Id.*

19. USER MANUAL, *supra* note 14, at 27.

20. REVISED GUIDANCE, *supra* note 3, Appendix 4-A.

21. *Id.*

22. *Id.*

5-5 Substantive Reporting Requirements

The LD-203 semiannual report has two core substantive components: (1) the disclosure of certain federal political contributions made by the filer and PACs the filer has established or controls, and other contributions and disbursements that might "honor" or otherwise assist a covered official in certain enumerated ways;[23] and (2) a certification that the filer has read and is familiar with the House and Senate gift and travel rules and has not provided, requested, or directed a gift, including travel, to a member of Congress or officer or employee of either the House or Senate knowing that the receipt of such a gift would violate the gift rules.[24] The following sections address each of these requirements in turn, with reference to substantive guidance provided by the Secretary and the Clerk where helpful.

5-5.1 Political Action Committee (PAC) Names

The first substantive disclosure required by section 1604(d) of the LDA is "the names of all political committees established or controlled by" the filer.[25] These should be listed in the "Political Action Committee Names" section of the LD-203 report.[26]

A filer must enter the name of a political committee in this section in order to report contributions from that political committee in the subsequent contribution reporting section, so any political committee whose contributions the filer is required to disclose in the semiannual report should be identified here.[27]

The Act does not define the term "established or controlled," but here the plain language of the provision is supplemented by the Revised Guidance. A registrant such as a corporation, trade association, or other organization that has established a connected PAC under the Federal Election Campaign Act (FECA)—that is, a separate segregated fund (SSF)—will generally need to identify the PAC here and disclose its reportable contributions.[28]

If a lobbyist filer has the ability to control the flow of a PAC's funds, and especially if this is somehow formalized in writing, that PAC would probably qualify as "controlled" by the filer for the purposes of this disclosure. For example, the Revised Guidance indicates that serving as a board member or treasurer of a PAC is enough to establish "control":

Example 10: *Lobbyists "C" and "D" serve on the board of a PAC as member and treasurer respectively. As board members, they are in positions that control direction of the PAC's contributions. Since both are controlling to whom the PAC's contributions are given, they must disclose applicable contributions of the PAC on their semi-annual LD-203 reports.*[29]

---

23. 2 U.S.C. § 1604(d)(1); *see also* REVISED GUIDANCE, *supra* note 3, Appendix 4-A.

24. 2 U.S.C. § 1604(d)(1)(G).

25. 2 U.S.C. § 1604(d)(1)(C).

26. USER MANUAL, *supra* note 14, at 36–37.

27. *Id.* at 38. This is because only political committees entered in this section will be available in the drop-down list for "contributor name" in the subsequent contribution reporting section (other than "self").

28. REVISED GUIDANCE, *supra* note 3, Appendix 4-A. For more information about SSFs, see Chapter 23.

29. REVISED GUIDANCE, *supra* note 3, Appendix 4-A.

However, the Revised Guidance also carves out an important exception to this rule for lobbyists who serve on the board of a registrant's SSF:

> *If "C" and "D" serve on the board of a Separate Segregated Fund (SSF), they may report that they are board members of an SSF in lieu of reporting the SSF's applicable contributions as long as the SSF's contributions are reported in the connected organization's LD-203 report.*[30]

Accordingly, a lobbyist who sits on the board of an SSF can opt out of identifying and disclosing the SSF's contributions on his or her LD-203 report as long as (1) the SSF's contributions are already being disclosed on the connected organization's LD-203 report; and (2) the lobbyist notes his or her board membership in the "Comments" section of the LD-203 report, discussed in Section 5-5.3.

SSFs are not the only type of political committees whose contributions are relevant for LD-203 purposes. The Revised Guidance also provides that "a leadership PAC (as defined by FECA) or former leadership PAC (for example, in the case of a lobbyist who was previously a covered official) may be a political committee established, financed, maintained or controlled by a lobbyist."[31]

Finally, the User Manual instructs that filers should only include PACs on a report if they were established or controlled during the selected filing period.[32] This permits a lobbyist who has severed ties with a PAC to exclude the PAC's activities from the lobbyist's personal report.

5-5.2 Contributions and Disbursements

Section 1604(d) of the LDA describes six general categories of contributions or disbursements made by the filer or a PAC it has established or controlled during the reporting period that must be disclosed. Specifically, it requires disclosure of the date, recipient, and amount of funds contributed or disbursed:

1. for political contributions to federal candidates or officeholders, leadership PACs, or political party committees if the aggregate to the recipient equals or exceeds $200 during the reporting period;[33]
2. to pay the cost of an event to honor or recognize a covered legislative branch official or covered executive branch official;
3. to an entity that is named for a covered legislative branch official, or to a person or entity in recognition of such official;
4. to an entity established, financed, maintained, or controlled by a covered legislative branch official or covered executive branch official, or an entity designated by such official;
5. to pay the costs of a meeting, retreat, conference, or other similar event held by, or in the name of, one or more covered legislative branch officials or covered executive branch officials;[34] or

---

30. *Id.*
31. *Id.*
32. User Manual, *supra* note 14, at 36.
33. 2 U.S.C. § 1604(d)(1)(D) (2015); *see also* Revised Guidance, *supra* note 3, Appendix 4-A.
34. 2 U.S.C. § 1604(d)(1)(E)(i)–(iv) (2015); *see also* Revised Guidance, *supra* note 3, Appendix 4-A.

6. for contributions to a Presidential library foundation or Presidential inaugural committee equal to or exceeding $200 during the reporting period.[35]

These statutory categories are represented by five "contribution types" for LD-203 reporting purposes:

1. "FECA," which corresponds to category 1 above;
2. "Honorary Expenses," which captures 2, 3, and 4;
3. "Meeting Expenses," which corresponds to 5;
4. "Presidential Library Expenses"; and
5. "Presidential Inaugural Committee," which together represent 6.[36]

In addition to identifying a "contribution type" for each reported contribution, the LD-203 also requires the filer to select a "contributor name," "date," "contribution amount," "payee name," and "honoree name."[37] Multiple honorees may be entered for a single contribution or disbursement.[38] The filer's choices for contributor name will be limited to "self" or the name of any PAC established or controlled by the filer and listed in the previous section, "Political Action Committee Names."[39]

If a lobbyist makes a reportable payment (other than a FECA contribution) and is reimbursed by a registrant, the registrant should report the payment as its own, rather than the lobbyist.[40] Note that in-kind contributions of goods and services are reportable.

We discuss each of the major categories of giving below.

5-5.2.1 Federal Election Campaign Act (FECA) Contributions

The LDA requires filers to disclose "the name of each Federal candidate or office-holder, leadership PAC, or political party committee, to whom aggregate contributions equal to or exceeding $200 were made by the person or organization, or a political committee established or controlled by the person or organization within the semiannual period, and the date and amount of each such contribution made within the semiannual period."[41] The Revised Guidance provides that, pursuant to this section, the filer must disclose for itself, and for any political committee the filer established or controls:

> The date, recipient, and amount of funds contributed (including in-kind contributions) to any Federal candidate or officeholder, leadership PAC, or political party committee (registered with the Federal Election

---

35. 2 U.S.C. § 1604(d)(1)(F) (2015); *see also* Revised Guidance, *supra* note 3, Appendix 4-A.

36. User Manual, *supra* note 14, at 38.

37. *Id.* at 39. On its face, section 1604(d) of the LDA only requires disclosure of the "recipient" of a reportable contribution or disbursement, but this will not always reveal which covered official or officials the expenditure was intended to "honor" or assist. It is probably for this reason that the LD-203 requires filers to identify both a "payee" and "honoree" for each contribution.

38. Revised Guidance, *supra* note 3, Appendix 4-A (Example 11).

39. See Section 5-5.1.

40. Revised Guidance, *supra* note 3, Appendix 4-A. The exception here for FECA contributions by a lobbyist that are reimbursed by a registrant probably reflects the fact that such a reimbursement would violate one or more federal laws. *See, e.g.,* 52 U.S.C. § 30122 (2015) (contributions in the name of another prohibited); 52 U.S.C. § 30118(a) (2015) (corporate contributions prohibited).

41. 2 U.S.C. § 1604(d)(1)(D) (2015).

Commission), if the aggregate during the period to that recipient equals or exceeds $200…. Contributions to state and/or local candidates and committees not required to be registered with the Federal Election Commission need not be disclosed.[42]

In line with this guidance, only contributions to federal candidate committees, leadership PACs,[43] national political party committees, the "federal" accounts of state political party committees, and federal joint fundraising committees organized by any these committees should be reported as FECA contributions. Contributions to other types of federally registered PACs—such as the SSF of a corporation or trade association, or a multicandidate committee not registered as a leadership PAC—do not need to be reported as FECA contributions. Contributions to federally registered, independent expenditure-only committees, commonly referred to as "super PACs," are also excluded from disclosure under this category.[44]

5-5.2.1.2 "Payee" and "Honoree"
The Secretary and the Clerk have provided informal guidance on the correct "honoree" to designate for each type of contribution:

- For contributions to a *candidate's authorized campaign committee*, filers should report the name of the committee as the payee, and the name of the candidate as the honoree.
- For contributions to *party committees*, filers should report the name of the committee as both the payee and the honoree.
- For contributions to *leadership PACs*, filers should report the name of the committee as the payee, and the PAC's sponsor (as identified in the committee's Federal Election Commission Statement of Organization) as the honoree.
- For contributions to *joint fund-raising committees*, filers should report the name of the committee as both the payee and the honoree.[45]

5-5.2.2 Honorary Expenses
The User Manual describes "honorary expenses" as an "expansive category designed to capture many required disclosures."[46] It includes a variety of payments made by the filer or a PAC established or controlled by the filer that might

---

42. *Id.*

43. As defined by FECA, a leadership PAC is "a political committee that is directly or indirectly established, financed, maintained or controlled by a candidate for Federal office or an individual holding Federal office but which is not an authorized committee of the candidate or individual and which is not affiliated with an authorized committee of the candidate or individual, except that leadership PAC does not include a political committee of a political party." 52 U.S.C. § 30104(i)(8) (2015); *see also* 11 C.F.R. § 100.5(e)(6) (2015). Leadership PACs are required to identify themselves to the FEC on their Statement of Organization, and the FEC makes a list of registered leadership PACs available on its website. *See* FEDERAL ELECTION COMMISSION, Leadership PACs and Sponsors, *available at* http://www.fec.gov/data/Leadership.do.

44. 2 U.S.C. § 1604(d)(1)(D) (2015).

45. Allocations among the committees participating in the joint fundraising committee do not need to be disclosed as such, though the filer may include allocation information if desired.

46. USER MANUAL, *supra* note 14, at 55.

"honor" or otherwise assist a covered official in certain enumerated ways,[47] but does not include any disbursement that is already reportable under federal campaign finance laws as a political contribution on the contribution recipient's FEC report.[48]

5-5.2.2.1 Payment for the Costs of an Event to Honor or Recognize a Covered Legislative or Executive Branch Official

Payments for the costs of events to honor or recognize covered officials are probably the most common type of non-FECA disbursements reported by filers. They also receive the most attention in the Revised Guidance, which at the time of publication devoted no less than nine of twelve hypothetical examples to various aspects of such payments. But despite the relative wealth of official guidance, this category of payments regularly presents some of the more difficult interpretative questions for filers. Trying to determine whether a payment is reportable is a fact-dependent inquiry, and filers are advised to carefully examine relevant hypothetical examples from the Revised Guidance, reproduced in Section 5-5.2.2.1.2, and to seek knowledgeable counsel when necessary. Even so, a few general principles are clearly discernable, as discussed below.

5-5.2.2.1.1 When Does an Event "Honor" or "Recognize"?

An event does not necessarily honor or recognize a covered official simply because the official has a speaking role at the event or is listed on the speaking program in event materials.[49] Similarly, an event does not automatically honor or recognize a covered official because the official is listed on event materials as an "attendee" or "special invitee," or even an "honorary co-host."[50] The Revised Guidance explains that merely listing officials' anticipated attendance or their "passive allowance of their names to be used as 'co-hosts,' in and of itself, is not sufficient [for them] to be considered 'honored or recognized.'"[51] Use of the title "The Honorable" in front of a covered official's name also does not indicate the official is being honored or recognized if its use is consistent with widely accepted notions of protocol applicable to referencing certain very senior government officials.[52] In each of these cases however, additional facts may warrant the conclusion that the event is honoring or recognizing the covered official. For example, if the covered official is "given a special award, recognition, or honor (which may not necessarily be through the receipt of a physical object) by the organization at the event, the cost of the event would have to be reported, even if the invitation did not indicate that such would be given."[53]

For an organization that donates money, goods, or services to another to fund an event (see discussion below), counsel can be helpful in reviewing invitations and event promotional materials to determine whether the event "honors" or "recognizes" a covered official within the parameters of the law.

---

47. 2 U.S.C. § 1604(d)(1)(E)(i)–(iv) (2015).
48. *Id.* § 1604(d)(1)(E)(iv); *see also* Revised Guidance, *supra* note 3, Appendix 4-A.
49. Revised Guidance, *supra* note 3, Appendix 4-A (Example 6).
50. *Id.* (Examples 7, 8).
51. *Id.*
52. *Id.* (Example 8).
53. *Id.* (Example 6).

5-5.2.2.1.2 What Constitutes "Payment of the Cost of an Event"?

Any payments specifically and knowingly designated by a filer for a cost of an event honoring or recognizing a covered official—such as catering costs, venue rental, or floral arrangements—must be reported, even if the filer wouldn't qualify as an event sponsor under House or Senate gift rules and isn't publicly held out as a sponsor in any way.[54] On the other hand, the purchase of a ticket or table to another entity's event, by itself, is not enough to be considered paying for the cost of an event for reporting purposes.[55]

Here too though, supplemental facts might require reporting payments associated with the event, as discussed more fully in Example 9, *infra*. Particularly difficult questions often arise when event organizers bundle the sale of tickets or tables into sponsorship packages that may include additional perquisites such as public acknowledgement of the purchaser's "sponsorship" of the event on event invitations or materials. And the Revised Guidance cautions that the purchase of tickets or tables may become reportable where registrants "purchase enough tickets/tables so that it would appear that they are paying the costs of the event and/or would not appear to be just ticket or table-buyers." It goes on to counsel for a case-by-case analysis of these situations "to determine if the quantity is such that it would appear that the filer is paying the costs of the event."[56]

The following examples from the Revised Guidance address this type of reportable honorary expense:

Example 1: *In State "A," a group of constituents involved in widget manufacturing decide to honor Senator "Y" and Representative "T" with the "Widget Manufacturing Legislative Leaders of 2008" plaques. Registrant "B" is aware that "Y" has checked with the Senate Select Committee on Ethics regarding her ability to accept the award and attend the coffee, and "T" has checked with the House Committee on Ethics. "B" pays caterer "Z" $500 and Hotel "H" $200 to partially fund the event. "B" would report that it paid $500 to "Z" and $200 to "H" on November 20, 2008 for the purpose of an event to honor or recognize "Y" and "T" with the plaques.*

Example 4: *There is a large regional conference on "Saving Our River," sponsored by three 501(c)(3) organizations. Senator "Y" and Representative "T" are given "Champions of Our River" awards at a dinner event that is part of the conference. Registrant "B" contributes $3,000 specifically for the costs of the dinner event, paying one of the sponsors directly. At the time of the specific or restricted contribution, "B" was aware that "Y" and "T" would be honorees. Regardless of whether "B" is a sponsor under House or Senate gift rules and although B is not listed on the invitation as a sponsor (or the like) nor is publicly held out as a sponsor (or the like), since "B" partially paid for the cost of the event, "B" would disclose a payment of $3,000 on the relevant date payable to the sponsor with the notation that "Y" and "T" were honored.*

Example 5: *Registrant "B," an industry organization, hosts its annual gala dinner and gives a "Legislator of the Year" award to Representative "T." Revenues from the gala*

---

54. *Id.* (Example 4, 5).
55. *Id.* (Example 9).
56. *Id.*

dinner help fund Registrant "B's" activities throughout the year. Registrant "B" must report: 1) the cost of the event (hotel, food, flowers, etc., but not indirect costs such as host staff salaries and host office overhead); 2), the payee(s) (as a convenience to filers, separate vendors may be aggregated by using the term "various vendors"); and 3) that the event honored Representative "T." Please note that "B" must still separately report the cost of any item that "B" gave "T." The fact that the event helped raise funds for the organization does not change the reporting requirement, though it could be noted in the filing.

Example 6: *Registrant "B," an industry organization, has an annual two-day "Washington fly-in" for its members. Among the events for its members is an event on "The Importance of Industry G to the U.S. Economy." Senator "T" is listed on the invitation as a speaker at the event. Based on these facts alone, Registrant "B" would not need to report the event under this section. For a covered official to speak at such an event would not, in and of itself, form the basis for concluding that the official is to be honored or recognized. Supplemental facts might require reporting the cost of the event. For example, if Senator "T" were given a special award, recognition, or honor (which may not necessarily be through the receipt of a physical object) by the organization at the event, the cost of the event would have to be reported, even if the invitation did not indicate that such would be given. Simply designating a covered official as a "speaker" at an event at which the covered official receives a special award, recognition or honor, will not permit the filer to avoid or evade reporting the expenses of the event.*

Example 7: *Senator "Y" and Representative "T" are "honorary co-hosts" of an event sponsored by Registrant "R" to raise funds for a charity, which is not established, financed, maintained, or controlled by either legislator. "Y" and "T's" passive allowance of their names to be used as "co-hosts," in and of itself, is not sufficient to be considered "honored or recognized." The purpose of the event is to raise funds for Charity "V," not to honor or recognize "Y" or "T." Nor are these facts (i.e. being passive honorary co-hosts), in and of themselves, sufficient to treat the event as being held "by or in the name" of "Y" or "T." Supplemental facts might require reporting the cost of the event.*

Example 8: *Registrant "R" sponsors an event to promote "Widget Awareness." "The Honorable Cabinet Secretary Z" is listed on the invitation as an "attendee" or "special invitee" but will not receive an honor or award at the event. Based on these facts alone, "R" would not need to include the costs of this event on "R's" disclosure under this section. Mere listing of "Z's" anticipated attendance at an event the purpose of which is to promote Widget Awareness, in and of itself, is not sufficient to be considered "honored or recognized". Use of the phrase "The Honorable" in this context is consistent with widely accepted notions of protocol applicable to referencing certain very senior government officials. Supplemental facts might require reporting the cost of the event. For instance, if "Z" received a special, award, honor, or recognition by "R" at the event, "R" would have to report the costs of the event noting that "Z" was being honored or recognized.*

Example 9: *Registrant "B" buys a table at a dinner event sponsored by a 501(c) organization to honor Representative "T" but Registrant "B" is not considered a sponsor of the event under House and Senate gift rules. Lobbyist "C" pays the $150 individual ticket cost* *to attend the dinner, but is not considered a sponsor of the event under House and Senate gift rules. The purchase of a table or ticket to another entity's event, in and of itself, is not sufficient to be considered paying the "cost of an event." Supplemental facts might require reporting the cost of the event. For example, if (1) "B" or "C" undertake activities such that "B" or "C" becomes a sponsor of the event for House and/or Senate gift rule purposes; or (2) "B" or " C" purchase enough tickets/tables so that it would appear that they are paying the costs of the event and/or would not appear to be just ticket or table-buyers (regardless of whether "B" or "C" is a sponsor under House or Senate gift rules), then "B" or "C" would need to report the costs incurred by "B" or "C" (as the case may be) for the event, noting that Representative "T" was the honoree. In the case of filers purchasing multiple tickets and/or tables to an event, a case-by-case analysis will be needed to determine if the quantity is such that it would appear that the filer is paying the costs of the event.*

Example 11: *Registrant "L" holds an annual fundraising event that honors one person from each of the 50 states whom "L" deems to have played a significant role for the cause "L" supports. In 2009, four of the honorees were covered legislative and executive officials. "L" must disclose the total amount that it paid for the event, disclosing in the payee section "various vendors," and disclosing the names of the four covered officials. Although not required, and thus at its option, "L" could note in the comments section that 4 of the 50 honorees were covered officials. Section 5(d) of the LDA does not contemplate a breakdown, delineation or separation of expenses.*

Example 12: *Registrant "O" is a university. In June 2009, in conjunction with its commencement event, "O" conferred an honorary degree upon Senator "P." "O" would report all payments relating to the commencement event (chair rental, lunch for honorees, etc.) on its LD-203 report, listing "various vendors" as the payee, and Senator "P" as the honoree. Although not required, and thus at its option, "O" could comment that "P" received an honorary degree.[57]*

5-5.2.2.2 Payment to an Entity Named for or in Recognition of a Covered Legislative Branch Official

Honorary expenses also include payments to an entity named for a covered legislative branch official, or to a person or entity in recognition of a covered legislative branch official.[58] Unlike the other types of honorary expenses, this category only applies to covered *legislative* branch officials, and not to executive branch officials.

The Revised Guidance offers the following example of this type of honorary expense:

Example 2: *After checking to discover if the activity is permissible, Lobbyist "C" contributes $300 on June 1, 2008 to Any State University toward the endowment of a chair named for Senator "Y." "C" would report the information above noting that the payment was made to Any State for the endowment of "Y's" chair.[59]*

---

57. *Id.*
58. 2 U.S.C. § 1604(d)(1)(E)(ii) (2015); *see also* REVISED GUIDANCE, *supra* note 3, Appendix 4-A.
59. *See* REVISED GUIDANCE, *supra* note 3, Appendix 4-A.

Note that a contribution to a federally registered, independent expenditure-only committee, or super PAC, named after a covered legislative official would not be reportable as an honorary expense. This is because super PACs—while able to solicit and accept unlimited contributions from individuals, political committees, corporations, and labor organizations—are still required to report such contributions to the FEC[60] and therefore still qualify under the statutory exception for entities "required to report the receipt of the funds under [FECA]."[61]

5-5.2.2.3 Payment to Entity Established, Financed, Controlled, Maintained, or Designated by Covered Legislative or Executive Official

As with events "honoring or recognizing" a covered official, determining whether an entity is "established, financed, controlled, maintained or designated"[62] by a covered official for reporting purposes is ultimately a fact-dependent inquiry. Fortunately the Revised Guidance provides direction for several of the key terms.

A charitable organization will not be considered to be "established" by a covered official if the official established the organization before becoming a covered official and had no further relationship with the organization after becoming a covered official.[63]

A de minimis contribution to a charity (in proportion to the charity's overall receipts of contributions) by a covered official does not, without more, make the charity one that is "financed, maintained, or controlled" by the covered official.[64] The Revised Guidance notes that a covered official serving as a nonvoting board member, such as an honorary or ex-officio member, does not "control" an entity for reporting purposes.[65] This begs the question whether the inverse is also true; that is, whether the service of a single covered official as a *voting* member on an entity's board means that the entity is "controlled" by that covered official for reporting purposes. The Revised Guidance doesn't answer this question, but the Secretary and the Clerk have informally advised that an entity will generally be considered to be "controlled" by covered officials through its board if covered officials make up 20 percent or more of the board's voting membership.[66]

A contribution will be considered "designated" to an entity when, for instance, a covered official directs a charitable contribution in lieu of an honoraria pursuant to House, Senate, or executive branch ethics rules. A payment directed to an entity by a covered official who is also on the board of the entity will also be considered "designated" for reporting purposes. On the other hand, a contribution given in response to a fundraising solicitation by a covered official is not sufficient to deem the contribution "designated" by that covered official. The Revised Guidance

---

60. *See generally* Federal Election Commission, Adv. Ops. 2010-09 (Club for Growth) & 2010-11 (Commonsense 10).

61. 2 U.S.C. § 1604(d)(1)(E)(iv) (2015); *see also* Revised Guidance, *supra* note 3, Appendix 4-A.

62. 2 U.S.C. § 1604(d)(1)(E)(iii) (2015); *see also* Revised Guidance, *supra* note 3, Appendix 4-A.

63. *Id.*

64. *Id.*

65. *Id.*

66. This guidance was probably originally derived from the definition of "[i]n whole or major part" in section 3 of the Revised Guidance. *See* Revised Guidance, *supra* note 3, Appendix 4-A. Note, also, that additional circumstances may indicate that an entity is "controlled" through its board even though less than 20 percent of the voting board is composed of covered officials, such as when a covered official is also serving as an officer or other leadership position on the board.

states that "a contribution following a mere statement of support or solicitation does not necessarily constitute a reportable event ... without some further role by a covered official."[67] Not that this should happen often: as any serious student of the congressional gift rules knows, if a lobbyist were to give a contribution to a charity in response to a direct solicitation from a member of Congress, that contribution would be viewed as an unlawful gift.[68] The Revised Guidance provides the following example of a contribution "designated" by a covered official:

Example 3: *Senator "Y" has been asked to speak at a conference held in Washington, DC, sponsored by a professional association of which Registrant "B" is a member. "B" makes a donation of $100 to Charity "X" in lieu of the association paying a speaking fee (i.e., a contribution in lieu of honoraria). "B" would disclose a contribution of $100 on the date of the payment, with the notation that the payment was made as a contribution in lieu of honoraria to an entity designated by "Y."[69]*

As with the other categories of honorary expenses, a contribution to a federally registered independent expenditure-only committee (super PAC) that is established, financed, maintained, or designated by a covered official should not be reported here, because it would be exempt under the statutory exception for contributions reportable by contribution recipients under federal campaign finance law.[70] It should be expected, however, that this type of reporting question will not often arise, given that most covered officials are prohibited by federal law from establishing, financing, or maintaining a super PAC in the first place.[71]

5-5.2.3 Meeting Expenses

This category covers any payment for a meeting, retreat, conference, or other similar event held by, or in the name of, one or more covered legislative or executive branch officials.[72] The Revised Guidance explains that having covered officials passively serve as "honorary co-hosts" of an event is not sufficient by itself to treat the event as being held "by or in the name of" the officials.[73] Costs related to nonpreferential sponsorship of multicandidate primary or general election debates

---

67. *Id.*

68. *See* U.S. House, Committee on Ethics, Rule XXV (114th Cong.) ("House Rule XXV"); U.S. Senate, Select Committee on Ethics Rule XXXV (114th Cong.) ("Senate Rule XXXV"). These rules generally provide that members, officers, and employees of the House or the Senate may only accept gifts that fall within one of the categories of acceptable goods or services described in the rules. Although the gift rules for each House of Congress contain many similarities, there are some important differences. Copies of these rules, which include specific enumerated exceptions, are included as Appendix 8-B. See Chapter 8 for further discussion of these rules.

69. *See* Revised Guidance, *supra* note 3, Appendix 4-A.

70. See discussion in Section 5-5.2.2.2.

71. *See* 52 U.S.C. § 30125(e) (2015); 11 C.FR. §§ 300.61, 300.60(d) (2015). While some covered officials *are* permitted to establish, finance, and maintain other types of political committees, such as candidate committees and leadership PACs, contributions to these entities should be reported on the LD-203 as FECA Contributions, see Section 5-5.2.1, and not as honorary expenses.

72. 2 U.S.C. § 1604(d)(1)(E)(iii) (2015); *see also* Revised Guidance, *supra* note 3, Appendix 4-A.

73. Revised Guidance, *supra* note 3, Appendix 4-A (Example 7).

also do not need to be disclosed.[74] The same statutory exception for funds report-able to the FEC applies here as well.[75]

5-5.2.4 Presidential Library Foundation and Presidential Inaugural Committee Contributions

The final category of disbursement disclosure required under section 1604(d) of the LDA is "the name of each Presidential library foundation, and each Presiden-tial inaugural committee, to whom contributions equal to or exceeding $200 were made by the person or organization, or a political committee established or con-trolled by the person or organization, within the semiannual period, and the date and amount of each such contribution within the semiannual period."[76] Accord-ingly, contributions to any presidential library foundation, or presidential inaugu-ral committee, that equal or exceed $200 during the semiannual reporting period must be disclosed as "Presidential Library Expenses" or expenses for a "Presiden-tial Inaugural Committee."[77] The latter category includes payments to the official inaugural committees for tickets to inaugural events, as well as contributions to an official Presidential Transition Organization.[78]

5-5.3 Comments Box

Individual lobbyists serving on the board of a registrant's SSF who wish to opt out of disclosing FECA contributions personally because the registrant will disclose them on its own report must indicate their board membership in the comments box.[79] This box may also be used to clarify an entry.[80]

5-5.4 Certification of Compliance with House and Senate Gift Rules

The final component of the LD-203 is a certification that the filer has read and is familiar with the House and Senate gift and travel rules[81] and has not provided, requested, or directed a gift, including travel, to a member of Congress or officer or employee of either the House or Senate knowing that the receipt of such a gift would violate the gift rules.[82]

Certification is provided by clicking a checkbox; the User Manual instructs that "[o]nly the registrant or lobbyist listed on the form can check the certification

---

74. *Id.*

75. 2 U.S.C. § 1604(d)(1)(E)(iv) (2015).

76. *Id.* § 1604(d)(1)(F).

77. 2 U.S.C. § 1604(d)(1)(F); USER MANUAL, *supra* note 14, at 38.

78. REVISED GUIDANCE, *supra* note 3, Appendix 4-A.

79. See Section 5-5.1.

80. USER MANUAL, *supra* note 14, at 60; *see also* REVISED GUIDANCE, *supra* note 3, Appendix 4-A (Examples 5 and 12).

81. *See* Senate Rule XXXV (114th Cong.); House Rule XXV (114th Cong.). See Chapter 8 for a dis-cussion of the congressional gift rules.

82. 2 U.S.C. § 1604(d)(1)(G) (2015). The congressional rules that are the subject of the certification technically apply only to members of Congress and staff and not, by their terms, to outsiders such as registrants and lobbyists; hence the phrasing of the certification that focuses on knowledge by the filer that the "*receipt* of the gift" would violate those rules. Note also that the certification does not extend to the rules governing executive branch employees.

portion of the form and file it,"[83] but the Revised Guidance indicates otherwise by specifically providing for the filing of reports by third-party filers, as long as they retain appropriate documentation demonstrating that they have authorization to make such filings.[84]

Though the LD-203 certification requirement does not pose the same interpretative difficulties as the contribution and disbursement reporting requirement, and requires only a few key strokes and a click to complete, the burdens associated with certification can nonetheless be considerable for organizational registrants. While individual lobbyists provide certification only as to their own individual compliance with the rules, organizational registrants must provide certification for the entity as a whole, including all directors, officers, and employees. An untruthful certification may be punishable by criminal and civil penalties.[85] To guard against this, many registrants implement and maintain education programs on congressional gift rules for employees to ensure compliance.[86]

5-5.5 Sample Form LD-203

Data entered into CRS does not immediately show how the LD-203 will appear upon filing; the form as filed can be viewed and printed after being filed electronically.[87] Figure 5-1 illustrates what a filed LD-203 looks like:

---

83. User Manual, *supra* note 14, at 50.

84. Revised Guidance, *supra* note 3, Appendix 4-A.

85. To the extent a "defective" filing includes a false certification, a registrant as well as a lobbyist can be prosecuted under the LDA both criminally and civilly if the violation was knowingly committed. They could also be prosecuted under the False Statements Accountability Act of 1996 (FSAA). *Id.* Because the signatory for a registrant "is an individual responsible for the accuracy of the information contained in the filing," according to the Revised Guidance, a false certification could also subject this individual to prosecution under the FSAA.

86. See Chapter 8 on the congressional gift rules and Chapter 30 on building a thorough compliance program.

87. User Manual, *supra* note 14, at 52.

LOBBYING CONTRIBUTION REPORT

Clerk of the House of Representatives • Legislative Resource Center • 135 Cannon Building • Washington, DC 20515
Secretary of the Senate • Office of Public Records • 232 Hart Building • Washington, DC 20510

FILER TYPE AND NAME

Type:
☑ Organization ☐ Lobbyist

Organization Name:
Big Company, Inc.

IDENTIFICATION NUMBERS

House Registrant ID:
32533

Senate Registrant ID:
31213

REPORTING PERIOD

Year:
2015

☑ Mid-Year (January 1 - June 30)
☐ Year-End (July 1 - December 31)
☐ Amendment

POLITICAL ACTION COMMITTEE NAMES

• Big Company, Inc. PAC

CONTRIBUTIONS

☐ No Contributions

#1.

Contribution Type:	**Contributor Name:**	**Amount:**	**Date:**
FECA	Big Company, Inc. PAC	$1,000.00	01/08/2015
Payee:	**Honoree:**		
Bill for Congress	Rep. Bill Brown		

#2.

Contribution Type:	**Contributor Name:**	**Amount:**	**Date:**
Honorary Expenses	Self	$60,000.00	05/10/2015
Payee:	**Honoree:**		
Widget Industry Association	Sen. Sam Smith		

COMMENTS

CERTIFICATION AND SIGNATURE

☑ I certify that I have read and am familiar with the provisions of the Standing Rules of the Senate and the Standing rules of the House of Representatives relating to the provision of gifts and travel. I have not provided, requested or directed a gift, including travel, to a Member of Congress or an officer or employee of either House of Congress with knowledge that receipt of the gift would violate rule XXXV of the Standing Rules of the Senate or rule XXV of the Rules of the House of Representatives during this filing period.

Digitally Signed By:
Janet Jones, 7/20/2015 10:22:46 AM

Figure 5-1 Lobbying Contribution Report

CHAPTER 6

Public Access to Lobbying Records: The Online Lobbying Disclosure Database

BY CRAIG HOLMAN*

6-1 Introduction

The Lobbying Disclosure Act of 1995 (LDA or the act),[1] as amended by the Honest Leadership and Open Government Act of 2007 (HLOGA),[2] mandates that public records of lobbying registration and lobbying activity, as well as records of gifts and travel for lawmakers and post-employment restrictions applicable to former members of Congress, be placed online in an easily accessible format. Online disclosure requirements apply also to lobbying records of agents of foreign principals lobbying the federal government under the Foreign Agents Registration Act of 1938 (FARA).[3]

The principal sources for providing these online lobbying databases are governmental entities, which are subject to the LDA's and FARA's statutory requirements. However, several private entities also provide online access to much of this data, often in a more user-friendly format.

---

*This chapter was written with assistance from Victoria Hall-Palerm and Adam Alba, legal research associates, and Anthony Szewczyk and Kendra-Pierre-Louis, research assistants, Public Citizen.

1. 2 U.S.C. §§ 1601–1612. For a full discussion of the LDA's filing requirements, see Chapter 4.
2. Pub. L. No. 110–81, 121 Stat. 735 (2007).
3. 22 U.S.C. §§ 611–621. See Chapter 19 for a discussion of the FARA generally.

For registration and activity reports for domestic lobbyists, the LDA requires the Secretary of the Senate and the Clerk of the House to make the information "available to the public over the Internet, without a fee or other access charge, in a searchable, sortable and downloadable manner."[4] HLOGA also included provisions requiring the Secretary and the Clerk to post the beginning and ending dates of the post-employment prohibitions that apply to a member, officer, or employee of Congress in a similarly searchable manner.[5] The same is true with regard to the travel and gift information for each member and congressional employee.[6] For registration and lobbying activity reports for lobbyists of foreign agents and foreign principals, the law directs the Department of Justice (DOJ) to post its FARA records online, also in a searchable, sortable, and downloadable format.[7]

The law only requires this information to be made available, however, "to the extent technically practicable."[8] This phrase allows some flexibility for the Secretary, the Clerk, and DOJ to work within the confines of technological limits. This chapter provides an overview of the accessibility and performance of these disclosure databases.

6-2 The Secretary of the Senate's Lobbying, Post-Employment, and Gift Databases

As required by statute, the Secretary makes the quarterly reports and registrations required under the LDA available to the public over the Internet without a fee or access charge. To access the lobbying information on the Secretary's website, the user clicks on the "Public Disclosure" link on the Senate's home page,[9] and then a link called "Lobbying Disclosure Act Databases"[10] (see Figure 6-1). From the database page, the user selects "Search the Lobbying Database (LD-1, LD-2)." This is a relatively easy navigation process and there is, as required, no fee or charge to access the database.

Searching the Secretary's database is relatively straightforward. The database operates by means of a simple interface and allows a user to search for individual reports and registrations by selecting subcategories within six main categories: "Registrants," "Clients," "Lobbyists," "Filings," "Affiliated Organizations," and "Foreign Entities."[11] Each of these categories has various subcategories by which the user searches the database[12] (see Figure 6-2). The user may select only five subcategories out of twenty-six to perform a search.[13] To perform a search with the

---

4. 2 U.S.C. § 1605(a)(9) (2015).

5. *Id.* § 4702 (a). For a discussion of the congressional post-employment restrictions, see Chapter 28.

6. *Id.* §§ 4712, 4727. For a discussion of the congressional gift rules, please see Chapter 8.

7. 22 U.S.C. § 616(d) (2015).

8. *See, e.g.*, 2 U.S.C. § 1605(a)(9) (2015); 22 U.S.C. § 616(d)(1) (2015).

9. U.S. Senate, http://www.senate.gov (last visited Sept. 25, 2015).

10. U.S. Senate, Legislative Records, Public Disclosure, http://www.senate.gov/legislative/lobbyingdisc.htm#lobbyingdisc=lda (last visited Sept. 25, 2015).

11. U.S. Senate, Query the Lobbying Disclosure Act Database, http://soprweb.senate.gov/index.cfm?event=selectfields (last visited Sept. 25, 2015).

12. *Id.*

13. *Id.*

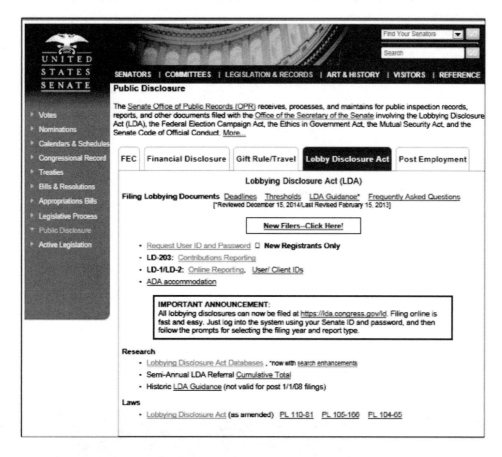

Figure 6-1 Link to Lobbying Disclosure Act Database

subcategory "amount reported" or "foreign entity ownership percentage," the user is required to enter a number value. Searches are limited to 3,000 results.[14]

After performing a search, users may select individual registrations or reports in PDF format (or some similar file format) from a table that contains their search terms. The results returned by the search are generally sortable. Once users perform a search, the database produces a table from which they may select individual reports or registrations. The table divides and sorts the filings by six categories: "Registrant Name," the "Client Name," the "Filing Type [either a report or a registration]," the "Amount Reported," "Date Posted," and "Filing Year" (see Figure 6-3). Users may click on the headings of the categories they wish to use in sorting the filings and can choose whether to sort them alphabetically or numerically. The table also allows for multicolumn sorting and filtering. Users may also export search results to an Excel spreadsheet or PDF and can print the results. The table always produces the same six columns. For example, if a user searches exclusively for a lobbyist's name, the table produces all the documents that contain the name, but not a separate column showing the name.

---

14. *Id.*

Query the Lobbying Disclosure Act Database

Search Lobbying Database | Search Contributions Database | Search Giftrule Database | Disclosure Home

Search Filings

Step 1 of 3: choose up to five search options

Registrants
- Registrant Name
- Registrant Country
- Registrant PPB Country
- Registrant ID

Clients
- Client Name
- Client State
- Client Country
- Client PPB Country
- Client ID

Lobbyists
- Lobbyist Name
- Covered Position Description (electronic filings only)
- Covered Govt Position Indicator (yes or no)

Filings
- Report Type
- Amount Reported
- Date Filing Posted
- Filing Period
- Filing Year
- Govt Entity Contacted
- Issue Area (lobbying activity)
- Specific Lobbying Issue (electronic filings only)

Affiliated Organizations
- Affiliated Org Name
- Affiliated Org Country

Foreign Entities
- Foreign Entity Name
- Foreign Entity Country
- Foreign Entity PPB Country
- Foreign Entity Ownership Percentage

Submit

(Please note that your search results will be limited to the first 3000 records returned.)

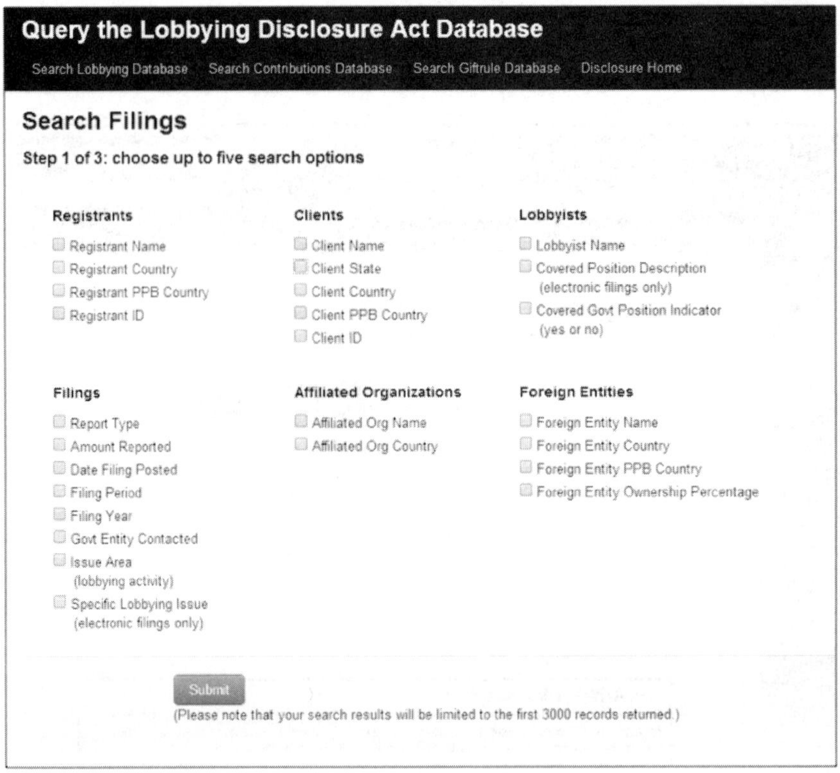

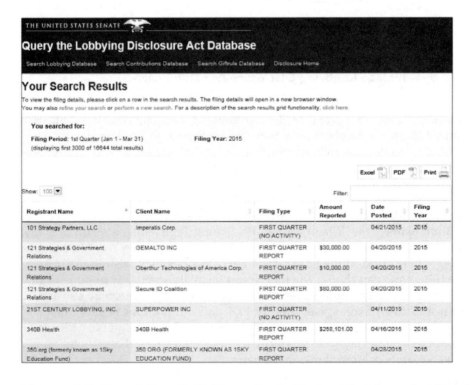

Figure 6-2 Search Options for the Lobbying Disclosure Act Database

THE UNITED STATES SENATE

Query the Lobbying Disclosure Act Database

Search Lobbying Database | Search Contributions Database | Search Giftrule Database | Disclosure Home

Your Search Results

To view the filing details, please click on a row in the search results. The filing details will open in a new browser window.
You may also refine your search or perform a new search. For a description of the search results grid functionality, click here.

You searched for:

Filing Period: 1st Quarter (Jan 1 - Mar 31) **Filing Year:** 2015
(displaying first 3000 of 16644 total results)

Excel | PDF | Print

Show: 100 Filter:

Registrant Name	Client Name	Filing Type	Amount Reported	Date Posted	Filing Year
101 Strategy Partners, LLC	Imperatis Corp.	FIRST QUARTER (NO ACTIVITY)		04/21/2015	2015
121 Strategies & Government Relations	GEMALTO INC	FIRST QUARTER REPORT	$30,000.00	04/20/2015	2015
121 Strategies & Government Relations	Oberthur Technologies of America Corp.	FIRST QUARTER REPORT	$10,000.00	04/20/2015	2015
121 Strategies & Government Relations	Secure ID Coalition	FIRST QUARTER REPORT	$80,000.00	04/20/2015	2015
21ST CENTURY LOBBYING, INC.	SUPERPOWER INC	FIRST QUARTER (NO ACTIVITY)		04/11/2015	2015
340B Health	340B Health	FIRST QUARTER REPORT	$258,101.00	04/16/2015	2015
350.org (formerly known as 1Sky Education Fund)	350 ORG (FORMERLY KNOWN AS 1SKY EDUCATION FUND)	FIRST QUARTER REPORT		04/28/2015	2015

Figure 6-3 Search Results Table on the Lobbying Disclosure Act Database

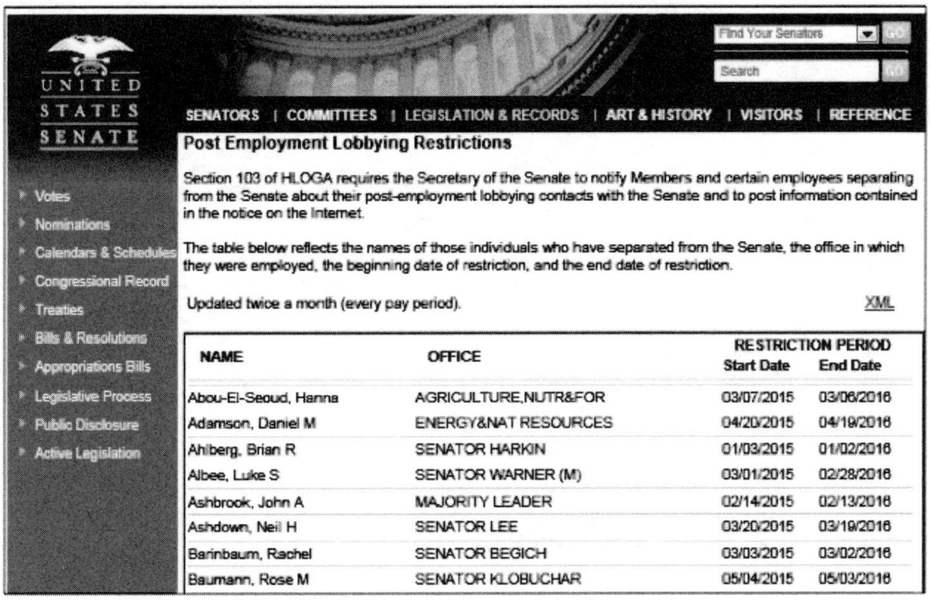

Post Employment Lobbying Restrictions

Section 103 of HLOGA requires the Secretary of the Senate to notify Members and certain employees separating from the Senate about their post-employment lobbying contacts with the Senate and to post information contained in the notice on the Internet.

The table below reflects the names of those individuals who have separated from the Senate, the office in which they were employed, the beginning date of restriction, and the end date of restriction.

Updated twice a month (every pay period). XML

NAME	OFFICE	RESTRICTION PERIOD Start Date	End Date
Abou-El-Seoud, Hanna	AGRICULTURE,NUTR&FOR	03/07/2015	03/06/2016
Adamson, Daniel M	ENERGY&NAT RESOURCES	04/20/2015	04/19/2016
Ahlberg, Brian R	SENATOR HARKIN	01/03/2015	01/02/2016
Albee, Luke S	SENATOR WARNER (M)	03/01/2015	02/28/2016
Ashbrook, John A	MAJORITY LEADER	02/14/2015	02/13/2016
Ashdown, Neil H	SENATOR LEE	03/20/2015	03/19/2016
Barinbaum, Rachel	SENATOR BEGICH	03/03/2015	03/02/2016
Baumann, Rose M	SENATOR KLOBUCHAR	05/04/2015	05/03/2016

Figure 6-4 Database for Post-Employment Lobbying Restrictions

To find the database for post-employment restrictions, a user clicks on the "Public Disclosure" link on the Senate's homepage, then a link entitled "Post Employment."[15] The user must then select a year to examine. The website then displays a prefabricated table listing the employee, the office, the restriction period start date, and the restriction period end date.[16] The table is sorted in alphabetical order by the employee's name and is updated twice a month, according to the website[17] (see Figure 6-4). The user may also download the database in XML format.

The Secretary's travel and gift database is found by clicking on the "Public Disclosure" link on the Senate's homepage, and then on the "Gift Rule/Travel" tab.[18] Users may then search the database, or download the entire database in compressed XML format.[19] When searching the database, users may select up to five fields out of seven: filer's last name, filer's first name, office name, filing/report type, reporting year, travel dates, or filing received date.[20] Searching the database produces a table that is sortable by the same categories (see Figure 6-5). Clicking on an individual result produces a single PDF-like document.

The Secretary's lobbying, post-employment, and gift databases allow users to download all the information that is searchable in large XML files. For the

15. *Id.*

16. U.S. Senate, Legislative Records, Post Employment Lobbying Restrictions, http://www.senate.gov/legislative/termination_disclosure/report2015.htm (last visited Sept. 25, 2015).

17. *Id.*

18. *See* U.S. Senate, *supra* note 9.

19. U.S. Senate, Legislative Records, Senate Rule 35 Requirements, http://www.senate.gov/legislative/lobbyingdisc.htm#lobbyingdisc=grt (last visited Sept. 25, 2015).

20. U.S. Senate, Query the Senate Gift Rule Database, http://soprweb.senate.gov/giftrule/ (last visited Sept. 25, 2015).

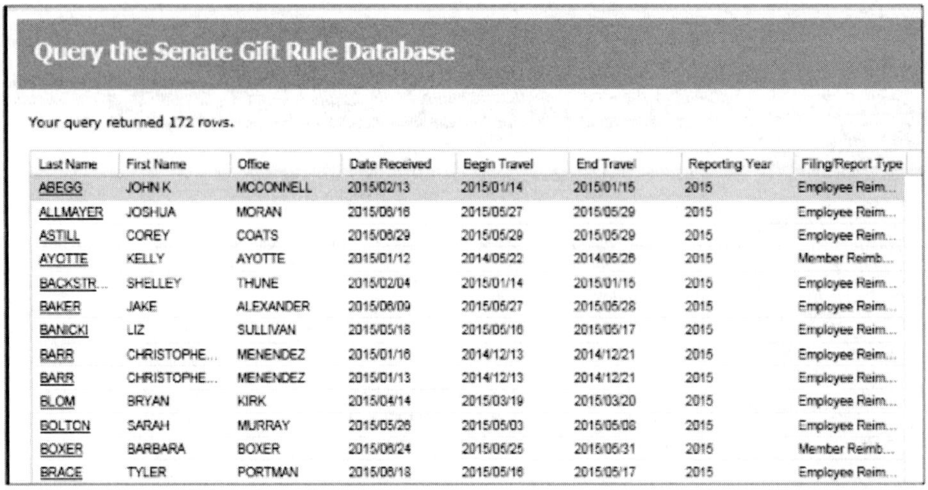

Query the Senate Gift Rule Database

Your query returned 172 rows.

Last Name	First Name	Office	Date Received	Begin Travel	End Travel	Reporting Year	Filing/Report Type
ABEGG	JOHN K	MCCONNELL	2015/02/13	2015/01/14	2015/01/15	2015	Employee Reim...
ALLMAYER	JOSHUA	MORAN	2015/06/16	2015/05/27	2015/05/29	2015	Employee Reim...
ASTILL	COREY	COATS	2015/06/29	2015/05/29	2015/05/29	2015	Employee Reim...
AYOTTE	KELLY	AYOTTE	2015/01/12	2014/05/22	2014/05/26	2015	Member Reimb...
BACKSTR...	SHELLEY	THUNE	2015/02/04	2015/01/14	2015/01/15	2015	Employee Reim...
BAKER	JAKE	ALEXANDER	2015/06/09	2015/05/27	2015/05/28	2015	Employee Reim...
BANICKI	LIZ	SULLIVAN	2015/05/18	2015/05/16	2015/05/17	2015	Employee Reim...
BARR	CHRISTOPHE...	MENENDEZ	2015/01/16	2014/12/13	2014/12/21	2015	Employee Reim...
BARR	CHRISTOPHE...	MENENDEZ	2015/01/13	2014/12/13	2014/12/21	2015	Employee Reim...
BLOM	BRYAN	KIRK	2015/04/14	2015/03/19	2015/03/20	2015	Employee Reim...
BOLTON	SARAH	MURRAY	2015/05/26	2015/05/03	2015/05/08	2015	Employee Reim...
BOXER	BARBARA	BOXER	2015/06/24	2015/05/25	2015/05/31	2015	Member Reimb...
BRACE	TYLER	PORTMAN	2015/06/18	2015/05/16	2015/05/17	2015	Employee Reim...

Figure 6-5 Example of Search Results on U.S. Senate Gift Rule Database

experienced researcher with access to sophisticated software, the large files should not be a problem. The lay user with only average computer experience will have considerable difficulty downloading the database, especially the massive lobbying activities database. The Secretary of the Senate provides the information in enormous XML files that are far too large to import into a spreadsheet program. Therefore, to actually make use of the data, users must have a sophisticated software program to accommodate the download. However, even with these shortcomings, the Secretary is still technically compliant with the law, as it requires the office to make the information downloadable *only to the extent that is technologically practicable*. Considering the large amount of data, XML format may be the best means for letting users download the information.

In sum, the Secretary generally complies with the language of the law in making the information available to the public. The databases are relatively simple to use and include the basic functionalities expected of any database. They will comply with the demands of the civic-minded citizen who would like to perform a cursory search and are also accessible to the more experienced researcher.

6-3 The Clerk of the House's Lobbying, Post-Employment, and Gift Databases

The Clerk's system for making lobbying information (registrations and quarterly reports) available generally follows a similar format to the Secretary's. Lobbyist information may be found by clicking on a "Lobbying Disclosure" tab on the home page of the Clerk's website.[21] From the main Lobbying Disclosure page,[22] the user

21. U.S. House of Representatives, Office of the Clerk, http://www.clerk.house.gov/(last visited Sept. 25, 2015).

22. U.S. House of Representatives, Office of the Clerk, http://lobbyingdisclosure.house.gov/ (last visited Sept. 25, 2015).

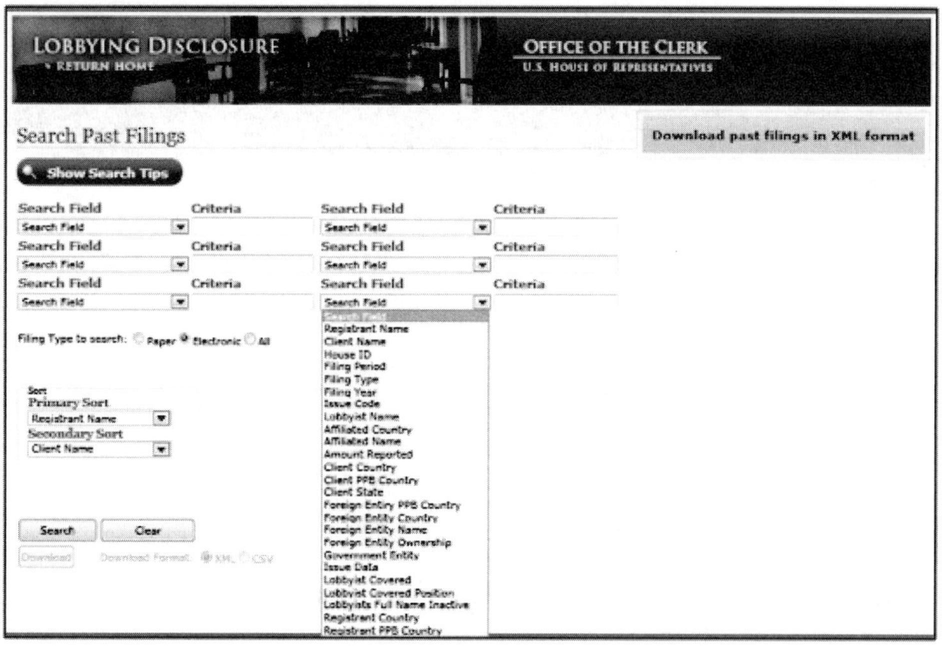

Figure 6-6 **Lobbying Disclosure Search Page on Office of the Clerk Website**

may click on the "Lobbying Disclosure Filing Search" link to reach the search query page.[23] This is a relatively easy navigation process and there is no fee or charge to access the database.

Searching the Clerk's database is also easy. When performing a search, users may select up to six "Search Fields" to search the lobbying reports and registrations.[24] Within the search fields, they may select one of twenty-five categories from the drop-down menu;[25] and to the right of each "Search Field" is an empty "Criteria" box where users may type the search terms.[26] Two subcategories—the lobbying "amount reported" and the foreign entity's "ownership percentage"—permit users to enter a number value. Neither function allows the use of "greater than" or "less than" symbols, but results returned show all amounts greater than or equal to the amount entered. Before performing the search, users must select one of thirteen categories by which to sort the results.[27] Finally, users can choose to search only paper filings, electronic filings, or both[28] (see Figure 6-6).

The results yielded by the Clerk's database are sortable. The table returned after users perform a search varies in relation to the categories they have chosen.

---

23. U.S. House of Representatives, Office of the Clerk, Lobbying Disclosure, http://disclosures.house.gov/ld/ldsearch.aspx (last visited Sept. 25, 2015).

24. *Id.*

25. *Id.*

26. *Id.*

27. *Id.*

28. *Id.*

House ID	Registrant Name	Client Name	Filing Year	Filing Period	Lobbyist Full Name	Amount Reported
411360003	3 Click Solutions, LLC	National Border Patrol Council	2015	2nd Quarter	murphy, patrick ▼	$30,000.00
428370001	9b Group, Inc.	American Farmland Trust	2015	2nd Quarter	Straughn, Pelham ▼	$20,000.00
428370002	9b Group, Inc.	Pheasants Forever, Inc	2015	2nd Quarter	Straughn, Pelham ▼	$10,000.00
329700006	AB MANAGEMENT ASSOCIATES	LOCKHEED MARTIN	2015	2nd Quarter	Barnett, Larry ▼	< $5,000
413970000	ACHILLEAN GROUP INC.	International Association of LGBT Investors and Private Business Owners	2015	2nd Quarter	None ▼	< $5,000
328650000	ALLETE, INC	ALLETE, INC	2015	2nd Quarter	Libro, William ▼	$52,000.00
330030000	AMERICAN ASSOCIATION FOR CLINICAL CHEMISTRY	AMERICAN ASSOCIATION FOR CLINICAL CHEMISTRY	2015	2nd Quarter	Stine, Vincent ▼	$40,000.00
352230000	AMERICAN COLLEGE OF CLINICAL PHARMACY	AMERICAN COLLEGE OF CLINICAL PHARMACY	2015	2nd Quarter	Webb, C. Edwin ▼	$127,250.00
310170000	AMERICAN FOUNDATION FOR THE BLIND	AMERICAN FOUNDATION FOR THE BLIND	2015	2nd Quarter	Richert, Mark ▼	< $5,000

Figure 6-7 Example of Lobbying Disclosure Search Results on Office of the Clerk Database

For example, if a user searched by "amount," the table would reflect the search by providing a column that lists the amount. Users may sort the filings by one of the thirteen categories required at the beginning of the search (see Figure 6-7). Search results are also downloadable in either XML or CSV format.

The post-employment data on the Clerk's database is also available to the public. On the Clerk's "Public Disclosure" page, users may click on the "Post-Employment Notifications" link to access the database.[29] The entire database may be downloaded in a zip file that contains the data in both TXT and XML format, or users may click on the "Search Post-Employment Notifications" link to search the records.[30] The database is searchable by the employee's last name, the employing office, and the termination date[31] (see Figure 6-8). A search produces a table with four columns: employee's last name, employing office, termination date, and eligibility date. By clicking on the header for any one of these columns, users may sort the results alphabetically or numerically.

The Clerk also maintains a database that allows users to search among gift and travel filings. Users navigate from the Clerk's main web page to the "Public Disclosure" web page, where they can select the "Gift and Travel Filings" link to access the Clerk's database, which contains reports received during the past six years.[32]

29. U.S. HOUSE OF REPRESENTATIVES, OFFICE OF THE CLERK, PUBLIC DISCLOSURE, http://clerk.house.gov/public_disc/index.aspx (last visited Sept. 25, 2015).
30. U.S. HOUSE OF REPRESENTATIVES, OFFICE OF THE CLERK, POST-EMPLOYMENT NOTIFICATIONS, http://clerk.house.gov/public_disc/postemployment.aspx (last visited Sept. 25, 2015).
31. U.S. HOUSE OF REPRESENTATIVES, OFFICE OF THE CLERK, POST EMPLOYMENT DATABASE, http://clerk.house.gov/public_disc/employment.aspx (last visited Sept. 25, 2015).
32. U.S. HOUSE OF REPRESENTATIVES, OFFICE OF THE CLERK, PUBLIC DISCLOSURE, http://clerk.house.gov/public_disc/index.aspx (last visited Sept. 25, 2015).

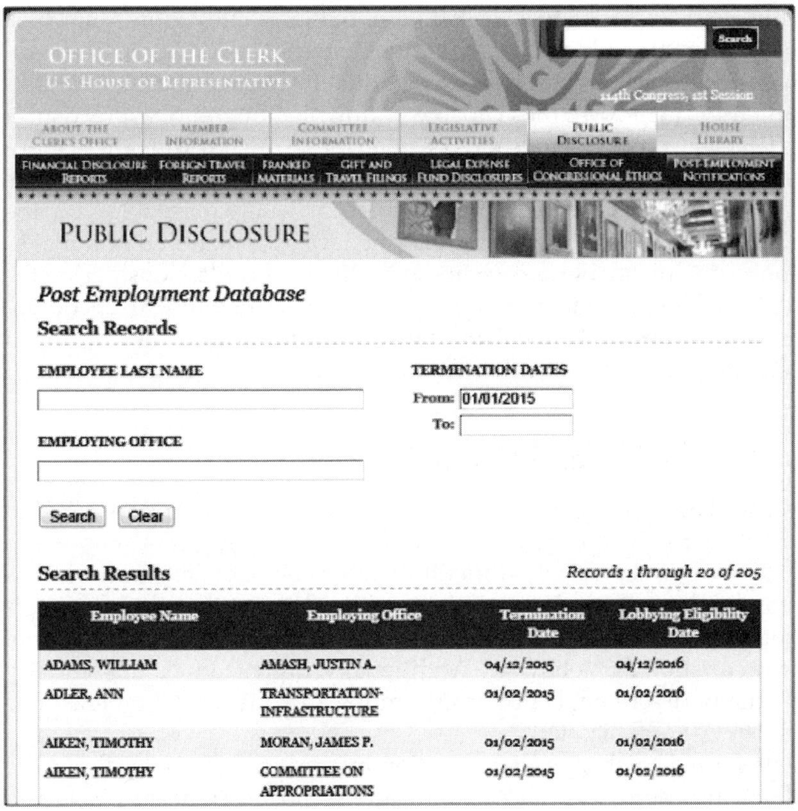

Figure 6-8 Office of the Clerk Public Disclosure Page with Example Search Results

Reports can be downloaded by year in a zip file that contains the data in TXT and XML format, or users may click on the "Search Gift & Travel Filings" link to search the records.[33]

Users can search using a member's name, destination, sponsor, or travel dates.[34] The main flaw in this database, however, is that there is no way to easily search for the amount of money spent on the gift or travel. To obtain that information, users must open results (in the form of a PDF) one by one and scroll down in the document to find the amount of money.[35] Strictly speaking, this database is still in compliance with the law.

While users can download specific search results in a fairly manageable manner, downloading the entire database for a year is only possible in large TXT or XML files, as with the Secretary of the Senate's data. Again, for the experienced

---

33. U.S. HOUSE OF REPRESENTATIVES, OFFICE OF THE CLERK, GIFT AND TRAVEL FILINGS, http://clerk.house.gov/public_disc/giftTravel.aspx (last visited Sept. 25, 2015).

34. U.S. HOUSE OF REPRESENTATIVES, OFFICE OF THE CLERK, GIFT AND TRAVEL FILINGS DATABASE, http://clerk.house.gov/public_disc/giftTravel-search.aspx (last visited Sept. 25, 2015).

35. *Id.*

researcher with access to sophisticated software, the large files should not be a problem. The lay user with only average computer experience will find download-ing the databases from the Clerk of the House difficult. Though the Clerk breaks up the database into small XML files capable of downloading into a spreadsheet program, the database comes in thousands of small files. Downloading these thou-sands of files requires a special software program that automatically downloads each file. However, as in the case of the Secretary's nearly unmanageable data, the Clerk's website is nevertheless compliant with the law's stipulation that it makes the information as downloadable as is technologically practicable. Considering the large amount of data, XML format might be the best means for letting users down-load the information, despite the challenges that poses to someone not equipped with the correct software to manage that volume of data.

6-4 Lobbyists and Campaign Contributions

Even though candidates, party committees, and political action committees (PACs) must all report their received contributions to the Federal Election Commission (FEC), it has always been extremely difficult to accurately track all contributions received from individuals (including, crucially, lobbyists). The greatest problem is that, when prompted on campaign finance disclosure forms, most lobbyists do not describe their occupation as "lobbyist." Additionally, organizations that employ lobbyists are usually described as nonprofit groups and advocacy organizations rather than as lobbyist organizations.

HLOGA attempted to change that situation by creating two new disclosure databases. Many consider these databases to be the most significant disclosure achievements of the statute, though both databases are currently falling short of their objectives due to the manner of their implementation.

The first database contains information on contributions "bundled" by lob-byists; this information must be filed by campaigns and committees on their FEC reports pursuant to federal campaign finance law. "Bundlers," or well-connected people (frequently CEOs or lobbyists) able to tap into the pocketbooks of hun-dreds of other individuals, represent one of the most influential driving forces in campaign financing. The bundler will amass many individual contributions of, say, $2,700 each into one large bundle of contributions on behalf of the company or special interest group the bundler represents. With 100 individual contribu-tions of $2,700 each, the bundler provides a campaign with over a quarter million dollars.

Public Citizen, a group advocating citizen interests, initiated a tracking web-site (www.WhiteHouseForSale.org) that has followed bundlers in the presiden-tial campaigns since 2000. The group relied exclusively on information that the presidential candidates voluntarily disclosed regarding their bundlers. (As such, the list is almost certainly incomplete.) Beginning in the 2010 election cycle, can-didates and committees were required to disclose their major lobbyist-bundlers on a separate reporting schedule to the FEC, which in turn made that data avail-able online.

On the FEC bundling disclosure website, users can either browse the data (which is organized alphabetically by the name of the committee) or customize their search by putting in a committee name, state, district, date, or contribution amount.[36] In the almost seven years since the implementation of these disclosure regulations (or, in other words, in the course of four federal election cycles), 632 bundlers were recorded as of June 2015.[37]

A second campaign contribution database (which itself is really two distinct databases) involving lobbyists is the LD-203 database, available as a result of amendments to the LDA affected by HLOGA. It is managed by the Clerk of the House and the Secretary of the Senate.[38] LD-203 is a special reporting form whereby LDA registrants and lobbyists listed on registrations and quarterly reports must report their own campaign contributions (as opposed to bundled contributions), as well as any contributions to a presidential library, events honoring a lawmaker, and expenses associated with a conference or a meeting in which lawmakers participate.[39]

In LD-203 reporting, a registrant organization is not responsible for reporting the personal contributions of its individual lobbyists. Rather, individual lobbyists file separate LD-203 reports listing their personal contributions. However, where a registrant organization reimburses a lobbyist employee for an honorary contribution, the organization must report the contribution as its own, rather than the lobbyist including the contribution on his or her individual LD-203 report.[40]

On the Secretary of the Senate's web page, two distinct links allow the user either to search the lobbyist contribution data or to download the full database[41] (see Figure 6-9).

As with the other LDA reports, downloading the database tends to be complicated, but the downloadable contribution database provided by the Secretary has been far easier to manage than the database provided by the Clerk. For the first 2008 filing period, for example, the Secretary's downloadable database consisted of eleven distinct files that had to be merged into a single data set. On the other hand, the Clerk's downloadable database consisted of thousands of individual files.

Searching the lobbyist contribution data on the Secretary's webpage is fairly straightforward. Users are provided three general search categories: registrants/lobbyists, types of filings, and contribution information. Users may search by the name of registrants and their lobbyists, registrants only, or lobbyists only.[42] The types of filings may be searched by original report or amended report as well as

---

36. Federal Election Commission, Bundled Contributions, http://www.fec.gov/data/LobbyistBundle.do?format=html (last visited Sept. 25, 2015).

37. *Id.*

38. *See* Lobbying Contributions Search (Office of the Clerk), http://disclosures.house.gov/lc/lcsearch.aspx (last visited Sept. 25, 2015); U.S. Senate, Office of the Secretary, Legislation and Records, LDA Reports, http://soprweb.senate.gov/index.cfm?event=lobbyistSelectFields&reset=1 (last visited Sept. 25, 2015).

39. 2 U.S.C. § 1604(d) (2015). See generally Chapter 5 for additional information regarding LD-203 reporting.

40. Sec'y of the Senate & Clerk of The House of Representatives, Lobbying Disclosure Act Guidance (revised February 15, 2013), *available at* http://lobbyingdisclosure.house.gov/amended_lda_guide.html. See also Appendix 4-A.

41. U.S. Senate, Public Disclosure, LDA Reports, http://www.senate.gov/legislative/Public_Disclosure/LDA_reports.htm (last visited Sept. 25, 2015).

42. U.S. Senate, Query the Lobbying Contributions Database, http://soprweb.senate.gov/index.cfm?event=lobbyistselectfields (last visited Sept. 25, 2015).

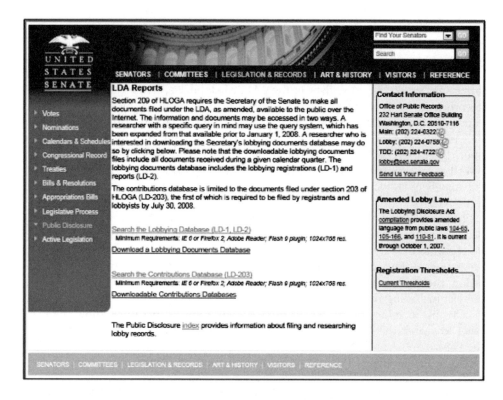

Figure 6-9 LDA Reports Page Showing Links to Lobbying Databases

by date and year.[43] Users may also search by a variety of contribution information, such as the name of the contributor (i.e., the registrant, lobbyist, or PAC), the amount of the contribution, and the date of the contribution.[44] Users may also search by contribution type, such as a campaign contribution (e.g., FECA), or an expense to honor a member of Congress, a contribution to pay for a meeting with a covered official, or a contribution to a presidential library fund[45] (see Figure 6-10).

The Clerk's webpage provides the same information, but in a very different format. Some users may find the Clerk's lobbyist contribution search engine easier to navigate. A user may search by organization or lobbyist name, PAC contributor, filing period, or recipient[46] (see Figure 6-11). The results of the search may be sorted by organization or lobbyist name, contribution type, and amount or filing period.[47] Searches and sorts may also be done by registrant or lobbyist identification number, for users who are seeking information on a specific registrant or lobbyist.[48]

---

43. *Id.*

44. *Id.*

45. *Id.*

46. U.S. HOUSE OF REPRESENTATIVES, OFFICE OF THE CLERK, LOBBYING CONTRIBUTION FILING SEARCH, http://disclosures.house.gov/lc/lcsearch.aspx (last visited Sept. 25, 2015).

47. *Id.*

48. *Id.*

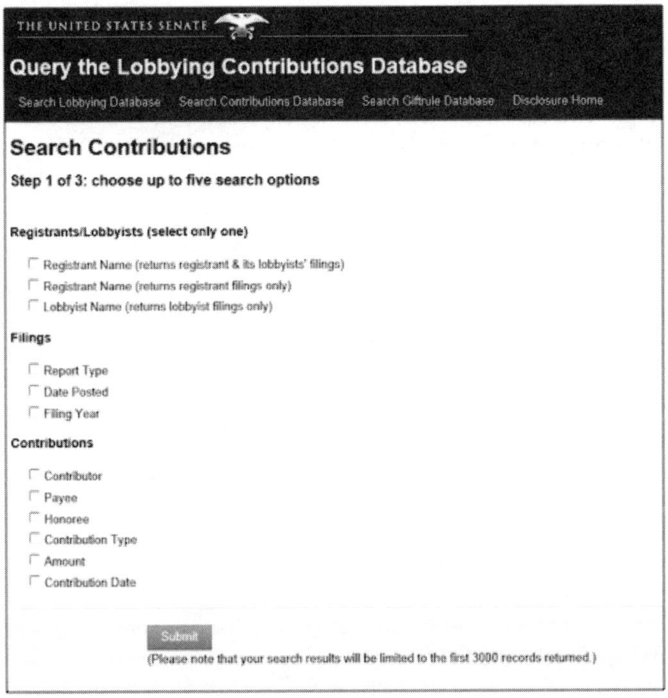

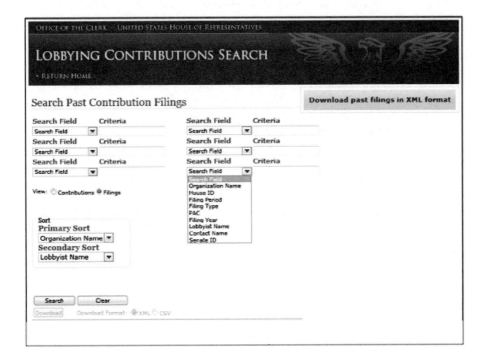

Figure 6-10 Secretary of the Senate's Lobbying Contributions Search Page

Figure 6-11 Office of the Clerk Lobbying Contributions Search Page

The first LD-203 disclosures (for the first half of 2008) were both surprising and somewhat confusing. The sheer amount of funds reported by lobbyists and lobbying organizations with regard to political events was far more than what most observers had expected. Approximately $200 million was reported as having been spent by lobbyists and lobbying organizations in the first six months of 2008 on everything from campaign contributions to meeting expenses. However, according to the Government Accountability Office (GAO), these days the LD-203 database paints a more complete picture of lobbyists' campaign contribution activity. A 2015 report found that only 4 percent of LD-203 reports omit reportable contributions documented in the FEC's database.[49]

The LD-203 database contains many duplicate filings that complicate any attempts to make sense of the data. When amendments to a report are filed, they are not synthesized into the original filing, but are instead listed as separate reports. No effort seems to be made by the Clerk or Secretary to remove duplicate or out-of-date filings. This ineffective maintenance has severely reduced the legitimacy of the LD-203 database as a disclosure mechanism.[50]

The database also distinctly lacks available summary statistics or any other broad overview of the information it contains. If a researcher wishes to know how much a particular industry's lobbyists contributed to campaigns or how many lobbyists contributed within a certain time frame, he or she has no alternative to manually sorting through hundreds of PDF files to find the relevant ones.

6-5 The FARA Database

The DOJ has in recent years made the public records of lobbying activity on behalf of foreign principals and foreign governments accessible to the public on the Internet.

FARA requires extensive reporting by agents of foreign principals regarding their lobbying efforts, including a day-by-day diary of each lobbying contact, money raised and spent for lobbying, and the issues, regulations, and legislation addressed.[51] FARA records are more extensive than required under the LDA for lobbying activity by domestic entities; however, these public records have been entrusted to the DOJ, an organization that has never considered itself a "disclosure" agency, for maintenance. As a result, until 2007, FARA records were kept solely in paper format tucked away in file cabinets in the agency's Washington, D.C., headquarters.

The DOJ invested so few resources into providing public access to FARA records that the database nearly perished. Responding to a Freedom of Information Act request for access to FARA records by the Center for Public Integrity, the DOJ announced in 2004 that the huge set of records (which serves as the lone window on lobbying activity by foreign governments) had been allowed to decay to the point that DOJ could not make electronic copies of its contents. In a letter from the agency, Thomas McIntyre, Chief of the Privacy Act Unit, said that simply

---

49. U.S. GOVERNMENT ACCOUNTABILITY OFFICE, 2014 LOBBYING DISCLOSURE: OBSERVATIONS ON LOBBYISTS' COMPLIANCE WITH DISCLOSURE REQUIREMENTS (March 2015), *available at* http://www.gao.gov/assets/670/669270.pdf.

50. Craig Holman, *The Tension Between Lobbying and Campaign Finance Laws: Rolling Back Gains Made Under the Honest Leadership and Open Government Act of 2007.* 13(1) ELECTION L.J. 45–65 (2014).

51. 22 U.S.C. § 612. See generally Chapter 19 for additional information regarding the Foreign Agents Registration Act of 1938.

attempting to make an electronic copy of the database "could result in a major loss of data, which would be devastating."[52]

HLOGA changed all this. As with LDA reports, the 2007 law required that the DOJ make FARA reports available to the public on the Internet in a "searchable, sortable and downloadable" format.[53] DOJ complied—and fairly well, as it turns out. HLOGA modified FARA by providing that the Attorney General must maintain and make available to the public over the Internet, without a fee or other access charge, an electronic database that

- Includes the information contained in registrations and reports filed under FARA;
- Provides a link to campaign finance reports filed with the Federal Election Commission under section 304 of the Federal Election Campaign Act of 1971; and
- Is searchable, sortable, and downloadable at a minimum, by each of the following categories:
  — Registrant's name, principal business address, and all other business addresses in the United States or elsewhere, and all residence addresses, if any;
  — Status of the registrant;
  — Nature of registrant's business;
  — Document type;
  — Contribution amount;
  — Type of activity; and
  — Name, business, and residence addresses of the foreign principal.

Each registration statement and update must be filed in electronic format[54] and made available to the public over the Internet "as soon as technically practicable after the registration statement or update is filed."[55]

The FARA database went live in May 2007 and is currently located on the FARA section of the DOJ website.[56] To access the database, the user clicks on the "Quick Search" or "Document Search" links. With the "Quick Search" function, the user may select from various subcategories of active and terminated primary registrants, short-form registrants, and foreign principals (see Figure 6-12).

Results are returned in a searchable, sortable list and can be further refined. For example, a "Quick Search for Active Registrants By Country or Location" can be refined to return only those registrants for Australia. Clicking on any of the column headers allows the user to sort the table by the column value, create breaks in the table according to column value, or hide the column[57] (see Figure 6-13).

---

52. Press Release, Center for Public Integrity, Kevin Bogardus, *Foreign Lobbyist Database Could Vanish* (July 28, 2004), *available at* http://www.publicintegrity.org/articles/entry/486/.

53. 22 U.S.C. § 616(d)(1) (2015).

54. 22 U.S.C. § 612(g) (2015).

55. 22 U.S.C. § 616(d)(2) (2015).

56. U.S. Department of Justice, Foreign Agents Registration Act, www.fara.gov (last visited Sept. 25, 2015).

57. U.S. Department of Justice, FARA Quick Search, http://www.fara.gov/quick-search.html (last visited Sept. 25, 2015).

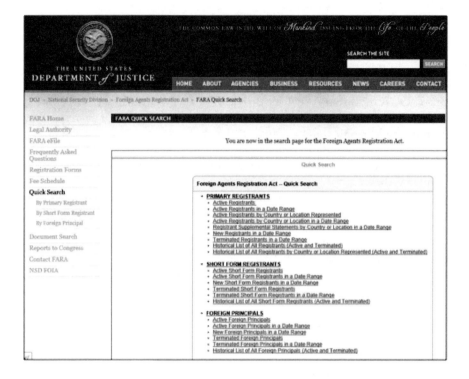

Figure 6-12 FARA Quick Search Page on Department of Justice Website

Figure 6-13 Sample Quick Search Results on FARA Database

Figure 6-14 View Options for FARA Quick Search Results

Clicking the "Actions" button next to the search field provides the user with additional search and sort options and also contains the option to download the database in CSV format. Via the blue "View" button, each filing is available for viewing and download as a PDF (see Figure 6-14).

With the "Document Search" function, users can conduct a more focused search. Users must first select a document type and choose a registration status (i.e., all, active, or terminated). Descriptions of each document type are provided at the bottom of the search page (see Figure 6-15).

Depending on the document type they select, users may further refine the search by registrant number, registrant name, short-form name, foreign principal name, foreign principal country, active/terminated date, and stamped/received date.

Results using the "Document Search" function are returned in grid format with sortable columns. Results can also be downloaded. By clicking where indicated in the "Document" column, users can view/save individual filings as PDF files (see Figure 6-16).

Not all FARA records, however, are available for public inspection over the Internet. The DOJ explains that "because some potential privacy issues remain under review, there are certain FARA documents not available via the Internet at this time, but which still can be accessed at the FARA public office."[58] This statement raises the question of why the information is accessible publicly at the FARA office, but not online if the information is indeed "public." In addition, the campaign finance link is not yet provided.

---

58. U.S. Department of Justice, FARA Document Search, http://www.fara.gov/search.html (last visited Sept. 25, 2015).

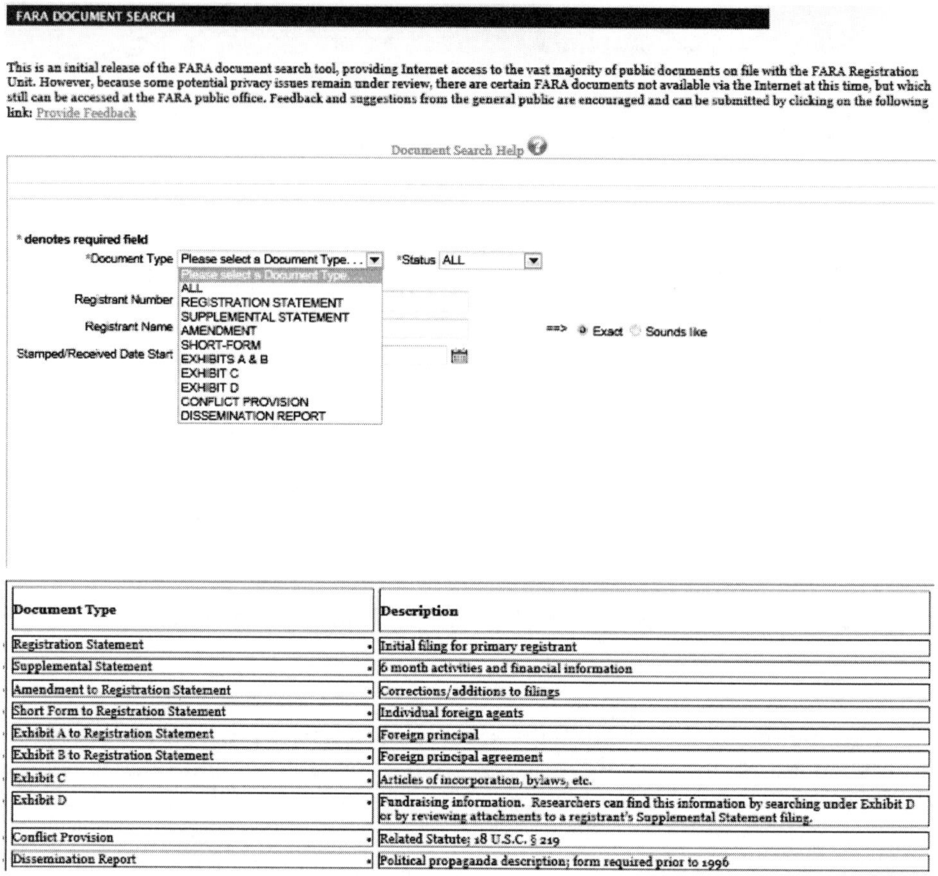

FARA DOCUMENT SEARCH

This is an initial release of the FARA document search tool, providing Internet access to the vast majority of public documents on file with the FARA Registration Unit. However, because some potential privacy issues remain under review, there are certain FARA documents not available via the Internet at this time, but which still can be accessed at the FARA public office. Feedback and suggestions from the general public are encouraged and can be submitted by clicking on the following link: Provide Feedback

Document Search Help

* denotes required field

*Document Type: Please select a Document Type. . . — *Status: ALL

Please select a Document Type. . .
ALL
REGISTRATION STATEMENT
SUPPLEMENTAL STATEMENT
AMENDMENT
SHORT-FORM
EXHIBITS A & B
EXHIBIT C
EXHIBIT D
CONFLICT PROVISION
DISSEMINATION REPORT

Registrant Number

Registrant Name ==> Exact / Sounds like

Stamped/Received Date Start

Document Type	Description
Registration Statement	Initial filing for primary registrant
Supplemental Statement	6 month activities and financial information
Amendment to Registration Statement	Corrections/additions to filings
Short Form to Registration Statement	Individual foreign agents
Exhibit A to Registration Statement	Foreign principal
Exhibit B to Registration Statement	Foreign principal agreement
Exhibit C	Articles of incorporation, bylaws, etc.
Exhibit D	Fundraising information. Researchers can find this information by searching under Exhibit D or by reviewing attachments to a registrant's Supplemental Statement filing.
Conflict Provision	Related Statute: 18 U.S.C. § 219
Dissemination Report	Political propaganda description; form required prior to 1996

Figure 6-15 Document Type Options for FARA Document Search

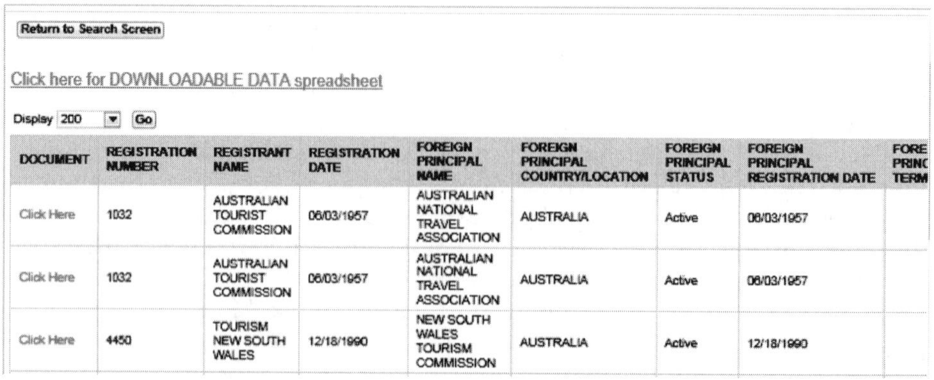

Return to Search Screen

Click here for DOWNLOADABLE DATA spreadsheet

Display 200 Go

DOCUMENT	REGISTRATION NUMBER	REGISTRANT NAME	REGISTRATION DATE	FOREIGN PRINCIPAL NAME	FOREIGN PRINCIPAL COUNTRY/LOCATION	FOREIGN PRINCIPAL STATUS	FOREIGN PRINCIPAL REGISTRATION DATE	FORE PRINC TERM
Click Here	1032	AUSTRALIAN TOURIST COMMISSION	06/03/1957	AUSTRALIAN NATIONAL TRAVEL ASSOCIATION	AUSTRALIA	Active	06/03/1957	
Click Here	1032	AUSTRALIAN TOURIST COMMISSION	06/03/1957	AUSTRALIAN NATIONAL TRAVEL ASSOCIATION	AUSTRALIA	Active	06/03/1957	
Click Here	4450	TOURISM NEW SOUTH WALES	12/18/1990	NEW SOUTH WALES TOURISM COMMISSION	AUSTRALIA	Active	12/18/1990	

Figure 6-16 Example of Search Results on FARA Database

The database also requires significant modernization. While the DOJ has provided a mechanism for online electronic filing, many registrants still file by paper, forcing the DOJ to manually scan the documents. This process is inefficient and results in loss of image quality to a point where the filings may be illegible and unusable (see Figure 6-17).

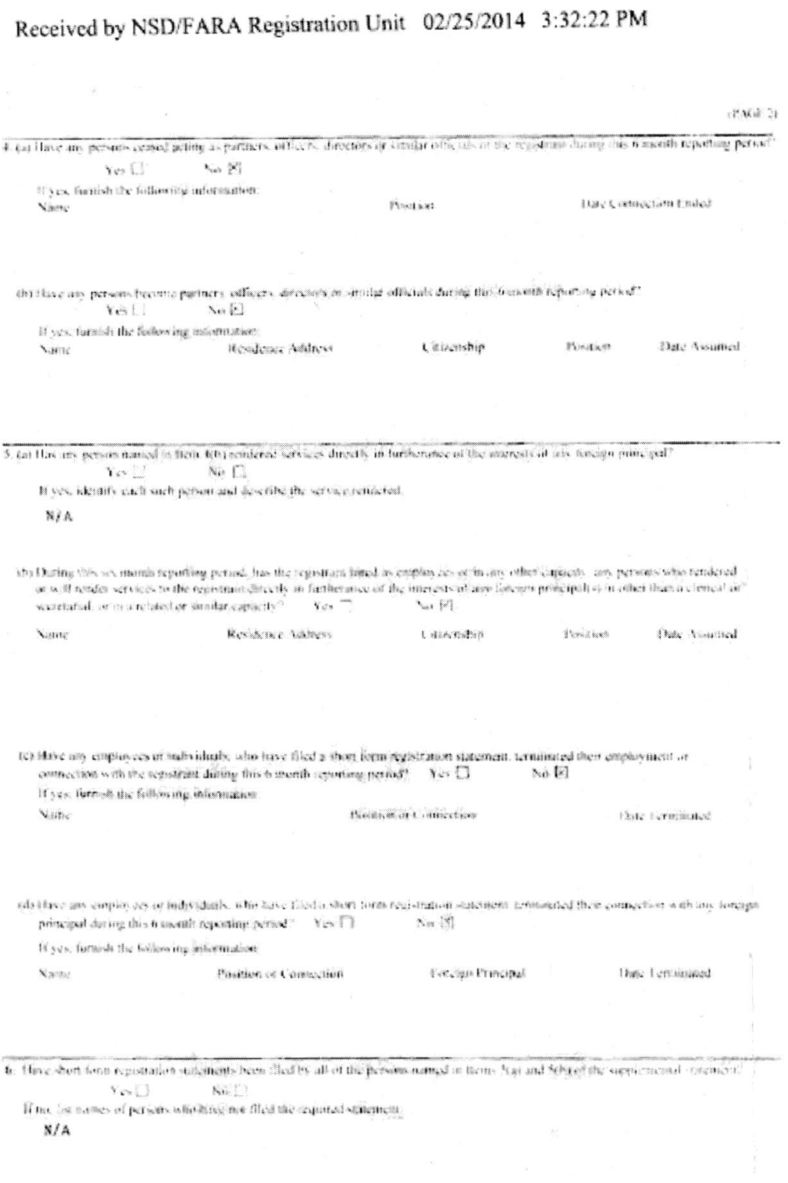
Received by NSD/FARA Registration Unit 02/25/2014 3:32:22 PM

N/A

N/A

Figure 6-17 Example of Scanned Paper Filing Received by DOJ for FARA Registration

Even the electronic uploading system forces users to convert their filings from structured data-set formats such as spreadsheets into PDF files, which have little searching and sorting functionality.

6-6 Nongovernmental Internet Sources of Lobbying Information

Throughout the years, a number of nongovernmental entities have sprung up to provide Internet access to government information. When it comes to lobbying data, some of the more useful nongovernmental sources include LegiStorm (www.legistorm.com), the Center for Responsive Politics (www.opensecrets.org), and Political Moneyline (http://www.politicalmoneyline.com).

LegiStorm, launched in 2006, provides information on various aspects of congressional public disclosure records, such as salaries and privately sponsored trips. Most pertinent to lobbying disclosure, LegiStorm also provides online access to all gifts provided to legislators and their staff while traveling overseas, as required for disclosure by the Foreign Gifts and Decorations Act.[59]

The Center for Responsive Politics (CRP) is the workhorse of nongovernmental entities when it comes to disclosure of governmental information. CRP provides easy and thorough access to all sorts of data involving money and politics and specializes in campaign finance data. But CRP also offers a lobbying database that allows users to

- Search by name for a company that is a lobbyist registrant or client of a lobbyist registrant;
- Search by name for a lobbying firm or individual lobbyist;
- Compile total spending records by a particular industry or sector;
- Search for specific bills or issues and the lobbyists working on those issues; and
- View the lobbying activity directed at a particular government agency.[60]

Political Moneyline is an online tool offered by CQ Roll Call. It provides a comparable, if not more extensive, database on money in politics, including lobbying activity. Most of the database from CQ Politics, however, is available only to paid subscribers.

6-7 Conclusion

The Secretary, Clerk, and to a lesser extent DOJ, are all generally compliant with the disclosure requirements of HLOGA. Experienced researchers will be able to locate the desired information and download it without problems. The lay user with average computer knowledge may experience difficulty downloading the information, as both the Clerk's and the Secretary's interface sort the downloadable files in XML format. However, for the average user who is simply interested in becoming generally knowledgeable about a certain bill or lobbyist, the online databases reviewed here provide a wealth of details.

---

59. 22 U.S.C. § 2625 (2015).
60. CENTER FOR RESPONSIVE POLITICS, LOBBYING DATABASE, http://www.opensecrets.org/lobby/ (last visited Sept. 25, 2015).

CHAPTER 7

GAO Audits of Compliance with the Lobbying Disclosure Act

BY BRIAN G. SVOBODA AND REBECCA H. GORDON

7-1 Background: The Statutory Mandate to Audit

The Lobbying Disclosure Act of 1995 (LDA) establishes an annual process by which the Government Accountability Office (GAO) randomly audits filings made by lobbyists, lobbying firms, and registrants.[1] Congress enacted the LDA's random audit provision as part of the Honest Leadership and Open Government Act of 2007 (HLOGA).[2] The random audit provision was one of multiple initiatives in HLOGA to improve LDA enforcement and compliance.[3]

The Comptroller General, who heads the GAO,[4] must annually "audit the extent of compliance or noncompliance" with the LDA "by lobbyists, lobbying firms, and registrants" through a random sampling of publicly available reports.[5] The reports reviewed include quarterly lobbying disclosure reports, which are filed by lobbying firms and other registrants, and semiannual political and honorary

---

1. *See* 2 U.S.C. § 1614 (2015).

2. *See* Pub. L. No. 110–81 § 213, 121 Stat. 735, Sept. 14, 2007.

3. *See* 2 U.S.C. § 1605(b) (2015) (requiring the attorney general to report to Congress semiannually on the numbers of enforcement actions taken and sentences imposed); *id.* § 1605(a)(11) (requiring the Clerk of the House and the Secretary of the Senate to report semiannually on the numbers of referrals made to the Department of Justice for enforcement).

4. *See* 31 U.S.C. § 702(b) (2015).

5. 2 U.S.C. § 1614(a) (2015).

expenditure reports, which are filed by lobbying firms, other registrants, and individual lobbyists as well.[6]

By April 1 of each year, the GAO must submit to Congress a report on the audit it has conducted.[7] The report must include

- An assessment of the extent of compliance or noncompliance;[8]
- Recommendations to improve compliance by lobbyists, lobbying firms, and registrants;[9]
- Recommendations to provide the Department of Justice with the resources and authorities needed for effective LDA enforcement;[10] and
- A specific assessment of compliance with the requirement to disclose so-called affiliated entities—that is, those who contribute more than $5,000 in a quarterly period to fund the registrant's lobbying activities, and who actively participate in the planning, supervision, or control of those activities.[11]

The statute authorizes the GAO to "request information from and access to any relevant documents" from registrants and individual lobbyists "if the material requested relates to the purposes of this section."[12] The statute also authorizes the GAO to request registrants and lobbyists "to submit in writing such information as the Comptroller General may prescribe."[13]

The LDA does not give the Comptroller General or the GAO subpoena power.[14] But registrants and individual lobbyists have a strong incentive to cooperate: the GAO may notify Congress in writing if the recipient of a particular request for information refuses to comply with the request.[15] Unsurprisingly, the GAO's report under the LDA's audit provision for calendar year 2015 (the last before the publication date of this manual) stated: "All lobbyists in our sample responded to our requests to discuss documentation with us."[16] Moreover, registrants and lobbyists have an incentive to cooperate truthfully. The general criminal prohibition on knowing and willful false statements to the government applies to statements, representations, and documents provided in "any investigation or review, conducted pursuant to the authority of any committee, subcommittee, commission or office of the Congress."[17]

When it passed HLOGA, Congress placed some express limits on the GAO's audit power. First, the GAO must comply with Congress's general warning that

---

6. *See id. See also* U.S. Gov't Accountability Office, 2015 Lobbying Disclosure: Observations on Lobbyists' Compliance with Disclosure Requirements, GAO 16-320 (March 24, 2016) [hereinafter GAO 2016 Report], *available at* http://www.gao.gov/assets/680/676053.pdf.

7. *See* 2 U.S.C. § 1614(b) (2015).

8. *See id.* § 1614(b)(1).

9. *See id.* § 1614(b)(1)(A).

10. *See id.* § 1614(b)(1)(B).

11. *See id.* § 1614(b)(2). See Chapter 4 for further discussion of affiliated entities.

12. *Id.* § 1614(c).

13. *Id.*

14. *See id.*

15. *See id.*

16. GAO 2016 Report, *supra* note 6, at 2.

17. 18 U.S.C. § 1001(c)(2) (2015).

nothing in HLOGA may be construed to "prohibit any expressive conduct protected from legal prohibition by, or any activities protected by the free speech, free exercise, or free association clauses of, the First Amendment to the Constitution."[18] Second, HLOGA's principal sponsors declared that there was no "authority for the GAO to obtain information protected by the attorney-client privilege."[19] Finally, the sponsors made clear that the GAO may not "audit the Secretary of the Senate or the Clerk of the House's activities under the LDA."[20]

Less clear, however, is how little—or how much—authority the GAO has to identify particular claims of misconduct by particular registrants or lobbyists in the reports it submits to Congress.[21] The GAO has said that its mandate under HLOGA "does not require us to identify lobbyist organizations that failed to register and report in accordance with LDA requirements."[22] (The scope of GAO's mandate is discussed in more detail later.) A separate provision of the LDA directs the attorney general to report to Congress semiannually on the numbers of LDA enforcement actions taken and sentences imposed, and that provision expressly prohibits the disclosure of nonpublic, personally identifiable information.[23] The audit provision lacks a prohibition of this kind. Moreover, the GAO's reports contain lists of those whose filings were reviewed.[24] These same reports occasionally contain anecdotes about filings that could be associated with a particular filer, if one were to invest the time and effort necessary to review the audited filings.

A summary follows of what a filer can expect when subjected to an audit.

7-2 The Audit Experience

The GAO's annual audit process has three parts. Only one of them, the LD-2 quarterly report review, directly involves the firms or organizations audited. The other parts of the process take place mainly within GAO, and registrants are contacted only when necessary.

7-2.1 Annual Review of Quarterly LD-2 Reports

Reviewing quarterly LD-2 reports is the "meat and potatoes" of the GAO audit process. The GAO identifies and reviews a random sample of approximately 100 LD-2 quarterly reports per year. For the registrant, the audit begins when GAO notifies it of the specific report to be reviewed. The audit culminates with an in-person meeting between a representative or representatives of the registrant (the registrant can choose who appears) and representatives from the GAO (there are usually two). At the meeting, the GAO representatives typically ask a series of questions about the report being reviewed.

---

18. Pub. L. No. 110–81 § 213, 121 Stat. 735, Sept. 14, 2007, 2 U.S.C. § 1601 Note, § 703 (2015).

19. 153 Cong. Rec. S10687, 10710 (daily ed. Aug. 2, 2007) (statement of Sen. Feinstein).

20. *Id.*

21. GAO sends these reports also to the Department of Justice, the Secretary of the Senate, the Clerk of the House "and interested congressional committees and members"—as well as publishing them on the Internet. *See* GAO 2016 Report, *supra* note 6, at 31.

22. GAO 2016 Report, *supra* note 6, at 3.

23. *See* 2 U.S.C. § 1605(b) (2015).

24. *See* GAO 2016 Report, *supra* note 6, at 39–46.

From the registrant's perspective, the audit concerns a single quarterly report. For a self-lobbying organization, that is fairly straightforward. However, for a lobbying firm, it is important to note that each audit covers only one report filed for a single client. The audit will not cover *all* reports filed for *all* clients during the quarter. However, because the audit sample is determined randomly, a single lobbying firm may have multiple client reports audited at the same time or in the same year.

After HLOGA first became effective, a targeted registrant who had not been through the audit process before would not typically know what the GAO might ask until the meeting began. This brought some angst and inefficiency into the process. The GAO has remedied this situation somewhat and streamlined the process by instituting a web-based survey before the in-person meeting. Under the common practice at this writing, a targeted registrant initially receives a survey to complete online, and the in-person meeting occurs later. This way the registrant is better prepared for the meeting, and the GAO representatives have more information on which to base their questions.

A few things about the audit process bear emphasis. First, the audits are random, not for cause. The GAO chooses its sample of reports to review through a random process by which it first identifies its sample time period—typically four quarterly reporting periods—and then its sample of approximately 80 to 100 reports.[25]

Second, the GAO takes the position that its mandate is only to review the compliance of "lobbyists," meaning those who are already registered with the House and the Senate pursuant to the LDA. "The mandate does not require us to identify lobbyist organizations that failed to register and report in accordance with LDA requirements."[26] As a result, the GAO reports present only a limited picture of compliance, focusing on those who have already registered while devoting comparably little attention to those who have not, even if they might have been required to do so.

Finally, the GAO does not believe the LDA requires it to "determine whether reported lobbying activity ... represented the full extent of lobbying activities that took place."[27] This is a limiting position that aims the audit process almost exclusively at confirming the accuracy of the information disclosed on the quarterly LD-2 report. Little or no time is spent identifying gaps in disclosure.

The questions in the online survey generally seek to confirm that the registrant can provide written documentation to support several main topics covered on the report:

- The amount of income (for a firm) or expenses (for a self-lobbying organization) reported;
- The issue area codes disclosed;
- The chamber or chambers of Congress reported as contacted;
- The executive branch agencies reported as contacted; and
- The individual registered lobbyists who are listed as having performed lobbying activities on the audited report during the quarter.

---

25. *See id.* at 1.
26. *See id.* at 3.
27. *See id.*

The in-person meeting allows the GAO representatives to confirm the accuracy of information disclosed on the survey by asking to review the written documentation. Therefore, one helpful way to prepare for the in-person meeting is to locate examples of each of the categories of documents to which the survey refers and ensure that copies of these documents are kept on hand for review at the time of the meeting. Information that is protected from disclosure or subject to privilege should be redacted. The GAO's practice has been not to keep copies of any such documentation presented at the in-person meeting.

Before the in-person meeting, GAO staff will conduct online searches about the careers of each listed lobbyist.[28] This is to confirm that every lobbyist's covered official positions have been properly disclosed, either on the selected LD-2 report, a prior report, or the initial registration for the client, as appropriate.[29] If a lobbyist appears to have omitted information about a covered position that should have been disclosed, the GAO representatives will generally ask about that during the in-person interview. If amendments are needed to correct any such omission, the filer may do so after the meeting.

GAO staff also prepare for the in-person meeting by reviewing the LD-203 reports filed during the one-year review period for the filer and by each lobbyist listed on the report.[30] If any of these reports has not yet been filed, the GAO representatives will generally ask about those reports as well. If additional reports must be filed, the filer may correct this oversight, or ensure that its lobbyists correct it, after the meeting.

7-2.2 Annual Review of Semiannual LD-203 Reports

As part of its annual audit process, the GAO reviews reports for compliance with the LD-203 reporting requirement. This review is undertaken principally internally within the GAO; filers are contacted only when necessary. The GAO identifies a random sample of LD-203 reports filed during the year in review to determine whether they fully reported federal political contributions as the LDA requires. For the period of time covered in the GAO 2016 Report, half of the reports sampled disclosed some political contributions, and half disclosed none.[31]

The GAO 2015 Report indicated that GAO staff analyzed the contents of the reports reviewed and compared them to data kept by the Federal Election Commission (FEC). When contributions reported in the FEC database were not disclosed on the LD-203, the GAO asked the filer to explain the absence, and some amended their reports.[32] For 2015 reports, the GAO indicated that only 4 percent of LD-203 reports reviewed omitted contributions that were contained in the FEC's database.[33]

Note that this review is limited to FEC-reportable contributions. It does not appear to reach the other honorary expenditures or other expenditures for which the LD-203 requires reporting.

---

28. *See id.* at 35.
29. For more information on required disclosure of covered official positions, see Chapter 4.
30. For more information on LD-203 disclosure, see Chapter 5.
31. *See* GAO 2016 REPORT, *supra* note 6, at 37.
32. *See id.* at 18.
33. *See id.*

7-2.3 Annual Review of First LD-2 Reports

The GAO also generally conducts a review to ensure that each registration is followed by a quarterly LD-2 for the period in which registration occurred. To do this for registrations made during the period covered by the GAO 2016 Report, the GAO used the Clerk of the House's data to match registrations with corresponding first-time LD-2 reports.[34] This was done electronically, by standardizing client and registration names and then matching reports and registrations using House identification numbers.

7-3 Other Objectives

The GAO uses the audit process as a way to solicit feedback and recommendations from the regulated community. A registrant that is subjected to an audit should expect to receive questions about the relative ease or difficulty it has in complying with the LDA. The registrant will also have an opportunity to submit in the survey any comments it has about the LDA filing process and to provide them again during the in-person meeting.

7-4 Reporting

The GAO does not publish specific findings about any organization or lobbyist subjected to an audit. Its annual reports provide general findings and statistical data compiled across each sample reviewed for the time period. Findings and conclusions are given at a high level of generality. For example, in the GAO 2016 Report, the GAO found that "For Most LD-2 Reports, Lobbyists Provided Documentation for Key Elements, but for Some LD-2 Reports, Lobbyists Rounded Their Income or Expenses Incorrectly."[35] The report shows by chart that in each year from 2010 to 2015, the GAO estimates that only a small percentage of filers (8 percent or less) lacked proper documentation to support the information on their reports.[36] The GAO 2016 Report does not identify the specific filers lacking documentation, nor does it identify those with adequate documentation. Information about rounding errors is handled the same way: statistics are given, but no filers are identified.[37]

The GAO does identify those organizations that are subject to an audit each year in a list printed at the end of the annual report.[38] It also identifies those individuals and registered organizations whose LD-203 reports are reviewed for disclosure of political contributions.[39] Two lists are given: one of sampled LD-203 filers who disclosed contributions on the sampled report, and one of sampled LD-203 filers who did not disclose contributions on the sampled report.

---

34. *See id.* at 36.
35. *See id.* at 9.
36. *See id.* at 9, fig. 3.
37. *See id.* at 11, fig. 4.
38. *See id.* at app. II, 39.
39. *See id.* at app. III, 42.

7-5 Conclusion

The GAO audit process can be intimidating for first-timers and the previously audited alike. An audit requires the filer to produce paperwork to support the information disclosed in the audited report. Most filers who have been through an audit find that the specter of another one provides added incentive to keep thorough contemporaneous records of their lobbying activities on an ongoing basis. Well-prepared filers sail through the audit process quickly. Those who cannot easily put their hands on documentation to support the reports filed often find the experience to be time-consuming, frustrating, and unpleasant.

CHAPTER 8

Congressional Ethics:
Gifts, Travel, and Outside Income

BY ROBERT F. BAUER AND REBECCA H. GORDON*

---

*Ellen L. Weintraub, formerly of counsel to Perkins Coie, was the coauthor of the version of this chapter that originally appeared in *The Lobbying Manual: A Compliance Guide for Lawyers and Lobbyists* (2nd ed.) (William Luneburg, ed., 1998).

8-1 Introduction

The late Senator Paul H. Douglas of Illinois, in his seminal book *Ethics in Government*, tells the following story: "[W]hen I once asked a policeman how some of his colleagues got started on the downward path, he replied, 'It generally began with a cigar.'"[1] Under current law, members of Congress would be obliged to decline the offer of a cigar if the hand extending it belonged to a lobbyist—and many would decline it even if it didn't. In the wake of ethics scandals involving Jack Abramoff, Tom DeLay, and Bob Ney, and a congressional election in which Democrats reclaimed the majority in part by promising sweeping ethics reform, both the Senate and the House enacted stringent new gift regulations in 2007. These rules are now simply part of the landscape; old-style lobbying, with its trademark wining and dining of members of Congress, is truly a thing of the past.

8-2 A Very Brief History of Congressional Ethics

Congressional ethics has a long and colorful history. Both the Senate and the House began their respective journeys down this road with gusto. After several challenges to the qualifications of various individuals to be seated, the Senate considered its first real ethics case in 1797. Within the space of a week, that body initiated an investigation of Senator William Blount of Tennessee for foreign intrigues and disloyalty to the United States,[2] expelled him, and then ordered him to appear to answer articles of impeachment for good measure.[3]

Before the Senate had time to resolve the case against Senator Blount, the House had occasion to consider the conduct of two of its own members. In January 1798, Representatives Roger Griswold (of Connecticut) and Matthew Lyon (of Vermont) taunted, spat, and finally went at each other with cane and fireplace tongs

---

1. PAUL H. DOUGLAS, ETHICS IN GOVERNMENT 44 (1952).

2. "In an apparent effort to extricate himself [from financial difficulties], Blount concocted a scheme for Indians and frontiersmen to attack Spanish Florida and Louisiana, in order to transfer those territories to Great Britain." ANNE M. BUTLER & WENDY WOLFF, UNITED STATES SENATE ELECTION, EXPULSION AND CENSURE CASES 1793–1990, S. DOC. NO. 103-33, at 13 (1995).

3. The actual trial took place almost a year and a half later, without Blount's presence, and the resolution declaring him an impeachable officer failed. *Id.* at 14.

on the House floor. A motion to expel fell a mere two votes short of the necessary two-thirds majority.[4]

Early congressional ethics cases were marked not only by the spirited nature of the underlying actions by the members but also by a certain lack of proportionality of the punishment to the crime. In 1832, for example, Representative William Stanberry (Ohio) was censured by the House for suggesting that the Speaker had presidential aspirations. Six years later, no punishment ensued after one member killed another in a duel over words spoken in debate.[5]

It was not until the mid-1800s that prosaic charges of financial misconduct, such as public corruption and bribery, began to come to the fore. Allegations that members have betrayed the public trust by allowing personal financial gain to sway their official actions have been a recurrent theme of congressional ethics from those days to the present. One can see it in its 19th-century incarnations, such as the 1853 enactment of the federal bribery law and the 1873 Crédit Mobilier scandal, through its more recent iterations, such as the Korean influence investigation of the 1970s, the Abscam cases of the 1980s, the Keating Five inquiry of the 1990s, the series of scandals coming to light in 2005 surrounding Jack Abramoff and his associates, the investigation and conviction of Alaska Senator Ted Stevens in 2008, and the investigation and conviction of Congressman William Jefferson in 2009. These days, perhaps inspired by a Watergate-era "follow the money" fixation, ethics regulation tends to focus on financial concerns, such as the gift and income limits that are the subject of this chapter.

It is only in the last forty-five years that the House and the Senate have adopted formal codes of conduct and formed standing committees to interpret those rules and investigate charges of misconduct. As one scholar has noted: "For nearly two centuries, a simple and informal code of behavior existed. Prevailing norms of general decency served as the chief determinants of proper legislative conduct."[6] By the late 1960s, these were no longer deemed sufficient. Spurred by investigations into the conduct of Senate officer Bobby Baker and Representative Adam Clayton Powell Jr., ethics committees were formed (in the Senate in 1964 and in the House in 1966) and preliminary standards were adopted in both the Senate and the House in 1968. A model for the modern ethics committee can be found in the select committee constituted by the Senate to consider the 1954 resolution to censure Senator Joseph R. McCarthy—a committee comprised of three Republicans and three Democrats "whose members were notable for their impeccable reputations and legal expertise."[7]

The 1970s saw the beginnings of modern campaign finance regulation as well as the post-Watergate-era ethics reforms. More stringent ethics codes, including outside income and gift limits, were adopted, and public financial disclosure and franking restrictions were enacted into law. By 1989, a Speaker of the House had resigned in the face of an ethics investigation concerning his alleged circumvention

---

4. 2 ASHER C. HINDS, HINDS' PRECEDENTS OF THE HOUSE OF REPRESENTATIVES OF THE UNITED STATES, ch. 52, §§ 1642–1643, 1114–16 (1907).

5. *See* HOUSE COMM. ON STANDARDS OF OFFICIAL CONDUCT, HISTORICAL SUMMARY OF CONDUCT CASES IN THE HOUSE OF REPRESENTATIVES 1 (1992).

6. Richard A. Baker, *The History of Congressional Ethics, in* REPRESENTATION AND RESPONSIBILITY, EXPLORING LEGISLATIVE ETHICS 4 (1985).

7. BUTLER & WOLFF, *supra* note 2, at 405.

of honoraria and gift limits. Before the year was out, honoraria were outlawed and outside income further curtailed as part of the Ethics Reform Act of 1989.

In 1992, the House and the Senate adopted a uniform gift limit of $250 from any one source in a calendar year, with gifts worth up to $100 not counted toward the total. By 1995, that limit was seen as excessive, and the Senate and the House enacted a new set of rules. Those rules left room for lobbyists and their clients to offer things of value to members and staff as long as each gift had a value of less than $50, and the source funding the gift did not give the same member or staffer more than $99.99 in gifts in the aggregate in a calendar year. Twenty-four detail-bound exceptions remained that permitted the conveyance of certain items of value—primarily food, beverages, and travel expenses—under carefully defined circumstances.

Washington operated under this regime with limited drama until around 2005, when the tactics of lobbyist Jack Abramoff grabbed the attention of newspapers both inside and outside the Beltway. Mr. Abramoff had established a pattern of cozying up to his favorite members—among them, House Majority Leader Tom DeLay—by providing free meals and free trips to foreign destinations like Scotland and Saipan, in clear violation of the gift rules. Abramoff's sins were many and varied, extending well beyond abetting regulatory gift-rule violations, and effectively ended his career. Before he left Capitol Hill, though, his tale contributed to two important narratives that became virtual Washington mantras: lobbyists were entirely too close to members to ensure purely merit-based congressional decision making; and the congressional gift rules were neither closely followed nor amply enforced.

Cleaning up Washington thus became a Democratic battle cry in the 2006 elections, and, when the Democrats took the majority of both Houses, they made ethics reform legislation their first priority. In its first week in office, the new House of Representatives enacted House Resolution 6, which amended certain of the House's ethics rules to place significant new limitations on the interactions between House members and staff on the one hand, and the lobbyists and their clients on the other.[8]

The Senate quickly matched the House's actions on gifts and travel and tightened regulation of other aspects of the lobbying process as well. It drafted companion changes to its own gift and travel rules and placed them in legislation that would also amend a number of existing laws impacting the relationship between lobbyists and members, such as lobbyist disclosure, the "revolving door" between Capitol Hill jobs and lobbying shops, and the so-called K Street Project, the practice through which Republicans had used promises or threats of official action to influence lobbying firms' hiring decisions.[9] The House later passed its own version of ethics legislation addressing many of the same issues.[10]

The two chambers negotiated furiously in the ensuing months, finally passing the legislation in the late summer.[11] The president signed the bill on September 14,

---

8. *See* H.R. Res. 6, 110th Cong. (2007) (codified in several sections of the Rules of the House of Representatives).

9. *See* S.1, 110th Cong. (as introduced Jan. 4, 2007).

10. *See* H.R. 2316, 110th Cong. (2007).

11. *See* 153 Cong. Rec. S10687 (daily ed. Aug. 2, 2007); *see also* congressional action on S.1 (110th Cong.) and H.R. 2316 (110th Cong.) as reported at https://www.congress.gov.

2007. The resulting law, the Honest Leadership and Open Government Act of 2007 (HLOGA or the Act), was drafted entirely by compromise between the two houses of Congress. It was never referred to committee or submitted to conference.

The history of congressional gift restrictions is summarized in Appendix 8-A of this chapter. Copies of the congressional gift rules (House and Senate), current as of date of publication, are included as Appendix 8-B.

8-3 Gifts

As described above, the current era of gift regulation represents an environment in which lobbyists and their clients face notably heavier gift restrictions than the rest of the populace. Most significantly, these restrictions apply directly to lobbyists, prohibiting their conveyance of gifts as well as the members' and staffers' receipt of them.

This substantive restriction on the behavior of lobbyists was written into the Lobbying Disclosure Act (LDA) by HLOGA and so applies directly to any entity that is registered as a lobbying organization with the House and Senate (that is, a self-lobbying organization or a lobbying firm) as well as to any individual who is listed on an LDA registration or report as a "lobbyist." The provision bans any registrant or listed lobbyist from giving a gift or providing travel to a member or staffer of Congress if the registrant or lobbyist has knowledge that the gift or travel would be unlawful under the congressional gift rules.[12] Thus, the LDA restriction incorporates directly by reference the House and Senate gift rules. It also imposes potential criminal liability on persons who "knowingly and corruptly" fail to comply with the LDA.[13] It is crucial to note, however, that the House and Senate gift rules themselves are broader in reach than the LDA restriction: the gift rules prohibit members and staff from taking gifts not only from LDA registrants and lobbyists, but also from the non-registered clients of LDA registrants (i.e., clients of lobbying firms) over which the LDA does not have jurisdiction.

The gift rules of the two houses are identical to each other in structure: a ban on gifts from lobbyists and their clients, a monetary limit for all others, and a list of almost identical exceptions generally available to all. Each of these rules is exclusively interpreted and enforced by an ethics committee: the Senate Select Committee on Ethics (Senate Ethics Committee or Senate Committee) or the House Committee on Ethics (House Ethics Committee or House Committee).[14] The two committees have, on various occasions, adopted similar interpretations, but they are not bound to do so. Their rules do contain the same broad definition of what constitutes a "gift":

---

12. *See* 2 U.S.C. § 1613 (2015).
13. *See* 2 U.S.C. § 1606 (2015).
14. The House Committee published a revised House Ethics Manual in the Spring of 2008 that interprets the gift rule. The Senate Committee publishes memoranda periodically, and devoted a chapter to the gift rule in its September 2003 Senate Ethics Manual. Each committee has also issued numerous private letter rulings to members, employees, and others in response to particular written requests. These rulings are not publicly available, although the Senate Committee has historically published compilations of its redacted "interpretative rulings" from time to time. The website for the House Ethics Committee, which contains a variety of the materials discussed in this chapter, is http://ethics.house.gov/; the website for the Senate Ethics Committee is http://ethics.senate.gov/.

[T]he term "gift" means any ["a" in the House version] gratuity, favor, discount, entertainment, hospitality, loan, forbearance, or other item having monetary value. The term includes gifts of services, training, transportation, lodging, and meals, whether provided in kind, by purchase of a ticket, payment in advance, or reimbursement after the expense has been incurred.[15]

Incorporating the gift rules into the LDA in the way HLOGA directs creates some odd asymmetries. For example, as just noted, although the congressional gift rules prohibit a member from accepting a non-excepted gift from a lobbyist or its non-registrant client, the client—as a non-registrant—is not subject to a corresponding statutory restriction on his, her, or its own conduct in making a gift. Further, in a situation in which a lobbyist gives a gift to a member and both parties know the gift is illegal under the gift rules, the lobbyist can be held criminally liable, but the member cannot (at least not under a strict gift rule analysis; depending on the situation, however, there may be other criminal theories, such as bribery, under which to pursue him or her). But these asymmetries should not, of course, be exploited for the purpose of circumventing the law. For example, it would likely be illegal, and certainly unwise, for a lobbyist to direct a client to deliver a gift that the lobbyist personally could not; this is particularly true given that the member could not accept it in any event. Indeed, the LDA, as amended by HLOGA, requires that both registrants and listed lobbyists certify, under criminal penalties for false certification, that they have not "provided, *requested, or directed* a gift, including travel, to a member of Congress or an officer or employee of either House of Congress with knowledge that receipt of the gift" violates the House or Senate rules relating to the provision of gifts and travel.[16]

8-3.1 The Basic Rule: Senate

Senate Rule XXXV provides that a member, officer, or employee of the Senate may not accept any gift from a federal lobbyist or from an organization that employs or retains a lobbyist. He or she may take a gift from any other source as long as its value is less than $50 and the total value of gifts from any one source in a calendar year is less than $100. Gifts worth less than $10 do not count toward the $100 limit. The rule also lists twenty-four exceptions allowing Members and staff to accept gifts in various circumstances notwithstanding these limits.[17] The gift rules apply equally to members and staff. For ease in reading, we will use the term "Members" henceforth, with the understanding that staff and congressional employees are subject to the same rules.

8-3.1.1 A Brief Note on Value and Source
Gifts are generally valued at their lowest retail (not wholesale) fair market value. The question the ethics committees generally will ask is this: What would it cost a member of the public to obtain the same item or benefit? Thus, if the item can be

---

15. Senate Rule XXXV, cl. 1(b)(1) (114th Cong.); House Rule XXV, cl. 5(a)(2)(A) (114th Cong.).
16. 2 U.S.C. § 1604(d)(1)(G)(ii) (2015) (emphasis added). See also Chapter 5 of this manual.
17. Senate Rule XXXV, cl. 1(c) lists twenty-four exceptions, with the criteria for accepting travel reimbursements separately detailed in Senate Rule XXXV, cl. 2.

found at a discount outlet for $49.99 or less, a Member of the Senate may accept it if offeror does not employ or retain lobbyists. Tickets (including tickets to fund-raisers) are worth their face price; club memberships are worth what it would cost anyone else to join; season passes are worth their market value at the time of acceptance, regardless of how many events are subsequently attended.[18] The Senate does not permit "buy-downs"—that is, a senator may not accept a gift worth $55 by paying $5.01 to bring the value down below $50.[19]

Gifts comprised of multiple items present more of a challenge. If the gift is "divisible by nature (such as tickets, bottles of wine, etc.)," and the offeror does not employ or retain lobbyists, a Member may accept as many items as will not exceed $49.99 in value (and decline or pay for the rest).[20] However, "[g]ifts may not be artificially broken down."[21] And even gifts that clearly fall under the limits or fit within an exception may be deemed unacceptable if given too frequently or regularly.[22]

A commonly asked question concerns whether a gift from an employee of an organization counts against the individual's or the organization's limit. The Senate Committee counts it against both, unless the individual is a personal friend of the recipient and is not being reimbursed by the employer for the cost of the gift.[23] This would seem to mean that no employee of a lobbying firm or lobbying firm client, whether or not the individual is a "lobbyist," may give any gift of any value to a Member, *even if he or she does not receive reimbursement from the employer for the gift,* unless the "personal friendship" exception (or another exception) applies.

Allocating costs comes up frequently in the context of persons taking a Member out for a meal. The rules of engagement are arcane. Assuming that the meal does not qualify for the "personal friendship" exception (see the discussion in Section 8-3.4.1), if two persons from the same organization take a Member out for a meal, the total cost of the meal (minus tax and tip) will count against the limits of each of the employees as well as that of the organization. If two persons from different organizations take a Member out for a meal, the total cost should be attributed to one of the organizations and its employee.[24]

Groups of individuals who are not acting on behalf of any organization may "chip in" to buy a gift for a Member, in which case the value of the gift may be divided and apportioned among them. The Senate Committee contrasts, in this

---

18. Senate Select Comm. on Ethics, United States Senate, Senate Ethics Manual, at 59–60 (2003) [hereinafter Senate Ethics Manual]. Note that at the time of publication, the Senate Ethics Committee was undertaking an update to the 2003 Senate Ethics Manual.

19. *Id.* at 23.

20. *Id.*

21. *Id.* at 61. Determining when a gift is being "artificially broken down" is something of an art form. While it is apparently permissible to split up a case of wine and accept one or two bottles (to keep the gift under the limit), it is not similarly permissible, the Senate Committee informs us, to split up a set of golf clubs or the courses of a meal (although tax and tip need not be included). Generally, when multiple items are offered simultaneously and each item is, on its own, worth less than $50, the "gift" is the aggregate of all of the items. Moreover, a "goody bag," or collection of items from different sources that are packaged and presented together, is viewed as a single gift from whomever is presenting it, and valued at the total cost of all the contents. *Id.* at 23–24, 61.

22. Senate Select Comm. on Ethics Interpretative Ruling No. 94 (cited in Senate Ethics Manual, *supra* note 18, at 23).

23. Senate Ethics Manual, *supra* note 18, at 55.

24. *Id.*

context, a group of friends each chipping in $30 to buy a gift for a senator (permissible) with a trade association purporting to buy a $1,000 gift on behalf of its 100 members (excessive).[25]

8-3.2 The Basic Rule: House

As in the Senate, under this rule, a Member, officer or employee may not take a gift from a lobbyist or an organization that employs or retains a lobbyist.[26] He or she may accept a gift from a non-lobbying source if it has a value of less than $50, subject to a cumulative annual limitation of less than $100 in gifts from one source.[27] Again, for simplicity, we use the term "Members" herein, with the understanding that staff and congressional employees are generally subject to the same rules.

Many of the House Committee's interpretations are similar to those the Senate Committee has adopted. For example, as with the Senate rule, under the House rule items are valued at their retail price, and buy-downs are not allowed.[28] If a Member is given multiple "naturally divisible" items from a non-lobbying source, he or she may accept one or more items aggregating to less than $50 in value and pay for or decline to accept the remainder.[29]

In some cases the House Committee has added its own gloss to the rule. For example, in 2003 the House Committee amended its gift rule to clarify that perishable food, such as pizza, delivered to staffers in a Member's office should be allocated among the individual recipients and not attributed only to the recipient Member.[30] Each staffer must still comply with the ban on gifts from lobbyists and clients along with the $99.99 annual gift limit from a single non-lobbying source, so he or she must find out who sent the food and how much it cost. In light of the prohibition on private subsidization of official House activities, the food may not be accepted during any event sponsored by a House office, including a briefing.[31]

8-3.3 Gifts to Family Members

Under both the House and the Senate rules, a gift to a family member, or even a friend of a Member, may count against the gift limit if the Member knows about and acquiesces to the gift and has reason to believe it was given because of his or her official position.[32] This provision recognizes the reality that providing a gift (say, a television) to a member of the Member's household is tantamount to providing the gift to the Member.

The examples provided by the ethics committees deal with the most straightforward situation, that of a gift to a Member's spouse that is offered because of the Member's position.[33] The committees have not offered any guidance on the outer

25. *Id.* at 61.

26. House Rule XXV, cl. 5(a)(1)(A)(ii) (114th Cong.).

27. House Rule XXV, cl. 5(a)(1)(B) (114th Cong.). *See* COMMITTEE ON STANDARDS OF OFFICIAL CONDUCT, U.S. HOUSE OF REPRESENTATIVES, HOUSE ETHICS MANUAL (2008) [hereinafter HOUSE ETHICS MANUAL], at 63.

28. HOUSE ETHICS MANUAL, *supra* note 27, at 35–36.

29. *Id.* at 35.

30. *See* House Rule XXV, cl. 5(a)(1)(B) (114th Cong.).

31. *See* HOUSE ETHICS MANUAL, *supra* note 27, at 38.

32. Senate Rule XXXV, cl. 1(b)(2)(A) (114th Cong.); House Rule XXV, cl. 5(a)(2)(B)(i) (114th Cong.).

33. *See, e.g.,* SENATE ETHICS MANUAL, *supra* note 18, at 56.

reaches of this provision. Its broad wording suggests, however, that the provision could encompass any valuable favor or benefit conferred upon a friend or associate of a Member in an attempt to engender goodwill from that Member.

In an apparent bow to the spouses, one exception was carved in this rule of imputing to Members' gifts to their spouses—that is, for food or refreshments provided at the same time to the Member and his spouse or dependent. Thus, if the offeror is not a lobbyist and does not employ or retain one, he or she (or the employing organization) may take a Member and spouse out to dinner, as long as the Member's meal costs less than $50. The spouse's meal does not count.[34]

Under both the House and Senate rules, an odd result obtains if the Member is unable to attend the dinner. The rules exempt the value of the spouse's meal only when food is provided simultaneously to the Member and spouse. Thus, assume a non-lobbying organization invites a Member and spouse to dinner. The spouse may accept a free meal if the Member is present, but the spouse must pay for his own meal if the Member never shows up.

A spouse is, of course, free to accept any gift that is unrelated to the Member's official position. Benefits (such as food, refreshments, lodging, and transportation) arising from a spouse's employment are specifically exempt from the gift rules' reach.[35]

8-3.4 Exceptions

The heart of the gift rules is found in the exceptions, which some unkindly call "loopholes." The rules set out twenty-three (or twenty-four, depending on the house) exceptions, in addition to the section permitting privately funded travel. The provisions that have generated the most interest in the lobbying community are discussed in greatest detail below. All of the exceptions are set forth in the text of the rules themselves. As previously observed, the House and the Senate rules contain substantially the same exceptions. Differences in wording are noted.

8-3.4.1 Family and Friends

Both gift rules exempt gifts from relatives and personal friends. The definition of "relative" parrots that of the Ethics in Government Act of 1978 (EIGA), as amended, which establishes the annual personal financial disclosure obligations of federal officials, including Members, but excludes from that disclosure gifts from relatives. Thus, gifts from anyone in this group of family members may be accepted, regardless of value, even if given from lobbyists, and need not be disclosed.[36]

More interesting is the exception for anything "provided by an individual on the basis of a personal friendship unless the Member, officer, or employee has

---

34. Senate Rule XXXV, cl. 1(b)(2)(B) (114th Cong.); House Rule XXV, cl. 5(a)(2)(B)(ii) (114th Cong.).

35. Senate Rule XXXV, cl. 1(c)(7)(A) (114th Cong.); House Rule XXV, cl. 5(a)(3)(G)(i) (114th Cong.).

36. EIGA defines a "relative" as a "father, mother, son, daughter, brother, sister, uncle, aunt, great aunt, great uncle, first cousin, nephew, niece, husband, wife, grandfather, grandmother, grandson, granddaughter, father-in-law, mother-in-law, son-in-law, daughter-in-law, brother-in-law, sister-in-law, stepfather, stepmother, stepson, stepdaughter, stepbrother, stepsister, half brother, half sister, . . . the grandfather or grandmother of [one's] spouse . . . , and . . . [one's] fiancé or fiancee." 5 U.S.C. app. 4, § 109(16) (2015).

reason to believe that, under the circumstances, the gift was provided because of the official position . . . and not because of the personal friendship."[37]

As noted earlier, this exception has taken on even greater significance since Congress banned gifts from lobbyists and their clients. The most notable practical effect of the gift ban is to restrict one-on-one meals, drinks, entertainment, and other paid interactions between lobbyists (or their clients) and Members and staff of Congress, unless an exception applies. And the "personal friendship" exception is one of the few exceptions that facilitate one-on-one interaction between an individual and a Member.

The drafters of the exception apparently thought the Members needed some help in figuring out who their friends are, because the rule lists several factors for them to consider, such as

- The history of the relationship between the donor and the recipient, including any previous exchange of gifts;
- Whether the donor personally paid for the gift or, alternatively, sought a tax deduction or business reimbursement for it; and
- Whether the donor also gave similar gifts to other Members.[38]

The intent of these guidelines appears to have been to avoid the situation in which a lobbyist claims that every Member is a personal friend. Both committees have taken pains to point out that lobbyists and Members may well be personal friends, but even in situations in which the friendship is unquestionable, some gifts should be declined as based on the official position rather than the friendship (e.g., cases in which the lobbyist is sending gifts to many Members at the same time). The Senate Committee warns that even gifts from personal friends may run afoul of the bribery and illegal gratuities laws and concludes with the following ominous, if vague, caution: "Even in the absence of criminal intent, Senators must also be careful to ensure that gifts, including those from personal friends, do not raise issues of improper linkage to their official position or actions."[39]

Assuming one can clear the hurdle of establishing a bona fide friendship with no possible linkage to official actions, there is still the question of the value of the gift. Members are trusted to exercise their own judgment, armed with the aforementioned guidance, in determining who their friends are, only with respect to gifts worth $250 or less. More valuable gifts require the approval of the relevant ethics committee.[40] Thus, it is safer for a Member to accept a valuable gift from a great-uncle or first cousin than from a dear and trusted friend; gifts from relatives may be accepted, regardless of their value, without consulting the ethics committee.

---

37. Senate Rule XXXV, cl. 1(c)(4)(A) (114th Cong.); *see also* House Rule XXV, cl. 5(a)(3)(D)(i) (114th Cong.).

38. Senate Rule XXXV, cl. 1(c)(4)(B) (114th Cong.); *see also* House Rule XXV, cl. 5(a)(3)(D)(ii) (114th Cong.).

39. Senate Ethics Manual, *supra* note 18, at 29. See Chapter 21 of this manual (dealing with criminal prosecution of officials for bribery and gratuity statute violations).

40. Senate Rule XXXV, cl. 1(e) (114th Cong.); House Rule XXV, cl. 5(a)(5) (114th Cong.).

8-3.4.2 Personal Hospitality

Both gift rules exempt "personal hospitality" as long as it is offered by someone other than a registered lobbyist or an agent of a foreign principal.[41] (The carve-out of lobbyists predated HLOGA's differentiation of lobbyists from the rest of the population where the gift rules are concerned.) Personal hospitality is defined by reference to the EIGA as "hospitality extended for a nonbusiness purpose by an individual, not a corporation or organization, at the personal residence of that individual or his family or on property or facilities owned by that individual or his family."[42]

This provision was intended to allow Members to accept invitations to dine at other people's homes or to stay overnight (or longer). There have been personal hospitality exceptions as long as there have been gift rules in Congress. Both committees require that personal hospitality be offered on nonbusiness premises (e.g., neither a stay at a corporate condo nor one at an individually owned bed and breakfast would qualify).[43] As long as the stay otherwise meets these criteria, however, the host need not be present.[44] The personal hospitality exemption covers food and lodging; it does not extend to travel expenses or entertainment outside of the home. Note, however, that the "nonbusiness purpose" requirement prohibits the use of this exception for the discussion of official business.

While the personal hospitality exception specifically excludes that offered by lobbyists, a lobbyist who is a bona fide personal friend may, under the personal *friendship* exception, invite a Member or congressional employee for a home-cooked meal or a visit. The ethics committees have determined that such hospitality would be subject to the $250 limit, in the absence of specific committee approval for a more valuable stay.[45] The House Ethics Committee has, however, urged additional caution in these circumstances. In its view, a lobbyist who wishes to offer a Member personal hospitality may do so under circumstances that comply with both the "personal hospitality" and the "personal friendship" exceptions. This means that, among other things, the property must be individually owned, the stay must be offered for a nonbusiness purpose, and there must be a history of reciprocal gift exchange between the offeror and recipient.[46]

8-3.4.3 Political Contributions

The House and Senate adopted two separate exceptions to insulate Members' political activities from the gift rules. The first, not surprisingly, exempts lawful political contributions for any federal, state, or local campaign and tickets to political fundraisers, that is, "attendance at a fundraising event sponsored by a political organization described in section 527(e) of the Internal Revenue Code of

---

41. Senate Rule XXXV, cl. 1(c)(17) (114th Cong.); House Rule XXV, cl. 5(a)(3)(P) (114th Cong.).

42. 5 U.S.C. app. 4, § 109(14) (2015).

43. *See* SENATE ETHICS MANUAL, *supra* note 18, at 37; HOUSE ETHICS MANUAL, *supra* note 27, at 61–63.

44. *See* SENATE ETHICS MANUAL, *supra* note 18, at 37; HOUSE ETHICS MANUAL, *supra* note 27, at 62.

45. *See* SENATE ETHICS MANUAL, *supra* note 18, at 37; HOUSE ETHICS MANUAL, *supra* note 27, at 62–63.

46. See HOUSE ETHICS MANUAL, *supra* note 27, at 63.

1986."[47] Section 527(e) includes political parties, campaign committees, multican-didate committees, political action committees, and other organizations that raise or spend funds to influence federal, state, or local elections.

A second provision exempts "[f]ood, refreshments, lodging, [transportation in the House rule,] and other benefits . . . provided by a political organization . . . in connection with a fundraising or campaign event sponsored by such an organization."[48] Both ethics committees agree that, under this provision, long-distance transportation and hotel expenses to attend a fundraiser may only be paid by the sponsoring political organization.[49]

House guidance indicates that only the sponsor of the fundraiser may actually hand out tickets to Members.[50] The Senate Committee has interpreted this exception more expansively, stating that anyone may provide "attendance" to political fundraisers to Members, and defining "attendance" to include "food, refreshments, entertainment, and local transportation in connection with the campaign event."[51]

The House Ethics Committee has clarified when a lobbyist and Member may share a meal during which a campaign contribution is delivered and treat the meal as if it were a fundraising or campaign event under the gift rules. According to the committee, such a meal "is not a fundraising or campaign event ... unless the meal is sponsored and paid for by a political organization, and the expenditures are reported" to the Federal Election Commission as such.[52] This suggests that corporate funds may not be used for such a meal, even if a Political Action Committee (PAC) check is delivered, but that a PAC could pay the expense.

8-3.4.4 Widely Attended and Charity Events

Among the primary goals of the gift regulations was to put an end to a practice by which, it was perceived, a Washington lobbyist could, for the price of an elegant meal or a round of golf, obtain access to a Member of Congress in a private setting during which relationships could be cultivated, information could be exchanged, and deals could be struck. Large events, with lots of people present, were thought not to present the same risk of behind-the-scenes deal making. Even the restrictive executive branch gift regulations, upon which the 1996 congressional rules were based, allow for attendance at certain traditional Washington events, such as the annual correspondents' dinners.[53]

For ease of administration, both ethics committees have arbitrarily settled on the number twenty-five as the definition of "widely attended." That is, for an event to qualify as widely attended, there must be an expectation of at least twenty-five

---

47. Senate Rule XXXV, cl. 1(c)(2) (114th Cong.); House Rule XXV, cl. 5(a)(3)(B) (114th Cong.). The House Rule expressly exempts contributions for state and local elections. The Senate Rule, by its terms, deals only with federal contributions and is silent on state and local campaigns, but the ethics committee has deemed them to be encompassed within this provision. See SENATE ETHICS MANUAL, *supra* note 18, at 27–28.

48. Senate Rule XXXV, cl. 1(c)(7)(C) (114th Cong.); House Rule XXV, cl. 5(a)(3)(G)(iii) (114th Cong.).

49. SENATE ETHICS MANUAL, *supra* note 18, at 32; HOUSE ETHICS MANUAL, *supra* note 27, at 47.

50. HOUSE ETHICS MANUAL, *supra* note 27, at 48.

51. SENATE ETHICS MANUAL, *supra* note 18, at 28.

52. HOUSE ETHICS MANUAL, *supra* note 27, at 48.

53. See 5 C.F.R. § 2635.204(g)(2) (2015). For a full discussion of these rules, see Chapter 26.

non-congressional guests. In addition, there is a diversity requirement: Attendance at the event must be open to members from throughout a given industry or profession, or those in attendance must represent a range of persons interested in the subject matter.[54] The types of events that might qualify include a "convention, conference, symposium, forum, panel discussion, dinner, viewing, reception, or similar event."[55]

Under both the Senate and House rules, a Member may accept free admission to such an event only from its sponsor, that is (as explained by the House Ethics Committee), "the person, entity, or entities that are primarily responsible for organizing the event."[56] The committees have pointed out that merely purchasing a table or buying a block of tickets to an event does not suffice to make one a "sponsor."[57]

The rules also require an official nexus to justify a Member's acceptance of free attendance to an event. A Member may satisfy this criterion by speaking at the event, participating on a panel, presenting information related to Congress or matters before Congress, performing a ceremonial function appropriate to her official position, or by determining that attendance is appropriate to the performance of her official duties or representative function.[58] If the invitation complies, a Member may accept free attendance, a waiver of any conference fee, the provision of *local* transportation (i.e., carfare, not airfare), and food, refreshments, entertainment, and any instructional materials furnished to all attendees as an integral part of the event. The Member may not accept private meals or entertainment away from the rest of the group.[59]

The Member may also accept an unsolicited offer by the sponsor to bring one companion (be it spouse, child, friend, or staff member) to a widely attended event. The Senate rule (although not the House rule) restricts a Member's ability to accept a second ticket for a companion to situations in which other guests will be similarly accompanied or in which the Member determines that the companion's attendance is appropriate to assist in the representation of the Senate.[60]

A Member may accept a sponsor's unsolicited offer to attend a charity event, regardless of the number of people expected. House Members may only accept travel or lodging in conjunction with such an event under particular circumstances: (1) the net proceeds of the event must go to a section 501(c)(3) charity; (2) that the sponsoring organization must reimburse the transportation and lodging expenses; and (3) that organization must extend the offer of free attendance.[61] Senators may accept travel and lodging from the sponsor of a charity event only if the event is not substantially recreational.[62] Thus, a Member of the House could accept transportation and lodging to participate in a charity golf tournament if all of the

54. SENATE ETHICS MANUAL, *supra* note 18, at 38; HOUSE ETHICS MANUAL, *supra* note 27, at 41–42.

55. Senate Rule XXXV, cl. 1(d)(1) (114th Cong.); House Rule XXV, cl. 5(a)(4)(A) (114th Cong.).

56. HOUSE ETHICS MANUAL, *supra* note 27, at 42; *see also* SENATE ETHICS MANUAL, *supra* note 18, at 38.

57. HOUSE ETHICS MANUAL, *supra* note 27, at 42; SENATE ETHICS MANUAL, *supra* note 18, at 38.

58. Senate Rule XXXV, cl. 1(d)(1) (114th Cong.); House Rule XXV, cl. 5(a)(4)(A) (114th Cong.).

59. Senate Rule XXXV, cl. 1(d)(4) (114th Cong.); House Rule XXV, cl. 5(a)(4)(D) (114th Cong.).

60. *Compare* Senate Rule XXXV, cl. 1(d)(2) (114th Cong.), *with* House Rule XXV, cl. 5(a)(4)(B) (114th Cong.).

61. House Rule XXV, cl. 5(a)(4)(C) (114th Cong.).

62. SENATE ETHICS MANUAL, *supra* note 18, at 39.

conditions of the rule are met, but a senator could not under any circumstances. Both a Member of the House and a Member of the Senate could accept airfare and hotel expenses from the sponsor to attend a charity dinner. A Member of either the House or the Senate could accept from the sponsor an unsolicited offer to bring a spouse or dependent to the charity event.[63] For reasons that are unknown, a Member may bring the companion of his or her choice to a widely attended event, but may bring only a spouse or child (at the sponsor's expense) to a charity event.

8-3.4.5 Food of Nominal Value

Another popular exception is that for "[f]ood or refreshments of a nominal value offered other than as a part of a meal."[64] This exception allows anyone, including lobbyists, to offer Members refreshments in settings that might not qualify as widely attended events. It has been construed by both the Senate and House committees to include sodas, coffee, or doughnuts offered at meetings, as well as hors d'oeuvres and drinks at receptions.[65]

Although the provision speaks in terms of nominal value, both committees have managed to avoid being drawn into a debate over appropriate catering costs per person. Rather, they have focused on the nature of the food presented—that it not appear too much like a meal. By offering this rather vague guidance, the committees elicited from the lobbying community some questions that were arcane, bordering on the comical. For example, may utensils and cloth napkins be provided or are receptions now limited to paper plates and food that can be speared on the end of a toothpick? Answer: Utensils and napkins of any composition may be used. Does the doughnut exception encompass croissants and bagels? Answer: yes. The Senate Ethics Committee has gone so far as to require that reception fare be consumed "while standing up," to differentiate it from "a sit-down meal," although continental breakfasts are acceptable, even if consumed sitting, as long as no hot food is served.[66] The goal here seems to be to avoid the gestalt of the one-on-one interaction between individual and Member that used to afford a favor-seeker with an uninterrupted block of time to plead a cause with a Member. The House Ethics Committee has taken pains to clarify that this exception is available for group events only and that one-on-one food, drinks, or other refreshments are not permitted under this exception, even if the fare offered is only of "nominal value."[67]

8-3.4.6 Market Value Transactions

Both rules reasonably enough exclude from the scope of the gift restrictions "[a]nything for which the Member, officer, or employee pays the market value, or does not use and promptly returns to the donor."[68] This provision responds to the inevitable question: What should a Member do with a gift that does not comply with the rule? The answer: *Pay for it or give it back!*

---

63. Senate Rule XXXV, cl. 1(d)(3) (114th Cong.); House Rule XXV, cl. 5(a)(4)(C) (114th Cong.).

64. Senate Rule XXXV, cl. 1(c)(22) (114th Cong.); House Rule XXV, cl. 5(a)(3)(U) (114th Cong.).

65. SENATE ETHICS MANUAL, *supra* note 18, at 42; HOUSE ETHICS MANUAL, *supra* note 27, at 50–51.

66. SENATE ETHICS MANUAL, *supra* note 18, at 42.

67. *See* HOUSE ETHICS MANUAL, *supra* note 27, at 51.

68. Senate Rule XXXV, cl. 1(c)(1) (114th Cong.); *see also* House Rule XXV, cl. 5(a)(3)(A) (114th Cong.).

Establishing the fair market value of a good or service, particularly when dealing with admittance to events, is not always easy. The ethics committees have each developed detailed guidance on valuation of tickets to events, including entry to luxury boxes. The Senate requires tickets to be valued at their face value. If there is no face value on the ticket, it should be given the value of the ticket with the highest face value at the event.[69] The Senate offers an opportunity to seek advance approval from the Ethics Committee to establish a lower value.

The House rule is similar, requiring tickets to be valued at their face price, but *only if* that is the price at which the issuer offers the ticket to the public. If there is no face price, the ticket should be valued the same as the ticket with the highest face value for the event.[70]

8-3.4.7 Opportunities Open to the Public

The gift rules also allow a Member to accept offers that are widely available to others and are not being provided solely on the basis of the individual's status as a Member of Congress. Thus, Members may take advantage of offers that are available to the entire public or to large segments thereof, such as government rates, benefits of professional associations, benefits offered by credit unions, and bank loans.[71] A separate provision exempts "[a]wards or prizes which are given to competitors in contests or events open to the public, including random drawings."[72] Apparently even Members of Congress dream of winning the lottery and are unwilling to foreclose the possibility of retiring on their winnings.

8-3.4.8 Gifts from Governments

The gift rules assume that there is no conflict of interest in accepting something from a governmental entity, be it federal, state, or local.[73] Thus, a Member may accept, with impunity, dinner at a governor's mansion or transportation from a local government. Similar reasoning underlies the exception for gifts from other Members, officers, and employees of the Congress.[74]

With respect to gifts from foreign governments, the Constitution prohibits those, except as specifically authorized by Congress.[75] Congress has specifically authorized Members to accept certain gifts of travel, food, lodging, and entertainment under the auspices of the Foreign Gifts and Decorations Act (FGDA)[76] and Section 108(A) of the Mutual Educational and Cultural Exchange Act (MECEA).[77] Items provided in conformity with those statutes are similarly exempted from the gift rules.[78]

---

69. SENATE ETHICS MANUAL, *supra* note 18, at 59–60.
70. House Rule XXV, cl. 5(a)(1)(B)(ii) (114th Cong.).
71. Senate Rule XXXV, cl. 1(c)(19) (114th Cong.); House Rule XXV, cl. 5(a)(3)(R) (114th Cong.).
72. Senate Rule XXXV, cl. 1(c)(10) (114th Cong.); *see also* House Rule XXV, cl. 5(a)(3)(J) (114th Cong.).
73. Senate Rule XXXV, cl. 1(c)(16) (114th Cong.); House Rule XXV, cl. 5(A)(3)(O) (114th Cong.).
74. Senate Rule XXXV, cl. 1(c)(6) (114th Cong.); House Rule XXV, cl. 5(A)(3)(F) (114th Cong.).
75. U.S. CONST. art. I, § 9, cl. 8.
76. 5 U.S.C. § 7342 (2015).
77. 22 U.S.C. § 2458a (2015).
78. Senate Rule XXXV, cl. 1(c)(15) (114th Cong.); House Rule XXV, cl. 5(a)(3)(N) (114th Cong.).

The FGDA authorizes Members to accept gifts of "minimal value" intended as souvenirs or marks of courtesy[79] and gifts of food, travel, lodging, and entertainment provided by a foreign government on foreign soil.[80] It does not authorize the Member to accept overseas transportation to and from the foreign country. The MECEA enables Members to accept invitations from foreign governments to travel abroad on cultural exchange trips approved by the State Department.[81] It does not authorize travel for Members' spouses.

Both types of travel are publicly disclosed. FGDA travel is reported separately on specialized forms for that purpose. MECEA travel is reported on Members' annual personal financial disclosure statements that are required under the EIGA.

8-3.4.9 Informational Materials and Training
The gift rules were not intended to interfere with Members' receipt of any information that might be useful to them in the performance of their official duties. Hence, the rules exempt "[i]nformational materials that are sent to the office of the Member, officer, or employee in the form of books, articles, periodicals, other written materials, audiotapes, videotapes, or other forms of communication."[82] The Senate Committee has limited this exception to "informational material received from the publisher, author, or producer" and has precluded "the acceptance of specialized reporting services or other collections which are periodically updated."[83] The House has addressed specifically the provision of software, drawing a distinction between application or development software (impermissible) and informational software that is self-contained on a disc (permissible).[84]

For similar reasons, the rules exempt training that is deemed to be in the interest of the House or Senate.[85] This determination appears to be left to the participant, in consultation with the employing Member if the attendee is a staffer.[86] As an added incentive to attend, food and refreshments may be accepted, if they are provided "to all attendees as an integral part of the training."[87]

The Senate recognizes two types of acceptable training. The first comprises "educational programs, seminars, and fellowships sponsored by universities and institutions of higher learning." The second is defined broadly to include "any event where information is presented to Members and staff by an outside group, so long as the event is expected to be attended by at least twenty-five persons

---

79. In another quirk, neither the House nor the Senate has consistently availed itself of the statutory authorization to adjust the "minimal value" figure every three years for inflation. Thus, the Senate defines "minimal value," for this purpose, as $100 and the House defines it as $335. HOUSE ETHICS MANUAL, *supra* note 27, at 58; SENATE ETHICS MANUAL, *supra* note 18, at 50.

80. 5 U.S.C. § 7342 (2015).

81. 22 U.S.C. § 2458a (2015); SENATE ETHICS MANUAL, *supra* note 18, 51; *see also* 22 U.S.C. § 6551 (2015) (in light of governmental reorganization, statutory references to the U.S. Information Agency should be read to refer to the Department of State).

82. Senate Rule XXXV, cl. 1(c)(9) (114th Cong.); *see also* House Rule XXV, cl. 5(a)(3)(I) (114th Cong.).

83. SENATE ETHICS MANUAL, *supra* note 18, at 33.

84. HOUSE ETHICS MANUAL, *supra* note 27, at 55.

85. Senate Rule XXXV, cl. 1(c)(13) (114th Cong.); House Rule XXV, cl. 5(a)(3)(L) (114th Cong.).

86. *See, e.g.*, SENATE ETHICS MANUAL, *supra* note 18, at 35.

87. Senate Rule XXXV, cl. 1(c)(13) (114th Cong.); House Rule XXV, cl. 5(a)(3)(L) (114th Cong.).

from more than one Senate office or Committee," in addition to any non-Senate attendees.[88]

The House Committee has issued limited guidance as to what might constitute training. It has noted that the training exception may apply to vendor promotional training, but suggests that Members and staff consult the committee before accepting such training since doing so may violate the prohibition on the private subsidy of official activity.[89] In addition, in exercising its waiver authority, it has shown an attitude that differs markedly from the Senate's with respect to food in the context of legislative briefings. The House Committee has issued a general waiver permitting Members and employees to attend events that are

1. Educational (e.g., lectures and seminars); and
2. Sponsored by nonprofit, non-advocacy organizations, like universities or think tanks.

However, the House Committee has limited this waiver to clarify that Members may not accept meals "in connection with presentations sponsored by lobbyists, lobbying firms, or advocacy groups [or] . . . meals in connection with legislative briefings or strategy sessions."[90] Thus, while the Senate Committee allows meals to be provided at legislative briefings, as long as a critical mass of staff from more than one office is present, the House Committee reads the intent behind the gift-rule revision to preclude meals in the same context.

8-3.4.10 Items of Little Value, Plaques, and Commemoratives

In a number of provisions, the gift rules indicate that certain gifts are too insignificant to matter and that Members should not be put to the trouble of keeping track of them or to the embarrassment of having to decline them. The final exception in the laundry list of exceptions is for items of "little intrinsic" (in the Senate version) or "nominal" (in the House version) value. The drafters of the rules, without defining "little intrinsic" or "nominal" value, give as examples a baseball cap, a T-shirt, and, remarkably, a greeting card.[91]

The House Committee reads the provision narrowly, stating: "Members and staff should not rely on the nominal value provision in accepting any item having a value of ten dollars or more, except for the items that are explicitly referred to in that provision (i.e., a baseball cap or a T-shirt)."[92]

Along similar lines, the gift rules exempt plaques, trophies, and other items that are "substantially commemorative in nature" and are "intended . . . for presentation."[93] Although the rule does not set any limit on the value of a commemorative item, the committees have both apparently inferred one, at least in a general sense. The House has adopted the Senate view that a commemorative item may not have "significant utilitarian or artistic value."[94] Both committees thus

88. SENATE ETHICS MANUAL, *supra* note 18, at 35.
89. HOUSE ETHICS MANUAL, *supra* note 27, at 67.
90. HOUSE ETHICS MANUAL, *supra* note 27, at 48.
91. Senate Rule XXXV, cl. 1(c)(23) (114th Cong.); House Rule XXV, cl. 5(a)(3)(W) (114th Cong.).
92. HOUSE ETHICS MANUAL, *supra* note 27, at 53.
93. Senate Rule XXXV, cl. 1(c)(20) (114th Cong.); House Rule XXV, cl. 5(a)(3)(S) (114th Cong.).
94. HOUSE ETHICS MANUAL, *supra* note 27, at 54; SENATE ETHICS MANUAL, *supra* note 18, at 40.

agree that a television could never qualify as a commemorative item. The House Committee has gone on to specify that "a framed photo or print, a figurine, or a clock" might be commemorative if appropriately inscribed (although presumably the clock would be utilitarian in that it would tell time).[95]

To ensure that an item is appropriately commemorative, the donor should, according to the House Committee, inscribe the item "with the Member's name, the name of the presenting organization, and the date of presentation."[96] The House Committee further opined that presenting a Member with a pen at an event would generally not suffice to make the pen a commemorative item. This reasoning appears to exclude pens from the category of permissible commemorative items since it would be difficult to inscribe such a small item with as much information as the House Committee appears to require. Both the House and Senate Committees agree that a commemorative item must be personally presented to the Member and may not be mailed after the fact.

Drawing still other fine distinctions, the rules specify that Members may accept donations of home state products "that are intended primarily for promotional purposes, such as display or free distribution, and are of minimal value to any . . . recipient."[97] The Senate Committee has explained that the provision of such items by home state producers or distributors for the enjoyment of constituents and other visitors represents "a time-honored tradition."[98] Thus, the gift rule protects the rights of Capitol Hill visitors to roam the hallways, popping into offices of the Washington delegation for apples, the Iowa delegation for handfuls of popcorn, and the Georgia delegation for airline-size bags of peanuts.

8-3.4.11 Meals Incidental to Site Visit, and Constituent Events

Often a company or other constituent organization that wishes to invite Members to its conferences or meetings, or to tour its facilities, will also want to offer the Member a beverage, local transportation, or some refreshment while he or she is on site. The House and Senate both authorize means to accomplish this in different ways.

Under an exception for food or beverage "incidental" to a site visit, the House permits its Members and staff to accept local transportation, food, and beverages when offered as part of a site visit or tour of a facility.[99] Any food offered, however, must be presented in a group setting with other employees of the host, such as in a plant cafeteria.[100] The Senate rules contain a companion exception for food and beverages offered under similar circumstances. However, the Senate's exception has a number of additional specific criteria. For example, the cost of the meal provided to the Member must be less than $50; the host must be a constituent, and the event must be in the senator's home state; no lobbyist may attend; and at least five constituents must be present. This exception is primarily useful to permit a senator to attend a constituent's conference or symposium, or to tour a business site.[101]

---

95. HOUSE ETHICS MANUAL, *supra* note 27, at 54.
96. HOUSE ETHICS MANUAL, *supra* note 27, at 53.
97. Senate Rule XXXV, cl. 1(c)(12) (114th Cong.); House Rule XXV, cl. 5(a)(3)(V) (114th Cong.).
98. SENATE ETHICS MANUAL, *supra* note 18, at 34.
99. HOUSE ETHICS MANUAL, *supra* note 27, at 52.
100. HOUSE ETHICS MANUAL, *supra* note 27, at 52.
101. Senate Rule XXXV, cl. 1(c)(24), cl. 1(g) (114th Cong.).

8-3.4.12 Miscellaneous Other Exceptions

Two other exceptions seem so clearly beyond the scope of "gift" regulation that it is a testament to the thoroughness of the drafters that they felt compelled to include them. In case there was any doubt, the rules spell out that Members retain the right to keep their pensions "and other benefits resulting from continued participation in an employee welfare and benefits plan maintained by a former employer."[102] Moreover, perhaps recognizing that there is little chance of a conflict arising in accepting a gift from a deceased donor, the rules exempt "[b]equests, inheritances, and other transfers at death."[103]

8-3.4.13 Waivers

Both the House and Senate rules contain an "escape hatch" in the form of the waiver authority retained by the respective committees.[104] The House Committee has granted a general waiver, for example, for the acceptance of wedding and baby gifts, and has stated that it will grant waivers in other "unusual case[s]."[105] The Senate Committee also routinely grants waivers for wedding gifts.[106]

8-3.5 Additional Special Restrictions on Lobbyists

The most recent gift-rule revisions (2007) arose primarily from a sense that lobbyists were using gift opportunities to wield undue influence over the legislative process. In fact, even before the passage of HLOGA, a few provisions in the preexisting gift rules singled out lobbyists and agents of foreign principals for particularly disfavored status.

As in HLOGA's gift rule restrictions, "lobbyist" for these purposes includes any individual lobbyist or lobbying firm that is registered pursuant to the Lobbying Disclosure Act of 1995.[107] Unlike HLOGA's gift rule restrictions, however, these special restrictions on lobbyists do *not* apply to organizations that retain or employ lobbyists to lobby only for their own interests (like trade associations and corporations). For these "self-lobbying organizations," only individual employees who qualify as "lobbyists" under the LDA will be subject to these separate restrictions. Self-lobbying organizations thus have extra incentive to avoid identifying as "lobbyists" on their LDA reports any individuals who do not meet the statutory definition. (For more discussion about avoiding over-disclosure, see Chapter 4.)

As noted in Section 8-3.4.2, a Member may not accept personal hospitality from a lobbyist unless that person is a bona fide personal friend.[108] Lobbyists may not provide travel expenses to Members to enable them to give speeches, make fact-finding trips, or conduct other business in connection with their official duties.[109]

---

102. Senate Rule XXXV, cl. 1(c)(8) (114th Cong.); House Rule XXV, cl. 5(a)(3)(H) (114th Cong.).

103. Senate Rule XXXV, cl. 1(c)(14) (114th Cong.); House Rule XXV, cl. 5(a)(3)(M) (114th Cong.).

104. Senate Rule XXXV, cl. 1(c)(21) (114th Cong.); House Rule XXV, cl. 5(a)(3)(T) (114th Cong.).

105. House Ethics Manual, *supra* note 27, at 70–71.

106. Senate Ethics Manual, *supra* note 18, at 41.

107. Senate Rule XXXV, cl. 5(a) (114th Cong.); House Rule XXV, cl. 5(g)(1) (114th Cong.). See also Chapters 3 and 4.

108. Senate Rule XXXV, cl. 1(c)(4)(A) and 1(c)(17) (114th Cong.); House Rule XXV, cl. 5(a)(3)(D) and cl. 5(a)(3)(P) (114th Cong.).

109. Senate Rule XXXV, cl. 2(a)(1) (114th Cong.); House Rule XXV, cl. 5(b)(1)(A) (114th Cong.).

Although there is a general exception for contributions to Members' legal expense funds, this exception does not extend to contributions by lobbyists.[110]

The rules have also historically presumed that certain contributions by lobbyists, while not donated directly to or subject to the unfettered control of Members, are of such benefit to them that they should be deemed gifts to the Members. The rules thus effectively prohibit lobbyists from contributing to entities that are maintained or controlled by Members, charities that are recommended by Members (other than by means of a mass mailing or other wide-scale solicitation or in lieu of an honorarium), or to conferences or retreats sponsored by congressional organizations for the benefit of Members.[111] Accordingly, some of the contributions and disbursements that must be reported in semiannual LDA reports filed by lobbyists (see Section 5-5.2 of this manual) are, in fact, not permitted under the House and Senate rules. If such reports do reflect such contributions, they may constitute proof of violation of the prohibition of the LDA against lobbyist gifts in contravention of the Senate and House gift rules and would, moreover, directly contradict a certification that no gifts were offered in violation of the rules, thereby triggering potential liability for both criminal and civil penalties.

The House has cautioned that Members should take particular care when accepting gifts from lobbyists, even from those who are also personal friends.[112] Specifically, the House Committee advises that a Member or staff person not accept a gift from a lobbyist under the personal friendship exception unless (1) the lobbyist has paid for the gift personally, and (2) the relationship history between the lobbyist and the recipient has included "reciprocal gift exchange."[113]

8-4 Travel

The House and Senate gift rules impose significant restrictions on privately funded, officially connected travel. These are travel expenses, food, and lodging provided to allow Members and staff to attend conventions, site visits, or other fact-finding events in their official capacities, but for which the federal government will not generally pay. Specifically, the rules limit the ability of corporations and other outside groups to pay for Members and staff to take these trips, which are often viewed as ways for private organizations to lavish attention on, and gain legislative favor with, Members and staff.

8-4.1 Restrictions on Travel Paid by Lobbyists' Clients—In General

Lobbyists and lobbying firms are entirely prohibited from providing Members and staff with privately funded travel. The rules do allow an organization or corporation that has lobbyists, whether in-house or through the retention of a lobbying firm, to pay for travel for Members and staff. However, the length of the trip may not exceed one day, and the corporation or organization may not provide more than a single night's stay. (With advance approval, two nights may be permitted

---

110. Senate Rule XXXV, cl. 1(c)(5) and cl. 3(c) (114th Cong.); House Rule XXV, cl. 5(a)(3)(E) and cl. 5(e)(3) (114th Cong.).

111. Senate Rule XXXV, cl. 3 (114th Cong.); House Rule XXV, cl. 5(e) (114th Cong.).

112. HOUSE ETHICS MANUAL, *supra* note 27, at 39.

113. HOUSE ETHICS MANUAL, *supra* note 27, at 39–40.

if the extra night is necessary, for logistical or other reasons, to participate in the event.[114])

In addition—and very significant for lobbyists—the lobbyists themselves generally may not participate in putting the trips together. Both the House and Senate explicitly prohibit lobbyists from "plan[ning], organiz[ing], or arrang[ing]" privately funded travel (although de minimis involvement is permitted in certain circumstances).[115] Nor may a lobbyist generally accompany the Member on the travel. Lobbyists are not, by and large, barred from attending these out-of-town events with Members; they may not, however, book a plane or train ride alongside the Member and use the travel time with the captive congressional audience as a lobbying opportunity.[116]

House and Senate guidance makes clear that extravagant, vacation-like trips are not what the committees have in mind. Corporate jets generally may not be provided for this kind of travel—the House allows it only under exceptional circumstances, and the Senate doesn't allow it at all—and first-class airfare is permissible only in certain very limited circumstances.[117] Hosts are similarly constrained with respect to the kinds of food they may provide; they are counseled, for example, in the House to refer to GSA per diem rates when choosing menus for events planned specifically for Members.[118]

Organizations that do not employ lobbyists, and certain nonprofit entities (501(c)(3) organizations in the Senate, and universities in the House) may provide travel expenses pursuant to limited time periods: three days in the Senate and four days in the House for travel inside the United States, and seven days for international travel.[119]

8-4.2 Purpose of Travel

Members travel for a variety of reasons, and the purpose of the trip determines who is permitted to pay the expenses. For example, Members travel at official expense to do congressional business. Usually this involves travel back and forth between Washington and the home state or district, but it may involve other destinations as well (e.g., the state capital for a House Member whose district lies elsewhere, or the location of a field hearing). Members may travel for campaign purposes at the expense of campaign committees, political parties, or political action committees. They may travel at private expense for officially connected purposes. And they may travel for personal purposes at personal expense.

---

114. Senate Rule XXXV, cl. 2(a)(2)(A)(i) (114th Cong.); House Rule XXV, cl. 5(b)(1)(C)(ii) (114th Cong.).

115. Senate Rule XXXV, cl. 2(d) (114th Cong.); House Rule XXV, cl. 5(c)(2) (114th Cong.).

116. Senate Rule XXXV, cl. 2(d) (114th Cong.); House Rule XXV, cl. 5(c)(1) (114th Cong.).

117. *See* Committee on Standards of Official Conduct, U.S. House of Representatives, *Memorandum to all Members, Officers, and Employeess (sic) on Travel Guidelines and Regulations* at 2 (Feb. 20, 2007); *see also* Select Committee on Ethics, U.S. Senate, *Senate Select Committee on Ethics Regulations and Guidelines for Privately-Sponsored Travel*, 6.

118. *See* Committee on Standards of Official Conduct, U.S. House of Representatives, *Memorandum to all Members, Officers, and Employeess (sic) on Travel Guidelines and Regulations* at 3 (Feb. 20, 2007); *see also* Select Committee on Ethics, U.S. Senate, *Senate Select Committee on Ethics Regulations and Guidelines for Privately-Sponsored Travel*, 6. General Services Administration (GSA) per diem rates can be found at http://www.gsa.gov/portal/content/104877.

119. *See* Senate Rule XXXV, cl. 2(f) (114th Cong.); House Rule XXV, cl. 5(b)(4)(A) (114th Cong.).

Sometimes Members will be offered rides on corporate jets. The House does not permit House Members to accept such rides for most purposes (other than, in very limited circumstances, for privately funded, officially connected travel subject to advance approval and disclosure).[120] Senators and Senate staff may accept rides on corporate planes (except for privately funded, officially connected travel), but whether the ride is for political or personal purposes, the owner of the jet must be reimbursed. To avoid receiving an impermissible gift for personal travel, the standard for reimbursement is generally the Member's pro rata share of the fair market value of the charter cost of a similar plane.[121] If such travel is for campaign purposes, the Federal Election Campaign Act (FECA) requires that the campaign or other political committee reimburse the service provider the campaign travelers' pro rata share of the fair market value of the flight.[122]

Within the narrow boundaries discussed in this section (e.g., on source of payment, time period, mode of travel, and character of amenities provided), the gift rules permit a Member to accept private reimbursement for necessary travel expenses to attend a meeting, speaking engagement, fact-finding trip, or similar event in connection with official duties and not substantially recreational in nature. Expenditures for recreational activities or entertainment other than that provided to all attendees as an integral part of the event are not covered under the travel provisions, but may be accepted *only subject to the other gift rules*. The Member may accept transportation, lodging, food and refreshments, conference fees, and materials. This permission is conditioned on complying with the following limitations.

8-4.3 Who May Pay

The gift rules are explicit that registered lobbyists and agents of foreign principals may not pay for Members' travel expenses.[123] Included within that prohibition are "lobbying firms," as defined by the LDA.[124] Travel expenses may be provided by trade associations, corporations, labor unions, foundations, or anyone else who is not a lobbyist (or an agent of a foreign principal) and has some connection to the purpose of the trip. Indeed, the absolute ban *does not* extend to organizations that retain lobbying firms or employ in-house lobbyists who lobby only on the employing organization's behalf. However, as noted previously, these organizations that employ or retain lobbyists are subject to the restrictive time limits discussed in Section 8-4.5. And, regardless of who pays, a lobbyist may not plan, request, or arrange any privately funded trip.

8-4.4 Who May Accompany

A House Member may bring a spouse or child along at the expense of the sponsor.[125] A senator may also bring a spouse or child at the expense of the sponsor, but only if the Member determines that "the attendance of the spouse or the child

120. *See* House Rule XXIII, cl. 15 (114th Cong.). By its terms, this restriction does not extend to House staff.
121. *See* Senate Rule XXXV, cl. 1(c)(1)(C) (114th Cong.).
122. *See* 52 U.S.C. § 30114 (2015).
123. Senate Rule XXXV, cl. 2(a)(1) (114th Cong.); House Rule XXV, cl. 5(b)(1)(A) (114th Cong.).
124. See Chapter 4 of this manual.
125. House Rule XXV, cl. 5(b)(4)(D) (114th Cong.).

is appropriate to assist in the representation of the Senate."[126] A Member may not bring a staffer in lieu of a spouse or child; staffers may travel if they are independently invited by the sponsor to participate in the event.

8-4.5 Time Limits

If an organization that employs or retains lobbyists pays, the trip may last no longer than one day and one night (two nights may be approved in advance if a one-night stay is not practical). For trips paid for by any other organization, or by those organizations offered an exception under the applicable rule (501(c)(3) organizations in the Senate, and universities in the House), time limits for privately paid travel depend on the chamber in which the traveler serves. In the Senate, the limits are as follows: three days within the contiguous forty-eight states, and seven days for trips that take place outside the contiguous forty-eight states. A day is defined as a twenty-four-hour period, and travel time does not count against the limits.[127]

Travel on the House side is subject to a four-day limit for domestic travel (i.e., within the contiguous forty-eight states) and a seven-day limit on foreign travel. The House measures the four days from the time of departure for the trip to the time of departure back to Washington or the Member's next duty station. Thus, the return trip does not count against the four-day limit. In the case of foreign travel, the House allows for jet lag time and does not count any part of a day in which the Member travels to or from the foreign destination. Thus, the seven days start on the first full day at the foreign destination and run until the day before departure.[128]

In both the House and the Senate, travel may be extended at the Member's own expense. Independently arranged events with separate purposes and separate sponsors may be scheduled back-to-back.[129] Both the House and the Senate Committees retain the authority to grant permission in advance for a privately funded trip to exceed the three-, four-, or seven-day limit. Such waivers are not routinely granted; the House Committee, in particular, has been reluctant to authorize extended trips in the past.

8-4.6 Disclosure

Privately funded travel must be disclosed, with certain exceptions (e.g., for political travel) on all Members' annual EIGA reports. The gift rules impose additional travel disclosure requirements as well.

For travel paid for by an entity that employs or retains lobbyists, both houses require robust disclosure, *in advance*, of the expenses to be provided, and the appropriate ethics committee must review and approve those expenses before the trip. There are extensive forms to be filled out by the sponsor, as well as a form for the traveler to complete and submit to the ethics committee in advance. Among the details requested on these forms are explanations of why the congressional travelers are being invited; certifications as to lobbyist involvement (or noninvolvement)

---

126. Senate Rule XXXV, cl. 2(f)(4) (114th Cong.).
127. *Id.* cl. 2(f)(1) (114th Cong.).
128. House Rule XXV, cl. 5(b)(4)(A) (114th Cong.); House Ethics Manual, *supra* note 27, at 93.
129. Senate Ethics Manual, *supra* note 18, at 47; House Ethics Manual, *supra* note 27, at 95.

in the trip; and details about the method of transportation and type of expenses provided.

Additional disclosure attaches to staff travel. A staffer wishing to embark on a privately funded trip must receive authorization in writing and in advance from a supervising Member.

All travel expenses for Members and staff must be itemized and disclosed within fifteen days of return (thirty days in the Senate). All such disclosures for Members and staff must be signed by Members. The disclosure forms, which are available from the ethics committees, the Clerk of the House, and the Secretary of the Senate, include a description of the expenses provided and a certification that the travel was in connection with official duties and did not create the appearance of using public office for private gain.[130]

8-4.7 Other Privately Funded Travel

In addition to permissible travel to conduct fact-finding or make speeches, the gift rules authorize Members to accept transportation, lodging, food, refreshments, and other benefits in connection with

- Campaign events;
- Job interviews; and
- Outside business, employment, or other unofficial activities of the Member or spouse, provided that these benefits "have not been offered or enhanced because of the official position of the Member . . . and are customarily provided to others in similar circumstances."[131]

This provision allows Members, for example, to accompany their spouses on the spouses' business trips. In addition, Members may accept travel, food, refreshments, and entertainment in connection with the receipt of an honorary degree.[132]

8-5 Honoraria and Other Outside Income

Both the Senate and the House have had some rules limiting the outside earnings of Members for decades. ("Unearned" or passive income is unlimited, but subject to public financial disclosure.) Congress adopted its most stringent limits by statute, in the Ethics Reform Act of 1989 (ERA),[133] later amended, notably by the Legislative Branch Appropriations Act for Fiscal Year 1992.[134] In these laws, the Members of Congress embraced the philosophy that the public should be their only paymaster. Thus, they foreswore honoraria and substantially reduced their opportunities for private remuneration. The House Bipartisan Task Force on Ethics, which drafted the ERA, explained that "[t]he earned income limitation was intended to assure the

---

130. Senate Rule XXXV, cl. 2(c) (114th Cong.); House Rule XXV, cl. 5(b)(1)(A) (114th Cong.); *see also* http://clerk.house.gov/public_disc/financial-search.aspx and https://efdsearch.senate.gov/search/home/ for disclosure forms.

131. Senate Rule XXXV, cl. 1(c)(7) (114th Cong.); SENATE ETHICS MANUAL, *supra* note 18, at 31–32; *see also* House Rule XXV, cl. 5(a)(3)(G) (114th Cong.).

132. Senate Rule XXXV, cl. 1(c)(11) (114th Cong.); House Rule XXV, cl. 5(a)(3)(K) (114th Cong.).

133. Pub. L. No. 101–94, 103 Stat. 1716 (1989).

134. Pub. L. No. 102–90, 105 Stat. 447 (1991).

public that (1) Members are not using their positions of influence for personal gain or being affected by the prospects of outside income, and (2) outside activities are not detracting from a Member's full-time attention to his or her official duties."[135]

8-5.1 Honoraria

Honoraria have been banned for Members and staff of Congress since 1991. The ban took effect on January 1, 1991, for House Members and on August 14, 1991, for Members of the Senate. The House Bipartisan Task Force frankly stated that the ban was prompted by public concerns that honoraria had become "a way for special interests to try to gain influence or buy access to Members of Congress, particularly since interest groups most often give honoraria to Members who serve on committees which have jurisdiction over their legislative interests."[136]

Both the House and the Senate have rules banning honoraria, in addition to the federal law that attempted to ban honoraria for all federal employees. The rules are similar in the House and the Senate. The rules are important because the Supreme Court has found the ERA unconstitutional, at least with respect to the class of executive branch employees who were party to the suit.[137] (No legislative branch employees participated.) Although the Office of Legal Counsel of the Department of Justice has opined that the Department cannot enforce the honoraria ban against any federal employee in any branch of government, both the House and the Senate Ethics Committees continue to enforce their rule-based bans against House and Senate Members and employees.[138]

The Senate Committee continues to use the definition contained in the ERA:

> The term "honorarium" means a payment of money or anything of value for an appearance, speech, or article (including a series of appearances, speeches, or articles if the subject matter is directly related to the individual's official duties or the payment is made because of the individual's status with the Government) by a Member, officer or employee, excluding any actual and necessary travel expenses incurred by such individual (and one relative).[139]

The House Committee's definition is similar, but, in the case of Members and senior staff, the rule's plain language would include any series of appearances, speeches, or articles, whether or not related to the individual's duties.[140] Thus, a Member of the House may not accept a payment for an individual speech or article on any subject. A senator may, however, accept payment for a *series* of appearances, speeches, or articles provided the series is unrelated to the individual's official

135. Rules Comm., Report of the Bipartisan Task Force on Ethics on H.R. 3660, Government Ethics Reform Act of 1989, 101st Cong., at 12 (Comm. Print 1989) [hereinafter Bipartisan Task Force Report].

136. *Id.* at 13.

137. United States v. Nat'l Treasury Employees Union, 513 U.S. 454 (1995).

138. Senate Rule XXXVI (114th Cong.); House Rule XXV (114th Cong.); *see also* Senate Ethics Manual, *supra* note 18, at 98–99.

139. 5 U.S.C. app. 4, § 505(3) (2015); Senate Rule XXXVI (114th Cong.).

140. House Rule XXV, cls. 1, 4 (114th Cong.).

duties or position (e.g., a three-part series of articles on numismatics by a Member with an established reputation as a coin collector).

Although a Member will not generally be able to accept a banned honorarium payment personally, he may ask that up to $2,000 be donated to a charity in honor of his speech, appearance, or article. The charity must be qualified under Section 170(c) of the Internal Revenue Code to receive tax-deductible contributions.

8-5.1.1 Disclosure

Members must disclose on their annual financial disclosure reports under EIGA the fact of any charitable contributions made in lieu of honoraria. (The semiannual reports filed under the LDA by registrants and lobbyists will also have to reflect such payments made by them in recognition of a Member or staff. See Section 5-5.2.2 of this manual.) The disclosure must include the date of the contribution, the name of the person or organization making the contribution, the event it commemorates, and the amount of the contribution. The name of the charity receiving the contribution need not be publicly disclosed, but must be reported confidentially to the appropriate ethics committee.[141] If the person making the contribution is a registered lobbyist or agent of a foreign principal, there is an additional public disclosure within thirty days of the request for the donation. The Member must disclose the name and address of the lobbyist, the date and amount of the contribution, and the name and address of the charity recommended.[142] Forms for this purpose are available from the ethics committees, the Secretary of the Senate, and the Clerk of the House.

8-5.2 Other Outside Income

Members and staff of the Senate and the House are subject to a plethora of other limitations on the type and amount of income they may earn, restrictions that vary according to the body with which they are associated, and their governmental salary level. These limits are summarized in Appendix 8-C. Key provisions are discussed below.

The principal statutory limits derive from the ERA and address potential conflicts of interest that are perceived to arise when Members, acting in their private capacities, undertake fiduciary responsibilities. By taking on such responsibilities, a Member could place himself or herself in the position of having to choose between the obligation to act in the best interests of her private clients and the responsibility of all public officials to act in the best interests of the general public or her constituents. An additional problem could arise when a private firm or organization seeks to associate itself with a Member, either to trade on the Member's and the institution's prestige or to gain financial influence with the Member.[143]

To avoid these dilemmas, the ERA prohibits Members from accepting compensation for professional services involving a fiduciary relationship. A firm that provides such services may not employ a Member in any capacity or use the Member's name (e.g., by listing the Member on the firm letterhead as "of counsel") regardless of whether that use is compensated. Members may not serve for compensation as

---

141. *See* 5 U.S.C. app. 4, § 102(a)(1)(A) (2015).
142. Senate Rule XXXV, cl. 4 (114th Cong.); House Rule XXV, cl. 5(f) (114th Cong.).
143. *See* Bipartisan Task Force Report, *supra* note 135, at 14.

officers or members of the board of any organization. Compensation for teaching must be approved in advance by the governing ethics committee to ensure that honoraria for speeches do not creep back in under the guise of teaching.[144]

This part of the ERA also restricts the outside activities of Members and those staff persons who are presumed, based on the salaries they earn, to hold influential policy-making positions. A legislative employee is subject to these restrictions if, for ninety days in a calendar year, his congressional salary exceeds 120 percent of the base rate paid to executive branch employees at the GS-15, step 1 level (without taking into account locality pay or other adjustments). In 2016, employees who earned at or above $123,175 are covered. These persons must also file publicly available, annual financial disclosure statements.

Members and staff who earn at this level must limit their annual outside earnings from all sources to 15 percent of the Member's base salary rate. The cap was $27,495 in 2016.

Beyond these income limitations, there are also restrictions on the post-employment activities of Members and staff (addressed in detail in Chapters 27 and 28). Ethics rules separately restrict, and require disclosure of, negotiations for future employment. These are also addressed in Chapters 27 and 28.

8-5.2.1 Government-Wide Restrictions

The criminal laws bar Members of Congress and all federal employees from accepting compensation for representing others, outside of their official duties, in particular matters in which the government is a party or has a direct and substantial interest, before federal agencies, courts, and officers.[145] It is similarly illegal to *offer* compensation for such representational services by a Member or employee. Even without being compensated, a federal employee (although not a Member) is prohibited from prosecuting any claim against the government, outside his or her official duties, or from acting as agent or attorney for anyone before any agency, court, or officer in any particular matter in which the government is a party or has a direct and substantial interest.[146]

Members, as well as federal employees, are subject to a constitutional bar against accepting compensation from foreign governments.[147] In addition, regardless of compensation, a public official may not act as an agent or lawyer for a foreign principal required to register under the Foreign Agents Registration Act of 1938.[148]

8-5.2.2 Senate Income Restrictions

Senate rules that predate the ERA impose fiduciary restrictions on Members and on all employees earning at least $25,000 a year in Senate salary that are similar to the ones the ERA imposes.[149] In addition, all employees must notify their supervising officer or senator, in writing, before accepting any outside employment.[150]

---

144. 5 U.S.C. app. 4, § 502(a) (2015).
145. 18 U.S.C. § 203 (2015).
146. 18 U.S.C. § 205 (2015).
147. U.S. Const. art. I, § 9, cl. 8.
148. 18 U.S.C. § 219 (2015). See also Chapter 19 addressing the FARA.
149. Senate Rule XXXVII, cl. 5(a) (114th Cong.).
150. *Id.* cl. 3 (114th Cong.).

Moreover, long-standing Senate rules impose their own post-employment restrictions, lasting one year from the date of termination for senators and one year for staff and employees who become registered lobbyists or are employed by LDA registrants for the purpose of influencing legislation.[151] It is not clear how this particular restriction can be enforced, since, by definition, only a former Member or employee is covered by the provision, and the Senate Ethics Committee has jurisdiction over only current Members, officers, and employees of the Senate.

8-5.2.3 House Income Restrictions: Book Publishing

As an outgrowth of the investigation into former Speaker Newt Gingrich's publishing activities, the House adopted a rule, effective in 1996, prohibiting Members and employees who earn at least 120 percent of the GS-15 rate of pay (in 2016, $123,175) from accepting advances in connection with writing books.[152] An attempt to subject all royalties to the outside earned income limit failed. Instead, Members and these employees may accept copyright royalties, provided that they are from established publishers pursuant to usual and customary contractual terms and that the House Ethics Committee approves the book contract in advance.

---

151. *Id.* cls. 8, 9 (114th Cong.).
152. House Rule XXV, cl. 3 (114th Cong.).

APPENDIX 8-A

History of Congressional Gift Restrictions

Year	House	Senate
1968	No gift of substantial value from a source with a direct interest in legislation.[153]	Confidential report to Comptroller General of gifts of $50 or more.[154]
1977	Limit of $100 from a source with a direct interest in legislation; gifts worth $35 or less do not count toward limit; public financial disclosure (by House rule) of gifts worth more than $100 or travel worth more than $250.[155]	Limit of $100 from a source with a direct interest in legislation; gifts worth $35 or less do not count toward limit; public financial disclosure (by Senate rule) of gifts worth more than $100 or travel worth more than $250.[156]
1978	Financial disclosure requirements enacted into law.[157]	Financial disclosure requirements enacted into law.
1987	Limit of $100 from a source with a direct interest in legislation; gifts worth $50 or less do not count toward limit.[158]	No change.
1990	Limit of $200 from any source other than a relative; gifts worth $75 or less do not count toward limit.[159]	Limit of $100 from a source with a direct interest in legislation; $300 from any source other than a relative; gifts worth $75 or less do not count toward limits.[160]
1992	Limit of $250 from any source other than a relative; gifts worth $100 or less do not count toward limit.[161]	Limit of $250 from any source other than a relative; gifts worth $100 or less do not count toward limit.[162]

(continued)

---

153. H.R. Res. 1099, 90th Cong. (1968).

154. S. Res. 266, 90th Cong., 114 Cong. Rec. 6672–73 (1968).

155. H.R. Res. 287, 95th Cong. (1977).

156. S. Res. 110, 95th Cong. (1977).

157. Ethics in Government Act of 1978 (EIGA), Pub. L. No. 95–521, § 101, 92 Stat. 1824 (1978) (codified at 5 U.S.C. app. 4, §§ 101–111 (2015)).

158. H.R. Res. 5, 100th Cong. (1987).

159. Ethics Reform Act of 1989, Pub. L. No. 101–94, § 801(a), 103 Stat. 1716, 1771–72 (1989) (amending House Rule XLIII, cl. 4 (110th Cong.)).

160. Ethics Reform Act of 1989, Pub. L. No. 101–94, § 901(a), 103 Stat. 1778-80.

161. Legislative Branch Appropriations Act for Fiscal Year 1992, Pub. L. No. 102–90, § 314(d), 105 Stat. 447, 470 (1991).

162. Legislative Branch Appropriations Act for Fiscal Year 1992, Pub. L. No. 102–90, § 314(c).

History of Congressional Gift Restrictions

Year	House	Senate
1996	No gifts allowed, except as specifically provided in twenty-four enumerated exceptions.[163]	Limits of less than $50 for single gifts, less than $100 for total gifts from any source other than a relative; gifts worth less than $10 do not count toward limit; twenty-four exceptions.[164]
1999	Limits of less than $50 for single gifts, less than $100 for total gifts from any source other than a relative; gifts worth less than $10 do not count toward limit; twenty-four exceptions.[165]	No change.
2007	Absolute ban on gifts from lobbyists, lobbying firms, and entities that employ or retain lobbyists; exceptions still permitted.	Absolute ban on gifts from lobbyists, lobbying firms, and entities that employ or retain lobbyists; exceptions still permitted.

---

163. H.R. Res. 250, 104th Cong. (1995) (enacting House Rule LII, which became House Rule LI in 1997, House Rule XXVI in 1999, and was renumbered as House Rule XXV in 2001).

164. S. Res. 158, 104th Cong. (1995) (amending Senate Rule XXXV).

165. 145 CONG. REC. H208–H211 (daily ed. Jan. 6, 1999).

APPENDIX 8-B

RULES OF THE HOUSE OF REPRESENTATIVES—GIFTS

Gifts 5. (a)(1)(A)(i) A Member, Delegate, Resident Commissioner, officer, or employee of the House may not knowingly accept a gift except as provided in this clause.

(ii) A Member, Delegate, Resident Commissioner, officer, or employee of the House may not knowingly accept a gift from a registered lobbyist or agent of a foreign principal or from a private entity that retains or employs registered lobbyists or agents of a foreign principal except as provided in subparagraph (3) of this paragraph.

(B)(i) A Member, Delegate, Resident Commissioner, officer, or employee of the House may accept a gift (other than cash or cash equivalent) not prohibited by subdivision (A)(ii) that the Member, Delegate, Resident Commissioner, officer, or employee reasonably and in good faith believes to have a value of less than $50 and a cumulative value from one source during a calendar year of less than $100. A gift having a value of less than $10 does not count toward the $100 annual limit. The value of perishable food sent to an office shall be allocated among the individual recipients and not to the Member, Delegate, or Resident Commissioner. Formal recordkeeping is not required by this subdivision, but a Member, Delegate, Resident Commissioner, officer, or employee of the House shall make a good faith effort to comply with this subdivision.

(ii) A gift of a ticket to a sporting or entertainment event shall be valued at the face value of the ticket or, in the case of a ticket without a face value, at the highest cost of a ticket with a face value for the event. The price printed on a ticket to an event shall be deemed its face value only if it also is the price at which the issuer offers that ticket for sale to the public.

(2)(A) In this clause the term "gift" means a gratuity, favor, discount, entertainment, hospitality, loan, forbearance, or other item having monetary value. The term includes gifts of services, training, transportation, lodging, and meals, whether provided in kind, by purchase of a ticket, payment in advance, or reimbursement after the expense has been incurred.

(B)(i) A gift to a family member of a Member, Delegate, Resident Commissioner, officer, or employee of the House, or a gift to any other individual based on that individual's relationship with the Member, Delegate, Resident Commissioner, officer, or employee, shall be considered a gift to the Member, Delegate, Resident Commissioner, officer, or employee if it is given with the knowledge and acquiescence of the Member, Delegate, Resident Commissioner, officer, or employee and the Member, Delegate, Resident Commissioner, officer, or employee has reason to believe the gift was given because of the official position of such individual.

(ii) If food or refreshment is provided at the same time and place to both a Member, Delegate, Resident Commissioner, officer, or employee of the House and the spouse or dependent thereof, only the food or refreshment provided to the Member, Delegate, Resident Commissioner, officer, or employee shall be treated as a gift for purposes of this clause.

(3) The restrictions in subparagraph (1) do not apply to the following:

(A) Anything for which the Member, Delegate, Resident Commissioner, officer, or employee of the House pays the market value, or does not use and promptly returns to the donor.

(B) A contribution, as defined in section 301(8) of the Federal Election Campaign Act of 1971 (2 U.S.C. 431) that is lawfully made under that Act, a lawful contribution for election to a State or local government office, or attendance at a fundraising event sponsored by a political organization described in section 527(e) of the Internal Revenue Code of 1986.

(C) A gift from a relative as described in section 109(16) of title I of the Ethics in Government Act of 1978 (5 U.S.C. App. 109(16)).

(D)(i) Anything provided by an individual on the basis of a personal friendship unless the Member, Delegate, Resident Commissioner, officer, or employee of the House has reason to believe that, under the circumstances, the gift was provided because of the official position of such individual and not because of the personal friendship.

(ii) In determining whether a gift is provided on the basis of personal friendship, the Member, Delegate, Resident Commissioner, officer, or employee of the House shall consider the circumstances under which the gift was offered, such as:

(I) The history of the relationship of such individual with the individual giving the gift, including any previous exchange of gifts between them.

(II) Whether to the actual knowledge of such individual the individual who gave the gift personally paid for the gift or sought a tax deduction or business reimbursement for the gift.

(III) Whether to the actual knowledge of such individual the individual who gave the gift also gave the same or similar gifts to other Members, Delegates, the Resident Commissioners, officers, or employees of the House.

(E) Except as provided in paragraph (e)(3), a contribution or other payment to a legal expense fund established for the benefit of a Member, Delegate, Resident Commissioner, officer, or employee of the House that is otherwise lawfully made in accordance with the restrictions and disclosure requirements of the Committee on Ethics.

(F) A gift from another Member, Delegate, Resident Commissioner, officer, or employee of the House or Senate.

(G) Food, refreshments, lodging, transportation, and other benefits—

(i) resulting from the outside business or employment activities of the Member, Delegate, Resident Commissioner, officer, or employee of the House (or other outside activities that are not connected to the duties of such individual as an officeholder), or of the spouse of such individual, if such benefits have not been offered or enhanced because of the official position of such individual and are customarily provided to others in similar circumstances;

(ii) customarily provided by a prospective employer in connection with bona fide employment discussions; or

(iii) provided by a political organization described in section 527(e) of the Internal Revenue Code of 1986 in connection with a fundraising or campaign event sponsored by such organization.

(H) Pension and other benefits resulting from continued participation in an employee welfare and benefits plan maintained by a former employer.

(I) Informational materials that are sent to the office of the Member, Delegate, Resident Commissioner, officer, or employee of the House in the form of books, articles, periodicals, other written materials, audiotapes, videotapes, or other forms of communication.

(J) Awards or prizes that are given to competitors in contests or events open to the public, including random drawings.

(K) Honorary degrees (and associated travel, food, refreshments, and entertainment) and other bona fide, nonmonetary awards presented in recognition of public service (and associated food, refreshments, and entertainment provided in the presentation of such degrees and awards).

(L) Training (including food and refreshments furnished to all attendees as an integral part of the training) if such training is in the interest of the House.

(M) Bequests, inheritances, and other transfers at death.

(N) An item, the receipt of which is authorized by the Foreign Gifts and Decorations Act, the Mutual Educational and Cultural Exchange Act, or any other statute.

(O) Anything that is paid for by the Federal Government, by a State or local government, or secured by the Government under a Government contract.

(P) A gift of personal hospitality (as defined in section 109(14) of the Ethics in Government Act) of an individual other than a registered lobbyist or agent of a foreign principal.

(Q) Free attendance at an event permitted under subparagraph (4).

(R) Opportunities and benefits that are—

(i) available to the public or to a class consisting of all Federal employees, whether or not restricted on the basis of geographic consideration;

(ii) offered to members of a group or class in which membership is unrelated to congressional employment;

(iii) offered to members of an organization, such as an employees' association or congressional credit union, in which membership is related to congressional employment and similar opportunities are available to large segments of the public through organizations of similar size;

(iv) offered to a group or class that is not defined in a manner that specifically discriminates among Government employees on the basis of branch of Government or type of responsibility, or on a basis that favors those of higher rank or rate of pay;

(v) in the form of loans from banks and other financial institutions on terms generally available to the public; or

(vi) in the form of reduced membership or other fees for participation in organization activities offered to all Government employees by professional organizations if the only restrictions on membership relate to professional qualifications.

(S) A plaque, trophy, or other item that is substantially commemorative in nature and that is intended for presentation.

(T) Anything for which, in an unusual case, a waiver is granted by the Committee on Ethics.

(U) Food or refreshments of a nominal value offered other than as a part of a meal.

(V) Donations of products from the district or State that the Member, Delegate, or Resident Commissioner represents that are intended primarily for promotional purposes, such as display or free distribution, and are of minimal value to any single recipient.

(W) An item of nominal value such as a greeting card, baseball cap, or a T-shirt.

(4)(A) A Member, Delegate, Resident Commissioner, officer, or employee of the House may accept an offer of free attendance at a widely attended convention, conference, symposium, forum, panel discussion, dinner, viewing, reception, or similar event, provided by the sponsor of the event, if—

(i) the Member, Delegate, Resident Commissioner, officer, or employee of the House participates in the event as a speaker or a panel participant, by presenting information related to Congress or matters before Congress, or by performing a ceremonial function appropriate to the official position of such individual; or

(ii) attendance at the event is appropriate to the performance of the official duties or representative function of the Member, Delegate, Resident Commissioner, officer, or employee of the House.

(B) A Member, Delegate, Resident Commissioner, officer, or employee of the House who attends an event described in subdivision (A) may accept a sponsor's unsolicited offer of free attendance at the event for an accompanying individual.

(C) A Member, Delegate, Resident Commissioner, officer, or employee of the House, or the spouse or dependent thereof, may accept a sponsor's unsolicited offer of free attendance at a charity event, except that reimbursement for transportation and lodging may not be accepted in connection with the event unless—

(i) all of the net proceeds of the event are for the benefit of an organization described in section 501(c)(3) of the Internal Revenue Code of 1986 and exempt from taxation under section 501(a) of such Code;

(ii) reimbursement for the transportation and lodging in connection with the event is paid by such organization; and

(iii) the offer of free attendance at the event is made by such organization.

(D) In this paragraph the term "free attendance" may include waiver of all or part of a conference or other fee, the provision of local transportation, or the provision of food, refreshments, entertainment, and instructional materials furnished to all attendees as an integral part of the event. The term does not include entertainment collateral to the event, nor does it include food or refreshments taken other than in a group setting with all or substantially all other attendees.

(5) A Member, Delegate, Resident Commissioner, officer, or employee of the House may not accept a gift the value of which exceeds $250 on the basis of the personal friendship exception in subparagraph (3)(D) unless the Committee on Ethics issues a written determination that such exception applies. A determination under this subparagraph is not required for gifts given on the basis of the family relationship exception in subparagraph (3)(C).

(6) When it is not practicable to return a tangible item because it is perishable, the item may, at the discretion of the recipient, be given to an appropriate charity or destroyed.

(b)(1)(A) A reimbursement (including payment in kind) to a Member, Delegate, Resident Commissioner, officer, or employee of the House for necessary transportation, lodging, and related expenses for travel to a meeting, speaking engagement, factfinding trip, or similar event in connection with the duties of such individual as an officeholder shall be considered as a reimbursement to the House and not a gift prohibited by this clause when it is from a private source other than a registered lobbyist or agent of a foreign principal or a private entity that retains or employs registered lobbyists or agents of a foreign principal (except as provided in subdivision (C)), if the Member, Delegate, Resident Commissioner, officer, or employee—

(i) in the case of an employee, receives advance authorization, from the Member, Delegate, Resident Commissioner, or officer under whose direct supervision the employee works, to accept reimbursement; and

(ii) discloses the expenses reimbursed or to be reimbursed and the authorization to the Clerk within 15 days after the travel is completed.

(B) For purposes of subdivision (A), events, the activities of which are substantially recreational in nature, are not considered to be in connection with the duties of a Member, Delegate, Resident Commissioner, officer, or employee of the House as an officeholder.

(C) A reimbursement (including payment in kind) to a Member, Delegate, Resident Commissioner, officer, or employee of the House for any purpose described in subdivision (A) also shall be considered as a reimbursement to the House and not a gift prohibited by this clause (without regard to whether the source retains or employs registered lobbyists or agents of a foreign principal) if it is, under regulations prescribed by the Committee on Ethics to implement this provision—

(i) directly from an institution of higher education within the meaning of section 101 of the Higher Education Act of 1965; or

(ii) provided only for attendance at or participation in a one-day event (exclusive of travel time and an overnight stay). Regulations prescribed to implement this provision may permit a two-night stay when determined by the committee on a case-by-case basis to be practically required to participate in the one-day event.

(2) Each advance authorization to accept reimbursement shall be signed by the Member, Delegate, Resident Commissioner, or officer of the House under whose direct supervision the employee works and shall include—

(A) the name of the employee;

(B) the name of the person who will make the reimbursement;

(C) the time, place, and purpose of the travel; and a determination that the travel is in connection with the duties of the employee as an officeholder and would not create the appearance that the employee is using public office for private gain.

(3) Each disclosure made under subparagraph (1)(A) shall be signed by the Member, Delegate, Resident Commissioner, or officer (in the case of travel by that Member, Delegate, Resident Commissioner, or officer) or by the Member, Delegate, Resident Commissioner, or officer under whose direct supervision the employee works (in the case of travel by an employee) and shall include—

(A) a good faith estimate of total transportation expenses reimbursed or to be reimbursed;

(B) a good faith estimate of total lodging expenses reimbursed or to be reimbursed;

(C) a good faith estimate of total meal expenses reimbursed or to be reimbursed;

(D) a good faith estimate of the total of other expenses reimbursed or to be reimbursed;

(E) a determination that all such expenses are necessary transportation, lodging, and related expenses as defined in subparagraph (4);

(F) a description of meetings and events attended; and

(G) in the case of a reimbursement to a Member, Delegate, Resident Commissioner, or officer, a determination that the travel was in connection with the duties of such individual as an officeholder and would not create the appearance that the Member, Delegate, Resident Commissioner, or officer is using public office for private gain.

(4) In this paragraph the term "necessary transportation, lodging, and related expenses"—

(A) includes reasonable expenses that are necessary for travel for a period not exceeding four days within the United States or seven days exclusive of travel time outside of the United States unless approved in advance by the Committee on Ethics;

(B) is limited to reasonable expenditures for transportation, lodging, conference fees and materials, and food and refreshments, including reimbursement for necessary transportation, whether or not such transportation occurs within the periods described in subdivision (A);

(C) does not include expenditures for recreational activities, nor does it include entertainment other than that provided to all attendees as an integral part of the event, except for activities or entertainment otherwise permissible under this clause; and

(D) may include travel expenses incurred on behalf of a relative of the Member, Delegate, Resident Commissioner, officer, or employee.

(5) The Clerk of the House shall make all advance authorizations, certifications, and disclosures filed pursuant to this paragraph available for public inspection as soon as possible after they are received.

(c)(1)(A) Except as provided in subdivision (B), a Member, Delegate, Resident Commissioner, officer, or employee of the House may not accept a reimbursement (including payment in kind) for transportation, lodging, or related expenses for a trip on which the traveler is accompanied on any segment by a registered lobbyist or agent of a foreign principal.

(B) Subdivision (A) does not apply to a trip for which the source of reimbursement is an institution of higher education within the meaning of section 101 of the Higher Education Act of 1965.

(2) A Member, Delegate, Resident Commissioner, officer, or employee of the House may not accept a reimbursement (including payment in kind) for transportation, lodging, or related expenses under the exception in paragraph (b)(1)(C)(ii) of this clause for a trip that is financed in whole or in part by a private entity that retains or employs registered lobbyists or agents of a foreign principal unless any involvement of a registered lobbyist or agent of a foreign principal in the planning, organization, request, or arrangement of the trip is de minimis under rules prescribed by the Committee on Ethics to implement paragraph (b)(1)(C) of this clause.

(3) A Member, Delegate, Resident Commissioner, officer, or employee of the House may not accept a reimbursement (including payment in kind) for transportation, lodging, or related expenses for a trip (other than a trip permitted under paragraph (b)(1)(C) of this clause) if such trip is in any part planned, organized, requested, or arranged by a registered lobbyist or agent of a foreign principal.

(d) A Member, Delegate, Resident Commissioner, officer, or employee of the House shall, before accepting travel otherwise permissible under paragraph (b)(1) of this clause from any private source—

(1) provide to the Committee on Ethics before such trip a written certification signed by the source or (in the case of a corporate person) by an officer of the source—

(A) that the trip will not be financed in any part by a registered lobbyist or agent of a foreign principal;

(B) that the source either—

(i) does not retain or employ registered lobbyists or agents of a foreign principal; or

(ii) is an institution of higher education within the meaning of section 101 of the Higher Education Act of 1965; or

(iii) certifies that the trip meets the requirements specified in rules prescribed by the Committee on Ethics to implement paragraph (b)(1)(C)(ii) of this clause and specifically details the extent of any involvement of a registered lobbyist or agent of a foreign principal in the planning, organization, request, or arrangement of the trip considered to qualify as de minimis under such rules;

(C) that the source will not accept from another source any funds earmarked directly or indirectly for the purpose of financing any aspect of the trip;

(D) that the traveler will not be accompanied on any segment of the trip by a registered lobbyist or agent of a foreign principal (except in the case of a trip for which the source of reimbursement is an institution of higher education within the meaning of section 101 of the Higher Education Act of 1965); and

(E) that (except as permitted in paragraph (b)(1)(C) of this clause) the trip will not in any part be planned, organized, requested, or arranged by a registered lobbyist or agent of a foreign principal; and

(2) after the Committee on Ethics has promulgated the regulations mandated in paragraph (i)(1)(B) of this clause, obtain the prior approval of the committee for such trip.

(e) A gift prohibited by paragraph (a)(1) includes the following:

(1) Anything provided by a registered lobbyist or an agent of a foreign principal to an entity that is maintained or controlled by a Member, Delegate, Resident Commissioner, officer, or employee of the House.

(2) A charitable contribution (as defined in section 170(c) of the Internal Revenue Code of 1986) made by a registered lobbyist or an agent of a foreign principal on the basis of a designation, recommendation, or other specification of a Member, Delegate, Resident Commissioner, officer, or employee of the House (not including a mass mailing or other solicitation directed to a broad category of persons or entities), other than a charitable contribution permitted by paragraph (f).

(3) A contribution or other payment by a registered lobbyist or an agent of a foreign principal to a legal expense fund established for the benefit of a Member, Delegate, Resident Commissioner, officer, or employee of the House.

(4) A financial contribution or expenditure made by a registered lobbyist or an agent of a foreign principal relating to a conference, retreat, or similar event, sponsored by or affiliated with an official congressional organization, for or on behalf of Members, Delegates, the Resident Commissioner, officers, or employees of the House.

(f)(1) A charitable contribution (as defined in section 170(c) of the Internal Revenue Code of 1986) made by a registered lobbyist or an agent of a foreign principal in lieu of an honorarium to a Member, Delegate, Resident Commissioner, officer, or employee of the House is not considered a gift under this clause if it is reported as provided in subparagraph (2).

(2) A Member, Delegate, Resident Commissioner, officer, or employee who designates or recommends a contribution to a charitable organization in lieu of an honorarium described in subparagraph (1) shall report within 30 days after such designation or recommendation to the Clerk—

(A) the name and address of the registered lobbyist who is making the contribution in lieu of an honorarium;

(B) the date and amount of the contribution; and

(C) the name and address of the charitable organization designated or recommended by the Member, Delegate, or Resident Commissioner. The Clerk shall make public information received under this subparagraph as soon as possible after it is received.

(g) In this clause—

(1) the term "registered lobbyist" means a lobbyist registered under the Federal Regulation of Lobbying Act or any successor statute;

(2) the term "agent of a foreign principal" means an agent of a foreign principal registered under the Foreign Agents Registration Act; and

(3) the terms "officer" and "employee" have the same meanings as in rule XXIII.

(h) All the provisions of this clause shall be interpreted and enforced solely by the Committee on Ethics. The Committee on Ethics is authorized to issue guidance on any matter contained in this clause.

(i)(1) Not later than 45 days after the date of adoption of this paragraph and at annual intervals thereafter, the Committee on Ethics shall develop and revise, as necessary—

(A) guidelines on judging the reasonableness of an expense or expenditure for purposes of this clause, including the factors that tend to establish—

(i) a connection between a trip and official duties;

(ii) the reasonableness of an amount spent by a sponsor;

(iii) a relationship between an event and an officially connected purpose; and

(iv) a direct and immediate relationship between a source of funding and an event; and

(B) regulations describing the information it will require individuals subject to this clause to submit to the committee in order to obtain the prior approval of the committee for any travel covered by this clause, including any required certifications.

(2) In developing and revising guidelines under subparagraph (1)(A), the committee shall take into account the maximum per diem rates for official Government travel published annually by the General Services Administration, the Department of State, and the Department of Defense.

Claims against the Government 6. A person may not be an officer or employee of the House, or continue in its employment, if acting as an agent for the prosecution of a claim against the Government or if interested in such claim, except as an original claimant or in the proper discharge of official duties.

7. A Member, Delegate, or Resident Commissioner shall prohibit all staff employed by that Member, Delegate, or Resident Commissioner (including staff in personal, committee, and leadership offices) from making any lobbying contact (as defined

in section 3 of the Lobbying Disclosure Act of 1995) with that individual's spouse if that spouse is a lobbyist under the Lobbying Disclosure Act of 1995 or is employed or retained by such a lobbyist for the purpose of influencing legislation.

8. During the dates on which the national political party to which a Member (including a Delegate or Resident Commissioner) belongs holds its convention to nominate a candidate for the office of President or Vice President, the Member may not participate in an event honoring that Member, other than in the capacity as a candidate for such office, if such event is directly paid for by a registered lobbyist under the Lobbying Disclosure Act of 1995 or a private entity that retains or employs such a registered lobbyist.

RULES OF THE SENATE—GIFTS

1. (a)(1) No Member, officer, or employee of the Senate shall knowingly accept a gift except as provided in this rule.

(2)(A) A Member, officer, or employee may accept a gift (other than cash or cash equivalent) which the Member, officer, or employee reasonably and in good faith believes to have a value of less than $50, and a cumulative value from one source during a calendar year of less than $100. No gift with a value below $10 shall count toward the $100 annual limit. No formal recordkeeping is required by this paragraph, but a Member, officer, or employee shall make a good faith effort to comply with this paragraph.

(B) A Member, officer, or employee may not knowingly accept a gift from a registered lobbyist, an agent of a foreign principal, or a private entity that retains or employs a registered lobbyist or an agent of a foreign principal, except as provided in subparagraphs (c) and (d).

(b)(1) For the purpose of this rule, the term "gift" means any gratuity, favor, discount, entertainment, hospitality, loan, forbearance, or other item having monetary value. The term includes gifts of services, training, transportation, lodging, and meals, whether provided in kind, by purchase of a ticket, payment in advance, or reimbursement after the expense has been incurred.

(2)(A) A gift to a family member of a Member, officer, or employee, or a gift to any other individual based on that individual's relationship with the Member, officer, or employee, shall be considered a gift to the Member, officer, or employee if it is given with the knowledge and acquiescence of the Member, officer, or employee and the Member, officer, or employee has reason to believe the gift was given because of the official position of the Member, officer, or employee.

(B) If food or refreshment is provided at the same time and place to both a Member, officer, or employee and the spouse or dependent thereof, only the food or refreshment provided to the Member, officer, or employee shall be treated as a gift for purposes of this rule.

(c) The restrictions in subparagraph (a) shall not apply to the following:

(1)(A) Anything for which the Member, officer, or employee pays the market value, or does not use and promptly returns to the donor.

(B) The market value of a ticket to an entertainment or sporting event shall be the face value of the ticket or, in the case of a ticket without a face value, the value of the ticket with the highest face value for the event, except that if a ticket holder can establish in advance of the event to the Select Committee on Ethics that the ticket at issue is equivalent to another ticket with a face value, then the market value shall be set at the face value of the equivalent ticket. In establishing equivalency, the ticket holder shall provide written and independently verifiable information related to the primary features of the ticket, including, at a minimum, the seat location, access to parking, availability of food and refreshments, and access to venue areas not open to the public. The Select Committee on Ethics may make a determination of equivalency only if such information is provided in advance of the event.

(C)(i) Fair market value for a flight on an aircraft described in item (ii) shall be the pro rata share of the fair market value of the normal and usual charter fare or rental charge for a comparable plane of comparable size, as determined by dividing such cost by the number of Members, officers, or employees of Congress on the flight.

(ii) A flight on an aircraft described in this item is any flight on an aircraft that is not-

(I) operated or paid for by an air carrier or commercial operator certificated by the Federal Aviation Administration and required to be conducted under air carrier safety rules; or

(II) in the case of travel which is abroad, an air carrier or commercial operator certificated by an appropriate foreign civil aviation authority and the flight is required to be conducted under air carrier safety rules.

(iii) This subclause shall not apply to an aircraft owned or leased by a governmental entity or by a Member of Congress or a Member's immediate family member (including an aircraft owned by an entity that is not a public corporation in which the Member or Member's immediate family member has an ownership interest), provided that the Member does not use the aircraft anymore than the Member's or immediate family member's proportionate share of ownership allows.

(2) A contribution, as defined in the Federal Election Campaign Act of 1971 (2 U.S.C. 431 et seq.) that is lawfully made under that Act, or attendance at a fundraising event sponsored by a political organization described in section 527(e) of the Internal Revenue Code of 1986.

(3) A gift from a relative as described in section 109(16) of title I of the Ethics Reform of 1989 (5 U.S.C. App. 6).

(4)(A) Anything, including personal hospitality, provided by an individual on the basis of a personal friendship unless the Member, officer, or employee has reason to believe that, under the circumstances, the gift was provided because of the official position of the Member, officer, or employee and not because of the personal friendship.

(B) In determining whether a gift is provided on the basis of personal friendship, the Member, officer, or employee shall consider the circumstances under which the gift was offered, such as:

(i) The history of the relationship between the individual giving the gift and the recipient of the gift, including any previous exchange of gifts between such individuals.

(ii) Whether to the actual knowledge of the Member, officer, or employee the individual who gave the gift personally paid for the gift or sought a tax deduction or business reimbursement for the gift.

(iii) Whether to the actual knowledge of the Member, officer, or employee the individual who gave the gift also at the same time gave the same or similar gifts to other Members, officers, or employees.

(5) A contribution or other payment to a legal expense fund established for the benefit of a Member, officer, or employee, that is otherwise lawfully made, subject to

the disclosure requirements of the Select Committee on Ethics, except as provided in paragraph 3(c).

(6) Any gift from another Member, officer, or employee of the Senate or the House of Representatives.

(7) Food, refreshments, lodging, and other benefits

(A) resulting from the outside business or employment activities (or other outside activities that are not connected to the duties of the Member, officer, or employee as an officeholder) of the Member, officer, or employee, or the spouse of the Member, officer, or employee, if such benefits have not been offered or enhanced because of the official position of the Member, officer, or employee and are customarily provided to others in similar circumstances;

(B) customarily provided by a prospective employer in connection with bona fide employment discussions; or

(C) provided by a political organization described in section 527(e) of the Internal Revenue Code of 1986 in connection with a fundraising or campaign event sponsored by such an organization.

(8) Pension and other benefits resulting from continued participation in an employee welfare and benefits plan maintained by a former employer.

(9) Informational materials that are sent to the office of the Member, officer, or employee in the form of books, articles, periodicals, other written materials, audiotapes, videotapes, or other forms of communication.

(10) Awards or prizes which are given to competitors in contests or events open to the public, including random drawings.

(11) Honorary degrees (and associated travel, food, refreshments, and entertainment) and other bona fide, nonmonetary awards presented in recognition of public service (and associated food, refreshments, and entertainment provided in the presentation of such degrees and awards).

(12) Donations of products from the State that the Member represents that are intended primarily for promotional purposes, such as display or free distribution, and are of minimal value to any individual recipient.

(13) Training (including food and refreshments furnished to all attendees as an integral part of the training) provided to a Member, officer, or employee, if such training is in the interest of the Senate.

(14) Bequests, inheritances, and other transfers at death.

(15) Any item, the receipt of which is authorized by the Foreign Gifts and Decorations Act, the Mutual Educational and Cultural Exchange Act, or any other statute.

(16) Anything which is paid for by the Federal Government, by a State or local government, or secured by the Government under a Government contract.

(17) A gift of personal hospitality (as defined in section 109(14) of the Ethics in Government Act) of an individual other than a registered lobbyist or agent of a foreign principal.

(18) Free attendance at a widely attended event permitted pursuant to subparagraph (d).

(19) Opportunities and benefits which are

(A) available to the public or to a class consisting of all Federal employees, whether or not restricted on the basis of geographic consideration;

(B) offered to members of a group or class in which membership is unrelated to congressional employment;

(C) offered to members of an organization, such as an employees' association or congressional credit union, in which membership is related to congressional employment and similar opportunities are available to large segments of the public through organizations of similar size;

(D) offered to any group or class that is not defined in a manner that specifically discriminates among Government employees on the basis of branch of Government or type of responsibility, or on a basis that favors those of higher rank or rate of pay;

(E) in the form of loans from banks and other financial institutions on terms generally available to the public; or

(F) in the form of reduced membership or other fees for participation in organization activities offered to all Government employees by professional organizations if the only restrictions on membership relate to professional qualifications.

(20) A plaque, trophy, or other item that is substantially commemorative in nature and which is intended solely for presentation.

(21) Anything for which, in an unusual case, a waiver is granted by the Select Committee on Ethics.

(22) Food or refreshments of a nominal value offered other than as a part of a meal.

(23) An item of little intrinsic value such as a greeting card, baseball cap, or a Tshirt.

(24) Subject to the restrictions in subparagraph (a)(2)(A), free attendance at a constituent event permitted pursuant to subparagraph (g).

(d)(1) A Member, officer, or employee may accept an offer of free attendance at a widely attended convention, conference, symposium, forum, panel discussion, dinner, viewing, reception, or similar event, provided by the sponsor of the event, if

(A) the Member, officer, or employee participates in the event as a speaker or a panel participant, by presenting information related to Congress or matters before Congress, or by performing a ceremonial function appropriate to the Member's, officer's, or employee's official position; or

(B) attendance at the event is appropriate to the performance of the official duties or representative function of the Member, officer, or employee.

(2) A Member, officer, or employee who attends an event described in clause (1) may accept a sponsor's unsolicited offer of free attendance at the event for an accompanying individual if others in attendance will generally be similarly accompanied or if such attendance is appropriate to assist in the representation of the Senate.

(3) A Member, officer, or employee, or the spouse or dependent thereof, may accept a sponsor's unsolicited offer of free attendance at a charity event, except that reimbursement for transportation and lodging may not be accepted in connection with an event that does not meet the standards provided in paragraph 2.

(4) For purposes of this paragraph, the term 'free attendance' may include waiver of all or part of a conference or other fee, the provision of local transportation, or the provision of food, refreshments, entertainment, and instructional materials furnished to all attendees as an integral part of the event. The term does not include entertainment collateral to the event, nor does it include food or refreshments taken other than in a group setting with all or substantially all other attendees.

(5) During the dates of the national party convention for the political party to which a Member belongs, a Member may not participate in an event honoring that Member, other than in his or her capacity as the party's presidential or vice presidential nominee or presumptive nominee, if such event is directly paid for by a registered lobbyist or a private entity that retains or employs a registered lobbyist.

(e) No Member, officer, or employee may accept a gift the value of which exceeds $250 on the basis of the personal friendship exception in subparagraph (c)(4) unless the Select Committee on Ethics issues a written determination that such exception applies. No determination under this subparagraph is required for gifts given on the basis of the family relationship exception.

(f) When it is not practicable to return a tangible item because it is perishable, the item may, at the discretion of the recipient, be given to an appropriate charity or destroyed.

(g)(1) A Member, officer, or employee may accept an offer of free attendance in the Member's home State at a conference, symposium, forum, panel discussion, dinner event, site visit, viewing, reception, or similar event, provided by a sponsor of the event, if--

(A) the cost of meals provided the Member, officer, or employee is less than $50;

(B)(i) the event is sponsored by constituents of, or a group that consists primarily of constituents of, the Member (or the Member by whom the officer or employee is employed); and

(ii) the event will be attended primarily by a group of at least 5 constituents of the Member (or the Member by whom the officer or employee is employed) provided that a registered lobbyist shall not attend the event; and

(C)(i) the Member, officer, or employee participates in the event as a speaker or a panel participant, by presenting information related to Congress or matters before Congress, or by performing a ceremonial function appropriate to the Member's, officer's, or employee's official position; or

(ii) attendance at the event is appropriate to the performance of the official duties or representative function of the Member, officer, or employee.

(2) A Member, officer, or employee who attends an event described in clause (1) may accept a sponsor's unsolicited offer of free attendance at the event for an

accompanying individual if others in attendance will generally be similarly accompanied or if such attendance is appropriate to assist in the representation of the Senate.

(3) For purposes of this subparagraph, the term 'free attendance' has the same meaning given such term in subparagraph (d).

2.(a)(1) A reimbursement (including payment in kind) to a Member, officer, or employee from an individual other than a registered lobbyist or agent of a foreign principal or a private entity that retains or employs 1 or more registered lobbyists or agents of a foreign principal for necessary transportation, lodging and related expenses for travel to a meeting, speaking engagement, factfinding trip or similar event in connection with the duties of the Member, officer, or employee as an officeholder shall be deemed to be a reimbursement to the Senate and not a gift prohibited by this rule, if the Member, officer, or employee complies with the requirements of this paragraph.

(2)(A) Notwithstanding clause (1), a reimbursement (including payment in kind) to a Member, officer, or employee of the Senate from an individual, other than a registered lobbyist or agent of a foreign principal, that is a private entity that retains or employs 1 or more registered lobbyists or agents of a foreign principal shall be deemed to be a reimbursement to the Senate under clause (1) if-

(i) the reimbursement is for necessary transportation, lodging, and related expenses for travel to a meeting, speaking engagement, factfinding trip, or similar event described in clause (1) in connection with the duties of the Member, officer, or employee and the reimbursement is provided only for attendance at or participation for 1 day (exclusive of travel time and an overnight stay) at an event described in clause (1); or

(ii) the reimbursement is for necessary transportation, lodging, and related expenses for travel to a meeting, speaking engagement, factfinding trip, or similar event described in clause (1) in connection with the duties of the Member, officer, or employee and the reimbursement is from an organization designated under section 501(c)(3) of the Internal Revenue Code of 1986.

(B) When deciding whether to preapprove a trip under this clause, the Select Committee on Ethics shall make a determination consistent with regulations issued pursuant to section 544(b) of the Honest Leadership and Open Government Act of 2007. The committee through regulations to implement subclause (A)(i) may permit a longer stay when determined by the committee to be practically required to participate in the event, but in no event may the stay exceed 2 nights.

(3)For purposes of clauses (1) and (2), events, the activities of which are substantially recreational in nature, shall not be considered to be in connection with duties of a Member, officer, or employee as an officeholder.

(b) Before an employee may accept reimbursement pursuant to subparagraph (a), the employee shall receive advance written authorization from the Member or officer under whose direct supervision the employee works. Each advance authorization to accept reimbursement shall be signed by the Member or officer under whose direct supervision the employee works and shall include--

(1) the name of the employee;

(2) the name of the person who will make the reimbursement;

(3) the time, place, and purpose of the travel; and

(4) a determination that the travel is in connection with the duties of the employee as an officeholder and would not create the appearance that the employee is using public office for private gain.

(c) Each Member, officer, or employee that receives reimbursement under this paragraph shall disclose the expenses reimbursed or to be reimbursed, the authorization under subparagraph (b) (for an employee), and a copy of the certification in subparagraph (e)(1) to the Secretary of the Senate not later than 30 days after the travel is completed. Each disclosure made under this subparagraph of expenses reimbursed or to be reimbursed shall be signed by the Member or officer (in the case of travel by that Member or officer) or by the Member or officer under whose direct supervision the employee works (in the case of travel by an employee) and shall include--

(1) a good faith estimate of total transportation expenses reimbursed or to be reimbursed;

(2) a good faith estimate of total lodging expenses reimbursed or to be reimbursed;

(3) a good faith estimate of total meal expenses reimbursed or to be reimbursed;

(4) a good faith estimate of the total of other expenses reimbursed or to be reimbursed;

(5) a determination that all such expenses are necessary transportation, lodging, and related expenses as defined in this paragraph; and

(6) a description of meetings and events attended; and

(7) in the case of a reimbursement to a Member or officer, a determination that the travel was in connection with the duties of the Member or officer as an officeholder and would not create the appearance that the Member or officer is using public office for private gain.

(d)(1) A Member, officer, or employee of the Senate may not accept a reimbursement (including payment in kind) for transportation, lodging, or related expenses under subparagraph (a) for a trip that was-

(A) planned, organized, or arranged by or at the request of a registered lobbyist or agent of a foreign principal; or

(B)(i) for trips described under subparagraph (a)(2)(A)(i) on which a registered lobbyist accompanies the Member, officer, or employee on any segment of the trip; or

(ii) for all other trips allowed under this paragraph, on which a registered lobbyist accompanies the Member, officer, or employee at any point throughout the trip.

(2) The Select Committee on Ethics shall issue regulations identifying de minimis activities by registered lobbyists or foreign agents that would not violate this subparagraph.

(e) A Member, officer, or employee shall, before accepting travel otherwise permissible under this paragraph from any source-

(1) provide to the Select Committee on Ethics a written certification from such source that-

(A) the trip will not be financed in any part by a registered lobbyist or agent of a foreign principal;

(B) the source either-

(i) does not retain or employ registered lobbyists or agents of a foreign principal and is not itself a registered lobbyist or agent of a foreign principal; or

(ii) certifies that the trip meets the requirements of subclause (i) or (ii) of subparagraph (a)(2)(A);

(C) the source will not accept from a registered lobbyist or agent of a foreign principal or a private entity that retains or employs 1 or more registered lobbyists or agents of a foreign principal, funds earmarked directly or indirectly for the purpose of financing the specific trip; and

(D) the trip will not in any part be planned, organized, requested, or arranged by a registered lobbyist or agent of a foreign principal and the traveler will not be accompanied on the trip consistent with the applicable requirements of subparagraph (d)(1)(B) by a registered lobbyist or agent of a foreign principal, except as permitted by regulations issued under subparagraph (d)(2); and

(2) after the Select Committee on Ethics has promulgated regulations pursuant to section 544(b) of the Honest Leadership and Open Government Act of 2007, obtain the prior approval of the committee for such reimbursement.

(f) For the purposes of this paragraph, the term 'necessary transportation, lodging, and related expenses'

(1) includes reasonable expenses that are necessary for travel for a period not exceeding 3 days exclusive of travel time within the United States or 7 days exclusive of travel time outside of the United States unless approved in advance by the Select Committee on Ethics;

(2) is limited to reasonable expenditures for transportation, lodging, conference fees and materials, and food and refreshments, including reimbursement for necessary transportation, whether or not such transportation occurs within the periods described in clause (1);

(3) does not include expenditures for recreational activities, not does it include entertainment other than that provided to all attendees as an integral part of the event, except for activities or entertainment otherwise permissible under this rule; and

(4) may include travel expenses incurred on behalf of either the spouse or a child of the Member, officer, or employee, subject to a determination signed by the Member or officer (or in the case of an employee, the Member or officer under whose direct supervision the employee works) that the attendance of the spouse or child is appropriate to assist in the representation of the Senate.

(g) The Secretary of the Senate shall make all advance authorizations, certifications, and disclosures filed pursuant to this paragraph available for public inspection as soon as possible after they are received, but in no event prior to the completion of the relevant travel.

3. A gift prohibited by paragraph 1(a) includes the following:

(a) Anything provided by a registered lobbyist or an agent of a foreign principal to an entity that is maintained or controlled by a Member, officer, or employee.

(b) A charitable contribution (as defined in section 170(c) of the Internal Revenue Code of 1986) made by a registered lobbyist or an agent of a foreign principal on the basis of a designation, recommendation, or other specification of a Member, officer, or employee (not including a mass mailing or other solicitation directed to a broad category of persons or entities), other than a charitable contribution permitted by paragraph 4.

(c) A contribution or other payment by a registered lobbyist or an agent of a foreign principal to a legal expense fund established for the benefit of a Member, officer, or employee.

(d) A financial contribution or expenditure made by a registered lobbyist or an agent of a foreign principal relating to a conference, retreat, or similar event, sponsored by or affiliated with an official congressional organization, for or on behalf of Members, officers, or employees.

4. (a) A charitable contribution (as defined in section 170(c) of the Internal Revenue Code of 1986) made by a registered lobbyist or an agent of a foreign principal in lieu of an honorarium to a Member, officer, or employee shall not be considered a gift under this rule if it is reported as provided in subparagraph (b).

(b) A Member, officer, or employee who designates or recommends a contribution to a charitable organization in lieu of honoraria described in subparagraph (a) shall report within 30 days after such designation or recommendation to the Secretary of the Senate

(1) the name and address of the registered lobbyist who is making the contribution in lieu of honoraria;

(2) the date and amount of the contribution; and

(3) the name and address of the charitable organization designated or recommended by the Member.

The Secretary of the Senate shall make public information received pursuant to this subparagraph as soon as possible after it is received.

5. For purposes of this rule

(a) the term 'registered lobbyist' means a lobbyist registered under the Federal Regulation of Lobbying Act or any successor statute; and

(b) the term 'agent of a foreign principal' means an agent of a foreign principal registered under the Foreign Agents Registration Act.

6. All the provisions of this rule shall be interpreted and enforced solely by the Select Committee on Ethics.

APPENDIX 8-C

Outside Income Restrictions[166]

Income Level	Restriction
All members, officers, and employees of the House and Senate	*May not receive honoraria* for appearances, speeches, or articles.[167]
	May not use official influence to further personal financial interests.[168]
	May not represent others in a private capacity before the government.[169]
	May not accept compensation of any kind from a *foreign* government or act as an agent for a foreign principal.[170]
House and Senate: members only	*May not contract* with the federal government.[171]
	May not practice in the United States Court of Federal Claims or the Court of Appeals for the Federal Circuit.[172]
House and Senate: members and those employees paid at least 75 percent of a member's rate of basic pay ($130,500 in 2016)	*May not lobby* former colleagues (Senate and House for Members) for one year after leaving House; two years after leaving Senate (criminal penalties).[173]
House and Senate: members and those employees earning at least 120 percent of the GS-15 rate of basic pay ($123,175 in 2016)	*May not* receive more than 15 percent of the Member's base salary in total outside earned income ($27,495 in 2016).[174]
	May not receive compensation for providing professional services involving a fiduciary relationship, or for being employed by an organization that provides such services.
	May not allow their *names* to be used, regardless of compensation, by organizations providing fiduciary services.
	May not accept compensation for serving as a *board member or officer* of any organization.

(continued)

166. Adapted from SENATE ETHICS MANUAL, *supra* note 18, at 95–96; HOUSE ETHICS MANUAL, *supra* note 27; 102d Cong., 2d Sess. 83–84 (1992).

167. 5 U.S.C. app. 4, § 501(b) (2015); House Rule XXV, cl. 1 (114th Cong.); Senate Rule XXXVI (114th Cong.).

168. House Rule XXIII (114th Cong.); Senate Rule XXXVII, cls. 1, 4 (114th Cong.).

169. 18 U.S.C. § 203 (2015) (for compensation, applies to Members, officers, and employees); *id.* § 205 (regardless of compensation, applies to officers and employees only).

170. U.S. Const. art. I, § 9, cl. 8; 18 U.S.C. § 219 (2015).

171. 18 U.S.C. §§ 431–32 (2015); see also 41 U.S.C. § 6306 (2015).

172. 18 U.S.C. § 204 (2015).

173. 18 U.S.C. § 207(e) (2015).

174. 5 U.S.C. app. 4, § 501(a) (2015); House Rule XXV (114th Cong.); Senate Rule XXXVI (114th Cong.).

Outside Income Restrictions

Income Level	Restriction
House and Senate: members and those employees earning at least 120 percent of the GS-15 rate of basic pay ($123,175 in 2016)	*May not* accept compensation for *teaching*, without prior written approval from supervising ethics committee.[175] *Must file* annual financial disclosure forms.[176] Absent waiver from supervising Member, employee *may not contact* executive or judicial branch on non-legislative matters affecting their own significant financial interests.[177]
Senate only: all members, officers, and employees	*May not engage* in outside activities that are inconsistent with the conscientious performance of official duties.[178] *May not lobby* former colleagues for one year after leaving office (Senate Rule).[179] *May not hold* outside jobs without prior approval of supervising officer or Senator (officers and employees only).[180]
Senate only: members, officers, and those employees earning at least $25,000 a year	*May not affiliate* for the purpose of providing professional services for compensation.[181] *May not allow* their *names* to be used by organizations providing professional services for compensation.[182] *May not practice* a profession for compensation on Senate time.[183] *May not serve as officer or board member* of any publicly held or regulated entity, except 1) a 501(c) organization, if unpaid; 2) an organization principally available to Senators, officers, or employees of the Senate, or their families, if unpaid; 3) an organization on whose board the person served for at least 2 years before coming to Senate, if time required is minimal and person is not on committee with legislative jurisdiction over relevant regulatory body.[184] *Committee staff must divest* of substantial holdings affected by actions of employing committee, without permission of Select Committee and supervising Senator.[185]
House only: members and those employees earning at least 120 percent of the GS-15 rate of basic pay ($123,175 in 2016)	*May not receive book advances.* *May only receive book royalties* from established publishers pursuant to usual and customary contractual terms; contract must be approved by House Ethics Committee.[186]

---

175. 5 U.S.C. app. 4, § 502(a) (2015); House Rule XXV (114th Cong.); Senate Rule XXXVII (114th Cong.).
176. 5 U.S.C. §§ 101–11 (2015); House Rule XXVI (114th Cong.); Senate Rule XXXIV (114th Cong.).
177. House Rule XXIII cl. 12 (114th Cong.); Senate Rule XXXVII, cl. 12 (114th Cong.).
178. Senate Rule XXXVII, cl. 2 (114th Cong.).
179. Id. cls. 8, 9 (114th Cong.).
180. Id. cl. 3 (114th Cong.).
181. Id. cl. 5(a)(1) (114th Cong.).
182. Id. cl. 5(a)(2) (114th Cong.).
183. Id. cl. 5(a)(3) (114th Cong.).
184. Id. cl. 6(a) (114th Cong.).
185. Id. cl. 7 (114th Cong.).
186. House Rule XXV, cl. 3 (114th Cong.).

CHAPTER 9

Laws Governing Interactions with the Executive Branch

BY KIP F. WAINSCOTT

9-1 LDA Contacts and the Impact of the IRC Election

As discussed in Chapter 4, the Lobbing Disclosure Act (LDA) creates a framework pursuant to which lobbying activities undertaken before Congress and certain executive branch officials must be reported and publicly disclosed.[1] As the previous discussion of the LDA notes, the law's registration and reporting obligations may be triggered by making lobbying contacts and satisfying the law's monetary threshold for lobbying expenditures.[2] This chapter examines the LDA's definition of "lobbying contacts" in the context of executive branch lobbying, and also the impact of making the "the IRC election" on an organization's registration and reporting obligations under the LDA.

---

1. See Chapter 4 of this manual.
2. *Id.*

9-1.1 Executive Branch Lobbying Contacts under the LDA

The LDA defines "lobbying contact" to include a broad range of interactions with executive branch officials. Under the statute, the term means (1) an oral or written communication (2) directed to a covered executive branch official (3) that is made on behalf of a client (4) with regard to any of the following types of government action:

- The formulation, modification, or adoption of federal legislation, including legislative proposals (which would include appropriations measures or earmarking funds for a particular purpose);
- The formulation, modification, or adoption of a federal rule, regulation, executive order, or any other program, policy, or position of the U.S. government;
- The administration or execution of a federal program or policy (including the negotiation, award, or administration of a federal contract, grant, loan, permit, or license); and
- The nomination or confirmation of a person for a position subject to confirmation by the Senate.[3]

This definition is expansive, but it includes some notable exceptions. In particular, a lobbying contact under the LDA does not include communications directed to members of the public in an effort to encourage them to contact government officials (often characterized as "grassroots" or "indirect" lobbying). Moreover, the statute includes several specific exceptions that may be particularly applicable in the context of executive branch interactions, including

- Statements in response to a subpoena or administrative demand, or otherwise compelled by law;
- Statements made to agency officials regarding law enforcement investigations or proceedings;
- Statements made in compliance with formal agency adjudicatory procedures;
- Petitions for agency action;
- Statements in response to *Federal Register* notices or similar agency publications;
- Comments made on the public record during public proceedings;
- Requests for meetings or similar administrative requests, if the request does not include an attempt to influence a covered official; and
- Statements made during the meetings of federal advisory committees.[4]

As previous chapters have covered, the term "lobbying activities" is broader than the lobbying contacts described here; lobbying activities also include "efforts in support of such contacts, including preparation and planning activities, research and other background work that is intended, at the time it is performed, for use in

---

3. 2 U.S.C. §§ 1602(8)(A)(i)–(iv) (2015).
4. 2 U.S.C. §§ 1602(8)(B)(v)–(vi), 1602(8)(B)(ix)–(x), 1602(8)(B)(xii)–(xv) (2015).

contacts," as well as "coordination with the lobbying activities of others."[5] For a complete discussion of "lobbying activities" under the LDA, see Chapter 4 of this manual.

9-1.2 Who Is a Covered Executive Branch Official under the LDA?

The LDA defines the term "covered executive branch official" to include any of the following:

- The president, vice president, and any person functioning in the capacity of an officer or employee in the Executive Office of the President;
- Any officer or employee serving in a position in level I-V of the Executive Schedule, such as agency heads and equivalent officials, as well as certain members of the uniformed services at high pay levels (equivalent to, or exceeding, pay grade O-7);
- Any other employee serving in a position of a "confidential, policy-determining, policy-making, or policy-advocating character." This includes Schedule C employees who play a significant role in the formulation of policy.[6]

When interacting with an executive branch official, it may be difficult to discern whether the official is covered under the LDA definition. If an official's status is unclear, just ask; covered officials are required to inform persons or entities of their covered status upon request.[7]

9-1.3 What Is the IRC Election?

The "IRC election" is an option the LDA makes available that allows some entities to use Internal Revenue Code definitions instead of LDA definitions for purposes of determining whether they must register and, if so, what they must report.[8] The different ways of measuring lobbying activity have the largest impact on the expense figure reported on the LDA form, and the impact is most significant for organizations that conduct sizable amounts of executive branch direct or grassroots lobbying, political activity, or legislative grassroots lobbying or ballot measure activity. Any such organization may be interested in investigating the option to determine whether using it might help it meet its reporting objectives.

9-1.4 Who Is Eligible for the IRC Election?

As a general matter, the IRC election is available only to organizations that lobby on their own behalves; it is not available to lobbying firms. Among these self-lobbying organizations, two types of entities may permissibly opt to use the IRC election:

---

5. *Id.* § 1602(7).
6. *Id.* § 1602(3).
7. *Id.* § 1609(c).
8. *See* 2 U.S.C. § 1610 (2015).

- First, the IRC election is available to organizations that are subject to section 162(e) of the IRC and tax-exempt organizations that use section 162(e) to calculate their lobbying expenses for IRS purposes.[9] This generally includes any organization that uses section 162(e) for calculating tax-deductible business expenses, including both for-profit companies and nonprofit organizations such as trade associations that track and report their lobbying under section 162(e). Collectively, organizations in this category will be referred to as "Section 162(e) Organizations."[10]
- Second, the IRC election is available to public charities organized under section 501(c)(3) of the IRC that have made the lobbying election under sections 501(h) and 4911 of the Internal Revenue Code.[11] Throughout this chapter, organizations in this category are referred to as "Qualifying Public Charities."[12]

An entity using the IRC election must do so on a calendar year basis, and must apply the applicable IRC definitions consistently on all LDA reports and related calculations.[13] In addition, an electing organization must report for LDA purposes all lobbying expenses that fall within the applicable IRC definition.[14]

9-2 The IRC Election for Section 162(e) Organizations

As noted above, section 162(e) organizations eligible for the IRC election will include both taxable businesses (other than lobbying firms) and tax-exempt organizations like trade associations.[15]

9-2.1 Section 162(e) Expenses

When calculating lobbying expenses for its quarterly LD-2 report, an electing Section 162(e) Organization must use figures derived from its nondeductible "lobbying and political expenditures" as defined by section 162(e), rather than a calculation based on the LDA definitions.[16] This framework will include expenses that would not necessarily be included in calculations made under the LDA framework and will exclude certain expenses that the LDA would require to be included.

---

9. *Id.* § 1610(b).

10. For additional information regarding lobbying by nonprofit organizations, see Chapter 11.

11. 2 U.S.C. § 1610(a).

12. For a complete discussion of lobbying by section 501(c)(3) entities, see Chapter 11.

13. Sec'y of the Senate & Clerk of the House of Representatives, Lobbying Disclosure Act Guidance (revised Feb. 15, 2013) [hereinafter Revised Guidance], *available at* http://lobbyingdisclosure.house.gov/amended_lda_guide.html and contained in Appendix 4-A.

14. *Id.* As described in greater detail below, this amount may include grassroots lobbying and federal and state government lobbying; however, all of these expenses will be reported in one total amount, so the quarterly LD-2 report will not indicate the amount related to different levels of government and types of lobbying activities.

15. The Secretary of the Senate and Clerk of the House of Representatives have advised that this definition may also include certain trade associations that are not required by the IRC to report nondeductible lobbying expenses to their members (i.e., those whose members are tax exempt). Revised Guidance, *supra* note 13, and Appendix 4-A.

16. 2 U.S.C. § 1610(b)(1) (2015).

Section 162(e) requires organizations to track amounts paid or incurred in connection with four principal categories of expenses:

1. Direct legislative lobbying;
2. Direct lobbying with certain covered executive branch officials regarding their official actions or positions;
3. Grassroots lobbying (including attempting to influence ballot initiatives); and
4. Intervention in political campaigns.[17]

Direct legislative lobbying includes "any attempt to influence any legislation through a lobbying communication . . . with any member or employee of a legislative body or with any government official or employee who may participate in the formulation of the legislation."[18] A communication is an "attempt to influence" if it "refers to specific legislation and reflects a view on that legislation," or if it "clarifies, amplifies, modifies, or provides support for views reflected in a prior lobbying communication."[19]

"Legislative bodies" includes federal and state legislatures, but does not include local councils.[20] "Legislation" includes most legislative proposals, including bills that have not yet been formally introduced.[21]

Direct legislative lobbying for section 162(e) purposes thus overlaps with certain of the reporting categories the LDA requires. With respect to communications with federal legislative branch officials, it is narrower than the LDA because it only covers communications about legislation. It does not reach communications on other topics, like executive branch action. With respect to communications with federal executive branch officials, it reaches much more broadly, beyond LDA-covered officials to communications with anyone at all in the executive branch if the communication is an attempt to influence legislation and the individual "may participate in the formulation of legislation." And direct lobbying as measured by section 162(e) is broader than the LDA in one other significant respect: it covers state-level lobbying as well as federal.

Section 162(e) covers more than just direct legislative lobbying, however. It reaches direct communications with certain covered federal executive branch officials on their official positions, including non-legislative topics. Like the LDA, this provision of section 162(e) enumerates only certain officials for coverage. They are

1. The president and vice president;
2. A cabinet officer, including anyone designated as cabinet-level status, and anyone serving in level I of the Executive Schedule;
3. Immediate deputies of cabinet-level officers;
4. The two most senior-level officers of each agency within the Executive Office of the President; and
5. Any officer or employee of the White House Office within the Executive Office of the President.[22]

---

17. *See* I.R.C. § 162(e).
18. Treas. Reg. § 1.162-29(b).
19. *Id.* § 1.162-29(b)(3).
20. *Id.* § 1.162-29(b)(6).
21. *Id.* § 1.162-29(b)(5).
22. I.R.C. § 162(e)(6).

Another significant difference between the LDA and section 162(e) definitions is that the Internal Revenue Code requires inclusion of certain grassroots lobbying expenses, both at the state and federal level. For these purposes, grassroots lobbying includes "any attempt to influence the general public, or segments thereof, with respect to elections, legislative matters, or referendums."[23] This includes attempts to "urge or encourage the public to contact members of a legislative body for the purpose of proposing, supporting, or opposing legislation."[24] This definition can encompass all kinds of communications, including issue-based television advertising and communications aimed at company employees about pending legislation.

Finally, as noted above, section 162(e) requires tracking and reporting of expenses for political intervention as well. These would include any expenses incurred for administration of a company's political action committee (PAC),[25] as well as direct corporate political contributions to candidates at the state or local level.

A Section 162(e) Organization that elects to use its section 162(e) nondeductible figure for purposes of calculating its quarterly LD-2 expenses must report the whole amount of lobbying-related section 162(e) expenses incurred for the relevant quarter on its LD-2 report. Thus, the figure may include expenses for state and grassroots lobbying that the LDA would not otherwise require the organization to report.

9-2.2 Triggering Lobbying Registration

Most organizations find the impact of the section 162(e) election to be most significant when calculating the quarterly lobbying expense figure. However, opting to use the section 162(e) definitions also has an impact on determining whether to register in the first place and, once registered, in determining which individuals meet the definition of "lobbyist."

An organization deciding whether it must register may opt to use section 162(e) definitions for determining whether it has met the monetary expense threshold for registration.[26] When determining whether direct contacts meet the two-contacts threshold, the LDA definitions will continue to apply to federal legislative branch lobbying activities, but the IRC definitions will apply to executive branch activities.[27]

9-3 The IRC Election for Qualifying Public Charities

A Qualifying Public Charity may also use the IRC election. Public charities must already report several lobbying-related expense amounts to the IRS as part of their annual reporting obligations on IRS Form 990. The IRC election permits the electing charity to substitute the lobbying expenditure amounts reported to the IRS for

---

23. *Id.* § 162(e)(1)(C).
24. Treas. Reg. § 1.162-20(c)(4).
25. I.R.S. Tech. Adv. Mem. 82-02-019; I.R.S. Tech. Adv. Mem. 82-02-021.
26. 2 U.S.C. § 1610(b)(1) (2015).
27. *Id.* § 1610(b)(2).

tax purposes as a means of determining whether the LDA expense threshold has been met and to calculate its lobbying expenditures for quarterly reporting.[28]

Moreover, the IRC election permits a Qualifying Public Charity to import certain IRC definitions for purposes of determining whether a lobbying contact has been made in the context of federal executive branch lobbying, as described below.

9-3.1 Calculating Expenses for Qualifying Public Charities

Under the IRC election, a Qualifying Public Charity will have the option of using the narrower IRC definition of "influencing legislation" for determining its lobbying expenditures, in lieu of a calculation derived from the LDA definitions.[29]

In this context, a "direct lobbying communication" means any attempt to influence any legislation through a communication with members or employees of a legislative body or any government official or employee who may participate in the formulation of legislation.[30]

The IRS defines "legislation" broadly here to include "action by the Congress, any state legislature, any local council, or similar legislative body, or by the public in a referendum, ballot initiative, constitutional amendment, or similar procedure."[31] This definition includes proposed treaties requiring Senate approval, as well as lobbying on nominations requiring Senate confirmation.[32]

Significantly, this definition includes grassroots legislative lobbying, as well as federal and state-level legislative lobbying;[33] however, it does not include federal direct or grassroots executive branch lobbying on non-legislative subjects.[34]

Qualifying Public Charities should also note that contacts with the organization's own members must, in some cases, be included when calculating lobbying expenses under the IRC definitions. In particular, the IRC definitions will apply when an organization asks its members to contact legislators directly in support of (or opposition to) specific legislation, or when an organization encourages its members to individually engage in grassroots lobbying.[35]

The IRC definitions applicable to a Qualifying Public Charity's executive branch contacts are appreciably narrower than the LDA definitions. In this context, the definition of a lobbying contact generally will not extend to communications directed to executive branch personnel unless the executive branch contact may play a role in the formulation of the specific legislation that is being discussed. More precisely, the definition extends to lobbying communications directed to an official or employee who may participate in the formulation of legislation, but only if the principal purpose of the executive branch communication is to influence legislation,[36] and only if the communication "refers to specific legislation

---

28. *Id.* § 1610(a).
29. 2 U.S.C. § 1610(a)(1) (2015); 26 U.S.C. § 4911(d) (2015).
30. Treas. Reg. § 56.4911-2(b).
31. *Id.* § 56-4911-2(d)(1)(i).
32. *Id.*
33. Treas. Reg. § 56.4911-2(b)(2).
34. *See* 26 U.S.C. § 4911(d)(2)(E) (2015) (excluding from the definition of "influencing legislation" any communication with an executive branch official or employee unless the communication's principal purpose is to influence legislation).
35. 26 C.F.R. §§ 56.4911-5(c), (d) (2015).
36. *See Id.* § 56.4911-2(b)(1)(i)(B).

[and] . . . reflects a view on such legislation."[37] The IRC definition would not, for example, extend to communications directed to an executive branch employee regarding an administrative rulemaking.

9-3.2 Triggering Lobbying Registration

Under the IRC election, the LDA definitions will continue to apply to a Qualifying Public Charity's federal legislative branch lobbying activities for purposes of determining whether lobbying activities may result in lobbying contacts triggering LDA registration.[38] However, the IRC definitions will apply when reviewing executive branch activities for this purpose.[39]

9-4 Impact of the IRC Election on Executive Branch Lobbying Contacts

The option to calculate lobbying expenses using these alternative bases can have significant implications for an entity's registration and reporting obligations under the LDA.

For electing organizations, the IRC definitions will play a significant role in determining who is a listed lobbyist. This carries implications not only for registration and quarterly reporting purposes but also for purposes of LD-203 filing obligations and bundling disclosure.[40] This fact may be relevant to the initial decision as to whether to use the IRC definitions when registration is required.[41]

Although the IRC definitions can be more expansive in certain areas (they extend, for example, to state and local legislative lobbying activities), in the context of federal executive branch interactions, their scope is much narrower than that of their LDA counterparts. In particular, lobbying under the IRC definitions does not include most actions taken to influence administrative agencies.

By way of illustration, lobbying a federal agency on an administrative rulemaking may not result in a lobbying contact at all if done by an electing Qualifying Public Charity.[42] Similarly, an electing Section 162(e) Organization may lobby a federal agency regarding an administrative rulemaking without meeting the IRC definition of a lobbying contact if the contacts include only lower-level Schedule C employees. Only officials at the highest levels in an agency are deemed to be covered officials under the IRC's definitions applicable to non-legislative communications with the executive branch.[43] However, under the LDA definitions, an entity's communications with these same Schedule C employees (or any agency employee of a "confidential, policy-determining, policy-making, or policy-advocating character") would almost certainly result

---

37. *Id.* § 56.4911-2(b)(1)(ii).

38. 2 U.S.C. §§ 1610(a)(2), 1610(b)(2) (2015).

39. *Id.*

40. A complete discussion of LD-203 reporting can be found in Chapter 5 of this manual.

41. *See* William V. Luneburg and A. L. (Lorry) Spitzer, *Registration, Quarterly Reporting, and Related Requirements*, in 144 THE LOBBYING MANUAL (4th ed. 2009).

42. *See* U.S. GENERAL ACCOUNTING OFFICE, Federal Lobbying/Differences in Lobbying Definitions and Their Impact, GAO/GGD-99-38, App. II 40 (Apr. 1999).

43. *Id.*

in a lobbying contact if the subject matter pertained to such an administrative rulemaking.[44]

While these examples serve to illustrate important differences in the applicable definitions, in practice few entities engage in only discrete types of federal agency lobbying and other non-lobbying activities under the IRC definitions. It is therefore not particularly useful to think about the IRC election as a means of avoiding registration under the LDA; more accurately, the IRC election is an alternative framework under which to catalogue and disclose an entity's lobbying activities on the whole (while keeping in mind that the LDA definitions will continue to apply to an entity's federal legislative lobbying activities, irrespective of whether the IRC election is made).

9-5 Concluding Note

For eligible entities, the IRC election offers intriguing alternatives to the LDA's standard reporting and registration definitions, particularly in the context of executive branch interactions. However, as noted throughout this chapter, the broader implications of LDA registering and reporting under the IRC definitions can be complicated and, in certain cases, imprudent. In addition to requiring disclosure of lobbying expenses for state, local, and grassroots activities that are not implicated under the LDA definitions, entities' communications with their own members may qualify as lobbying under the IRC election if the communications ask the members to contact legislators in support of or opposition to specific legislation.[45] For many organizations, the IRC election would therefore subject them to reporting activities that, for LDA purposes at least, the entities do not intuitively understand to be lobbying activities.

Moreover, as noted above, the IRC election will not impact the application of the LDA definitions to any federal legislative branch lobbying that an electing organization may undertake. In light of this, organizations engaging in both legislative and executive branch lobbying may indeed complicate their federal lobbying compliance by implicating two different sets of governing definitions.

---

44. 2 U.S.C. §§ 1602(8)(A)(i)–(iv) (2015).
45. *See* 26 C.F.R. § 56.4911-5 (2015).

Part II
Federal Laws Related
to Specialized Areas
or Aspects of Lobbying

Introduction to Part II

Specialized federal laws pertain to various areas and aspects of federal government relations work. These include, for example: lobbying with regard to judicial decrees entered in antitrust cases; the use of federal funds for lobbying and lobbying with unappropriated funds to obtain federal contracts, grants, loans, and cooperative agreements; the tax treatment of lobbying expenses incurred by businesses and tax-exempt entities; the practice of political intelligence gathering; and lobbying on behalf of foreign entities. This Part II of the manual focuses on the statutes and regulations implicated in these specialized areas and aspects of federal government relations practice.

CHAPTER 10

Antitrust Consent Decree (Tunney Act) Lobbying

BY THOMAS M. SUSMAN

10-1 Introduction

Attempting to guarantee that settlements of antitrust actions brought by the government are actually in "the public interest," Congress, in 1974, passed the Antitrust Procedures and Penalties Act (Tunney Act).[1] With this legislation, Congress hoped to ensure "the integrity of and public confidence in procedures relating to settlements [of antitrust claims] via consent decree."[2]

---

1. 15 U.S.C. §§ 16(a)–(i) (2015). The legislation is popularly known as the "Tunney Act" in recognition of the bill's primary sponsor, the former U.S. senator from California, John Tunney. For another recent evaluation of the Act, *see* Warren S. Grimes, *Transparency in Federal Antitrust Enforcement*, 51 Buff. L. Rev. 937, 960–63 (2003). *See also* John J. Flynn & Darren Bush, *The Misuse and Abuse of the Tunney Act: The Adverse Consequences of the "Microsoft Fallacies,"* 34 Loy. U. Chi. L.J. 749 (2003).

2. H.R. Rep. No. 93-1463 (1974). *See* United States v. AT&T, 552 F. Supp. 131, 148 (1982), *aff'd*, Maryland v. United States, 460 U.S. 1001 (1983). For a critical assessment of "regulatory-style" antitrust consent decrees of the kind that the judicial review standards of the Tunney Act were designed to reach, *see* Richard A. Epstein, Antitrust Consent Decrees in Theory and Practice: Why Less is More (2007).

Accordingly, Congress drafted the Tunney Act to "transform a procedure which was generally accomplished in a series of private, informal negotiations between antitrust lawyers and attorneys for the defendant, into one that is exposed to the full light of public awareness and judicial scrutiny."[3]

This transformation was to occur through two major changes in antitrust consent decree processes. First, the statute was aimed at reducing secrecy surrounding consent decree negotiations by requiring the Department of Justice to disclose the rationale and terms of any consent decree proposal when filed with a court. This disclosure was then to be followed by a public comment period.[4] Second, the Tunney Act sought to eliminate judicial "rubber stamping" of consent decrees by requiring courts to impose independent review on the terms negotiated by the Department of Justice.[5]

In 1995, the U.S. Court of Appeals for the D.C. Circuit overturned the district court's use of its Tunney Act authority to refuse to approve a decree on substantive grounds. In what some considered to be judicial abrogation of the required role of the courts in reviewing consent decrees, the appellate court suggested that courts should accept all consent decrees that do not appear "to make a mockery of judicial power." The D.C. Circuit ordered the district court to enter the original consent decree.[6] In 2002 another Microsoft antitrust consent decree came before the D.C. District Court, which approved the decree with only minor changes, over the strong objections of competitors and customers.[7] The congressional response was reflected in enactment of legislation to amend the Tunney Act to enhance judicial scrutiny of antitrust consent decrees,[8] though the efficacy of the new provisions has been questioned.[9]

To ensure the integrity of the new process established by the 1974 act—and with one eye on the extensive lobbying undertaken by ITT Corp. seeking favorable resolution by consent decree of the antitrust challenges leveled against it by the Department of Justice[10]—Congress included a requirement (section 16(g)) for disclosing lobbying contacts made on behalf of antitrust defendants:

> Not later than 10 days following the date of the filing of any proposal for a consent judgment under subsection (b) of this section, each defendant shall file with the district court a description of any and all written or oral communications by or on behalf of such defendant, including any and all written or oral communications on behalf of such defendant by any officer, director, employee, or agent of such defendant, or other person, with any

3. See United States v. Central Contracting Co., 527 F. Supp. 1101, 1103 (E.D. Va. 1981) (quoting 119 Cong. Rec. 24,598 (July 18, 1973) (statement of Senator Tunney)). However, the act has been characterized as "an imperfect and incomplete means to achieve" its objectives. Lawrence M. Frankel, Rethinking the Tunney Act: A Model for Judicial Review of Antitrust Consent Decrees, 75 Antitrust L.J. 549, 575 (2008).

4. See AT&T, 552 F. Supp. at 148–49. See also R. Hewitt Pate, Antitrust Enforcement at the United States Department of Justice: Issues in Merger Investigations and Litigation, 2003 Colum. Bus. L. Rev. 411, 422.

5. See AT&T, 552 F. Supp. at 149.

6. United States v. Microsoft Corp., 56 F.3d 1448, 1462 (D.C. Cir. 1995), reversing 159 F.R.D. 318 (D.D.C. 1995).

7. United States v. Microsoft Corp., 231 F. Supp. 2d 144 (D.D.C. 2002), aff'd Massachusetts v. Microsoft Corp., 373 F.3d 1199 (D.C. Cir. 2004).

8. Pub. L. 108–237, title II, § 221(a)(1)(B), June 22, 2004, 118 Stat. 668.

9. See generally Joseph G. Krauss, David J. Saylor, and Logan M. Breed, The Tunney Act: A House Still Standing, The Antitrust Source (June 2007), available at http://www.americanbar.org/content/dam/aba/publishing/antitrust_source/Jun07_Krauss6_20f.authcheckdam.pdf.

10. See Section 10-2 of this chapter.

officer or employee of the United States concerning or relevant to such proposal, except that any such communications made by counsel of record alone with the Attorney General or the employees of the Department of Justice alone shall be excluded from the requirements of this subsection.[11]

Although the provision may appear straightforward, lawyers faced with the obligation to comply must come to grips with several crucial ambiguities: the length of the disclosure period is not clear, and there are no definitions of the terms "officer or employee of the United States" or "counsel of record." This chapter discusses the scope and application of the Tunney Act and addresses those ambiguities.

10-2 Background of Reporting Requirement

The impetus for the antitrust consent decree lobbying disclosure requirement came in 1972 with the revelation of the events surrounding the settlement of an antitrust case brought against International Telephone & Telegraph (ITT).[12] The government had filed three cases against ITT challenging its rapid corporate expansion through mergers. After losing twice, the Department of Justice reached a settlement with ITT in the third case. The settlement, without any details regarding the negotiations, was made public in 1971.[13] The announcement of the settlement led to some controversy,[14] but it was not until the 1972 confirmation hearings on Richard Kleindienst's nomination as attorney general that suspicions regarding the settlement were voiced, including "allegations linking settlement of the ITT cases with a commitment of $400,000 by ITT to assist the City of San Diego in preparation for the upcoming Republican National Convention."[15] Moreover, "[e]xtensive congressional hearings established that ITT had engaged in an extensive lobbying campaign throughout the Nixon Administration in an effort to obtain relief from the antitrust litigation."[16] Against the background of these allegations, Congress enacted section 16(g) of the Tunney Act to require public disclosure, subject to certain limitations, by antitrust defendants of written or oral communications by or on behalf of the defendants concerning consent decree proposals.[17]

---

11. 15 U.S.C. § 16(g) (2015).

12. *See* Note, *The ITT Dividend: Reform of Department of Justice Consent Decree Procedures*, 73 COLUM. L. REV. 594, 603 (1973).

13. *Id.* at 604.

14. *See id.* at 604–05 for details regarding Ralph Nader's involvement in challenging the ITT consent decree; *see also* United States v. ITT Corp., 1974-1 Trade Cas. (CCH) ¶ 74,872 (D. Conn. 1974) (ruling on request of amici curiae, Ralph Nader and Reuben Robertson).

15. United States v. Central Contracting Co., 537 F. Supp. 571, 574 (E.D. Va. 1982).

16. *Id. See also* 120 CONG. REC. 38,585 (Dec. 9, 1974) (statement of Senator Tunney):

> The genesis of this legislation came during the hearings held by the Senate Judiciary Committee . . . which quickly became known as the ITT hearings, because the major issue involved allegations that a massive behind-closed-doors campaign resulted in halting the Justice Department's prosecution of the ITT case and its hasty settlement favorable to the company.

See generally "Nomination of Richard G. Kleindienst," Exec. Rep. 92-19, 92d Cong., 2d Sess., Comm. on the Judiciary pt. 4 (May 31, 1972).

17. 15 U.S.C.A. § 16(g) (2015). *See also* United States v. Gillette Co., 406 F. Supp. 713, 715 (D. Mass. 1975) ("The legislative history shows clearly that Congress did not intend the court's action to be merely pro forma, or to be limited to what appears on the surface. Nor can one overlook the circumstances under which the act was passed, indicating Congress' desire to impose a check not only on the government's expertise—or at the least, its exercise of it—but even on its good faith.").

10-3 Communications Covered

The Tunney Act's lobbying disclosure requirement appears on its face to be quite broad; it includes non-exempted "written or oral communications by or on behalf of . . . defendant[s], or other person[s], with any officer or employee of the United States concerning or relevant to [the consent decree] proposal."[18] The only exempt communications are those that fall within the "counsel of record exemption," discussed below.[19] While the filing obligation falls solely on defendants, the defendant also has a duty to disclose any communications of which it has knowledge concerning the consent decree proposal, even if they were made on behalf of another person. This could cause special problems when there are multiple defendants. Moreover, the legislative history suggests that "reasonable efforts have to be made [by defendants] to find out what communications with Government officials took place. Otherwise, the main purpose of Section 16(g) would be thwarted, and defendants could wear blinders in making their disclosures to the court."[20] Defendants, however, are not responsible for disclosing unauthorized contacts; for example, "a corporation clearly should not be responsible for a letter written to the Department of Justice by an irate shareholder."[21]

10-3.1 Period of Covered Communications

Section 16(g) establishes a disclosure period: The end of the period occurs when the proposal for a consent decree is filed with the court. But when does the period begin? The statute is ambiguous. One might assume that the obligation begins with the filing of the complaint or, perhaps earlier, when a draft proposal of a decree is tendered to the defendant(s), but the answer is not that easy. The disclosure period does not commence upon any specific action; rather, it begins whenever there are communications "concerning or relevant to the proposal" that is ultimately filed.[22]

The legislative history of the Tunney Act indicates that Congress intended a broad construction of the phrase "concerning or relevant to the proposal" to include all non-exempted communications that may have had some effect on the

---

18. 15 U.S.C. § 16(g) (2015).

19. *See* Section 10-4 of this chapter.

20. 120 Cong. Rec. 36,342 (Nov. 19, 1974) (statement of Rep. Holtzman).

21. S. Rep. No. 93-298, at 3 (1973).

22. Although a disclosure period initiated by the filing of a complaint might make sense, it is not unusual for the Antitrust Division of the Department of Justice to file a proposed consent decree at the same time that it files a complaint. "This procedure permits the consent decree to incorporate prior negotiations between the Division and the parties." E. Thomas Sullivan, *The Antitrust Division as a Regulatory Agency: An Enforcement Policy in Transition*, 64 Wash. U. L. Rev. 997, 1041 (1986). Thus, if the disclosure clock was started by the filing of a complaint, the purpose of the section 16(g) requirement would be defeated in many instances.

The legislative history of section 16(g) indicates that Congress was well aware of the Department of Justice's practice of negotiating first and filing later and wanted to cover that practice. Congress, therefore, noted that the filing requirements extended to "*prospective* defendants in those situations in which a simultaneous filing of a complaint and a proposed settlement occurs." H.R. Rep. No. 93-1463 (1974) (emphasis added). Given the tenor of the legislative history, and because defendants cannot foresee how a "case" will end, lawyers must advise clients that pre-complaint communications that wind up leading to a settlement will have to be disclosed.

settlement of antitrust suits that culminate in consent decrees.[23] This inclusiveness was noted during the House debate:

> There is of course nothing wrong with trying to negotiate a settlement, but certainly there is something wrong in not having the public and other interested parties, such as the competitors affected, know about the nature of the contacts made, if those contacts go beyond the mere technical negotiation among the lawyers to the parties. Accordingly, Section 16(g) . . . requires defendants in these consent decree cases to file with the court a description of all contacts the defendant had with Government officials concerning the settlement.[24]

Consistent with this legislative history, the courts have reached the conclusion that the disclosure period begins with the first nonexempt communication. For instance, *United States v. Assoc. Milk Producers Inc. (AMPI)*,[25] one of the first cases to implement the requirements of the Tunney Act, supports coverage of pre-filing lobbying contacts. In *AMPI*, the defendant had been engaged in intensive lobbying activities before the filing of the antitrust complaint. Although the court said that it would not be necessary to add those communications to the defendant's section 16(g) statement, its reasoning suggests that it was unnecessary to expand the disclosure statement only because the additional information on lobbying activities had already been exposed in pretrial discovery.[26] The *AMPI* court did request, however, that the defendant "amplify the Section 16(g) information" and include "any and all contacts which may have been made in connection with earlier unsuccessful attempts to negotiate a specific consent decree in this case."[27] In other words, in keeping with the expansive scope of section 16(g) suggested in its legislative history, the court indicated that the disclosure requirement goes beyond communications concerning the specific consent decree ultimately filed.

United States v. Central Contracting Co.[28] provides additional support for commencing the disclosure period with the earliest nonexempt communication "concerning or relevant to" the consent decree. In *Central Contracting*, the court noted:

> In sum, the purpose and effect of . . . [the Tunney Act] procedures are to require public disclosure of all steps leading to the proposed consent

---

23. This broad interpretation is supported by numerous references in the legislative history of the Tunney Act. For example, H.R. Rep. 93-1463 at 6540 (1974) states that "defendants are required to describe *all* communications made by them or on their behalf but only *in connection with* cases subject to be settled by a consent decree." (emphasis added). Moreover, the same report notes that section 16(g) is to "insure that no loopholes exist in the obligation to disclose *all* lobbying contacts made by defendants *in antitrust cases culminating* in a proposal for a consent decree." *Id.* at 6543 (emphasis added). Rep. Seiberling stated that section 16(g) "requires defendants . . . to file . . . a description of all contacts the defendant had with government officials *concerning* the settlement." 120 CONG. REC. H. 36,342 (Nov. 19, 1974) (remarks of Rep. Seiberling) (emphasis added).

24. 120 CONG REC. 36,342 (Nov. 19, 1974) (remarks of Rep. Seiberling).

25. 394 F. Supp. 29 (W.D. Mo. 1975), *aff'd*, 534 F.2d 113 (8th Cir. 1976).

26. *AMPI*, 394 F. Supp. at 40.

27. *Id.* at 38.

28. 527 F. Supp. 1101 (E.D. Va. 1982).

judgment and thereby to encourage additional comment from the public, to which the Justice Department must respond.[29]

The "all steps" language of the court, although not specifically directed toward section 16(g) disclosure, when read together with the court's explication of the purpose of the act in general, indicates that the disclosure period has no particular procedural trigger. Rather, the objective is for the court and the public to have all relevant information regarding "negotiations." This would appear to include communications made before the presentation of any specific proposal or even before the filing of a complaint, if prospective defendants are on notice of an Antitrust Division investigation.[30]

This conclusion is also supported by *United States v. LTV Corp.*,[31] where the court specifically discussed some of the communications disclosed in the defendant's section 16(g) statement. Those communications included pre-filing negotiations conducted immediately following the Department of Justice's announced opposition to the defendant's proposal for a settlement.[32] The court viewed the reporting period as having begun as soon as the Antitrust Division's opposition was announced.[33]

In sum, there is nothing to suggest that any specific procedural event is necessary to trigger the start of the disclosure period. More than timing, the question is one of relevance. Lawyers should not assume that pre-complaint or pre-proposal communications will not have to be disclosed. In enacting the disclosure requirement, Congress intended to eliminate the "'excessive secrecy' of the consent decree process . . . [that had undermined] confidence in the legal system."[34] If defendants themselves are talking with government officials about any aspect of an antitrust investigation, those contacts may have to be disclosed when a proposal for a consent decree is filed.

10-3.2 Communications with "Officers or Employees of the United States"

While executive branch officers and employees are plainly covered by the Tunney Act's reporting requirements, the statute does not address whether members

---

29. *Id.* at 1104.

30. In a later proceeding concerning the *Central Contracting* settlement, 537 F. Supp. 571 (E.D. Va. 1981), the court addressed the government's obligation to disclose a letter sent to an Assistant U.S. Attorney from defendant's counsel. That obligation arose pursuant to section 16(b) of the Tunney Act, which requires the Department of Justice to file a competitive impact statement and a disclosure statement listing all "determinative" documents regarding the settlement. *Id.* at 573. The letter provided background information and also stated that the defendant's attorney was "prepared to recommend that Central settle the criminal case and all *future* litigation with the United States by agreeing, *inter alia*, to accept 'a consent decree similar to the one agreed to by [another party].'" *Id.* at 576 (emphasis added). In a footnote, the court pointed out that the letter would be exempt from section 16(g) disclosure because it was a communication between the attorney of record and the Department of Justice. *Id.* at 576, n.6. See Section 10-4 for a discussion of the "counsel of record" exemption. The correspondence itself indicates that, although a criminal case had begun, there was no pending civil action. Nevertheless, the court implies that, even if no civil case had been initiated, such a communication would fall within the section 16(g) disclosure requirement if it had been made by the defendant rather than by its lawyer.

31. 1984-2 Trade Cas. (CCH) ¶ 66,133 (D.D.C. 1984).

32. *Id.* at 66,335. The complaint and stipulation were later filed simultaneously.

33. *Id.* at 66,334–35.

34. *AT&T*, 552 F. Supp. at 148.

of Congress are to be considered "officers or employees of the United States." Although there is a provision of the Constitution indicating that members of Congress cannot serve as "officers" of the United States during their terms as members,[35] and a number of federal statutes exclude Congress from this class,[36] Senator Tunney's statements in the legislative history of section 16(g) are clear and direct:

> Included under this provision are contacts on behalf of a defendant by any of its officers, directors, employees or agents or any other person acting on behalf of the defendant, with any Federal official or employee. Thus, for example, the provision would include contacts with Members of Congress or staff, Cabinet officials, staff members of executive departments and White House staff.
>
> [The disclosure requirements] apply equally to contact with any branch of Government including the Congress. I believe it is important that we in the Congress accept the same scrutiny as we would impose on any other branch. Furthermore, I believe there is a great deal to be gained by having a corporate official who seeks to influence a pending antitrust case through congressional pressure, know that his activity is subject to public view.[37]

Senator Tunney's remarks are consistent with the purposes of the statute as a whole. Nonetheless, in a highly visible antitrust case against Microsoft Corporation involving extensive lobbying activities, the D.C. Circuit, affirming the district court, concluded that "the term 'United States' as used in Section16(g) refers only to the Executive Branch."[38] The Court of Appeals offered two grounds for its conclusion. First, since every one of the other seventeen references to "United States" in the Tunney Act denotes only the executive branch, under basic tenets of statutory construction, the reference in section 16(g) should be similarly read.[39]

---

35. *See* U.S. CONST. art. I, § 6, cl. 2.

36. For instance, title 5 of the United States Code does not contemplate members of Congress as officers or employees of the United States. *See also* 28 U.S.C. § 1391(e) (2015) (venue statute does not include members as officers or employees). However, there are specific statutes that have been interpreted to include members of Congress within the definition of officers or employees of the United States. In Lamar v. United States, 241 U.S. 103 (1916), the Supreme Court held that a congressman was an "officer or employee" of the United States for purposes of what is now 18 U.S.C. § 912 (prohibiting impersonation of an officer or employee of the United States). The Court stated that the question was not a constitutional one, but rather one of statutory interpretation. *See Lamar*, 241 U.S. at 112. In arriving at its interpretation, the Court looked primarily to the purpose of the statute but noted that, if the answer was still not apparent, it could also consider the common understanding of the terms, other statutes, and prior Court decisions. *Id.* at 112–13. *See also* Liberation News Serv. v. Eastland, 426 F.2d 1379, 1384 (2d Cir. 1970) (court looks to legislative history to determine who are "officers or employees" within the meaning of statute).

37. 118 CONG. REC. 31,676 (Sept. 21, 1972); 119 CONG. REC. 3453 (Feb. 6, 1973) (remarks of Senator Tunney). Senator Tunney even filed an Affidavit in the *Microsoft* case reiterating his perspective. *See* http://www.justice.gov/atr/cases/ms_tuncom/major/mtc-00032065.htm.

38. Commonwealth of Massachusetts v. Microsoft Corp., 373 F.3d 1199 (D.C. Cir. 2004), *affirming* United States v. Microsoft Corp., 215 F. Supp. 2d 1 (2002) (concluding that the proposed consent decree was ripe for a public interest determination).

39. 373 F.3d at 1249.

Second, "only contacts with the Executive Branch are relevant to the purpose of the Tunney Act—namely, to block settlements that are not in the public interest."[40]

The district court in *Microsoft* had articulated four additional grounds for its conclusion. First, no party had "identified any case in which the Section 16(g) disclosure has included contacts beyond those with the Executive Branch, nor has the Court located any such case."[41] Second, no case had been brought to the court's attention where the defendant was required to disclose communications with the legislative or judicial branches.[42] Third, the D.C. Circuit had approved an earlier consent decree involving Microsoft based upon a comparable disclosure statement that revealed no contacts with the legislative branch.[43] Finally, there was legislative history from the House (in contrast to Senator Tunney's statement quoted above) interpreting the section as encompassing communications with government agencies.[44] "Given the plain language of the statute and the manner in which it has been interpreted by the D.C. Circuit, the Court will construe the statute to apply to communications only with the Executive Branch."[45]

The first two editions of the *Lobbying Manual* had concluded unequivocally that, based on legislative history and apparent legislative intent, the Tunney Act should be read to encompass lobbying of the Congress when related to an antitrust consent decree.[46] The D.C. Circuit's affirmance in *Microsoft* casts doubt upon this conclusion, although the issue may well be litigated again, and an antitrust defendant may receive different guidance from a different court.

10-4 Exemption for Counsel of Record

Recognizing that lawyers for defendants and prospective defendants would have to communicate with the Department of Justice, Congress incorporated a "counsel of record" exemption into section 16(g): "any . . . communications made by counsel of record alone with the Attorney General or the employees of the Department of Justice alone shall be excluded from the [disclosure] requirements."[47] The exact scope of the exemption was the subject of some controversy during congressional debate. Fearing that a narrow exemption would "chill" legitimate negotiation, the Senate supported a "counsel of record" exemption

---

40. *Id.* As the district court put it, since neither the judicial nor legislative branch controls the nature or degree of enforcement of the antitrust laws, "application of the subsection (g) disclosure provision to the other two branches of government is counterintuitive." United States v. Microsoft, 215 F. Supp. 2d at 20. By contrast, in the Section 16(g) Statement filed by the American Bar Association in its antitrust settlement, the ABA listed communications with federal judges who served on the Association's Accreditation Committee. As the ABA filing observed: "Since federal judges are officers of the federal government, the ABA states that members of the Accreditation Committee received written materials and discussed issues relevant to the Department's investigation of the ABA's accreditation activities during the pendency of that investigation." United States v. American Bar Ass'n (D.D.C. Civ. No. 95-1211) (Section 16(g) Statement) (July 12, 1995).

41. 215 F. Supp. 2d at 20.

42. *Id.*

43. *Id.* at 20–21.

44. *Id.* at 20, n.18.

45. *Id.* at 21.

46. *See, e.g.,* THE LOBBYING MANUAL (2nd ed. 1998), Chapter 16, Section 16-3.2.

47. 15 U.S.C. § 16(g) (2015).

encompassing all communications made "by or in the presence" of such counsel.[48] It was the House version, however, that limited the exemption to "communications made by counsel of record *alone* with the Attorney General or employees of the Department of Justice alone," and it was that version that was ultimately enacted.

10-4.1 Definition of Counsel of Record

The definition of the term "counsel of record" is critical to the determination of the scope of the required disclosure, and yet it is left undefined in the Tunney Act. Ambiguity arises because there is no single definition of the term; it varies from context to context.[49] The narrowest definition would include only an "attorney whose appearance has been filed with court papers."[50] That definition, however, is inapposite in the section 16(g) context because, if the complaint and consent decree proposal are filed simultaneously, as they often are, there would be no "counsel of record" exemption, since, strictly speaking, there are no "court papers" before the filing of the decree. Such a narrow construction would thus chill the negotiations that the exemption was specifically designed to foster.[51]

A more reasonable definition in the Tunney Act context would include any lawyer (1) who will actually try the case or (2) who represents the party *and* has or would have authority to settle or enter into procedural stipulations. This definition is used in the settlement context when courts construe Rule 16 of the Federal Rules of Civil Procedure, regulating pretrial conferences.[52]

This definition is appropriate for the Tunney Act because the statute clearly envisions that lawyers will conduct settlement negotiations. Defining the term "counsel of record" on the basis of actual authority granted by the client is consistent with congressional intent, since this definition would eliminate attorneys who

---

48. *See* S. 782 as passed by the Senate ("communications made by or in the presence of counsel of record with the Attorney General or the employees of the Department of Justice shall be excluded"), 119 CONG. REC. 24,606 (July 18, 1973). See Section 10-4.2.

49. Outside the Tunney Act context, some courts employ the term to refer solely to the attorney who signed court papers. *See, e.g.*, Robideau v. Sec'y of HHS, No. 90-16V, 1990 U.S. Cl. Ct. LEXIS 372, at *1 (Cl. Ct. Sept. 17, 1990) (interpreting 42 U.S.C. §§ 300aa-10–17). Others use it to refer to the firm representing a party. *See In re* Globe Transp. & Trading, Ltd. v. Guthrie Latex, Inc., 722 F. Supp. 40, 48 (S.D.N.Y. 1989) (interpreting 9 U.S.C. § 1, relating to the actions of an arbitrator that would form the basis to vacate an arbitration award). Still others, interpreting specific statutes, use the term to refer to members of the bar of the court in which the case is pending. *See* Ormento v. United States, 328 F. Supp. 246, 261 (S.D.N.Y. 1971) (interpreting 28 U.S.C. § 144, relating to bias or prejudice of a judge).

50. BLACK'S LAW DICTIONARY 138, 374 (8th ed. 2004) (defining "attorney of record" as well as "counsel of record").

51. As Senator Tunney stated, "[t]he exception is designed so as to avoid interference with legitimate settlement negotiations between attorneys representing a defendant and Justice Department attorneys handling the litigation." 119 CONG. REC. 3453 (Feb. 6, 1973).

52. *See, e.g., In re* Novak, 932 F.2d 1397, 1407 n.19 (11th Cir. 1991) ("to ensure further that the responsible individuals attend such conferences, the local rules for many district courts require the attorney actually trying the case, or other attorneys empowered to enter into binding agreements for the parties, to appear at pretrial conferences"). In support of this proposition, the court cites to the Local Rules for the Southern District of Georgia: "Counsel who will actually try the case, or other counsel of record with authority to define issues, make stipulations, and discuss settlement, shall attend the pretrial conference." *Id.*

are brought into cases merely for their political clout as lobbyists.[53] It would also eliminate a potential loophole of concern to Senator Tunney—that merely signing court papers could qualify a "horde" of attorneys as counsel of record for purposes of the exemption.[54] The issue arose in the *Microsoft* case, where one lawyer had been a lobbyist, but was reported by Microsoft—and accepted by the court—as having represented the corporation as a "counsel of record."[55]

10-4.2 Scope of Exemption

The scope of the counsel of record exemption is described plainly in the House Report:

> The only communications with any officer or employee of the Government exempted from [the disclosure requirements] . . . are those made by counsel of record for defendants who meet alone *with members of the Department of Justice*. The limited exemption provided reflects a balancing test judgment distinguishing "lawyering" contacts of defendants from their "lobbying contacts." Numerous contacts by counsel of record with antitrust enforcers occur as an incident to the filing of a case: these, and these alone, are excepted from disclosure. A "lobbying" contact includes a communication to antitrust enforcers by counsel of record accompanied by corporate officers or employees; or by attorneys not counsel of record whether or not they are accompanied by officers or employees of defendants or prospective defendants in those situations in which a simultaneous filing of a complaint and a proposed settlement occurs.[56]

---

53. Of course, the line between lawyering and lobbying is not easy to draw in many contexts. *See, e.g.,* Section 22-2 of this manual. Lawyers can, in their lawyering capacity, appropriately attempt to convince the opposition that a case does not merit trial or prosecution, which is the same type of effort that may be launched by lawyers acting as paid lobbyists who besiege the Antitrust Division to influence the result of a pending or contemplated prosecution. The legislative history of the Tunney Act indicates that there is a distinction between lawyering and lobbying even for the "counsel of record" exemption, *see infra* note 56, and Congress decided to "draw the line" by allowing all counsel of record communications with the Department of Justice to go undisclosed.

54. *See* 119 Cong. Rec. 3453 (Feb. 6, 1973) (remarks of Senator Tunney) (the counsel of record exception "is not intended as a loophole for extensive lobbying by a horde of 'counsel of record'"). While not purporting to be counsel of record, a "horde" of attorneys was reported as communicating with government officials regarding the case of United States v. American Bar Ass'n, No. 95-1211, 2001 U.S. Dist. LEXIS 2279 (D.D.C. Feb. 16, 2001). Not surprisingly, officers, members of the Board of Governors of the ABA, and Council members and staff of the Section of Legal Education and Admissions to the Bar all made forays into both the Justice and Education Departments before the antitrust investigation relating to the ABA's accreditation process was settled through consent judgment. *See* Section 16(g) Statement of the American Bar Association (July 12, 1995); Supplemental Section 16(g) Statement and Certification of Compliance of Defendant American Bar Association (D.D.C. Civ. No. 95-1211 (CR)) (Oct. 16, 1995).

55. *Microsoft*, 215 F. Supp. 2d at 22 n.22.

56. H.R. Rep. No. 93-1463 (1974) (emphasis added). The report acknowledges "the difficulties of legislating legal ethics confining communications by counsel of record to 'lawyering' and not 'lobbying.'"

The intent is clear: the exemption will only cover communications between the attorneys of record alone and members of the Department of Justice alone. The underlying assumption is that those communications are necessarily "lawyering," not "lobbying" contacts.[57] In practice, Department of Justice staff often requests that clients attend negotiating sessions. Therefore, under the final version of the statute, communications during such sessions would be subject to the reporting requirements.

10-5 Filing of Disclosure

A section 16(g) filing is the defendant's obligation, and the filing must be accomplished "[n]ot later than 10 days following the date of the filing of any proposal for a consent judgment." The procedure, which allows the court and possible intervenors to review the statement before the entry of the decree, is also applied to consent decree modifications.[58] There is, however, one specific occasion when an antitrust proceeding ends consensually without implicating the filing requirements of the Tunney Act: the Tunney Act does not apply to stipulations of dismissal.[59]

The district court in the *Microsoft* case found "of less concern than the sufficiency and detail of Microsoft's disclosures" the argument that those disclosures were untimely. Having already noted that "the disclosures required by Section 16(g) serve primarily to assist the Court in assessing the public interest, rather than to inform public comment," it was not surprising that the court found the late filing to be "not prejudicial to the parties, the Court, or the public."[60]

10-6 Form of Disclosure

Section 16(g) requires a disclosure of oral and written communications, but it does not specifically state what information about these communications must be disclosed. Senator Tunney noted that the "disclosure intended is a disclosure of the fact of the meeting and the general subject matter. It obviously does not envision an outline of the conversation. But [it must include] the essential data, that is, the

---

57. The Senate bill as reported from Committee excepted communications made "by counsel of record, with any officer or employee of the United States." An amendment by Senator Philip Hart, which was adopted by voice vote, was intended "to close what may have been an inadvertent but gaping hole" that would have allowed counsel, "so long as he does not have his client with him," to "wander through the White House and Department of Commerce and the Department of Treasury and any other agency of government and lobby against the merits of pending legislation." 119 Cong. Rec. 24,602–603 (July 18, 1973). On the other hand, Senator Hart believed it entirely appropriate for counsel to take his client along when engaging in settlement negotiations; in fact, he quoted Assistant Attorney General Kauper's testimony in arguing that this ought to be encouraged. *Id.* at 24,603.

58. 1 A Legislative History of the Federal Antitrust Laws and Related Statutes 6536 (Earl W. Kintner, ed. 1984) (citing United States v. Motor Vehicle Mfg. Ass'n, 1981-2 Trade Cas. (CCH) ¶ 64,370 (C.D. Cal. 1981)) [hereinafter Kintner].

59. *In re* IBM Corp., 687 F.2d 591, 601 (2d Cir. 1982).

60. *Microsoft*, 215 F. Supp. 2d at 22.

date, the participants, and the fact that antitrust matters were discussed."[61] Thus, *specific* data regarding the participants and the dates of any communications must be disclosed along with *generalities* describing the subject matter. If any written communications need to be disclosed, the same standard should apply: correspondence would not have to be appended to the disclosure form; a listing of the dates, the correspondents, and the general subject matter should suffice.

10-7 Certification

Section 16(g) requires the defendant to "certify to the district court that the requirements of [the] subsection have been complied with and that such a filing is a true and complete description of such communications known to the defendant or which the defendant reasonably should have known." This includes communications made on the defendant's behalf, but does not extend to unauthorized contacts. Apparently some attorneys are "reluctant to sign the certification because of the possibility of a communication made by one of defendant's employees, concerning or relevant to the proposal, which would be a communication 'known to the defendant,' but not known to the attorney."[62] There appears to be no escape from the certification requirement on this basis, however, and defense counsel often query government counsel to verify that the list of communications to be reported is complete.

10-8 Enforcement

The primary enforcement mechanism for the defendant disclosure requirement is embodied elsewhere in the Tunney Act. Section 16(e) requires that, before entering any consent decree, the court "shall determine that such a judgment is in the public interest."[63] In making this determination, courts have a range of alternative procedures and factors to consider.[64]

---

61. *Id.* 119 Cong. Rec. 3451 (Feb. 6, 1973) (remarks of Senator Tunney). In United States v. LTV, 1984-2 Trade Cas. (CCH) ¶¶ 66,133, 66,335 (D.D.C. 1984), the decision summarizes what was disclosed in the defendant's section 16(g) statement:

> As reflected in the [section 16(g)] certifications . . . defendants met several times with the DOJ between March 5 and March 21, 1984 concerning the pending transaction and kept [Commerce Secretary Malcolm] Baldrige regularly informed as to the status of the discussions with the DOJ. They also discussed with [United States Trade Representative William] Brock the matter of an alleged voluntary restraint agreement with the Japanese and the impact on domestic prices of Japanese imports and the European Economic Community Arrangement (EEC). All these conversations took place in face-to-face meetings or by telephone. Communications made solely by counsel of record with the Attorney General or with employees of the DOJ alone were not required to be reported. No written communications were reported.

62. ABA Section of Antitrust Law, Antitrust Consent Decree Manual 8 n.29 (1979) [hereinafter Consent Decree Manual].

63. 15 U.S.C. § 16(e) (2015).

64. *See* United States v. SBC Comm., Inc. and AT&T, 489 F. Supp. 2d 1, 17 (D.D.C. 2007) (noting the factors that the court must consider in making its public interest determination).

Of considerable significance (in the defendant disclosure context) is the broad authority granted the court to permit participation in the proceedings by "interested" persons, opening the way for a wider range of information and assistance to reach the court for use in determining whether entry of a consent decree will be in the public interest. Under the law, interested persons who were not originally parties to the litigation but who wish to participate in the proceedings are no longer limited to the traditional alternatives of seeking to intervene as parties under Rule 24 of the Federal Rules of Civil Procedure, or playing the narrow role of amicus curiae. The Clayton Act, section 16(f)(3), provides that the court may authorize participation by such a person in a broad range of capacities, on a "full or limited" basis, and in whatever "manner and [to whatever] extent" the court finds to be appropriate.[65]

Subject to leave of court, interested persons can exert a good deal of influence "by reviewing the pertinent documents,[66] examining witnesses, filing briefs, and requesting that the court take testimony of government officials or expert witnesses."[67] In theory, they can review the defendant's disclosure statement and, if the court allows, question the veracity of the statement and even produce witnesses to contradict it. In the end, they can argue that a defendant's violation of its section 16(g) disclosure requirement obligations justifies the court's refusal to give deference to the government's determination that the settlement is in the public interest.[68] However, the conclusion of the district court in *Microsoft* that "the disclosures required by Section 16(g) serve primarily to assist the Court in assessing the public interest, rather than to inform public comment"[69] would, if accepted generally, undermine this potential use of the disclosure requirements.

10-9 Experience under the Act

Curiously, the only available study suggests that the section 16(g) requirements have not produced many disclosures,[70] despite legislative recognition that "[t]here is . . . nothing wrong with trying to negotiate a settlement."[71] One explanation is that, while the scope, adequacy, and timing of the defendant's section 16(g) disclosure were hotly contested, the *Microsoft* courts opted for the narrowest interpretation possible on all the issues presented. If that approach is followed in other circuits, the extent of disclosure under the Tunney Act will likely remain of modest

---

65. Kintner, at 6536 (quoting The Clayton Act, 15 U.S.C. § 16(f)(3) (2015)).

66. Section 16(b) of The Clayton Act requires the publication in the *Federal Register* of a competitive impact statement regarding the proposed consent decree. That publication is followed by a sixty-day comment period. Section 16(c) requires the government to publish summaries of the proposed settlement in newspapers. These procedures not only notify possible intervenors and other interested persons but also allow them access to much of the information relied upon by the Department of Justice in reaching settlement. 15 U.S.C. §§ 16(b), 16(c) (2015).

67. Kintner, at 6537.

68. *See* oral argument on behalf of the American Antitrust Institute in the settlement hearing of United States v. Microsoft Corp., No. 98-1232 (D.D.C. Mar. 8, 2002), *available at* http://www.antitrustinstitute.org/content/aais-oral-argument-microsoft-settlement-hearing-attorney-mike-lenetts-ten-minute-amicus (last visited September 15, 2015).

69. *Microsoft*, 215 F. Supp. 2d at 18.

70. *See, e.g.*, Consent Decree Manual, *supra* note 62, at 8.

71. See, e.g., *id.*

proportions even in cases where the behind-the-scenes lobbying may have been substantial. But there is a possible second explanation; as one authoritative treatise puts it: "In practice, the Tunney Act's sunshine provision means that most defendants will refrain from making lobbying contacts and that they will have nothing to report."[72] Finally, yet one more rationale might explain the absence of many lobbying disclosures under the Tunney Act:

> A defendant willing to engage in improprieties to influence the DOJ would not necessarily hesitate either to do so in a way that would not need to be disclosed, or to simply ignore the Act's requirements. Similarly, improperly influenced officials are unlikely to confess improprieties in a court filing.[73]

Commentators have suggested that the combined procedures of the Tunney Act seem to have had a prophylactic effect.[74] There can be no doubt that Congress, with the enactment of the Tunney Act, intended, in the words of Justice Brandeis, to use sunlight as a disinfectant to sanitize the antitrust consent decree process[75] that had been tainted by the revelations surrounding the *ITT* case. Whether this had been a problem before the *ITT* case, and whether it would have been a problem thereafter in the absence of section 16(g), is impossible to assess.

---

72. AMERICAN BAR ASSOCIATION, THE MERGER REVIEW PROCESS 423 (4th ed.) (*citing* ABA SECTION OF ANTITRUST LAW, ANTITRUST LAW DEVELOPMENTS 401-12 (7th ed.)).

73. *Frankel, supra* note 3, at 576.

74. CONSENT DECREE MANUAL, *supra* note 62, at 8.

75. *See* 119 CONG. REC. 24,599 (July 18, 1973) (remarks of Senator Tunney quoting New York Times Co. v. Sullivan, 376 U.S. 254, 305 (1964)).

CHAPTER 11

501(c)(3) Internal Revenue Code Lobbying Limits

BY EZRA REESE

11-1 Two Methods of Calculating Legislative Lobbying Limits

11-1.1 Substantial Part Test

Under the Internal Revenue Code (the Code), a section 501(c)(3) organization that is not a private foundation[1] may engage in some legislative lobbying, but it must limit its attempts to influence legislation to maintain its exempt status to "no substantial part" of its activities. If the organization does not opt into the section 501(h) expenditure test, or if it is not eligible, the determination of whether a "substantial part" of the activities of a section 501(c)(3) organization involve legislative

---

1. For the rules regarding private foundations, see Section 11-4 of this chapter.

lobbying activities will be based on an examination of all the pertinent facts and circumstances.

There is no definitive formula or percentage for determining whether a "substantial part" of the activities of an organization involve legislative lobbying activities. "Neither the legislative history of section 170(c)(2) and 501(c)(3), nor the cases that have arisen thereunder, provide specific guidance."[2] However, one court has found lobbying activities that constitute 5 percent or less are generally not considered substantial.[3] Conversely, activities constituting 16 to 20 percent generally have been considered substantial.[4]

Note that the Code provides for a 5 percent penalty on the lobbying activities of a section 501(c)(3) organization if they are so large as to lead to the revocation of the tax-exempt status of the organization; there is also a separate penalty levied on the managers of the organization who agreed to making of expenditures.[5] The penalty structure does not apply to organizations that elect the 501(h) expenditure test; are ineligible for that test; or are private foundations (for which a separate penalty structure for lobbying expenditures applies).[6]

11-1.2 501(h) Election

Section 501(h) and the applicable regulations provide an *optional* mechanical expenditure test for the amount of legislative lobbying activity that may be conducted by an organization. An organization that stays within these limitations suffers no adverse tax consequences as a result of its lobbying activities. The permissible amount of tax-free lobbying expenditures is determined by a percentage of the organization's "exempt purpose expenditures," defined in the regulations as money the organization spends in furtherance of an exempt purpose.[7]

"Exempt purpose expenditures" include funds spent on exempt purposes as well as funds spent on lobbying.[8] However, there are a few exclusions from the exempt-purpose expenditure calculation. Two in particular are of note.[9]

First, while in general fund-raising expenditures are included,[10] amounts expended for a separate fund-raising unit (defined in the regulations as two or more individuals, the majority of whose time is devoted to fund-raising activities) are excluded.[11] Exempt-purpose expenditures also do not include amounts paid to a person who is not an employee, or an organization that is not an affiliated organization, if paid or incurred primarily for fund-raising and if the person or organization engages in fund-raising or fund-raising counseling.[12]

Exempt-purpose expenditures include transfers to another section 501(c)(3) organization in furtherance of the transferor's exempt purpose, and not earmarked for any purpose other than those described in I.R.C. section 170(c)(2) (e.g.,

---

2. *See* Haswell v. United States, 500 F.2d 1133, 1142 (Ct. Cl. 1974).
3. *See* Seasongood v. Comm'r, 227 F.2d 907, 912 (6th Cir. 1955).
4. *See Haswell*, 500 F.2d at 1146–47.
5. I.R.C. § 4912(a), (b) (2015).
6. *Id.* § 4912(c).
7. Treas. Reg. § 56.4911-4(b).
8. *Id.*
9. For the full list of exclusions, *see* Treas. Reg. § 56.4911-4(c).
10. *Id.* § 56.4911-4(b)(8).
11. *Id.* § 56.4911-4(b), (c)(3).
12. *Id.* § 56.4911-4(c)(4).

educational or charitable purposes), and a "controlled grant," to the extent amounts paid or incurred by the transferee would be exempt-purpose expenditures by the transferor.[13] However, transfers do not count as exempt-purpose expenditures if they are made to a member of an "affiliated group,"[14] if the IRS determines that a substantial purpose of the transfer is to artificially inflate the transferor or transferee's exempt-purpose expenditures, or if a transfer is made to an organization that is not a section 501(c)(3) organization and that does not attempt to influence legislation, and outside of a controlled grant context.[15]

An organization elects to be governed by section 501(h) by filing a Form 5768. An organization may elect into section 501(h) any time before the end of its current fiscal year;[16] however, revocation of that election for a fiscal year must be made before the beginning of that fiscal year.[17]

Some types of section 501(c)(3) organizations—including private foundations and churches—may not elect to be regulated by section 501(h).[18]

11-2 Lobbying Limits under Section 501(h)

11-2.1 Section 501(h) Limits

Section 501(h) and accompanying regulations use a sliding-scale percentage test to determine the amount of an organization's permissible tax-free lobbying expenditures for those organizations that have elected the section 501(h) expenditure test. Under this test, an organization can spend the following amounts in furtherance of lobbying (both direct and grassroots lobbying) with no tax consequences: 20 percent of the first $500,000 exempt-purpose expenditures, 15 percent of the next $500,000, 10 percent of the next $500,000, and 5 percent of any remaining expenditures.[19] Organizations are subject to the following two additional yearly limitations: (1) an organization may not spend more than $1 million in any given year on lobbying activities without being taxed; and (2) an organization may only spend 25 percent of the above-determined amount in grassroots lobbying without being taxed.[20]

Exempt-Purpose Expenditures	Total Nontaxable	Grassroots Nontaxable
Up to $500,000	20%	5%
$500,000 to $1,000,000	$100,000 + 15% of excess over $500,000	$25,000 + 3.75% of excess over $500,000
$1,000,000 to $1,500,000	$175,000 + 10% of excess over $1,000,000	$43,750 + 2.5% of excess over $1,000,000
$1,500,000 to $17,000,000	$225,000 + 5% of excess over $1,500,000	$56,250 + 1.25% of excess over $1,500,000
Over $17,000,000	$1,000,000	$250,000

13. *Id.* § 56.4911-4(d).
14. *Id.* § 56.4911-4(e), *id.* § 56.4911-7(e).
15. *Id.* § 56.4911-4(e).
16. I.R.C. § 501(h)(6)(A) (2015).
17. *Id.* § 501(h)(6)(B).
18. *Id.* § 501(h)(3).
19. *Id.* § 4911-1(c)(2).
20. *Id.*

This is purely an expenditure test, unlike the "no substantial part" test. For instance, while the costs associated with recruiting volunteers, and for preparing material, in connection with a grassroots lobbying effort would be counted, the un-reimbursed expenses incurred by the volunteers would not be considered.[21] More importantly, the fact that many unpaid volunteers are conducting lobbying activities is simply not a factor under section 501(h).[22]

An organization that elects under section 501(h) and exceeds either permitted level of expenditures for grassroots or overall lobbying in any given year is subject to a 25 percent excise tax on the greater of the two excesses.[23] If, over a four-year period, the sum of an electing organization's lobbying expenditures exceeds the sum of 150% of either limitation, the organization will lose its tax-exempt status.[24]

11-2.2 Affiliation Rules

As noted above, the total amount of nontaxable lobbying expenditures permitted under section 501(h) is subject to a sliding scale as well as an overall $1,000,000 cap. Therefore, smaller organizations are able to spend a larger percentage of their exempt-purpose expenditures on direct and grassroots lobbying. To prevent circumvention of these rules by creating multiple smaller organizations, the Code includes an anti-abuse rule that, for the purpose of calculating the total amount of permitted lobbying expenditures, combines the lobbying expenditures of affiliated organizations and the total amount of lobbying actually conducted.[25]

Two or more organizations are considered to be affiliated if they have interlocking governing boards or if one organization is able to control action on legislative issues by the other organization because of provisions in the governing instruments of the controlled organization.[26] Organizations have "interlocking governing boards" if one organization has sufficient representatives on the board of the other to cause or prevent action on legislative issues by the controlled organization (by constituting a majority on the board, by constituting a quorum, or by constituting enough representatives to prevent a quorum).[27] A "representative" includes an individual from one organization specifically designated to serve on the board of the controlled organization; or an individual on the board of the controlled organization who is a board member, officer, or executive staff member of the other organization.[28] Organizations may be indirectly affiliated.[29] Only section 501(c)(3) organizations that are eligible to elect the section 501(h) expenditure test are included in an affiliated group; however, only one organization in the group need actually elect the expenditure test for the affiliated rules to apply.[30]

---

21. Treas. Reg. § 56.4911-2(b)(4)(ii)(C), Example 8.
22. *Id.* § 1.501(h)-3(e), Example 5.
23. I.R.C. § 4911(b) (2015); Treas. Reg. § 56.4911-1(b).
24. I.R.C. § 501(h)(1), (2) (2015); Treas. Reg. § 1.501(h)-3(b).
25. I.R.C. § 4911(f) (2015).
26. Treas. Reg. § 56.4911-7(a)(1). Note, however, that there is an exception for a "limited affiliated group of organizations" that do not have interlocking boards and that is bound by decisions on legislative issues only with respect to national legislative issues. *See generally id.* § 56.4911-10.
27. *Id.* § 56.4911-7(b).
28. *Id.* § 56.4911-7(b)(5). *See id.* § 56.4911-7(b)(5)(v) for a definition of an executive staff member.
29. *Id.* § 56.4911-7(d)(1).
30. *Id.* § 56.4911-7(e)(1).

An affiliated group is treated as one organization for purposes of determining the permissible nontaxable lobbying limits under section 501(h).[31] If there are excess lobbying expenditures, members of the affiliated group who have elected to be governed by the expenditure test will owe a portion of the tax on excess lobbying expenditures.[32] Only the members of the affiliated group that actually elect to be governed by section 501(h) are liable for the tax on excess lobbying.

11-2.3 Direct Lobbying Definitions

The regulations define direct lobbying to include a communication that:

- Refers to specific legislation[33] and reflects a view on such legislation; and
- Is made with:
  - "A member or employee of a legislative body"; or
  - With any other government official or employee who has a role in legislation, but only if the "principal purpose" is to influence legislation.[34]

Communication with government officials only counts as direct lobbying if it refers to and reflects a view on *legislation*. A letter sent to a legislative official asking that she write an administrative agency regarding proposed regulations, for instance, would not be considered direct lobbying, because the subject is not legislative in nature.[35] Neither is the delivery of a paper on a state's environmental problems if it does not reflect a view on a specific legislative proposal to address those problems.[36]

If a government official is a subscriber to a widely distributed newsletter, communications in the newsletter do not need to be counted as direct lobbying, because the official is receiving the material as a subscriber rather than as an official.[37] However, material in the newsletter may have to be counted as grassroots lobbying material. Furthermore, if the official is sent the newsletter without requesting it, the communication may have to be counted as a direct lobbying expense.

Communications regarding referenda or ballot initiatives with members of the voting public count as direct lobbying; in this case, the regulations treat voters who consider referenda to be the equivalent of legislators.[38] A ballot initiative becomes "specific legislation" when it is first circulated among voters for signature.[39]

11-2.4 Grassroots Lobbying Definitions

The regulations define grassroots lobbying to include any communication with the general public that (1) refers to specific legislation, (2) reflects a particular view of

---

31. I.R.C. § 4911(f)(1) (2015).
32. Treas. Reg. § 56.4911-8(d). The tax allocation rules are complex and depend on whether an electing organization has made direct or grassroots expenditures.
33. Note that "specific legislation" includes a specific proposal that an organization supports or opposes, even if it has not yet been introduced in the legislative body. Treas. Reg. § 56.4911-2(d)(1)(ii).
34. *Id.* § 56.4911-2(b)(1).
35. *Id.* § 56.4911-2(b)(4)(i), Example 2.
36. *Id.* § 56.4911-2(b)(4)(i), Example 3.
37. *Id.* § 56.4911-2(b)(4)(i), Example 7.
38. *Id.*
39. *Id.* § 56.4911-2(d)(1)(ii).

the legislation, and (3) includes a "call to action."[40] An example of grassroots lobbying is where an organization attempts to persuade the public to take particular action with respect to a bill that is pending before the legislature.

A "call to action" includes any of the following:

- A request that the recipient contact a government official or employee;
- The inclusion of contact information for a legislative official or employee;
- The inclusion of a way for the recipient to communicate with a government official or employee (including a petition, a postcard, or a link to an e-mail system); and
- The identification of legislators who will vote on the legislation and who are on a relevant committee or subcommittee, who represent the recipient, who oppose the organization's views, or who are undecided.[41]

Examples of a grassroots lobbying communication include

- A pamphlet that asks readers to "write or call your senators and representatives and tell them to vote for the President's plan" *or* that merely lists the members of the committee considering the bill;[42]
- A newsletter that endorses and opposes bills and lists legislators who are undecided on the bills;[43] and
- A fund-raising letter that discusses opposition to a bill and that includes the name of the recipient's congressional representative.[44]

Examples of communications that are not grassroots lobbying communications include

- A letter that refers to a pending bill and praises it, but that does not ask readers to take any action;[45]
- A pamphlet that asks readers to send legislators a message stating, "I support a drug-free America" (so long as that phrase is not associated with a specific pending legislative proposal);[46] and
- A newsletter that discusses pending legislation and identifies by name two legislators who support it, but not the names of legislators who oppose it, who are undecided, who represent the recipient, or who are on a relevant committee or subcommittee.[47]

There is, however, a "mass media" exception: If a paid advertisement appears in the mass media within two weeks before a vote on "highly publicized" legislation, there is a presumption that it will be considered grassroots lobbying if it both

40. *Id.* § 56.4911-2(b)(2)(i), (ii).
41. *Id.* § 56.4911-2(b)(2)(iii).
42. *Id.* § 56.4911-2(b)(2)(4)(ii)(B), Examples 1 and 2.
43. *Id.* § 56.4911-2(b)(2)(4)(ii)(B), Example 4.
44. *Id.* § 56.4911-2(b)(2)(4)(ii)(B), Example 7.
45. *Id.* § 56.4911-2(b)(2)(4)(ii)(A), Example 2.
46. *Id.* § 56.4911-2(b)(2)(4)(ii)(A), Example 4.
47. *Id.* § 56.4911-2(b)(2)(4)(ii)(A), Example 7.

reflects a view on the general subject and either refers to the highly publicized legislation or else encourages the public to contact legislators on the general subject.[48] "Highly publicized" means that legislation has received frequent coverage on television, on radio, and in newspapers during the two weeks preceding the vote.[49] The presumption can be rebutted by demonstrating that the paid advertisement is a type of mass media communication that the organization regularly makes without regard to the timing of legislation or that the timing of the paid advertisement was unrelated to the upcoming legislative action.[50]

Reports in the news media need not be counted as grassroots lobbying expenses.[51]

11-2.5 Supporting Activities

The IRS has long held that supporting activities (including studying issues before taking a position and formulating and agreeing upon positions) should be included when determining the scope of legislative lobbying activities.[52] Under section 501(h), all costs—including both direct and indirect costs, such as allocable staff time and "administrative, overhead, and other general expenditures" attributable to a direct or grassroots lobbying communication—must be included when calculating lobbying expenditures.[53]

11-2.6 Transfers

A transfer earmarked[54] for grassroots lobbying is treated as a grassroots expenditure.[55] A transfer earmarked for direct lobbying purposes, or for mixed direct and grassroots activities, is treated as a grassroots expenditure in full except to the extent the organization can demonstrate that funds were used for direct lobbying purposes.[56]

A transfer for less than fair market value to a non-section 501(c)(3) organization that lobbies will be considered a grassroots lobbying expenditure, up to the lesser of the amount of the grant or the amount of the transferee's grassroots lobbying expenditures; the remainder of the grant will be considered a direct lobbying expenditure up to the amount of the transferee's direct lobbying expenditures.[57]

11-2.7 Member Communications

A "member" is a person who pays dues or makes contributions of "more than a nominal amount," or who volunteers more than a nominal amount of time.[58]

---

48. *Id.* § 56.4911-2(b)(5).

49. *Id.* § 56.4911-2(b)(5)(iii)(C).

50. *Id.* § 56.4911-2(b)(5)(ii).

51. *Id.* § 56.4911-2(b)(4)(i), Example 6.

52. *See* League of Women Voters of the United States v. United States, 180 F. Supp. 379 (Ct. Cl. 1960), *cert. denied*, 364 U.S. 882 (1960).

53. Treas. Reg. § 56.4911-3(a)(1).

54. *See id.* § 56.4911-4(f)(4) for the definition of "earmarked."

55. *Id.* § 56.4911-3(c)(1).

56. *Id.* § 56.4911-3(c)(2).

57. *Id.* § 56.4911-3(c)(3).

58. *Id.* § 56.4911-5(f)(1).

A communication that is directed *only* or *primarily* to members (where members are more than half of the distribution) will not count as lobbying (including the portion sent to nonmembers) if

- The legislation discussed is of direct interest to the organization and its members; and
- The communication does not *directly* encourage the member to engage in direct or grassroots lobbying.[59] Direct encouragement includes
  — For direct lobbying, direct encouragement includes requests to contact government officials or employees, the contact information for legislators of legislative employees, or the inclusion of a way for the recipient to communicate with a government official or employee.[60]
  — For grassroots lobbying, direct encouragement includes requests to provide any of the above to nonmembers.[61]

If a membership communication sent only to members does include direct encouragement to engage in direct lobbying, it will count as direct lobbying.[62] If it includes direct encouragement to engage in grassroots lobbying, it will count as grassroots lobbying.[63]

If a membership communication sent primarily to members (i.e., at least half of the recipients are members, but it is also sent to nonmembers) includes direct encouragement to engage in direct lobbying (but not in grassroots lobbying), the cost may be allocated between direct and grassroots lobbying depending on the percentage of the communication that was distributed to nonmembers.[64] If a membership communication sent also to nonmembers includes direct encouragement to engage in grassroots lobbying, the entire cost of the communication is counted as grassroots lobbying.[65]

11-2.8 Exceptions

The Code provides a few exceptions to the definition of lobbying; communications that fall under these exceptions will not count as "influencing legislation" even if they otherwise meet the lobbying definitions. Note that these exceptions apply to *both* direct and grassroots lobbying efforts.

- Nonpartisan analysis, study, or research.[66]
  — *Definition.* Materials in this category "may advocate a particular position or viewpoint so long as there is a sufficiently full and fair exposition of the pertinent facts to enable the public or an individual to form an independent opinion or conclusion."[67] For material presented in a

59. *Id.* § 56.4911-5(b), (e)(4).
60. *Id.* § 56.4911-5(f)(6)(i)(A).
61. *Id.* § 56.4911-5(f)(6)(ii).
62. I.R.C. § 4911(d)(3)(A).
63. *Id.* § 4911(d)(3)(B).
64. Treas. Reg. § 56.4911-5(e)(2).
65. *Id.* § 56.4911-5(e)(3).
66. I.R.C. § 4911(d)(2)(A) (2015).
67. Treas. Reg. § 56.4911-2(c)(1)(ii).

series, the series as a whole can meet the definition of nonpartisan research even if an individual presentation does not;[68] however, if an organization times or channels a part of a series to influence the public or a legislative body to influence a particular legislative proposal, the expense of preparing and distributing that presentation will count as a direct or grassroots lobbying communication.[69]

Nonpartisan analysis, study, or research materials may name undecided legislators; however, they may not ask recipients to contact government officials or employees, give contact information for legislative officials or employees, or include a way for recipients to contact government officials.[70]

— *Distribution.* Nonpartisan analysis, study, or research may be distributed in a number of ways, including oral or written presentations, or distribution with or without charge. However, communications may not be limited to, or directed toward, people who are interested solely on one side of an issue.[71]

— *Subsequent use.* Nonpartisan analysis, study, or research may be treated as a grassroots lobbying expense under the "subsequent use" rules described below.

- *Communications in response to a request for technical advice from a governmental body.*[72] The request must be in writing and from a legislature, a committee, or a subcommittee; requests from individual members of the legislature do not qualify for this exception.[73]

- *Communications in defense of the organization's existence* (the self-defense exception). Communications before or with a legislative body with respect to a possible action that might affect the existence of the organization, its powers or duties, its tax-exempt status, or the deductibility of contributions to the organization do not count as direct lobbying expenditures.[74] By its terms, this exception does not apply to grassroots lobbying.

- *Communications that do not reflect a view on legislation.* In general, such communications do not meet the definition of direct or grassroots lobbying in the first place; moreover, there is a specific regulatory exception for "examinations and discussions of broad social, economic, and similar problems" so long as the discussion does not address a specific legislative proposal or encourage recipients to take action with respect to legislation.[75]

11-2.9 Mixed-Purpose Activity

If the "primary purpose" of preparing a communication is not lobbying, then the expenses for preparing it need not be counted, even if it is later used for lobbying

---

68. *Id.*
69. *Id.* § 56.4911-2(c)(1)(vii), Example 7.
70. *Id.* § 56.4911-2(c)(1)(vi).
71. *Id.* § 56.4911-2(c)(1)(iv).
72. *Id.* § 56.4911-2(c)(3).
73. *Id.* § 53.4945-2(d)(2).
74. *Id.* § 56.4911-2(c)(4).
75. *Id.* § 56.4911-2(c)(2).

purposes; however, direct costs for the later lobbying use, such as the transportation, photocopying, and other expenses, should be counted as lobbying.[76]

For nonmember communications, a communication with both a lobbying and non-lobbying purpose may allocate the costs, but all expenses for the portions of the communication that address the same specific subject as the lobbying message must be counted as lobbying.[77] The "same specific subject" includes discussion of an activity or issue that would be directly affected by the specific legislation that is the subject of the lobbying message.[78] For instance, if a communication is divided into two sections, one on subject "X" and one on subject "Y," and it includes a lobbying message regarding subject X, the entire subject X portion must be counted as lobbying, no matter how small the lobbying message.

For communications sent primarily to members (defined above), the allocation between the lobbying and non-lobbying purposes need only be "reasonable" and need not include all expenses associated with the same subject as the lobbying message.[79] For instance, in the above example, only the lobbying message portion need be allocated as a lobbying cost.

Lobbying expenditures that have both direct and grassroots lobbying components will be treated as grassroots expenditures in full, unless the organization can demonstrate that the communication was made primarily for direct lobbying purposes and makes a reasonable allocation between the purposes served by the communication.[80]

11-2.10 Subsequent Use

Subsequent use of a nonpartisan analysis or other communications or research materials may render the expenses to create them to be grassroots lobbying expenses if:

- It reflects a view on specific legislation, but in its initial form does not include a direct encouragement for recipients to take action;[81]
- The "primary purpose" of its creation is for lobbying.[82] The IRS will consider "all of the facts and circumstances," including the extent of the organization's non-lobbying distribution of the materials and whether the subsequent lobbying is conducted by the organization or a related organization, or by an unrelated organization (in which case "clear and convincing evidence" of cooperation or collusion between the two organizations is required to establish that the primary purpose of its creation was for lobbying).[83] The IRS has also established a safe harbor for a primary purpose determination: If, before or contemporaneously with the direct encouragement to action, the organization makes a "substantial non-lobbying distribution" (determined by reference to the facts and cir-

---

76. *Id.* § 56.4911-2(b)(4)(i), Example 5.
77. *Id.* § 56.4911-3(a)(2)(i).
78. *Id.*
79. *Id.* § 56.4911-3(a)(2)(ii).
80. *Id.* § 56.4911-3(a)(3).
81. *Id.* § 56.4911-2(b)(2)(v)(B).
82. *Id.* § 56.4911-2(b)(2)(v)(C).
83. *Id.* § 56.4911-2(b)(2) (v)(G).

cumstances, including the normal distribution of other similar materials), the materials will not be considered developed for the primary purpose of lobbying.[84] For materials that do not qualify for the definition of "non-partisan analysis, study or research," the distribution must be at least as extensive as the lobbying distribution to meet the safe harbor;[85] and

- It is later accompanied by a cover letter or other communication that includes a direct encouragement for recipients to take action.[86]

Two caveats apply. First, this rule regarding subsequent use will not cause expenses to become direct lobbying expenses; the rule applies only to grassroots lobbying.[87] Second, only expenditures that are paid less than six months before the subsequent lobbying use can be retroactively considered to be grassroots lobbying; earlier expenditures need not be considered.[88]

11-3 Action Organizations

Even if an organization stays within section 501(c)(3) legislative lobbying limits, Treasury regulations hold that it will not be eligible for section 501(c)(3) status if it is an "action organization." The definition of an action organization includes entities that engage in excessive legislative lobbying, but also includes an organization whose "main or primary objective or objectives (as distinguished from its incidental or secondary objectives) may be attained only by legislation or a defeat of proposed legislation" and that "advocates, or campaigns for, the attainment of such main or primary objective or objectives as distinguished from engaging in nonpartisan analysis, study, or research and making the results thereof available to the public."[89] In other words, an entity could be an action organization based on its primary objective being too closely tied to legislation, even if it does not engage in an excessive amount of lobbying to achieve that goal.

11-4 Private Foundations

While private foundations are subject to the "no substantial part" test for purposes of determining whether they qualify under section 501(c)(3),[90] they are also subject to a tax on *any amount* paid or incurred to "carry on propaganda" or otherwise attempt to influence legislation.[91] That tax is levied on both the private foundation and on any manager who willfully agrees to make a taxable lobbying expenditure,[92] and includes additional fines on both the foundation and manager if the taxable expenditure is not corrected within the fiscal year.[93] Thus, for practical purposes

---

84. *Id.* § 56.4911-2(b)(2) (v)(E).
85. *Id.* § 56.4911-2(b)(2)(v)(F).
86. *Id.* § 56.4911-2(b)(2)(v)(C).
87. *Id.* § 56.4911-2(b)(2)(v)(A).
88. *Id.* § 56.4911-2(b)(2)(v)(D).
89. *Id.* 1.501(c)(3)-1(c)(3)(iv).
90. *See* Staff of the Joint Committee on Internal Revenue Taxation, General Explanation of the Tax Reform Act of 1969, 49 n.21 (1969).
91. I.R.C. § 4945(d)(1) (2015).
92. *Id.* § 4945(a).
93. *Id.* § 4945(b).

private foundations should be treated as having no ability to engage in legislative lobbying at all.

The definition of lobbying for private foundations is largely identical to the definition for section 501(c)(3) organizations that elect to be governed by the section 501(h) expenditure test.[94] However, there is no rule for membership communications; all communications are governed by the rules for communicating with the public even if they are sent to the foundation's membership.[95]

A grant from a private foundation to a public charity will not be considered a taxable lobbying expenditure, even if the public charity engages in legislative lobbying, if either of the following applies:

- The grant is a "general support grant" and is not earmarked to be used for legislative lobbying.[96] This type of grant is not a taxable lobbying expenditure on the part of the private foundation even if the recipient public charity uses the funds to support its own lobbying efforts.
- The grant is earmarked for a specific project of the public charity, and
  — The grant is not earmarked for legislative lobbying, and
  — The amount of all grants by the foundation for this project does not exceed the amount budgeted by the public charity for non-legislative lobbying activities.[97]

On the other hand, a grant by a private foundation that is earmarked for legislative lobbying, or that is for a specific project and exceeds the project's non-lobbying budget, will be a taxable expenditure by the private foundation.

11-5 Form 990 Reporting

A section 501(c)(3) organization, on its annual IRS Form 990, must report on Schedule C the total amount of funds it has spent on legislative lobbying.[98] Section 501(c)(3) organizations that have elected to be governed by the section 501(h) expenditure test must report their grassroots and direct lobbying expenses; other section 501(c)(3) organizations currently must report expenses in seven different categories.[99]

11-6 No Specific Limit for Administrative Lobbying

The above limits apply only to attempts to influence "action by the Congress, by any State legislature, by any local council or similar governing body, or by the public in a referendum, initiative, constitutional amendment, or similar procedure."[100] The section 501(h) regulations specifically exclude actions by "executive, judicial,

---

94. *See* Treas. Reg. § 53.4945-2(a)(1).
95. *Id.* § 53.4945-2(a)(2).
96. *Id.* § 53.4945-2(a)(6)(i).
97. *Id.* § 53.4945-2(a)(6)(ii).
98. *See* IRS Form 990 Schedule C, *available at* http://www.irs.gov/pub/irs-pdf/f990sc.pdf.
99. *Id.*
100. Treas. Reg. § 1.501(c)(3)-1(c)(3)(ii).

or administrative bodies."[101] Thus, advocacy to affect executive branch action does not count against section 501(c)(3) lobbying limits, even if the action taken by the executive branch may necessitate legislative approval. However, this exclusion does not apply to attempts to influence legislation through the executive branch. For example, asking an executive agency to make a purchase of land for a park is not legislative lobbying, even if that purchase will require appropriated funds from the legislature to support it; however, attempting to affect the budget the executive agency submits to the legislature will count as legislative lobbying.[102]

Keep in mind, however, that even though there are no specific limits to administrative advocacy by a section 501(c)(3) organization, it is still subject to the general rule that all but an insubstantial part of its activities must be in furtherance of an exempt purpose.[103]

101. *Id.* § 56.4911-2(d)(3).
102. *Id.* § 56.4911-2(d)(4).
103. *See id.* § 1.501(c)(3)-1(c)(1).

CHAPTER 12

Tax Laws That Apply to Lobbying for Businesses and Other Nonprofits

BY TYLER HAGENBUCH

Lobbying for 501(c)(4), (5), and (6) Organizations: An Introduction

Other 501(c) tax-exempt organizations are not subject to the same restrictions on lobbying activities as 501(c)(3) organizations. In general, an entity organized and operated under sections 501(c)(4), (5), or (6) of the Internal Revenue Code (the Code) may engage in an unlimited amount of lobbying activity related to the organization's exempt purpose.[1] This includes both direct and grassroots lobbying.[2] However, as explained below and in more detail in Chapter 13 of this manual, lobbying expenditures are generally not deductible, and certain tax-exempt organizations that lobby may be required to either inform dues payers that a corresponding portion of their dues and similar payments are not deductible as business expenses or else pay a proxy tax on their nondeductible lobbying and political activity.

Section 501(c)(4) of the Internal Revenue Code makes a "social welfare" organization exempt from federal taxation if the organization has the primary purpose of bringing about civic betterments or public improvements.[3] Social welfare organizations typically spend a large portion of their budgets on lobbying. A social welfare organization may qualify as a tax-exempt 501(c)(4) organization even if it is an "action" organization.[4] An "action" organization is one involved in political or legislative activities to such an extent that it does not qualify as a 501(c)(3) charitable organization, or whose primary objectives are only achievable through legislation and who lobbies for the attainment of those objectives.[5] Thus, provided that a 501(c)(4) organization meets the general requirement that "it is primarily

---

1. I.R.S. Pub. 4221-NC, Compliance Guide for Tax Exempt Organizations (Other Than 501(c)(3) Public Charities and Private Foundations) 5 (Dec. 2010).

2. *See* I.R.S. Tech. Adv. Mem. 81-15-024 (Dec. 31, 1980) (recognizing the ability of a 501(c)(6) tax-exempt organization to engage in grassroots lobbying activities).

3. Treas. Reg. § 1.501(c)(4)-1(a)(2)(i).

4. *Id.* § 1.501(c)(4)-1(a)(2)(ii).

5. *Id.* § 1.501(c)(3)-1(c)(3)(iv).

engaged in promoting in some way the common good and general welfare of the people of the community,"[6] the organization may engage in an unlimited amount of lobbying activity related to its exempt purpose,[7] even if lobbying comprises 100 percent of the organization's activities.[8]

The Supreme Court has recognized the ability of a single organization to establish both a 501(c)(3) entity to carry out its non-lobbying activity and a separate 501(c)(4) affiliate to lobby in favor of those same charitable goals.[9] Organizations that choose such a structure must maintain the 501(c)(3) and 501(c)(4) affiliates as separate entities to ensure that the 501(c)(3) organization does not subsidize the 501(c)(4) organization.[10] Note that a 501(c)(4) organization that engages in lobbying activity becomes ineligible to receive any federal award, grant, loan, or other federal funds under the Lobbying Disclosure Act.[11] However, a 501(c)(4) may establish a separate lobbying affiliate to conduct lobbying activities using nonfederal funds.[12] The affiliate organization can then lobby without jeopardizing the 501(c)(4)'s ability to receive federal grants.[13]

Section 501(c)(5) labor organizations and section 501(c)(6) trade associations may similarly engage in an unlimited amount of lobbying that is related to the organization's exempt purpose.[14] A 501(c)(5) or 501(c)(6) organization may qualify for tax-exempt status whether lobbying to promote legislation related to its primary purpose constitutes only a part of the organization's activities,[15] or if its sole activity is to introduce and promote such legislation.[16] Both kinds of organizations are typically membership organizations, and both tend to spend a significant amount of their budgets on lobbying.

Despite the allowance of many tax-exempt organizations to engage in lobbying activity, Internal Revenue Code section 162(e) prohibits the deduction of lobbying and political expenses, including the portion of dues or similar payments paid to certain tax-exempt organizations that is allocable to nondeductible lobbying expenditures.[17] In other words, an entity may not deduct the proportion of dues or similar payments it makes to a covered tax-exempt organization that the organization uses to lobby. "Similar payments" in addition to dues that are nondeductible include any voluntary payments made to cover basic operating costs and any special assessments imposed by the tax-exempt organization used to conduct lobbying activities.[18] These payments are discussed in more detail in Chapter 13.

Internal Revenue Code section 6033(e)(1) requires certain tax-exempt organizations that receive dues or similar payments and engage in lobbying activities

---

6. *Id.* § 1.501(c)(4)-1(a)(2)(i).

7. Rev. Rul. 67-293, 1967-1 C.B 185.

8. Rev. Rul. 71-530, 1971-2 C.B. 237.

9. Regan v. Taxation with Representation, 461 U.S. 540, 544 (1983).

10. *See id.*

11. 2 U.S.C. § 1611 (2015).

12. H.R. Rep. 104-339 at 24 (1995).

13. *Id.*

14. *See* Rev. Rul. 61-177, 1961-1 C.B. 117; Rev. Rul. 71-530, 1971-2 C.B. 237.

15. Rev. Rul. 71-504, 1971-2 C.B. 231.

16. Rev. Rul. 61-177.

17. I.R.C. § 162(e) (2015); Rev. Proc. 98-19, 1998-7 I.R.B. 30. For additional discussion of tax laws governing the deductibility of lobbying expenses, see Chapter 13 of this manual.

18. Rev. Proc. 98-19, 1998-7 I.R.B. 30.

to notify dues payers at the time dues or similar payments are collected with an estimate for the portion of such dues that the organization reasonably estimates are allocable to lobbying activity, and, therefore, are not deductible.[19] As discussed in more detail in Chapter 13, if a covered tax-exempt organization does not provide such notification, or if the notification does not include the amount spent on lobbying and political activity, section 6033(e)(2)(A) requires the organization to pay a tax on the amount of its lobbying and political expenditures (to the extent it exceeds the amount included in notices to dues payers, if any) at the highest corporate tax rate currently imposed by the Internal Revenue Code.[20] The tax imposed on organizations that do not provide the required notice is commonly known as the "proxy tax." The proxy tax is capped at the amount of dues and other similar payments received by the organization during the taxable year.[21]

To be effective, an estimate must be reasonably calculated to provide dues payers with adequate notice of the nondeductible portion of their dues.[22] The notice must be provided either at the time of assessment or upon payment of the dues.[23] If an organization elects to give notice but underestimates its actual amount of lobbying expenditures, it is subject to the proxy tax on the amount of the underestimate.[24]

The requirement to notify dues payers of the non-deductibility of dues or pay the proxy tax is applicable to the following tax-exempt organizations: all 501(c)(4) social welfare organizations other than veterans organizations; all 501(c)(5) agricultural and horticultural organizations (but not labor organizations); and all trade associations and other organizations exempt under section 501(c)(6).[25] However, a 501(c)(4) social welfare organization or 501(c)(5) agricultural and horticultural organization can establish a safe harbor exemption from the notice and proxy tax requirement if more than 90 percent of its annual dues are received from (1) dues payers paying annual dues of $111 or less (as of 2015);[26] (2) 501(c)(3) organizations or state or local governments; or (3) 501(c)(4) veterans organizations or 501(c)(5) labor organizations.[27] A trade association or other organization exempt under section 501(c)(6) may establish a safe harbor if more than 90 percent of its annual dues are received from (1) 501(c)(3) organizations or state or local governments, or (2) 501(c)(4) veterans organizations or 501(c)(5) labor organizations.[28]

The registration and reporting requirements of the LDA also apply to tax-exempt organizations that lobby. For a full discussion of these requirements, see Chapters 4 and 5.

---

19. I.R.C. 6033(e)(1)(A)(ii) (2015).
20. *Id.* § 6033(e)(2).
21. *See* 2014 Instructions for Schedule C (Form 990 or 990-EZ).
22. *See* IRC § 6033(e)(1)(A)(ii) (2015).
23. I.R.C. § 6033(e)(1)(A)(ii) (2015).
24. I.R.C. § 6033(e)(2)(A)(ii) (2015).
25. *Id.; see also* Rev. Proc. 98-19, 1998-7 C.B. 547, § 4.01.
26. *See* Rev. Proc. 14-61, 2014-47 I.R.B. 860. This amount will continue to be indexed for inflation.
27. Rev. Proc. 98-19, 1998-7 C.B. 547, § 4.02.
28. *Id.*

CHAPTER 13

Tax Rules Limiting Deductibility of Lobbying Expenses by Businesses and Trade Associations

BY JOSEPH SANDLER

13-1 Introduction

A recurrent theme of this manual is that lobbying is a valid exercise of basic First Amendment rights for individuals and organizations.[1] Certainly businesses and the trade groups that advocate for the interests of their industries find it necessary to have a voice in shaping the laws, rules, and policies that regulate their

---

1. *See also* D. R. Gelak, *Communicating with Congress, in* Chapter 29, THE LOBBYING MANUAL 606 (4th ed. 2009) ("Lobbying . . . is not only a necessary reality, but a healthy part of our Nation's effective governance").

operations. Undoubtedly, businesses regard the costs of lobbying as an "ordinary and necessary" business expense. The federal tax laws, however, do not. At various times in the last century, and since 1993, businesses have been unable to deduct expenses for "influencing legislation," "participation in, or intervention, any political campaign," "any attempt to influence the general public . . . with respect to elections, legislative matters or referendums," or "any direct communication with" certain senior officials of the federal government.[2]

The result is that, for businesses, the decision to lobby Congress and state legislatures, or to support or oppose ballot initiatives or referendums—common and essential activities for so many companies—requires a willingness to create a cash hole: the money is expended, but the expenditure cannot be deducted for income tax purposes.

The provisions of the Internal Revenue Code and IRS regulations limiting the deductibility of lobbying expenses are complex. The definitions of what counts as lobbying or political—nondeductible—are in certain respects not clear and, notably, do not match the definitions used in the rules limiting lobbying by nonprofit organizations exempt under section 501(c)(3) of the Code.[3] A wide range of costs must be accounted for and disallowed in determining the nondeductible amounts spent for lobbying. And, sometimes to the surprise of groups and their members, to the extent trade associations or certain other types of nonprofit groups engage in lobbying, that portion of the contributions made or dues paid to those groups that is allocable to lobbying becomes nondeductible to the donors and members.

13-2 History

The evolution of the current rules on tax deductibility of lobbying expenses has not followed a straight line. In 1915, the Treasury Department issued regulations disallowing any deduction for lobbying expenses of corporations—specifically, no deduction would be allowed for expenses for "lobbying purposes, the promotion or defeat of legislation, the exploitation of propaganda, including advertising other than trade advertising."[4] In 1941, the Supreme Court upheld the regulation, ruling that the plain meaning of "ordinary and necessary" would not necessarily include lobbying expenses because lobbying itself is disfavored by the law as a matter of policy: lobbying contracts "to spread such insidious influences through legislative halls have long been condemned."[5]

Almost two decades later, in the case of *Cammarano v. United States*, the Supreme Court ruled that the Treasury Department could properly apply the regulation to disallow contributions from a beer wholesaler to a special fund formed to defeat a Washington State initiative to permit retail sale of beer and wine solely by the state government.[6] The Court held that the IRS had reasonably interpreted "lobbying"

---

2. Internal Revenue Code of 1986 as amended (I.R.C.) § 162(e)(1) (2015).

3. See Chapter 11 for a discussion of those definitions.

4. T.D. 2137, 17 Treas. Dec. Int. Rev. 48, 57–58 (1915) (cited and discussed in Shannon King, *Note: The Lobbying Deduction Disallowance: Policy Considerations, Comparisons and Structuring Activities Under Amended Section 162(e)*, 15 Va. Tax. Rev. 551, 553 (1996). These regulations remained largely unchanged but were renumbered over the years before the Revenue Act of 1962. *Id.*

5. Textile Mills Securities Corp. v. Comm'r of Internal Revenue, 314 U.S. 326, 338 (1941).

6. 358 U.S. 498 (1959).

and "legislation" to include efforts to support or oppose referenda and initiatives. The Court rejected the arguments that denying a deduction for "sums expended by a taxpayer to preserve his business from destruction" are necessarily included in the plain meaning of "ordinary and necessary and business expenses" and that the IRS's regulation, as so applied, would raise a First Amendment issue.[7] To the contrary, the Court reasoned, the IRS regulation simply put businesses in the same position as everyone else engaged in lobbying on legislation—with no special tax benefit to subsidize the expense of such lobbying. The regulation "appears to us to express a determination by Congress that since purchased publicity can influence the fate of legislation which will affect, directly or indirectly, all in the community, everyone in the community should stand on the same footing as regards its purchase."[8]

In response, Congress in 1962 enacted as part of the Revenue Act of 1962 a provision effectively repealing the Treasury regulations and partially reversing the result in *Cammarano* by specifically allowing the deduction, as an "ordinary and necessary business expense," of all expenses incurred by a business entity in *direct* lobbying—that is, appearing before or communicating with Congress or a state legislature "with respect to legislation or proposed legislation of direct interest to" the business.[9] The new provision disallowed any deduction, however, for anything spent to participate in a political campaign or for grassroots lobbying, defined as "any attempt to influence the general public, or segments thereof, with respect to legislative matters, elections or referendums."[10] The Senate Finance Committee Report on the provision that became law explains that it would be anomalous to disallow a deduction for lobbying the legislative branch, but not for attempts to influence executive branch and agency officials or for litigation in the courts; that as a policy matter it is "desirable" that business taxpayers "who have information bearing on the impact of present laws, or proposed legislation, on their trades or businesses, not be discouraged in making this information available to" members of Congress and legislators; and that deductibility of direct lobbying expenses is necessary to determine a business's true income given that "making sure that legislators are aware of the effect of proposed legislation may be essential to the very existence of a business."[11]

The provision allowing deductibility of lobbying expenses remained in effect for the next thirty years. Then, in 1993, as part of his proposals for campaign finance and ethics reform, President Clinton in his first State of the Union Address proposed to eliminate the deduction for lobbying expenses, asking the Congress, along with a request to pass comprehensive campaign finance reform, "to deal with the undue influence of special interests by passing a bill to end the tax deduction for lobbying."[12]

---

7. *Id.* at 507.

8. *Id.* at 513.

9. Revenue Act of 1962, P.L. 87-834, 76 Stat. 973, § 3, codified as amended as I.R.C. § 162(e)(2) (2015).

10. *Id.* codified as amended as I.R.C. § 162(e)(1) (2015).

11. S. Rep. No. 87-221 § III(A) (1962).

12. State of the Union Address (Feb. 17, 1993) (Miller Center, University of Virginia Presidential Speech Archive).

In May 1993, the House of Representatives passed its version of the Omnibus Budget Reconciliation Act of 1993, eliminating the deduction for lobbying expenses and defining lobbying to include only attempts to influence legislation—not executive branch action.[13] In June 1993, the Senate passed its version of the House bill, which would have broadened the definition to include contacts with certain high-ranking federal executive branch officials made to influence federal executive branch actions.[14] The Conference Committee adopted the Senate approach to the definition of lobbying, but excluded attempts to influence any local council or legislative body and added a number of other provisions, discussed below, that differed in important respects from both the Senate and House versions.[15] The Conference Report version of the bill was adopted, and Congress enacted the current version of section 162(e), effective as of January 1, 1994.[16]

13-3 Scope of Nondeductibility

The costs of three types of activities are made nondeductible by section 162(e): lobbying (including direct and grassroots, and certain efforts to influence executive actions as well as legislation), influencing ballot measures and political activity. These costs are discussed in this section, in turn. What *types* of costs associated with each activity are subject to disallowance are discussed in Section 13-4.

13-3.1 Lobbying

13-3.1.1 Direct Lobbying
The costs of two types of direct lobbying are disallowed: (1) "influencing legislation"[17] and (2) "any direct communication with a covered executive branch official in an attempt to influence the official actions or positions of such official."[18]

13-3.1.2 "Influencing Legislation"
The statutory language itself defines "influencing legislation" to mean "any attempt to influence legislation through communication with any member or employee of a legislative body, or with any government official or employee who may participate in the formulation of legislation."[19] Several points should be noted in connection with this familiar and seemingly straightforward concept of direct lobbying.

First, the statute provides that "legislation" is defined in the same way as in the IRC provisions prohibiting lobbying by private foundations and limiting lobbying by nonprofit organizations that are public charities exempt from taxation under IRC section 501(c)(3).[20] Under that definition, "legislation" includes specific bills, resolutions, or similar items under consideration by a *legislative* body, and a specific

13. H.R. 2264, 103d Cong. (1993).
14. S. 1134, 103d Cong. (1993), passed June 23, 1993, as Senate Amendment to H.R. 2264.
15. H.R. Conf. Rep. No. 103-213, at 598–608 (1993).
16. Omnibus Budget Reconciliation Act of 1993, Pub. L. No. 103–66. 107 Stat. 312 § 13222 (codified at I.R.C. § 162(e)) (2015).
17. I.R.C. § 162(e)(1)(A) (2015).
18. *Id.* § 162(e)(1)(D).
19. *Id.* § 162(e)(4)(A).
20. *Id.* § 162(e)(4)(B), referencing I.R.C. § 4911(e)(2) (2015).

legislative proposal, even if it has not yet been introduced.[21] The significance of this definition is that, except for specific contacts with certain high-level federal officials as discussed below, attempts to influence executive branch or administrative agency action at the federal, state, or local level do *not* count as "influencing legislation," and the costs of such efforts remain deductible.[22]

Second, under implementing IRS regulations, again mirroring the 501(c)(3) rules, influencing legislation requires a "lobbying communication," which means to count as a lobbying contact, a communication must *reflect a view about specific legislation.*[23] If a communication with a legislator, staffer, or government official communicates support for or opposition to a general policy, or policy proposal, that has not taken the form of a specific legislative proposal or a bill, the costs of that communication are deductible.

Third, unlike the 501(c)(3) rules, section 162(e) excludes from the scope of influencing legislation any *direct* communication with a member or staffer of a *local* legislative body—including city or county council, county supervisors, and local agencies such as school boards, housing authorities, zoning boards and planning commissions, and sewer and water districts.[24]Attempts to influence either legislation or agency action at the local level through direct lobbying do not count as influencing legislation, and the costs are deductible. Costs incurred by an organization to contact its members to get them in turn to contact local legislators are also deductible;[25] costs of other grassroots lobbying at the local level are not.

Finally, under IRS rules, influencing legislation includes not only the actual act of communicating with a member or staffer of Congress or a state legislature, but also all "activities, such as research, preparation, planning and coordination . . . engaged in for a purpose of making or supporting a lobbying communication, even if not yet made."[26] Thus, researching and preparing fact sheets, arranging meetings and following up on meetings with additional materials and e-mail, all count as part of influencing legislation.

But what about background research on an issue that was conducted before there was any legislation to take a position on, or before any decision was made to undertake any lobbying effort? Or fact sheets that are used to educate legislators, staff, the media, and coalition partners generally about an issue? The IRS rules call for a factual analysis to determine the purpose of an activity, taking into account factors including the proximity in time to a lobbying communication, whether the activity was requested by the company's lobbying operation, whether the results were used for a non-lobbying purpose, and whether specific legislation was pending when the activity was carried out.[27] Thus, for example, if a company analyzes the potential impact on its business of a proposal well before it becomes legislation, then uses that analysis much later when there is a bill pending on the same subject,

---

21. I.R.C. § 4911(e)(2); Treas. Reg. § 56.4911-2(d)(1).

22. Treas. Reg. § 1.162-29(b)(7)(examples); *see* H.R. Conf. Rep No. 103-213, at 605 (1993); Lloyd Mayer, *What Is This "Lobbying" That We Are So Worried About?* 26 Yale L. & Pol'y Rev. 485, 555 (2008).

23. *Id.* § 1.162-29(b)(3)(1995); compare Treas. Reg. § 56.4911-2(b)(i)(1990) (definition of direct lobbying communication for public charities electing the "expenditure" test for determining permissible amount of lobbying).

24. I.R.C. § 162(e)(2); H.R. Conf. Rep. No. 102-213 at 605 (1993).

25. *Id.* § 162(e)(2)(B)(ii).

26. Treas. Reg. § 1.162-29(b)(1)(ii) (1995).

27. *Id.* § 1.162-29(c)(1) (1995).

the costs of the analysis would not be considered to be for a lobbying purpose.[28] If an activity is carried out for a lobbying purpose but also clearly used for a non-lobbying purpose, the costs can be allocated.

Monitoring the status of and summarizing legislation, if not carried out to support lobbying communications or undertaken before any decision to lobby, is not considered to be "influencing legislation."

13-3.1.3 Communications with Covered Federal Executive Branch Official

In addition to disallowing a deduction for the costs of influencing legislation, section 162(e) disallows a deduction for the costs of "any direct communication with a covered executive branch official in an attempt to influence the official actions or positions of such official."[29] "Covered executive branch officials" include the president; the vice president; any employee of the White House Office; the top two officials in any other agency of the Executive Office of the President, such as the Office of Management and Budget or the Council on Environmental Quality; any individual serving at level I of the Executive Schedule—generally meaning Cabinet Secretaries and other persons given Cabinet rank—and their immediate deputies, generally meaning the Deputy Secretaries of the Cabinet agencies.[30] Note that the number of covered officials is considerably less than the number included in the definition of covered Executive Branch officials for purposes of the Lobbying Disclosure Act.[31]

Note also that a deduction is disallowed for the costs of any communication with these covered officials to influence any action within their official duties, whether the subject matter is legislation or executive action, rulemaking, an executive order, contracting, or virtually anything else.

13-3.1.4 Grassroots Lobbying

As noted, the 1962 law passed by Congress to allow a business deduction for direct lobbying specifically excluded "any attempt to influence the general public, or segments thereof, with respect to legislative matters, elections or referendums."[32] That language—understood to disallow any deduction for the expenses of grassroots, as opposed to direct, lobbying—was retained in the 1993 law that enacted section 162(e) in its current form. As the Conference Report on the bill that became the 1993 law explained, "The present-law rules disallowing business deductions for expenses of grass roots lobbying . . . will remain in effect."[33]

But what are those "present-law rules"? This turns out to be a difficult question because the Code does not define "grassroots lobbying" for purposes of subsection 162(e). A nonprofit organization that is exempt under section 501(c)(3) and that is a public charity is forbidden from making lobbying a "substantial" part of its activities.[34] To steer clear of having its lobbying activities treated as substantial, such

---

28. *Id.* § 1.162-29(c)(4) (Examples).

29. I.R.C. § 162(e)(1)(D) (2015).

30. *Id.* § 162(e)(6).

31. *See* Lobbying Disclosure Act, 2 U.S.C. § 1602(4) (2015) (listing of "covered executive branch officials" for LDA purposes).

32. I.R.C. § 162(e)(2)(B) (1962).

33. H.R. Conf. Rep. No. 103-213, at 605 (1993).

34. I.R.C. § 501(c)(3) (2015).

an organization can elect to subject its lobbying activities to an expenditure test, which allows the organization to expend up to a specific dollar limit each year on lobbying without facing a tax penalty.[35] Of that dollar amount, only 25 percent can be spent on grassroots lobbying.[36] The Code and IRS regulations define grassroots lobbying, for this purpose, as a communication with the *general public* that refers to legislation or a specific legislative proposal, reflects a view on it, and encourages the recipient to take some action on the legislation or proposal.[37] It would seem logical to apply the same definition for purposes of section 162(e).

The IRS, however, in issuing the proposed regulations defining "influencing legislation" as used in subsection 162(e), stated that "it should not be inferred that the IRS will adopt the definition of grassroots lobbying communication under the section 4911 regulations for purposes of" subsection 162(e).[38] Moreover, in 1980, the IRS issued proposed regulations—never finalized—defining grassroots lobbying under the pre-1993 law (which, as noted, already disallowed a deduction for the expenses of grassroots lobbying).[39] Under those Proposed Regulations, to be considered grassroots lobbying, a communication basically has to meet the first two prongs of the definition for 501(c)(3) groups: the communication has to refer to specific legislation (or a legislative proposal) and it has to reflect a view on that legislation. But it does *not* have to encourage the recipient to take any action; rather, it merely needs to be "communicated in a form and distributed in a manner so as to reach individuals as members of the general public, that is, as voters or constituents."[40] Given the IRS's admonition, and the reference to present-day rules in the legislative history, it seems likely that the IRS would apply the broader definition of grassroots lobbying in the 1980 Proposed Regulations, rather than the narrower one used in measuring the lobbying activity of 501(c)(3) organizations. But that is far from certain.

13-3.1.5 De Minimis Exception

A business may deduct certain lobbying expenses if they do not exceed $2,000 for the taxable year.[41] Expenses to be included in that number consist of the costs of the time of employees engaged in lobbying and direct activity costs such as reproducing materials; overhead costs associated with the employee time do not need to be included.[42] Two significant limitations should be noted. First, third-party payments for lobbying, including payments to lobbying firms and trade association dues allocable to lobbying, cannot be included in the $2,000 and are always nondeductible regardless of amount.[43] Second, if the expenses that do count toward the $2,000

35. I.R.C. §§ 501(h), 4911(b) (2015).

36. I.R.C. § 4911(c)(4) (2015).

37. Treas. Reg. § 56.4911-2(b)(2) (1990).

38. Dept. of the Treasury, 59 Fed. Reg. 24992-01, 24994 (proposed May 13, 1994) (to be codified at Treas. Reg. § 1.162-29).

39. Dept. of the Treasury, 45 Fed. Reg. 78167 (proposed Nov. 25, 1980) (to be codified at Treas. Reg. § 1.162(a), (b) & (c)).

40. *Id.* (to be codified at Treas. Reg. 1.162(c)(4)).

41. I.R.C. § 162(e)(5)(B) (2015).

42. *Id.*

43. H.R. Conf. Rep. No. 103-213, at 606 (1993).

exceed that number, all of the expenses become nondeductible—in other words, the company cannot simply subtract the first $2,000.[44]

13-3.2 Initiatives and Referenda

Many ballot initiatives and referenda affect business interests, and companies and their trade associations expend significant resources supporting or opposing ballot measures. By one estimate, in the 2014 election cycle, more than $196 million was spent on television advertising alone, supporting or opposing 158 different statewide initiatives and referenda, much of it by business groups and trade associations.[45]

Section 162(e) disallows a deduction for "any attempt to influence the general public, or segments thereof, with respect to . . . referendums." [46] It is clear, then, that the costs of advertising and other public communications advocating support or opposition to a ballot measure are nondeductible under section 162(e).

More complicated is the question of how to treat costs expended before a ballot measure qualifies for the ballot—or is even first circulated for signature. Such activities may include, for example, polling on the viability of a ballot measure, legal research and assistance in drafting an initiative, polling with respect to potential language and ballot titles and summaries, formulating ballot titles and summaries, and litigation with respect to ballot titles and summaries. On the one hand, under the definitions of lobbying for purposes of determining the amount of lobbying in which a 501(c)(3) public charity can engage, attempts to influence ballot measures count as direct, not grassroots lobbying—on the theory that in a referendum or initiative, the members of the public are the "legislators."[47] And, under IRS regulations, a ballot measure does not become "legislation" until it is first circulated for signatures.[48] Further, even before the 1993 legislation, the costs of grassroots lobbying were nondeductible; "influencing referenda" was lumped with grassroots lobbying,[49] by contrast with treatment of influencing ballot measures as direct lobbying for purposes of measuring lobbying by public charities. The term "legislation" was defined to include "action . . . by the public in a referendum, initiative, constitutional amendment or similar procedure."[50] And the current version of section 162(e) as amended by the 1993 law provides that the "term 'legislation' has the meaning given such term by section 4911(e)(2),"[51] the provision applicable to 501(c)(3) groups that are public charities. As interpreted by the IRS, that provision does not treat a ballot measure as legislation until it is circulated for signature.

---

44. *Id.*

45. Center for Public Integrity, *Ballot Measure Backers Spend Big, Win Big* (Nov. 6, 2014), http://www.publicintegrity.org/2014/11/06/16229/ballot-measure-backers-spend-big-win-big (last visited Dec. 22, 2014).

46. I.R.C. § 162(e)(1)(c) (2015).

47. Treas. Reg. § 56.4911-2(b)(1(iii) (1990).

48. *Id.* § 56.4911-2(d)(1)(ii) (1990).

49. I.R.C. § 162(e)(2) (1962).

50. *Id.* (to be codified at Treas. Reg. § 1.162-20(c)(2)(ii)(A)).

51. I.R.C. § 162(e)(4)(B) (2015).

On the other hand, all costs incurred for "preparing" a direct lobbying communication are treated as lobbying expenditures.[52] The IRS rules provide that "all expenditures for researching, drafting, reviewing, copying, publishing and mailing" a direct lobbying communication are included as lobbying expenditures.[53]

Thus, whether a public charity can engage in activities related to formulating and preparing the groundwork for a ballot measure, without having the costs count as lobbying at all, depends on a number of factors, which may include the extent to which the product of those activities is actually used in the ballot measure campaign.

13-3.3 Political Activity

Section 162(e) defines political activity, the costs of which are nondeductible, in exactly the same language as that used to define political activity that is prohibited for 501(c)(3) organizations: "participation in, or intervention in, any political campaign on behalf of (or in opposition to) any candidate for public office." There have been extensive interpretations of that language in section 501(c)(3) in IRS rulings and training materials,[54] and those will not be reviewed in detail here. In general, it is clear that businesses cannot take deductions—not only for direct political contributions, but for the costs of advertising that praises or criticizes public officials who are candidates—in an election year, depending on the timing, content, and circumstances of the advertising, and the costs of other communications that imply support for or opposition to a candidate.

13-4 What Types of Costs Are Nondeductible?

Payments by a business to a lobbying firm or contract lobbyist are all nondeductible.[55] So are payments of trade association dues to the extent those dues are used for nondeductible lobbying—a subject treated in Section 13-6 of this chapter.

IRS regulations address in detail the determination of a business's in-house costs that have to be included in the nondeductible amount. The regulations allow use of "any reasonable method," but recognize four specific methods as "reasonable":[56]

1. The "ratio" method, in which the ratio of "lobbying labor hours" to the hours worked by all employees is multiplied by the business's total operating costs. In calculating "lobbying labor hours," only time spent in direct lobbying contacts—not background research, preparing materials, scheduling, and the like—is counted.[57] And the time of any employee who spends less than 5 percent of her time on such direct lobbying activity can be excluded altogether.[58]

---

52. Treas. Reg. § 56.4911-3(a)(1).
53. *Id.*
54. *See, e.g.,* Rev. Rul. 2007-41, 2007-1 C.B. 1421; IRS 2002 Exempt Organizations Continuing Professional Education Text (2002).
55. Treas. Reg. 1.162-28(d) (1995).
56. *See generally* King, *supra* note 4, at 575–78.
57. Treas. Reg. § 1.162-28(d) (1995).
58. *Id.* § 1.162-28(g)(1).

2. "Gross-up" method—Under this method, in-house lobbying costs are determined simply by taking 175 percent of lobbying labor hours of, times the hourly rate paid to, the employees engaged in direct lobbying and supporting administrative and clerical employees, but without including payroll burden.[59]
3. Alternative gross-up method, in which the in-house lobbying costs are determined by taking 225 percent of lobbying labor hours of, times the hourly rate paid to, only those employees directly engaged in lobbying activities, not including support staff, and again excluding payroll burden.[60]
4. "Section 263A method," in which the lobbying function is treated as a department of the company, and direct and overhead costs are allocated based on one of several methods spelled out in that section and its implementing regulations.[61]

These methods do not apply to allocation of the costs of grassroots lobbying, all of which—including associated overhead costs—must be allocated on some reasonable basis.

13-5 Anti-Cascading: Professional Lobbyists

Payments by a business to a lobbying firm or contract lobbyist are clearly nondeductible. The law recognizes, however, that the amount that lobbying firm or contract lobbyist itself spends to lobby on behalf of its client must be deductible—that those expenses, in other words, are legitimate business expenses of the professional lobbyist. Section 162(e), therefore, as amended by the 1993 law, includes an "anti-cascading" rule that bars deductibility only at one level—client to lobbyist—and does not prevent the professional lobbyist from then deducting her own expenses of conducting lobbying on behalf of clients.[62]

As explained in the Conference Report for the 1993 law, deductibility of the professional lobbyist's expenses is allowed only "where there is a direct, one-on-one relationship between the taxpayer and the entity conducting the lobbying activity."[63] Thus, the anti-cascading rule does not, for example, permit deductibility of dues paid to trade associations, which lobby on behalf of multiple entities. Further, the IRS has taken the position that professional lobbyists cannot deduct political contributions, because those by definition could not lawfully be made to promote the interests of a specific client.[64]

13-6 Dues Payments and Other Contributions to Trade Associations and Nonprofit Organizations

Businesses conduct much of their lobbying, of course, through trade associations, to which they pay dues and may make additional contributions for special projects

---

59. *Id.* § 1.162-28(e)(1).
60. *Id.* § 1.162-28(e)(2).
61. *Id.* § 1.162-28(f); *see* I.R.C. § 263A (2015).
62. I.R.C. § 162(e)(5)(A) (2015).
63. H.R. Conf. Rep. No. 103-213, at 607–10 (1993).
64. 2002 IRS Non Docketed Service Advice Review 21070 (May 24, 2002).

and campaigns of advocacy for or against particular legislation or other actions. Businesses also frequently contribute to nonprofit organizations—charities and educational organizations exempt under section 501(c)(3) of the Code and issue advocacy organizations exempt under section 501(c)(4). This section addresses the extent to which these contributions are nondeductible, and the obligations of the recipient nonprofit organizations.

13-6.1 Trade Associations: Flow-through and Proxy Tax

A business may not deduct that portion of its dues, or other payment or contribution, to a trade association that is allocable to expenditures that would be nondeductible for the business itself under section 162(e)[65]—that is, the nondeductible expenses for lobbying and political activity described above, using all the definitions and allocation rules discussed earlier.

At the time a business member or contributor pays dues or makes a contribution to the trade association, the trade association must provide to the business an estimate of the portion of those dues or that payment that is allocable to nondeductible lobbying expenses and must notify the business that such portion is nondeductible.[66] The amounts allocable to lobbying expenses include not only dues but also any special assessment or even a one-time contribution to the association.[67] In determining this allocation, the association must treat the nondeductible lobbying expenses as being paid entirely out of the business dues and contributions, rather than out of other revenue.[68] In other words, if an association receives $600,000 in dues and contributions, and $400,000 from other revenue, and expends $300,000 on lobbying expenses, it must count all $300,000 toward the dues portion, and it must notify its members that 50 percent of their dues is nondeductible. If the amount of nondeductible lobbying expenses incurred during the year exceeds the total amount of dues, the excess is carried over to the next year and treated as part of the nondeductible lobbying expenses for that next year.[69]

The association must disclose in its annual information return—the Form 990—the amount of nondeductible lobbying expenses and the amount of dues allocable to those expenses.[70]

If the association fails to provide the required notice when the dues were paid or contributions made, or the actual nondeductible amount exceeds the estimated amount on which the notice to the business was based, then the association must pay a special "proxy tax." The tax is calculated by applying the highest corporate tax rate to the amount of the excess.[71] Taking the prior example, if the 50 percent estimate was based on estimated lobbying expenses of $300,000, but the actual expenses were $400,000, then the association would owe a tax of 35 percent of the excess $100,000—in this case, $35,000. The tax is treated as an income tax for

---

65. I.R.C. § 162(e)(3) (2015).
66. I.R.C. § 6033(e)(1)(A)(ii) (2015).
67. H.R. Conf. Rep. No. 103-213, at 607 n.64 (1993).
68. I.R.C. § 6033(e)(1)(C)(i) (2015).
69. *Id.* § 6033(e)(1)(C)(ii).
70. *Id.* § 6033(e)(1)(A)(i).
71. *Id.* § 6033(e)(2). *See generally* Bruce R. Hopkins, The Law of Tax Exempt Organizations 597–98 (10th ed. 2011).

purposes of all other provisions of the tax code, including penalties for failure to file.[72] An association faced with this tax, however, can apply to the IRS for a waiver of the tax in exchange for agreeing to adjust the following year's estimate to account for the excess.[73]

13-6.2 Other Noncharitable Exempt Organizations

Businesses may contribute to other types of nonprofit organizations in addition to paying dues or contributing to their trade associations. Charitable organizations exempt under section 501(c)(3) present a special case, discussed in the next section. Section 501(c)(4) organizations, in general, are treated exactly the same way as trade associations: They must notify donors what portion of their contribution is allocable to nondeductible lobbying and political activity, at the time the contribution is made. Agricultural and horticultural associations exempt under section 501(c)(5) are also generally treated the same as trade associations, but labor unions are not. Labor unions, veterans' organizations, and other 501(c) organizations are exempt from the notification requirement altogether.[74]

Section 501(c)(4) and other nonprofits generally subject to the notification requirement, however, are exempted from that requirement if more than 90 percent of the organization's annual dues come from members who each pay less than $103.[75] In determining if that test is met, local chapters of a national organization and the national organization itself are all treated as one entity—so that only the amount received as dues from members is counted as dues received, not transfers from the local to the national or vice versa.[76]

Finally, a section 501(c)(4) or other nonprofit subject to the notification requirement (other than a trade association) can be exempted from that requirement if it can establish that 90 percent of the dues it received would not have been deducted because the dues were paid by individuals or entities that would not have deducted the dues as business expenses.[77] To get this exemption, the organization must note that it is eligible on the Form 990.[78]

13-6.3 Section 501(c)(3) Organizations

As noted, section 501(c)(3) organizations are permitted to engage in a certain amount of lobbying, as long as it is not a substantial portion of their activity, measured either by all of the facts or circumstances or by the optional dollar expenditure test. Businesses may make contributions to section 501(c)(3) organizations that are deductible as charitable contributions.[79] Section 501(c)(3) organizations do not have to notify donors that any portion of their dues allocable to lobbying is

---

72. *Id.* § 6033(e)(2)(C).

73. *Id.* § 6033(e)(2)(B).

74. Rev. Proc. 98-19, 1998-1 C.B. 547 § 4.01.

75. *Id.* § 4.02. The amount in the Revenue Procedure is actually $75, but that amount has been adjusted for inflation to $103. Rev. Proc. 2010-40, 2010-46 I.R.B. 2.

76. Rev. Proc. 98-19, 1998-1 C.B. 547 §§ 5.03–5.04.

77. *Id.* § 5.06.

78. *Id.* § 5.06(ii).

79. *See* I.R.C. § 170(b)(2) (2015) (corporate deduction limited to 10% of taxable income).

nondeductible.[80] However, the Code does provide that a contribution by a business to a section 501(c)(3) organization will not be deductible, either as a charitable contribution or as a business expense, if (1) the contribution was used to conduct lobbying of "direct financial interest" to the contributor, and (2) a "principal purpose of the contribution was to avoid" loss of the deduction that the donor would have been saddled with if the donor business had engaged in the lobbying directly.[81]

---

80. Rev. Proc. 98-19, 1998-1 C.B. 547 § 4.01.

81. I.R.C. § 170(f)(9) (2015). For a full discussion of the tax treatment of lobbying expenses by section 501(c)(3) organizations, see Chapter 11 of this manual.

CHAPTER 14

Office of Management and Budget Regulations Governing Lobbying Costs Incurred by Nonprofit Organizations

BY THOMAS M. SUSMAN*

14-1 Introduction
14-2 Prohibitions under OMB Circulars
14-3 Allowed Exceptions
14-4 Required Cost-Accounting Procedures
14-5 Recordkeeping
14-6 Enforcement

14-1 Introduction

While the Federal Acquisition Regulation (FAR) governs the contractual interactions between commercial contractors and the government,[1] guidance issued by the Office of Management and Budget (OMB), titled "Uniform Administrative Requirements, Cost Principles, and Audit Requirements for Federal Awards" (the Uniform Guidance or OMB Circular A-81), governs whether nonprofit organizations may use federal award funds to reimburse lobbying costs.[2] The relevant provisions of the Uniform Guidance are almost identical to the FAR, but the Uniform Guidance has a broader scope, covering grants and cooperative agreements along with contracts. The Uniform Guidance defines "nonprofit organization" as:

---

*Clayton S. Marsh, formerly with Ropes & Gray LLP, was a contributor to an earlier version of this chapter as it appeared in THE LOBBYING MANUAL: A COMPLIANCE GUIDE FOR LAWYERS AND LOBBYISTS (2nd ed.) (William Luneburg, ed., 1998). Leslie Thornton, an associate with Ropes & Gray LLP, contributed to the current revision.

1. See Chapter 17 on FAR as it applies to lobbying costs.

2. *Uniform Administrative Requirements, Cost Principles, and Audit Requirements for Federal Awards,* 2 C.F.R. pt. 200 (2014) [hereinafter UNIFORM GUIDANCE], superseded OMB Circular A-122, *Cost Principles for Nonprofit Organizations,* 45 Fed. Reg. 46022 (July 8, 1980), official correction 46 Fed. Reg. 17185 (Mar. 17, 1981), amended 49 Fed. Reg. 18260 (Apr. 27, 1984), amended 49 Fed. Reg. 19,588 (May 29, 1984), amended 52 Fed. Reg. 19788 (May 27, 1987), amended 60 Fed. Reg. 52516 (Oct. 6, 1995), amended 62 Fed. Reg. 45934 (Aug. 29, 1997), amended 63 Fed. Reg. 29794 (June 1, 1998), amended 69 Fed. Reg. 25970 (May 10, 2004).

[A]ny corporation, trust, association, cooperative, or other organization, not including [Institutions of Higher Education], that: (1) is operated primarily for scientific, educational, service, charitable, or similar purposes in the public interest; (2) is not organized primarily for profit; and (3) uses net proceeds to maintain, improve, or expand the operations of the organization.[3]

The Uniform Guidance seeks to prevent use of appropriated funds for lobbying that diverts resources from the purpose for which the grant or contract was awarded. Any federal subsidy of lobbying threatens to distort the political process by favoring the goals of some organizations over others and by giving the appearance of federal support for private lobbying. OMB has tried to avoid the appearance that the government has "endorsed, fostered, or prescribe[d as] orthodox" any one political view.[4]

14-2 Prohibitions under OMB Circulars

Like the FAR, the Uniform Guidance sets forth general factors that determine the allowability of costs. To be allowable (and thus reimbursable) under a federal award, unless otherwise authorized by statute, costs must (1) be reasonable and necessary for performance of the federal award and be allocable thereto; (2) conform to any limitations or exclusions set forth in the Uniform Guidance or in the federal award as to types or amount of cost items; (3) be consistent with policies and procedures applicable to both federally financed and non-federally financed activities of the nonprofit entity; (4) be treated consistently as either a direct cost or an indirect cost; (5) be determined in accordance with generally accepted accounting principles; (6) not be included as a cost or used to meet cost-sharing or matching requirements of any other federally financed program in either the current or a prior period; and (7) be adequately documented.[5]

The lobbying provision in OMB Circular A-122, a predecessor to the Uniform Guidance, was added on April 27, 1984.[6] The provision bars the use of federal award funds to reimburse the costs associated with most types of lobbying and political activities. Formerly found at section 25 of Appendix B to OMB Circular-122, the lobbying provision now appears at section 200.450 of the Uniform Guidance. Like the FAR, however, the Uniform Guidance does not restrict lobbying paid with nonfederal funds.

According to regulatory commentary accompanying OMB Circular A-122, the express lobbying prohibitions now within the Uniform Guidance were originally drafted to mirror the FAR prohibitions.[7] With some exceptions, costs associated with the following categories of activity are unallowable under the Uniform

---

3. UNIFORM GUIDANCE, *supra* note 2, at § 200.70. An "Institution of Higher Education" is defined at 20 U.S.C. § 1001 (2015).

4. 49 Fed. Reg. 18260, 18262 (Apr. 27, 1984) (quoting W.Va. State Bd. of Educ. v. Barnette, 319 U.S. 624, 645 (1943)).

5. UNIFORM GUIDANCE, *supra* note 2, at § 200.403; *see generally* UNIFORM GUIDANCE, at Appendix IV, *Indirect (F&A) Costs Identification and Assignment, and Rate determination for Nonprofit Organizations.*

6. 49 Fed. Reg. 18260 (Apr. 27, 1984) (originally classified as "paragraph B21").

7. *Id.*, at pmbl. VII § B.

Guidance and thus are not reimbursable. Note that these categories generally align with the categories of lobbying activities deemed unallowable under the FAR.[8]

1.   Attempts to influence the outcomes of any federal, state, or local election, referendum, initiative, or similar procedure, through in-kind or cash contributions, endorsements, publicity, or similar activity.[9]

2.   Establishing, administering, contributing to, or paying the expenses of a political party, campaign, political action committee, or other organization established for the purpose of influencing the outcomes of elections in the United States.[10]

3.   Any attempt to influence[11]
    a.   The introduction of federal or state legislation.[12]
    b.   The enactment or modification of any pending federal or state legislation through communication with any member or employee of the Congress or state legislature (including efforts to influence state or local official to engage in similar lobbying activity).[13] This provision does not apply to executive branch lobbying, with the exception of (1) attempts to influence a decision to sign or veto legislation and (2) attempts to use state and local officials as conduits for grantee and contractor lobbying of Congress or state legislatures.[14] The provision is somewhat more limited than the parallel FAR provision, in that it does not apply to legislative lobbying at the state or local level except to the extent that the organization lobbies state and local officials to become conduits to accomplish other lobbying activities defined in the section.[15]
    c.   The enactment or modification of any pending federal or state legislation by preparing, distributing, or using publicity or propaganda, or by urging members of the general public, or any segment thereof, to contribute to or participate in any mass demonstration, march, rally, fund-raising drive, lobbying campaign, or letter-writing or telephone campaign (i.e., "grassroots lobbying").[16] Grassroots lobbying is by definition an effort to obtain concerted action by the public and does not apply to efforts

---

8. See Section 17-2 of this manual (setting forth the categories for which costs may not be reimbursed under 48 C.F.R. § 31.205-22(a)(1)–(a)(6) (2015)).

9. Uniform Guidance, *supra* note 2, at § 200.450(c)(1)(i); *see also* 48 C.F.R. § 31.205-22(a)(1) (2015).

10. Uniform Guidance, *supra* note 2, at § 200.450(c)(1)(ii); *see also* 48 C.F.R. § 31.205-22(a)(2) (2015).

11. The phrase "attempt to" requires "intent or conduct with the reasonably foreseeable consequence of initiating legislative action or to support or facilitate such ongoing action." 49 Fed. Reg. 18260, at pmbl. VII § C (Apr. 27, 1984).

12. Uniform Guidance, *supra* note 2, at § 200.450(c)(1)(iii)(A); *see also* 48 C.F.R. § 31.205-22(a)(3)–(a)(4) (2015).

13. Uniform Guidance, *supra* note 2, at § 200.450(c)(1)(iii)(B); *see also* 48 C.F.R. § 31.205-22(a)(3) (2015).

14. 49 Fed. Reg. 18260, at pmbl. VII § C (Apr. 27, 1984).

15. *Id.*

16. Uniform Guidance, *supra* note 2, at § 200.450(c)(1)(iii)(C); *see also* 48 C.F.R. § 31.205-22(a)(4) (2015).

"to affect the *opinions* of the general public" if these efforts are not intended to have the reasonably foreseeable consequence of leading to concerted action.[17]

d. Any government official or employee in connection with a decision to sign or veto enrolled legislation.[18]

4. Legislative liaison activities, including attendance at legislative session or committee hearings, gathering information regarding legislation, and analyzing the effect of legislation, when such activities are carried on in support of or in knowing preparation for an effort to engage in unallowable lobbying.[19] In contrast to the Department of Defense FAR Supplement, which makes reimbursement for all legislative liaison activities unallowable, this section of the Uniform Guidance seems to allow costs associated with some activities not directly associated with lobbying.[20] The requirement of "knowing preparation" is intended to avoid the retroactivity problem whereby auditors automatically disallow legislative liaison costs when associated with later lobbying efforts. Only legislative liaison activities that, from their "timing and subject matter, can reasonably be inferred to have had a clearly foreseeable link with later lobbying fall within the 'knowing preparation' standard of [this provision]."[21]

In May 2004, language was added to OMB Circular A-122, now found at section 200.450(b) of the Uniform Guidance, to declare unallowable those "costs incurred in attempting to improperly influence, either directly or indirectly, an employee or officer of the executive branch of the federal government to give consideration or to act regarding a Federal award or a regulatory matter."[22] Unlike other lobbying activities outlined in this Section, 14, executive lobbying costs are not excepted from disallowance under any of the circumstances outlined in the following Section 14-3.

14-3 Allowed Exceptions

The Uniform Guidance provides exceptions to the lobbying disallowances outlined in Section 14-2 above. Again, the exceptions are almost identical to those in the FAR.[23] These exceptions do not necessarily make the costs of these excluded activities allowable, but rather the excluded activities are not forbidden expressly.[24] In other words, in these instances, costs incurred for lobbying are allowable and may be reimbursed *if* they meet the more general allowability criteria described

17. 49 Fed. Reg. 18260, at pmbl. VII § C (Apr. 27, 1984) (emphasis in original).

18. UNIFORM GUIDANCE, *supra* note 2, at § 200.450(c)(1)(iii)(D); *see also* 48 C.F.R. § 31.205-22(a)(3) (2015).

19. UNIFORM GUIDANCE, *supra* note 2, at § 200.450(c)(1)(iv); *see also* 48 C.F.R. § 31.205-22(a)(5) (2015).

20. 49 Fed. Reg. 18260, at pmbl. VII § D (Apr. 27, 1984).

21. *Id.*

22. UNIFORM GUIDANCE, *supra* note 2, at § 200.450(b); 69 Fed. Reg. 25970, 25992 (May 10, 2004); *see also* 48 C.F.R. § 31.205-22(a)(6) (2015). "Improper influence means any influence that induces or tends induce a Federal employee or officer to give consideration or to act regarding a Federal award or regulatory matter on any basis other than the merits of the matter." UNIFORM GUIDANCE at § 200.450(b).

23. See Section 17-3 of this manual.

24. 49 Fed. Reg. 18260, at pmbl. VII § B (Apr. 27, 1984).

above (Section 14-2). These activities could still be unallowable if the activities were not reasonable to perform the activity funded by the contract or grant in question.

Section 200.450(c)(2)(i) of the Uniform Guidance excepts costs associated with technical and factual presentations to specific legislative audiences on topics directly related to the contract or grant under which reimbursement is sought and only when offered in response to a documented request by the nonprofit entity's member of Congress, legislative body or subdivision, or a cognizant staff member. The information supplied to the legislative recipient must be readily obtainable and in a deliverable form. The exception is meant to allow the organization to respond to specific informational needs of legislators and their staffs.[25] For the costs to be reimbursable, however, the services rendered must be predominantly informational in purpose and content and not advocatory. The fact, however, that an advocatory conclusion is reached does not, in itself, take the activity out of this exception, providing that conclusion flows from the technical and factual data presented and is only a minor aspect of the presentation.[26] The data can be provided through "hearing testimony, statements or letters" and need not necessarily take the form of formal testimony. Costs for travel, lodging, and meals are allowable only if they result from the offer of testimony at a regularly scheduled congressional hearing pursuant to a written request from the chairman or ranking minority member of the committee or subcommittee conducting the hearing.[27]

Section 200.450(c)(2)(ii) of the Uniform Guidance excepts costs associated with lobbying to "influence state legislation in order directly to reduce the cost, or to avoid impairment of the [nonprofit entity's] authority to perform the grant, contract, or other agreement." This exception does not, however, "permit the use of Federal funds to lobby state legislatures to promote an organization's ideological objectives merely because those objectives are consonant with the purposes of the grant or contract."[28]

Section 200.450(c)(2)(iii) of the Uniform Guidance excepts any activity that is "specifically authorized by statute to be undertaken with funds from the Federal award."

Finally, section 200.450(c)(2)(iv) of the Uniform Guidance excepts any activity that is excepted from the definitions of "lobbying" or "influencing legislation" by the Internal Revenue Code provisions requiring nonprofit entities to limit participation in direct and "grassroots" lobbying activities in order to retain their charitable deduction status and avoid punitive excise taxes.[29] These activities include nonpartisan analyses, studies, or research reports; examinations and discussions of broad social, economic, or similar problems; and information provided upon request by a legislator for technical advice and assistance.[30]

25. 49 Fed. Reg. 18260, at pmbl. VII § F (Apr. 27, 1984).
26. *Id.*
27. Uniform Guidance, *supra* note 2, at § 200.450(c)(2)(i).
28. 49 Fed. Reg. 18260, at pmbl. VII § G (Apr. 27, 1984).
29. *See* I.R.C. §§ 501(c)(3), 501(h), 4911(a) (2015).
30. As to technical advice and assistance, *see* I.R.C. § 4911(d)(2) (2015) and 26 C.F.R. § 56.4911-2(c)(1)–(c)(3) (2015).

14-4 Required Cost-Accounting Procedures

Unallowable lobbying costs include not only the costs of the actual lobbying activities but also the costs of tangential activities, such as consultation and preparation.[31] Section 200.450(c)(2)(v) of the Uniform Guidance follows existing accounting practice and emphasizes that total lobbying costs must be separately identified in the indirect (Facilities and Administration, or F&A) cost rate proposal, and thereafter must be treated as other unallowable activity costs according to the direct cost procedures set forth at section 200.413 of the Uniform Guidance. Again, organizations are exempt from this section if they do not seek reimbursement of their indirect costs from federal grants and contracts.[32]

14-5 Recordkeeping

Pursuant to section 200.450(c)(2)(vi), nonprofit entities receiving federal award funds must, as part of the annual indirect (F&A) cost rate proposal, certify that they have complied with the requirements and standards of the above lobbying restrictions. As do the parallel provisions of the FAR, section 200.450(c)(2)(vii) of the Uniform Guidance relaxes the recordkeeping requirements when an employee's lobbying activities comprise 25 percent or less of the employee's compensated hours of employment for a given calendar month *and*, within the preceding five-year period, the nonprofit entity has not materially misstated allowable or unallowable costs, including legislative lobbying costs. General recordkeeping requirements are set forth at section 200.302 of the Uniform Guidance, formerly of OMB Circular A-110.[33]

14-6 Enforcement

As under the FAR,[34] whether the policy goals underlying the Uniform Guidance are achieved depends largely upon voluntary compliance by contractors and grantees,[35] as the Uniform Guidance does not contain an independent enforcement mechanism. Section 200.450(2)(c)(viii) of the Uniform Guidance requires federal awarding agencies to establish procedures for advance resolution of significant questions or disagreements arising under the lobbying provisions, which must be binding in any subsequent settlements, audits, or investigations as to a particular grant or contract. This provision is intended to prevent interpretational problems and to allow organizations to engage in activities without fear of uncertain application of the guidance by federal agencies.

OMB considered and rejected as too stringent a penalty provision requiring the "return to the Federal government of all grant or contract funds received by a

---

31. 49 Fed. Reg. 18260, at pmbl. VII § J (Apr. 27, 1984).

32. *Id.* at pmbl. VII § K.

33. OMB Circular A-110, *Uniform Administrative Requirements for Grants and Agreements with Institutions of Higher Education, Hospitals, and Other Non-Profit Organizations*, 62 Fed. Reg. 45933 (Aug. 29, 1997).

34. See Section 17-6 of this manual.

35. 49 Fed. Reg. 18260, at pmbl. IX § 1 (Apr. 27, 1984).

nonprofit organization found to be using Federal funds [for] lobbying."[36] Nevertheless, the Uniform Guidance does have some degree of enforceability. The principal sanction in the event of minor or unintentional violations is cost recovery or reimbursement.[37] In more serious cases, contracts or grants may be terminated or contractors and grantees may be debarred from further awards.[38] In addition, the audit requirements that the rules currently impose on contractors and grantees, along with expanded Inspector General and agency audit staffs now in place, have increased the likelihood that improper expenditures on lobbying activities will be detected.

36. *Id.* at pmbl. IX § 2.
37. *Id.*
38. *Id.*

CHAPTER 15

The Byrd Amendment

BY THOMAS M. SUSMAN*

15-1 Introduction

The Byrd Amendment prohibits the use of funds appropriated by Congress to lobby for any type of a federal award—a federal contract, grant, loan, or cooperative

---

*Clayton S. Marsh, formerly with Ropes & Gray LLP, was a contributor to an earlier version of the chapter as it appeared in *The Lobbying Manual: A Compliance Guide for Lawyers and Lobbyists* (2nd ed.) (William Luneburg, ed., 1998).

agreement. It also requires a recipient of a federal award to disclose to the award-ing agency certain payments made to influence the award. The Byrd Amendment applies equally to nonprofit entities, state and local governments, and businesses, and it reaches subcontractors (subgrantees and the like) at any tier. This chapter addresses the impact of the Byrd Amendment on lobbyists for government con-tractors and other government awardees.

The Byrd Amendment was enacted with some fanfare, but it has been criticized as being both unclear in some respects and undesirably broad in others.[1] Initial reports filed with Congress by federal agencies also revealed widespread confu-sion and inconsistent interpretations concerning the amendment's requirements.[2] Interim regulations implementing the amendment have not resolved all questions of its scope and application, but have reduced its potential coverage. Only a few of the uncertainties have been addressed by the Government Accountability Office (GAO). In *United States v. Nat'l Training & Info. Center, Inc.*, the one federal court that has addressed the constitutionality of this statute upheld it against charges of being unconstitutionally vague and overbroad, but it began its assessment of the constitutional issues by observing: "The Byrd Amendment of 1989 is a strange bird."[3] As a result, awardees should not be faulted for erroneously interpreting, twenty-five years after its enactment, the still uncertain aspects of Byrd Amend-ment requirements.

15-2 Background of the Byrd Amendment

The Byrd Amendment was added by the Senate at the last minute, without hear-ings, to the 1990 Department of the Interior Appropriations Act to address Appro-priations Committee Chairman Robert Byrd's concerns over the use of lobbyists by contractors and grantees.[4] With few, though significant, revisions by the conference committee,[5] the Byrd Amendment was approved and enacted into law.[6]

The impetus behind the Byrd Amendment included scandals at the Depart-ment of Housing and Urban Development during the late 1980s and Senator Byrd's anger over a constituent educational institution's nonpublic hiring of an outside lobbyist to obtain specially earmarked funds for the institution from the Appropriations Committee.[7] As a result, the law covers lobbying of both Congress and the executive branch.

---

1. *See, e.g.,* Thomas M. Susman & Clayton S. Marsh, *Byrd Shot: Congress Takes a Broad Aim at Gov-ernment Contract Lobbyists,* 37 FED. B. NEWS & J. 387 (1990); OMB, *Lobbying Guidance Creates "Untenable Burden," CODSIA Charges,* 55 FED. CONT. REP. 362–63 (1990).

2. Requirements for semiannual reports to Congress by federal agencies and annual reports by Inspectors General were discontinued by the Lobbying Disclosure Act of 1995, Pub. L. No. 104–65, § 10(b)(1), 109 Stat. 691, 700 (1995) (codified as amended in scattered sections of 2 U.S.C.); 31 U.S.C. § 1352 nt. (2015).

3. 532 F. Supp. 2d 946, 951 (N.D. Ill. 2007) (citing this chapter of the 3rd edition of the LOBBYING MANUAL).

4. *See* 135 CONG. REC. 16245-47 (July 26, 1989).

5. H.R. REP. No. 101-264 (1989). Both OMB and GAO worked closely with the committees on the drafting of the legislation. For a summary of the significant revisions made in the conference commit-tee, *see* Thomas M. Susman, *Lobbying for Government Contracts,* 52 FED. CONT. REP. 927, 932 (1989).

6. Pub. L. No. 101–121, § 319, 103 Stat. 701, 750 (1989) (codified as amended at 31 U.S.C. § 1352 (2015)).

7. ROLL CALL, Aug. 14–20, 1989, at 12.

Congress appeared to give no attention to coordinating the Byrd Amendment with the federal laws that governed contractors' lobbying activities. The Byrd Amendment overlaps, without coordination, with the Federal Acquisition Regulation (FAR) provisions that prohibit the use of federal funds for lobbying Congress.[8] (FAR also requires contractors with proposals for settlement and indirect costs over $500,000 to certify compliance with regulations.)[9] However, the Byrd Amendment's prohibition against expenditure of appropriated funds for lobbying and its required certification of compliance not only duplicate the FAR and other rules, but also extend beyond them to reach executive branch lobbying.

The legislative history of the Amendment is sparse, but contains rhetoric about "influence peddlers [who] sell themselves as hired guns to the highest bidder . . . [and] claim that they know the password to the back doors on Capitol Hill."[10] This sentiment indicated a congressional belief that lobbying encouraged federal agencies to elevate political favoritism over objective evaluation of the merits of prospective awardees.[11] Congress seemed to think that the sunshine of mandatory disclosure would be the best disinfectant to alleviate this kind of favoritism.

15-3 Description of the Byrd Amendment

The Byrd Amendment contains both a *prohibition* on the use of "appropriated" federal funds to lobby for federal awards and *disclosure requirements* for those who use non-appropriated funds to pay lobbyists for assistance in obtaining federal contracts, grants, loans, and cooperative agreements.[12]

Although the targets of the Byrd Amendment are lobbying and the use of influential consultants to obtain federal awards, nowhere do the words "lobbying," "lobbyist," or "consultant" appear. Instead, the Byrd Amendment applies to "influencing or attempting to influence" major federal awards.[13] Activities subject to the amendment include efforts by an entity's officers, directors, partners, employees, lawyers, associations, or even friends and relatives—as well as those who hold themselves out as "lobbyists" or "consultants"—as long as they are paid by the awardee to influence federal awards.

The essential features of the Byrd Amendment are as follows:

- No *appropriated* funds may be expended (1) by the recipient of an award (2) to pay any person (3) to influence Congress or an agency regarding

---

8. 48 C.F.R. § 31.205–22 (2015); see Chapter 17.

9. 10 U.S.C. § 2324(h)(1), (*l*)(1)(A) (2015).

10. 135 Cong. Rec. S8762, 8779 (daily ed. July 26, 1989). As Senator Byrd opined:

In recent months, there has been a constant stream of news articles relating to lobbyists who exert undue influence to steer the executive branch decision-making process away from merit selection and toward political favoritism; or who collect exorbitant fees to create projects and have them earmarked in appropriation bills and reports for the benefit of their clients, oftentimes before the prospective recipients have filed their application for such grants.

Id.

11. *See* S. Rep. No. 101-85, 125 (1989).

12. 31 U.S.C. § 1352 (2015); *see also* 55 Fed. Reg. 24540, 24541–42 (June 15, 1990). The Byrd Amendment applied to all awards made on or after December 23, 1989. *See* 31 U.S.C. § 1352 nt. (2015).

13. *Id.* § 1352(a)(1). The Lobbying Disclosure Act, however, does not use the term "influence" in defining "lobbying activity." 2 U.S.C. § 1602(7) (2015).

(4) the making of an award (including any "extension, continuation, renewal, amendment or modification" of a prior award), subject to specific exceptions noted below.[14]

- If *non-appropriated* funds are expended for uses that would be prohibited for appropriated funds (or for loan insurance or loan guarantees by the United States), then anyone who "initiates agency consideration" or receives the award (including any subcontract) must file a declaration with the agency (in the case of a subcontract, with the prime contractor or next-highest subcontractor, which in turn must file it with its contracting partner, and so on up the contractual chain to the agency contracting officer), again subject to exceptions noted below.[15]

- The declaration must be filed (1) with each submission that initiates agency consideration; (2) upon receipt of the award (if there has been no prior filing); and (3) quarterly, if any event has occurred that materially affects information in a previous declaration.[16]

- The declaration must (1) state the name of any registrant under the Lobbying Disclosure Act of 1995 who has made lobbying contacts[17] regarding the award on behalf of the offeror or awardee; and (2) contain a certification that the declarant has not made and will not make any prohibited payment.[18]

- Sanctions may involve the imposition of civil penalties of $10,000–$100,000 per violation (and each failure to report is a separate violation).[19]

- Excepted from the *prohibition* on expenditure of appropriated funds are (1) "payment of reasonable compensation" to an awardee's officers or employees for lobbying "not directly related" to any award,[20] and (2) "any reasonable payment" to a consultant or "payment of reasonable compensation" to officers or employees for "professional or technical services rendered directly in the preparation, submission, or negotiation" of the award, or for meeting requirements imposed by law as a condition of receiving the award.[21]

- Excepted from the *reporting* requirements are (1) reasonable compensation to regularly employed officers and employees,[22] and (2) payments where the contract, grant, or cooperative agreement sought does not exceed $100,000 ($150,000 in the case of a loan, loan insurance, or a guarantee).[23]

- In addition to private entities, state and local governments (but not Indian tribes) are covered by the Byrd Amendment.[24]

---

14. 31 U.S.C. § 1352(a) (2015).

15. *Id.* § 1352(b).

16. *Id.* § 1352(b)(4)(A)–(C).

17. See Chapter 4 of this manual, Section 4-1 (overview) and Section 4-2.2 (definition of "lobbying contact").

18. 31 U.S.C. § 1352(b)(2)(A)–(B) (2015).

19. *Id.* § 1352(c).

20. *Id.* § 1352(d)(1)(A).

21. *Id.* § 1352(d)(1)(B).

22. *Id.* § 1352(d)(2)(A).

23. *Id.* § 1352(d)(2)(B)–(C).

24. *Id.* § 1352(g)(3).

15-4 OMB Rules for All Federal Agencies

On December 20, 1989, the Office of Management and Budget (OMB) published interim final regulations (*Government-wide Guidance for New Restrictions on Lobbying*) implementing the Byrd Amendment and clarifying how certain requirements would apply in practice.[25] These were added to the FAR (for all federal agency procurement contracts) on January 30, 1990,[26] and were adopted for all other federal agency awards on February 26, 1990.[27] In June 1990, January 1992, and January 1996, OMB amended or supplemented this guidance.[28] However, after initial publication of the interim regulations, OMB has still not made the "interim" final rules a final common rule for all agencies. Agencies have adopted separate rules codifying application of OMB Byrd Amendment guidance.[29]

Among the more significant clarifications emerging from OMB are the following:

- *Actions not covered by the prohibition.* With respect to the exemption under the Byrd Amendment for payments made to employees "for agency and legislative liaison activities not directly related to a Federal action,"[30] OMB has noted that "providing any information specifically requested by an agency or Congress is allowable at any time."[31] OMB further provided that employee discussions with an agency regarding product qualities, or adaptation of products for agency use, are allowable when not related to a specific (existing) solicitation for a federal award.[32] It also provided that furnishing certain unsolicited information necessary for informed agency decision making regarding a federal award is permissible "*prior to* formal [agency] solicitation of any covered Federal action."[33]
- *Exemption from prohibition—routine communications and requests for clarifications.* In the June 1990 notice, OMB stated that "nothing in the statute or OMB's guidance limits Federal agencies" from responding to requests from cities and counties for information or clarification about federal grants to such authorities.[34] OMB stated that this clarification would be reflected through an addition to the interim rules made in the course of

---

25. 54 Fed. Reg. 52306 (Dec. 20, 1989).
26. 55 Fed. Reg. 3190 (Jan. 30, 1990).
27. OMB interim final rule § ____.100(c), 55 Fed. Reg. 6736, 6738 (Feb. 26, 1990). The OMB interim rule has been adopted government-wide. *See, e.g.,* 7 C.F.R. § 3018 (2015) (Department of Agriculture); 32 C.F.R. § 28 (2015) (Department of Defense); 49 C.F.R. § 20 (2015) (Department of Transportation).
28. 55 Fed. Reg. 24540 (June 15, 1990); 57 Fed. Reg. 1772 (Jan. 15, 1992); 61 Fed. Reg. 1412 (Jan. 19, 1996).
29. *See* Codification of Governmentwide Grants Requirements by Department, OMB, http://www.whitehouse.gov/omb/GRANTS_chart.
30. 31 U.S.C. § 1352(d)(1)(A) (2015).
31. OMB interim final rule § ____.200(b), 55 Fed. Reg. at 6739.
32. *Id.* § ____.200(c), 55 Fed. Reg. at 6739.
33. *Id.* § ____.200(d), 55 Fed. Reg. at 6739 (emphasis added).
34. 55 Fed. Reg. at 24541.

finalizing those rules.[35] OMB also indicated in that notice that its final rules would make clear that communications in the nature of routine and ongoing post-award administration of grants and contracts are not "influencing activities" and fall within the exemption for "Professional and Technical Services."[36]

- *The prohibition and program lobbying.* In the June 1990 notice, OMB proposed certain changes to its February 1990 interim rules. First, OMB attempted to clarify the applicability of the Byrd Amendment to "program lobbying," as distinguished from "award lobbying," by stating that the prohibition on the use of appropriated funds did not apply to lobbying activities relating to a "program versus a specific covered Federal action."[37] However, in the January 1992 notice, OMB stated that it was concerned that this language "may have been interpreted too broadly to exclude most disclosure requirements on 'program lobbying,' even when such activity results in influencing covered Federal actions."[38] Accordingly, the agency proposed to revoke its June 1990 guidance on the matter and directed that "[a]ctivities to influence Congressional or Executive Branch action on a provision of a bill or report that would direct the funding of, or indicate an intent to fund, a covered Federal action" cannot be undertaken with appropriated funds and must be included in any disclosures required under the Amendment.[39] According to OMB, this new guidance means that "activities to influence the earmarking of funds for a particular *program*, project or activity in an appropriation, authorization or other bill or in report language would be included within that Act's restrictions" and, it would follow, declarations.[40]

- *Disclosure.* In the January 1992 notice, OMB also proposed to clarify when lobbying activities covered by the Byrd Amendment and paid for with non-appropriated funds must be disclosed. According to OMB, disclosure should be required only when "the influencing relates to covered Federal action for a specifically identifiable party or parties, and not for funds distributed to a broad class of parties."[41] It therefore would appear that the cost of membership in an organization that lobbies for its members is not an expenditure required to be reported, unless the organization specifically seeks to influence an award to a particular member (the declarant).

- *Updating declarations.* With respect to the requirement under the amendment that disclosure updates be filed "at the end of each calendar quarter in which there occurs any event that materially affects the accuracy of the information contained in any declaration previously filed,"[42] OMB

---

35. *Id.* While the agency stated that this conclusion would be reflected in future versions of the Byrd Amendment rules, there was nothing in the June 1990, January 1992, or January 1996 notices to indicate that OMB would not consider the conclusion to apply *until* these rules are announced. As noted previously in the text, the interim final rules have not yet been replaced by final rules.

36. *Id.*

37. *Id.* at 24,542.

38. 57 Fed. Reg. 1772 (Jan. 15, 1992); see also Section 15-6.3 of this chapter.

39. 57 Fed. Reg. 1772.

40. *Id.* (emphasis added).

41. *Id.* at 1773.

42. 31 U.S.C. § 1352(b)(4)(C) (2015).

has explained that material changes in information would include (1) an increase of $25,000 or more in the amount paid or expected to be paid in connection with lobbying related to a federal award, (2) any change in the persons doing the lobbying, and (3) any change in the "officer(s), employee(s), or Member(s) contacted to influence or attempt to influence a covered Federal action."[43]

- *Civil penalties.* An agency considering imposing penalties must also consider the nature and circumstances surrounding the failure to comply with the requirements of the amendment; first-time offenders generally will not be assessed a civil penalty in excess of $10,000.[44]

15-5 Modification by the Lobbying Disclosure Act of 1995

The Byrd Amendment was substantially changed by the Lobbying Disclosure Act of 1995 (LDA). Before enactment of the LDA, the Byrd Amendment had required contractors and awardees to file with the awarding agency a complicated disclosure certification stating that no appropriated funds were used for prohibited purposes and detailing payments made by the contractor's or awardee's own funds to influence awards.[45] For awards made on or after January 1, 1996, the LDA simplified the disclosure requirements by requiring only a declaration. The declaration must (1) state the name of any lobbyist who has made lobbying contacts on behalf of the contractor and (2) contain a certification that the declarant has not made, and will not make, any prohibited payments.

The LDA also repealed the requirements for semiannual reports from agency heads to Congress and annual reports from the Inspectors General to Congress. These changes were reflected in OMB's guidelines in January 1996.[46] The Standard Form LLL must be filed to disclose lobbying paid for with non-federal funds, to comply with the Byrd Amendment, as amended by the LDA. (The LDA is discussed in greater detail in Chapters 3 through 6.)

15-6 Uncertainty Regarding the Prohibition on Appropriated Funds

Numerous questions remain regarding the Byrd Amendment's prohibition on the use of appropriated funds for the purpose of influencing a federal award. Over two-and-a-half decades after enactment of the Byrd Amendment, many of these still cannot be answered.

15-6.1 What Are "Appropriated Funds"?

The words "appropriated funds" are not defined in the Byrd Amendment or in the regulations. Nor do any of the several definitions of "appropriations" appearing in the United States Code address whether funds retain their "appropriated"

---

43. OMB interim final rule § ____.110(c), 55 Fed. Reg. 6736, 6739 (Feb. 26, 1990).
44. *Id.* § ____.400(d)–(e), 55 Fed. Reg. at 6740.
45. 31 U.S.C. § 1352 nt. (2015).
46. 61 Fed. Reg. 1412 (Jan. 19, 1996).

status for any period or in any way after they are received and commingled by a recipient.[47]

"Appropriate," according to the *American Heritage Dictionary*, means "to set apart for a specific use," and "appropriation" means a "legislative act authorizing the expenditure of an amount of public funds" for a specific use.[48] Thus, it could be argued that, once federal payments are received for a specific use and the use has been performed, the funds should no longer be considered appropriated. Under this interpretation, the prohibition in the Byrd Amendment would only mean that awardees could not pass the costs of influencing covered federal actions on to the government, such as by including them under cost-reimbursable contracts or in cost pools that are otherwise reimbursed or that may influence the amount of future contract prices. In short, the proscribed lobbying expenditures could be treated under the Byrd Amendment simply the same way that unallowable costs are treated by the present FAR.[49]

Unfortunately, Congress muddied this issue in the conference report's Statement of Managers, noting that "[i]n the case of a payment, or progress payment, received by a contractor for performance of a contract, the *portion* of the payment properly allocable to the contractor's *profit* is not appropriated funds."[50] This statement may imply that funds other than the portion allocated to contractor profit somehow remain appropriated even after payment to a contractor or awardee.

The OMB regulations implementing the Byrd Amendment follow this reasoning, describing *non-appropriated* funds "to include *profit*s from any covered Federal action"; the 2007 (and current) version of the FAR makes the same point in the negative: "For purposes of this subpart the term 'appropriated funds' does not include profit or fee from a covered Federal action."[51] And OMB's June 1990 guidance states that "[t]o the extent a person can demonstrate that the person has sufficient monies, other than Federal appropriated funds, the Federal Government shall assume that these other monies were spent for any influencing activities" subject to the Byrd Amendment.[52]

These passages suggest that the congressional managers and the regulation drafters assumed that the cost "portion" of a payment *is* an appropriated fund—a sensible rule up to the time the money changes hands, but not thereafter. Thus the key question becomes: At what point do funds cease to be appropriated? It would appear reasonable to impose some constraint upon a sweeping interpretation

---

47. *See, e.g.,* 5 U.S.C. § 5721(5) (2015) (regarding federal employees' travel, transportation, and subsistence expenses); 31 U.S.C. § 1101(2) (2015) (regarding budget and fiscal program information); 31 U.S.C. § 1511(a) (2015) (regarding apportionments for accounting); and 41 U.S.C. § 6101 (2015) (regarding administrative expenses in public contracts).

48. AM. HERITAGE DICTIONARY (5th ed. 2015). Numerous state courts have, in the absence of a statutory definition, relied on the dictionary definition of "appropriation" or "appropriate" in interpreting state laws. *See, e.g.,* Almond v. Day, 89 S.E.2d 851, 856 (Va. 1955); Davis v. Eggers, 91 P. 819, 823 (Nev. 1907); Brown v. Honiss, 68 A. 150, 158 (N.J. 1907).

49. 48 C.F.R. §§ 31.201-2, 31.201-6 (2015). See Chapter 17 of this manual. But the court in *Nat'l Training & Info. Center* specifically rejected "the government's attempt to conflate the prohibitions of the Byrd Amendment with the unallowable costs of the OMB's Cost Principles." 532 F. Supp. 2d at 959.

50. H.R. REP. No. 101-264 (1989) (emphasis added).

51. OMB interim final rule § ____.100(c), 55 Fed. Reg. 6736, 6738 (Feb. 26, 1990); 48 C.F.R. § 3.802(a)(1) (2015).

52. 55 Fed. Reg. 24540, 24542 (June 15, 1990); 55 Fed. Reg. 3190, 3194 (Jan. 30, 1990), carried forward in FAR regulations at 48 C.F.R. § 3.801(a)(2) (2015).

that appropriated funds retain their appropriated character, perhaps forever, in the bank accounts of contractors and awardees. Yet the question has never been answered by OMB, GAO, or the courts.

15-6.2 Bid Protests and Contract Dispute Costs

The Byrd Amendment arguably could be read to prohibit recovery from federal agencies of bid protest expenditures otherwise recoverable under the FAR[53] and the Competition in Contracting Act (CICA).[54] These protests are clearly an attempt to influence a covered federal award. Therefore, it would follow that all unrecovered payments to lawyers, consultants, and the like would be required to be reported. Similarly, the Byrd Amendment prohibition seems contrary to the reimbursement by federal agencies of certain litigation costs of small businesses mandated by the Equal Access to Justice Act (EAJA).[55] Payments to lawyers and consultants for contract dispute litigation may often be an attempt to influence the modification or renewal of a contract. However, the implementing regulations have not clarified these issues.

In its June 1990 notice, OMB stated that contracts subject to the FAR are covered by the January 1990 FAR interim final rule, Federal Acquisition Circular (FAC) 84-55, not OMB's interim rules for the Byrd Amendment.[56] According to the June 1990 notice, OMB rules apply only to "contracts not subject to the FAR (generally nonprocurement contracts) as well as to grants, loans, cooperative agreements, loan guarantee commitments, and loan insurance commitments."[57] FAC 84-55 is silent on the issue of reimbursement for bid protest expenses, and from this one might conclude that no change was intended regarding the recoverability of bid protest expenses. Nevertheless, in the face of agency silence, it remains unclear whether the Byrd Amendment, separate and apart from OMB and FAR implementing regulations, precludes the recovery of these expenditures.

With respect to the recovery of expenses under the CICA and EAJA, neither the interim final rules nor OMB guidelines address or resolve the conflict among statutory provisions. And so far, there appears to have been no effort by a federal agency to avoid its statutory obligations to reimburse contract-related litigation expenses by invoking the Byrd Amendment.

15-6.3 Program (Earmark) Lobbying

Excepted from the Byrd Amendment's prohibition on the use of appropriated funds for lobbying is the "payment of reasonable compensation made to an officer or employee . . . to the extent that the payment is for agency and legislative liaison activities not directly related to a Federal [award]."[58] Since the prohibition in the amendment applies in the first instance only to activities "in connection with" the

---

53. *See* 48 C.F.R. § 33.104(h) (2015).
54. 31 U.S.C. § 3554(c)(1) (2015).
55. 5 U.S.C. § 504(a) (2015); *see also* 28 U.S.C. § 2412 (2015).
56. 55 Fed. Reg. at 24,542 (June 15, 1990).
57. *Id.*
58. 31 U.S.C. § 1352(d)(1)(A) (2015).

award, the effect of this exception is unclear,[59] unless it is possible for an activity to be "in connection with" but "not directly related to" the award.

The February 1990 interim final rules and the January 1992 proposal to amend those rules attempted to clarify the meaning of this provision; it is no surprise that they have not succeeded. While OMB in 1990 indicated that "program" lobbying—as distinguished from lobbying related to a "specific covered Federal action"—would not be covered by the Byrd Amendment,[60] the January 1992 proposal suggested that program lobbying would be covered: "[a]ctivities to influence the earmarking of funds for a particular program, project or activity in an appropriation, authorization or other bill or in report language would be included within that Act's restrictions."[61] However, this proposed change was not fully adopted, and, as a result, the meaning and effect of the exemption under the amendment remain unclear, and some observers have reasonably concluded that lobbying for earmarks is arguably not covered by the Byrd Amendment.[62]

15-6.4 Distinguishing "Liaison" from "Influence"

It may prove difficult to distinguish between, on the one hand, "influencing" an award—or, especially, the extension, continuation, or modification of an award—and, on the other hand, securing approval of periodic releases of funds, arranging renewals, responding to agency inquiries, and processing modifications and amendments initiated by the agency. These efforts might, for example, be seen as efforts to "influence" the "continuation" of a contract, which would be subject to the prohibition and reporting requirements. They would not be exempt as "agency and legislative liaison activities" since they plainly would be "directly related to a covered Federal action."[63] Nor would these activities be exempt as "professional or technical services" or legally required services, as interpreted in the interim regulations.[64] Fortunately, OMB's June 1990 guidance resolves this ambiguity for certain *post-award* communications: "[R]outine and ongoing post-award activities to administer grants and contracts . . . are not influencing activities."[65] But OMB has not clarified whether communications regarding possible modifications, price adjustments, exercise of options, and the like are subject to the Byrd Amendment.

15-6.5 Lobbying for Contract Specifications

Efforts to influence the contents of a specification or solicitation to allow or to require the use of a particular product would seem to qualify as an attempt to influence a particular award—a future award for that product. In fact, OMB's June 1990 guidance created a useful, bright-line rule that solved this problem, though in a

59. *But see* Nat'l Training & Info. Center, 532 F. Supp. 2d at 949 (providing a general analysis of the Byrd Amendment and specifically noting that the meaning of the phrase "in connection with," as used in the Byrd Amendment, is easily determinable, even if only on a case-by-case basis).

60. 55 Fed. Reg. at 24542.

61. 57 Fed. Reg. 1772 (Jan. 15, 1992).

62. *See, e.g.*, DLA Piper Memorandum, "Byrd Amendment Overview" (May 2009), *available at* http://images.politico.com/global/2013/06/18/byrd_amendment_overview_may09.pdf.

63. 31 U.S.C. § 1352(d)(1)(A) (2015); OMB interim final rule § _____.200(a), 55 Fed. Reg. 6736, 6739 (Feb. 26, 1990).

64. OMB interim final rule § _____.205, 55 Fed. Reg. at 6739; 48 C.F.R. § 52.203-12(c)(2) (2015).

65. 55 Fed. Reg. at 24541 (to be incorporated in a future version of interim final rules or final rules).

fashion contrary to what might otherwise be expected. Discussions of a product or service, and its uses or adaptations, are *not* subject to the Byrd Amendment before the release of a solicitation by an agency.[66] OMB has concluded that pre-solicitation discussions are not attempts to influence a specific award. The FAR and OMB rules should, for consistency, be amended to state this guidance clearly.

15-6.6 Payments By and To Third Parties

The Byrd Amendment's lobbying prohibition does not apply to lobbying paid for *by* a third party, such as where a state agency pays for lobbying directed at the award of a grant to a specific institution or where a city hires a consultant to influence the award to a private developer. A similar coverage gap may also allow a law firm, for example, to contract with a lobbyist to persuade an agency to make an award for the firm's client. As long as the cost of payments is not passed through to the awardee, these third-party payments appear to be outside the scope of the amendment. The Byrd Amendment does, however, expressly cover a potential subcontractor who hires a lobbyist to assist in influencing the prime contract award, because the prohibition applies to payments by the "recipient"—which covers subcontractors.[67]

The January 1992 clarification by OMB proposed that third-party lobbying by associations be exempt where it related to a broad class of potential awardees, but covered where it related to a particular awardee.[68] Where third-party lobbying occurs without any payment to the third party by an awardee, however, there is no Byrd Amendment requirement for reporting the third-party expenditure in any event. Conversely, in deciding a bid protest that predated OMB's January 1992 proposed guidance, GAO appeared to assume that, if payments had been made to a lobbyist by the state of Israel (the third party), they would be treated as having been made by the awardee, an entity wholly owned by the state of Israel.[69] But, since GAO found no evidence that a payment had been made to the lobbyist by either the awardee or the state of Israel, it did not reach this issue. It does not stretch the imagination to conclude that payments to a lobbyist by the owner of a business or the parent of a subsidiary should be attributed to the business or subsidiary, rather than treating the payments as having been made by a third party. However, making such an attribution in the absence of an ownership or controlling relationship would seem to be beyond the reach of the Byrd Amendment.

Just as the Byrd Amendment does not apply to payments by a third party, it likewise does not apply to payments made *to* a third party who is not involved in lobbying. The government argued in *National Training & Information Center* that payments made by the defendant directly to vendors, such as airlines, for bringing subgrantees to Washington to lobby Congress constituted lobbying expenditures under the Byrd Amendment. Citing the language of the statute, legislative history, and the OMB regulations, the court concluded that payments for food, lodging, airfare, and the like paid by the defendant to vendors did not constitute lobbying

---

66. *Id.* at 24542 (with respect to independent sales representatives); *see also* OMB interim final rule § _____.200(c)(1)–(2), 55 Fed. Reg. at 6739 (with respect to employees).
67. 31 U.S.C. § 1352(g)(1)(A) (2015); OMB interim final rule § _____.105(o), 55 Fed. Reg. at 6738.
68. 57 Fed. Reg. 1772, 1773 (Jan. 15, 1992).
69. *In re* Construccionnes Aeronauticas, S.A., 71 Comp. Gen. 81 (1991).

expenses: "We do not see how payments to service providers on behalf of employees or association members lobbying Congress constitutes prohibited payments under the specific language of the Act. It would be a different matter if the payments were reimbursements to the sub-recipient doing the lobbying, but that is not what is alleged here."[70]

15-7 Questions Regarding Disclosure Requirements

In addition to the questions raised by the Byrd Amendment's *prohibition*, many questions and issues are raised by the *disclosure requirements* of the law. The significance of these is magnified because the Byrd Amendment requires redundant reports by awardees and all of their lower-tier partners, which makes agencies, prime awardees, and sub-awardees at every level potentially responsible for maintaining and collating hundreds of thousands of documents. Moreover, these requirements overlap with some other reporting provisions.

15-7.1 Reporting Non-reportable Payments

The exemption covering payments for technical or professional services, at least on its face, applies only to the Byrd Amendment's prohibition on appropriated funds and not to the reporting requirement. Yet, in the Byrd Amendment itself, the reporting requirement is limited to lobbying that would not be permitted with appropriated funds.[71] Must an awardee that pays non-appropriated funds to consultants or lawyers for bid preparation and negotiation file a declaration describing the payments made? The statute would suggest that filing is *not* required, since reporting is required by the Byrd Amendment only where the use of appropriated funds would be prohibited. Initially the FAR rule governing federal procurement contracts provided otherwise, but the provision was dropped from the 2007 version.[72]

Furthermore, the Byrd Amendment, as initially enacted, appeared to require a contractor to file a report stating that no expenditures were made that would have been prohibited if made with appropriated funds: "A declaration . . . shall contain . . . a statement setting forth *whether* such person . . . has made any payment . . . which would be prohibited . . . if the payment were paid for with appropriated funds."[73] The OMB interim final rule, on the other hand, requires reporting only "*if* such person has made or has agreed to make any payment using nonappropriated funds . . . which would be prohibited . . . if paid for with appropriated funds."[74] However,

---

70. 532 F. Supp. 2d at 959. The Comptroller General had held in *In re* Construcciones Aeronauticas, S.A., 71 Comp. Gen. 81 (1991), that expenses such as telephone calls and airline tickets incurred in connection with employee lobbying did not fall within the prohibition of the Byrd Amendment since the payments were not made to those vendors to cause them to influence agency or congressional officials.

71. 31 U.S.C. § 1352(b) (2015); *see also* OMB interim final rule § ____.100(c), 55 Fed. Reg. at 6738.

72. The Federal Acquisition Regulation initially required reporting of *any* non-appropriated expenditure to influence a covered federal action, with no express exception for expenditures that would have been permitted with appropriated funds, 48 C.F.R. § 3.802(b)(2) (2015), but that clause no longer appears in the subsection, 48 C.F.R. § 3.802(b).

73. 31 U.S.C. § 1352 nt. (2015) (emphasis added).

74. OMB interim final rule § ____.100(c), 55 Fed. Reg. at 6738 (emphasis added).

the Standard Form LLL contains no mechanism for reporting that *no* expenditures were made that would have been prohibited with appropriated funds.[75]

This inconsistency is largely removed for awards made on or after January 1, 1996, the effective date of the LDA. That statute altered the reporting requirements simply to require the name of any registrant under the LDA who has made lobbying contacts on behalf of the awardee and a certification that no prohibited payment has been or will be made.[76] It appears reasonably certain that professional and technical services are not "prohibited" for purposes of this amended certification, although the fact that this exception is not stated in the FAR still leaves the nature of this certification somewhat vague for procurement contractors.

15-7.2 Reasonable Compensation Not Reportable

The Byrd Amendment initially exempted from reporting "reasonable compensation" paid to an officer or employee of an entity who lobbies for a contract. Again, this no longer applies to reports for awards made on or after January 1996. For prior awards, this exception appeared not to exempt, and thus required, reporting of non-salary *costs* of lobbying by an employee (which may be as minor as transportation and office space or as major as a massive grassroots campaign), as well as "unreasonable compensation" of employees. Although GAO has held that payments made to airlines, telephone companies, couriers, and the like in support of lobbying efforts are not payments to third parties for influencing an award,[77] this reasoning, confirmed in *Nat'l Training & Info. Center*, would not apply when such costs of an employee engaged in influencing an award were reimbursed by the awardee. Reporting of all such costs appears literally to have been required for awards made before 1996, since no exception squarely applied.

15-7.3 Defense Department

The Byrd Amendment allows the Department of Defense (DOD) to exempt "a Federal action" from reporting requirements by transmitting the written exception to Congress, but there are no standards for this determination and no indication whether the exemption must be made public. In short, Congress provided no guidance on how the DOD's available exemption procedure should work, and OMB's interim final rule adds nothing more than to note that DOD "may issue supplemental regulations to implement" this exemption.[78] Such supplemental regulations do not exist at the present time.

15-7.4 The Need for Clarification

The January 1990 Notice of Proposed Guidance under the Byrd Amendment noted that the first four reports to Congress indicated widespread confusion and

---

75. An electronic version of Standard Form LLL is available online at http://www.whitehouse .gov/omb/grants/sflllin.pdf (last visited Sept. 25, 2015).

76. Pub. L. No. 104–65, § 10(a)(1), 109 Stat. 691, 700 (1995) (codified as amended in scattered sections of 2 U.S.C.); 31 U.S.C. § 1352(b)(2) (2015).

77. *See In re* Construccionnes Aeronauticas, S.A., 71 Comp. Gen. 81 (1991).

78. OMB interim final rule § _____.500, 55 Fed. Reg. at 6739.

inconsistent interpretation of that statute.[79] Similarly, a survey of implementation of that law by the General Accounting Office (now called the Government Accountability Office) found widespread noncompliance and inadequate compliance, observing that OMB guidance was "confusing." GAO recommended that OMB guidance and instructions be refined and improved.[80]

It was not until after enactment of the LDA in 1995 that OMB and the FAR updated guidance and regulations to "improve clarity" of the Byrd Amendment regulations.[81] Nonetheless, even after these largely editorial changes, most of the questions raised in this chapter remain. Plainly, clarifying regulations that address these lingering questions would ensure more uniform compliance with the Byrd Amendment's prohibition and reporting requirements and would avoid unfair penalties or even prosecutions of awardees that do their best to interpret them.

15-8 Penalties and Enforcement

Civil penalties are required to be assessed for each "failure" to file a required declaration. Implementing regulations limit first offenders to the minimum $10,000 penalty, "absent aggravating circumstances," while repeat offenses are subject to fines up to $100,000.[82] However, since "each such expenditure" is a separate violation[83] and since there is no requirement that a failure be knowing or willful, this first-offender protection might prove illusory. In fact, imposition of even the minimum $10,000 penalty for an inadvertent failure to file, especially by a losing bidder, would seem harsh. Perhaps this best explains why the penalty provisions have not been invoked; rather, two enforcement actions brought by the government challenging contractor's failures to comply with the Byrd Amendment were grounded on the False Claims Act.[84]

In *Nat'l Training & Info. Center*, the government argued that a challenge to the constitutionality of the Byrd Amendment was misplaced because the government's suit was for false certifications under the False Claims Act.[85] The decision does not reflect the ultimate outcome of the case, but the court refused to dismiss the government's claims as to unreported payments made by the defendant that contravened the Byrd Amendment.

In 2011, the Department of Justice intervened in a whistleblower lawsuit against Fluor Hanford LLC and its parent company alleging that Fluor violated the False Claims Act by using federal funds to lobby the Department of Energy

---

79. *See, e.g.,* 57 Fed. Reg. 1772 (Jan. 15, 1992).

80. "Lobbying the Executive Branch," Statement of Bernard L. Ungar, Director, Federal Human Resource Management Issues, General Government Division, U.S. General Accounting Office, before the Subcomm. on Oversight of Government Management, Comm. on Governmental Affairs, U.S. Senate (Sept. 25, 1991), *available at* http://www.gao.gov/assets/110/104122.pdf.

81. *See* 72 Fed. Reg. 46327 (Aug. 17, 2007) (FAR amendments).

82. OMB interim final rule § _____.400(e), 55 Fed. Reg. at 6740.

83. 31 U.S.C. § 1352(c)(1)(2015); OMB interim final rule § _____.400(a), 55 Fed. Reg. at 6740.

84. 31 U.S.C. § 3729 (2015).

85. *National Training & Information Center* at 951.

(DOE).[86] Fluor had contracted to manage and operate an emergency response center for DOE and was alleged to have used DOE funds to lobby Congress and other federal officials to increase funding for the center in violation of the Byrd Amendment. The government did not seek penalties under the Byrd Amendment, but sought treble damages and civil penalties pursuant to the False Claims Act, as well as damages and reinstatement for the relator. The case was settled without a determination of liability when Fluor agreed to pay $1.1 million to settle the allegations in the complaint.[87]

15-9 Incomplete Coverage

Problems in applying the Byrd Amendment are exacerbated by the incomplete, and possibly inconsistent, coverage of the law. The following examples are illustrative.

15-9.1 Employee Lobbying

By excepting from coverage communications and efforts made by "regularly employed officers or employees,"[88] the Byrd Amendment excludes coverage of lobbying by employees that may be as subject to abuse as the engagement of outside consultants or lobbyists. This exception also appears to ensure that any compilations of data regarding implementation of the Byrd Amendment will not provide even reasonably accurate information about who is doing what to lobby for awards.

15-9.2 Non-appropriated Federal Benefits

Only direct federal funding—through contracts, grants, and loans—is addressed by the Byrd Amendment.[89] The provision completely ignores tax credits, many subsidies, and a myriad of other kinds of federal benefits where lobbying that affects substantial federal appropriations routinely occurs.

15-10 Public Availability of Disclosure Reports

OMB guidance and agency rules for Byrd Amendment compliance specifically refer to the requirement for filing "a disclosure form," and the form itself is entitled "Disclosure of Lobbying Activities."[90] Nonetheless, agencies do not appear to compile forms in a central location, to enable the public to access filings online, or even to make efforts to respond to specific Freedom of Information Act requests for

86. Complaint, United States ex rel. Rambo v. Fluor Hanford, LLC, No. 2:11-cv-5037 (E.D. Wash. Feb. 23, 2011). While the government intervened with respect to Fluor, it declined to intervene with respect to the two lobbying firms that were also named defendants. The case is discussed in Dickstein Shapiro LLP, "Government Contractors Beware—DOJ is Now Using the Byrd Amendment to Bring FCA Cases for Alleged Lobbying Violations," *available at* http://www.dicksteinshapiro.com/news-and-views/government-contractors-beware-doj-now-using-byrd-amendment-bring-fca-cases-alleged.

87. DEPT. OF JUSTICE, *Justice News*, "Fluor Hanford Agrees to Pay $1.1 Million to Resolve Allegations of Improper Lobbying" (April 3, 2013), *available at* http://www.justice.gov/opa/pr/2013/April/13-civ-379.html.

88. 31 U.S.C. § 1352(d)(2)(A) (2015).

89. *Id.* § 1352(a)(1)–(2).

90. Disclosure of Lobbying Activities, *available at* http://www.whitehouse.gov/sites/default/files/omb/grants/sflll.pdf.

the filed LLL forms. When a reporter for *Politico* endeavored to obtain filings from various agencies, some press officers responded that they had never heard of the form, some agencies said that forms submitted as part of classified contracts may not be available, and others seemed uncertain whether they had ever received the forms. In short, the half-dozen agencies from which the LLL form was requested "declined to provide them or did not respond."[91] For its part, the CIA responded that it could "neither confirm nor deny the existence or nonexistence of records" on the ground that "the existence or nonexistence of requested records is currently and properly classified and is intelligence sources and methods information that is protected from disclosure."[92]

As a lobbying disclosure statute, the Byrd Amendment has proved, in short, an utter failure.

15-11 Constitutionality

The court in *Nat'l Training & Info. Center* was faced with a head-on attack by a grantee with regard to the constitutionality of the Byrd Amendment. The government had sued the grantee, seeking reimbursement of grant funds used for lobbying on the basis of the grantee's allegedly false and fraudulent certifications that it had not used federal funds for lobbying purposes. The defendant moved to dismiss, arguing that the Byrd Amendment is unconstitutionally vague and overbroad on its face. The court recognized the shortcomings of the Byrd Amendment—many of which have been explored in this chapter—but concluded by rejecting the constitutional challenge.

Two key arguments made by the defendant were that the term "lobbying" is unconstitutionally overbroad and nowhere defined in the statute or regulations, while the phrase "influencing or attempting to influence" is unconstitutionally vague. The court analyzed these words in light of the language of the amendment, its legislative history, OMB regulations, and case law, and rejected the defendant's assertions, in part concluding that "any opaqueness . . . can be clarified on a case-by-case basis."[93]

15-12 Conclusion

After scarcely two years of life, the Byrd Amendment was pronounced "ineffective,"[94] and legislation was introduced (but not passed) to repeal the disclosure portions

91. Byron Tau, *Contractor Lobbying Info under Wraps*, Politico (July 7, 2013), *available at* http://www.politico.com/story/2013/07/thank-you-for-contacting-nsa-we-do-not-have-anything-for-you-93752.html.

92. Byron Tau, *CIA Won't Disclose Lobbying Reports*, Politico (Sept. 16, 2013), *available at* http://www.politico.com/blogs/under-the-radar/2013/09/cia-wont-disclose-lobbying-reports-172733.html.

93. 532 F. Supp. 2d at 958.

94. *See generally Disclosure of Executive Branch Lobbying, Hearings Before the Subcomm. on Oversight of Government Management, Senate Comm. on Governmental Affairs*, 102d Cong., 111 (Sept. 25, 1991).

of the amendment.[95] This criticism is not entirely surprising, since, as explained above, the amendment was drafted without benefit of hearings or debate. Based upon its first few years of operation, the Byrd Amendment appeared to be more of a distraction for government agencies and contractors than either an inhibition on undesirable political influence peddling or a source of enlightenment regarding the federal award process. The Lobbying Disclosure Act of 1995 reduced the requirements on agencies to create and file reports to Congress and reduced the reporting requirements on awardees and potential awardees, but it did not reduce the flow of required reports to agencies.

OMB has shown no inclination either to issue "final final" rules in place of its incrementally published "interim final" rules and guidances or to resolve the many ambiguities of the Byrd Amendment that have been highlighted in this chapter. The result in *Nat'l Training & Info. Center* appears not to provide any incentive to OMB to move expeditiously to change that situation.

The Byrd Amendment has somehow survived the reinvention of government, regulatory reform, paperwork reduction, and the overhaul of the general lobbying law and its subsequent amendment. It continues to remain a vague prohibition and to impose a confusing paperwork requirement that awardees and potential awardees must honor at the peril of penalty, even though federal agencies themselves seem generally to ignore the provisions of this opaque statute. The mandate, contained in the Byrd Amendment, that "The head of each Federal agency shall take such actions as are necessary to ensure that the provisions of this section are vigorously implemented and enforced in such agency," remains an empty promise.

---

95. An earlier version of the LDA, approved by the Senate Committee on Governmental Affairs in 1992, would have replaced the disclosure provisions of the Byrd Amendment entirely with the new disclosure provisions applicable to both Congress and the executive. *See* S. Rep. No. 102-354 (1992). The Senate never acted on this proposal, and the impact of the LDA on the Byrd Amendment was the limited one described in Section 15-5 of this chapter.

CHAPTER 16

Contingent Fee Lobbying

BY THOMAS M. SUSMAN*

16-1 Introduction

Many lobbyists believe that contingent fee lobbying is or should be prohibited,[1] while others actively lobby Congress on contingent fee contracts.[2] Advocates on both sides of the contingent fee lobbying issue can make persuasive arguments for their positions. Those in favor of permitting lobbyists to work under contingent fee arrangements argue that the contingent fee can provide access to effective representation before Congress and agencies for those with fewer financial resources,[3]

---

*Margaret H. Martin coauthored this chapter in the fourth edition of *The Lobbying Manual*.

  1. *See, e.g.,* T. R. Goldman, *Contingent Fees: Why the Bad Rap?,* INFLUENCE, May 30, 2001.

  2. *See id.* (describing the contingent fee contracts that some lobbyists use).

  3. Stacie L. Fatka & Jason Miles Levien, *Protecting the Right to Petition: Why a Lobbying Contingency Fee Prohibition Violates the Constitution*, 35 HARV. J. ON LEGIS. 559, 559 (1998). Fatka and Levien argue that not having access to a professional lobbyist can shut a citizen or group of citizens out of the political process:

> The daily schedules of congressional members and their staffs are filled with meetings attended by professional lobbyists who have established personal relationships with policymakers. The problem with this system is not that there are too many lobbyists, but that the skilled lobbyists are linked only to the large and powerful business and social issue groups that can afford them. Thus the voices of individual citizens, minorities, and under-funded causes are shut out of political discourse because they cannot be heard without the intermediary of a professional lobbyist.

Id. at 567–68.

that contingent fee lobbying is constitutionally protected by the First Amendment right to petition the government, and that a contingent fee for lobbying is no more dangerous or corrupting than the contingent fees regularly collected for representation of clients in litigation.[4] Opponents of the use of a contingent fee arrangement for lobbying argue that contingent fees have a strong tendency to tempt lobbyists to use corrupt means and improper influences to achieve their goals, whether or not any illegitimate methods are actually used,[5] and that use of those means will turn legislators from the consideration of the public good that should be their primary consideration. Opponents also argue that all the evils arising from the use of a contingent fee in a litigation setting apply to the use of the contingent fee for lobbying, that avoiding corruption or the appearance of corruption in public policy is a substantial government interest justifying a ban on contingent fee compensation, and that the use of the contingent fee for lobbying will result in increased costs to the taxpayer.[6]

This chapter surveys the law governing the use of a contingent fee for federal lobbying services and addresses the basis for the perception that it is prohibited, why that perception persists, and, even where there is no legal prohibition on contingent fee lobbying, whether ethical norms militate against the use of this kind of compensation structure.

16-2 Statutory Prohibitions

There are several *federal* statutory prohibitions applicable to contingent fee lobbying in certain contexts; state laws on the subject are not uniform.[7] Some federal

---

4. *See, e.g.,* Stroemer v. Van Orsdel, 74 Neb. 132 (1905).

5. Contingent fee agreements for lobbying "furnish the strongest incentive to the exertion of corrupting and sinister influences to the end that the desired legislation may be secured. . . ." 51 AM. JUR. 2D *Lobbying* § 4 (2015).

6. *See, e.g.,* T. R. Goldman, *supra* note 1 ("You are arguing for the appropriation of dollars not in relation to an identified need, but so you can make more money. If an institution of higher learning needs $10 million for some facility and you go argue for $15 million because you'll get more money, then that's really at the expense of the federal taxpayer.") (quoting the comments of a former appropriations staffer).

7. Many states have legislated contingent fee lobbying bans. These are Alabama, ALA. CODE § 36-25-23 (2015); Alaska, ALASKA STAT. § 24.45.121 (2015); Arizona, ARIZ. REV. STAT. § 41-1233 (2015); California, CAL. GOV'T CODE § 86205 (2015); Colorado, COLO. REV. STAT. § 24-6-308 (2015); Connecticut, CONN. GEN. STAT. § 1-97 (2015); Delaware, DEL. CODE ANN. tit. 29, § 5834 (2015); Florida, FLA. STAT. ANN. §§ 11.047, 112.3217 (2015); Georgia, GA. CODE ANN. § 28-7-3 (2015); Hawaii, HAW. REV. STAT. § 97-5 (2015); Idaho, IDAHO CODE § 67-6621 (2015); Illinois, 25 ILL. COMP. STAT. 170/8 (2015); Indiana, IND. CODE § 2-7-5-5 (2015); Kansas, KAN. STAT. ANN. § 46-267 (2015); Kentucky, KY. REV. STAT. ANN. § 6.811 (2015); Maine, ME. REV. STAT. ANN. tit. 3, § 318 (2015); Maryland, MD. GEN. PROVIS. § 5-714 (2015); Massachusetts, MASS. GEN. LAWS ch. 3, § 42 (2015); Michigan, MICH. COMP. LAWS § 4.421 (2015); Minnesota, MINN. STAT. § 10A.06 (2015); Mississippi, MISS. CODE ANN. § 5-8-13 (2015); Nebraska, NEB. REV. STAT. § 49-1492 (2015); Nevada, NEV. REV. STAT. § 218H.930 (2015); New Jersey, N.J. STAT. ANN. § 52:13C-21.5 (2015); New Mexico, N.M. STAT. ANN. § 2-11-8 (2015); New York, N.Y. LEGIS. LAW § 1-k (2015); North Carolina, N.C. GEN. STAT. § 120C-300 (2015); North Dakota, N.D. CENT. CODE § 54-05.1-06 (2015); Ohio, OHIO REV. CODE ANN. § 101.77 (2015); Oklahoma, OKLA. STAT. tit. 21, § 334 (2015); Oregon, OR. REV. STAT. § 171.756 (2015); Pennsylvania, 65 PA. CONS. STAT. § 13A07 (2015); Rhode Island, R.I. GEN. LAWS § 22-10-12 (2015); South Carolina, S.C. CODE ANN. § 2-17-110 (2015); South Dakota, S.D. CODIFIED LAWS § 2-12-6 (2015); TENN. CODE. ANN. § 3-6-304(k) (2015); Texas, TEX. GOV'T CODE ANN. § 305.022 (2015); Utah, UTAH CODE ANN. § 36-11-301 (2015); Vermont, VT. STAT. ANN. tit. 2, § 266 (2015); Virginia, VA.

procurement laws prohibit or severely restrict the use of contingent fee arrangements for the procurement of government contracts for goods and services.[8] And the Foreign Agents Registration Act (FARA) prohibits registrants from entering into contracts for fees contingent upon the success of political lobbying.[9] However, beyond particular, limited enactments, there exists no general *statutory* ban on lobbying for contingent compensation, and Congress has from time to time recognized this by proposing legislation to create a general proscription.[10]

CODE ANN. § 2.2-432 (2015); Washington, WASH. REV. CODE § 42.17A.655 (2015); and Wisconsin, WIS. STAT. § 13.625 (2015).

Pennsylvania's lobbying disclosure statute was invalidated on grounds that the statute unconstitutionally interfered with the judicial branch's governance of the practice of law in the state, Gmerek v. State Ethics Comm'n, 807 A.2d 812 (Pa. 2002), but a subsequent rules change by the state supreme court authorized regulation of lawyer-lobbyists. *See* PA. RULES OF PROF'L CONDUCT § 1.19 (2015). The Pennsylvania legislature then enacted a new lobbying statute. *See* 65 PA. CONS. STAT. ANN. §§ 13A01–13A11 (2015). West Virginia appears specifically to permit contingent fee lobbying. The statute regulating lobbying expressly states that any contingent fee being charged by the lobbyist must be disclosed. *See* W. VA. CODE § 6B-3-2(a)(4) (2015) ("The registration statement shall contain . . . [a] statement as to whether . . . the registrant's compensation . . . is or will be contingent upon the success of his or her lobbying activity.").

Courts have heard challenges to the contingent fee prohibition on First Amendment grounds. The Montana Supreme Court held the prohibition unconstitutional in Mont. Auto. Ass'n v. Greely, 632 P.2d 300 (Mont. 1981); the Kentucky Supreme Court held the prohibition constitutional in Associated Indus. of Ky. v. Commonwealth, 912 S.W.2d 947 (Ky. 1995); a federal court upheld the Florida prohibition as constitutional, albeit reluctantly, in Fla. League of Prof'l Lobbyists, Inc. v. Meggs, 87 F.3d 457 (11th Cir. 1996); and a Maryland appellate court upheld the constitutionality of the prohibition in Bereano v. State Ethics Comm'n, 920 A.2d 1137 (Md. App. 2007), *rev'd on other grounds*, 944 A.2d 538 (2008). A comprehensive discussion and catalogue of cases considering the enforceability of contingent fee lobbying agreements in the states are found in William M. Howard, *Validity, Construction and Application of State and Municipal Enactments Regulating Lobbying and of Lobbying Contracts*, 35 A.L.R. 6th 1, §§ 29, & 30 (2008, Supp. 2014).

8. *See* 10 U.S.C. § 2306(b) (2015) (military procurement statute; requires a warranty that contingent fees were not used in procuring contracts); 31 U.S.C. § 1352 (2015) (Byrd Amendment prohibiting the recipients of federal grants, contracts, loans, or cooperative agreements from using federally appropriated funds to pay any person to influence or attempt to influence any executive or legislative branch official); 41 U.S.C. § 3901 (2015) (formerly cited as 41 U.S.C. § 254) (general federal procurement statute requiring a warranty that contingent fees were not used in procuring a contract); 48 C.F.R. §§ 3.400–3.406 (2015) (policies and procedures restricting contingent fee arrangements in obtaining government contracts; requires insertion of covenant against contingent fees in all contracts exceeding a certain threshold, and includes actions for violations of covenant); and 48 C.F.R. § 52.203–5 (2015) (covenant against contingent fees). For an examination of the Byrd Amendment, see Chapter 15 of this manual.

9. 22 U.S.C. §§ 611–621 (2015):

It shall be unlawful for any agent of a foreign principal required to register under this subchapter to be a party to any contract, agreement, or understanding, either express or implied, with such foreign principal pursuant to which the amount or payment of the compensation, fee, or other remuneration of such agent is contingent in whole or in part upon the success of any political activities carried on by such agent.

Id. § 618(h). For a general overview of the FARA, see Chapter 19 of this manual.

10. See Section 16-2.4 of this chapter. Even where state or other statutory bans on lobbying exist, exceptions have been crafted. For instance, some courts have held that lobbying for "debt" legislation—legislation necessary to bring to closure an existing private claim—may be reimbursed on a contingent basis, where "favor" legislation may not. *See, e.g.*, Gesellschaft fur Drahtlose Telegraphine M.B.H. v. Brown, 78 F.2d 410 (D.C. Cir. 1935); Jack Maskell, Congressional Research Service Memorandum: Contingency Fees for Lobbying Activities (Sept. 21, 2000) at CRS-5. The rationale in *Brown* for permitting

16-2.1 "Covenant Against Contingent Fees" in Federal Contracts

The general federal procurement statute requires a "suitable warranty" that, with some exceptions, contingent fees or commissions have not been used to secure any contract other than one awarded based on sealed-bid procedures. The full provision reads:

> Except as provided in section 3905 of this title, contracts awarded after using procedures other than sealed-bid procedures may be of any type which in the opinion of the agency head will promote the best interests of the Federal Government. Every contract awarded after using procedures other than sealed-bid procedures shall contain a suitable warranty, as determined by the agency head, by the contractor that no person or selling agency has been employed or retained to solicit or secure the contract on an agreement or understanding for a commission, percentage, brokerage, or contingent fee, except for bona fide employees or bona fide established commercial or selling agencies the contractor maintains to secure business. For the breach or violation of the warranty, the Federal Government may annul the contract without liability or deduct from the contract price or consideration the full amount of the commission, percentage, brokerage, or contingent fee. Paragraph (1) does not apply to a contract for an amount that is not greater than the simplified acquisition threshold or to a contract for the acquisition of commercial items.[11]

The Federal Acquisition Regulation (FAR) requires the contracting officer to insert a standard Covenant Against Contingent Fees in solicitations and contracts, fulfilling the statutory requirement for a "suitable warranty."[12] The term "contingent fee" is defined in the FAR as including "any commission, percentage, brokerage, or other fee that is contingent upon the success that a person or concern has in securing a Government contract."[13] The penalties for violation of the Covenant Against Contingent Fees include rejection of a proposal if before the award,

---

contingent fees for lobbying for debt legislation was to allow a person the means of asserting a legitimate and existing legal claim. Other exceptions to these bans include services rendered in the normal course of client representation by an attorney where the services were not expressly contemplated by the original contract, Maskell at CRS-5; a contract for "legitimate professional services" such as "the drafting of legislative language" rather than doing anything that would be considered "lobbying," that is, the use of any pressure or influence with legislators, *id.*; and other activities that are hard to square with the literal language of the statutory bans on contingency fees, *see generally* 51 Am. Jur. 2D *Lobbying* § 4 (2015).

   11. 41 U.S.C. § 3901 (2015). Similar language is found in the military procurement statute, 10 U.S.C. § 2306(b) (2015). Cases interpreting the elements of this provision in the government contracting context are explored in James Lockhart, Annotation, *Requirement Under Defense Procurement and General Procurement Statutes (10 U.S.C. § 2306(b); 41 U.S.C. § 254 (a)) and Regulations Promulgated Thereunder (32 CFR § 1-1500 et seq.; 41 CFR § 1-1.500 et seq.) that Government Contract for Property and Services Contain Warranty Against Commissions or Contingent Fees*, 60 A.L.R. Fed. 263 (1982).

   12. 48 C.F.R. § 3.402 (2015). The full text of the currently applicable Covenant Against Contingent Fees is found at 48 C.F.R. § 52.203-5 (2015).

   13. *Id.* § 3.401.

annulment of the contract or recovery of the fee after the award, initiation of a suspension or debarment action, and a criminal referral to the Department of Justice.[14]

The Covenant Against Contingent Fees dates back to 1918, when Attorney General J. W. Gregory issued a series of press releases calling attention to the Supreme Court's condemnation of contingent fee lobbying[15] and declaring that the "no contract no fee arrangement suggests an attempt to use sinister and corrupt means."[16]

According to a later Senate Report, the early provisions were adopted at a time when there was "increasing evidence of the growth of an unsavory fraternity of individuals who represented to businessmen that they could affect Government decisions by pressure or influence."[17] The term used to describe these lobbyists was "5-percenters" because they were employed on a contingent basis and received a fee amounting to 5 percent or more of any contract they succeeded in obtaining.[18] It was not uncommon for the 5-percenter to have more than one client competing for the same contract, so that he was virtually assured of receiving some compensation when the contract was awarded.[19] The Senate Report concluded that the service these 5-percenters offered was collusion with government officials.[20] "The mere existence of such a condition tends to destroy good government."[21]

Executive Order No. 9001, issued in 1941 and establishing methods for wartime procurement, required that every contract entered into contain a warranty by the contractor in substantially the following terms: "The contractor warrants that he has not employed any person to solicit or secure this contract upon any agreement for a commission, percentage, brokerage, or contingent fee."[22]

This same covenant was subsequently prescribed in the Armed Services Procurement Act of 1947 and the Federal Property and Administrative Services Act of 1949,[23] and it later was applied government-wide by General Services Administration General Regulation No. 12.[24] The objectives of this broad new regulatory ban on contingent fee lobbying included the "prevention of improper influence in connection with the obtaining of Government contracts; the elimination of arrangements which encourage the payment of inequitable and exorbitant fees bearing no reasonable relationship to the services actually performed; and the prevention of unwarranted expenditure of public funds which inevitably results therefrom."[25]

The "suitable warranty" requirement imposed in the procurement statute[26] is fulfilled by the Covenant Against Contingent Fees clause that must be inserted in

---

14. *Id.* § 3.405.

15. See discussion in Section 16-3 of this chapter.

16. Paul A. Barron & William Munves, *The Government Versus the Five-Percenters: Analysis of Regulations Governing Contingent Fees in Government Contracts*, 25 Geo. Wash. L. Rev. 127, 129 (1956–1957).

17. *The 5-Percenter Investigation*, Interim Report submitted to the Comm. on Expenditures in the Executive Depts., S. Rep. No. 81-1231, at 1 (1950).

18. *Id.* at 4.

19. *Id.* at 6.

20. *Id.* at 1.

21. *Id.*

22. Exec. Order No. 9001, Dec. 27, 1941, 6 Fed. Reg. 6,787 (1941).

23. Barron & Munves, *supra* note 16, at 137. Federal Property and Administrative Services Act of 1949 § 304, 41 U.S.C. § 3901 (2015), is quoted in text *supra* note 11.

24. 41 C.F.R. § 1–1.500 (Supp. 1956), issued Dec. 29, 1952. *See* Barron & Munves, *supra* note 16, at 141.

25. Barron & Munves, *supra* note 16, at 142.

26. 41 U.S.C. § 3901 (2015).

government contracts in accordance with the FAR.[27] This Covenant Against Contingent Fees, with roots in Attorney General Gregory's campaign against the 5-percenters, was originally created to respond to corruption in the federal procurement process. In its current, statutorily required iteration, the covenant is intended to prevent that corruption from recurring.

16-2.2 Foreign Agents Registration Act (FARA)

FARA prohibits registrants from entering into contracts for fees contingent upon the success of lobbying or other covered activities:

> It shall be unlawful for any agent of a foreign principal required to register under this subchapter to be a party to any contract, agreement, or understanding, either express or implied, with such foreign principal pursuant to which the amount or payment of the compensation, fee, or other remuneration of such agent is contingent in whole or in part upon the success of any political activities carried on by such agent.[28]

In 1935, a special committee of the House of Representatives was commissioned to investigate Nazi and other subversive propaganda in the United States.[29] Three years later, FARA was enacted, based in part on the special committee's report.[30]

FARA is basically a disclosure statute—"intended to protect the interests of the United States by requiring complete disclosure by persons acting for or in the interests of foreign principals where their activities are political in nature or border on the political."[31] Inclusion of the ban on contingent fee lobbying reflected the contemporary distrust of contingent fee lobbying by Congress and the desire to target illicit lobbying activity.[32]

---

27. 48 C.F.R. 3.404, 52.203–5 (2015).

28. 22 U.S.C. § 618(h) (2015). "Political activities" are defined as any activity that a person "intends to, in any way influence any agency or official of the Government of the United States . . . with reference to formulating, adopting, or changing the domestic or foreign policies of the United States." *Id.* § 611(o) (2015).

29. H.R. Rep. No. 74-153 (1935). The House special committee recommended:

> That the Congress shall enact a statute requiring all publicity, propaganda, or public relations agents or other agents who represent in this country any foreign government or a foreign political party or a foreign industrial organization to register with the Secretary of State of the United States, and to state name and location of such employer, the character of the service to be rendered, and the amount of compensation paid or to be paid therefore.

Id. at 23.

30. See generally Chapter 19 of this manual.

31. H.R. Rep. No. 89-1470 (1966).

32. *See Hearing on S.693 Before the Senate Comm. on Foreign Relations*, 89th Cong. 22 (Feb. 16, 1965) (testimony of Senator Hickenlooper) ("I think what we are trying to reach are these surreptitious gumshoes . . . that slip around cocktail parties and the back door of some offices, and this that, or the other thing."). *See also* Amoruso e Figli v. Fisheries Dev. Corp., 499 F. Supp. 1074, 1084 n.30 (S.D.N.Y. 1980) ("[a]lthough there are no cases construing the specific contingent fee prohibition of section 618(h) of FARA, there is no reason to believe that Congress intended this prohibition to differ significantly from the common law rule. Indeed, there is evidence that FARA too was directed at illicit lobbying activity.").

16-2.3 Byrd Amendment

By prohibiting the use of appropriated funds to lobby for any award of a federal contract, the Byrd Amendment addresses at least one element of a contingent fee arrangement: It prevents payment for the lobbying costs from any amounts paid under the contract.[33] It would not matter whether the payment is to be calculated as a percentage of the contract or simply a lump sum paid upon the award; the key is that the payment may not be made from the government funds received by the contractor.

That means, of course, that the Byrd Amendment does not prevent payment to a lobbyist from funds available to the contractor other than those paid by the federal government. In theory, in the absence of the Covenant Against Contingent Fee Lobbying discussed above,[34] a business could pay for contract lobbying on a contingent basis as long as the payment was made from corporate funds that had not been received from the government. The Byrd Amendment would, in that case, require disclosure through the filing of a declaration.[35]

16-2.4 Congressional Recognition that There Is No General Ban

Congress itself does not appear to believe that a general federal ban on contingent fee lobbying exists. First, in 1950 Senate hearings, several lobbyists testified regarding their contingent fee arrangements.[36] Despite the disfavor voiced by some of the members of Congress at the hearing and the condemnation of this arrangement in the committee's report,[37] the use of the contingent fee agreement in lobbying Congress was not considered illegal at the time.

Second, there have been several attempts to legislate a broad ban on contingent fee lobbying, but none has succeeded. For example, Senator Strom Thurmond proposed free-standing bills[38] and amendments to bills[39] prohibiting contingent fee lobbying in several Congresses. (Representative Schumer introduced similar legislation in 1994.[40]) Substantive debate on legislation to ban contingent lobbying fees occurred only once, centering on what types of fee arrangements would be swept into the purview of the bill, whether a contingent fee for lobbying was like a contingent fee for legal services, and whether it was appropriate for the federal government to step into a contract between two private parties.[41]

Third, Lobbying Disclosure Act (LDA) guidance posted on the website of the Secretary of the Senate states that "[l]aw other than the LDA governs whether a

---

33. See generally Chapter 15 of this manual. The Byrd Amendment's proscription applies to federal contracts, grants, loans, and cooperative agreements.

34. *See* Section 16-2.1 of this chapter.

35. 31 U.S.C. § 1352(b) (2015), discussed in Section 15-3 of this manual.

36. *Contingent Fee Lobbying: Hearings before the House Select Committee on Lobbying Activities*, 81st Cong. (1950).

37. See S. REP. No. 81-1231 (1950).

38. S. 2733, 100th Cong. (1988); S. 91, 101st Cong. (1989); S. 170, 102d Cong. (1991); S. 44, 103d Cong. (1993); S. 53, 104th Cong. (1995).

39. Amendment No. 2553 to the National Defense Authorization Act for Fiscal Year 1991 (1990); Amendment No. 492 to S. 1241 (1991).

40. H.R. 4108, 103d Cong. (1994).

41. 136 CONG. REC. S12,055-01 (daily ed. Aug. 3, 1990).

firm may be retained on a contingent-fee basis."[42] The guidance indicates that a lobbyist retained on a contingent fee basis must register under the LDA.

Thus the notion that contingent fee contracts for lobbying may presently be illegal as a matter of federal law did not arise from either legislative enactments or congressional sentiment. The answer appears to lie with the judicial branch of government.

16-3 Judicial Pronouncements on Contingent Fee Lobbying

While there is no statutory prohibition on the use of contingent fee compensation for lobbying Congress (except when representing a foreign interest) or for lobbying the executive branch outside the procurement arena, this does not settle the question whether a contingent fee lobbying contract might be unenforceable if compensation under such a contract is contested in court. The perception of unenforceability—often repeated in legal encyclopedias, lower-court decisions, and informal dialogue—is grounded on a series of Supreme Court decisions dating back to the 19th century. Some of the Court's opinions were written with a broad enough brush to forbid not only contingent fee lobbying, but all contracts for lobbying to obtain favors from government. Contingent fee lobbying was viewed as especially heinous because it made the purportedly evil practice of lobbying even more corrupt.[43] The historical context of these old cases and the nature of much of the reported lobbying as it existed at that time explain much about the Court's crabbed perspective on lobbying.

Although pressure groups had been a part of the fabric of American politics since before the Revolution, the growth of the industrial state led to a hundredfold increase in the practice of lobbying the federal government.[44] Civil War era lobbyists were a far cry from today's professionals. In its early days, lobbying and all the activities surrounding it were completely unregulated.[45] Many of the early lobbyists, and their congressional targets as well, appeared to have no compunction about trading votes for dollars or using other nefarious means to reach their goals; at times, these means included payment of a contingent fee.[46] So reviled was the lobbyist in general that "many states had criminalized the act of lobbying by the end of the nineteenth century."[47] The Supreme Court's pronouncements were

---

42. Sec'y of the Senate & Clerk of the House of Representatives, Lobbying Disclosure Act Guidance (revised Feb. 15, 2013) [hereinafter Revised Guidance], *available at* http://lobbying disclosure.house.gov/amended_lda_guide.html, which guidance is also contained in Appendix 4-A to this manual.

43. Some of these cases dealt with lobbyists paid on a contingent basis attempting to win contracts from the government; that is, the lobbyists were lobbying the executive branch, not the legislative branch. However, the Supreme Court repeatedly remarked that these two activities were largely equivalent for purposes of the relevant analysis. *See, e.g.*, Providence Tool Co. v. Norris, 69 U.S. 45, 56 (1864).

44. *See generally* Karl Schriftgiesser, The Lobbyists: The Art and Business of Influencing Lawmakers (1951). See also Section 3-2 of this manual.

45. Schriftgiesser, at 8–15.

46. *Id.*

47. Fatka & Levien, *supra* note 3, at 569.

written against this backdrop—a context that can be seen as alien to both the lobbying profession and legislators of today.[48]

16-3.1 The Cases

The first Supreme Court ruling on contingent fee lobbying, *Marshall v. Baltimore and Ohio Railroad Co.*,[49] held that "all contracts for a contingent compensation for obtaining legislation, or to use personal or any secret or sinister influence on legislators, [are] void by the policy of the law."[50] The rationale for the Court's condemnation has become the linchpin of subsequent objections to contingent fee lobbying—that a lobbyist will be tempted to use any means necessary, including improper or illicit means, to achieve his goals when his own compensation is on the line.[51]

The Supreme Court's next visit to this issue, *Providence Tool Co. v. Norris*,[52] included condemning contingent fee lobbying, but primarily involved a broader condemnation of the evils of receiving compensation for lobbying in general, regardless of its form.

In its most famous opinion on contingent fee lobbying, *Trist v. Child*,[53] as in *Tool Co.*, the Court condemned lobbying itself as illegitimate and went on to criticize the use of a contingent fee arrangement for exacerbating the already illegitimate means contemplated by the agreement.

Thus in *Marshall*, *Tool Co.*, and *Trist*, the Supreme Court equated "lobbying" and "lobby agent" with the secret, venal, and forbidden use of personal influence, rather than reason, to sway legislators. Lobbying, an already condemned activity, is only made worse by contingent compensation; professional representation involving use of professional skills and relying on reason might be secured on a contingent fee precisely because it is not the same as lobbying. Unfortunately, the Court does not draw a clear line between lobbying and professional services and appears to condemn any form of compensation for lobbying in general terms.[54]

Finally, in *Hazelton v. Sheckels*,[55] the Supreme Court's most recent (1906) condemnation of contingent fee lobbying, the Court replays the theme that lobbying is inherently bad and use of a contingent fee exacerbates an already corrupt situa-

---

48. The early cases addressing the legality of lobbying contracts, including contingent fee lobbying contracts, are discussed in Richard Briffault, *The Anxiety of Influence: The Evolving Regulation of Lobbying*, 13 ELECTION L.J. 160, 166–69 (2014), and Zephyr Teachout, *The Forgotten Law of Lobbying*, 13 ELECTION L.J. 4, 7–19 (2014).

49. 57 U.S. 314 (1853).

50. *Id.* at 336.

51. *Id.* at 335.

52. 69 U.S. 45 (1864).

53. 88 U.S. 441 (1874).

54. The Court noted:

> We have said that for professional services in this connection, a just compensation may be recovered. But where they are blended and confused with those which are forbidden, the whole is a unit and indivisible. That which is bad destroys that which is good, and they perish together. Services of the latter character, gratuitously rendered, are not unlawful. The absence of motive to wrong is the foundation of the sanction. The tendency to mischief, if not wanting, is greatly lessened. The taint lies in the stipulation for pay. Where that exists, it affects fatally, in all its parts, the entire body of the contract.

Id. at 452.

55. 202 U.S. 71, 78 (1906).

tion: "In its inception, the offer, however intended, necessarily invited and tended to induce improper solicitations, and it intensified the inducement by the contingency of the reward."[56]

The Court appeared to soften its condemnation of lobbying in its 1927 opinion in *Steele v. Drummond*.[57] There, the Court upheld an agreement (not involving a contingent fee) to obtain passage of ordinances, observing that "[d]etriment to the public interest will not be presumed where nothing sinister or improper is done or contemplated."[58] The Court distinguished *Tool Co.*, *Trist*, *Hazelton*, and similar cases not with reference to the issue of contingent fees, but with this comment: "The claims there considered were under contracts requiring or contemplating the obtaining of legislative or executive action as a matter of favor by means of personal influence, solicitation and the like, or by other improper or corrupt means."[59] Because there was nothing in the record to indicate that promoting enactment of the ordinances involved anything other than "the best standards of duty to the public,"[60] the Court found the agreement enforceable.

The early Supreme Court cases are still frequently cited in state court decisions for the proposition that contingent fee lobbying contracts are void and unenforceable, but several cases make it clear that state contract law, rather than federal common law, dictates the decision.[61] Lobbyists thus must look to state law governing the lobbying agreement to determine whether a contingent fee lobbying contract will be condemned or upheld.[62]

Analysis of these and other Supreme Court cases addressing use of contingent fees to secure government contracts has led two authors to conclude that not only would the lobbying contracts in these cases "have been held illegal even though the compensation was not contingent," but "in none of the cases where the contract was declared invalid was the person regularly engaged in the business of selling goods for his principal."[63] The conclusion to be drawn is that the target of the Court's condemnation, despite the sweeping language, was not contingent fee representation, but lobbying.

---

56. *Id.* at 79.

57. 275 U.S. 199 (1927).

58. *Id.* at 205.

59. *Id.* at 206.

60. *Id.*

61. *See, e.g.*, Rome v. Upton, 648 N.E.2d 1085, 1087–89 (Ill. App. Ct. 1995) (relying on Illinois common law and an Illinois statute prohibiting contingent fee lobbying contracts to void the contract). *See also* City of Hialeah Gardens v. John L. Adams & Co., 599 So. 2d 1322, 1324–25 (Fla. Dist. Ct. App. 1992) (analogizing contingent fee lobbying contracts to contingent fee contracts for obtaining public funding and relying on Florida statutory and common law to declare the contract void as against public policy).

62. Some state laws addressing contingent fee lobbying contracts are discussed in note 7. To the extent that contingent fee lobbying contracts are entered into in or subject to the laws of the District of Columbia, the latest pronouncement on the subject of enforceability was in 1939, one year after the *Erie* decision. *See* Brown v. Gesellschaft fur Drahtlose Telegraphy, M.B.H., 104 F.2d 227 (D.C. Cir. 1939) (citing Gesellschaft v. Brown, 78 F.2d 410 (D.C. Cir. 1935), and Noonan v. Gilbert, 68 F.2d 775 (D.C. Cir.1934) and holding the contract null and void as against public policy). See also Section 16-4 in this chapter discussing possible constitutional issues.

63. John W. Townsend & Lloyd Fletcher, Jr., *Contingent Fees in Procurement of Government Contracts*, 11 Geo. Wash. L. Rev. 37, 42–43 (1942–43). The authors discuss both Supreme Court and lower court cases involving contingent fee contracts either to effect legislation or to procure a government contract.

16-3.2 Evolution of Lobbying and the Case Law

The evolution of lobbying from reviled practice to accepted profession[64] has contributed to judicial reevaluation of whether contracts for lobbying should be enforceable. During the 20th century the lobbying landscape changed from one that routinely embodied secret and corrupting influences, if not outright bribery and blackmail, to one that relied more and more on open and generally accepted means of advocacy. As lobbying evolved, courts tended to ignore pronouncements in the earlier cases rejecting as improper all forms of "lobbying" and to embrace those holding that contracting for professional services before the legislature was legitimate—expanding the definition of professional services in the process. This evolution of lobbying from a corrupt practice to a legitimate one was noted as early as 1947. In observing that there was some discrepancy between the old cases that condemned lobbying and the newer cases that condemned contingent fee lobbying (but not lobbying as such), one commentator wrote:

> It is questionable if there is any functional basis for the distinction between the two types of lobbying contracts. It is more likely that courts denouncing lobbyists have thought in terms of the corrupt practices of the old lobby, while courts recognizing the less reprehensible lobbying of more recent times as a legitimate occupation have sought a ground for differentiation in the fact of contingent compensation.[65]

Lobbying is no longer generally considered a reviled or forbidden practice; indeed, the Supreme Court has recognized the constitutional foundation for the practice of lobbying.[66] Given the changed context, the earlier cases may not have the relevance ascribed to them for the past century.[67] In fact, the changed nature of lobbying, in conjunction with the Court's more recent First Amendment jurisprudence on political speech, may vitiate not only the perception that a contingent fee contract is unenforceable but also the basis for some of the existing state statutory bans.

---

64. The increased regulation of lobbying practices that evolved throughout the 20th century is detailed in Chapters 2 and 3 of this manual.

65. Improving the Legislative Process: Federal Regulation of Lobbying, 56 YALE L. J. 304 n.43 (1947) (citations omitted).

66. United States v. Harriss, 347 U.S. 612, 625 (1954) ("[t]hus construed, [the provisions at issue] also do not violate the freedoms guaranteed by the First Amendment—freedom to speak, publish, and petition the Government."). The Court reached this conclusion only after discussion of whether Congress had exercised its power of self-protection "in a manner restricted to its appropriate end"—the implication being that if the means were too extreme, any restriction on lobbying could be considered a violation of the First Amendment freedoms to speak and to petition the government. *Id.* at 625–26. See also Section 3-2.3 of this manual for a discussion of *Harriss*. This is a far cry from the Supreme Court that had, in earlier days, condemned the practice of lobbying in its entirety.

67. For a brief synopsis of the traditional view of the case law, *see* 51 AM. JUR. 2D *Lobbying* §§ 2, 4 (2015).

16-4 Supreme Court's First Amendment Jurisprudence

Since its first acknowledgment that lobbying had a constitutional basis in *United States v. Harriss*,[68] the Supreme Court has developed a branch of First Amendment jurisprudence striking down various restraints on political speech.[69] In *Buckley v. Valeo*,[70] *Village of Schaumburg v. Citizens for a Better Environment*,[71] *Meyer v. Grant*,[72] and *Riley v. National Federation of the Blind of North Carolina*,[73] the Supreme Court laid the foundation for viewing with deep suspicion a restriction on citizens' abilities to hire an advocate to engage in protected political speech, particularly when the restriction is quantitatively, rather than qualitatively, drawn. The Supreme Court's jurisprudence in *Buckley* and related cases indicates that the Court would probably not follow its own precedent from the early cases prohibiting contingent fee lobbying contracts on public policy grounds.

The modern Court's reasoning would more likely proceed as follows: The First Amendment guarantees the right to petition the government.[74] An infringement on that right should be addressed under *Buckley*'s exacting scrutiny standard, with an examination of the compelling governmental interest underlying the infringement. In the contingent fee lobbying context, the articulated compelling interest has been the prevention of corruption in the political process. However, the reasoning behind this purportedly compelling interest stems from an outdated view of lobbying.

The governmental interest in preventing corruption "remains vital," but the kinds of corruption that need to be prevented have changed.[75] Through the mid-twentieth century, any form of lobbying was considered corrupt, and contingent fees exacerbated the corrupt tendencies of lobbying. Now, however, lobbying is essential to the federal legislative process. Professional lobbyists are more effective

---

68. 347 U.S. 612 (1954). The constitutional issues implicated in lobbying and its regulation are discussed in Section 1-2.2 of this manual.

69. The Court's modern political speech jurisprudence that evolved during the 20th century has been addressed in lower court cases dealing with state bans on contingent fee lobbying. *See* note 7. The most extensive discussion of the difference in attitude appears in the briefs and the decision in Florida League of Prof'l Lobbyists, Inc. v. Meggs, 87 F.3d 457 (11th Cir. 1996) (holding the ban constitutional, albeit reluctantly).

70. 424 U.S. 1 (1976) (striking down certain campaign expenditure limitations that "impose direct and substantial restraints on the quantity of political speech"). *Id.* at 39.

71. 444 U.S. 620 (1980) (declaring unconstitutional an ordinance prohibiting in-person solicitation of contributions by charitable organizations that did not use at least 75 percent of their receipts for charitable purposes).

72. 486 U.S. 414 (1988) (holding unconstitutional a Colorado statute prohibiting paying people to circulate petitions for placing initiatives on a ballot).

73. 487 U.S. 781 (1988) (declaring unconstitutional a North Carolina statute prohibiting professional fundraisers from retaining an "unreasonable" or "excessive" fee).

74. *See* U.S. CONST. amend. I. *See also* Eastern R.R. Presidents Conference v. Noerr Motor Freight, Inc., 365 U.S. 127, 137 (1961) ("[T]o a very large extent, the whole concept of representation depends upon the ability of the people to make their wishes known to their representatives.").

75. Some argue that the modern perception of corruption stems at least in part from the impression that only the rich have access to Congress—that they have "purchased" access—via highly compensated lobbyists. Fatka & Levien, *supra* note 3, at 584–86 ("[A] ban on contingency fees has the perverse effect of creating a more exclusive system where only the wealthy are able to exercise their right to petition the government by employing a lobbyist. . . . In fact, rather than protecting the system from corruption, a ban on contingency fees may have the opposite effect.").

advocates than inexperienced citizens in 21st-century America and are sometimes the only effective advocates.[76] The professionalization of lobbying is not the only change affecting the analysis. The Lobbying Disclosure Act and other modern lobbying regulations have been widely adopted; these clearly represent a less burdensome restraint on the First Amendment–protected practice of lobbying than an outright ban.

Additionally, the Supreme Court's recent campaign finance jurisprudence not only reinforces the concept that money (political contributions and independent expenditures) is protected speech under the First Amendment, but also adopts an extremely narrow view of what kind of corruption must be found or threatened before reasonable government regulation may be imposed.[77] Both of these developments suggest the potential for stricter scrutiny of efforts to regulate fees, including contingent fees, paid to lobbyists.

Given the changes in both First Amendment jurisprudence and the practice of lobbying, the Supreme Court would more likely recognize constitutional protection for the right to lobby generally and the use of a contingent fee contract for lobbying in particular than invalidate a contract for contingent fee lobbying as contrary to public policy. Even if the Court found that a ban on contingent fee lobbying could prevent some quantity of corrupt speech, that ban would probably be considered overbroad because corrupt speech can be addressed by means other than imposing such a heavy burden on a First Amendment right. However, even if contingent fee lobbying contracts are legally permissible, is it an ethical practice for lobbyists and their clients to use them? That is the subject of the final section of this chapter.

16-5 Are Contingent Fee Lobbying Contracts Ethical?

While lobbying is, in various law review articles and compilations, included among examples of activities for which lawyers cannot ethically receive contingent fees,[78] the only prohibitions on contingent fees that appear in either the ABA Model Rules

---

76. *See, e.g.,* Fatka & Levien, *supra* note 3, at 567–68:

> Professional lobbyists are better able to influence legislation than non-lobbyists for several reasons. First, they have already formed relationships with government officials and their staffs. Second, many lobbyists are former legislative branch employees who have high levels of expertise regarding the legislative process and knowledge of the specific subject matters that congressional committees address. In fact, members of Congress have even relied on the expertise of lobbyists to draft legislation. Third, professional lobbyists have the time and resources to follow a bill through the legislative process, whereas most citizens do not have this capability. Therefore, hiring a professional lobbyist is the most effective means of communicating with lawmakers. The lobbyist serves as a link between congressional policymakers and citizens, thereby helping those groups and individuals that have the ability to pay to voice their concerns in an organized and effective manner.

Id. at 568. *See also id.* at 566 ("Today, if citizens wish to make their voice heard by their legislator, they must exercise their petition right by employing a lobbyist.").

77. Citizens United v. Fed. Election Comm'n, 558 U.S. 310, 365 (2010); McCutcheon v. Fed. Election Comm'n, 134 S. Ct. 1434, 1438 (2014).

78. *See, e.g.,* Peter Lushing, *The Fall and Rise of the Criminal Contingent Fee*, 82 J. CRIM. L. & CRIMINOLOGY 498, 503 (1991).

of Professional Conduct or the ABA Model Code of Professional Responsibility are restrictions on their use in domestic relations and criminal matters.[79]

Supporters of contingent fees litigation argue that they are vital for the prosecution of claims and advancement of interests by those who otherwise would not be able to afford representation; contingent fees, at times, provide the only way that the poor and middle class can gain access to the court system.[80] Opponents, however, believe that the contingent fee is already a plague on lawyering: "When lawyers take a percentage of the recovery as payment . . . they become financial partners in litigation. Where is the impetus not to push a frivolous lawsuit?"[81] Ultimately, as with the contingent fee agreement in the litigation context, whether it is ethical to accept a lobbying assignment on a contingent fee basis depends largely on one's views regarding the work for which the fee is received. For some people, preventing corruption or the appearance of corruption may warrant a ban on anything that might present a temptation to corruption—as contingent fee compensation for lobbying may. For others, the preemptive ban on possible corruptive tendencies is a less effective preventive measure than is the punishment of actual corruption.

Recognizing both the potential benefits to allowing contingent fee lobbying in some cases and the potential corrosive effect in others, the American Bar Association in August 2011 recommended prohibiting federally registered lobbyists from entering "into a contingent fee contract with a client to lobby for an earmark or other narrow financial benefit for that client."[82]

In the end, perhaps the most that can be said on the subject is that contingent fee lobbying, unless prohibited by statute, is legal and that a contract for contingent fee lobbying is likely, in the 21st century, to be considered enforceable. Whether an individual lobbyist or firm decides to engage in this activity may, for now, be simply a matter of conscience.[83]

---

79. MODEL CODE OF PROF'L RESPONSIBILITY, EC 2-20 (1980); MODEL RULES OF PROF'L CONDUCT, R. 1.5(d) (2008). Some have argued that, in any event, the ABA guidance is inadequate for legislative lawyers. *See* Michelle Grant, Note, *Legislative Lawyers and the Model Rules*, 14 GEO. J. LEGAL ETHICS 823 (2001). The Model Code does state that contingent fees should generally not be charged except to clients who are unable to pay a reasonable fixed fee, although the Code also acknowledges that there will be times and circumstances in which a contingent fee for someone who can pay a fixed fee is appropriate. It may make sense to use this measure in gauging whether any individual client should be charged a contingent fee for lobbying services; however, it does not answer the question whether a contingent fee should ever be charged for lobbying services. MODEL CODE OF PROF'L RESPONSIBILITY, EC 2-20. *See also* D.C. RULES OF PROF'L CONDUCT § 1.5 (2007).

80. Fatka & Levien, *supra* note 3, at 580.

81. Sara Rimensnyder, *Bashing Lawyers; Soundbite; Court TV Host Catherine Crier's New Book; Interview*, REASON, Oct. 1, 2002, at 15.

82. ABA House of Delegates Resolution 104B (Aug. 2011), *available at* http://www.americanbar.org/content/dam/aba/directories/policy/2011_am_104b.authcheckdam.pdf. The Report accompanying this proposal explained it as follows: "Where the lobbyist is seeking a narrow financial benefit for the client, the temptations for unethical behavior are probably at their greatest. The appearance of unseemliness, driven by public apprehensions about a possible corrupt exchange, is likely to be particularly strong in that setting also, as taxpayer dollars are directly involved." *Id., Report* at 14. The ABA Task Force that developed this recommendation also proposed to require that contingent fee lobbying contracts be filed accompanying LD-1 or LD-2 forms; this part of the recommendation was not adopted by the Association.

83. For a more detailed discussion of the relevant case law and ethical considerations, *see* Thomas M. Susman & Margaret H. Martin, *Contingent Fee Lobbying: Inflaming Avarice or Facilitating Constitutional Rights?*, 31 SETON HALL LEGIS. J. 311 (2007).

CHAPTER 17

Federal Acquisition Regulation Governing Lobbying

BY THOMAS M. SUSMAN*

17-1 Introduction and General Proscriptions

The Federal Acquisition Regulation (FAR), like its predecessors, the Defense Acquisition Regulation and the Federal Procurement Regulation, governs all aspects of contracting between government agencies and private businesses and contains limitations on the reimbursement of contractors' lobbying expenditures.[1]

The FAR is issued jointly by the Government Services Administration (GSA), the Department of Defense, and the National Aeronautics and Space Administration (NASA). It is periodically updated and revised by the Defense Acquisition Regulatory Council and the Civilian Agency Acquisition Council, all under the aegis of the Office of Federal Procurement Policy. Agency acquisition regulations that implement or supplement the FAR apply to (1) the military departments and defense agencies subject to the authority of the Secretary of Defense; (2) NASA activities subject to the authority of the administrator of NASA; and (3) civilian agencies other than NASA, subject to the overall authority of the GSA or any independent authority a particular agency may have.[2]

The applicable agency supplements should always be consulted for any modifications or additions to the basic regulations contained in the FAR.

---

*Clayton S. Marsh, formerly with Ropes & Gray LLP, was a contributor to the version of this chapter that appeared in The Lobbying Manual: A Compliance Guide for Lawyers and Lobbyists (2nd ed.) (William Luneburg, ed., 1998).

1. The Byrd Amendment also governs government contractor lobbying. See Chapter 15.

2. 48 C.F.R. § 1.301(d) (2015). Authority to supplement the FAR may be granted to an agency by Congress in specific instances.

None of the acquisition regulations expressly *prohibits* lobbying relating to government contracting.[3] To do so would potentially implicate the First Amendment rights of contractors.[4] Furthermore, the FAR does not regulate lobbying activities financed with *non-federal* funds. The FAR does, however, restrict what types of lobbying costs can be recovered from the federal government by contractors working for or selling to the covered government agencies.[5]

The FAR specifically proscribes reimbursement of certain lobbying costs associated with government contracts,[6] although the contractor is not prohibited from funding its lobbying activities out of its own pocket. The FAR also establishes guidelines relevant to determining the allowability of costs in general. The five essential factors to be considered in determining the allowability of commercial contractors' costs are (1) the reasonableness of the costs; (2) the allocability of the costs to the performance of the contract in question; (3) the amenability of the costs to standards promulgated by the Cost Accounting Standards Board (if applicable), and otherwise their compliance with generally accepted accounting principles (GAAP) and practices appropriate to the particular circumstances; (4) any limitations set forth in the cost principles stated in FAR Subpart 31.2; and (5) any specific contract provisions.[7]

Even if costs are not expressly prohibited by the FAR sections dealing specifically with lobbying activities, they may not be allowable under other cost principles of Part 31. A contracting officer, for example, may determine that a cost is "unreasonable" or only partially allocable to a contract even though it is not otherwise specifically prohibited under the FAR. In this case, the contractor has the right to appeal the contracting officer's final decision under the contract's procedures for resolving disputes.

17-2 Lobbying Costs Expressly Prohibited for Reimbursement

The FAR expressly disallows reimbursement for commercial contractors' costs for political activities and legislative lobbying associated with the following:

(1) Attempts to influence the outcomes of any Federal, State or local election, referendum, initiative, or similar procedure, through in kind or cash contributions, endorsements, publicity, or similar activities;

(2) Establishing, administering, contributing to, or paying the expenses of a political party, campaign, political action committee, or other organization established for the purpose of influencing the outcomes of elections;

(3) Any attempt to influence (i) the introduction of Federal, state, or local legislation, or (ii) the enactment or modification of any pending Federal,

---

3. The civilian and the military procurement statutes both require a contractor to include a warranty that no contingent fee has been paid for lobbying for the contract. 41 U.S.C. § 3901(b) (2015); 10 U.S.C. § 2306(b) (2015). The FAR also reflects this requirement. 48 C.F.R. Subpart 3.4 (2015). See Section 16-2 of this manual (dealing with contingent fee lobbying generally).

4. See generally chapter 1 of this manual.

5. 48 C.F.R. § 31.205-22 (2015).

6. *Id.* § 31.205-22(a) (disallowing costs associated with specific lobbying activities, discussed in Section 17-2 of this chapter).

7. *Id.* § 31.201-2(a).

state, or local legislation through communication with any member or employee of Congress or a state legislature (including efforts to influence state or local officials to engage in similar lobbying activity), or with any government official or employee in connection with a decision to sign or veto enrolled legislation;

(4) Any attempt to influence (i) the introduction of Federal, state, or local legislation, or (ii) the enactment or modification of any pending Federal, state, or local legislation by preparing, distributing, or using publicity or propaganda, or by urging members of the general public or any segment thereof to contribute to or participate in any mass demonstration, march, rally, fund-raising drive, lobbying campaign, or letter-writing or telephone campaign;

(5) Legislative liaison activities, including attendance at legislative sessions or committee hearings, gathering information regarding legislation, and analyzing the effect of legislation, when such activities are carried on in support of or in knowing preparation for an effort to engage in unallowable activities; or

(6) Costs incurred in attempting to improperly influence (see. 3.401) [defining "improper influence"], either directly or indirectly, an employee or officer of the Executive branch of the Federal government to give consideration to or act regarding a regulatory or contract matter.[8]

In addition, where the FAR applies to contracts with state, local, and Indian tribal governments, it prohibits reimbursement of "costs incurred to influence (directly or indirectly) legislative action on any matter pending before Congress, a State legislature, or a legislative body of a political subdivision of a State."[9]

There are, however, several exceptions to these broad prohibitions against contractors' charging lobbying costs to the federal government.

17-3 Exceptions to Reimbursement Prohibitions

In general, the exceptions to the FAR's proscription of lobbying-cost reimbursement address circumstances under which Congress or a state legislature expressly requires information concerning the performance of the contract. The exceptions also include instances when contract costs can directly be reduced or impediments to contract performance can be avoided through lobbying activity on the part of the contractor in the state legislature.

Specifically, the FAR allows reimbursement for the following activities:

1. Providing a technical and factual presentation of information on a topic directly related to the performance of a contract through hearing testimony, statements or letters to Congress or a state legislature, or subdivision, member, or cognizant staff member thereof, in response to a documented request (including a Congressional Record notice requesting testimony or statements for the record at a regularly scheduled hearing)

made by the recipient member, legislative body or subdivision, or a cognizant staff member thereof; provided such information is readily obtainable and can be readily put in deliverable form; and further provided that costs under this section for transportation, lodging or meals are unallowable unless incurred for the purpose of offering testimony at a regularly scheduled congressional hearing pursuant to a written request for such presentation made by the chairman or ranking minority member of the committee or subcommittee conducting such hearing.

2. Any lobbying made unallowable by paragraph (a)(3) of this subsection (see Section 17-2) to influence state or local legislation in order to directly reduce contract cost, or to avoid material impairment of the contractor's authority to perform the contract.

3. Any activity specifically authorized by statute to be undertaken with funds from the contract.[10]

17-4 Executive Branch Lobbying Costs

The FAR separately disallows reimbursement for "[c]osts incurred in attempting to improperly influence . . . , either directly or indirectly, an employee or officer of the Executive branch of the Federal Government to give consideration to or act regarding a regulatory or contract matter."[11] "Improper influence" is defined vaguely to mean "any influence that induces or tends to induce a Government employee or officer to give consideration or to act regarding a Government contract on any basis other than the merits of the matter."[12] In practice, the regulation may be a catchall for costs that a federal contracting officer or auditor might wish to disallow for policy reasons.

17-5 Reporting Requirements

When a contractor seeks reimbursement for indirect costs, total lobbying costs must be separately identified in the contractor's indirect cost rate proposal and treated like other unallowable activity costs.[13] The contractor must maintain adequate records to demonstrate that its certification of costs as allowable or unallowable is proper and accurate.[14] In addition, Department of Defense contractors with noncompetitive (sole-source) awards over $100,000 must certify compliance with the FAR prohibition.[15]

17-6 Enforcement

Enforcement of the FAR's lobbying proscriptions generally is sporadic and somewhat indiscriminate. The government has the ability to perform audits to identify

10. 48 C.F.R. § 31.205-22(b)(1)–(b)(3) (2015).
11. Id. § 31.205-22(a)(6).
12. Id. § 3.401.
13. Id. § 31.205-22(c).
14. Id. § 31.205-22(d).
15. 10 U.S.C. § 2324(h)(1) (2012).

unallowable costs through organizations like the Defense Contract Audit Agency,[16] but this is not always done. Although there is no guarantee that unallowable lobbying costs will be discovered, the likelihood of detection is great through reviews of specific contracts (particularly cost-type contracts) or through audits of a contractor's general accounting system.

The government relies on contractors to comply voluntarily with the regulations, and urges contractors to resolve in advance any significant questions or disagreements they might have about reimbursement for lobbying costs.[17] However, compliance with the FAR is not optional, and the regulations impose sanctions on violators. The remedy for receiving reimbursement for unallowable lobbying costs is usually restitution, sometimes by means of an administrative setoff against contract payments due.[18] The FAR also authorizes the suspension of a contractor in the case of gross or recurring violations and, where misconduct is of a serious or compelling nature such that it affects the contractor's present responsibility, the FAR authorizes debarment.[19] Finally, any claims for payment of costs that are unallowable may be actionable as civil[20] or even criminal[21] false claims.

---

16. 48 C.F.R. §§ 42.101–42.102 (2015) (defines the policy and procedure for interagency contract audit services).

17. *Id.* § 31.205-22(e).

18. *Id.* § 42.803.

19. *Id.* §§ 9.407-2(c), 9.406-2(c).

20. 31 U.S.C. § 3729(a) (2015).

21. 18 U.S.C. § 287 (2015).

CHAPTER 18

Political Intelligence

BY MARY C. MOYNIHAN, BRIAN G. SVOBODA, AND BARAK COHEN*

18-1 Introduction

Washington politicians and policy makers have exchanged political intelligence since the birth of the Republic. However, the emergence of the political intelligence business is a relatively new phenomenon.[1] The political intelligence industry took off after the 2008 financial crisis and the enactment of the Dodd-Frank Act of 2010.[2] Although many businesses and industries are consumers of political intelligence, Wall Street investors in particular have increasingly appreciated how valuable an understanding of Washington's inner workings can be to their trading and investment strategies.

---

*The authors gratefully acknowledge the contributions of Marc Elias and Luis Mejia, partners at Perkins Coie LLP, to this article.

    1. *See, e.g.,* Brody Mullins & Susan Pullman, *Hedge Funds Pay Top Dollar for Washington Intelligence,* WALL STREET JOURNAL (Oct. 4, 2011), *available at* http://www.wsj.com/articles/SB10001424053111904070604576514791591319306.

    2. Dodd-Frank Wall Street Reform and Consumer Protection Act, Pub. L. No. 111–203, 124 Stat. 1376.

Perceiving the risk of insider trading and other abuses that could arise from the exchange of information about Washington policy making with Wall Street traders, while responding also to claims of self-dealing by elected officials and their staffs, Congress enacted the Stop Trading on Congressional Knowledge Act (the STOCK Act)[3] in 2012.

Because of their existing relationships with Washington policy makers, lobbyists and the firms they associate with often find they have a natural affinity for political intelligence work. However, lobbyists must know and understand the rules that relate to political intelligence. There are numerous pitfalls for the unwary. The routine exchange of information common within the Washington policy world can impose unique risks when information is shared with investors. This chapter discusses those unique risks and rules of the road for those who engage in the political intelligence industry.

The chapter first describes the business generally and discusses the federal and state securities laws that apply, especially in the context of insider trading and recent investigations by the Securities and Exchange Commission (SEC). The chapter concludes by recommending best practices that firms engaged in political intelligence may wish to follow to reduce the potential for liability under the STOCK Act and the federal and state securities laws.

18-2 Political Intelligence and Passage of the STOCK Act

The concept of political intelligence is somewhat amorphous. It is generally understood to be the provision of data regarding what is likely to occur on some government-related issue. Its practitioners include not only lobbyists, but law firms, registered broker-dealers, and registered investment advisers, among others. In addition, many former government officials have opened small firms that provide advice in their particular areas of expertise, and these services are often seen as including the provision of political intelligence.

The STOCK Act defines political intelligence as information that is "derived by a person from direct communications with an executive branch employee, a member of Congress, or an employee of Congress; and provided in exchange for financial compensation to a client who intends, and who is known to intend, to use the information to inform investment decisions."[4] This is a good functional definition of political intelligence, but it encompasses both information derived from confidential sources and information that is public and widely disseminated.

A 2012 study required by the STOCK Act and performed by the Government Accountability Office (the GAO Study)[5] provided detailed information about the political intelligence industry and made several findings:

- The prevalence of the sale of political intelligence is not known and is therefore difficult to quantify.

---

3. STOCK Act, Pub. L. No. 112–105, 126 Stat. 291.
4. *Id.* § 7(b).
5. U.S. GOVERNMENT ACCOUNTING OFFICE, Political Intelligence: Financial Market Value of Government Information Hinges on Materiality and Timing (2013) [hereinafter GAO STUDY].

- Political intelligence is often bundled and provided to clients with other information such as research, opinion, and policy analysis.
- Compensation structures vary. Firms are often paid through monthly retainers or for information relating to a general topic (like health care reform), but not based on specific sources of information or in connection with specific investment decisions.
- There is a lack of consensus on the meaning of several different terms included in the STOCK Act when applied to the activities of political intelligence firms, particularly with respect to information that is conveyed in public settings or meetings, but might be directly communicated.
- Although it is often difficult to link the provision of particular information by a political intelligence firm to a particular investment decision, it is clear that this can and does occur.[6]

The GAO Study also summarized several of the practical and policy considerations that would be involved in regulating the political intelligence industry, including important issues under the First Amendment and the "Speech or Debate" clause of the U.S. Constitution.[7]

Concerns that the growing political intelligence industry was helping only a privileged few at the expense of others prompted the introduction of the STOCK Act in 2006.[8] As one of the bill's principal sponsors, Representative Brian Baird, told the House Rules Committee shortly after the bill was introduced:

> Clearly, the buying or selling of stock based on nonpublic information has the potential to profit some private parties at the expense of others who may not have access to this same information ... I am very concerned that privileging a handful of investors with confidential information about congressional activity is not only a misuse of a congressional office, but also undermines investor confidence in the fairness and integrity of the securities market.[9]

Representative Baird asserted that a "loophole in our law ... allows members of Congress and their staffs, as well as those outside Congress with key contacts or influence in Congress, to trade on nonpublic information."[10]

These types of concerns highlighted the inherent tension between the appropriate desire to regulate potential abuses within the political intelligence industry and the nonetheless valuable function that the industry performs in making information about potential government action available to the investing public. Without the expertise provided by political intelligence firms, this information might not be well understood and digestible by the markets. While most consumers of political intelligence are institutional investors, not retail investors, many

---

6. *Id.* 8–12.

7. *Id.* 7, 15.

8. H.R. 5015, 109th Cong. (2006).

9. *Rep. Baird Testifies Before Rules Committee on Insider Trading 72 Hour Proposals*, U.S. Fed. News (Mar. 30, 2006) (statement of Rep. Baird).

10. *Id.*

institutional investors manage pension plans and widely held mutual funds whose ultimate beneficiaries are smaller investors.

Further, notwithstanding the concerns voiced about the political intelligence industry's impact on the integrity of markets, Congress had long understood that the use of nonpublic information by members and employees for private gain was prohibited—potentially by the securities laws, and certainly by congressional ethics rules.[11] But uncertainty about how the main theories of insider trading under the securities laws might apply to members and their staff, together with cynicism about Congress's ability to police itself through the ethics process, lent credibility to the concerns about potential abuse and the need for regulatory action.

The STOCK Act was reintroduced in the House in 2007, and again in 2009 and 2011, without generating major congressional action. Then, in November 2011, the CBS News investigative program *60 Minutes* aired a story alleging that "members of Congress and their aides have regular access to powerful political intelligence, and [that] many have made well-timed stock market trades in the very industries they regulate. For now, the practice is perfectly legal, but some say it's time for the law to change."[12] Congress reacted with alacrity. When the *60 Minutes* segment aired, the STOCK Act had been sitting in the House for more than five years, and it had nine cosponsors.[13] Less than five months later, the House bill had acquired 286 cosponsors and the president signed its Senate companion into law.[14]

Among its major provisions, the STOCK Act affirmed that government officials and employees are not exempt from the securities laws' insider trading prohibitions, and that they have the fiduciary duty necessary for insider trading liability.[15] It prohibited them from using material nonpublic information to trade in the commodities markets as well.[16] It required members, senior congressional staff, and senior executive branch personnel to file periodic transaction reports for transactions in stocks, bonds, commodities futures, and other securities that exceed $1,000;[17] restricted their ability to participate in initial public offerings or

---

11. *See, e.g.*, Code of Ethics for Government Service, H. Con. Res. 175 (85th Cong.) ¶ 8 (requiring members, officers and employees of Congress never to "use any information coming ... confidentially in the performance of governmental duties as a means for making private profit"). *See also* U.S. HOUSE OF REPRESENTATIVES COMMITTEE ON ETHICS, *Rules Regarding Personal Financial Transactions* (Nov. 29, 2011), *available at* http://ethics.house.gov/sites/ethics.house.gov/files/fin%20trans%20pink%20sheet. pdf (last visited Sept. 14, 2015) (summarizing laws and standards of conduct that may apply to personal financial transactions).

12. *60 Minutes: Insiders* (CBS television broadcast Nov. 13, 2011), *available at* http://www.cbsnews. com/news/congress-trading-stock-on-inside-information/ (last visited Sept. 14, 2015). The segment drew heavily from a book written by Peter Schweizer, a research fellow at the Hoover Institution at Stanford University. *See* Peter Schweizer, *Throw Them All Out: How Politicians and Their Friends Get Rich Off Insider Stock Tips, Land Deals, and Cronyism That Would Send the Rest of Us to Prison* (2011). The segment's claim that it was "perfectly legal" for members and staff to trade off confidential information was, at the very least, overstated. *See supra* note 11.

13. *See* H.R. 1148, 112th Cong. (2011).

14. *See* Pub. L. 112–105 (2012).

15. *See id.* §§ 3, 9.

16. *See id.* § 5.

17. *See id.* § 6.

"IPOs";[18] and required their personal financial disclosure reports to be made available online.[19]

The STOCK Act did not require registration of political intelligence firms, as some had proposed.[20] Instead, it authorized the GAO Study, discussed above.[21]

18-3 The STOCK Act and Insider Trading

The main target of the STOCK Act,[22] insider trading, is a complicated area of the law that remains a focus of both federal prosecutors and the SEC. Very generally, insider trading refers to "buying or selling a security, in breach of a fiduciary duty or other relationship of trust and confidence, while in possession of material, nonpublic information about the security."[23] Illegal insider trading[24] is prohibited by section 10(b) of the U.S. Securities Exchange Act of 1934, as amended (Exchange Act), and Rule 10b-5 thereunder.

Insider trading liability generally requires five elements: (1) a duty of trust and confidence is owed to the source of the information; (2) the duty must be breached by revealing the information; (3) the information itself must be material nonpublic information (MNPI); (4) the trading must take place while in possession of the MNPI; and (5) if the recipient of the information is not the trader, but "tips" the information, there must be a benefit to the tipper (and for the person making the trade, knowledge that the tipper received a benefit).[25] Proving insider trading, in the context of political intelligence, poses certain unique questions. This section discusses how the elements of insider trading may apply to political intelligence.

---

18. *See id.* § 12.

19. *See id.* §§ 8, 11. The requirement for Internet publication of personal financial disclosure reports triggered a lawsuit on behalf of a number of federal employees, contending that the STOCK Act had made them "easy targets for identity theft, financial fraud, and even kidnapping when the nature, extent, and location of their financial assets became freely available worldwide." Complaint, Senior Executives Ass'n et al. v. United States, Civ. No. 8:12-cv-02297-AW ¶ 2 (D. Md., filed Aug. 2, 2012). Congress responded by limiting the online posting requirement. *See* Pub. L. 113–7 (2013).

20. *See* 158 CONG. REC. 17, S295-97 (daily ed. Feb. 2, 2012) (statement of Sen. Grassley).

21. *See* GAO STUDY, *supra* note 5. The Study provided much useful information about the industry but made no specific recommendations. Among other matters, the Study concluded that before requiring registration Congress would need to "address the lack of consensus on the meaning of the terms "direct communication" and "investment decision" to provide clarity regarding the definition of political intelligence as well as guidance to specify the purpose of disclosure, who would be required to file, how often disclosures would be required, and who would manage the disclosure process.

22. "Send me a bill that bans insider trading by members of Congress; I will sign it tomorrow." Remarks by the President in State of the Union Address (Jan. 12, 2012), *available at* http://www.white house.gov/the-press-office/2012/01/24/remarks-president-state-union-address (last visited Sept. 14, 2015).

23. http://www.sec.gov/answers/insider.htm.

24. Note that insider trading is not necessarily illegal. Corporate insiders, such as officers, directors, and employees, may legally buy and sell stock in their own companies. This form of insider trading is decidedly legal, although corporate insiders who trade in their own securities must report the trades to the SEC.

25. *See, e.g.*, United States v. Newman, 773 F.3d 438 (2d Cir. 2014), *cert. denied*, 136 S. Ct. 242 (Oct. 5, 2015); *but see* United States v. Salman, 792 F.3d 1087, 1093 (9th Cir. 2015) (declining to follow Newman to the extent that "[d]oing so would require us to depart from the clear holding of Dirks that the element of breach of fiduciary duty is met where an 'insider makes a gift of confidential information to a trading relative or friend.'), *granting cert.*, 2016 WL 207256 (Jan. 19, 2016).

18-3.1 Existence of Duty

Much of the law surrounding insider trading is based on the breach of a presumed duty not to disclose or trade on confidential information. There are two primary theories for how breaches may occur.

The *classical theory* of insider trading involves trading by insiders of an issuer (including temporary insiders, such as lawyers and accountants). In *Chiarella v. United States*, the Supreme Court held that the relationship of trust and confidence that exists between corporate insiders and shareholders imposes a duty to disclose or abstain from trading when the insiders have obtained confidential information vis-à-vis the issuer.[26] Trading in breach of this duty constitutes a fraud or deceit on the issuer's shareholders under section 10(b) and Rule 10b-5.

The *misappropriation theory* of insider trading covers persons who are not insiders, but who nonetheless owe a duty of trust and confidence that is breached when they misappropriate confidential information to trade securities. Case law has primarily imposed this duty in circumstances involving fiduciary relationships, but also where persons may have contractually assumed a duty of nondisclosure. Rule 10b5-2 under the Exchange Act provides a nonexclusive definition of circumstances in which a person has a duty of trust or confidence for purposes of the misappropriation theory. Under Rule 10b5-2, a duty of trust or confidence may exist whenever (1) a person agrees to maintain information in confidence; (2) people have a history, pattern, or practice of sharing confidences; and (3) a person receives or obtains material nonpublic information from his or her spouse, parent, child, or sibling.

Before the STOCK Act took effect, it was not clear when government officials owed a duty of trust and confidence under the misappropriation theory and, if so, to whom that duty was owed. For example, it could be argued that an officeholder *should* communicate material information to stakeholders or constituents. The STOCK Act explicitly applies the federal prohibitions on insider trading to members of Congress, congressional staff, executive branch officials, and judicial officers and employees (covered officials).[27] It says further that covered officials owe a duty arising from a relationship of trust and confidence to the United States and its citizens (and in the case of members of Congress and staff, to the Congress as well) with respect to MNPI derived from the officials' positions or gained from the performance of their responsibilities. Finally, the STOCK Act affirms that covered officials may not use such information to make a profit.

Lobbyists or other nongovernment officials typically are not themselves subject to a duty of confidentiality. However, they run the risk of being part of a tipper/tippee chain if they receive or pass on information under certain circumstances, as discussed below. In addition, under the misappropriation theory they may become subject to a duty where they have agreed to keep information confidential or have a history, pattern, or practice of sharing confidences such that a person providing the information would expect them to maintain its confidentiality.

26. Chiarella v. United States, 445 U.S. 222 (1980).
27. STOCK Act, Pub. L. No. 112–105, § 18, 126 Stat. 291.

18-3.2 Is the Information MNPI?

Determining whether information is MNPI is a complicated fact-specific analysis, and recent insider trading prosecutions have focused extensively on the point.[28] Congress itself has left the definition somewhat uncertain, and only the House of Representatives has so far provided guidance in the context of the STOCK Act. The House Committee on Ethics has opined that "A good rule of thumb to determine whether information may be MNPI is whether or not the release of that information to the public would have an effect on the price of the security or property." While helpful, this standard does not entirely align with case law.

In the context of political intelligence, there are two major hurdles to determining whether information is MNPI.

What is material? Political intelligence is likely to be material if it relates to specific information that is likely to affect the stock price of a particular issuer or group of issuers. Traditional analyses of materiality relate to whether the information would be material to an investment decision concerning a specific issuer. Political intelligence, however, rarely focuses on a specific company because legislation and policy usually do not link to specific issuers. Political intelligence instead generally deals with broader factors that affect an entire industry or market segment. In addition, political intelligence often depends on opinion and conjecture, and thus may not rise to the requisite level of materiality.

What is confidential in Washington? Washington is full of rumors and leaked information, some of which are deliberately planned as so-called trial balloons to gauge public reaction to new policies and thus arguably are not confidential by their nature. Further, much of what Congress does (e.g., floor debate, committee hearings, markups of legislation, and speeches) is inherently public. And lawmakers and staff meet routinely with lobbyists, citizens, and others in settings that may not be public but are nonetheless intended to promote a free exchange of information between policymakers and stakeholders. In such situations, it is hard to apply a bright-line test to decide when information is or is not public.

For this reason, there have been very limited prosecutions involving MNPI in the public sector. Those that have been pursued have involved very specific government information tied to a specific company or specific security that was used before a clearly defined public announcement. For example, the SEC brought an enforcement action related to trading based on nonpublic information about the U.S. Treasury's decision to cease issuance of the thirty-year bond. In that case, a consultant attended a Treasury Department briefing and tipped clients before the news was made public.[29] In a second case, the SEC sued a chemist working for the Food and Drug Administration (FDA) for trading in advance of twenty-eight different announcements concerning FDA decisions on drug applications by specific companies.[30] A current case involving political intelligence pertains to a release of

---

28. "Information is material when there is a substantial likelihood that a reasonable investor would find it important in making an investment decision." United States v. Contorinis, 692 F.3d 136, 143 (2d Cir. 2012) (citation omitted). "To be material, information must alter[ ] the total mix of information available." *Id.* (citation and internal quotation marks omitted).

29. SEC v. Davis, No. 03-CV-6672 (NRB), (S.D.N.Y., filed Sept. 4, 2003); *available at* http://www.sec.gov/litigation/litreleases/lr18453.htm.

30. SEC v. Cheng Yi Liang, No. 8:11-cv-00819-RWT (D. Md., Filed March 29, 2011); *available at* http://www.sec.gov/litigation/litreleases/2011/lr21907.htm.

information affecting a small industry segment that occurred very shortly before the public announcement.[31] In another recently settled SEC administrative proceeding, the SEC asserted that the political intelligence firm had failed to "establish, maintain and enforce written policies and procedures reasonably designed to prevent the misuse of [MNPI] consistent with the nature of its business." The case related to two different incidents involving in the first case, information obtained from a source at the Centers for Medicare and Medicaid Services regarding a pending coverage decision for a particular drug, and in the second, information relating to FDA approval of a new drug application.[32]

While the type of information typically provided by political intelligence firms is not so specific, and likely would not qualify as MNPI, it is clear that information can in some cases qualify as MNPI and result in regulatory action against the firms or persons who have tipped or traded on it.

18-3.3 Tipper/Tippee and the Benefit Requirement

Because political intelligence firms convey information to traders, liability for insider trading involving political intelligence would most likely arise in the context of a tip. For example, a political intelligence firm might be viewed as having received a tip from a government insider that it then passed to its clients whom it knew would trade. *Dirks v. SEC,*[33] the seminal insider trading case addressing tipper and tippee liability, makes clear that tippee liability derives from tipper liability.

Critically, a breach of the duty of confidentiality occurs only if the information is disclosed in breach of a duty of confidentiality *and* for the personal benefit of the tipper.

The question of personal benefit to the tipper has been an elusive one.[34] The *Dirks* court explained that a personal benefit could include "a pecuniary gain or a reputational benefit that will translate into future earnings" or be inferred from "a relationship between the insider and the recipient that suggests a *quid pro quo* from the latter, or an intention to benefit the particular recipient."[35]

Over time, it seemed that even the remotest of relationships between the tipper and the tippee might rise to a level sufficient to infer a personal benefit, and courts applied a "knew or should have known" standard with respect to whether the tippee must know that the tipper had received a benefit. However, in December 2014, the federal Court of Appeals for the Second Circuit issued an important opinion in *United States v. Newman*[36] holding that a tippee can be liable for insider trading only if he or she had knowledge that the tipper obtained a personal benefit. The decision

---

31. SEC v. The Comm. on Ways and Means of the U.S. House of Representatives, No. 14-mc-00193 (S.D.N.Y., filed June 20, 2014). The case concerned the alleged leak of information shortly before an announcement by the Centers for Medicare and Medicaid Services relating to reimbursement rates for the Medicare Advantage program that would benefit health insurance plans. The leak sparked trading by hedge fund and asset managers that reaped profits when the decision was made public.

32. In re Marwood Group Research, LLC, Exchange Act Rel. No. 76512 (Nov. 24, 2015).

33. Dirks v. SEC, 463 U.S. 646 (1983).

34. "Determining whether an insider personally benefits from a particular disclosure, a question of fact, will not always be easy for courts." *Dirks*, 463 U.S. at 664–65.

35. *Id.*

36. United States v. Newman, 773 F.3d 438, 455 (2d Cir. 2014), *reh'g denied* (2d Cir. 2015).

also significantly tightened the criteria for what constitutes a personal benefit. The Second Circuit held that the government may not "prove the receipt of a personal benefit by the mere fact of a friendship, particularly of a casual or social nature," but that "the personal benefit received in exchange for the confidential information must be of some consequence."[37] On July 30, 2015, the U.S. Department of Justice petitioned the Supreme Court to review *Newman*, but the Second Circuit's decision remains intact as of this writing.

The *Newman* case applied to a criminal matter and is binding only in the Second Circuit.[38] Nonetheless, the case is significant to the political intelligence world, in which the day-to-day exchange of information, even if the information is MNPI, typically involves very little that would amount to the giving of a personal benefit, other than the uniquely Washington bragging rights of "being in the know."

It would likely be difficult to show that a remote tippee knew or should have known that information was obtained in breach of a duty created under the STOCK Act. Similarly, it would be a high hurdle to prosecute a covered official as a tipper if he or she conveyed information to someone not known to be a potential trader (e.g., to trade groups, unions, or a policy group), who then tips a trader. Even under *Dirks*, the sifting and distilling of information from various sources that political intelligence firms typically perform raises significant barriers to meeting the burden of proof in an insider trading case. Political intelligence firms generally mix public information and opinion with slivers of information that may have been gleaned directly from a covered official. Moreover, there may be only an attenuated connection between a particular piece of information provided by a public official that is filtered through a political intelligence firm and a trader's investment decision. Covered officials also provide information to stakeholders, interest groups, and lobbyists for many purposes other than stock market investing. Thus, it is likely that a covered official may have had no knowledge that the information would find its way to a trader's desk. If the tipper lacks intent, there is likely no actionable breach.

18-3.4 Other Issues

The STOCK Act's insider trading provisions raise unique public policy and constitutional issues. These issues implicate the Speech or Debate clause of the U.S. Constitution,[39] as well as assertions of sovereign immunity[40] by covered officials.

The Speech or Debate clause protects words spoken during legislative debates. In addition, "Committee reports, resolutions, and the act of voting are equally covered, as are 'things generally done in a session of the House by one of its members

---

37. *Id.* at 452.

38. *See* United States v. Salman, 792 F.3d 1087, cert. granted, 136 S. C. 99 (Jan 19, 2016) (No. 15-628) (9th Cir. 2015), in which the Ninth Circuit declined to accept an expansive reading of *Newman*, holding that to do so would contradict *Dirks* ("Proof that the insider disclosed material nonpublic information with the intent to benefit a trading relative or friend is sufficient to establish the breach of fiduciary duty element of insider trading.").

39. U.S. Const. art. 1, § 6, cl.1.

40. FDIC v. Meyer, 510 U.S. 471, 475 (1994) ("Absent a waiver, sovereign immunity shields the Federal Government and its agencies from suit.").

in relation to the business before it.'"[41] Generally, courts have held that the clause extends to cover legislators "acting in the sphere of legitimate legislative activity."[42]

The clause's application to the STOCK Act turns on whether particular conduct potentially covered by the act would be considered "an integral part of the deliberative and communicative processes by which members participate in committee and House proceedings with respect to the consideration and passage or rejection of proposed legislation or with respect to other matters which the Constitution places within the jurisdiction of either House."[43] If so, the argument would be that the conduct was protected, or for this purpose immune from prosecution. The key questions here are whether tipping is an integral part of the deliberative and communicative process and whether disclosure of MNPI outside of Congress is a legitimate legislative activity.

In the case of sovereign immunity, the issue hinges on whether sovereign immunity is limited to suits brought by private parties. If so, then legislators and their employees cannot claim sovereign immunity as a defense against DOJ and SEC subpoenas relating to alleged STOCK Act violations. But if sovereign immunity does shield legislators and their employees from such demands for information, then it may prove difficult to investigate violations of the STOCK Act.

At this writing, several investigations involving alleged insider trading in connection with the political intelligence business are under way.[44] The resolution of these and other cases will provide greater clarity into the applicable legal standards.

18-4 Regulatory Status Issues

Providing political intelligence to investors implicates the federal securities laws on several other levels besides insider trading.

18-4.1 Broker-Dealers

Generally, political intelligence can be viewed as investment research. This then raises the question of whether a political intelligence firm must be a registered broker-dealer in order to provide that service. Although the purchase of investment research by investment firms has a complicated regulatory background with historical connections with the broker-dealer industry, there is generally no requirement that political intelligence firms register as broker-dealers.

For historical reasons, however, the dissemination of investment research has been largely the province of broker-dealers. Until the elimination of fixed commissions in 1975,[45] broker-dealers sought to gain market share by offering superior service to their customers. A party executing a trade would thus receive not only execution but also other services that included investment research. Thus, broker-

---

41. Powell v. McCormack, 395 U.S. 486, 502 (1969), quoting Kilbourn v. Thompson, 103 U.S. 168, 204 (1880).

42. Spallone v. United States, 493 U.S. 265, 645–46 (1990) (citations omitted).

43. Gravel v. United States, 408 U.S. 606, 625 (1972).

44. *E.g.*, SEC v. The Comm. on Ways and Means of the U.S. House of Representatives, No. 14-mc-00193 (S.D.N.Y., filed June 20, 2014).

45. *See* http://www.sec.gov/rules/interp/2006/34-54165.pdf, pp. 8–9.

dealers often employed investment analysts whose job was to produce investment research reports for customers of the broker-dealer. With the elimination of fixed commissions in 1975, brokers began competing more aggressively over prices, and they began to question how they could continue to provide such research services. In response, Congress included a safe harbor in the law, codified as section 28(e) of the Exchange Act. The safe harbor provides generally that a money manager does not breach its fiduciary duties under state or federal law solely because it has paid brokerage commissions to a broker-dealer for effecting securities transactions in excess of the amount another broker-dealer would have charged, if the money manager determines in good faith that the amount of the commissions paid is reasonable in relation to the value of the brokerage and research services provided by such broker-dealer.[46] Adoption of the safe harbor allowed broker-dealers to continue to be compensated through commissions for investment research. The portion of the commission that pays for the additional services is colloquially referred to as "soft dollars."

Traditionally, these soft dollars could be paid only to broker-dealers for their proprietary research. Through a series of regulatory reforms and guidance, the SEC has permitted third-party research arrangements in which the research services and products are developed by third parties, but funded out of commission dollars. Much, but not all, political intelligence purchased by investment firms is purchased with soft dollars through such commission-sharing arrangements. This practice has both advantages and disadvantages to the business. On the one hand, the investment management firms have soft dollars available to pay for political intelligence (and it thus may not affect their bottom line, as commissions are often paid by customer accounts). On the other hand, allocations of soft dollars are made by so-called broker votes in which broker-dealers solicit votes on the "value" of the research services from institutional clients. As a result, if information provided by a political intelligence firm is not deemed valuable, the payment to the firm may be decreased or not made at all after the research has been provided.

Some broker-dealer firms do provide Washington-based research as one of their proprietary research services. These firms must be registered with the SEC and the Financial Regulatory Authority (FINRA), and the individuals providing such research must also hold certain licenses with FINRA.

18-4.2 Investment Advisers

A second question arises in connection with the regulatory status of political intelligence firms under the Investment Advisers Act of 1940, as amended (the Advisers Act). The Advisers Act defines an investment adviser as any person who "engages in the business of advising others, either directly or through publications or writings, as to the value of securities or as to the advisability of investing in, purchasing, or selling securities, or who, for compensation and as part of a regular business, issues or promulgates analyses or reports concerning securities."[47] While there is a risk that political intelligence activities might trigger the registration requirements

---

46. 15 U.S.C. § 78bb(e)(1) (2015).
47. 15 U.S.C. § 80b-2(11) (2015).

of the Advisers Act or, more likely, of state laws covering investment advisers,[48] most firms take the position that they should not be defined as investment advisers under the Advisers Act.

In the first instance, many firms only provide general information with respect to public policy; in other words, they do not provide advice as to "securities." "Mission creep" can arise, however, and investment firm clients will tend to seek security-specific binary information[49] when available. Therefore, in certain circumstances, research provided by a political intelligence firm could be considered advice as to the "value of securities or as to the advisability of investing in, purchasing, or selling securities."

Even where advice could be construed as pertaining to securities, however, there are available exclusions to the definition of investment adviser under the Advisers Act that would likely apply to the provision of political intelligence. Where the political intelligence is provided under the auspices of a law firm, lobbying firm, or accounting firm, the so-called professional exclusion would apply, provided that the service can be construed as "incidental" to the practice of the profession.[50]

Most independent research firms, however, rely on the "publisher's" exclusion, so called because the definition of investment adviser specifically excludes "the publisher of any bona fide newspaper, news magazine or business or financial publication of general and regular circulation." The U.S. Supreme Court addressed the scope of the publisher's exclusion in *Lowe v. SEC*.[51] In that case, Lowe, who had been barred from acting as an investment adviser, was publishing a newsletter. The Court held that the Advisers Act "was designed to apply to those persons engaged in the investment-advisory profession—those who provide personalized advice attuned to a client's concerns, whether by written or verbal communication."[52] The Court determined that Lowe was not an investment adviser because the newsletters did "not offer individualized advice attuned to any specific portfolio or to any client's particular needs."[53]

While the interpretation may be aggressive, most research firms take the position that they provide only impersonal advice, that is, advice not tailored to the individual needs of a specific client. They argue that, following *Lowe*, they are excluded from the definition of investment adviser and thus not required to register as such. While this position is reasonable, firms that seek the flexibility to provide advice on specific securities, or that may seek engagements for more bespoke

---

48. Requirements to register under the Advisers Act are linked generally to the assets under management of the adviser. Typically, political research firms do not manage client accounts and thus would not qualify for federal registration.

49. "Binary" refers here to information that is potentially actionable in an investment context. In other words, rather than a generalized policy view that health care costs will increase under a certain legislative provision, this would be information suggesting that a governmental act would have a direct and immediate impact on the stock of a particular issuer or issuers. This is seen frequently, for example, for actions of the Centers for Medicare and Medicaid Services, the agency responsible for decisions covering Medicare and Medicaid reimbursements, whose actions have formed the basis of alleged insider trading in several cases receiving widespread media attention.

50. 15 U.S.C. § 80b-2(a)(11).

51. Lowe v. SEC, 472 U.S. 181 (1985).

52. *Id*. at 207–08.

53. *Id*. at 208.

projects relating to specific investment strategies, should consult qualified counsel. These firms should carefully consider their regulatory status under the state and federal laws governing investment advisers.

In conclusion, while the provision of political intelligence likely does not require registration, political intelligence firms may include firms that are registered broker-dealers or registered investment advisers. For investment managers, using a regulated firm may somewhat reduce the risk of potential exposure to claims of insider trading or other regulatory infractions, as registered firms are required to have in place robust policies and procedures covering compliance with the securities laws.

18-5 Best Practices

Political intelligence firms, regardless of how they are organized, should adopt basic policies and procedures to ensure that their activities fully comply with the law. In the first instance, depending on the nature of the services they provide, firms should consult with counsel to determine if any of their activities might subject them to regulation as either a broker-dealer or investment adviser. They should also be fully conversant with laws applicable to lobbying activities, and carefully distinguish lobbying or policy advocacy work from that which is done specifically in connection with provision of political intelligence to investment firms.[54] Work done for investment firms will require additional compliance safeguards.[55]

18-5.1 Political Intelligence Firms

Political intelligence firms would be well served by adopting basic policies and procedures covering insider trading and the STOCK Act.[56] These policies should include regular staff training on the issues involved, including

- *How to identify whether information is public or nonpublic.* For example, was the information obtained under circumstances suggesting that it is public (i.e., at a widely attended gathering rather than a private one-on-one meeting)?
- *How to identify if the information is material.* For example, does the information represent the views of leadership, or is it more likely immaterial or unreliable (e.g., a trial balloon, view of member not in leadership, or a staff member's opinion)? Is the information specific and factual, or opinion, analysis, and spin? Is the information related to a specific company or financial instrument, or otherwise likely to move the market? Put

---

54. See Chapter 4 of this manual for a general discussion of the Lobbying Disclosure Act.

55. It is noteworthy that one case that has attracted regulatory scrutiny involved the alleged transmission of information from a government official to a lobbyist, who conveyed the information to a related business involved in providing information to trading firms, who allegedly traded on the information. Had appropriate safeguards been in place when the information moved from the lobbying side of the firm to those involved with investing, the subsequent issues could potentially have been avoided. *See* SEC v. The Comm. on Ways and Means of the U.S. House of Representatives et al., No. 14-mc-00193 (S.D.N.Y., filed June 20, 2014).

56. Policies must not only be adopted, but they should be rigorously maintained and enforced. *See Marwood, supra* note 32.

differently, would the information be significant to the decision to buy or sell a stock? What is the timing of the information with respect to any expected public announcements or disclosure?

- *How to identify red flags.* For example, is the source of the information an insider or someone who may have a duty of trust and confidence not to disclose the information?[57] Is the information being communicated in a manner suggesting that a breach of confidentiality could be involved (i.e., is the information conveyed along with language such as, "this is confidential," "don't tell anyone," or "this is off the record"?) Is the informant seeking a personal benefit (e.g., employment or money) by disclosing the information?

Staff should also understand and be required to communicate their role to sources—that they are gathering information for clients who are likely to trade on the information. Where practical, they should inquire whether the information being exchanged is confidential.

Finally, a firm should establish an escalation procedure so that an individual who may have obtained MNPI has a clear process for seeking counsel regarding whether such information must be embargoed or other appropriate actions taken.

18-5.2 Covered Officials

Covered officials should understand the limits placed on them by the STOCK Act and insider trading rules. This is new territory for members of Congress and their staff, who may not fully appreciate that information they provide to one person may find its way into the hands of investors who will trade on it. Covered officials should *never* seek personal financial benefit while performing their official duties. Moreover, like political intelligence firms, covered officials should carefully consider whether they may have a duty not to disclose certain information and whether that information could constitute MNPI.

18-5.3 Investors

Investment firms who wish to avail themselves of the services of a political intelligence firm should conduct due diligence of the firm before retaining it. They should ask whether the firms have compliance policies and training in place, as described above. In addition, they should consider contractual provisions including (1) an acknowledgment that information may be used as a basis for investment decisions and (2) an agreement from the political intelligence firm not to convey MNPI.

---

57. Note that even government officials not covered by the STOCK Act are covered by their own rules governing duties of confidentiality. For example, confidentiality laws cover branches of the military, intelligence agencies, the Internal Revenue Service, the Centers for Medicare and Medicaid Services, and numerous other federal agencies.

18-6 Conclusion

Few images show the impact of Washington decisions on financial markets more clearly than the pictures of "Wall Street traders huddling around television screens" while the House of Representatives debated financial bailout legislation at the height of the financial crisis on September 29, 2008.[58] The traders "watched lawmakers denounce the bailout legislation, and then sent the Dow plummeting."[59]

Yet even in ordinary times, every day sees a torrent of initiatives and decisions emanating from Washington that can impact the bottom lines of issuers, market segments, and entire industries. Understanding Washington politics and the complicated processes of legislation, rulemaking, and administration can be daunting to the uninitiated. Political intelligence firms perform a vital role in increasing the amount and clarity of information available to investment firms. In doing so, they may positively impact the investment returns of their clients, including indirectly the investment and retirement accounts of millions of Americans.

However, like all businesses involved in the markets, they must be attentive to the regulatory regime in place to prohibit manipulation of the markets through illegal insider trading. When advising their clients, they must also ensure that they stay within the available exemptions or exclusions from registration as an investment adviser or broker-dealer, or, if required, register and comply with the applicable rules. Finally, they should ensure that their operations are conducted with an understanding of other rules that may apply, including those connected to lobbying. The role of political intelligence will only become more important, as the economy and government become ever more entwined and complex. At the same time, compliance in the field of political intelligence will only become more challenging, as laws both old and new are increasingly applied to this emerging industry.

Lobbying firms and lobbyists in particular may be faced with a blurring of the lines between influencing policy and communicating the information gleaned through interaction with Washington policy makers to individuals and firms involved in trading securities. A knowledge of the risks related to political intelligence and best practices are important tools for ensuring compliance with all applicable law and regulations.

---

58. Jonathan Weisman, *House Rejects Financial Rescue, Sending Stocks Plummeting*, Wash. Post, Sep. 30, 2008, *available at* http://www.washingtonpost.com/wp-dyn/content/article/2008/09/29/AR2008092900623.html.

59. *Id.*

CHAPTER 19

Foreign Agents Registration Act

BY RONALD I. MELTZER*

19-1 Introduction

Lawyers and lobbyists who represent foreign clients may be subject to the Foreign Agents Registration Act (FARA),[1] enacted in 1938 to require public disclosure of Nazi propaganda efforts in the United States.[2] It was amended in 1966 to cover lobbying and political activities undertaken in the United States on behalf of foreign

---

*The author is grateful to Marik String of WilmerHale for his valuable assistance in updating this chapter.

    1. 22 U.S.C. § 621 (2015).

    2. *See, e.g.,* Viereck v. United States, 318 U.S. 236, 241 (1943); THE REGISTRATION OF FOREIGN AGENTS IN THE UNITED STATES: A PRACTICAL AND LEGAL GUIDE 4–5, 18–21 (Joseph E. Pattison & John L. Taylor, eds., 1981) [hereinafter REGISTRATION OF FOREIGN AGENTS IN THE UNITED STATES].

business and governmental interests.[3] FARA was further amended by the Lobbying Disclosure Act of 1995 (LDA), the Lobbying Disclosure Technical Amendments Act of 1998 (LDTAA), and the Honest Leadership and Open Government Act of 2007 (HLOGA).[4] These amendments have revised the scope of FARA with respect to registrable and exempted activities and have limited its registration requirements in relation to the LDA. In addition, the amended FARA now has provisions seeking to increase public access to required filings.

Under FARA, a person who acts as an "agent of a foreign principal" must register with the Department of Justice within ten days of agreeing to become an agent and before performing any registrable activity on behalf of the foreign principal. Foreign principals include foreign governments, foreign political parties, foreign companies, and any other person outside the United States. FARA registration is a significant undertaking, requiring the submission of initial registration statements, as well as detailed supplemental filings for each six-month period following registration.

FARA covers a wide range of activities. It applies to any attempt to influence Congress, federal agencies, or U.S. public opinion "with reference to formulating, adopting, or changing the domestic or foreign policies of the United States or with reference to the political or public interests, policies, or relations of a government of a foreign country or a foreign political party."[5] During the 1990s, Congress considered major reform of FARA[6] and ultimately amended the Act in connection with its enactment of the LDA and LDTAA. The most significant changes involved broadening the definition of political activities, tightening the terms of the exemption for legal representation, removing the exemption for domestic subsidiaries of foreign-owned companies, and limiting FARA's application (in most instances) to persons acting as agents of foreign governments or foreign political parties. Moreover, in the wake of the Jack Abramoff scandal,[7] Congress amended the act intending to provide greater transparency and public access to FARA filings.

19-2 Persons Subject to Registration

FARA is applicable to any person who acts "as an agent of a foreign principal."[8]

---

3. Pub. L. No. 89–486, 80 Stat. 244 (1966).

4. Lobbying Disclosure Act of 1995, Pub. L. No. 104–65, 109 Stat. 691, Lobbying Disclosure Technical Amendments Act of 1998, Pub. L. No. 105–166, 112 Stat. 38, and Honest Leadership and Open Government Act of 2007, Pub. L. No. 110–81, 121 Stat. 735, September 14, 2007 (codified at 2 U.S.C. §§ 1601–1614 and in scattered sections of the U.S.C.) (2015).

5. 22 U.S.C. § 611(o) (2015).

6. *See, e.g.,* GENERAL ACCOUNTING OFFICE, *Foreign Agent Registration: Justice Needs to Improve Program Administration,* GAO/NSIAD-90-250 (July 1990); Congressional Research Service, *Foreign Interest Lobbying* 2–4 (Dec. 1991); *Federal Lobbying Disclosure Laws, Hearings on Enforcement and Administration of the Foreign Agents Registration Act Before the Senate Comm. on Governmental Affairs,* 102d Cong. (1991); S. 2279, 102d Cong. (1992); H.R. 3579, 102d Cong. (1992). *See generally* Charles Lawson, *Shining the "Spotlight of Pitiless Publicity" on Foreign Lobbyists? Evaluating the Impact of the Lobbying Disclosure Act of 1995 on the Foreign Agents Registration Act,* 29 VAND. J. TRANSNAT'L L. 1151 (1996).

7. See Chapter 21 of this manual.

8. 22 U.S.C. §§ 612(a), 614 (2015).

19-2.1 Definition of a Foreign Principal

The term "foreign principal" is defined to include a government of a foreign country; a foreign political party; any person, association, or corporation "outside the United States," except U.S. citizens domiciled within the United States and U.S. corporations with their principal place of business in the United States; and any corporation, association, or other organization "organized under the laws of or having its principal place of business in a foreign country."[9]

In addition, the term "agent of a foreign principal" includes any person who acts on behalf of an entity whose "activities are directly or indirectly supervised, directed, controlled, financed, or subsidized in whole or in major part by a foreign principal."[10] This means that the term "agent of a foreign principal" may include U.S. subsidiaries of foreign companies in certain circumstances (i.e., if the foreign parent directs the U.S. subsidiary to engage in registrable activity on its behalf or otherwise controls or finances its performance of such activity).

19-2.2 Agent of a Foreign Principal

An "agent of a foreign principal" includes anyone who:
  (i) engages within the United States in political activities for or in the interests of a foreign principal;
  (ii) acts within the United States as a public relations counsel, publicity agent, information-service employee, or political consultant for or in the interests of a foreign principal;
  (iii) solicits, collects, disburses, or dispenses contributions, loans, money, or other things of value within the United States for or in the interests of a foreign principal; or
  (iv) represents within the United States the interests of a foreign principal before any agency or official of the Government of the United States.[11]

19-2.2.1 Political Activities

The term "political activities" is key to understanding the scope of FARA. The term covers not only actual political contacts with U.S. government officials but also any other activity that a person believes will or intends to influence such officials or the U.S. public with respect to covered matters. Specifically, political activities are defined as:

> any activity that the person engaging in believes will, or that the person intends to, in any way influence any agency or official of the Government of the United States or any section of the public within the United States with reference to formulating, adopting, or changing the domestic or foreign policies of the United States or with reference to the political or public interests, policies, or relations of a government of a foreign country or a foreign political party.[12]

---

9. 22 U.S.C. § 611(b) (2015).

10. *Id.* § 611(c)(1); 28 C.F.R. § 5.100(a)(8) (2015).

11. 22 U.S.C. § 611(c) (2015).

12. *Id.* § 611(o).

Several points should be noted about the definition of political activities. First, the legislative history and regulations indicate that this term covers efforts to influence the formulation of policy, rather than the interpretation or administration of existing policy. Thus, political activities do not include "making a routine inquiry of a Government official or employee concerning a current policy or seeking administrative action in a matter where such policy is not in question."[13]

Second, political activities encompass attempts to maintain an existing policy, as well as efforts to seek a change in that policy.[14]

Third, the term covers the design, supervision, or facilitation of another person's attempts to influence the U.S. government or public opinion. Thus, a practitioner may be subject to FARA registration requirements, regardless whether that person has any direct dealings or personal contacts with federal officials for activities such as:

1. Organizing a "grassroots" campaign to promote U.S. public awareness of policy issues;
2. Devising a strategy and plan of action for others to carry out concerning how to influence U.S. government policy; or
3. Arranging and preparing materials for meetings by others with U.S. government officials for that purpose.[15]

On the other hand, persons who merely monitor, inform about, analyze, or predict the course of U.S. policymaking or legislation for foreign clients are not required to register under the act, even if they make direct contacts with U.S. government officials in connection with those activities. Interpretation versus formulation of policy appears to be a key distinction from the legislative history in this respect.[16]

19-2.2.2 Public Relations Counsel, Publicity Agent, Information-Service Employee, and Political Consultant

A person may become an "agent of a foreign principal" under FARA if he or she acts as a public relations counsel, publicity agent, information-service employee, or political consultant.

- The term "public relations counsel" covers any person who "engages directly or indirectly in informing, advising or in any way representing a principal in any public relations matter pertaining to political or public interests, policies or relations of such principal."[17]
- The term "publicity agent" includes any person who "engages directly or indirectly in the publication or dissemination of oral, visual, graphic,

---

13. 28 C.F.R. § 5.100(e) (2015); REGISTRATION OF FOREIGN AGENTS IN THE UNITED STATES, *supra* note 2, at 60–62.

14. *Id.* at 60.

15. *See* Letter from Joseph Clarkson, Chief of Registration Unit, Internal Security Section, Criminal Division, Department of Justice, to Thomas M. Susman, Feb. 6, 1992 [hereinafter Letter from Joseph Clarkson], reproduced in Appendix 19-A following this chapter.

16. REGISTRATION OF FOREIGN AGENTS IN THE UNITED STATES, *supra* note 2, at 60–62.

17. 22 U.S.C. § 611(g) (2015).

written, or pictorial information or matter of any kind, including publication by means of advertising, books, periodicals, newspapers, lectures, broadcasts, motion pictures, or otherwise."[18]

- The term "information-service employee" means any person who is "engaged in furnishing, disseminating, or publishing accounts, descriptions, information, or data with respect to the political, industrial, employment, economic, social, cultural, or other benefits, advantages, facts, or conditions of any country other than the United States or of any government of a foreign country or of a foreign political party or of a partnership, association, corporation, organization, or other combination of individuals organized under the laws of, having its principal place of business in, a foreign country."[19]
- The term "political consultant" means any person who "engages in informing or advising any other person with reference to the domestic or foreign policies of the United States or the political or public interest, policies, or relations of a foreign country or of a foreign political party."[20]

Obviously, these definitions are extremely broad and require analysis beyond the professional title of the potential registrant. For example, the legislative history suggests that persons engaging in these roles are not required to register under FARA unless they "engaged in political activities . . . for [the] foreign principal" or where the purpose "is to effect a change in existing policy," and they are not otherwise exempted.[21] One Committee report noted its intention that the definition of "political consultant" would not cover cases "in which a lawyer merely advises a client concerning the construction or application of an existing statute or regulation."[22]

19-2.2.3 Representation

Any person representing a foreign principal before the U.S. government (which the regulations define as every unit of the executive and legislative branches, including congressional committees, as well as members and officers of Congress)[23] is an "agent of a foreign principal" under the act. However, as discussed below, FARA registration requirements applicable to such representation, and to other lobbying activities in the United States, are subject to various exemptions set forth within the act.

---

18. *Id.* § 611(h).
19. *Id.* § 611(i).
20. *Id.* § 611(p).
21. *See* Registration of Foreign Agents in the United States, *supra* note 2, 63–66 (citing H. Rep. No. 89-1470, at 9 (1966), S. Rep. No. 88-875, at 9 (1964)).
22. *Id.* (citing S. Rep. No. 88-875, at 9 (1964)).
23. 28 C.F.R. § 5.100(c)-(d) (2015).

19-3 Exemptions

FARA contains several exemptions that significantly affect its scope and registration requirements.[24] Three such exemptions are particularly relevant to lawyers and lobbyists.

19-3.1 Registration under the LDA

FARA exempts from registration persons who are engaged in lobbying activities and who register (even if not required to) under the LDA in connection with their representation of foreign clients, except if the latter are foreign governments or foreign political parties.[25] This exemption means that FARA is applicable only to:

1. persons who act as agents of foreign governments or foreign political parties; and
2. persons who act as agents of other foreign principals (i.e., foreign companies, foreign associations, or foreign individuals), but who do not register under the LDA.

The legislative history indicates that this exemption was enacted to create uniform standards for reporting lobbying activities and to avoid overlapping registration requirements for persons subject to both FARA and the LDA. During the legislative process leading to the LDA's enactment, the Department of Justice expressed concern that this exemption would "significantly reduce public disclosure" about the influence of foreign interests on U.S. policy. This is because, in relation to the LDA, FARA covers a broader range of activities and requires the submission of far more information about a consultant's work in the United States.

Moreover, section 613(h) of FARA exempts from registration an agent of a foreign company, association, partnership, or individual "if the agent has engaged in lobbying activities and has registered" under the LDA "in connection with the agent's representation of such person or entity." At a minimum, the exemption means that registration of such agents under the LDA avoids the need for FARA registration. And it is clear that where such persons do not meet LDA thresholds for registration (i.e., more than one lobbying contact, the 20 percent of time requirement, and requisite income or expense amounts; see Chapter 4 of this manual), they have a choice to register under either the LDA or FARA.[26]

The question arises whether an agent who meets LDA thresholds that would require registration under that statute may lawfully choose to register under FARA rather than the LDA. Although section 613(h) provides an exemption from FARA registration, it does not, by its terms, compel LDA registration. Exemptions can often be waived in other circumstances, creating areas for choice. Before 2007, this question would have been seen as largely academic because the FARA reporting burdens were far greater than those imposed by the LDA at that time. However, the congressional gift restrictions and political contribution and other reporting obligations created by the 2007 HLOGA that apply to LDA registrants and lobbyists

---

24. 22 U.S.C. § 613 (2015).
25. *Id.* § 613(h).
26. *See* S. Rep. No. 105-147 (1997), at 4.

(see Chapters 4 and 5 of this manual), along with recent Obama administration restrictions that apply by their terms to those same persons and entities (see Chapter 29) without express inclusion of FARA registrants, may create incentives to register under FARA where lawful choice exists.

On this point, the legislative history is clear: If an agent of a "foreign principal" qualifies for exemption under FARA and also meets LDA thresholds, it *must* register under the LDA and not FARA. Support for this requirement can be found in congressional statements, including the following language taken from the House Report on the bill that was enacted in 1995 as the LDA:

> The Foreign Agents Registration Act of 1938 (FARA) is amended in four ways: (1) FARA is limited to agents of foreign governments and political parties. *Lobbyists of foreign corporations, partnerships, associations, and individuals are required to register under the Lobbying Disclosure Act, where applicable, but not under FARA. . . .*[27]

Similar statements are found in the legislative history of the 1998 technical amendments to the LDA that created the option to register under the LDA for agents of foreign companies and individuals that do not meet LDA thresholds.[28]

19-3.2 Legal Representation

FARA includes an exemption for lawyers who provide legal representation to foreign principals in certain judicial and administrative proceedings. Specifically, the act exempts:

> [a]ny person qualified to practice law, insofar as he engages or agrees to engage in the legal representation of a disclosed foreign principal before any court of law or any agency of the Government of the United States: *Provided*, That for the purposes of this subsection legal representation does not include attempts to influence or persuade agency personnel or officials other than in the course of judicial proceedings, criminal or civil law enforcement inquiries, investigations, or proceedings, or agency proceedings required by statute or regulation to be conducted on the record.[29]

Several key points should be considered in determining the limited application of this exemption. First, it applies only to lawyers representing foreign clients in certain types of proceedings—in courts, during criminal or civil law enforcement investigations, and before U.S. government agencies. This includes representation in covered agency proceedings in which disclosure of the lawyer's appearance on behalf of the foreign principal is not otherwise required as a matter of established agency procedure. In those cases, the regulations provide that the lawyer still must

---

27. H.R. Rep. No. 104-339, Part 1 (1995), at 21 (emphasis added). *See also* S. Rep. No. 103-37 (1993), at 39; H.R. Rep. No. 103-750 (1994) (Conf. Rep.), at 61.

28. *See* H.R. Rep. No. 104-699 (1996), at 3–4; S. Rep. No. 105-147 (1997), at 4.

29. 22 U.S.C. § 613(g) (2015) (emphasis added).

disclose the identity of his client "to each of the agency's personnel or officials before whom and at the time his legal representation is undertaken."[30]

Second, the only agency proceedings covered by the exemption are those "required by statute or regulation to be conducted on the record."[31] Agency proceedings that are not required to be conducted on the record are not covered by the exemption.

Third, although the legislative history is ambiguous on this point, the Department of Justice has taken the position that the exemption does not apply to the lobbying of Congress by lawyers, nor to legal representation of a foreign client before Congress—except in connection with a formal appearance before an investigative committee.[32]

Fourth, although the legislative history again provides little guidance on the matter, the phrase "in the course of" suggests that the exemption applies only to legal representation during the pendency of a specific judicial, investigative, or agency proceeding that has already commenced—*not* to political activities undertaken in anticipation of such proceedings or to efforts pursued outside of a covered proceeding that attempt to influence its course or outcome.[33]

Fifth, although FARA attempts to draw a line between political activities requiring registration and exempted legal representation, the distinction is often difficult to make in practice. The statute indicates that a lawyer may engage in political activities and still be covered by the exemption if those attempts to influence U.S. policy are "in the course of" legal representation of a foreign client in court, during a criminal or civil enforcement investigation, or before an agency in proceedings legally required to be conducted on the record. However, the Department of Justice has stated that the exemption does not cover all political activities undertaken by a lawyer in connection with those proceedings, such as:

- a lawyer's use of a case or proceeding "as a vehicle for generating propaganda";
- a lawyer's "activities outside the courtroom or hearing room [that] go beyond the bounds of normal legal representation of his client's case and amount to efforts to influence public opinion"; or
- a lawyer's *"ex parte* attempts to influence a political decision."[34]

19-3.3 Commercial Activities

FARA exempts any person who engages or agrees to engage "only in private and nonpolitical activities in furtherance of the bona fide trade or commerce" of foreign

---

30. 28 C.F.R. § 5.306(b) (2015).

31. *Id.* at § 5.306(a).

32. *See* REGISTRATION OF FOREIGN AGENTS IN THE UNITED STATES, *supra* note 2, at 104–06; Statement of Mark Richard, Deputy Assistant Attorney General, Criminal Division, Before the Subcommittee on Oversight of Government Management, Committee on Governmental Affairs, United States Senate, June 20, 1991, at 9 [hereinafter Statement of Mark Richard]; Letter from Joseph Clarkson, *supra* note 15.

33. *See* REGISTRATION OF FOREIGN AGENTS IN THE UNITED STATES, *supra* note 2, at 107–08.

34. Statement of Mark Richard, *supra* note 32, at 9.

principals.[35] The exemption broadly covers "the exchange, transfer, purchase, sale of commodities, services, or property of any kind."[36] To qualify for the exemption, an agent's activities must be "private" and "nonpolitical." According to the legislative history, private activities are those that have a "commercial end" and do not directly advance government interests.[37] The regulations make clear that this exemption includes the representation of foreign governments in purely commercial matters, such as real estate acquisitions or the operation of government enterprises, as long as that representation does "not directly promote the public or political interests of the foreign government."[38]

The statute and regulations do not define the term "nonpolitical activities." The legislative history indicates that this phrase covers all activities that do not fall within the statutory definition of political activities.[39] This means that, as long as lawyers are not attempting to influence U.S. policy or public opinion, and are not telling others how to do so with respect to covered matters, they can represent foreign clients broadly in private trade and commercial matters without triggering registration requirements under FARA.

19-3.4 Deletion of "Domestic Subsidiary" Exemption

FARA also exempts "activities not serving predominantly a foreign interest."[40] FARA registration is not required in these circumstances as long as (1) those activities further the bona fide commercial, industrial, or financial operations of the foreign corporation; (2) those activities are not directed by a foreign government or foreign political party; and (3) those activities do not directly promote the public or political interests of a foreign government or foreign political party.[41]

This exemption has been attributed to a concern raised by U.S. corporations with foreign subsidiaries (and foreign corporations with U.S. subsidiaries) that routine activities involving contacts with government officials related to matters affecting their foreign subsidiary/parent would require registration.[42] The legislative history suggests that this exemption would extend to activities having "some political complexion" or "some foreign interest" so long as the activity does not serve "predominantly" a foreign interest.[43] The exemption thus generally covers representation of a U.S. corporation engaged in business in the United States, even though it has a foreign affiliate, so long as the affiliate is not directed or controlled by a foreign political body.[44] The purpose, in other words, was to exempt activities involving "the normal, above-board representation of legitimate U.S. commercial interests," even if some foreign governmental interest was also implicated.[45]

35. 22 U.S.C. § 613(d)(1) (2015).
36. 28 C.F.R. § 5.304(a) (2015).
37. S. Rep. No. 89-143, at 2, 11 (1965).
38. 28 C.F.R. § 5.304(b) (2015).
39. S. Rep. No. 89-143, at 11.
40. 22 U.S.C. § 613(d)(2) (2015).
41. 28 C.F.R. § 5.304(c) (2015).
42. Registration of Foreign Agents in the United States, *supra* note 2, at 85–87.
43. *Id.*
44. *Id.*
45. *Id.*

In these and other matters, however, the burden of establishing the availability of any given exemption from registration under the act rests with the person benefiting from such exemption.[46]

19-4 Registration and Reporting Requirements

Persons required to register under FARA must do so at the Department of Justice within ten days after becoming an "agent of a foreign principal" and before undertaking registrable activities.[47] As a practical matter, this means that any person, including a law firm or lobbyist, that enters into an agreement to represent a foreign client in a way that requires FARA registration must register within ten days of that agreement—even if the firm does not actually perform any work on behalf of the client until much later.[48] The initial FARA registration entails two sets of forms. The first set of forms requires the disclosure of certain information about the registrant (including a list of its partners and officers), together with exhibits that identify each foreign principal and disclose the nature of the registrant's agreement with the foreign principal, as well as the types of activities to be performed on its behalf. In addition, the registrant must report certain financial information, including all political contributions made by the registrant and receipts from, and disbursements for, any foreign principal identified in the registration form during the period beginning sixty days before the date of the registrant's obligation to register to the date of registration.[49]

The second set of forms required to be filed in the initial FARA registration deals with every individual who performs registrable activities on behalf of the foreign principal. This "short-form registration statement" requires the disclosure of certain information about all individuals performing registrable activities, including occupation, relationship to the registrant, the types of services rendered on behalf of the foreign principal, the amounts of compensation received for such services, and political contributions made during the period beginning sixty days before the date of the registrant's obligation to register to the date of registration.[50] If any pertinent information included in such forms changes, the registrant must file a new short-form registration statement within ten days of that occurrence.[51]

HLOGA amended FARA to mandate the filing of any registration statement or supplement in electronic form,[52] and the Department of Justice unveiled its "FARA eFile" system in early 2011.[53] The 2007 legislation also directed the Department of Justice to establish a fully searchable electronic database that is publicly accessible

---

46. 28 C.F.R. § 5.300 (2015); *see also* 28 C.F.R. § 5.2 (2015) for provisions by which persons with inquiries about the application of the act may submit confidential written review requests to the Department of Justice for the purpose of resolving those questions. In addition, the Registration Unit of the Department of Justice often will provide informal telephone guidance as to the terms and application of the act.

47. 22 U.S.C. § 612(a) (2015). The Department of Justice maintains a webpage dedicated to the FARA, *see* http://www.fara.gov/, where forms and other information are available.

48. *See* REGISTRATION OF FOREIGN AGENTS IN THE UNITED STATES, *supra* note 2, at 122–23.

49. 28 C.F.R. §§ 5.200, 5.201 (2015).

50. *Id.* § 5.202.

51. 28 C.F.R. § 5.202 (2015).

52. 22 U.S.C. § 612(g) (2015).

53. The FARA eFile form can be accessed at http://www.fara.gov/efile.html.

over the internet and that contains updated FARA filings.[54] See also Chapter 6 of this manual.

FARA also requires the submission of a "supplemental statement" for each six-month period following the initial registration.[55] This requirement applies even if the registrant did not engage in any activity on behalf of the foreign principal during the covered period. In filing the supplemental statement, registrants must describe all activities (i.e., both registrable and non-registrable) performed on behalf of foreign principals during that six-month period and disclose, inter alia, the total amounts of compensation received from each foreign principal during that time (whether or not such payments were for registrable activities). This requirement has caused considerable concern for registrants and their foreign clients because it means that registrants must reveal detailed information about all of their work for, and total compensation from, foreign clients in these supplemental statements, even though such reported activities and payments may have nothing to do with FARA. Some registrants have sought to address this concern by separating specific amounts received for FARA-related activities from their overall reported compensation.

If the registrant ceases performing registrable activities on behalf of a foreign principal during a specific six-month period and does not contemplate undertaking such activities in the future, it may report a termination of the relationship requiring registration in the supplemental statement covering that period. Likewise, if the relationship is terminated by agreement or explicit action between the agent and foreign principal, the registrant should file a final statement on a supplemental statement form within thirty days of the termination.[56]

Registrants who continue an agency relationship with foreign principals also may file for termination of registration if the activities they perform for such foreign principals are confined to those for which exemptions are available under FARA.[57] This provision has become less relevant in the years since the enactment of the LDA and LDTAA because many law firms and lobbyists have taken advantage of the LDA exemption, where possible.

19-5 Dissemination of Informational Materials

FARA also contains filing and labeling requirements for the dissemination of "informational materials" for or in the interests of foreign principals by persons who are required to register under the Act.[58] The filing requirement occurs whenever a registrant in the United States transmits or causes to be transmitted in the U.S. mails or by any means or instrumentality of interstate or foreign commerce any informational materials for or in the interests of such foreign principal (1) in

---

54. 22 U.S.C.. § 616(d) (2015). The FARA document search tool can be accessed at http://www .fara.gov/search.html.

55. 28 C.F.R. § 5.203 (2015).

56. 28 C.F.R. § 5.205(a) (2015).

57. *Id.* § 5.205(c).

58. Before enactment of the LDA, such materials were called "political propaganda." The term was changed to "informational materials" to lessen the stigma previously associated with FARA registration. *See* Pub. L. No. 104–65, § 9(4)(A), 109 Stat. 691, 700 (Dec. 19,1995). *See also* H.R. REP. No. 104-339, at 31.

the form of prints, or (2) in any other form that is reasonably adapted to being, or that he or she believes will be, or that he or she intends to be, disseminated or circulated among two or more persons.[59] Examples of informational materials include press releases, e-mails sent to multiple recipients, white papers, and public letters.

Registrants must file one copy of the informational materials with the Department of Justice within forty-eight hours after such dissemination. Informational materials may be filed electronically and will be made available for public inspection.[60] In addition, all such materials must be labeled with "a conspicuous statement" indicating that they are being disseminated by an agent of a foreign principal and that "additional information is on file with the Department of Justice."[61] Furthermore, if any informational material is given to a member of Congress or staff or to a U.S. government official by a person within the United States who is required to register under FARA, it must include a statement that the person distributing the material is registered as an agent of a foreign principal under the act.[62] Similarly, whenever an agent of a foreign principal required to register under FARA appears before any committee of Congress to testify for or in the interest of that foreign principal, the person must furnish to the committee the most recent FARA registration statement as part of that testimony.[63]

19-6 Recordkeeping and Inspection

The act also requires every registrant to preserve "books of account and other records" related to its FARA activities for a period of three years following the termination of the registration.[64] Such records include "correspondence, memoranda, cables, telegrams, teletype messages, and other written communications" relating to the activities, as well as contracts, financial records, and minute books.[65] These materials may be reviewed by any FARA enforcement official.[66]

19-7 Contingent Fee Prohibition

FARA also prohibits any registrant to be a party to a contract or other arrangement with a foreign principal under which the fee is in whole or in part continent upon the success of any political activities carried out by the registrant.[67] This prohibition was partly motivated by the notion that such fees would "impair the propriety of an advocate's presentation of the issue."[68]

---

59. 22 U.S.C. § 614(a) (2015).
60. *Id.* § 614(c).
61. *Id.* § 614(b).
62. *Id.* § 614(e).
63. *Id.* § 614(f).
64. 22 U.S.C. § 615 (2015).
65. 28 C.F.R. § 5.500(a) (2015).
66. *Id.*
67. 22 U.S.C. § 618(h) (2015).
68. Registration of Foreign Agents in the United States, *supra* note 2, at 246–47. For a discussion of contingent fee arrangements generally, see Chapter 16 of this manual.

19-8 Enforcement

Violations of FARA, including the failure to register and the willful making of false material statements or material omissions in FARA filings, can result in fines of up to $10,000 and up to five years imprisonment.[69] In cases in which the Department of Justice determines that a FARA registration is deficient, the FARA Registration Unit may inform the registrant of the deficiency, in which case the registrant may not act as the agent of a foreign principal for more than ten days without amending the registration.[70] We provide a brief summary here, but for more discussion of enforcement of FARA, see Chapter 20 of this manual.

From 1966 until quite recently, prosecutors rarely used FARA, and only a handful of FARA-based indictments were issued.[71] In recent years, however, the Department of Justice has announced a series of high-profile FARA enforcement actions related to terrorism and espionage and initiated audits of various entities suspected of failing to register under FARA or making incomplete submissions.

In 2010, former U.S. Congressman and U.S. Ambassador Mark Deli Siljander pleaded guilty to obstruction of justice and to acting as an unregistered foreign agent for his work for a Sudan-based Islamic charity, which had been designated as a terrorist organization.[72] Congressman Siljander was accused of lobbying for the charity's removal from a Senate Finance Committee list of entities with suspected links to terrorism and of concealing the funds paid to him without registering under FARA. He was sentenced to one year and one day in prison.

In 2011, Syed Ghulam Nabi Fai, a U.S. citizen, pleaded guilty to conspiracy and other violations related to a scheme to conceal the transfer of approximately $3.5 million from the Pakistani Government to fund his lobbying efforts relating to the territory of Kashmir, after failing to register under FARA and making false statements to federal agents.[73] He agreed to forfeit $142,851 and was sentenced to two years in prison.

Finally, media reporting has raised questions concerning the lack of registration by nonprofit research organizations receiving foreign government funding.[74] It remains unclear whether such reports will alter enforcement practices by the Department of Justice.

19-9 Conclusion

FARA originally was enacted at a time that was strikingly different from today. However, its purpose has continuing relevance, and the Department of Justice has recently increased FARA enforcement activity. The act attempts to inform the American public and its lawmakers about the nature and source of information

---

69. 22 U.S.C § 618(a) (2015).

70. *Id.* § 618(g).

71. *See* UNITED STATES ATTORNEYS' MANUAL, DEPARTMENT OF JUSTICE, Foreign Agents Registration Act Enforcement.

72. News Release, Office of the U.S. Attorney for the Western District of Missouri, *Former Congressman Pleads Guilty to Obstructing Justice, Acting as Unregistered Foreign Agent* (July 7, 2010).

73. News Release, Department of Justice, *Virginia Man Sentenced to 24 Months for Scheme to Conceal Pakistan Government Funding for His U.S. Lobbying Efforts* (Mar. 30, 2012).

74. Eric Lipton, Brooke Williams, & Nicholas Confessore, *Foreign Powers Buy Influence at Think Tanks*, N.Y. TIMES, Sep. 6, 2014.

intended to influence U.S. government policies and public opinion. As these means
of potential influence evolve, including through use of nontraditional lobbying or
consultant arrangements, it is reasonable to expect FARA enforcement activities
to adapt accordingly. In doing so, FARA reflects a long-standing perceived need
for legislation to ensure adequate public disclosure of lobbying activities and to
protect the integrity of the U.S. policymaking process.

APPENDIX 19-A

U.S. Department of Justice
Criminal Division

Washington, D.C. 26530

Thomas M. Susman, Esquire
Ropes & Gray
1001 Pennsylvania Avenue, N.W.
Suite 1200 South
Washington, D.C. 20004

Dear Tom:

Before responding to the questions raised in your letter of July 18, 1991, let me first apologize for the delay in our answering you.

Your first question seeks our view of the role of the S 3(g) exemption in an attorney's activities *vis a vis* the Congress. We view this exemption as having a particularly narrow scope in this area. Essentially, we see S 3(g) applying only in a situation where the attorney is acting to protect the legal right of a client who has been called to appear before a non-legislative committee of the Congress.

Your second question raises the issue of whether political consultants that do not directly lobby Executive Agencies or the Congress are covered by FARA. Political consultants need not engage in political activity to fall within the registration requirements of FARA. They need only engage in activity whose purpose is to further political activity. Thus, those who plan strategy or, to cite your example, arrange meetings must register even though they do not engage directly in political activity. It is obvious that Congress intended to reach beyond those who directly lobby and include within the Act those others whose actions fall short of direct lobbying but whose purpose is to affect the political process.

In answer to your last question, the fact of who pays the agent is of little if any import. The test of whether it is the domestic interest that is being furthered is, if there is a domestic interest that is cognizable and independent of the foreign interest. By independent we mean an interest that is directly in issue and not some consequential result that flows from the effect of the policy or legislation on the foreign interest.

We hope these answers are useful in your research and to your audience. It is important to bear in mind, however, that whether a particular exemption applies always depends on the specific facts in a given situation. Thus, any general guidance is always of limited value. Once again, we apologize for our delay in responding.

Sincerely,

Joseph E. Clarkson, Chief
Registration Unit
Internal Security Section
Criminal Division

CHAPTER 20

DOJ FARA Enforcement

BY JIM CHRISTIAN AND TARYN FRIDERES*

20-1 Introduction

The Foreign Agents Registration Act (FARA) is a disclosure statute that affects a small subset of people, generally in Washington, D.C. However, the history of the statute foretells its importance—Congress passed FARA in 1938 to prevent agents of Nazi Germany from disseminating "propaganda" to unsuspecting Americans under false pretenses. Since the WWII era, the statute has undergone numerous amendments, and efforts to enforce the statute have been enhanced by digital advancements. Today, "agents" of foreign governments and other qualifying entities include private practice attorneys, government relations professionals, public relations professionals, members of a diaspora, and other interested parties. Agents may represent more than one foreign principal.

Enforcement policies and procedures have evolved in accordance with changing times and the legislative history of the statute,[1] but a focus on voluntary

---

*The authors gratefully acknowledge Dan Waltz, FARA Compliance Partner at Squire Patton Boggs LLP, for his invaluable assistance with this article

1. U.S. Department of Justice, Criminal Resource Manual § 2062, *available at* http://www.justice.gov/usao/eousa/foia_reading_room/usam/title9/crm02062.htm.

compliance has characterized recent practice. Presently, the FARA Registration Unit of the Counter Intelligence and Export Control Section in the National Security Division of the Department of Justice (DOJ), the entity of the U.S. Government (USG) responsible for the administration and enforcement of the act, remains committed to the overarching goal of seeking to obtain voluntary compliance with the statute.

20-2 Obligations and Penalties

As discussed in Chapter 19, FARA is a disclosure statute that requires "agents" of "foreign principals" to:

(1) Register with DOJ and file forms every six months outlining their agreements with, income from, and expenditures on behalf of the foreign principal;
(2) Identify oneself in dealings with USG officials and in the media as a registered foreign agent under FARA, label informational materials (formerly called "propaganda") disseminated on behalf of the foreign principal, and provide a copy of such materials to DOJ;
(3) Keep records of all contacts with covered federal officials, submit them to DOJ, and preserve them for three years; and
(4) If testifying before a committee of Congress, provide a copy of the "agent's" most recent registration statement.[2]

Though the FARA Registration Unit focuses most of its resources on securing voluntary compliance, there are criminal penalties for willful violations of FARA. Failure to register, comply with FARA's disclosure requirements, keep accounts, mark informational materials, or provide a congressional committee with a copy of an agent's most recent registration are all violations of the act, subject to criminal penalties.[3] The act also prohibits either express or implied contingent fee arrangements between an agent and a foreign principal.[4] Moreover, any person who willfully makes a false statement of material fact or omits any material fact in filings with DOJ could also be subject to criminal penalties.[5] The threshold for a criminal investigation under the FARA statute is the presence of reason to believe that a significant FARA offense has been committed and that sufficient evidence exists to prove it.[6] The government may also seek civil injunctive relief in the form of a U.S. District Court temporary or permanent injunction enjoining violations or requiring compliance.[7] The threshold for a civil action is sufficient credible evidence of a significant FARA violation for which the civil injunctive remedy is judged appropriate in light of surrounding circumstances.[8]

---

2. U.S. DEPARTMENT OF JUSTICE, FARA Frequently Asked Questions, *available at* http://www.fara.gov/fara-faq.html#4; 22 U.S.C. § 615 (2015).
3. FARA Frequently Asked Questions, *available at* http://www.fara.gov/fara-faq.html.
4. 22 U.S.C. § 618(h) (2015).
5. 22 U.S.C. § 618(a) (2015).
6. CRIMINAL RESOURCE MANUAL, *supra* note 1.
7. 22 U.S.C. § 618(f) (2015).
8. CRIMINAL RESOURCE MANUAL, *supra* note 1.

20-3 DOJ Enforcement History

From the statute's passage in 1938 until its amendment in 1966, enforcement of FARA was focused on the alleged "propagandists" that prompted the statute's initial passage.[9] During the WWII era, the U.S. government successfully prosecuted some twenty-three criminal cases.[10] Near the end of WWII, after administration of the act was transferred from the Department of State to the Department of Justice in 1942, DOJ developed the practice of working to achieve voluntary compliance with the statute (particularly in instances that did not seem to warrant prosecution) by sending letters advising prospective agents of the existence of the FARA statute and their possible obligations thereunder.[11] Though DOJ intended the letters to invoke compliance, they could also be used to help prove "willfulness" should the recipient subsequently fail to register under and comply with the act.[12]

Since amendments to the statute and regulations adding a civil injunctive remedy (similar to that in U.S. securities law) and a "Rule 2" review request mechanism, criminal prosecutions have drastically decreased.[13] However, there are recent examples. In 2010, Mark Deli Siljander, former congressman and U.S. Ambassador to the United Nations, pled guilty in federal court to obstruction of justice and to acting as an unregistered foreign agent in relation to his work for an Islamic charity with suspected ties to international terrorism.[14] This case is discussed in more detail below.

20-4 DOJ Enforcement Today

For a myriad of reasons—including the high threshold required for criminal prosecutions, the nature of the statute, and the changing demographic subject to the statute—the DOJ FARA Registration Unit is first and foremost focused on obtaining voluntary compliance. DOJ's FARA Unit attempts to encourage compliance among both registrants and potential registrants through a number of informal and formal tools. With respect to potential registrants, the FARA Unit encourages both informal and formal dialogue. In close cases, the FARA Unit moreover encourages the submission of a review request, which will typically result in a Rule 2 "advisory opinion."

In recent years, review requests have increasingly been used as a tool for political opponents to submit allegations to the DOJ FARA Unit that another is acting as a "foreign agent" without registering and should therefore be investigated or forced to register. To date, such attempts to politicize the FARA Unit have apparently been unsuccessful.

In addition to accepting review requests, the FARA Unit proactively engages in investigatory work to identify potential "agents" that have failed to fulfill their obligations under the act, and submits inquiries to those potential agents regarding

9. *Id.*
10. *Id.*
11. *Id.*
12. *Id.*
13. *Id.*
14. News Release, Office of the United States Attorney, Western District of Missouri (July 7, 2010), *available at* http://www.fara.gov/docs/siljander_press_070710.pdf.

their failure to register. Conversely, with respect to persons that have affirmatively registered under the act, the FARA Unit reviews registrant statements and issues notices of deficiency for noncompliant submissions. Finally, the FARA Unit also reviews the subsequent filings of registrants and informs them of any instances of noncompliance.

20-4.1 Informal Discussions

Before the submission of a registration statement or review request to DOJ, the FARA Unit welcomes the initiation of informal dialogue by prospective agents, "foreign principals," and their lawyers to determine whether registration is required. Such informal dialogue can be initiated via phone call or e-mail,[15] and may or may not result in a request from the FARA Unit that the prospective agent or foreign principal submit a request for an advisory opinion. Although at this stage, the FARA Unit recognizes that the requesting party may not want to reveal all of the details regarding a prospective representation, a certain level of detail is required for the FARA Unit to make an informed recommendation.

20-4.2 Rule 2 Review Requests

Section 5.2 of the FARA regulations offers a procedure by which interested parties can submit a "review request" to the FARA Registration Unit.[16] Section 5.2 specifically provides any present or prospective agents or foreign principals (or their respective attorney) with the opportunity to request a statement of the present enforcement intentions of the DOJ under the act, informally referred to as an "advisory opinion."[17] Such a request must be specific and relate to an actual—not hypothetical—situation, and must involve disclosed, not anonymous agents and principals.[18] All requests must be submitted in accordance with the regulations and must be accompanied by a filing fee.[19]

Upon receipt of a review request, the FARA Unit may respond with a formal statement regarding its present enforcement intentions under the act, or may decline to state its present enforcement intentions.[20] In general, the FARA Unit tries to respond to all review requests that include the required level of detailed information. The FARA regulations require that the FARA Unit respond to any review request within thirty days of receipt of the review request and any requested additional information,[21] although this deadline is not always met in practice. In the interim, according to the regulations, the pending review request does not absolve the interested parties from compliance with the statute.[22] However, in practice, if an agent refrains from registration until receipt of an "advisory opinion" mandating

---

15. Contact information for the FARA Unit can be accessed on its website: http://www.fara.gov /contact.html.

16. Administration and Enforcement of Foreign Agents Registration Act of 1938, As Amended, 28 C.F.R. § 5.2 (2015).

17. 28 C.F.R. § 5.2(a) (2015).

18. 28 C.F.R. § 5.2(b) (2015).

19. 28 C.F.R. § 5.2(c)–(f) (2015).

20. 28 C.F.R. § 5.2(h) (2015).

21. 28 C.F.R. § 5.2(i) (2015).

22. 28 C.F.R. § 5.2(l) (2015).

such registration, the FARA Registration Unit will generally focus solely on getting the agent into compliance.

Previously issued advisory opinions are not publicly available, though they can be requested under the Freedom of Information Act (FOIA)—something that anyone submitting a review request should keep in mind. However, any written material submitted pursuant to a review request may be exempt from disclosure. Once advisory opinions are issued, recipients can take it upon themselves to share them if they wish to do so.

20-4.3 Letter of Inquiry

A handful of the FARA Unit's seven-member permanent staff spend a portion of their time proactively reviewing filings under the Lobbying Disclosure Act (LDA),[23] news clippings, and so on to determine whether certain persons have mistakenly refrained from filing under FARA. If the FARA Unit determines the likely existence of a registration obligation, it will typically send a "Letter of Inquiry" advising the individual or entity of the existence of FARA and the person's possible obligations thereunder. The letter usually cites to or provides the information prompting the inquiry. Typically, the vast majority of persons who receive such a letter respond within a reasonable amount of time and either register or convincingly explain that they are not properly characterized as a foreign agent under the statute or that an appropriate exemption is available to them.[24] If a person receiving a Letter of Inquiry fails to respond or submits a false response, the FARA Unit will likely refer the matter to the Federal Bureau of Investigation (FBI) for investigation. Similar to Notices of Deficiency or Noncompliance, a Letter of Inquiry could serve as evidence that the recipient has been put on notice of the existence and reach of the act.[25]

20-4.4 Notice of Deficiency

Once an agent files a registration statement, the FARA Registration Unit will review the statement to ensure compliance with the applicable statute and regulations. Should the Registration Unit determine that a registration statement filed with the FARA Unit is not in compliance, the FARA Unit may submit a "Notice of Deficiency" to the registrant, requiring compliance within ten days of receipt.[26] If the registrant subsequently files an amendment to its registration statement pursuant to the notice, it may continue to act as an agent of a foreign principal unless it receives a "Notice of Noncompliance" from the FARA Unit.[27] Should a registrant either refuse to amend its registration statement after receiving a Notice of Deficiency or continue to act as an agent after receiving a Notice of Noncompliance, the

---

23. The Lobbying Disclosure Act of 1995 amended FARA to exempt certain agents of foreign principals required to register under the LDA from registration under FARA. Lobbying Disclosure Act of 1995, Pub. L. No. 104–65 (1995). This exemption often covers agents of certain multinational corporations, but the FARA Unit may review an agent's decision to file under LDA rather than FARA.

24. CRIMINAL RESOURCE MANUAL, *supra* note 1.

25. *Id.*

26. 22 U.S.C. § 618(g) (2015).

27. 28 C.F.R. § 5.801 (2015).

FARA Unit could rely on such notices to support a criminal prosecution for willful violation of the act.

20-4.5 Section 5 Inspection

Section 5 of the Public Law (codified at 22 U.S.C. § 615) requires every agent of a foreign principal registered under FARA to "keep and preserve while he is an agent of a foreign principal such books of account and other records with respect to all his activities, the disclosure of which is required."[28] The act further provides that "such books and records shall be open at all reasonable times to the inspection of any official charged with the enforcement of this subchapter."[29] In practice, the FARA Unit does not descend upon a registrant's place of business to review his or her records (although the language of the statute suggests that it could do so). Rather, the FARA Unit periodically engages in "Section 5 inspections" of a registrant's filings with the FARA Unit to ensure compliance.[30]

Section 12 of the act (codified at 22 U.S.C. § 612) provides that, in addition to a registration statement, agents must file every six months a supplemental statement detailing its activities during the six-month review period.[31] Upon receiving an agent's supplemental statement, the FARA Unit reviews the statement—with a specific focus on item numbers 11 (Activities and Services), 12 (Political Activities), 14 (Receipts), and 15 (Disbursements)—to ensure it is consistent with the agent's previous filings. If a review of an agent's supplemental statement raises concerns about potential noncompliance, the FARA Unit generally corresponds with the registrant to address those concerns and get the registrant into compliance.

20-5 Exemptions

The act provides for numerous exemptions from registration, though they are often misunderstood. For example, the exemption available for "persons qualified to practice law" is limited to lawyers engaging in the legal representation of a foreign principal in the course of judicial proceedings, criminal or civil law enforcement inquiries, investigations, or agency proceedings conducted on the record.[32] Separately, in 1995, the LDA amended FARA to exempt from registration agents of nongovernmental foreign principals that register under the LDA.[33] This exemption typically covers agents of privately owned foreign or multinational corporations, though registrants should carefully consider whether the structure of the principal or the type of lobbying proposed triggers FARA registration. As underscored in the regulations implementing the statute, "[i]n no case where a foreign government

---

28. 22 U.S.C. § 615 (2015).

29. *Id.*

30. In February 2014, Covington & Burling LLP released data showing that the Department of Justice has conducted fifteen audits of FARA registrants in each of the last four years. Brian D. Smith, *Covington Releases New Data on FARA Audits Conducted by the Department of Justice, Inside Political Law,* Covington & Burling LLP (Feb. 6, 2014), *available at* http://www.insidepoliticallaw.com/2014/02/06/covington-releases-new-data-on-fara-audits-conducted-by-the-department-of-justice/.

31. 22 U.S.C. § 612(b) (2015). Filings are required within one month of the six-month period that is based upon the date of a person's first FARA registration.

32. 22 U.S.C. § 613(g) (2015).

33. Lobbying Disclosure Act of 1995, Pub. L. No. 104–65 (1995).

or foreign political party is the principal beneficiary will the exemption . . . be recognized."[34] The regulations also state that the burden of establishing the availability of any exemption from registration under the act rests upon the person who claims it.[35]

20-6 Recent Enforcement Actions, Media Pressure, and Congressional Oversight

Examples of recent enforcement actions and media scrutiny underscore the importance of FARA compliance. As noted above, in July 2010, Mark Siljander pled guilty in federal court to violations of FARA in relation to his work on behalf of the Islamic American Relief Agency (IARA), an Islamic charitable organization with suspected ties to international terrorism.[36] IARA was located in Missouri and served as the U.S. office of the Islamic African Relief Agency headquartered in Khartoum, Sudan (IARA in Sudan). According to the plea agreement between Siljander and the U.S. Attorney's Office for the Western District of Missouri, at all times IARA in Sudan controlled the office in Missouri—a fact concealed from the state and federal government.[37] In 2004, Siljander advocated for IARA with individuals and agencies of the U.S. government but failed to register or report his activity. During this period, he knew that IARA was controlled by its headquarters in Sudan and willfully agreed to mischaracterize his efforts and relationship with IARA.[38] In January 2012, Siljander was sentenced to a year and a day in federal prison.[39]

In a comparable, but perhaps more severe example, in December 2011, Syed Ghulam Nabi Fai pled guilty in federal court to conspiracy and tax violations in connection with a long-term scheme to conceal the transfer of millions from the Government of Pakistan to fund his lobbying efforts in the United States. He was later sentenced on March 30, 2012, to serve two years in prison.[40] Fai was the director of the Kashmiri American Council, a nonprofit organization that held itself out to be financed by Americans, but court documents show that it was secretly funded by officials employed by the government of Pakistan—including the Inter-Services Intelligence Directorate (ISI). Despite receiving funding and direction from the government of Pakistan—indeed even submitting strategy documents and proposed budgets to Pakistani government officials for approval—Fai did not register with DOJ under FARA. In fact, in his written response to a DOJ letter in the spring of 2010 telling him that the Indian press had reported that he was a Pakistani agent and notifying him of his possible obligation to register under FARA, Fai falsely asserted that the Kashmiri American Council was not funded by the government

---

34. 28 C.F.R. § 5.307 (2015).

35. 28 C.F.R. § 5.300 (2015).

36. News Release, *supra* note 14.

37. Plea Agreement, United States v. Mark Deli Siljander, No. 07-CR-00087-07-W-NKL (W.D. Mo. 2010), *available at* http://www.fara.gov/docs/DE%20539_Siljander%20Plea.pdf.

38. *Id.*

39. Press Release, FBI, *Former Congressman Sentenced for Obstructing Justice, Acting as Unregistered Foreign Agent* (Jan. 11, 2012), *available at* http://www.fbi.gov/kansascity/press-releases/2012/former-congressman-sentenced-for-obstructing-justice-acting-as-unregistered-foreign-agent.

40. Press Release, FBI Washington Field Office, *Treasurer of Charitable Organization Pleads Guilty to Making False Statements* (Jan. 9, 2014), *available at* http://www.fbi.gov/washingtondc/press-releases/2014/treasurer-of-charitable-organization-pleads-guilty-to-making-false-statements.

of Pakistan. Fai moreover denied to the IRS on a tax return for the Kashmiri American Council that it had received any money from foreign sources that year.[41]

In another example, in August 2014, Prince Asiel Ben Israel of Chicago, Illinois, was sentenced to seven months in prison after pleading guilty to violating FARA. Ben Israel signed a $3.4 million "consulting agreement" in November 2008 to assist Zimbabwe President Robert Mugabe and others in an effort to lift U.S. sanctions against Zimbabwe. The FBI commenced an investigation into Ben Israel and his codefendant, C. Gregory Turner, after President Elect Obama's transition team informed the FBI of a contact by someone who had participated in a delegation trip to Zimbabwe and raised questions about whether the trip may have violated sanctions.[42] Despite a written agreement with the government of Zimbabwe and several contacts with U.S. government officials, Ben Israel failed to register with DOJ under FARA.[43]

In recent years, the DOJ FARA Unit has posted FARA filings on its website. While these filings are always a possible source of potentially scandalous "inside the Beltway" news stories, journalists have only recently recognized them as an attractive and easily available source of news stories. Short of enforcement action, media attention surrounding the issue of FARA registration can result in negative reputational impact—regardless of whether an actual violation has occurred.

As an example, a couple of months after the Sunlight Foundation first questioned the Monitor Group's adherence to FARA in a blog post back in March 2011, the international consulting firm issued a statement acknowledging its breach of FARA. The Monitor Group had a multimillion-dollar contract with Libyan leader Muammar Gaddafi, a relationship heavily criticized after the start of the Libyan revolution in February 2011.[44] Deloitte acquired Monitor in January 2013, after the firm filed for bankruptcy in 2012. Though Monitor insists that its controversial contract with Gaddafi had nothing to do with the company's deteriorating financial situation, it is conceivable that the bad press had a negative impact on the firm.[45]

41. Press Release, FBI Washington Field Office, *Virginia Man Pleads Guilty in Scheme to Conceal Pakistan Government Funding for his U.S. Lobbying Efforts* (Dec. 7, 2011), *available at* http://www.fbi. gov/washingtondc/press-releases/2011/virginia-man-pleads-guilty-in-scheme-to-conceal-pakistan -government-funding-for-his-u.s.-lobbying-efforts; Kim Barker et al., *The Man Behind Pakistan Spy Agency's Plot to Influence Washington*, PROPUBLICA (Oct. 3, 2011), *available at* http://www.propublica.org /article/the-man-behind-pakistani-spy-agencys-plot-to-influence-washington.

42. Press Release, U.S. Attorney's Office, Northern District of Illinois, *Chicago Man Convicted of Conspiracy to Violate U.S. Sanctions by Providing Services to Zimbabwean President Mugabe and Others* (Oct. 10, 2014), *available at* http://www.justice.gov/usao/iln/pr/chicago/2014/pr1014_01.html.

43. Press Release, Department of Justice, Office of Public Affairs, *Chicago Man Sentenced to 15 Months in Prison for Violating U.S. Sanctions Against Zimbabwe President Mugabe and Others* (Jan. 20, 2015), *available at* http://www.justice.gov/opa/pr/chicago-man-sentenced-15-months-prison-violating-us -sanctions-against-zimbabwe-president.

44. *Monitor Group Admits Breaking Federal Law with Illegal Lobbying for Libya,* EXAMINER (May 6, 2011), http://www.examiner.com/article/monitor-group-admits-breaking-federal-law-with-illegal -lobbying-for-libya; Paul Blumenthal, *Monitor Group Admits Violating FARA Law,* SUNLIGHT FOUND. (May 6, 2011), http://sunlightfoundation.com/blog/2011/05/06/monitor-group-admits-violating -fara-law/; Peter Overby, *U.S. Firm Under Fire for Gadhafi Makeover Contract,* NPR (Mar. 10, 2011), http://www.npr.org/2011/03/10/134411798/mass-firms-libya-work-may-have-violated-fara-act.

45. Farah Stockman, *Why Did the Smartest Guys in the Room Go Bankrupt?* BOSTON GLOBE (Jan. 20, 2013), http://www.bostonglobe.com/opinion/2013/01/20/when-smartest-guys-room-bankrupt /lUYj7Nl8vAHhlL1iWVpSoK/story.html.

More recently, following media reports that New York–based public relations firm MCSquared promoted protests on behalf of the government of Ecuador at a May 2014 shareholders meeting of Chevron oil company without registering under FARA, the firm's spokesperson denied that it had a current engagement with the government of Ecuador. However, weeks later, the firm filed a FARA registration disclosing a multimillion-dollar contract with the government of the Republic of Ecuador.[46] There is no clear evidence that MCSquared violated FARA, but the media frenzy surrounding the firm's activities and whether it was FARA-registered suggests that DOJ can increasingly rely on the support of journalists to enhance its enforcement activities.

In addition to isolated news stories, journalists and nongovernmental organizations (NGOs) have recently engaged in more holistic reviews of FARA compliance and enforcement. For example, in December 2014, after reviewing four years' worth of registration documents, reports, and informational materials filed with DOJ, the Project on Government Oversight released a report critical of lobbyists' compliance with FARA and DOJ's FARA enforcement efforts. Citing lax compliance with the statute's filing requirements, the report alleged that enforcement—particularly related to the timely filing of informational materials—is "difficult if not impossible," and it cited several specific examples of documents that appear to have been submitted late by registrants.[47]

In addition to media and NGO oversight, Congress continues to be active in its oversight of FARA. In June 2014, the House Appropriations Committee approved a State-Foreign Operations Appropriations bill for fiscal year 2015 and an accompanying committee report stating the following:

> *Lobbying restrictions.*—The Committee remains concerned about the perception that former senior United States Government diplomatic officials are representing foreign entities or governments that the Department of State has determined to be a state sponsor of terrorism or a country of particular concern after leaving government service. The Committee urges the Secretary of State to examine this matter and to take appropriate steps, either administratively or through a legislative proposal, to ensure that appropriate rules are in place.[48]

Reports suggest that the language was added at the behest of Congressman Frank Wolf (R–VA), who had initially sought legislative text mandating a ten-year

---

46. Megan Wilson, *Ecuador's Eye-Popping PR Deal Revealed*, THE HILL (July 10, 2014), http://thehill.com/business-a-lobbying/lobbying-contracts/211938-ecuadors-eye-popping-pr-deal-revealed; *see also* Lachlan Markay, *PR Firm's Undisclosed Work for Ecuadorian Government Raises Legal Questions*, WASH. FREE BEACON (June 17, 2014), http://freebeacon.com/issues/pr-firms-undisclosed-work-for-ecuadorian-government-raises-legal-questions/.

47. Ben Freeman & Lydia Dennett, *Project on Government Oversight, Loopholes, Filing Failures, and Lax Enforcement: How the Foreign Agents Registration Act Falls Short* (Dec. 16, 2014), http://www.pogo.org/our-work/reports/2014/loopholes-filing-failures-lax-enforcement-how-the-foreign-agents-registration-act-falls-short.html.

48. H.R. Rep. No. 113-499, at 13 (2014), *available at* https://www.congress.gov/congressional-report/113th-congress/house-report/499/1.

"cooling off" period before diplomats could work for countries that sponsor terrorists or are egregious violators of religious freedom.[49]

In another action not directly attributed to FARA enforcement, the House of Representatives recently adopted a new rule requiring witnesses before House Committees to disclose foreign government payments to them or their relevant clients.[50] Members of the House of Representatives passed this rule on the heels of a September 2014 article published by the *New York Times* that highlighted relationships between foreign government donors and prominent U.S. think tanks and NGOs and suggested that certain such relationships may go as far as to trigger FARA.[51] The question at issue in considering whether entities receiving foreign government grants should register under FARA as an "agent of a foreign principal" typically turns on whether the entity is acting under the "direction or control" of a foreign principal. These terms are not defined within the statute, leaving the DOJ FARA Unit to consider the facts on a case-by-case basis.

20-7 Conclusion

In summary, although the DOJ FARA Unit has the legal authority to pursue criminal and civil actions in appropriate circumstances, the FARA Unit's driving principle is to ensure voluntary compliance with the statute. While respecting the requirements of the statute, practitioners should appreciate this modus operandi of the FARA Unit and consider engaging the FARA Unit if questions about registration or other filing requirements arise.

---

49. Tim Starks, *Should Ex-Spies, Diplomats Be Able to Go Straight to Work for Shady Foreign Governments?* ROLL CALL (June 27, 2014), http://blogs.rollcall.com/five-by-five/should-ex-spies-diplomats-be-able-to-going-straight-to-work-for-shady-foreign-governments/?dcz=.

50. H.R. Res. 5, 114th Cong., 1st Sess. (Jan. 6, 2015).

51. Eric Lipton, Brooke Williams, & Nicholas Confessore, *Foreign Powers Buy Influence at Think Tanks,* N.Y. TIMES (Sept. 6 2014), http://www.nytimes.com/2014/09/07/us/politics/foreign-powers-buy-influence-at-think-tanks.html?_r=0.

Part III
Related Bodies of
Federal Law of
Particular Interest
to Lobbyists

Introduction to Part III

Modern-day federal government relations work often implicates laws other than lobbying-specific provisions like the LDA, congressional gift rules, or tax law. Lobbyists and their clients or employers are increasingly called upon to make political contributions to candidates, participate in fundraising for candidates, and/or fund candidate advocacy communications. Lobbyists and lobbying entities must be aware of the extent to which campaign finance laws address or limit their ability to undertake these activities. This Part III therefore includes fulsome discussions of campaign finance laws as they impact corporate political activity.

At the same time, prosecutors have begun to take much more interest in ensuring government decisions are made on the merits of the matters considered. We have therefore included a chapter on criminal prosecution of lobbyists. A separate chapter addresses so-called pay-to-play laws, which are aimed at ensuring political contributions are not made for the purpose of obtaining government contracts. Another one summarizes the ethics rules related to giving gifts to federal executive branch officials. Finally, for lawyers who lobby, we include here a chapter addressing the peculiar ethics issues relevant to your relationship with your clients.

CHAPTER 21

Criminal Prosecution of Lobbyists and Lawmakers for Bribery, Gratuities, and Honest Services Fraud

BY VIRGINIA E. DAVIS HORTON AND JAMES B. CHRISTIAN JR.

21-1 Introduction

In recent years, concern over public corruption has been on the rise, both in the press and in the minds of the American people. Newspapers have been filled with stories of politicians stashing tens of thousands of dollars in their home freezers,[1] or passing cash in boxes of cereal.[2] Television series like *House of Cards* and *Scandal* have kept (fictional) political corruption in its long-standing position of national entertainment. More than half of Americans surveyed believe that public officials and civil servants are corrupt, and 59 percent believe the government's actions in the fight against corruption are ineffective.[3]

---

1. David Stout, *Ex-Rep. Jefferson Convicted in Bribery Scheme*, N.Y. TIMES (Aug. 5, 2009), at A14, *available at* http://www.nytimes.com/2009/08/06/us/06jefferson.html.

2. David M. Halbfinger, *44 Charged by U.S. in New Jersey Corruption Sweep*, N.Y. TIMES (July 23, 2009), at A1, *available at* http://www.nytimes.com/2009/07/24/nyregion/24jersey.html?pagewanted=all.

3. TRANSPARENCY INT'L, *Global Corruption Barometer 2013: United States*, http://www.transparency.org/gcb2013/country/?country=united_states (last visited May 6, 2014).

In September 2004, Jack Abramoff's "*Sopranos*-like" e-mail messages were revealed in a hearing before the United States Senate Committee on Indian Affairs.[4] The e-mails showed a continuous pattern of payoffs, kickbacks, and manipulated tribal elections, and they set off a downward spiral that ultimately led to over twenty people being found guilty in various corruption investigations.[5] The news cycle was filled with tales of $100,000 golf trips to Scotland and cash payments to politicians' wives. Abramoff himself called the experience "Kafkaesque."[6] "All of a sudden," he told the *New York Times*, "in an almost Job-ian fashion, my whole world collapsed."[7]

Ultimately, Abramoff admitted to defrauding four of his Native American tribal clients out of millions of dollars, conspiring to bribe public officials, and evading taxes.[8] He was sentenced to four years in prison after prosecutors argued in favor of a reduced sentence due to his cooperation with investigators.[9] Abramoff's conduct was part of a broad pattern of corruption, but for some of the people who went down with him, it only took a few relatively minor violations to run afoul of the law. For example, Fraser Verrusio, a former aide to Representative Don Young, was convicted of three felonies stemming from accepting tickets to Game 1 of the Yankees–Marlins World Series from a construction equipment rental company.[10] Mr. Verrusio was convicted of accepting a gratuity, conspiring to accept a gratuity, and failure to report gifts on his financial disclosure statement.[11] The gift rules that applied to Verrusio at the time required him to disclose any gifts exceeding $285— his trip to New York was valued at approximately $1,300.[12]

The public's reaction to the Abramoff scandal was one of the impetuses for the 2007 passage of the Honest Leadership and Open Government Act,[13] which increased lobbying disclosure requirements and tightened gift rules as they apply to lobbyists and their clients. Then Senator Barack Obama called the bill "the most sweeping ethics reform since Watergate."[14] Under the law, lobbyists must submit quarterly reports that include, among other things, a list of specific issues for which lobbying work was performed. They also have to submit semiannual reports disclosing certain political and honorary contributions. This information all becomes

---

4. *A Lobbyist in Full*, N.Y Times Mag. (May 1, 2005), at 1, *available at* http://www.nytimes.com/2005/05/01/magazine/01ABRAMOFF.html?pagewanted=1&_r=0.

5. United States v. Ring, 706 F.3d 460 (D.C. Cir. 2013).

6. *A Lobbyist in Full, supra* note 4, at 2.

7. *Id.* at 6.

8. James V. Grimaldi & Susan Schmidt *Abramoff Pleads Guilty to 3 Counts*, Wash. Post (Jan. 4, 2006), at A04, *available at* http://www.washingtonpost.com/wp-dyn/content/article/2006/01/03/AR2006010300474.html.

9. Neil A. Lewis, *Abramoff Gets 4 Years in Prison for Corruption*, N.Y. Times (Sept. 5, 2008), at A13, *available at* http://www.nytimes.com/2008/09/05/washington/05abramoff.html?_r=0.

10. Jennifer Epstein, *Former Aide Jailed for Yankees Trip*, Politico (Aug. 5, 2011, 1:25 PM, EDT), http://www.politico.com/news/stories/0811/60744.html.

11. Warren Richey, *Fresh Conviction in Abramoff Scandal: Aide Traded Favors for World Series Trip*, Christian Sci. Monitor (Feb. 10, 2011), http://www.csmonitor.com/USA/Justice/2011/0210/Fresh-conviction-in-Abramoff-scandal-aide-traded-favors-for-World-Series-trip.

12. *Id.*

13. Pub. L. No. 110–81, 121 Stat. 735, *codified at* 2 U.S.C. §§ 1601–1614 (2015).

14. Charles Babington, *Bush Signs Lobby-Ethics Bill*, Wash. Post (Sept. 15, 2007), http://www.washingtonpost.com/wp-dyn/content/article/2007/09/15/AR2007091500589.html.

publicly available.[15] Under certain circumstances, the law also prohibits registered lobbyists from giving gifts or providing travel to any legislative official covered by the Rules of the House of Representatives or the Standing Rules of the Senate if the lobbyist knows the gifts are prohibited.[16] Lobbyists who have failed to comply with the act's registration and reporting requirements, such as Alexandria lobbyist Alan Mauk, have faced fines of up to $5.2 million.[17]

The climate of corruption and the increased scrutiny it has brought should give anyone involved in politics, fund-raising, or lobbying pause to consider the legal risks of activities that may seem perfectly innocent. At one time, it may have been common practice for a lobbyist to buy a lawmaker dinner or give him the occasional social gift as an act of hospitality. However, when government officials are involved, lobbyists must temper politeness with an understanding of laws and gift rules that are complex and, at times, counterintuitive.

21-2 The Legal Landscape

Members of Congress and the executive branch or their employees are heavily regulated in receiving gifts from lobbyists.[18] Federal judges have another set of gift rules; state and local governments each have their own rules, too. The resulting regulatory scheme is Byzantine at best, but it is crucial for lobbyists to understand the applicable policies before offering anything—even modest food or drink—to a government official.[19]

However, Chapter 18, Section 201 of the United States Code trumps all of these gift rules and regulations. Even when a lobbyist follows all applicable ethics rules, he or she can still be subject to prosecution of bribery or offering an illegal gratuity under section 201 if the thing of value was given "to influence an official act" or "for or because of any official act."[20] While the gift rules focus on an official's acceptance of a gift, section 201 criminalizes both offer and acceptance. The applicable ethics rules regulate the specifics of gift giving—what can be given, to whom, and when—but section 201 addresses the purpose of giving gifts—*why* the gift was

---

15. 2 U.S.C. § 1603 (2015); see also Chapter 5 of this manual.

16. 2 U.S.C. § 1613 (2015); see also Chapter 8.

17. Holly Yeager, *Lobbyist Faces $5 Million Fine for Allegedly Failing to File Disclosure Reports*, Wash. Post (Mar. 18, 2014), at A13, *available at* http://www.washingtonpost.com/politics/lobbyist-faces -5-million-fine-for-allegedly-failing-to-file-disclosure-reports/2014/03/18/10bd8ad0-aee3-11e3-96dc -d6ea14c099f9_story.html.

18. *See* 5 U.S.C. §§ 7342, 7351, 7353 (2015) (Federal employees); 5 C.F.R. § 2635.201–2635.205 (2015) (Executive Branch employees and employees of independent agencies); Senate Manual, Standing Rules of the Senate, Rule XXXV, S. Doc. No. 112-1 at 62–75 (2012) (Senators and Senate Employees); House Manual, Rules of the House of Representatives, Rule XXV, H. Doc. No. 112-161 at 951–980 (2013) (Representatives and House employees); *see also* U.S. Senate Select Comm. on Ethics, *Gifts*, http://www.ethics.senate.gov/public/index.cfm/gifts (last visited July 22, 2015); U.S. House Comm. on Ethics, *Gifts*, http://ethics.house.gov/gifts (last visited July 22, 2015); U.S. Office of Gov't Ethics, *Gifts & Payments*, http://www.oge.gov/Topics/Gifts-and-Payments/Gifts---Payments (last visited July 22, 2015). Note that these rules can be changed by the bodies themselves at any time without the need for legislation. See Chapter 8 of this manual for a full discussion of the congressional gift rules, and Chapter 26 for an overview of the rules that apply to giving gifts to executive branch officials.

19. Small quantities of food or drink are allowed in some cases. *See* Ethics Rules cited in note 18, *supra*, and Chapters 8 and 26 of this manual for more detailed information.

20. United States v. Sun-Diamond Growers of Cal., 526 U.S. 398, 404 (1999).

given. In other words, an otherwise legal gift can become illegal when it is given for an improper purpose.

Lobbyists should also be aware of the honest services fraud law found at 18 U.S.C. § 1346. This statute extends the mail fraud and wire fraud statutes to include schemes to defraud the public of their intangible right to the honest, impartial services of their leaders. Even if there is no proof that a bribe or kickback actually resulted in a loss of funds from the public coffers, all parties involved may still be guilty of a federal offense under section 1346. For example, former Virginia governor Bob McDonnell and his wife Maureen were convicted in 2014 of honest services wire fraud for using their political positions to promote dietary supplements in exchange for gifts and loans.[21]

This chapter first discusses section 201, the distinction between bribery and gratuities, and some of the major cases tried under the statute. Then, it will discuss the honest services fraud law and some of its notable cases.

21-3 Section 201: Bribery and Illegal Gratuity

At first glance, it can be difficult to distinguish between bribery and offering an illegal gratuity. After all, the two crimes are regulated by the same statute, and both involve giving things of value to officeholders and former officeholders for improper purposes. However, a closer examination highlights the key differences. "In their simplest forms . . . a bribe says 'please,' and a gratuity says 'thank you.'"[22]

Section 201(a) sets forth a set of definitions shared by both the bribery and gratuities subsections, including the definition of "public official"[23] and "official act."[24] It is important to note that section 201 only applies to public officials—it does not cover private officials like corporate directors or executives. It is also important to realize that "thing of value" is defined quite broadly. A "thing of value" is anything the official believes has subjective worth. It includes not only cash, but gifts, promises of future employment for the official or members of his family, sexual favors, or loans given on unusually favorable terms.[25]

---

21. Andrew Zajac & William Selway, *Ex-Virginia Governor McDonnell Indicted with Wife*, Bloomberg (Jan. 22, 2014 1:41 PM, ET), http://www.bloomberg.com/news/2014-01-21/ex-virginia-governor-mcdonnell-indicted-with-wife-in-fraud-scam.html; Valerie Bauerlein & Dawn Chase, *Former Virginia Gov. McDonnell and Wife Found Guilty*, Wall St. J. (Sept. 4, 2014 8:22 PM, ET), http://online.wsj.com/articles/former-virginia-gov-bob-mcdonnell-and-wife-found-guilty-on-public-corruption-charges-1409858382.

22. Randall D. Eliason, *Criminal Law: Surgery with a Meat Axe: Using Honest Services Fraud to Prosecute Federal Corruption*, 99 J. Crim. L. & Criminology 929, 938 (2009).

23. 18 U.S.C. § 201(a)(1) (2015) ("[T]he term 'public official' means Member of Congress, Delegate, or Resident Commissioner, either before or after such official has qualified, or an officer or employee or person acting for or on behalf of the United States, or any department, agency, or branch of Government thereof, including the District of Columbia, in any official function, under or by authority of any such department, agency, or branch of Government, or a juror.").

24. *Id.* § 201(a)(3) ("[T]he term 'official act' means any decision or action on any question, matter, cause, suit, proceeding or controversy, which may at any time be pending, or which may by law be brought before any public official, in such official's official capacity, or in such official's place of trust or profit.").

25. Eliason, at 935.

The next two subsections set forth two related but distinct crimes: bribery and illegal gratuity. The chart below is similar to one found in the United States Attorneys' Manual[26] that differentiates the two crimes.

	§ 201(b): Offering a Bribe	§ 201(c): Offering a Gratuity
Status of Officials	"to any public official or person selected to be a public official,"	"to any public official, former public official, or person selected to be a public official,"
Intent	Corruptly	[n/a]
Act	"directly or indirectly … gives, offers, or promises anything of value … or offers or promises to give anything of value to any other person or entity,"	"otherwise than as provided by law for the proper discharge of official duty—directly or indirectly gives, offers, or promises anything of value,"
Thing	Anything of value	Anything of value
For Whom	To the official "personally or for any other person or entity"	To the official "personally"
Purpose	"with intent— (A) to influence any official act; or (B) to influence [the recipient] to commit or aid in committing, or collude in, or allow, any fraud, or make opportunity for the commission of any fraud, on the United States; or (C) to induce [the recipient] to do or omit to do any act in violation of [their] lawful duty"	"for or because of any official act performed or to be performed by such official or person"

Bribery requires the corrupt intent of both parties, while gratuity requires only one party to behave improperly. For example, a representative of Widgets, Inc. could give a legislator new luggage bearing the Widgets, Inc. logo. If the representative intends for the luggage to be a gesture of thanks for a recent favorable vote on zoning laws, then the Widgets, Inc. representative has given an illegal gratuity, even if the legislator sees the luggage as merely a friendly gesture, unrelated to his official duties.

Bribery requires a quid pro quo, a corrupt intent to receive some favorable treatment in exchange for the gift. Gratuity merely requires that the gift be given "for or because of any official act" and includes gifts given before or after the official act takes place. This distinction is key. A lobbyist violates section 201(b) by offering a bribe if he takes a senator out for a steak dinner and says, "My client, the National Association of Elvis Presley Fan Clubs, has become aware that a bill is pending before your subcommittee to change the national anthem to 'All Shook

---

26. *See* U. S. Att'ys' Manual Title IX, Criminal Resource Manual § 2043 (1998), *available at* http://www.justice.gov/usao/eousa/foia_reading_room/usam/title9/crm02043.htm.

Up.' We hope you'll do everything you can to get this bill to a floor vote. If you can help us out, then we'd like to offer you and your family a free trip to Hawaii next month where we can discuss this matter further with our executive director, and, of course, have a screening of rare lost video footage from Elvis's 'Aloha from Hawaii' concert." In this scenario, the lobbyist is hoping he and the senator will reach an agreement, and it's clear that the trip to Hawaii is a quid pro quo for making sure the national anthem bill makes it out of committee.

On the other hand, the same lobbyist violates section 201(c) by offering an illegal gratuity if he takes the senator out for dinner and says, "My client, the National Association of Elvis Presley Fan Clubs, is truly grateful for your work last month to change the national anthem to 'All Shook Up.' As a token of our appreciation, we'd like to invite you and your family to take an all-expenses paid trip to Hawaii with our executive director next week." Here, the trip to Hawaii is being given because of the senator's official acts in supporting the bill, but there was never a meeting of the minds or a direct quid pro quo.[27]

There are other key differences between bribery and gratuities. A gift to a former public official can be an illegal gratuity, but it cannot be a bribe. Because a bribe requires a quid pro quo, a former official would not be in a position to uphold his end of the bargain if he were offered a bribe. However, he could still receive an illegal gratuity as a gesture of thanks for actions he took while in office. Another core difference is that illegal gratuities must be accepted personally while bribes can be accepted "personally or from any other person or entity." Since things of value given to political parties, aides, or committees can all be prosecuted as bribes (but not gratuities), bribery can often be easier to prosecute, even though it is the more serious offense—bribery carries a maximum sentence of fifteen years in prison, while gratuities carries a maximum sentence of two years in prison.[28]

Bribes and gratuities can be given either for an official action or an official's failure to act in a certain way. The key issue is not whether the official acted or omitted, but rather whether the official gave treatment that is better than what would be expected if not for the bribe or gratuity.[29]

Finally, it is important to note that while many "pure gratuities" are given after an official act has taken place (such as the Elvis Presley Fan Clubs example above), other "looking forward gratuities" may be given before an official act occurs. For example, if a senator was already a cosponsor of a bill to change the national anthem to "All Shook Up" and had run on the anthem change as a major part of her campaign platform, it would be difficult to argue that she voted in favor of the bill because of a trip from the National Association of Elvis Presley Fan Clubs. However, the Fan Clubs would still be offering her an illegal gratuity if they thanked her for her support thus far by offering her a trip to Hawaii before the vote took place.[30]

---

27. For further explanation and examples, *see* Charles B. Klein, *What Exactly Is an Unlawful Gratuity after United States v. Sun-Diamond Growers?*, 68 Geo. Wash. L. Rev. 116 (1999); Eliason, at 938; Alex Stein, *Adjudicating the Guilty Mind: Corrupt Intentions: Bribery, Unlawful Gratuity, and Honest Services Fraud*, 75 Law & Contemp. Probs. 61 (2012); Klein, at 116.

28. Eliason, *supra* note 22, at 935–38; Klein, *supra* note 27, at 119.

29. Stein, *supra* note 27, at 63; *see also* James Lindgreen, *The Theory, History, and Practice of the Bribery-Extortion Distinction*, 141 U. Pa. L. Rev. 1695, 1699 (1993).

30. For further explanation and examples, see Eliason, *supra* note 22, at 938.

21-4 *Sun-Diamond*: **Strengthening the Nexus Requirement**

While it takes a lower level of intent to be guilty of offering a gratuity than a bribe, there still must be a link, or nexus, between the gratuity and the official act for which it was given. One of the more significant developments in illegal gratuities law came in 1999 in *United States v. Sun-Diamond Growers*,[31] a case involving a trade association of raisin, prune, and fig growers in California.[32] In a unanimous decision, the Supreme Court held that the government must prove a link between the thing of value given to a public official and the specific official act for which the gratuity was given.

Sun-Diamond was charged with giving approximately $5,900 in illegal gratuities to the then Secretary of Agriculture, including meals, luggage, a framed print, a crystal bowl, and tickets to the 1993 U.S. Open Tennis Tournament.[33] The indictment alluded to two matters pending before the Secretary in which Sun-Diamond had an interest: a grant program administered by the Department of Agriculture and the federal government's regulation of methyl bromide, an inexpensive pesticide used by many of the association's growers.[34] However, the indictment did not allege a *specific* connection between the matters before the Secretary and the gratuities offered.

The District Court instructed the jury that "it is sufficient if Sun-Diamond provided [Secretary] Espy with unauthorized compensation simply because he held public office,"[35] and the jury convicted Sun-Diamond. However, the Supreme Court disagreed with this instruction and remanded the case. In his opinion for the unanimous Court, Justice Scalia pointed out the absurd results that would come to pass if the District Court's interpretation of the statute prevailed. For example, a championship sports team would be committing a criminal offense if it gave the president a commemorative jersey on a White House visit, because at any point in time there is some proposed rule or regulation that would affect the professional sports industry. A high school principal would be committing a federal crime if he gave the Secretary of Education a school baseball cap during a ceremonial visit to the school, as would a group of local farmers who took the Secretary of Agriculture out to lunch following a speech in a nearby town.[36]

The Court reasoned that these "absurdities" would be eliminated if gratuities were defined as being linked to an official act of the government official. After a discussion of the statutory language and its context, Justice Scalia concluded that "a statute in this field that can linguistically be interpreted to be either a meat axe or a scalpel should reasonably be taken to be the latter."[37]

Sun-Diamond rejected a proposed broad interpretation of the gratuities statute by strengthening the required link between a thing of value given to a public official and the official act for which it is given.[38] However, *Sun-Diamond* did not significantly limit the applicability of the gratuities statute, and it remained clear that

---

31. 526 U.S. 398 (1999).
32. *Id*. at 400–01.
33. *Id*. at 401.
34. *Id*. at 401–02.
35. *Id*. at 403.
36. *Id*. at 406–07.
37. *Id*. at 412.
38. *Id*. at 414.

an otherwise legal gift can still be a bribe or gratuity if it is given for an improper purpose.[39]

21-5 *Valdes*: Narrowing the Definition of an Official Act

In *Valdes v. United States*,[40] the D.C. Court of Appeals reached a surprising result, reversing the gratuities conviction of a police officer whose conduct seemed unabashedly corrupt. The unlikely decision was a result of the differences between the elements of the bribery and gratuities statutes. Valdes's conduct would have almost certainly fit within bribery's intent requirement to "corruptly . . . induce [the recipient] to do or omit to do any act in violation of [their] lawful duty," but the jury had convicted him of accepting illegal gratuities. He was ultimately acquitted because his conduct did not fit within section 201(c)'s intent requirement "for or because of an official act."

Nelson Valdes, a detective with the Washington, D.C. Metropolitan Police Department, was introduced to an undercover FBI informant posing as a judge at a local nightclub. Valdes met the "judge" several times over the course of the following weeks and provided him with license plate numbers for people who allegedly owed him money in exchange for cash payments.[41]

Valdes was indicted on three counts of bribery—the jury acquitted him of bribery, but convicted him of three counts of the lesser-included offense of receiving illegal gratuities.[42] The appellate court was closely divided (seven to five), and one of the points on which some of the dissenting justices differed from the majority was whether Valdes's queries were a police investigation. The key issue was whether Valdes was performing "official acts" or moonlighting outside of his job responsibilities.[43]

The D.C. Court of Appeals referred to *Sun-Diamond*'s admonition that section 201 should be interpreted as a scalpel rather than a meat axe, saying "this adjuration led the Court to reject the government's theory that 18 U.S.C. § 201(a)(3) covers any action taken in an official capacity."[44] "Thus, both our precedent and the language of the statute make clear that section 201 is not about officials' moonlighting, or their misuse of government resources, or the two in combination."[45] Valdes's conduct was potentially illegal under numerous statutes and regulations (such as those banning the conversion of government property or restricting federal employees' receipt of gifts).[46] However, the court found that section 201's definition of a "question" or "matter" before a public official must refer to a question the official is capable of deciding as part of his official duty. "Questions like 'Should this person receive a contract or disability benefit, and for how much?' are simply

39. *See, e.g.*, United States v. McCarter, 219 Fed. App'x 921 (11th Cir. 2007); United States v. Bucheit, 134 Fed. App'x 842 (6th Cir. 2005); United States v. Alfisi, 308 F.3d 144 (2d Cir. 2002); United States v. Ahn, 231 F.3d 26 (D.C. Cir. 2000).
40. 475 F.3d 1319 (D.C. Cir. 2007).
41. *Id.* at 1321–22.
42. *Id.* at 1322.
43. *Id.* at 1325–26.
44. *Id.* at 1323.
45. *Id.* at 1324.
46. *Id.*

in a different class from questions like 'Where do you live?' and 'What kind of car do you drive?' Section 201(a)(3) clearly encompasses the former, but not the latter."[47]

The majority wrote that if *any* question that even paralleled an official's work was covered by section 201, then a Department of Justice lawyer who used a government Westlaw account to look up a legal question for a friend would be "deciding" a "question" that might "be brought before [him]," which would be an absurd result.[48] Ultimately, the court found that Valdes' actions violated his official duties as a police officer, but they were not official acts. The court elaborated on its construction of section 201:

> We believe that § 201 thus reflects a kind of balance between the bribery and gratuity violations. For the former, it defines the predicate acts broadly, but the required compensatory link narrowly; culpability attaches for "any official act," "any fraud," or "any act in violation of [a] lawful duty," but the payment at issue must actually influence the act or omission. For gratuities, the reverse is true; the predicate acts are defined narrowly (excluding, for instance, mere violation of an official duty), and the required compensatory link is defined more broadly ("for or because of," even where the compensation has had no influence).[49]

Violating an official duty is a predicate act of bribery but not for gratuity. Since Valdes had already been acquitted of bribery, the Court of Appeals only dealt with the charge of accepting an illegal gratuity and was left with no choice but to overturn his conviction.

Although bribery is a more serious offense than accepting an illegal gratuity, *Valdes* (and bribery's lack of a personal acceptance requirement) shows how bribery cases can sometimes be easier to prosecute than cases of accepting an illegal gratuity. *Valdes* is somewhat of an anomaly, and it is likely that since it was decided, some juries may be instructed only on bribery *or* gratuity to prevent cases from slipping through the cracks.

21-6 *Jefferson*: The Continued Force of Section 201

Despite the ruling in *Valdes*, the bribery and illegal gratuities statutes remain powerful tools for prosecutors. In 2005, Congressman William Jefferson of the Second District of Louisiana made national news when an FBI raid uncovered $90,000 in marked bills in his basement freezer.[50] Jefferson was alleged to have participated in numerous self-dealing bribery, money laundering, and fraud schemes reaching from the United States to Nigeria and Ghana.

Jefferson was alleged to have (among other things) received direct payments, shares in revenue, and transfers of stock to his wife's company from American and Nigerian telecommunications firms in exchange for promoting joint business

---

47. *Id.* at 1325.
48. *Id.* at 1326.
49. *Id.* at 1327 (internal citations omitted).
50. David Stout, *Ex-Rep. Jefferson Convicted in Bribery Scheme*, N.Y. TIMES (Aug. 5, 2009), at A14, *available at* http://www.nytimes.com/2009/08/06/us/06jefferson.html.

ventures by sending letters on official congressional letterhead, conducting official travel, and meeting with American and Nigerian government officials.[51] During his trips to Nigeria, he was accompanied by congressional staff and used them to create trip itineraries and to coordinate with the Department of State to arrange official meetings. He was also accompanied by U.S. embassy security and "introduce[ed] himself as a U.S. congressman in charge of overseeing affairs of Nigeria or Africa."[52] Jefferson engaged in similar schemes on behalf of companies that hoped to open sugar factories, build fertilizer plants, and develop so-called marginal oil fields in Nigeria.[53] Jefferson also worked through a lobbyist to solicit bribes from a businessperson in return for his assistance in resolving a dispute over oil exploration rights off the coast of São Tomé and Príncipe.[54] Ultimately, Jefferson was arrested after an FBI informant gave him a briefcase filled with $100,000 in marked bills that Jefferson said he intended to use to bribe the vice president of Nigeria. Two days later, FBI agents seized $90,000 of the marked cash from a freezer in Jefferson's basement.[55]

In August 2009, Jefferson was convicted of eleven charges including bribery, wire fraud, money laundering, racketeering, and conspiracy.[56] On appeal, Jefferson argued, among other things, that the jury was not instructed properly on the definition of an "official act" or the requirement for a quid pro quo in regard to the bribery statute.[57]

He first argued that the definition of an "official act" in 18 U.S.C. § 201(a)(3) should be limited to activities involving questions pending or brought before Congress, such as voting on proposed legislation or conducting committee work, citing *Sun-Diamond* and *Valdes* as precedent.[58] At trial, the prosecution had presented evidence that Jefferson's meetings with public officials on behalf of his bribers were "constituent services" and therefore a part of his official duties.[59]

In *United States v. Birdsall*,[60] the Supreme Court had analyzed a predecessor bribery statute and held that it prohibited more than just those acts that are "prescribed by a written rule," but rather that "[e]very action that is within the range of official duty comes within the purview of these sections."[61] The *Jefferson* court noted that the only difference between the bribery statute at issue in *Birdsall* and the current bribery statute is that section 201(b) describes the conduct reached by bribery as "official acts," while the predecessor version used the phrase "decision or action on any question, matter, cause, or proceeding which may at any time be pending, or which may by law be brought before him in his official capacity, or in his place of trust or profit." However, section 201(a)(3) defines "official act" with substantively the same language as the predecessor statute. Therefore, the court

---

51. United States v. Jefferson, 674 F.3d 332, 341–44 (4th Cir. 2012).
52. *Id.* at 344.
53. *Id.* at 346–49.
54. *Id.* at 349–50.
55. *Id.* at 346.
56. *Id.* at 335.
57. *Id.*
58. *Id.* at 336, 338.
59. *Id.* at 337.
60. 233 U.S. 223 (1914).
61. *Id.* at 230–31.

reasoned that there was no substantive distinction between the two bribery laws and looked to *Birdsall*'s interpretation of an official act.[62]

Jefferson had argued that *Sun-Diamond* put forth a more restricted definition of "official act" and that his activities more closely mirrored the "moonlighting" in *Valdes* than official acts related to his congressional office.[63] In rejecting this argument, the *Jefferson* court noted that "[t]here is simply no indication that *Sun-Diamond* sought to undermine *Birdsall*'s holding. Indeed, *Sun-Diamond* did not mention *Birdsall* at all—a curious omission if the Court intended to overturn its landmark decision on the definition of 'official act.'"[64] The *Jefferson* court interpreted the Supreme Court's decision in *Sun-Diamond* as embracing a narrow reading of the gratuity statute by requiring a nexus between the act and the thing of value received, but found that it did not change the definition of "official act."[65] It also quickly dismissed Jefferson's comparisons to *Valdes* because of Jefferson's extensive use of congressional resources in carrying out his scheme.[66]

Ultimately, the Fourth Circuit found that the trial court did not err in instructing the jury that acts performed as a part of settled practice (here, constituent services) fit the statutory definition of "official acts" because the instruction was consistent with *Birdsall*. However, it elaborated, "Inasmuch as the trial court gave its 'settled practice' instruction in tandem with the statutory definition of 'official act,' the jury was not authorized to ignore the directive that Jefferson's official acts must pertain to a pending question, matter, or cause that was before him. In other words, the jury could not rely exclusively on Jefferson's settled practices."[67] Jefferson's conviction complied with this requirement because "the jury was free to find, first of all, that performing constituent services was a settled official practice of Jefferson's congressional office and, second, that African trade issues were 'matters' or 'causes' that were pending before him."[68]

Jefferson also argued that the trial court was incorrect in its jury instructions when it said that the quid pro quo element of the bribery charge "could be satisfied by proof that Jefferson had agreed to perform unspecified official acts on an 'as-needed basis,'" saying this instruction was contrary to *Sun-Diamond*'s nexus requirement.[69] The Fourth Circuit rejected this argument, citing *United States v. Quinn*,[70] *United States v. Ganim*,[71] and *United States v. White*[72] to assert that the quid pro quo requirement is satisfied if an official adopts a particular course of conduct in exchange for a thing of value and it is not necessary to link each individual act or omission with a particular payment.[73] If the prosecution can establish that a

---

62. *Jefferson*, 674 F.3d at 353.
63. *Id*. at 353–54.
64. *Id*. at 355.
65. *Id*. at 355–56.
66. *Id*. at 356–57.
67. *Id*. at 357.
68. *Id*.
69. *Id*. at 339.
70. 359 F.3d 666 (4th Cir. 2004).
71. 510 F.3d 134 (2d Cir. 2007).
72. 665 F.3d 560, 568 (3d Cir. 2012) ("The bribery theory does not require that each *quid*, or item of value, be linked to a specific *quo*, or official act. Rather, a bribe may come in the form of a 'stream of benefits.'").
73. *Jefferson*, 674 F.3d at 358–59.

particular course of conduct was done as a quid pro quo, then the defense will likely be unsuccessful in any efforts to pick apart which payments were allegedly given for which deeds.

Sun-Diamond and *Valdes* can still be used as defense tools in cases where the conduct complained of is not clearly linked to the thing of value or the official's duties. However, *Jefferson's* holding that "official act" can include constituent services strengthens section 201's reach and shows that *Sun-Diamond* and *Valdes* are not sweeping decisions. Their scope is still relatively limited, and the addition of constituent services to the range of covered official acts has the potential to include a broad range of conduct simply because "constituent services" is a fluid and somewhat amorphous concept.

21-7 Honest Services Fraud Prosecutions

Although the news reports surrounding the Jack Abramoff scandal described conduct that sounded like classic bribery, almost none of the convictions in the Abramoff ring were for bribery or illegal gratuities. Instead, honest services mail fraud and wire fraud were among the most frequently charged offenses.[74] More recently, former Virginia governor Bob McDonnell and his wife were both convicted of honest services wire fraud for accepting gifts and loans from the CEO of a dietary supplement company while using their political positions to promote the company's products.[75] The McDonnells hosted events at the governor's mansion and arranged meetings for the CEO with several state officials.[76] Both Bob and Maureen McDonnell were sentenced to prison, but as of this writing, their case is pending before the U.S. Supreme Court.[77]

The federal mail and wire fraud statutes, 18 U.S.C. §§ 1341 and 1343, prohibit the use of the mail or wires (including telephone and internet) "to devise any scheme or artifice to defraud," or to "obtain[ ] money or property by means of false or fraudulent pretenses." These two statutes are applied extremely broadly. Nearly any fraud or scheme imaginable involves mailing something, calling somebody, or sending an e-mail. As soon as one of those contacts happens, an otherwise small-time local swindle becomes a federal crime. For example, the Supreme Court held in *Schmuck v. United States* that a local used car salesman who sold cars with rolled-back odometers committed federal mail fraud when title applications were sent to the state Department of Transportation for the vehicles with fraudulent mileage readings. Mailings can be sent innocently by a third party and may be only incidentally linked to an essential part of the scheme, and the defendant can still be convicted of mail or wire fraud.[78]

---

74. Eliason, *supra* note 22, at 929.

75. Andrew Zajac & William Selway, *Ex-Virginia Governor McDonnell Indicted with Wife*, BLOOMBERG (Jan. 22, 2014 1:41 PM), http://www.bloomberg.com/news/2014-01-21/ex-virginia-governor-mcdonnell -indicted-with-wife-in-fraud-scam.html; Valerie Bauerlein & Dawn Chase, *Former Virginia Governor McDonnell and Wife Found Guilty*, WALL ST. J. (Sept. 4, 2014 8:22 PM), http://online.wsj.com/articles /former-virginia-gov-bob-mcdonnell-and-wife-found-guilty-on-public-corruption-charges-1409858382.

76. Bauerlein & Chase, *supra* note 21.

77. Robert Barnes, Supreme Court will Review Corruption Conviction of Former Va. Governor Robert McDonnell, WASHINGTON POST (Jan 15, 2016), https://www.washingtonpost.com/politics /courts_law/supreme-court-will-review-corruption-conviction-of-former-va-governor-robert -mcdonnell/2016/01/15/e281ede0-b3c8-11e5-a76a-0b5145e8679a_story.html

78. Schmuck v. United States, 489 U.S. 705 (1989).

The honest services fraud statute, 18 U.S.C. § 1346, defines "scheme or artifice to defraud" as it is used in the mail and wire fraud statutes to include "a scheme or artifice to deprive another of the intangible right of honest services." In other words, prosecutors do not have to prove that citizens were cheated out of money or property—they can meet their burden of proof by showing that the public was deprived of its right to the fair, honest, and impartial services of its public officials.[79]

Like the bribery and gratuities statutes, both payors and payees can be indicted under section 1346. The statute applies to both public officials, such as legislators, and private officials, such as corporate officers. Honest services fraud also applies equally to federal, state, and local officials, whereas the bribery and gratuities laws typically need a separate "jurisdictional hook" to apply to state or local officials.[80]

This intangible rights theory of mail fraud was first presented many decades ago in *Shushan v. United States*,[81] which held "[a] scheme to get a public contract on more favorable terms than would likely be got otherwise by bribing a public official would not only be a plan to commit the crime of bribery, but would also be a scheme to defraud the public."[82]

Honest services fraud prosecutions were abruptly halted by the Supreme Court in 1987 in *McNally v. United States*.[83] McNally was a Kentucky state official who selected the state's insurance agent and arranged to take a share of the agent's commissions for himself in a kickback scheme.[84] The prosecutor in the case argued that McNally's conduct defrauded the state's citizens of their right to have their government's affairs conducted honestly, but he did not argue that the state would have paid less in insurance costs or secured better coverage if the kickback scheme had not occurred.[85] Ultimately, the Supreme Court read the mail fraud statute "as limited in scope to the protection of property rights,"[86] deliberately excluding the intangible right to honest services.

The next year, Congress responded to *McNally* by passing 18 U.S.C. § 1346. With the passage of this single-sentence definition of "scheme or artifice to defraud" to include "a scheme or artifice to deprive another of the intangible right of honest services," prosecutors could once again use the mail and wire fraud[87] statutes to go after officials involved in bribes, kickbacks, and other frauds even when they could not prove that the citizenry paid higher costs as a direct result of the scheme. Following the strengthening of the nexus requirement in *Sun-Diamond*, honest services fraud became an increasingly popular tool for federal prosecutors.[88]

In 2010, the Supreme Court limited the application of section 1346 to cover only bribes and kickback schemes in order to keep the statute from being void for vagueness in *Skilling v. United States*.[89] Former Enron executive Jeffrey Skilling

---

79. *Id.*

80. *Id.*

81. 117 F.2d 110 (1941).

82. *Id.* at 115; *see also* United States v. Dixon, 536 F.2d 1388, 1400 (2d Cir. 1976).

83. 483 U.S. 350 (1987).

84. *Id.* at 360.

85. *Id.* at 353.

86. *Id.* at 360.

87. 18 U.S.C. §§ 1341–1351 also cover bank fraud, health care fraud, securities and commodities fraud, and fraud in foreign labor contracting, but the vast majority of prosecutions of lobbyists under this chapter are as mail fraud or wire fraud.

88. Eliason, *supra* note 22, at 931.

89. 561 U.S. 358 (2010).

was convicted of conspiracy to commit honest services wire fraud under 18 U.S.C. §§ 1371, 1343, and 1346 for his role in the now infamous scheme to inflate Enron's short-run stock prices by misleading investors about the company's financial well-being.[90] At trial, Skilling was acquitted of nine counts of insider trading, but convicted of nineteen counts, including the honest services wire fraud charge. He was sentenced to over twenty-four years in prison and ordered to pay $45 million in restitution.[91]

Skilling argued that the statute was unconstitutionally vague or, in the alternative, that his conduct was not covered by the statute. Writing for a unanimous court, Justice Ginsburg said that "In the main, the pre-*McNally* cases involved fraudulent schemes to deprive another of honest services through bribes or kickbacks supplied by a third party who had not been deceived. Confined to these paramount applications, section 1346 presents no vagueness problem."[92] The Court held that Congress *at least* intended to reach bribes and kickback schemes in passing section 1346, but that including a wider range of conduct "would raise the due process concerns underlying the vagueness doctrine."[93] Therefore, section 1346 was held to only criminalize "the bribe-and-kickback core of the pre-*McNally* case law."[94] Based on this interpretation, the Court found that Skilling's conviction was flawed and remanded it to the lower courts for further proceedings.

Since *Skilling*, more honest services fraud convictions have been overturned. Fewer cases are tried under section 1346 than they were before *Skilling*. However, in the cases of clear bribes or kickbacks, the statute remains a favorite tool for prosecutors, as evidenced by *United States v. Ring*[95] and *United States v. Jefferson*.

Kevin Ring, a lobbyist who worked for Jack Abramoff's team, was indicted on multiple counts of illegal gratuities and honest services wire fraud.[96] Ring's first trial ended in a hung jury, and prosecutors decided to wait for the Supreme Court to decide *Skilling* before retrying him.[97]

Ring was ultimately convicted on multiple counts, and on appeal he argued that the district court's instructions on honest services fraud misstated the law post-*Skilling*. The D.C. Court of Appeals upheld his convictions. The court held that under *Skilling*, the prosecution had to prove each element of bribery, including that Ring "gave gifts with an 'intent to influence an official act' by way of a corrupt quid pro quo" as described in *Sun-Diamond*.[98] Ring argued that the jury instructions on the quid pro quo element failed to clarify that (1) an explicit quid pro quo was required and (2) the official must agree to the exchange.[99]

The court held that the "explicitness" instruction required to show a quid pro quo in campaign contributions is not required to show a quid pro quo in honest services fraud. While receiving things of value is "inevitable" in financing a campaign, "accepting free dinners is certainly not." Furthermore, the court wrote,

90. *Id.* at 368–69.
91. *Id.* at 375.
92. *Id.* at 404.
93. *Id.* at 408.
94. *Id.* at 409.
95. 706 F.3d 460 (D.C. Cir. 2013).
96. *Id.* at 463.
97. *Id.* at 464–65.
98. *Id.* at 465 (citing United States v. Sun-Diamond Growers of Cal., 526 U.S. 398, 404 (1999)).
99. *Id.* at 465.

"although providing information, commenting on proposed legislation, and other lobbying activities implicate First Amendment speech and petition rights, the First Amendment interest in giving hockey tickets to public officials is, at least compared to the interest in contributing to political campaigns, de minimis."[100]

The court also disagreed with Ring's argument that the district court should have instructed the jury that the government official must agree to the exchange in order for honest services fraud to have been committed. The court noted that both parties agreed that the bribery statute, section 201, serves as the "benchmark" for honest services bribery. Under section 201, offering a bribe and soliciting a bribe are two separate crimes, which makes it clear that criminal bribery can occur as a preparatory offense without a mutual agreement. Just as offering a bribe is itself a crime under the bribery statute, offering a bribe is a crime under the honest services fraud statute when the mail or wires are involved.[101] For example, former Illinois governor Rod Blagojevich was convicted of ten counts of wire fraud for his attempts to sell Barack Obama's former Senate seat even though his "sale" was unsuccessful.[102]

United States v. Jefferson[103] also tackled issues of honest services fraud. Jefferson challenged his honest services wire fraud conviction by arguing that *Skilling* discredited the theory that he committed a federal crime by failing to disclose his interests in the businesses he was promoting to foreign and domestic public officials.[104]

Jefferson's honest service wire fraud charges were based on the theory that he failed to disclose his self-dealing and conflicts of interest in his long-running Nigerian bribery scheme.[105] Even though the jury instructions indicated that undisclosed self-dealing was sufficient to find a violation of section 1346 (which was no longer true post-*Skilling*), the court found that the jury could have reasonably found that Jefferson violated section 1346 through the overt bribery discussed above. Therefore, it found that any error was harmless, and Jefferson's honest services fraud convictions were upheld.[106]

21-8 Conclusion

Bribery, illegal gratuities, and honest services fraud are constantly changing parts of the legal landscape. Although some decisions, such as *Sun-Diamond*, *Valdes*, and *Skilling*, have set more firm parameters around the laws, cases like *Jefferson* and *Ring* show that sections 201 and 1346 remain powerful tools. Lobbyists and public officials must also remember that these laws function alongside applicable gift rules, creating a complex web of laws, rules, and regulations. Lobbyists should do

---

100. *Id.* at 466 (internal citations omitted).

101. *Id.* at 466–67.

102. *Blagojevich Convicted on Corruption Charges*, CNN Wire (June 27, 2011, 8:54 PM, EDT), http://www.cnn.com/2011/POLITICS/06/27/blagojevich.trial/.

103. 674 F.3d 332 (4th Cir. 2012). See also Section 21-6 of this chapter (discussing United States v. Jefferson).

104. *Id.* at 339.

105. *Id.* at 360. See also Section 21-6 (discussing the Nigerian bribery scheme).

106. *Id.* at 361–62.

more than err on the side of caution in their interactions with legislators and other government officials.

Communication with elected officials by private interests is long ingrained in our democratic process and often provides information that is vital to the efficient function of our government.[107] The continued free exercise of the First Amendment rights at the core of lobbying ultimately depends on the probity of those who practice in this arena. The effective and informed practitioner is aware of the risks and liabilities to all parties and values long-term interests over potentially risky short-term gains.

---

107. Nicholas W. Allard, *The Law of Lobbying: Lobbying is an Honorable Profession: The Right to Petition and the Competition to Be Right*, 19 STAN. L. & POL'Y REV. 23 (2008).

CHAPTER 22

Ethics Law and the Lawyer-Lobbyist

BY THOMAS ROSS

22-1 Introduction

With regard to lawyers who engage in lobbying, this manual is a testament to the large and complex body of law that regulates the lawyer-lobbyist's practice. This chapter is concerned, however, with a particular part of that legal terrain, namely, the ethics law.[1]

"Ethics law" as used in this chapter means the law of each jurisdiction that applies specifically and solely to lawyers. While these laws vary somewhat from jurisdiction to jurisdiction, most have modeled their laws on the model formulations

---

1. This chapter does not address the larger ethical issue of the lobbyist-lawyer's sense of social responsibility. For a thoughtful consideration of this issue, *see* Thomas M. Susman, *Private Ethics, Public Conduct: An Essay on Ethical Lobbying, Campaign Contributions*, 19 STAN. L. & POLICY REV. 10 (2008).

of the American Bar Association. This chapter uses the current ABA Model Rules as the template for analysis.[2] Lawyers should, of course, always consult the current ethics law of the applicable jurisdiction. This chapter will provide the basic orientation that should allow the lawyer to discern the presence of risk in these matters. This discernment of risk, whenever it arises, should trigger the necessary research of the then current applicable ethics law and/or consultation with an expert.

The ethics law can be significant to the lawyer engaged in lobbying in two basic ways. First, any lawyer-lobbyist who violates the ethics law risks professional discipline. Thus, for example, a lawyer engaged in lobbying on behalf of a client who deposits unearned advances from the client into the lawyer's own account violates the "no commingling" command of Model Rule 1.15. Such a violation of the ethics law could lead to professional discipline ranging from a private reprimand up to disbarment. Second, apart from the specter of professional discipline, the ethics law may influence the application of other parts of the regulatory law. In an extreme version of this effect, the Pennsylvania courts in 1999 voided the Pennsylvania Lobbying Disclosure Act on the ground that the act attempted to regulate the conduct of lawyers that, the court held, was solely within the jurisdiction of the judiciary.[3] In the more typical case, courts applying some other body of law may look to the ethics law for guidance in judging the lawyer's conduct. For example, if a lawyer-lobbyist is sued for malpractice by a former client, the court may look to ethics law rules relating to the duty to communicate, confidentiality, and so forth in judging whether the lawyer-lobbyist failed to render reasonable care.

22-2 Application of the Ethics Law to Lawyers Engaged in Lobbying

First, a lawyer engaged in lobbying may simply be deemed to have entered into a lawyer-client relationship. If so, all the protections of the ethics law must be accorded to the client, including duties of confidentiality and conflict of interest proscriptions. The lobbying work in this case becomes simply another part of the services provided by the lawyer to the client.

Second, a lawyer can violate the ethics law even when he or she is engaged in non-lawyering activities. For example, a lawyer who, as part of his or her lobbying work, gives a speech that vilifies a judge with false accusations may violate Rule 8.2(a) forbidding a lawyer from falsely impugning the integrity of a judge. Perhaps more important for lawyer-lobbyists, a lawyer who violates the state's other laws may thereby also violate the ethics law. For example, a lawyer who violates criminal laws forbidding bribery of public officials also violates Rule 8.4(b), which prohibits a lawyer from "commit[ing] a criminal act that reflects adversely on the lawyer's honesty, trustworthiness or fitness as a lawyer." That the bribery may have occurred outside a formal lawyer-client representation is not a defense in this context. Thus, the lawyer-lobbyist who violates other laws risks professional discipline, including disbarment, as an additional sanction for the misconduct.

---

2. Because many lawyer-lobbyists practice in the District of Columbia, this chapter will also note any significant differences between the ABA Model Rules and the D.C. ethics law.

3. Gmerek v. State Ethics Comm'n, 751 A.2d 1241 (Pa. Commw. Ct. 1999), *aff'd by an equally divided* Pennsylvania Supreme Court, 569 Pa. 579, 807 A. 2d 812 (Pa. 2002).

A lawyer may, of course, function outside his professional capacity, for example, as a writer or a carpenter or a lobbyist. And when a lawyer acts in another capacity, most of the proscriptions of ethics law will cease to apply directly. For example, a lawyer who writes crime novels runs little risk of violating the ethics law.[4] But the activities of the lawyer-lobbyist, unlike the lawyer-novelist, pose serious risks in terms of the ethics law. The important point is that the lawyer must always be aware of the ethics law, even when the lawyer is acting outside an attorney-client relationship. The idea that "the ethics law simply doesn't apply when the lawyer isn't lawyering" is a dangerous myth.[5]

Four basic issues dominate ethics law generally, as well as the application of ethics law to the lawyer-lobbyist. Those issues are confidentiality, conflicts of interest, competence, and prohibited assistance. This chapter is primarily organized around those issues. But a threshold matter is the meaning and significance of ABA Model Rule 5.7, which addresses "law-related services" including lobbying. Some view this Rule as the basis on which lawyers doing lobbying work can "opt out" of the ethics law. As the next section will reveal, it is not quite that simple.

22-3 Model Rule 5.7 and "Opting Out" of the Ethics Law

From the ethics law perspective, the turn to lobbying by lawyers is connected to the larger debate regarding multidisciplinary practices (MDP). Lawyers for generations have offered services to clients that are not obviously and simply "legal services" (e.g., business advice, tax preparation, and so on). But beginning in the 1980s, law firms became increasingly involved in offering related services to clients that fell outside traditional legal services. These services included investment counseling, business strategy development, financial planning, public relations, environmental consulting, computer technology assistance, tax preparation, and lobbying. The bar explained this phenomenon as a response to client demand and, as importantly, a move to match the "one-stop shopping" that the large global accounting firms were then offering.

The organized bar, and thus the ethics laws, initially viewed MDP with disfavor, putting constraints on the lawyer's nonlegal services practice, requiring that any such "ancillary business" be wholly separate from the law practice. But, acknowledging the competitive pressures from the accounting firms as well as the reality of proliferating MDP, the ABA in 1994 adopted Rule 5.7, which recognized the lawyer's right to offer such ancillary business services either within the law firm or through a separate entity. (The ABA amended Rule 5.7 in 2002, although the basic thrust of the rule was unchanged.) A majority of states, including the

---

4. But if the lawyer writes nonfiction accounts of his work, the lawyer, absent adequate informed consent from the clients, risks violating the ethics law on confidentiality as well as a waiver of the attorney-client privilege. *See, e.g.,* In re von Bulow, 828 F.2d 94 (2d Cir. 1987) (court considered whether the disclosures in Alan Dershowitz's book, REVERSAL OF FORTUNE, constituted a waiver of the privilege).

5. Moreover, many of the basic constraints of the ethics law, e.g., confidentiality and conflict of interest precepts, have counterparts in the basic law of agency that presumably would apply to the lobbyist-client relationship in any event.

District of Columbia, have adopted Rule 5.7 or one similar to it; [6] other states have endorsed the ancillary business reality through ethics opinions.

Rule 5.7 provides:

(a) a lawyer shall be subject to the Rules of Professional Conduct with respect to the provision of law-related services, as defined in paragraph (b), if the law-related services are provided:

(1) by the lawyer in circumstances that are not distinct from the lawyer's provision of legal services to clients; or

(2) in other circumstances by an entity controlled by the lawyer individually or with others if the lawyer fails to take reasonable measures to assure that a person obtaining law-related services knows that the services are not legal services and that the protections of the client-lawyer relationship do not exist.

(b) The term "law-related services" denotes services that might reasonably be performed in conjunction with and in substance are related to the provision of legal services, and that are not prohibited as unauthorized practice of law when provided by a nonlawyer.

Lobbying work is clearly included within the definition of "law-related services."[7]

While Rule 5.7 does acknowledge that lawyers may provide law-related services and that, in certain circumstances, the Rules of Professional Conduct that govern the lawyer-client relationship will not apply, opting out is not a simple thing. Essentially, the lawyer-lobbyist may opt out of the ethics law governing the lawyer-client relationship only when the law-related services are kept separate and distinct from any legal services rendered to the client and when the lawyer satisfies the high threshold of disclosure set forth in Rule 5.7(a)(2).

Lawyer-lobbyists may have strong incentives for opting out of the constraints and obligations that apply to the lawyer–client relationship. While the ethics law imposes strict confidentiality rules, the lawyer-lobbyist may seek some greater degree of freedom to share information with other clients and third parties. Also, the ethics law's conflict of interest rules may get in the way of a lobbying practice that at times may advance conflicting goals. The constraints within ethics law on fee sharing with non-lawyers and non-lawyer ownership of the practice may interfere with desired partnerships with non-lawyer lobbyists.[8] And the ethics law rules regarding solicitation can be an impediment to vigorous marketing.[9] These sorts of considerations might lead the lawyer-lobbyist to seek to get out from under the ethics law.

---

6. *See* Variations of the ABA Model Rules of Professional Conduct (May 6, 2015), http://www.americanbar.org/content/dam/aba/administrative/professional_responsibility/mrpc_3_8_g_h.authcheckdam.pdf (last visited Sept. 25, 2015).

7. *See* MODEL RULES OF PROF'L CONDUCT R. 5.7 cmt. 9 (2008).

8. *See* MODEL RULES OF PROF'L CONDUCT R. 5.4 (2008). D.C. ethics law on this subject diverges from the Model Rules and permits non-lawyers providing law-related services to have an ownership interest in the law firm subject to certain conditions. *See* D.C. RULES OF PROF'L CONDUCT R. 5.4(b) (2007).

9. *See* MODEL RULES OF PROF'L CONDUCT R. 7.3 (2008).

Yet opting out of the ethics law through Rule 5.7 is tricky business. First, if the lobbying services are intertwined with the provision of legal services by the firm, the ethics law will apply to the rendition of services, both legal and lobbying. Rule 5.7(a)(1) so provides. And in jurisdictions without Rule 5.7, if the legal and lobbying services are not kept separate and distinct, the lawyer as a practical matter would likely be unable to create a representation free from the constraints of the ethics law. Any such agreement would likely be unenforceable as "unreasonable."[10] The rationale for this result is that, when the services are intertwined, the correct lawyer-client relationship, demanding trust and confidentiality, cannot be properly maintained when the lawyer feels free of the constraints of ethics law while performing the law-related services.

On the other hand, if the lawyer-lobbyist can truly separate the provision of services—most obviously by providing the lobbying services through an entity apart from the law firm—then opting out becomes a possibility. Rule 5.7(a)(2) provides, albeit implicitly, that the ethics law will not apply if the lobbying services are rendered through an entity distinct from the law practice, and if the lawyer takes "reasonable measures to assure that a person obtaining the law-related services knows that the services are not legal services and that the protections of the lawyer-client relationship do not exist."

The latter element, "reasonable measures," is a difficult and uncertainly defined hurdle, especially when the lobbying client is a preexisting legal services client. A preexisting lawyer-client relationship means that the ethics law is already in play. First, the very referral of the legal services client to the lobbying entity triggers conflict of interest rule consideration. Rule 1.7(a) defines a "concurrent conflict of interest" as arising whenever "there is a significant risk that the representation [of the client] will be materially limited by . . . a personal interest of the lawyer." The lawyer would routinely have an interest in the lobbying entity and thus would have a personal incentive to steer the client to that entity. The lawyer may, nonetheless, proceed to advise the client to retain the lobbying entity so long as the client gives informed consent, confirmed in writing.[11] Such informed consent would require the lawyer to advise the client of the lawyer's personal interests implicated in the referral.

In most jurisdictions (Maryland is an example of an exception to the rule), the ethics law will deem any agreement for lobbying services through a separate entity for a preexisting legal services client to be a "business transaction" with the client governed by Rule 1.8(a).[12] Rule 1.8(a) imposes three basic requirements: (1) the transaction must be substantively fair to the client; (2) the lawyer must advise the client of the advisability of getting independent representation in

---

10. *See* MODEL RULES OF PROF'L CONDUCT R. 1.2(c) (2008): "A lawyer may limit the scope of the representation *if the limitation is reasonable* under the circumstances and the client gives informed consent" (emphasis added).

11. *See* MODEL RULES OF PROF'L CONDUCT R. 1.7(b)(4) (2008).

12. "When a client-lawyer relationship exists with a person who is referred by a lawyer to a separate law-related service entity controlled by the lawyer, individually or with others, the lawyer must comply with rule 1.8(a)." MODEL RULES OF PROF'L CONDUCT R. 5.7 cmt. 5 (2008). *But see* Maryland Rules of Professional Conduct, Rule 5.7, Comment 5. "A lawyer is not required to comply with Rule 1.8(a) when referring a person to a separate law-related entity owned or controlled by the lawyer . . . If the lawyer also is providing legal services to the person, the lawyer must exercise independent professional judgment in making the referral." *Id.*

constructing the transaction; and (3) if the client is not independently represented, the lawyer must obtain the client's informed and written consent to proceed. "Informed consent" will require various disclosures, including the nature and extent of the lawyer's interest in the lobbying entity. Complying with Rule 1.8 can be especially difficult if the client is not independently represented.

In contrast, if the prospective lobbying client is not a preexisting legal services client, and if the lobbying services are offered through an entity distinct from the law firm, the lawyer-lobbyist can more easily navigate the demands of Rule 5.7. The rule would, nonetheless, require that the lawyer-lobbyist take those "reasonable measures" to make sure that the client understood that the representation was being undertaken outside the protections of the ethics law. The logic of this rule is that a client who is likely aware of the lawyer-lobbyist's professional status as a lawyer might assume that the relationship carried the ordinary protections of the attorney-client relationship. It is the lawyer's responsibility to make clear to the client, even when lobbying services alone are being rendered, that the relationship is not that of attorney-client and that the ordinary protections of ethics law are inapplicable. To discharge this responsibility, the lawyer would need to disclose to the client not merely the fact of the inapplicability of the ethics law but also the practical significance of that fact.[13] Thus, for example, the lawyer-lobbyist would need to explain the practical effect of the loss of the confidentiality and conflicts rules. The Official Comments do acknowledge that a "sophisticated user" of law-related services may need less detailed disclosure of the practical effects, although the burden is always on the lawyer-lobbyist to make sure that the disclosures are sufficient.[14]

In theory, if a client becomes both a legal services client and a lobbying client of the lawyer-lobbyist, the lawyer may assume that the two relationships are distinct and that the ethics law generally is inapplicable to the lobbying relationship. But in practice this would be enormously tricky to pull off. For example, the ethics law says that everything the lawyer comes to know about the legal services client is protected by the rules on confidentiality. How then would the lawyer effectively compartmentalize that duty and somehow feel free to disclose confidences when engaged in the lobbying services?

All of this boils down to a simple pragmatic road map. If the lawyer-lobbyist is offering only lobbying services to the client and not legal services, the lawyer must simply make sure that she has made all this clear to the client, describing in particular the aspects of ethics law that will not apply to the relationship, and that the client has consented to all this in writing. If, on the other hand, the lawyer-lobbyist is mixing the provision of legal services with lobbying services, even when done through a separate lobbying entity, the safest and most sensible approach is simply to assume that the ethics law, including duties of confidentiality and conflict of

---

13. "In taking the reasonable measures referred to in paragraph (a)(2) to assure that a person using law-related services understands the practical effect or significance of the inapplicability of the Rules of Professional Conduct, the lawyer should communicate to the person receiving the law-related services, in a manner sufficient to assure that the person understands the significance of the fact, that the relationship of the person to the business entity will not be a client-lawyer relationship. The communication should be made before entering into an agreement for provision of or providing law-related services, and preferably should be in writing." MODEL RULES OF PROF'L CONDUCT R. 5.7 cmt. 6 (2008).

14. *See* MODEL RULES OF PROF'L CONDUCT R. 5.7 cmt. 7 (2008).

interest rules, applies. If the lawyer-lobbyist has good reason to seek a suspension of those rules in any particular circumstance, he may determine whether the client's informed consent can be appropriately sought and, if so, obtain that informed consent in writing. Seeking instead, at the outset of the relationship, a blanket waiver of the ethics law is a difficult and perilous path.

> **Example 1.** Law firm controls a separate lobbying services entity. Partner with the firm, who also does lobbying work within the structure of the separate entity, undertakes an engagement with a new lobbying client. The law firm has no formal relationship with the client. Partner explains to client that he is providing only lobbying and not legal services. Client says that she understands and is not seeking legal services. The lawyer then proceeds with the lobbying engagement.
>
> *The lawyer has not satisfied the opt-out provision of Rule 5.7, which demands informed consent in writing. The hypothetical sets forth no effort by the lawyer to explain the inapplicability of the ethics law and the practical significance of the absence of the protections of the ethics law. Thus, even though the client expresses acceptance of the lobbying only engagement, this is insufficient under Rule 5.7. The full protections and constraints of the ethics law will apply to this engagement.*

Finally, it is critical to recall that, even if a lawyer successfully opts out of the ordinary provisions of the ethics law, certain provisions of the ethics law still apply. For example, a lawyer who engages in any of the forms of misconduct proscribed in Rule 8.4 is subject to discipline, even when providing only law-related services. Also, the relationship with the lobbying client is still governed by the basic law of agency, which has its own rules on confidentiality and conflicts. Finally, evading the constraints of ethics law does nothing to dilute the lawyer-lobbyist's obligations under civil liability law to render services in a competent manner.

22-4 Confidentiality

The ethics law treats confidentiality as what one ethics scholar has called the "constitutional norm."[15] The basic rule, Model Rule 1.6, provides for an expansive ethical duty of confidentiality with very limited exceptions. The significance of confidentiality can also be seen in the law of attorney-client privilege, a part of the law of evidence.

These two bodies of law, the ethics law of confidentiality and the law of attorney-client privilege, are different in their scope and function. The ethics law imposes a duty upon lawyers that, if transgressed, exposes the lawyer to professional discipline. Also, as explained below, violation of the ethics law on confidentiality can become part of the analysis of other legal issues, most obviously, a negligence claim grounded in the lawyer's disclosure of client confidences. In contrast, the law of attorney-client privilege is a part of evidence law that allows lawyers and clients to resist compelled disclosure of protected communications. The consideration of confidentiality begins with the law of attorney-client privilege.

---

15. Susan P. Koniak, *The Law Between the Bar and the State*, 70 N.C. LAW REV. 1389 (1992).

22-4.1 The Attorney-Client Privilege

Although the precise formulation of the privilege varies somewhat among jurisdictions, the general principle is that communications between lawyer and client (or certain agents thereof) made in confidence for the purpose of seeking legal advice are generally protected from compelled disclosure. The protections of the privilege are often critical to the client. Thus, the lawyer must understand the basic principles of this body of law.

A threshold issue exists for the lawyer-lobbyist—that is, whether the privilege applies at all to communications with the lobbying client. Lawyers who interact with clients in capacities other than a straightforward legal services context risk the loss of the privilege. For example, this has been an issue for many years for lawyers who serve on the client's board of directors. Courts may deem communications between the lawyer-director and the client constituents to be outside the privilege.[16] Recent case law has extended an analogous rationale to lawyer-lobbyists who are providing primarily lobbying or public relations services.[17]

The issue of the lawyer-lobbyist and the attorney-client privilege was at the forefront of a legal challenge to President Clinton's "eleventh hour" pardon of the fugitive financier Marc Rich.[18] In the wake of a public outcry over the pardon, the Southern District of New York empaneled a grand jury to investigate the circumstances of the pardon. The lawyers who had represented Rich in the pardon matter resisted complying with a subpoena demanding the production of documents and the disclosure of attorney-client communications, asserting the attorney-client privilege, as well as work product protection. The court rejected the lawyers' arguments and granted the motion to compel production. The court explained: "The Marc Rich Lawyers were acting principally as lobbyists, working with public relations specialists and individuals—foreign government officials, prominent citizens, and personal friends of the president—who had access to the White House. They were not acting as lawyers or providing legal advice in the traditional sense. Accordingly, the objections based on the work product doctrine and attorney-client privilege are overruled."[19] Thus, the case exemplifies the principle that lawyers rendering lobbying services may not simply assume that the privilege will apply.

The case law on the attorney-client privilege as applied to lobbyist-lawyers reflects a divergence in approach, but there is a persistent suggestion that the issue is "fact specific."[20] Thus, on the one hand, the fact that the person performing the lobbying services is also a licensed attorney does not mean that communications with the lawyer-lobbyist are necessarily protected by the privilege. On the other hand, courts recognize that a lawyer retained to perform lobbying services may

---

16. *See, e.g.,* SEC v. Gulf & Western Industries, Inc., 518 F. Supp. 675 (D.D.C. 1981).

17. "Thus, O'Hara [the lawyer-lobbyist] was wearing multiple hats and if he was advising NXIVM on anything and everything other than legal services, whether business, media, public relations, or lobbying, there is no attorney-client privilege." NXIVM Corp. v. O'Hara, 241 F.R.D 109, 130 (N.D.N.Y. 2007).

18. *In re* Grand Jury Subpoenas, 179 F. Supp. 2d 270 (S.D.N.Y. 2001).

19. *Id.* at 274.

20. *See, e.g.,* Black v. Southwestern Water Conservation District, 74 P.3d 462 (Ct. App. CO. 2003) (asserting that the inquiry is "fact specific" and that the essential question is whether the communications were made for the purpose of seeking legal advice as opposed to lobbying services).

also at times be consulted by the client on legal matters and that such communications may well be within the privilege.[21]

As a practical matter, the lawyer-lobbyist who is mixing legal and lobbying services runs an inescapable risk that, if challenged, a court applying a fact-specific analysis may conclude that the protections of the attorney-client privilege do not apply to communications with the client. This risk should be explained to the lobbying services client at the outset of the representation. And if the lawyer-lobbyist chooses to construct a representation restricted to lobbying in an effort to evade the constraints of the ethics law, the attorney-client privilege presumably will be inapplicable to her communications.

> **Example 2.** Client retains lawyer-lobbyist to push for the passage of a particular amendment to the Internal Revenue Code. Lawyer and client jointly develop a lobbying strategy. Lawyer-lobbyist contacts key legislative staffers and sends client updates on each of these contacts. Contemporaneously, lawyer engages a public relations specialist on behalf of the client to seek favorable press coverage of the proposed amendment. While this work is ongoing, the IRS undertakes an investigation of possible tax fraud by the client and serves lawyer with a subpoena compelling the lawyer to produce various documents related to the representation and to appear at a deposition.
>
> *Although any actual case would involve a more complete set of facts, the facts of this hypothetical suggest that the privilege is inapplicable. The privilege demands that the communications be for the purpose of seeking or providing legal services. These facts suggest that the lawyer is providing merely lobbying services.*

Even when the privilege applies, it can be waived by disclosure or by other acts.[22] Thus, the lawyer-lobbyist must be aware that the disclosure of otherwise privileged communications as part of a lobbying activity, even in a nonpublic setting (e.g., a letter to a regulator or elected official), likely waives protection of the privilege in any future context.

---

21. "The fact that a lawyer occasionally acts as a lobbyist does not preclude the lawyer from acting as a lawyer and having privileged communications with a client who is seeking legal advice. Many lawyers 'have expertise in special areas of knowledge that enhances their skill as lawyers, and that does not diminish their legal status.'" *In re* Grand Jury Subpoenas, 179 F. Supp. 2d at 285 (quoting Montgomery Co. v. MicroVote Corp., 175 F.3d 296, 302 (3d Cir. 1999)).

However, "if a lawyer happens to act as a lobbyist, matters conveyed to the attorney for the purpose of having the attorney fulfill the lobbyist role do not become privileged by virtue of the fact that the lobbyist has a law degree or may under other circumstances give legal advice to the client, including advice on matters that may also be the subject of lobbying efforts." *In re* Grand Jury Subpoenas, 179 F. Supp. 2d at 285 (quoting Edna Stein Epstein, THE ATTORNEY-CLIENT PRIVILEGE & THE WORK PRODUCT DOCTRINE 239 (2001)). "Summaries of legislative meetings, progress reports, and general updates on lobbying activities do not constitute legal advice and therefore are not protected by the attorney-client privilege or work product doctrine." Black v. Southwestern Water Conservation District, 74 P.3d at 468.

22. *See generally* George A. Davidson & William H. Voth, *Waiver of the Attorney-Client Privilege*, 64 OR. L. REV. 637 (1986).

22-4.2 The Ethical Duty of Confidentiality

Model Rule 1.6 is the central confidentiality rule of the ethics law. It provides:

(a) A lawyer shall not reveal information relating to the representation of a client unless the client gives informed consent, the disclosure is impliedly authorized in order to carry out the representation or the disclosure is permitted by paragraph (b).

(b) A lawyer may reveal information relating to the representation of a client to the extent the lawyer reasonably believes necessary:

 (1) to prevent reasonably certain death or substantial bodily harm;

 (2) to prevent the client from committing a crime or fraud that is reasonably certain to result in substantial injury to the financial interests or property of another and in furtherance of which the client has used or is using the lawyer's services;

 (3) to prevent, mitigate or rectify substantial injury to the financial interests or property of another that is reasonably certain to result or has resulted from the client's commission of a crime or fraud in furtherance of which the client has used the lawyer's services;

 (4) to secure legal advice about the lawyer's compliance with these Rules;

 (5) to establish a claim or defense on behalf of the lawyer in a controversy between the lawyer and the client, to establish a defense to a criminal charge or civil claim against the lawyer based upon conduct in which the client was involved, or to respond to allegations in any proceeding concerning the lawyer's representation of the client;

 (6) to comply with other law or a court order; or

 (7) to detect and resolve conflicts of interest arising from the lawyer's change of employment or from changes in the composition or ownership of a firm, but only if the revealed information would not compromise the attorney-client privilege or otherwise prejudice the client.

(c) A lawyer shall make reasonable efforts to prevent the inadvertent or unauthorized disclosure of, or unauthorized access to, information relating to the representation of a client.[23]

The ethical duty of confidentiality emanates from values and concerns that also support the attorney-client privilege, namely, the concern that clients be able to trust their lawyers to keep confidences. This trust, it is supposed, facilitates open and frank communications between clients and lawyers, which in turn facilitate more effective representation. Client candor also allows the lawyer to more fully inform the client of the client's legal obligations.

---

23. The D.C. ethics law on confidentiality sets forth more detailed text addressing certain specific confidentiality issues, but the essential principles of the D.C. rule are consistent with the ABA Model Rule. *See* D.C. RULES OF PROF'L CONDUCT R. 1.6 (2007).

The ethical duty of confidentiality, however, importantly differs from the privilege. First, the duty of confidentiality covers everything that a lawyer knows with regard to the client and the client's affairs, whatever the source of the information. In contrast, the privilege extends only to certain lawyer-client communications. Second, the ethical duty of confidentiality obliges the lawyer to keep the client's confidences unless the client consents or the disclosure is impliedly authorized or the disclosure falls into one of the narrowly drawn exceptions of Rule 1.6(b). The duty applies in all settings, unlike the privilege which operates only in circumstances of compelled disclosure, (e.g., responses to subpoenas, depositions, and trial testimony).

While all lawyers must take care to conform their conduct to the ethics law on confidentiality, the lawyer-lobbyist, by the nature of the practice, will routinely run into situations that call for careful attention to the confidentiality rules. The very idea of lobbying is to communicate with third parties on behalf of the client. These communications will often involve explanations of the client's interests and conduct, information presumptively protected by the duty of confidentiality. Communicating to the client the lobbying strategy and the likely disclosures and obtaining client consent to such disclosures are key to navigating this domain of ethics law. While some disclosures are surely impliedly authorized (e.g., the fact that the client has retained the lawyer-lobbyist or strategically driven responses to inquiries from legislators and others "on the spot"), any disclosures that are not so obviously authorized and that involve sensitive data should ideally be the subject of client consent.

Lawyers are ceaselessly making choices to disclose information that falls within the broad zone of confidential information protected by Rule 1.6. As a practical matter, many, if not most, of those disclosures are done pursuant to implied authority. In such cases, the demands of the ethics law on confidentiality overlap with the duty of competent representation. That is, the lawyer's reliance on implied authority to reveal confidences will likely pose little risk so long as the decision to make such disclosures is reasonable and well within the range of competent lawyering.

Other laws regulating the conduct of the lawyer-lobbyist may require disclosure of confidential information as part of a registration and disclosure process (including that created by the Lobbying Disclosure Act, which mandates disclosure of, among other information, fees paid to lobbying firms and contributions from third parties used to pay for lobbying services on behalf of the client[24]). While Rule 1.6 (b)(6) does permit a lawyer to make disclosures "to comply with other law," the lawyer-lobbyist should nonetheless make sure that the client is aware of any such necessary disclosures. Also, the ethically permitted disclosure in these cases is limited by the phrase, "to the extent the lawyer reasonably believes [the disclosure is] necessary."

22-5 Conflicts of Interest

The second major set of concerns within the ethics law is conflict of interest. Lawyers cannot make their way without conflicts. The very engagement of the lawyer

---

24. See Section 4-4 of this manual.

puts into play a potential conflict between the client's interests and the lawyer's interests. At the simplest level, the client wishes to pay less for more service, while the lawyer wishes to be paid more for less service. The ethics law on conflicts of interest thus does not command the lawyer to refrain from working in the presence of conflict—a practical impossibility—but rather specifies and precludes certain circumstances that pose serious risks of the subordination of the client's interests.

Lawyers often struggle with the conflicts rules. Ethics law on conflicts is a complex and uncertain domain. Large law firms with multiple offices and a long list of firm clients must pay careful attention to potential conflicts.[25] When those firms take on lobbying work, the problems compound. In conventional practice, the outcomes obtained for a particular client are unlikely to harm the interests of another client. Winning a lawsuit or concluding a commercial transaction on behalf of a client rarely affects directly and negatively the position of another client not a party to the litigation or the deal. But a successful lobbying initiative often shapes the laws of general application in ways that, while beneficial to the lobbying client, may well harm the interests of other firm clients. Thus, the lawyer-lobbyist must take care to understand the ethics law on this subject and to be watchful for conflicts issues.

Combining a law practice with lobbying services on behalf of trade associations or other industry groups creates special risks of conflicts. If the lawyer-lobbyist is deemed to have entered into a lawyer-client relationship with each corporate member of such a trade group, the list of firm clients to whom duties of loyalty and confidentiality are owed multiplies, as the important case discussed in the next section demonstrates.

22-5.1 The *Westinghouse* Case as Illustrative

Westinghouse Elec. Corp. v. Kerr-McGee Corp.[26] well illustrates the risks of conflicts for the lawyer-lobbyist. In this case, the D.C. office of Kirkland & Ellis represented the American Petroleum Institute (API) in lobbying efforts to defeat proposals in the mid-1970s to break up the oil companies. API was a nonprofit corporation with over 300 corporate members and thousands of individual members. In the course of this representation, the Kirkland lawyers reviewed questionnaires completed by API members and conducted interviews with various oil company executives. Their work culminated in a lengthy and substantially documented report from Kirkland to API that asserted essentially that the energy industry in each of its segments was highly competitive.

On the same day that the D.C. Kirkland office delivered its final report to API, the Chicago office of Kirkland filed an antitrust action on behalf of Westinghouse against various corporate defendants connected with the uranium industry. The

---

25. In Westinghouse Elec. Corp. v. Kerr-McGee Corp., 580 F. 2d 1311 (7th Cir. 1978), to be discussed in Section 22-5.1 of this chapter, the law firm sought to defend its conduct by noting that it was a large law firm with multiple offices and that the lawyers working for one client were resident in the D.C. office while the lawyers in the second matter worked from the Chicago office. The Seventh Circuit was unimpressed with the argument. *Id.* at 1318. *But see* U.S. for Use and Benefit of Lord Elec. Co. v. Titan Pac. Const. Corp., 637 F. Supp. 1556, 1564 (W.D. Wash. 1986) (noting that the Seventh Circuit's post-*Westinghouse* cases established that the presumption that lawyers working together within a firm will share confidential information is a rebuttable presumption).

26. 580 F. 2d 1311 (7th Cir. 1978).

gist of Westinghouse's complaint was that the uranium industry was monopolistic in nature and that the defendants had violated the antitrust law. Several of these defendants were corporate members of API. These API member corporations had completed questionnaires that were provided to the law firm as part of the research for the API report. Also their executives had participated in interviews with the firm's lawyers. These defendants brought a disqualification motion against the law firm in the Westinghouse litigation. While the district court denied the motion, the Seventh Circuit reversed and held that Westinghouse had to either fire their lawyers or dismiss the API corporations from the lawsuit. The client chose ultimately to find new representation.

The Seventh Circuit opinion addresses several issues critical to the lawyer-lobbyist. The corporate defendants argued that they were clients of the Kirkland firm and, as such, the firm's filing of the antitrust action represented the law firm suing one client on behalf of another—a blatant conflict of interest and a clear basis for disqualification. The lawyers argued that the client was only API, noting that the corporations had paid no fee directly to the law firm and that there was no explicit agreement for representation between the law firm and the corporations. But the Seventh Circuit noted that fees or formal agreements, while common indicia of the lawyer-client relationship, are not essential to the formation of the relationship.[27] In fact, the court considered the possibility of imposing upon the law firm an attorney-client relationship with each and every member of the API, but decided instead to resolve the issue on a "more narrow ground."[28]

While choosing not to impose a formal attorney-client relationship, the court nonetheless concluded that the sharing of confidential information with the lawyers on the corporations' reasonable assumption that the information would not be used against them was sufficient to ground an "implied professional relation" between the law firm and the API member defendants.[29] Although not a formal attorney-client relationship, this implied professional relationship, the court concluded, was a sufficient basis for the disqualification of the firm.[30]

The Seventh Circuit also rejected the notion that the law firm's size and use of multiple offices justified a more lenient conception of the conflicts rules.[31] In fact, the court applied a blunt rule of imputation, concluding that the knowledge of confidential information possessed by the D.C. Kirkland lawyers involved in the API representation should be imputed to all Kirkland lawyers, including those in the Chicago office representing Westinghouse.[32] The court rejected the firm's argument that "screening" of the D.C. lawyers and the Chicago lawyers was a sufficient protection.[33]

The *Westinghouse* case also posed the issue of "positional conflict." That is, the position advanced by the law firm in the API report—that the energy industry, including the uranium industry, was fully competitive—was in direct conflict

---

27. *Id.* at 1317.

28. *Id.* at 1319.

29. *Id.*

30. The Seventh Circuit put Westinghouse to the choice—fire your lawyers or dismiss the API corporate defendants. Thus, the remedy was in effect a functional disqualification. *Id.* at 1322.

31. *Id.* at 1318.

32. *Id.* at 1321.

33. *Id.*

with the premises of the antitrust complaint filed on behalf of Westinghouse. The court merely noted this conflict, without analysis.[34] Presumably, the sufficiency of the "implied professional relationship" basis for disqualification made this analysis superfluous. (See the more general discussion of positional conflicts in Section 22-5.3 of this chapter.)

The lessons of *Westinghouse* are significant. First, the case illustrates that undertaking lobbying work on behalf of trade associations creates the possibility for dramatic expansion of the firm's ethical obligations. Although the court focused on the sharing of confidential information to build the implied professional relationship, the nature of lobbying work often involves the gathering of information from the constituents of a trade association. Second, the broad imputation rule recognized in the *Westinghouse* case and its rejection of the screening remedy suggest that a major law firm that conducts lobbying work can risk an imputation that would dramatically limit the firm's representation in any matters that relate to the lobbying work and that result in taking an adverse position against any of the trade association constituents.[35] Finally, the case is a reminder that the effects of the conflicts law can play out in ways other than the risk of professional discipline under the ethics law. In fact, the threat of disqualification motions is a more significant risk than professional discipline. And following any successful disqualification motion, a firm may have to contend with an unhappy client who must seek new counsel and who has a presumptive malpractice claim against the law firm.[36] After all, "reasonable care" in lawyering entails, among other things, avoiding ethically impermissible conflicts that cause harm to the client.

When sorting through the ethics law on conflicts, one must understand that it is not enough for the lawyer to be satisfied in her own head that she is able to fulfill her duties to all of her clients, current and former. Ethics law, as well as the law of civil liability, responds to actual breaches of loyal and competent representation. The ethics law rules on conflicts are directed to circumstances where the *risks* of such breaches are intolerably high. Those circumstances can exist even when the lawyer is convinced that loyalty and competent representation are maintained.

Analysis of conflicts under ethics law generally separates the topic into concurrent and successive conflicts. Concurrent conflicts can arise when the interests of current clients or third parties diverge. Successive conflicts arise when the lawyer's duty to a former client diverges from the interests of a current client. The following discussion begins with concurrent conflicts.

---

34. *Id.* at 1314.

35. At the time of the *Westinghouse* decision, the ABA Model Rules embodied a broad imputation rule. Model Rule 1.10(a) provided: "While lawyers are associated in a firm, none of them shall knowingly represent a client when any one of them practicing alone would be prohibited from doing so by Rules 1.7 [concurrent conflicts rule] or 1.9 [successive conflicts rule], unless the prohibition is based on a personal interest of the prohibited lawyer and does not present a significant risk of materially limiting the representation of the client by the remaining lawyers in the firm." In 2009 the ABA amended Model Rule 1.10 to allow screening as a remedy in successive conflict cases. *See* text at note 42 *infra*. The new "screening" version of Rule 1.10, however, applies only to successive conflicts scenarios. On its facts *Westinghouse* posed instead a concurrent conflicts problem.

36. In fact, in the *Westinghouse* case, the client did consider seeking a recovery of the approximately $3 million in fees paid to the law firm, although it chose not to pursue the claim. *See* Geoffrey Hazard et al., THE LAW AND ETHICS OF LAWYERING 408, n. 9 (4th ed. 2005).

22-5.2 Concurrent Conflicts

Although navigation of the ethics law on conflicts is often difficult, the central ideas form a basic orientation for the practicing lawyer. Generally, in concurrent conflicts, the duty of *loyalty* is the primary duty at risk. Loyalty is at risk when the interests of one client tug in one direction while the interests of another client push the opposite way. Thus, the focus generally should be on the degree of *adversity* among the interests of the clients involved.

For example, two clients seeking directly opposite outcomes with regard to a particular piece of legislation—one seeks its passage, the other its defeat—exhibit real adversity in their respective interests. A lawyer would struggle mightily (and likely to no avail) to maintain loyalty to each client while representing either of them in the lobbying work on that legislation. In contrast, if one client seeks passage of a particular tax deduction while the other client is indifferent to that particular tax issue, but is seeking an unrelated tax deduction, success for one client may make success for the second client incrementally more difficult. Thus, it would not be accurate to say that there is no adversity whatever in the clients' interests in that case. On the other hand, the adversity is contingent, and likely sufficiently diluted, to satisfy the ethics law.

The central conflicts rule for concurrent conflicts is embodied in Model Rule 1.7:

(a) Except as provided in paragraph (b), a lawyer shall not represent a client if the representation involves a concurrent conflict of interest. A concurrent conflict of interest exists if:

   (1) the representation of one client will be directly adverse to another client; or
   (2) there is a significant risk that the representation of one or more clients will be materially limited by the lawyer's responsibilities to another client, a former client or a third person or by a personal interest of the lawyer.

(b) Notwithstanding the existence of a concurrent conflict of interest under paragraph (a), a lawyer may represent a client if:

   (1) the lawyer reasonably believes that the lawyer will be able to provide competent and diligent representation to each affected client;
   (2) the representation is not prohibited by law;
   (3) the representation does not involve the assertion of a claim by one client against another client represented by the lawyer in the same litigation or other proceeding before a tribunal; and
   (4) each affected client gives informed consent, confirmed in writing.[37]

---

37. The text of D.C. Rule of Prof'l Conduct 1.7 differs in various respects from the ABA Model Rule. Yet, the essential obligations remain the same. For example, D.C. Rule of Prof'l Conduct 1.7(d) seems to permit the lawyer to continue the representation if a concurrent conflict arises after the representation commences and the conflict was not "reasonably foreseeable." But this only applies if the representation of the client is not likely to be adversely affected. Thus, the two rules essentially converge on this matter.

With regard to concurrent conflicts, ethics law identifies two kinds of conflicts: directly adverse conflicts under Rule 1.7(a)(1) and "material limitation" conflicts as described in Rule 1.7(a)(2). An example of a directly adverse conflict would be for a lawyer to represent a client as plaintiff in a litigation matter in which another client was a defendant. Such conflicts typically cannot be waived by consent of the client. That is, the ethics law presumes that the essential qualities of trust and commitment between lawyer and client cannot be maintained when the lawyer is suing one of his own clients. It would not be reasonable for the lawyer in such circumstances to seek client consent. Such directly adverse conflicts are not limited to litigation settings. A lawyer ordinarily may not represent the client in a transaction when another client is sitting across the table.

Directly adverse conflicts are uncommon because lawyers can ordinarily easily discern the potential of such a conflict. The *Westinghouse* case, however, illustrates the complexity that can arise in particular circumstances. In that case, the firm found itself suing on behalf of one client (Westinghouse) another set of parties to whom it owed fiduciary duties (the API corporate defendants). In other words, *Westinghouse* operates as a reminder that the conventional category of a fee-paying, explicit "client" does not exhaust the realm of parties to whom the lawyer-lobbyist may owe legally recognized duties that might translate into successful disqualification and potential civil liability.

The more commonly encountered conflict, and the one that the lawyer-lobbyist must be especially watchful for, is the material limitation conflict. The essential idea of this conflict is that a lawyer must avoid representation where the lawyer is likely to consider "pulling his punches" out of regard for another client. For example, if a lawyer representing the plaintiff in a litigation matter is offered an attractive settlement, but one that would work to the disadvantage of another client, the lawyer would be in an untenable position. Loyalty to the plaintiff client would dictate advising the client to take the deal. But loyalty to the other client would counsel resisting the settlement.[38]

A lobbying practice is likely to present such conflicts issues. For example, lobbying for tougher workplace safety regulations on behalf of a union client might conflict with duties of loyalty to other clients who oppose the regulations because their workplaces would be subject to stricter controls. Sometimes this type of conflict will be less direct and simple. Working to achieve particular tax credits for one industry, for example, may effectively thwart, or at least significantly hamper, efforts for tax reduction for other clients. Ethics law, however, takes account of the practical necessity for lawyers to sometimes act on behalf of one client in ways that may indirectly disadvantage another client. Thus, for example, the legal representation of two competing companies is not ordinarily deemed an impermissible conflict.[39]

As previously explained, the key to analyzing concurrent conflicts generally is to look to the degree of adversity among the clients and their interests and place that adversity within one of three basic categories. First, when the adversity is

---

38. This hypothetical is drawn from Fiandaca v. Cunningham, 827 F.2d 825 (1st Cir. 1987).

39. "[S]imultaneous representation in unrelated matters of clients whose interests are only economically adverse, such as representation of competing economic enterprises in unrelated litigation, does not ordinarily constitute a conflict of interest." MODEL RULES OF PROF'L CONDUCT R. 1.7 cmt. 6 (2008).

direct and significant, as when a lawyer proposes to sue one client on behalf of another client, the representation is ethically impermissible. Second, if the adversity is less confrontational, but nonetheless the risk of impaired representation is real, the lawyer must seek the informed written consent of each affected client. This presumably would be the case where the lawyer-lobbyist seeks passage of a bill that is opposed by another client. Finally, when the adversity is attenuated, as in the ordinary course of representation of competing businesses, the lawyer may proceed without seeking consent. This would probably encompass the situation where the lawyer-lobbyist simultaneously seeks tax relief of different sorts on behalf of multiple clients in a legislative environment where such relief is likely to be a very limited commodity as a practical matter.

Example 3. Lawyer undertakes to lobby on behalf of an environmental organization for a federal ban on concealed weapons in any federally controlled property including national parks. Lawyer also represents the Firearms Manufacturers Association on another legislative matter, a proposed bill to immunize handgun manufacturers from tort liability, but the Association strongly opposes the "concealed weapons" bill.

While the two clients, the environmental group and the Association, are not clearly in a directly adverse position, the lawyer's duties of loyalty to each client are in tension. This tension seems more than attenuated in the circumstances presented. While the actual best resolution would depend upon the development of a more complete set of facts, it seems that disclosure of the two representations to each client with informed consent from each would be the correct course of action. Note that consent in these matters must come from each client. The firearms group needs to know that its lawyers are actively pushing for legislation that it opposes. But the environmental organization needs to appreciate the risk of the lawyer pulling his punches in the lobbying work out of regard for the other client. Thus, each client must be informed and must consent. Moreover, even if a lawyer were to conclude that the applicable ethics law did not compel such disclosure and consent, the practical necessity of maintaining good client relations suggests disclosure will often be a good idea.

Example 4. Lawyer seeks a tax deduction for oil exploration on behalf of an energy company client. The chairperson of the critical legislative committee has agreed to sponsor the bill. Another client, a software developer, has asked the lawyer to represent it in lobbying efforts to get favorable changes to the copyright law. But the lawyer knows that the chairperson strongly opposes the copyright law amendments.

Depending upon a more complete elaboration of the factual setting, this case could fall within the third category of more attenuated conflicts. The reality is that legislative lobbying carries with it the potential, if not the certainty, of eliciting the ire or distrust of influential legislators whose support may be critical to initiatives that may be sought by other clients. On the other hand, while the risk of violating the ethics law may be slim, client relations are another matter. Thus, as in the previous example disclosure of this risk to each affected client may be simply good practice, even if the ethics law does not command seeking consent.

Within the lobbying context, as previously noted, category one conflicts, direct adversity, will be rare. Conflicts within the second category, however, are likely to arise more frequently. The lines between these categories are like other legal boundaries—inherently impossible to predict with precision and assurance, but nonetheless reasonably navigable. In circumstances where the lawyer is unsure, the safer course of action always will be to assume that the representation will be viewed in the more restrictive category. As a practical matter, this means seeking client consent when in doubt.

22-5.3 Positional Conflicts

Positional conflicts represent a particular form of concurrent conflict.[40] Positional conflicts arise when the lawyer takes inconsistent positions in two separate proceedings. The *Westinghouse* case provides an example. In one proceeding, the lobbying effort for the client API, the firm argued for the existence of a competitive market in the energy industry generally and the uranium industry specifically. In another contemporaneous proceeding, the litigation matter, the firm argued that the uranium industry was monopolistic in its structure. The two positions conflicted, hence the positional conflict.

The Official Comment to Model Rule 1.7 provides that a conflict exists whenever "a decision favoring one client will create a precedent likely to seriously weaken the position taken on behalf of the other client."[41]

While conventional wisdom suggests that positional conflicts are rarely problematic, reality is more complex, especially for the lawyer-lobbyist. The debate about positional conflicts tends to focus on litigation and the creation of case law precedents. Because the lobbyist often works outside the litigation realm, it is easy to dismiss the issue. But the underlying principles operate in the lobbying realm as well. The essential principle is that lawyers should not undertake representations that conflict with responsibilities owed to other clients. Pushing for a binding precedent on behalf of one client that would undercut the legal position of another client is the easy example. But consider the positional conflict in the *Westinghouse* case. Persuading Congress to back off regulation of the industry will not establish a legal precedent that would result in the dismissal of the antitrust claim in the litigation matter. On the other hand, publicly arguing for the API stance on competitiveness and compiling and presenting factual evidence in support of that position could harm the litigation client's position. At a minimum, the trial lawyer on the other side of the litigation matter would likely seek to introduce the report into evidence and to make sure that the judge and jury noted its authorship. Of course the concerns run in the other direction as well. The lobbying client might easily find itself seeking to explain to the congressional committee why its lawyers had just filed a claim that contradicted the lobbying position taken.

None of this suggests that the lawyer-lobbyist will be in violation of Rule 1.7 whenever a client ends up disadvantaged by the lawyer's successful representation of another client. On the other hand, it is clear that the risks posed by positional conflicts are not restricted to litigation representations. Whenever in doubt,

---

40. *See generally* John Dzienkowski, *Positional Conflicts of Interest*, 71 Tex. L. Rev. 457 (1993).
41. *See* ABA Model Rules of Prof'l Conduct R. 1.7 cmt. 24 (2008).

the safer course of action will be to seek the informed written consent of each affected client. While the risk of professional discipline may be slight, the risks of engaging in two essentially contradictory representations without informing each client and getting consent are quite real. After all, one of the clients is likely to be disappointed in the outcome. The disappointed client who understands the nature of the two representations and consents is less likely to sue the lawyer (and less likely to have a viable claim) than the client kept out of the loop.

22-5.4 Successive Conflicts

Successive conflicts represent the second domain of conflict. These conflicts arise when a lawyer's obligations to a current client impermissibly conflict with the lawyer's obligations to a former client. It is generally said that lawyers owe duties of confidentiality, but not loyalty, to former clients. Thus, a lawyer may even sue a former client so long as the matter is sufficiently unrelated to the former representation that it poses no serious risk of the use of confidential information obtained through the former representation. For example, a lawyer who represented a client in a personal injury case presumably may subsequently represent the former client's landlord in a dispute with the former client over the payment of rent. The risk of the use of confidential information gathered in the personal injury case seems highly unlikely.

ABA Model Rule 1.9(a) is the principal rule governing successive conflicts.

> A lawyer who has formerly represented a client in a matter shall not thereafter represent another person in the same or a substantially related matter in which that person's interests are materially adverse to the interests of the former client unless the former client gives informed consent, confirmed in writing.

In successive conflicts, as a general matter, the duty of *confidentiality* to the former client is at risk. Thus, the focus is on the *relatedness* between the subject of the former representation and the subject of the current representation. The more related the subjects, the more likely that the lawyer will be able to use the confidential information gained from the former client in the new representation.

> **Example 5.** Consider the basic narrative of the *Westinghouse* case, but assume that the law firm had concluded the API lobbying representation and thus API was a former client. Thereafter, the firm files the antitrust claims against the corporate members of API.
> *Although the rule speaks of former clients, it is possible that the "implied professional relationship" found in the Westinghouse case could be sufficient to satisfy the conception of "client" as used in Rule 1.9. If so, the subject of the API representation, which included an analysis of the competitiveness of the uranium industry, and the subject of the litigation claim, a claim that challenged the competitiveness of that very industry, are substantially related. That is, the risk that the lawyers might use confidential information gathered from the API work to advance the antitrust claim against the corporate defendants seems quite high. Thus, this example would almost surely represent an ethically impermissible*

*representation under Rule 1.9(a), assuming again that the relationship was
deemed that of a client.*

*A more difficult question posed by the above problem above is whether the
firm might avoid the conflict problem by screening the firm's API lawyers from
the antitrust litigators. In 2009 the ABA amended Model Rule 1.10 to permit
screening as a potential solution to the successive conflicts problem. (Concurrent
conflicts remained subject to the blunt imputation rule.)*

*Reasons exist though to question the sufficiency of screening as a response to
the successive conflicts problem. First, most states, and D.C., have not adopted
the new version of Model Rule 1.10.*[42] *Second, the ethics laws do not bind judges
deciding disqualification motions. Although judges routinely turn to the ethics
law for guidance, a judge is free to conclude that other considerations override
the outcome apparently dictated by an application of the ethics law. On the
other hand, this judicial autonomy may be exercised to find that screening is an
adequate response, whatever the ethics law provides.*

Professional discipline for conflicts is rare. Much more likely is the use of such
conflicts as the basis for disqualification motions. If a firm performs both lobbying and legal services, including litigation work, for a large number of clients, the
risks of conflict and disqualification must be taken seriously. Today firms routinely
have systems in place to detect conflicts. But these systems must be sophisticated
enough to discern the non-obvious conflicts that any legal practice, but perhaps
especially a mixed legal/lobbying practice, pose.

Conflicted representation also enhances the lawyer's risks of civil liability. First, as previously described in the analysis of the *Westinghouse* case, the
lawyer who loses the disqualification motion is thereby exposed to a malpractice claim from the client who must bear the costs of seeking and obtaining new
representation. Second, if a client is unhappy with the prior representation and
its outcome and thus sues the lawyer for malpractice, the presence of a conflict
that might explain the lawyer's less than devoted and diligent effort can be relevant and influential in the malpractice case. For example, if a lobbying client
sued a law firm for negligence in its effort to obtain a casino license, and if the
law firm happened to represent on other matters the successful competitor in
the casino licensing matter, the presence of that conflict could be relevant in the
malpractice case.[43]

22-5.5 Former Government Lawyers

The ranks of lawyer-lobbyists include many former government lawyers. The
so-called revolving door between government service and private practice poses

---

42. *See* the ABA chart at http://www.americanbar.org/content/dam/aba/administrative
/professional_responsibility/lateral_screening.authcheckdam.pdf (last visited Sept. 25, 2015).

43. Malpractice claims are often joined with claims for breach of fiduciary duty. To engage in conflicted representation can be deemed a breach of this duty. Damages for such breach can, at a minimum,
include fee disgorgement.

important issues.[44] On the one hand, the law recognizes the utility of the tradition of citizen participation in government service in lieu of a purely lifetime civil service model. At the same time, the possibilities for corruption and abuse of power are real. The body of law that addresses these issues is large and complex. This chapter addresses only the ethics law's special rules for conflicts in the practice of former government lawyers.

The general principle of successive conflicts as reflected in Model Rule 1.9(a) is that a lawyer may not represent a client in any matter substantially related to a matter on which he or she worked for a former client when the new representation is adverse to the interests of the former client. In a sense, it is a "no switching sides" rule. The ethics law, however, treats former government lawyers differently.

Model Rule 1.11(a) embodies the basic conflicts rule applying to former government lawyers:

(a) Except as law may otherwise expressly permit, a lawyer who has formerly served as a public officer or employee of the government: (1) is subject to Rule 1.9(c) [forbidding the use of information against the interests of the former client]; and (2) shall not otherwise represent a client in connection with a matter in which the lawyer participated personally and substantially as a public officer or employee, unless the appropriate government agency gives its informed consent, confirmed in writing, to the representation.[45]

This section prohibits the former government lawyer from representing a client in a "matter" in which the lawyer "participated personally and substantially" while in government service unless the government agency consents. The rule on its face is not a simple ban against switching sides. In the absence of informed consent, the lawyer may not pursue a matter on which she worked as a government lawyer even when her new client's interests seem consistent with the government's interests in the matter. For example, when a former SEC lawyer who worked on a securities fraud matter while employed by the government entered private practice and then pursued the same defendants for securities fraud on behalf of the plaintiff in a private securities fraud case, the court disqualified the lawyer and his law firm.[46] The court explained the logic of this rule in this fashion:

---

44. For a detailed discussion of statutory and other post-employment restrictions applicable to congressional and executive branch employees, see Chapters 27 and 28 of this manual. Those subject to such restrictions should pay careful attention to instances where the governing non-ethics rule and the ethics rule differ (e.g., where conduct would not violate the applicable ethics rule regarding conflicts, but where a statute nevertheless forbids the conduct).

45. There are two important substantive differences between the ABA and D.C. ethics law on this subject. First, the D.C. rule does not provide for government agency consent for the former government lawyer to proceed personally with the representation. Under the D.C. ethics law, the former government lawyer is simply disqualified. Second, if a former government lawyer's firm wishes to screen the "tainted" lawyer and proceed with the representation, the D.C. rule requires the firm to notify both the government agency and the parties and to represent to the agency and parties that the firm will maintain the screening. *See* D.C. RULES OF PROF'L CONDUCT R. 1.11 (2007).

46. *See* SIPC v. Vigman, 587 F. Supp. 1358 (C.D. Cal. 1984).

[The rule seeks] to avoid the manifest possibility . . . [that a former government lawyer's] action as a public legal official might be influenced (or open to the charge it had been influenced) by the hope of later being employed privately to *uphold* or *upset* what he had done.[47]

The idea is that we do not want to allow the perception that government lawyers, while working for the government, are looking to the door and either undermining the case against the private party or pursuing the private party simply to set them up for a civil suit once the lawyer jumps to private practice. The rule thus reflects a concern for the appearance of impropriety in these "revolving door" representations.

On the other hand, the requirement of "personal and substantial participation" and the definition of "matter" limit the sweep of this conflicts rule. For example, a government lawyer with supervisory responsibilities who had merely been briefed on a matter that was handled by subordinate lawyers would not likely be deemed to have personally and substantially participated in the matter. Also, the reference to "specific party or parties" in the definition of "matter" in Rule 1.11(e) reflects the idea that a government lawyer's participation in broader policy matters, such as rulemaking or legislation, would likely not provide the basis for disqualifying the lawyer from working on related matters in a private practice setting.

Also, Rule 1.11(b) permits a law firm to screen the tainted former government lawyer from participation in the representation and thus presumably avoid the disqualification of the entire firm. The firm must also not share any fees earned from its representation with the former government lawyer, and the firm must notify the government agency of the representation.

> **Example 6.** Justice Department lawyer writes an appellate brief in opposition to a habeas petition brought by a person detained as an illegal alien. The lawyer leaves government and enters private practice. The detained person ultimately prevails in the habeas proceeding and thereafter asks the lawyer's new firm to represent him in a civil suit against the government and certain specific government actors for damages caused by the illegal detention. May the firm undertake this representation?
>
> *In the absence of DOJ consent, clearly the former government lawyer may not be involved in the representation. The other firm lawyers may do so only if the tainted lawyer is screened. Screening would entail not only no active involvement by the former government lawyer but also other measures to avoid contact between the lawyers and any situation that might suggest the possibility that the former government lawyer was sharing information with his colleagues. Also, the former government lawyer cannot share in the fees, and the DOJ must be notified. Recall also that, although all of these measures may effectively insulate the lawyer and the firm from the risk of professional discipline, this would not preclude any of the defendants in the civil suit from bringing a disqualification motion. The risk of losing that motion, if all these screening measures are undertaken, may be small. But because a residual risk of confronting and losing such a motion*

---

47. *Id.* at 1363–64 (court quoting in part ABA Formal Ethics Op. 37 (1931)) (emphasis in original).

remains, the law firm should explain this risk to the detainee client and seek his informed consent before proceeding with the representation.

Former government lawyers must also conform their conduct to the provisions of Rule 1.11(c) governing the use of "confidential government information." If the former government lawyer is in possession of nonpublic information about a person, that lawyer may not then represent a client in a matter where "the information could be used to the material disadvantage of that person." Again, the law firm may avoid imputation by screening and avoiding fee sharing with the former government lawyer.

22-6 Fees

The ethics law addresses fees in Model Rule 1.5, which essentially forbids "unreasonable fees" and offers a list of factors that may be relevant in determining the reasonableness of the fee (e.g., a lawyer's experience, the results obtained, and so on). The most important variable, however, is not on the list—namely, the sophistication of the client. As a general matter, if the client is a sophisticated, repeat consumer of legal services (such as a major national corporation), the courts will ordinarily enforce the fee agreed to by the lawyer and client, however large.[48]

The second basic form of regulation of fees is the ethics law's demand in Rule 1.5(b) that the fee arrangement be clearly explained and set forth in writing. (The rule actually reads "preferably in writing," but it would be pointlessly foolish to permit the fee arrangements to remain a verbal agreement only.)[49] Thus, however sophisticated the client, the lawyer-lobbyist must employ an engagement letter that sets forth the essential terms of the representation, including the fees to be charged.

The third category of regulation involves contingent fees. Importantly for the lawyer-lobbyist, if the applicable lobbying laws and regulations prohibit contingent fees, the use of such a fee would also be a violation of Rule 1.5(c)'s reference to contingent fees "prohibited by . . . other law."[50]

Finally, the ethics law addresses the common practice of referral fees. Referral fees occur typically when a lawyer lacks the expertise to represent the client in a particular matter and thus chooses to refer the client to another lawyer outside the firm. The two lawyers may agree that a percentage of the fee earned will go to the first referring lawyer. Rule 1.5(e) requires, among other things, that the lawyers obtain the client's informed consent in writing to any such fee division. Lawyer-lobbyists, because of the special nature of their practice, may well encounter such

---

48. *See, e.g.,* Brobeck, Phleger & Harrison v. Telex Corp., 602 F.2d 866 (9th Cir. 1979) (court enforced fee agreement between law firm and corporate client that gave firm a $1 million fee for drafting and filing a petition for certiorari).

49. The D.C. ethics law provides that unless the lawyer has "regularly represented" the client, the terms of engagement, including fees, must be provided to the client in writing. *See* D.C. Rules of Prof'l Conduct R. 1.5(b) (2007).

50. See Chapter 16 of this manual for a discussion of contingent fees (including the ramifications under the rules of professional responsibility). *See also generally,* Lynn A. Baker & Charles Silver, *Fiduciaries and Fees: Preliminary Thoughts,* 79 Fordham L. Rev. 1833 (2011).

fee division proposals and must take care to discern and comply with their jurisdiction's ethics rules on this subject.

22-6.1 The *Coudert Brothers* Case as Illustrative

In re Coudert Brothers[51] is a case that offers several lessons in the relevance of the ethics law to fee agreements. The client coal company retained the law firm in 1997 to bring litigation seeking tax refunds on export taxes paid by the client. The law firm's litigation work yielded refunds for taxes paid by the client from 1994 forward, but not for the taxes paid in earlier years. Pursuant to the engagement agreement, which provided for contingent fees, the law firm received payment for the litigation work that yielded these refunds.

Thereafter, the law firm continued its litigation efforts but also began what became a significant lobbying effort to obtain the tax refunds. Congress responded in 2008 with the passage of legislation that resulted in refunds for export taxes paid by the coal companies for the period 1991 through 1994. The refund to the client as a result of this legislation was approximately $59 million.

The law firm subsequently filed for bankruptcy and the administrator, the assignee of the law firm's claims against the client, brought this action against the former client to recover the fees earned by the firm's lobbying work. The former client resisted payment, arguing that the engagement agreement referenced only litigation services and not lobbying activities. In response to the client's summary judgment motions, the court granted summary judgment on the contract-based cause of action but denied the motion as to the quantum meruit claim.

The court's analysis of the contract-based claim is importantly illuminating. First, while the engagement agreement referenced only litigation-related services among the list of services to be provided, the administrator argued that the list was merely illustrative rather than exclusive as it was preceded by the phrase "may include." The administrator argued that this created an ambiguity that justified the consideration of extrinsic evidence in interpreting the agreement. The administrator also argued that the fact that the client was fully aware, and even involved in, the lobbying work being done by the firm formed the basis for an effective modification of the agreement to embrace the lobbying work as part of the agreement.

In its analysis of the contract-based claim, the court swept away each of the administrator's arguments, finding that the agreement was unambiguous and did not include as compensable services the lobbying work done by the firm, thus granting the former client's motion for summary judgment on the contract-based claim. In explaining the judgment, the court emphasized the "nature of the Agreement," namely, "an attorney-client engagement agreement which includes a contingent fee for services."[52]

A person with a working knowledge of legal ethics knows, or should know, that the terms of a contingent fee agreement must be clearly stated to the client in writing. [citing the N.Y. version of Rule 1.5(c) of the Rules of Professional Conduct][53]

---

51. 487 B.R. 375 (S.D.N.Y. 2013).
52. *Id.* at 391.
53. *Id.* at 392.

The court also cited *Shaw v. Manufacturers Hanover Trust Co.*,[54] which set forth a rebuttable presumption in favor of the client's interpretation of an ambiguity in any engagement agreement, whatever the fee arrangement. (Because the court in *Coudert Brothers* found no ambiguity, the *Shaw* principle was not directly applied.)

The court also noted that the very idea of contingent fees for lobbying work was problematic, raising what it called "imponderable questions of causation."[55] Contrasting the contingent fee arrangement in the litigation context, where the causal link between the lawyer's work and the verdict or ruling can be more easily traced, the court described the lobbyist's causal task in the following terms.

> In a city full of lobbyists, interest groups, congressional staffers, other purveyors of influence, and the media, it may well be open to debate—or an unanswerable metaphysical question—whose efforts caused the passage of particular legislation.[56]

In the concluding part of its analysis of the contracts claim, the court again referenced the connection between the resolution of the fee claim and the ethics law, noting: "A reasonably intelligent person, familiar with basic legal ethics, could not reasonably interpret the Agreement as covering lobbying work."[57]

The court denied the client's summary judgment motion on the quantum meruit claim, concluding that genuine factual disputes existed as to whether the elements of that claim might be successfully advanced by the administrator. The burden of proving the elements of the claim rested, of course, on the claimant.

The lessons of the *Coudert Brothers* case are important to the lawyer-lobbyist. The terms of any engagement agreement must be clear and as unambiguous as the context and the English language will permit. As a general principle, any ambiguity in the engagement agreement is likely to be construed in favor of the client's reasonable interpretation.

22-7 Competence

The ethics law demands competence. Model Rule 1.1 states: "A lawyer shall provide competent representation to a client. Competent representation requires the legal knowledge, skill, thoroughness and preparation reasonably necessary for the representation."

Although this rule is probably the most violated precept of ethics law, professional discipline for incompetent lawyering is rare. On the other hand, malpractice lawsuits abound.[58] The competence issue is especially important for lawyers who seek to provide law-related services. Legal education and training focus on conventional legal services. Lobbying, as with any law-related service, demands skills

---

54. 68 N.Y. 2d 172, 507 N.Y.S. 2d 610, 499 N.E. 2d 864 (1986).

55. 487 B.R. at 391.

56. *Id.*

57. 487 B.R. at 393.

58. "Although accurate data is hard to come by—most malpractice insurers do not report their data—most settlements are confidential and the ABA's studies are influenced by the profession's self-interest; reliable estimates place the annual cost of legal malpractice at $4 billion, a figure roughly equivalent to the overall cost of medical malpractice." Hazard et al., *supra* note 36, at 854.

and knowledge not usually part of a traditional law school curriculum. Thus, the lawyer-lobbyist is obliged to gain the knowledge and expertise required for this work "on the job."

As a practical matter, avoiding malpractice suits has as much to do with client relations as with actual performance. Put another way, certain practices, when combined with poor results, often trigger malpractice suits. Neglect is one of those triggers. Not communicating with clients and not returning phone calls are practices that invite clients to feel neglected. On the other hand, communications with the client that promise outcomes that are not achieved also trigger malpractice suits. The lawyer-lobbyist must be especially careful in this regard. To develop a client base, lawyers must always project confidence and capacity. But to promise a particular outcome in the legislative or regulatory arena is as problematic as the promise of a litigation outcome. Finally, whenever a lawyer chooses to sue a client over unpaid fees, a counterclaim for malpractice is a routine response.

22-8 Prohibited Assistance

Zealous representation is the hallmark of competent lawyering. Moreover, loyalty is a central tenet of the ethics law. But the law imposes limits on what a lawyer may do on behalf of a client. These limits come from both the ethics law and other domains of the law.

22-8.1 Ethics Rules

The lobbyist is an advocate. Ethics law imposes limitations on advocacy in trials and other adjudicative settings. But the lawyer-lobbyist may not operate in an adjudicative setting on most occasions. Thus, Model Rule 3.9 addresses the limitations on advocacy for the lawyer-lobbyist:

> A lawyer representing a client before a legislative body or administrative agency in a nonadjudicative proceeding shall disclose that the appearance is in a representative capacity and shall conform to the provisions of Rules 3.3(a) through (c), 3.4(a) through (c), and 3.5.

Rule 3.9 essentially selects particular provisions of the ethics law governing the lawyer in a litigation setting and drops them into the realm of the lawyer-lobbyist operating outside the adjudicative context.

Rules 3.3(a) through (c) express the lawyer's duty of candor to the tribunal, or in the case of the lawyer-lobbyist, to the legislative body or administrative agency. Put simply, the ethics law forbids the lawyer-lobbyist from offering testimony or evidence that the lawyer knows to be false. If the lawyer-lobbyist offers testimony or evidence (e.g., at a congressional or rulemaking hearing) that she believes to be accurate and true when given and later learns of the false nature of that testimony or evidence, the ethics law obliges her to take "reasonable remedial measures" to correct the record.[59] This remedial obligation, however, at least in the adjudicative

---

59. *See* Model Rules of Prof'l Conduct R. 3.3(a)(3) (2008).

setting, extends only to the "conclusion of the proceeding."[60] Concerns for finality in adjudication presumably drive this "practical time limit" in the litigation context.[61] How this should work in the legislative or agency non-adjudicative setting is less clear. (Indeed, even if the lawyer-lobbyist in such a circumstance concluded that the clock had run out under Rule 3.3 for taking remedial measures, the lawyer must still take account of any other laws that may address such conduct as well as the practical issue of professional reputation.)

> **Example 7.** Lawyer-lobbyist represents CEO of an energy corporation in the executive's appearance before a congressional committee examining the issue of executive compensation. The CEO testifies that her compensation for the last fiscal year—salary and all other forms of compensation included—was approximately $5 million. Several months after the hearing, the lawyer learns that the executive had failed to disclose the grant of stock options that would have increased the actual compensation figure to more than $20 million.
>
> *The lawyer has learned that his client offered material and false testimony before the committee. The threshold issue is whether the remedial obligations under Rule 3.3(a) still apply after the passage of time. Rule 3.3(c) states that these obligations persist until the "conclusion of the proceeding." A functional interpretation of this time limit would suggest that the obligations would continue until the committee had closed its consideration of the matter. If this interpretation applies, it may not be enough to note that the hearings are over. If the committee is still actively considering the issue of executive compensation as well as a possible legislative response (e.g., mark-up sessions on a proposed committee bill to deal with executive compensation are ongoing), the lawyer's remedial obligations may still be in play. If so, Rule 3.3(a)(3) would require the lawyer to "take reasonable remedial measures, including, if necessary, disclosure to the tribunal."*

Although references to "testimony" and "evidence" in these particular rules suggest that presentations of factual and other information outside the context of formal hearings are not subject to these obligations of candor, Rule 4.1 prohibits a lawyer from making a false statement of material fact or of law to any person. Moreover, a lawyer who makes such false statements risks liability to third parties under the civil liability doctrine such of fraud.

Rules 3.4(a) through (c), the second set of rules identified by Rule 3.9 to apply in the non-adjudicative setting, essentially forbid the lawyer from assisting or counseling the client to unlawfully destroy evidence or induce perjury. Rule 3.5, also made applicable to the lawyer-lobbyist through Rule 3.9, forbids bribery of an official or other forms of unlawful influence or contact with an official. These rules make clear that acts such as bribery, subornation of perjury, and so on, which are illegal under other laws,[62] are also transgressions of the ethics law. Put simply, if you bribe a legislator, in addition to going to jail, you will lose your law license.

---

60. *See* MODEL RULES OF PROF'L CONDUCT R. 3.3(c) (2008).
61. *See* MODEL RULES OF PROF'L CONDUCT R. 3.3 cmt. 13 (2008).
62. See Chapter 21 of this manual (dealing with bribery and illegal gratuities).

The inclusion of MR 3.5 in the list of rules that apply in these non-adjudicative proceedings does raise an issue. Rule 3.5 prohibits ex parte contact between the lawyer and the judge or other "official." Thus, Rule 3.9's inclusion of the prohibitions of Rule 3.5 could be read to suggest that ex parte, one-on-one contacts between the lawyer-lobbyist and the official would be prohibited. Because the nature of lobbying work often entails one-on-one contact, and because non-lawyer lobbyists are unconstrained in this regard, such an interpretation of Rule 3.9 would impose a crushing limitation on the lawyer acting as a lobbyist. But the Official Comments to Rule 3.9 make clear that the restrictions apply only to an "official hearing or meeting of a governmental agency or a legislative body to which the lawyer or the lawyer's client is presenting evidence or argument" and do not apply to ordinary "negotiations with a government agency."[63]

22-8.2 General Principles Outside Ethics Law

A lawyer, whether acting as a lobbyist or in any other professional capacity, is an agent for the client principal. This legal category of "agent" is also reflected in the common self-conception of the "lawyer as mere helper" or, in the less attractive colloquial expression, the lawyer as "hired gun." This ascription of role can mislead lawyers into supposing that, so long as they are following the directions of the client and sitting in their offices doing ordinary lawyering/lobbying tasks, they are essentially safe (i.e., not at personal risk of violating the law). This, however, is not the case. Acting as an agent is not a defense to charges of illegality—just ask the convicted getaway driver in a bank robbery.

The bulk of this manual is devoted to analyzing various laws that the lawyer-lobbyist must navigate at her own and her client's risk. In addition, certain basic principles of "prohibited assistance" are critical.

First, the legal domains of secondary liability (which include "aiding and abetting" for criminal law purposes and, on the civil side, "persons acting in concert" liability) are directed precisely at "mere helpers." While the precise content of the laws of secondary liability vary, the essential elements are (1) a client who is breaking the law; (2) a lawyer who knows or has good reason to know this is the case; and (3) the lawyer's rendering of assistance to the client in the unlawful activity.

Second, the liability of the party held legally responsible under theories of secondary liability are typically coextensive with primary liability. That is, if you "merely help" your client commit fraud and steal $100 million, your liability as a "person acting in concert" with the wrongdoer is for the entire $100 million.

Third, the basic principle of criminal liability is that the government must prove both actus rea (the criminal act) and mens rea (the criminal state of mind). In cases of lawyers being held criminally liable, the acts are typically conventional lawyering activities (i.e., doing deals, writing opinion letters, communicating with third parties, and so on). What makes these ordinary lawyering activities criminal is precisely that they are done with mens rea. While different criminal laws

---

63. *See* ABA M.R. 3.9, Comment 3. To make this interpretation more certain, Illinois, for example, amended its version of MR 3.9 to take out the reference to MR 3.5 for just this reason, namely, the concern that lawyer-lobbyists might otherwise be precluded generally from ex parte contacts with government officials. *See* Illinois Rules of Professional Conduct, Rule 3.9 (2010).

embody different forms of mens rea, the important point is that even ordinary lawyering can risk criminal liability.

22-9 Conclusion

This chapter has attempted to address only the most significant legal ethics issues for the lawyer-lobbyist. Other ethics rules may apply to the practice. To take just one example, Rule 4.2 forbids contact with a third party that the lawyer knows is represented by another lawyer in the matter. This rule has its most significant impact in litigation. On the other hand, legislators and agency officials are often represented by government lawyers. Within the conventional lobbying context where the attempt is to influence the decision on general matters of government policy, however, because of First Amendment considerations that protect the right to petition the government, as well as basic practical considerations, the "no contact" rule is likely inapplicable.[64]

As this manual reveals, multiple, significant, and complex bodies of law apply to the lawyer-lobbyist. The ethics law constrains the lawyer-lobbyist in particular ways. It also reminds the lawyer-lobbyist that any violation of any other part of the applicable jurisdiction's law may result in professional discipline as well.

The practice of law today, whatever the specialty, is difficult and filled with legal risk. The ethics law is an often underestimated source of risk. This chapter has sought to support that admonition as applied to the lawyer-lobbyist.

---

64. *See* ABA Formal Ethics Op. 97-408 (1997). This principle regarding contact with government actors is explicitly part of the D.C. ethics law. *See* D.C. RULES OF PROF'L CONDUCT R. 4.2(d) (2007).

CHAPTER 23

The Use of Corporate Resources in Connection with Federal Elections

BY ANDREW HARRIS WERBROCK

23-1 Introduction

Lobbyists—as well as their employers and clients—understand that participation in the electoral process in support of like-minded candidates can provide valuable support to their lobbying activities. Just as the lobbyist needs to understand the laws applicable to lobbying activities, the lobbyist who works for politically active corporations must understand the far more complex campaign finance regulations.

Federal law significantly limits the ways in which corporations may attempt to influence federal elections. Corporations may not make contributions, whether monetary or in kind, to federal candidates, party committees, and most other federal political committees. Nor may they, absent certain exceptions, use their resources or facilities to engage in fund-raising activities on behalf of these entities. And they are, by statute, prohibited from otherwise making expenditures in connection with federal elections. Though the Supreme Court's decision in *Citizens United v. Federal Election Commission*[1] invalidated the federal prohibition on corporate political spending to the extent that it prohibits corporations from engaging in certain election-influencing activities that are conducted entirely *independently* from candidates and the political parties,[2] the law still generally prohibits corporate political activity conducted in coordination or consultation with candidates, their campaigns, and the political parties.

Despite these restrictions, the law provides for several ways that corporations and their employees may participate in the political process. A corporation may establish a separate segregated fund (commonly referred to as an SSF or a PAC) that raises money from executives and stockholders and uses those funds to make contributions directly to candidates and party committees. Campaigns, individual corporate employees, and other federally permissible sources may use corporate facilities for their own fund-raising and political activities, provided that they pay the normal and usual charge for using those facilities and comply with certain other requirements. And, under certain circumstances, corporations may communicate directly to their executives and stockholders, and even to the general public, on election-related matters. This chapter describes the contours of these exceptions. It also describes how the rules apply to incorporated trade associations.

---

1. 558 U.S. 310, 365 (2010).
2. For a discussion of the ways in which corporations may engage in *independent* political activity, see Sections 24-2.1 through 24-3.1 of this manual.

This chapter only addresses the campaign finance laws that govern corporate activity in connection with *federal* elections. Many states and some localities have their own laws that limit or prohibit the use of corporate funds in connection with nonfederal elections in those jurisdictions.

23-2 Establishing a Corporate PAC

The Federal Election Campaign Act of 1971 (FECA), as amended, prohibits corporations from directly contributing to candidates, their campaigns, the national party committees, and most other federal political committees.[3] This prohibition covers not only monetary contributions but also in-kind contributions, which are things of value that are provided to a candidate or committee at less than the normal and usual charge.[4] That law, however, permits a corporation to use treasury funds to establish and to administer a political committee, referred to as an SSF. This committee collects voluntary contributions from its executives and shareholders and uses those funds to make contributions to federal candidates, political party committees, and other political committees.

This section addresses the general rules that apply when establishing a corporate SSF.[5] However, a corporation that wishes to establish an SSF should consult with counsel separately before doing so. Each corporation's structure is different and may raise unique legal issues that impact, among other things, the SSF's name and the universe of individuals that the SSF may solicit.

---

3. 52 U.S.C. § 30118(a) (2015). The law also prohibits unions and federal contractors from making contributions or expenditures in connection with federal elections, *id., id.* § 30119(a), and it prohibits national banks, corporations organized by authority of any law of Congress, and foreign nationals from making contributions or expenditures in connection with any federal, state or local election, *id.* §§ 30118(b), 30121(a). Unions, national banks, corporations organized by authority of a law of Congress, and federal contractors that are organized as corporations are generally subject to the same limitations, and enjoy the same exceptions, as corporations more generally. *See* 11 C.F.R. §§ 114.2(a) (1), 115.3(a) (2015). They may, for example, establish an SSF, just like any other corporation. However, foreign nationals—including corporations that are organized under the laws of, or have their principal place of business in, a foreign country—are subject to significantly stricter limitations. *See* 52 U.S.C. § 30121 (2015); 11 C.F.R. § 110.20 (2015). A foreign corporation may not, for example, establish an SSF, though a domestic subsidiary of a foreign corporation that is a discrete legal entity may under certain circumstances, provided that the SSF is not controlled, directed, or influenced by the foreign parent or foreign nationals and it does not solicit funds from foreign nationals. *See* Fed. Election Comm'n Adv. Op. 1999-28.

4. 11 C.F.R. § 100.52(d)(1) (2015). The law treats "coordinated communications," communications that are coordinated with a candidate, a candidate's campaign, a political party committee, or their agents and that contain certain types of content, as in-kind contributions. *Id.* § 109.21(b)(1). The rules for coordinated communications are described in greater detail in chapter 24.

5. SSFs may also be established by labor organizations, "membership organizations," as that term is defined by the FEC, cooperatives, and trade associations. 11 C.F.R. § 100.6(a). The rules that apply to trade associations are described in Section 23-5.2. Different rules apply to PACs that are established by partnerships, limited liability companies that are taxed as partnerships, or other unincorporated business entities.

23-2.1 Establishing an SSF and Paying Its Expenses

FECA authorizes a corporation to use its treasury funds to pay for the "establishment, administration, and solicitation" costs of a connected SSF.[6] These costs include the salaries of corporate employees who help administer the SSF, office space, phones, utilities, supplies, bank charges, and legal and accounting fees expended in connection with the political committee.[7] These payments are not considered contributions or expenditures and, therefore, are not subject to the act's contribution limits. Nor do they need to be reported on the SSF's reports that are filed with the Federal Election Commission (FEC).[8]

A corporation may generally not transfer treasury funds into an SSF's bank account. However, if the SSF pays any expense that could have been paid by a corporation, the corporation may reimburse the SSF within thirty days after the original payment by the SSF.[9] When a disbursement is made by the SSF, rather than by the corporation, it must be reported on the SSF's disclosure reports.

The act does not require a corporation to prepare bylaws for its political committee. Having a set of bylaws can a useful, however, to address specific internal management issues, guide decision making, and assure a disciplined decision-making process. If a corporation chooses to develop bylaws or other operating documents, these documents generally need not be made public.

23-2.2 Registering the SSF

An SSF must register as a political committee with the FEC within ten days after it is established. Establishment occurs when, for example, the corporation's board of directors votes to create a political committee, the political committee's initial operating expenses are paid, or the initial officers of the political committee are selected.[10]

To register, the SSF must file a Statement of Organization (FEC Form 1) with the FEC. Once the registration is received, the FEC assigns the SSF an identification number and, as discussed below, the SSF must then file periodic reports of its financial activity with the commission. Any changes or corrections in the Statement of Organization must be filed with the FEC within ten days of the change by filing an amended Statement of Organization.[11]

The official registered name of the SSF must include the full name of the sponsoring corporation, or "connected organization."[12] The SSF may use an abbreviated form of its official name on its stationery or checks, so long as this shorter form of name is an acronym or set of initials by which the corporation would be generally recognized.[13] The SSF must list any connected organizations and affiliated political committees on its Statement of Organization. The connected organization is

---

6. 52 U.S.C. § 30118(b)(2)(C) (2015).
7. *See* 11 C.F.R. § 114.1(a)(2)(iii), (b) (2015); *see also id.* § 114.5(b).
8. *See id.* § 114.5(e)(1).
9. *Id.* § 114.5(b)(3).
10. *Id.* § 102.1(c).
11. *Id.* § 102.2(a)(2).
12. *Id.* § 102.14(c).
13. *Id.* § 102.14(c).

the corporation establishing the SSF.[14] Affiliated committees include those political committees established by the parent or subsidiaries of the corporation, and other committees that are otherwise closely related.[15]

The Statement of Organization also requires that the SSF list its only statutorily required officer, the treasurer.[16] While not required, it is also prudent to name an assistant treasurer who can assume the duties of the treasurer when the treasurer is not available. When an SSF has no treasurer, it may not accept contributions or make expenditures.[17]

The SSF must also name a depository, a national bank or recognized and properly insured depository institution, such as a savings and loan or a credit union.[18] All receipts and disbursements of the SSF must pass through a designated depository, but there is no limit to the number of depositories an SSF may use or the number of accounts it may have within a particular depository.

23-2.3 Reporting Requirements

Once the SSF has registered, it must file periodic reports detailing its receipts and disbursements. The SSF must file reports electronically if it expects to raise or spend more than $50,000 in a calendar year.[19] If the SSF plans to support candidates for both House and Senate as well as president, the reports will be filed with the FEC.[20]

An SSF may choose to file either "quarterly" or "monthly" reports.[21]

If the SSF chooses to file quarterly, reports during an election year must be filed on April 15, July 15, and October 15, with the fourth quarterly or "year-end" report due on January 31 of the following year. In addition to these reports, the SSF must file a preelection report twelve days before any election in which the SSF has made contributions or expenditures not previously reported in connection with that particular election. Finally, the SSF must file a post-general election report thirty days after the general election. There is no requirement for any post-primary election report. During a nonelection year, an SSF on a quarterly schedule must file only two semiannual reports covering January through June (to be filed July 31) and July through December (to be filed January 31 of the following year). In addition to these regularly scheduled reports, a quarterly filer may also be required to file reports in connection with special elections, on a schedule to be determined by the FEC.

---

14. *Id.* § 100.6(a).

15. Committees established by a parent and its subsidiaries are per se affiliated; otherwise, the FEC rules require a close examination of the facts and circumstances of the relationship between the committees to determine if they are affiliated. *Id.* §§ 100.5(g), 110.3(a)(2). When a corporation has, or different corporations within the same corporate family have, multiple affiliated committees, the relationships raise issues under the contribution limits. All affiliated committees are subject to a single contribution limit when making contributions *to* federal candidates and when receiving contributions *from* donors. *See id.* § 110.3(a)(1).

16. 52 U.S.C. § 30102(a) (2015); 11 C.F.R. § 102.7(a) (2015).

17. 11 C.F.R. § 102.7(b) (2015).

18. 52 U.S.C. § 30102(h)(1) (2015); 11 C.F.R. § 103.2 (2015).

19. 11 C.F.R. § 104.18(a)(2) (2015).

20. *Id.* § 105.4. If the SSF will support only Senate candidates, it must file with the Secretary of the Senate. *Id.* § 105.2(a).

21. *See id.* § 104.5.

Monthly filing in an election year requires filing reports on the twentieth day after the last day of each month during the period January through September. For the last three months of an election year, in place of the monthly report, the SSF must file the same pre- and post-general election reports and year-end report as a quarterly filer. In a nonelection year, a monthly filer files a report by the twentieth day after the last day of each month, except for the year-end report covering the month of December, which is due on January 31 of the next year.

Monthly filing is advantageous if the SSF is planning to support candidates in numerous primary or special elections around the country. A quarterly filer must file pre-primary and special election reports in every election where a candidate is supported, and this can create administrative burdens if the political committee is active in primaries nationwide. Monthly filing obviates the need to track the coverage dates and deadlines for pre-primary and special election reports. An SSF may change its filing schedule from monthly to quarterly, or vice versa, once a calendar year.[22]

The FEC takes the matter of timely filings very seriously: Reports are due on the date specified and no later. Extensions of time to file are never granted for any reason. A late filing, by even a day, will result in an automatic administrative fine and even consideration by the FEC to undertake a full-scale audit of the committee.[23]

23-2.4 Contribution Limits

Contributions made both to and by the SSF are subject to monetary limits.

Contributions to the SSF are limited to $5,000 a year from individuals.[24] An SSF may not solicit or accept contributions from individuals who are not U.S. citizens or lawful permanent residents, or individuals who are Federal contractors.[25]

The amount that an SSF may contribute to candidates and other recipients will depend on whether it has achieved "multicandidate" status. When an SSF is first formed, it is subject to one set of limits. But once the committee has received contributions from at least fifty persons, has been registered with the FEC for at least six months, and has contributed to at least five federal candidates, it becomes a multicandidate committee and is subject to a different set of limits.[26] The limits that apply to each type of SSF are described below:[27]

- *Candidates:* For the 2015–2016 election cycle, contributions by a non-multicandidate SSF to a candidate or a candidate's committee are limited to

---

22. *See id.* § 104.5(c).

23. Administrative fines are based on a formula that takes into account the length of delinquency, the financial activity on the report, and the number of previous violations. *See id.* § 111.43.

24. 52 U.S.C. § 30116(a)(1)(C) (2015).

25. *Id.* §§ 30121, 30119.

26. 11 C.F.R. § 100.5(e) (2015). Once a committee qualifies as a multicandidate committee, it must notify each recipient of a contribution of its status. *Id.* § 110.2(a)(2). Most SSFs comply with this requirement by printing the words "XYZ PAC has qualified as a multicandidate committee" on its checks. For this reason, an SSF may wish to order only a limited number of pre-printed checks to use during the first six months of the SSF's existence.

27. *See* 52 U.S.C. § 30116(a)(1), (2) (2015); Fed. Election Comm'n, Contribution Limits for 2015–2016, *available at* http://www.fec.gov/pages/fecrecord/2015/february/contriblimits20152016.shtml.

$2,700 per election.[28] Multicandidate SSFs may contribute up to $5,000 per election. Elections for which a separate limit applies include, for example, a primary, a general, or a runoff. In certain cases a convention may also qualify as an election.

- *National Party Committees:* For the 2015–2016 election cycle, a non-multicandidate SSF may contribute up to $33,400 in a calendar year to a national party committee (e.g., the DNC, DSCC, DCCC, RNC, NRSC, and NRCC) for its general purposes.[29] In addition, each of the national political parties may establish a recount account, to pay expenses in connection with election recounts and contests; a headquarters account, to pay for expenses incurred with respect to the party's headquarters building; and, in the case of the DNC and the RNC, a convention account, to pay costs in connection with a presidential nominating convention. A non-multicandidate PAC may contribute up to $100,200 per year to each of these accounts.[30] A multicandidate SSF may contribute up to $15,000 per year to a national party committee's general fund, and up to $45,000 per year to a convention, recount, or headquarters account.
- *State Party Committees:* A non-multicandidate SSF may contribute up to $10,000 per year to the federal account of a state political party committee. A multicandidate SSF may contribute up to $5,000 per year.
- *Other Political Committees:* An SSF may contribute up to $5,000 per year to other noncandidate political committees regardless of whether the SSF has achieved multicandidate status. This includes, for example, contributions to ideological political committees not affiliated with a particular candidate and so-called leadership PACs.

The contribution limits apply jointly to all "affiliated" political committees.[31] Thus an individual may contribute an aggregate of $5,000 per calendar year to all affiliated SSFs. And affiliated SSFs may not make contributions to a particular candidate that aggregate in excess of $2,700 per election or $5,000 per election if any one of the affiliated political committees is a multicandidate committee. Affiliated political committees may make unlimited transfers to one another.[32]

23-2.5 Soliciting Contributions for the SSF

23-2.5.1 Who May Be Solicited: The Corporation's "Restricted Class"
FECA limits the class of individuals that a corporate political committee may solicit. A corporation may never solicit the general public.[33] While a corporation's political committee may accept unsolicited contributions from any person who is

---

28. The amount that a non-multicandidate committee may contribution to a candidate increases with the Consumer Price Index every two years. 52 U.S.C. § 30116(c) (2015).

29. A party's national committee, Senate campaign committee, and House campaign committee each enjoy their own, separate limits. 11 C.F.R. § 110.3(b) (2015).

30. The amount that a non-multicandidate committee may contribute to the different accounts of a national party committee increases with the Consumer Price Index every two years. 52 U.S.C. § 30116(c) (2015).

31. 11 C.F.R. § 110.3(a)(1) (2015).

32. *Id.* § 110.3(c)(1).

33. *See id.* § 114.5(g)(1).

not a prohibited source, informing such a person of the right to accept unsolicited contributions is itself considered to be a solicitation.[34]

A corporation may make unlimited solicitations of its executive and administrative personnel, stockholders, and the families of both groups—a group that the FEC refers to collectively as the corporation's "restricted class."[35] A corporation's restricted class also includes the executive or administrative personnel of its subsidiaries, branches, divisions, and departments, and their families.[36] Because corporate structures vary significantly, it is important to carefully identify those individuals who fall into this category before making any solicitations. Most organizations find the guidance of counsel to be helpful, and often necessary, in this endeavor. The following general guidelines set out which employees fall within the restricted class.

"Executive or administrative personnel" are individuals who are paid on a salary rather than an hourly basis and who have policymaking, managerial, professional, or supervisory responsibilities. These include individuals who run the corporation's business, such as officers, other executives, plant, division, and section managers, and employees who follow the recognized professions, such as lawyers and engineers.[37]

FEC regulations expressly *exclude* from the restricted class:[38]

- Professionals who are represented by a labor organization;
- Salaried foremen and other salaried lower-level supervisors having direct supervision over hourly employees;
- Former or retired personnel who are not stockholders; and
- Individuals who may be paid by the corporation, such as consultants, but who are not employees for federal withholding purposes.

A corporation's directors are members of the restricted class only if they receive a salary or retainer and are not paid on an hourly basis.[39] Employees paid on an hourly basis are, as a matter of law, excluded from the restricted class.[40]

In general, to determine whether an employee has the requisite policymaking, managerial, professional, or supervisory responsibilities, a corporation can use as a guideline the employee status determined in accordance with the Fair Labor Standards Act (FLSA) and related regulations.[41] Note, however, that reliance on the FLSA will not always result in a correct determination of membership in the restricted class. Salaried foremen, for example, may qualify as "exempt" for FLSA purposes, but are not solicitable under FEC rules.

A corporation's restricted class also includes its stockholders—though to qualify, a stockholder must meet a three-part test. The stockholder must (1) have a vested beneficial interest in corporate stock; (2) have the power to direct how that

---

34. Fed. Election Comm'n Adv. Op. 1983-38, n.2.
35. 11 C.F.R. §§ 114.1(j), 114.5(g)(1) (2015).
36. *Id.*
37. *Id.* § 114.1(c).
38. *Id.* § 114.1(c)(2).
39. *See, e.g.,* Fed. Election Comm'n Adv. Op. 1985-35.
40. 11 C.F.R. § 114.1(c) (2015).
41. *Id.* § 114.1(c)(4).

stock will be voted, if it is voting stock; and (3) have the right to receive dividends.[42] Corporate employees who are not executive and administrative personnel may be solicited as stockholders if they participate in a corporate stock option plan and meet these three requirements. If the plan automatically reinvests dividends, employees will be considered stockholders only if they have an unrestricted right to withdraw at least one share of stock.[43]

23-2.5.2 The Requirement that Contributions Be Voluntary and Disclaimer Requirements

The law imposes certain restrictions on the solicitation of contributions to an SSF to ensure that all contributions are voluntary. Contributions may not be secured by the use or "threat of physical force, job discrimination or financial reprisals."[44]

All solicitations for a political committee, whether oral or written, must inform the solicitee of the political purpose of the political committee and of the right to refuse to contribute without reprisal. A solicitation may also suggest or provide guidelines on how much an individual should contribute to the political committee. But those guidelines must be merely suggestions, and the solicitation must inform the recipients that they are free to contribute more or less than the guidelines suggest and that they may refuse to contribute without disadvantage to their position within the company.[45]

Solicitations must also contain certain other disclaimers. All written solicitations made by an SSF must contain a statement that the SSF must use "best efforts" to obtain and report the name, address, occupation, and employer of each contributor who contributes more than $200 in a calendar year.[46] And under the Internal Revenue Code, SSFs with annual gross receipts exceeding $100,000 must state in their solicitations, in a conspicuous and easily recognizable format, that contributions are not tax deductible as charitable contributions for federal income tax purposes.[47] Moreover, because solicitations may only be directed at the restricted class, it is advisable to include language on written solicitations stating that the solicitation is for the recipient only and should not be forwarded or copied. Solicitations for an SSF need not include a statement indicating who paid for the solicitation.[48]

23-2.5.3 Methods of Solicitation

The methods a corporation may use to solicit its restricted class are relatively unlimited.[49] All solicitations must, of course, contain the necessary notices, designed to assure that contributions are voluntary. The SSF may solicit members of the restricted class in person, by phone, or by mail, whether sent internally at the corporation or to an individual's residence. The SSF may also use a payroll deduction or checkoff plan to collect contributions from its executive and administrative employees, provided that the employee provides affirmative written approval in

---

42. *Id.* § 114.1(h).
43. *See, e.g.,* Fed. Election Comm'n Adv. Op. 1998-12.
44. 11 C.F.R. § 114.5(a)(1) (2015).
45. *Id.* § 114.5(a).
46. *Id.* § 104.7(b)(1)(i)(A).
47. 26 U.S.C. § 6113 (2015).
48. 11 C.F.R. § 110.11(f)(2) (2015).
49. *See id.* § 114.1(g)

advance.[50] A corporation may not use a "reverse checkoff" plan, whereby contributions are automatically deducted from an employee's paycheck unless the employee registers a specific objection.[51]

Solicitations may also be made through a corporation's internal publications. This type of solicitation, however, can pose problems if the publication is distributed beyond the corporation's solicitable class, such as to all corporate employees or to the general public. An article about the corporation's SSF contained in such a publication may inadvertently constitute a solicitation if it publicizes its right to receive unsolicited contributions, provides information on how to contribute to the SSF, or encourages support of the SSF.[52] An article that merely recites factual or statistical information about an SSF is not considered a solicitation.[53] Counsel can assist any organization trying to navigate the line demarcating what is a solicitation and what is not.

A corporation should be aware that any method it uses to solicit contributions for its SSF must also be made available to any labor organization that represents the corporation's employees or the employees of its parent, subsidiaries, or other affiliates, even if the SSF does not solicit those employees.[54] The method must be made available to the labor organization upon the labor organization's written request and at a cost sufficient only to reimburse the corporation for the expenses incurred in making the method available. If, for example, a corporation establishes a payroll deduction plan for contributions to its SSF, it must allow a labor organization to establish a payroll deduction plan for contributions from its members to the labor organization's SSF.[55]

23-2.5.4 Solicitation of Other Employees

In addition to its unlimited solicitation of the restricted class, a corporation may also solicit those employees who fall outside the restricted class and their families twice yearly.[56] These twice-yearly solicitations must be in writing and mailed to the recipient's residence.[57] The political committee must establish a custodial arrangement to receive the contributions in order to preserve the anonymity of individuals who do not wish to contribute or who wish to contribute small amounts.[58] This chapter does not discuss these requirements in detail. If a corporation wishes to undertake these solicitations, it should confer with counsel.

23-3 The Use of Corporate Facilities

While a corporation may use its resources to help establish, administer, and solicit funds for its own SSF, different rules apply to the use of corporate facilities to raise funds for candidates, political party committees, and other committees (including,

50. *See, e.g.*, Fed. Election Comm'n Adv. Op. 2001-04.
51. *Id.*
52. *See* Fed. Election Comm'n Adv. Ops. 1984-55, 1979-13.
53. *See* Fed. Election Comm'n Adv. Op. 1979-66.
54. 11 C.F.R. § 114.5(k) (2015).
55. *Id.* § 114.5(k)(1).
56. *Id.* § 114.6(a).
57. *Id.* § 114.6(c).
58. *Id.* § 114.6(d).

for example, a federal officeholder's leadership PAC). This section discusses the circumstances under which corporate facilities may be used to host fund-raising and other events for candidates and committees other than the corporation's own SSF. It also discusses the rules that govern an individual corporate employee's ability to conduct volunteer activities using corporate space and the rules that apply when individuals or SSFs "bundle" contributions for federal candidates.

23-3.1 Corporate "Facilitation"

As described earlier, the law prohibits corporations from "facilitating" the making of contributions, other than to the corporation's own PAC. "Facilitation" is defined as the use of corporate resources or facilities to engage in fund-raising activities in connection with any federal election.[59] The rules generally require that any use of corporate resources—including those of an incorporated lobbying firm—to support a candidate or committee (other than the corporation's own SSF) must be paid for *in advance*, at the full fair market value, by a source that may lawfully contribute under the federal campaign finance laws. This includes

- Any time that corporate employees spend to plan, organize, or carry out a fund-raising project as part of their work responsibilities;
- Any corporate lists of customers, clients, vendors, or others who are not in the corporation's "restricted class" used to solicit contributions or distribute invitations to a fund-raiser;
- Food or other catering or services provided or arranged by the corporation;
- Use of corporate meeting rooms that are not customarily made available to clubs, civic community organizations, or other groups; and
- Any office space or other corporate facilities used in connection with the fund-raising activities.[60]

The application of these rules may differ with respect to certain expenses, such as the payment by a lobbyist's employer for local transportation to and from fund-raising events, depending on the circumstances.

Corporations may not use coercion, such as the threat of a detrimental job action, financial reprisal, or force, to urge an individual to make a contribution or engage in fund-raising activities on behalf of a candidate or political committee.[61] Nor may the corporation, through its representatives, receive and deliver contributions or provide materials for the purpose of transmitting or delivering contributions, such as stamps and envelopes addressed to a candidate or political committee.[62]

---

59. *Id.* § 114.2(f)(1).

60. *Id.* § 114.2(f)(2)(i), 114.9(d). The one specific exception to the requirement that the use of corporate resources be paid for in advance is for use of office space and office equipment, such as telephones, typewriters, and copy machines. The costs for use of these facilities may be paid within a commercially reasonable time. *See id.* § 114.2(f)(2)(i)(B).

61. *See id.* § 114.2(f)(2)(iv).

62. *See id.* § 114.2(f)(2)(ii).

23-3.2 Permissible Uses of Corporate Resources for Fund-Raising and Other Events

Despite the prohibition on corporate facilitation, the rules provide two general ways in which corporate facilities may be used permissibly in connection with fund-raising events held for federal candidates, party committees, and other political committees. First, a campaign (or another federally permissible source) may sponsor an event held in corporate space, provided that the campaign (or another federally permissible source) reimburses the corporation in advance for the fair market value for the facilities used. Second, the corporation itself can host the fund-raising event, provided that attendance is limited to its restricted class and that certain other criteria are met. The rules for each type of event are described below.

23-3.2.1 Campaign-Sponsored Events

A campaign or committee can use corporate facilities or resources in connection with a fund-raising event provided that the campaign or another federally permissible source pays fair market value for all of the costs associated with the event, generally in advance.[63] This includes the use of corporate space, corporate lists, food and refreshments, and any corporate staff that are used to support the event. All contributions made in connection with the event must be collected by the candidate or a campaign representative; the corporation may not collect contributions for the campaign, nor may it provide stamps or envelopes so that attendees or others can remit contributions to the campaign.[64]

The costs of an event like this may be paid for by the campaign itself, or by another federally permissible source. If a PAC or individual pays for the costs of the event, the value of those costs will be treated as an in-kind contribution to the benefiting campaign or committee, and will be subject to the contribution limits. A federal PAC that has attained "multicandidate" status may contribute up to $5,000 per election to a federal candidate. Individuals and non-multicandidate PACs may currently contribute up to $2,700 per election.[65] Note that a campaign may generally not receive an in-kind contribution for the general election until the candidate has successfully won his or her primary election.[66]

Individual senior-level officers or employees may volunteer their time to help organize or support the event without the cost of their time being treated as a contribution to the campaign.[67] It should be clear to all, however, that these officers or employees are acting in their individual capacities, and not on behalf of the corporation. Thus, for example, volunteers should not be identified by their corporate titles in invitations or pre-event publicity, or at the event itself. Employees who support the event at the request or direction of their superiors are not truly acting in volunteer capacities, and their time must be paid for in advance, like other event expenses. And under no circumstance may corporate employees be coerced into

---

63. *See id.* § 114.2(f)(2)(i).
64. *See id.* § 114.2(f)(2)(ii).
65. For a discussion of the contribution limits, see Section 23-2.4.
66. *See* Fed. Election Comm'n Adv. Op. 1996-29.
67. The rules for individual volunteer activity are described in Section 23-3.3.

helping to arrange or staff a fund-raising event.[68] If an employee is asked to help staff an event, it should be made clear, preferably in writing, that the employee's participation is entirely voluntary and that the employee is free to decline participation without it affecting in any way his or her employment.

23-3.2.2 Restricted Class Events

The rules also permit a corporation to allow a candidate, a candidate's representative, or a party representative to attend a corporation-sponsored meeting, convention, or other function and address the corporation's restricted class.[69] Such events may be attended only by members of the corporation's restricted class, with the exception of employees necessary to administer the meeting; other guests who are being honored or speaking at, or who are participating in, the event; and representatives of the news media.[70]

At the event, the candidate, candidate's representative, or party representative may solicit contributions to his or her campaign or party. The corporation may also, through its representatives, "suggest that members of its restricted class contribute to the candidate or party committee."[71] However, the corporation may not facilitate the making of contributions by, for example, allowing its officers, directors, and other representatives to collect contributions and forward them to a candidate. All contributions must be accepted directly by the candidate or representative, either before, during, or after the event.[72]

The corporation may pay for the costs of the event, such as room rental, catering, and invitations.[73] These expenses are subject to the reporting requirements described below in Section 23-4.1.3. The invitations may suggest that the corporation's restricted class members make voluntary contributions to the candidate or party appearing at the event. Though the corporation may coordinate with a campaign in drafting the communications, the communications must represent the corporation's own speech—the corporation may not republish or redistribute materials prepared by the campaign or party committee.[74] Again, all contributions raised from such a solicitation must be sent directly to the benefiting committee; a corporation is prohibited from receiving or collecting contributions, or transmitting contributions to the candidate.

As a general rule, a restricted class communication that is paid for by a corporation need not include a "paid for by" disclaimer.[75] However, if the communication contains a solicitation, it may need to contain the FEC's "best efforts"

---

68. *See* 11 C.F.R. § 114.2(f)(2)(iv) (2015).
69. *Id.* § 114.3(c)(2). The composition of a corporation's restricted class is discussed in Section 23-2.5.1.
70. *Id.* § 114.3(c)(2)(i).
71. *Id.* § 114.3(c)(2)(iii).
72. *See id.* § 114.3(c)(2)(ii), (iii).
73. Note, however, that the House and Senate ethics rules may limit the refreshments that an incumbent member may accept at such an event. For a discussion of these rules, see Chapter 8 of this manual.
74. 11 C.F.R. § 114.3(c)(1)(ii).
75. *Id.* § 110.11(f)(2).

disclaimer[76] and an Internal Revenue Service disclaimer stating that contributions or gifts to the committee are not tax deductible for federal income tax purposes.[77]

23-3.3 Use of Corporate Facilities in Connection with Individual Volunteer Activity

Stat FEC regulations allow a corporation to permit its employees to use office space and equipment during and after working hours to conduct individual volunteer activities on behalf of a candidate, political party committee, or other political committee.[78] The activities permitted are activities an employee elects on his or her own to pursue, not activities required or directed at a senior management level to accomplish corporate objectives.

Generally, an individual's use of corporate resources for volunteer political activity must be limited to "occasional, isolated, or incidental" use.[79] Under the FEC's safe harbor, individual volunteer political activity that does not exceed one hour per week or four hours per month will be considered occasional, isolated, or incidental.[80] Even if the employee's activities exceed this de minimis limit, they may still be considered occasional, isolated, or incidental, so long as they do not prevent the employee from completing the normal amount of work that he or she usually carries out.[81]

The "one hour per week/four hours per month" rule does not apply to certain individual volunteer activities undertaken over the Internet, including drafting and sending e-mail, hyperlinking, blogging, and creating and hosting a website. An individual employee may make *unlimited* use of his or her office computer for such voluntary activities in support of a candidate or party as long as (1) doing so does not prevent him or her from completing the normal amount of work during the workday; (2) the activities do not increase the employer's overhead costs; and (3) the employer has not coerced the employee into undertaking the activity.[82]

If the employee uses corporate equipment, resources, or facilities, he or she must reimburse the corporation, at full fair market value, for any increase in overhead or operating expense related to that use, such as long-distance charges and printer paper.[83] Moreover, if an employee makes more than occasional, isolated, or incidental use of a corporation's facilities for individual volunteer activities, he or she must reimburse the corporation within a commercially reasonable time for the normal and usual rental charge for the use of such facilities.[84] If the individual's activities are coordinated with the benefiting candidate, the reimbursement will be an in-kind contribution from the individual to the candidate that is reportable by

---

76. *Id.* § 104.7(b)(1)(i).

77. 26 U.S.C. § 6113.

78. A corporation is not, however, *required* to permit employees to engage in volunteer activities using corporate facilities or resources.

79. 11 C.F.R. § 114.9(a)(1) (2015).

80. *Id.* § 114.9(a)(2)(i).

81. *Id.* § 114.9(a)(1)(i).

82. *Id.* § 114.9(a)(2)(ii).

83. *Id.* § 114.9(a)(1).

84. *Id.* § 114.9(a)(3).

the campaign. The use of the corporate name, logo, or trademark should also be avoided.[85]

Other company staff may not be required to support a corporate executive's or employee's volunteer activities under any circumstances. All such participation must be voluntary. The benefiting candidate or party must pay in advance for the staff time of any staff who voluntarily agree to help a corporate executive or employee in these efforts.[86]

23-3.4 Bundling

Individuals and PACs that help raise funds for federal candidates need to be aware of the rules regarding bundled contributions. The subject of bundling can be confusing because the FEC has two separate sets of rules governing bundled contributions, and the scope of activity regulated by each set is different. The first imposes certain reporting obligations on individuals and PACs that act as "conduits," receiving and transmitting contributions to other committees; the second requires candidates, leadership PACs, and party committees to file special reports for contributions that are bundled by lobbyists, Lobbying Disclosure Act (LDA) registrants, and their PACs. I discuss each in turn below.

23-3.4.1 Conduit Contributions

As described earlier, the law prohibits corporations, and corporate employees and officers acting on behalf of a corporation, from collecting and forwarding contributions to a federal campaign, even if the corporation receives advance payment.[87] An individual, acting in a volunteer capacity on his or her own time, *may* help collect and forward contributions to a candidate. However, corporate facilities or personnel should not be used to support the effort, such as by having contributions sent to corporate offices, using corporate stamps, envelopes, or letterhead for soliciting or forwarding the contributions, or requesting that clerical employees prepare transmittal envelopes for the contributions.[88] The activity must be undertaken by the individual in his or her personal capacity, using campaign or personal resources.

A corporation's SSF may also solicit and forward contributions from its restricted class. When the *corporation* pays for the solicitation of contributions earmarked for particular candidates, those contributions count against the overall contribution limits of both the individual and the SSF.[89] Alternatively, the *SSF* may itself pay for the solicitation of earmarked contributions from the restricted class, using the SSF's own funds.[90] Provided that the SSF does not direct or control the choice of the recipient candidate, the earmarked funds will not count against the SSF's contribution limits.[91] However, the costs of soliciting, collecting, and for-

---

85. *See* Fed. Election Comm'n Adv. Op. 2007-10.

86. 11 C.F.R. § 114.2(f)(2)(i)(A) (2015).

87. *Id.* §§ 114.2(f), 110.6(b)(2)(ii).

88. *See id.* § 114.2(f)(2)(ii).

89. *Id.* § 114.2(f)(2)(iii).

90. The FEC's commissioners have not been able to agree whether an SSF may pay to solicit those outside the restricted class for contributions earmarked for candidates. *See* Fed. Election Comm'n Adv. Ops. 2009-28, 2006-14.

91. 11 C.F.R. §§ 114.2(f)(3)(ii), 110.6(d) (2015).

warding the contributions will count as in-kind contributions from the SSF to the candidate benefited.

A conduit, whether an individual or an SSF, that receives a contribution ear-marked for a particular candidate must forward that contribution to the candidate's authorized committee within ten days of receiving it.[92] Moreover, with certain exceptions, a person who acts as a conduit must disclose to the FEC certain information about the conduit contributions.[93] While an SSF can comply with this requirement by including the additional information on its regular FEC reports, individuals who act as conduits must file special conduit reports. Excepted from this requirement are individuals who are expressly authorized by a candidate or campaign to engage in fund-raising and who occupy a "significant position" within the campaign organization.[94]

23-3.4.2 Reports of Contributions Bundled by Lobbyists

In addition to the restrictions on conduit contributions just described, the bundling disclosure rules that were introduced by the Honest Leadership and Open Government Act of 2007 require candidates, their leadership PACs, and political party committees to disclose certain contributions bundled by lobbyists registered under the LDA, organizations that register lobbyists ("registrants"),[95] and the PACs they establish or control (lobbyist/registrant PACs).[96] For purposes of the disclosure rules, contributions are treated as bundled if they are *forwarded* by a lobbyist, LDA registrant, or lobbyist/registrant PAC to the candidate committee; or *received* by the candidate committee and *credited* by the candidate committee to a lobbyist, registrant, or lobbyist/registrant PAC.[97]

This is a broader definition of "bundling" than the definition that applies to the restrictions on corporate conduit contributions. While contributions must be physically collected and then transmitted to the candidate to be subject to the restrictions on corporate conduit contributions, any contributions that are either forwarded by a lobbyist or received by a committee and credited by that committee to a lobbyist, registrant, or registrant PAC are subject to disclosure.[98] A contribution may be credited to a lobbyist, registrant, or registrant PAC through records, designations, or other means of recognizing that a certain amount of money has been raised, such as through:

- Titles assigned to persons who have raised a certain amount (e.g., "Pioneers" or "Rangers");
- Tracking identifiers assigned and included on contributions or contribution-related materials to maintain information about the amounts a person raises;

---

92. *Id.* §§ 102.8(a), 110.6(c)(1)(iv).
93. *Id.* § 110.6(c)(1).
94. *Id.* § 110.6(b)(2)(i)(E).
95. A registrant is an organization that employs one or more lobbyists; the term does not include an organization that merely retains an outside lobbyist or lobbying firm to lobby on the organization's behalf. See Chapter 4.
96. *See* 2 U.S.C. § 434(i) (2015).
97. *See* 11 C.F.R. § 104.22(a)(6) (2015).
98. *Id.*

- Access to events or activities given as a result of raising a certain amount; and
- Mementos, such as photographs with the candidate or autographed copies of books authored by the candidate.[99]

Under the rules, candidates, leadership PACs, and political party committees ("reporting committees") are required to disclose the name and address of each lobbyist, registrant, or lobbyist/registrant PAC that provides two or more bundled contributions aggregating in excess of $17,600 during a covered period, the lobbyist's employer, and the aggregate amount of contributions bundled by the lobbyist, registrant, or lobbyist/registrant PAC.[100] Ordinarily, a committee's covered period tracks its regular quarterly or monthly campaign finance reporting schedule. The semiannual periods beginning on January 1 and July 1 are also covered periods, requiring additional reports.[101] Thus, for example, a reporting committee that receives $17,600 or less in lobbyist-bundled contributions during a quarterly period will not have to disclose the total bundled contributions on its quarterly report. But it would have to report the lobbyist's bundling on its semiannual report if the aggregate amount of bundled contributions raised during the semiannual period exceeds $17,600. Neither contributions made by the lobbyist, registrant, or lobbyist/registrant PAC itself, nor those made by the lobbyist or registrant's spouse, count toward the reporting threshold.[102]

While these disclosure obligations fall primarily on the reporting committee that receives the bundled contributions, a lobbyist/registrant PAC must identify its status as such on the Statements of Organization that it files with the FEC.[103] A PAC will qualify as a lobbyist/registrant PAC if (1) the PAC is required to be disclosed by the lobbyist or registrant on its Form LD-203; (2) the PAC is the separate segregated fund of a registrant; (3) a lobbyist or registrant had a primary role in establishing the PAC; or (4) a lobbyist or registrant directs the governance or operations of the PAC.[104] This means that the SSF established by a corporation that employs in-house lobbyists will need to identify itself as a lobbyist/registrant PAC on its Statement of Organization.

23-4 Corporate Communications

The Federal Election Campaign Act and FEC rules provide for several specific ways in which corporations may communicate about federal elections without it resulting in a prohibited corporate contribution or an expenditure. The applicable rules depend on whether the communication is directed to the corporation's restricted

---

99. *Id.*

100. *Id.* § 104.22(b)(1). This is the reporting threshold for 2016. The threshold is increased annually with inflation. *Id.* § 104.22(g).

101. *See id.* § 104.22(a)(5)(i).

102. *See id.* § 104.22(a)(6)(iii).

103. *Id.* § 104.22(c).

104. *Id.* § 104.22(a)(4). See Chapter 4 of this manual for a discussion of the rules regarding registration and reporting under the LDA; see Chapter 5 for a discussion of the LD-203 reporting requirements.

class[105] or to individuals beyond the restricted class. This section describes the rules that apply to communications directed to each audience.[106]

Following *Citizens United*, corporations are now permitted to sponsor certain independent communications in connection with federal elections.[107] But these communications may not be coordinated with candidates in the way that restricted class communications may be. And communications that fall outside the exemptions described in this section may trigger reporting obligations with the FEC.[108] The rules governing corporate independent expenditures are described separately in Chapter 24 of this manual.

23-4.1 Communications to the Restricted Class

23-4.1.1 Restricted Class Communications and Candidate/Party Appearances
FECA permits a corporation to communicate on any subject, including partisan political matters, with its restricted class.[109] Thus, a corporation may spend treasury funds to send a mailing, e-mail, or other communication to its restricted class.[110] These communications may expressly advocate the election or defeat of a candidate or party and ask the recipient to make a contribution directly to a candidate or party. These communications may be fully coordinated with the benefiting candidate or party committee, but they must represent the corporation's own speech—the corporation may not republish or redistribute materials prepared by the campaign or party committee. Moreover, communications with a campaign over the contents of a restricted class communication could compromise the ability of the corporation to sponsor independent communications to those outside the restricted class at a later date.[111]

The rules also permit a corporation to allow a candidate, a candidate's representative, or a representative of a party committee to address the corporation's restricted class at a corporate-sponsored event.[112] The rules for these events were described earlier, in Section 23-3.2.2.

23-4.1.2 Restricted Class Voter Registration and Get-Out-the-Vote Drives
A corporation may also establish and operate a phone bank to urge members of its restricted class to register or vote for a particular candidate or candidates, or to register with a particular political party.[113] It may also conduct registration and get-out-the-vote drives aimed at its restricted class, including providing transportation to registration locations and to the polls. These drives may include communications containing express advocacy for a particular candidate or party, but if the drives are coordinated with a campaign or political party, information and assis-

---

105. The composition of a corporation's restricted class is described in Section 23-2.5.1.

106. This section only addresses the federal campaign finance rules that govern corporate communications. Other laws, such as the Internal Revenue Code, may impose additional restrictions.

107. Citizens United, 558 U.S. at 365; 11 C.F.R. § 114.10(a) (2015); *see also* 79 Fed. Reg. 62,797, 62,799 (Oct. 21, 2014).

108. *See* 52 U.S.C. § 30104(c) (2015).

109. 11 C.F.R. § 114.3(a)(1) (2015).

110. *Id.* § 114.3(c)(1).

111. *Id.* § 114.2(c).

112. *See id.* § 114.3(c)(2).

113. *Id.* § 114.3(c)(3).

tance regarding registering or voting cannot be withheld on the basis of support for or opposition to a particular candidate or party.[114]

23-4.1.3 Reporting Restricted Class Communications
A corporation must disclose to the FEC on Form 7 costs that are directly attributable to a restricted class communication that expressly advocates the election or defeat of a clearly identified candidate if those costs exceed $2,000 in any election.[115]

23-4.2 Communications Outside the Restricted Class

The rules also provide for certain ways in which corporations may communicate with—or permit candidates or officeholders to appear and communicate with—individuals outside of the restricted class on political matters. Some of these types of communications are described below. This list is not exhaustive; provided that they are conducted entirely independently of candidates, campaigns, and the political party committees, corporations may communicate with the general public about federal elections without following these guidelines.[116] However, activities that fall within these parameters will not be considered prohibited contributions, nor will they be treated as expenditures that trigger reporting obligations for the corporation.

23-4.2.1 Candidate and Party Appearances before a Corporation's Employees
A corporation may permit candidates, candidates' representatives, or representatives of a political party to address the corporation's employees—both those who fall within the restricted class and without—and their families on corporate premises or at a corporate meeting, convention, or other function.[117] However, when a candidate or party appearance is opened up to those beyond the restricted class, it is subject to a far stricter set of rules. As with a restricted class event, attendance at a candidate appearance is limited—in this case, to the corporation's employees, the corporation's other guests who are speaking or who are being honored, and representatives of the news media.[118] However, unlike a restricted class event, when a corporation permits a candidate or party representative to address employees outside of the restricted class, it must provide similar, substantially equal opportunities to the candidate or party's opponents upon request.[119]

Moreover, a corporation is limited in its ability to coordinate with candidates in connection with these appearances. While a corporation may discuss with the candidate or party representative the structure, format, and timing of the appearance, and the candidate's positions on issues, it may not discuss the candidate's campaign plans, projects, or needs.[120]

When appearing before a corporation's employees, a candidate or party may request contributions and may leave campaign materials or envelopes that

---

114. *Id.* § 114.3(c)(4). If information or assistance is so withheld, the drive may not be coordinated with a candidate or political party, and may trigger independent expenditure reporting. *See id.*

115. *Id.* §§ 100.134(a), 104.6(a), 114.3(b).

116. *See* 79 Fed. Reg. at 62,806; see Chapter 24 of this manual.

117. 11 C.F.R. § 114.4(b)(1) (2015).

118. *Id.*

119. *Id.* § 114.4(b)(1)(i)–(iii).

120. *Id.* § 114.4(b)(1)(vii).

members of the audience can use to remit contributions. However, unlike at a restricted class event, the candidate may not accept contributions before, during, or after the event. And the corporation sponsoring the appearance and its employees may not solicit funds for the candidate or party, expressly advocate the election of the candidate or party, or encourage corporate employees to do the same.[121]

23-4.2.2 Officeholder Appearances before the General Public

As a general rule, a corporation may not host an event that is open to the general public at which candidates appear to discuss campaign matters.[122] However, a corporation may host an appearance by an officeholder who is a candidate if he or she is appearing in his or her capacity as an officeholder and not as a candidate.[123] At such an appearance, the officeholder may talk about issues of interest to the sponsor, including ones that may also be issues in his or her campaign. But the appearance may not be campaign related: Neither the officeholder nor the host may expressly advocate the officeholder's election or defeat, solicit or accept contributions, or distribute campaign materials; and, in introducing the officeholder, the host may not refer to the officeholder's status as a federal candidate. Moreover, the host may not contribute to the officeholder in exchange for the officeholder's appearance.[124]

23-4.2.3 Voter Registration and Get-Out-the-Vote Communications and Drives

The rules permit a corporation to make communications to the general public that urge individuals to vote or to register to vote, provided that they do not expressly advocate the election or defeat of any clearly identified candidate or political party and they are not coordinated with any candidates or political parties.[125]

A corporation may also support or conduct voter registration and get-out-the-vote drives that are aimed at employees outside the restricted class or to the general public, including providing transportation to the polls or places of registration. These drives, too, may not contain express advocacy or be coordinated with candidates or political parties.[126] In addition, the drives must be nonpartisan. They may not be directed primarily to individuals based on past, present, or anticipated party registration. They must be made available without regard to a voter's political preference, information and other assistance may not be withheld on the basis of support for or opposition to particular candidates or a particular party, and individuals must receive written notification of this requirement at the time of the drive.[127] Individuals who conduct the drive may not be paid on the basis of the number of individuals registered or transported who support one or more particular candidates or political parties.[128]

---

121. *Id.* § 114.4(b)(1)(iv), (v).

122. Within certain parameters, however, broadcasters, newspapers, magazines and other bona fide periodicals, and nonprofit section 501(c)(3) and 501(c)(4) organizations may host candidate debates that are open to the public. *Id.* § 114.4(f). For-profit corporations may not host these debates, but may donate funds to nonprofit organizations in support of such efforts. *Id.* § 114.4(f)(3).

123. *See* Fed. Election Comm'n Adv. Op. 1996-11; *see also* Fed. Election Comm'n Adv. Op. 1992-6.

124. *Id.*

125. *Id.* § 114.4(c)(2).

126. *Id.* § 114.4(a), (d)(2).

127. *Id.* § 114.4(d)(4).

128. *Id.* § 114.4(d)(5).

23-4.2.4 *Voting Records and Voter Guides*

A corporation may prepare and distribute to the general public the voting records of members of Congress. The voting records may not expressly advocate the election or defeat of any clearly identified candidate, and the corporation may not coordinate with candidates or political parties on the content and distribution of the record.

Corporations may also prepare and distribute voter guides (including voter guides obtained from a section 501(c)(3) or (c)(4) organization), subject to the same general requirements: They may not contain express advocacy and may not be coordinated with candidates or political parties.[129] The coordination rules, however, permit a candidate or political party to respond to an organization's inquiry about that candidate's or party's positions on legislative or policy issues, provided that the response does not include a discussion of campaign plans, projects, activities, or needs.[130]

23-4.2.5 *Candidate Endorsements*

A corporation is permitted to endorse a candidate and may communicate that endorsement to the public. The corporation's disbursements to announce the endorsement to the general public are not considered a contribution or expenditure, provided that they are not coordinated with a candidate, his or her campaign, or the candidate's agents, and the press release and notice of the press conference are distributed only to the representatives of the news media that the corporation customarily contacts when issuing nonpolitical press releases or holding press conferences for other purposes.[131] The corporation may coordinate with candidates regarding the announcement of the endorsement to its own restricted class, but no more than a de minimis number of copies may be circulated beyond the restricted class.[132]

23-5 Rules for Trade Associations

Similar to their treatment of corporations, the FEC rules provide for a number of ways that different types of membership organizations, including trade associations, cooperatives, and corporations without capital stock, may engage in federal elections. This section addresses the rules that apply to trade associations specifically.

For the most part, trade associations may engage in the same types of activities as corporations, as discussed throughout this chapter.[133] The principal difference is the composition of the group of individuals from whom a trade association's SSF may solicit contributions and the group of individuals with whom a trade association may otherwise communicate about federal elections. In the case of most corporations, these two groups are one and the same. In the case of a trade association, the group that a trade association's SSF may solicit (the "solicitable class") is different from the group that the trade association may communicate with on other

---

129. *Id.* § 114.4(c)(5)(i).
130. *Id.* § 109.21(f).
131. *Id.* § 114.4(c)(6)(ii).
132. *Id.* § 114.4(c)(6)(i).
133. *Id.* § 114.8(g), (h).

political matters (the restricted class). The composition of each group is described below.

23-5.1 What Is a Trade Association?

Under the rules, a "trade association" is a membership organization of persons engaging in a similar or related line of commerce, organized to promote and improve business conditions in that line of commerce and not to engage in a regular business of a kind ordinarily carried on for a profit.[134] Trade associations are typically tax exempt under section 501(c)(6) of the Internal Revenue Code, though the FEC has, under certain circumstances, treated other nonprofit organizations as trade associations for purposes of the campaign finance laws.[135]

To qualify as a membership organization, and hence a trade association, an organization must meet six criteria. It must

- Entrust some or all of its members with the power and authority to operate and administer the organization, pursuant to its articles, bylaws, constitution, or other formal organizational documents;
- Expressly state its qualifications for membership in its articles, bylaws, constitution, or other formal organizational documents;
- Make its articles, bylaws, constitution, or other formal organizational documents available to its members upon their request;
- Expressly solicit persons to become members;
- Expressly acknowledge each member's acceptance of membership, such as with a membership card or inclusion of the member's name on a membership list; and
- Not be organized primarily for the purpose of influencing the nomination for election, or the election, of any individual to federal office.[136]

23-5.2 Trade Association SSFs and the "Solicitable Class"

A trade association may establish and operate an SSF, just as a corporation may, but the group of persons that the association or its SSF may solicit is different.[137] A trade association may solicit voluntary contributions to its SSF from its noncorporate members, the trade association's executive or administrative personnel, and their families.[138] To qualify as a member of a trade association, an individual or entity must (1) currently satisfy all requirements for membership as established in the membership organization's governing documents; (2) affirmatively accept the membership organization's invitation to become a member; and (3) either (a) have some significant financial attachment to the membership organization, such as a significant investment or ownership stake, (b) pay membership dues at least annually of a specific amount predetermined by the organization, or (c) have a significant organizational attachment to the membership organization, which includes

---

134. *Id.* § 114.8(a).
135. *See* Fed. Election Comm'n Adv. Op. 2005-17.
136. 11 C.F.R. § 114.1(e)(1) (2015).
137. *See id.* § 114.7(h).
138. *See id.* § 114.7(c), (e), (f).

an affirmation of membership on at least an annual basis and possession of direct participatory rights in the organization's governance.[139]

Determining who, precisely, qualifies as a member of a trade association for FEC purposes typically requires a close review of the association's governing documents. Even though an association may consider a person to be a member for its own purposes, that person may not be solicited for contributions to the trade association's SSF unless he or she meets the FEC's three-part test. In many cases, trade associations recognize multiple classes of members, each of which must be considered separately.

A trade association may not solicit contributions from its corporate members directly. Nor may it solicit contributions from the SSFs established by its member corporations.[140] However, it may seek and obtain prior approval from each corporate member to solicit that corporate member's own restricted class.[141] A member corporation's approval is effective only in the calendar year for which it is granted, and a member corporation may approve solicitation by only one trade association in a calendar year.[142] In its approval, the corporation may limit the class of individuals whom the trade association may solicit.[143] Once a corporation approves a solicitation, there is no limit to the number of times the association may solicit the corporation's restricted class, unless the corporation specifies otherwise in its approval.[144]

A member corporation may provide incidental services to help collect and forward contributions to the trade association's SSF, including the use of a payroll deduction or checkoff system. However, if the corporation provides these services to the trade association, the corporation and its subsidiaries and affiliates must, upon written request, make those same incidental services available to a labor organization that represents any members that work for the corporation or its subsidiaries and affiliates.[145] A member corporation may also make monetary and in-kind donations under certain circumstances to a trade association to help the association pay the administration and solicitation costs of its SSF.[146]

A trade association with foreign companies as members, or with foreign nationals involved in its activities, must be aware of the limitations the law places on foreign national involvement in political activity. These rules are complex and broad, and navigating them often requires the advice of counsel.

23-5.3 Trade Association Communications and Appearances

Like a corporation, a trade association may communicate on an unrestricted basis about federal elections with its own "restricted class" and may permit candidates and candidate and party representatives to appear at association-sponsored

---

139. *See id.* § 114.1(e)(2).

140. *Id.* § 114.8(c).

141. *See id.* § 114.8(c)(1).

142. *See id.* § 114.8(c)(2), (d)(4).

143. *See id.* § 114.8(d)(5).

144. *See id.* § 114.8(e)(1).

145. *See id.* § 114.8(e)(4). The rules for payroll deduction systems are described in greater detail in Section 23-2.5.3.

146. *See* Fed. Election Comm'n Adv. Ops. 1992-20, 1982-36.

events before the restricted class.[147] For purposes of this rule, a trade association's "restricted class" consists of its members (as that term is defined under the rules), its executive and administrative personnel, and their families.[148] When communicating with its corporate members, the association may communicate with the representatives of the corporation with whom the association normally conducts its activities.[149] It may not otherwise communicate with the restricted classes of its corporate members, except to solicit contributions for its own SSF after receiving authorization from the corporation, as described earlier.

An incorporated trade association may also communicate with, and host candidate or party appearances that are open to, its employees at large and the general public under the same conditions that a corporation may.[150]

---

147. *See* 11 C.F.R. § 114.8(h) (2015). The rules for restricted class communications and appearances are described in Sections 23-3.2.2 and 23-4.1.

148. 11 C.F.R. § 114.8(h) (2015).

149. *Id.*

150. *See id.* § 114.8(i)(1). The rules for communications and appearances directed outside of the restricted class are described in Section 23-4.2.

CHAPTER 24

Federal Election Activity by Corporations after *Citizens United*

BY TREVOR POTTER AND MATTHEW T. SANDERSON

Federal campaign finance law long prohibited corporations from using their treasury funds to influence elections for federal office,[1] though the prohibition's scope has been broadened[2] and narrowed[3] over time. Corporations are still not

---

1. 52 U.S.C. § 30118(a) (2015) ("It is unlawful . . . for any corporation whatever . . . to make a contribution or expenditure in connection with any [federal] election").

2. For example, in an attempt to broaden the corporate prohibition, the Bipartisan Campaign Reform Act of 2002 forbade corporations from using treasury funds for any "electioneering communication," a television or radio ad referencing a candidate or party shortly before an election. *See* Bipartisan Campaign Reform Act of 2002, Pub. L. 107–155 at § 203.

3. *See, e.g.,* Fed. Election Comm'n v. Wis. Right to Life, Inc., 551 U.S. 449, 470 (2007) (stating that corporate treasury funds were prohibited from financing "electioneering communications" only to the

permitted to use treasury funds to make monetary or in-kind contributions to federal candidates, national party committees, state and local party committees' federal accounts, and federal PACs' "contribution" accounts.[4] In 2010's *Citizens United v. Federal Election Commission* case, however, the United States Supreme Court held that corporations may make unlimited election expenditures for communications using corporate treasury funds, so long as those communications are created and distributed independently from candidates and political parties.[5]

This chapter explains the post-*Citizens United* legal rules that govern a corporation's ability to use treasury funds to sponsor, both directly and indirectly, independent communications that may influence federal elections. This chapter also describes special prohibitions that apply to particular categories of corporations, including federal government contractors, national banks, and federally chartered corporations.[6]

24-1 Corporations Generally—Directly Sponsoring Independent Communications That May Influence Federal Elections

A corporation may, as a direct sponsor, spend an unlimited amount of its treasury funds on advertisements that reference federal candidates and party committees, so long as it does not "coordinate" the ads with federal candidates and party committees. A corporation must also file certain disclosure reports about these advertisements, depending on a particular advertisement's content, medium, and distribution.

24-1.1 A Corporation Must Maintain Its Independence from Federal Candidates and Party Representatives When Sponsoring Certain Advertisements That Identify Federal Candidates or Party Committees

A corporation and its employees should carefully monitor their interactions with federal candidates, their campaigns, and party representatives when sponsoring advertisements that mention federal candidates or party committees. Federal law prohibits corporations from contributing to candidates and party committees. And a prohibited in-kind contribution could result if *any one* of the following is true

---

extent that they are the "functional equivalent of express advocacy"—a standard that is satisfied only if an "ad is susceptible of no reasonable interpretation other than as an appeal to vote for or against a specific candidate").

4. 11 C.F.R. § 114.2(b) (2015). A federal PAC may maintain a "non-contribution" account to be used for independent communications that may receive unlimited funds from corporations. Fed. Election Comm'n Adv. Op. 2013-09. *See also* Press Release, *FEC Statement on* Carey v. Fed. Election Comm'n: *Reporting Guidance for Political Committees that Maintain a Non-Contribution Account* (Oct. 5, 2011), *available at* http://www.fec.gov/press/press2011/20111006postcarey.shtml.

5. 558 U.S. 310, 365 (2010).

6. This chapter does not address the rules governing corporate involvement in state and local elections. While *Citizens United* recognized that corporations have a constitutional right to sponsor independent communications in connection with these elections, too, a number of states impose disclosure obligations and other restrictions on corporations that wish to do so. Thus, corporations should confer with counsel before sponsoring communications in connection with state elections, or donating to outside organizations for this purpose.

about a corporate-sponsored communication that mentions a federal candidate or party committee, depending on its content:

- A candidate, campaign, or party representative requests, suggests, or assents to the communication's creation, production, or distribution.[7]
- A candidate, campaign, or party representative is "materially involved in decisions regarding" the communication's content, intended audience, medium, timing, frequency, size, prominence, or duration.[8]
- A candidate, campaign, or party representative is involved in "substantial discussions" about the communication.[9]
- The commercial vendor hired to create, produce, or distribute the communication (1) provided during the previous 120 days media strategy, polling, fund-raising, media production, voter identification, list development, personnel, or consulting services to a candidate clearly identified in the communication, that candidate's opponent, or a political party committee; and (2) uses or conveys information about "campaign plans, projects, activities, or needs" that is "material to the creation, production, or distribution of the communication."[10]
- An individual who, in the past 120 days, worked for a candidate clearly identified in the communication, that candidate's opponent, or a political party uses or conveys information about "campaign plans, projects, activities, or needs" that is "material" to the communication.[11]

If a corporation distributes a public communication following one of the above-described courses of conduct, it will result in a prohibited in-kind contribution to the benefiting candidate if it contains one of the following types of content:[12]

---

7. 11 C.F.R. § 109.21(d)(1) (2015).

8. 11 C.F.R. § 109.21(d)(2) (2015). The "material involvement" standard focuses on the factual nature of information conveyed by the candidate or party and its "importance, degree of necessity [and] influence" or the "effect of involvement" by a candidate or party. 68 Fed. Reg. 421, 433 (Jan. 3, 2003). A candidate or party need not be included in formal decision making or engage in discussion with the person paying for the communication to be "materially involved." A candidate asking a staffer to deliver a candidate-commissioned poll to the person paying for the communication is an example of "material involvement." *See id.* at 433–34.

9. 11 C.F.R. § 109.21(d)(3) (2015). A discussion is "substantial" if "information about the candidate's or political party committee's campaign plans, projects, activities, or needs is conveyed to a person paying for the communication" and the information conveyed is "material to the creation, production, or distribution of the communication." 68 Fed. Reg. at 435.

10. 11 C.F.R. § 109.21(d)(4) (2015). However, "coordination" will not result if the vendor establishes and uses an adequate "firewall" to prevent information sharing between those employees or consultants providing services to the person paying for the communication and those employees or consultants providing services to the candidate identified in the communication, her opponent, the candidates' authorized committees, or a political party committee. 11 C.F.R. § 109.21(h) (2015). *See also* FEC Matter Under Review 5506, First General Counsel's Report at 6–7 (Aug. 9, 2005) (noting firewall policy for EMILY's List); Coordinated Communications, 71 Fed. Reg. 33,190, 33,206 (June 8, 2006) (endorsing firewall approach used by EMILY's List).

11. 11 C.F.R. § 109.21(d)(5) (2015).

12. Despite this general rule, a corporation may make certain communications to its so-called restricted class—its stockholders, executive and administrative employees, and their families—in full coordination with candidates and political party committees. These rules are described in detail in Chapter 23 of this manual.

- The communication "expressly advocates" the election or defeat of a clearly identified federal candidate.[13] An "express advocacy" communication is one that either (1) includes so-called magic words, such as "vote for," "reelect," "support," or "oppose" with respect to a federal candidate; or (2) when, taken as a whole and with limited reference to external events, could only be interpreted by a reasonable person as containing express advocacy of "the election or defeat of a clearly identified candidate."[14]
- The communication contains the "functional equivalent of express advocacy"—a communication that is susceptible of no reasonable interpretation other than as an appeal to vote for or against a clearly identified federal candidate.[15]
- The communication "disseminates, distributes or republishes" a candidate's own campaign materials.[16]
- The communication is an "electioneering communication," as that term is defined in Section 24-1.2, below.[17]
- The communication merely refers to a clearly identified candidate for the United States House or Senate and is publicly distributed or disseminated in that candidate's jurisdiction within the ninety days before that candidate's primary, general, special, or runoff election.[18]
- The communication merely refers to a clearly identified presidential or vice presidential candidate and is publicly distributed or disseminated in a jurisdiction during the time period beginning 120 days before the candidate's primary or preference election in that jurisdiction and ending on the day of the general election.[19]
- The communication refers to a clearly identified political party close to an election, depending on the composition of the ballot in the jurisdiction where the communication is disseminated.[20]

24-1.2 A Corporation May Need to File Disclosure Reports for Advertisements That Mention Federal Candidates or Party Committees

As a result of directly sponsoring advertisements that mention federal candidates or party committees, a corporation may be required to file certain disclosure reports, depending on the advertisement's content, medium, and distribution. Two types of advertisements that mention federal candidates or party committees must be reported: "express advocacy" communications and "electioneering" communications. To disclose an independent express advocacy communication, otherwise known as an independent expenditure,[21] a corporation must file a report with

---

13. 11 C.F.R. § 109.21(c)(3) (2015).
14. 11 C.F.R. § 100.22 (2015).
15. 11 C.F.R § 109.21(c)(5) (2015).
16. *Id.* § 109.21(c)(2).
17. *Id.* § 109.21(c)(1).
18. *Id.* § 109.21(c)(4)(i).
19. *Id.* § 109.21(c)(4)(ii).
20. *See id.* § 109.21(c)(4)(iii).
21. 11 C.F.R. § 100.22 (2015).

the Federal Election Commission (FEC) at the end of the first reporting period in which communications with respect to a given election aggregated more than $250 in a calendar year and in any succeeding period during the same year in which additional communications are made.[22] In addition, a corporation must file reports within twenty-four and forty-eight hours of sponsoring independent expenditures under certain circumstances: expenditures aggregating $10,000 or more in a calendar year must be disclosed within forty-eight hours, when made up to and including the twentieth day before an election, and expenditures aggregating $1,000 or more must be disclosed within twenty-four hours when made less than twenty days before the election.[23] These reports must disclose, among other things, the identification of each contributor who made a contribution in excess of $200 "for the purpose of furthering the reported independent expenditure" and must contain a certification, signed under penalty of perjury, that the expenditures were not coordinated with any candidate, candidate's committee, or political party.[24]

"Electioneering" communications are broadcast, cable, or satellite-communication advertisements that

- Refer to a clearly identified candidate for federal office;
- Are publicly distributed[25] either—
  - Within sixty days before a general election for the office sought by the clearly identified candidate;
  - Within thirty days before a primary election, preference election, convention, or caucus of a political party that has authority to nominate the clearly identified candidate for the office she seeks, and the candidate is seeking the nomination of that political party; and
- In the case of a House or Senate candidate, can be received by more than 50,000 people in the district or state the candidate seeks to represent.[26]

If a corporation sponsors or contracts to sponsor "electioneering" communications totaling in excess of $10,000 in a calendar year, it must disclose to the FEC within twenty-four hours of each communication, among other things, (1) the communication sponsor's identity, (2) all candidates clearly identified by the communication, and (3) the name and address of each donor who, since the first day of the preceding calendar year, has donated $1,000 or more to the communication's sponsor.[27]

---

22. 11 C.F.R. § 109.10(b) (2015).

23. *Id.* § 109.10(c), (d).

24. *Id.* § 109.10(e).

25. "Publicly distributed means aired, broadcast, cablecast or otherwise disseminated through the facilities of a television station, radio station, cable television system, or satellite system." 11 C.F.R. § 100.29(b)(3)(i) (2015).

26. In the case of an advertisement that refers to a candidate for president or vice president, it will be an electioneering communication if it is distributed to 50,000 or more persons anywhere in the United States during the sixty days before the presidential general election. It will also be an electioneering communication if it is distributed to 50,000 or more persons (1) anywhere in the United States within the period from thirty days before a national nominating convention to the conclusion of the convention, or (2) in a state holding a presidential primary election, within thirty days of that primary. *Id.* § 100.29(b)(3)(ii).

27. 52 U.S.C. § 30104(f)(2)(E)–(F) (2015).

24-2 Corporations Generally—Indirectly Sponsoring Independent Communications That May Influence Federal Elections

Rather than serving as an advertisement's direct sponsor, a corporation may also choose to sponsor an advertisement indirectly by simply contributing money to another entity that then creates, produces, and distributes the advertisement. Again, a corporation may use an unlimited amount of its treasury funds for this purpose.

The types of entities to which a corporation may contribute treasury funds for this purpose are outlined in the table below.

Table 24.1 Legal Rules Associated with Certain Tax-Exempt Entities

	501(c)(4) Social Welfare Organizations and 501(c)(6) Trade Associations	Super PACs and 527 Political Organizations
General Characteristics	Operated for the promotion of social welfare (i.e., the good of the community as a whole, or the good of a particular industry, including issue education); *may not benefit one individual or limited group of individuals as its primary purpose.*	Exists to influence the selection, nomination, election, or appointment of political candidates; may conduct issue education efforts that further that goal.
Tax Status	Exempt from paying tax on income apart from unrelated business income; contributions to (c)(4)s/(c)(6)s are not generally tax deductible. The IRS is currently not enforcing the gift tax on donations to (c)(4)s.	Exempt from paying tax on their exempt function income but not on investment income; contributions to a 527 are not tax deductible and are not subject to gift tax.
Disclosure Requirements	Report organizational information annually on IRS Form 990; aggregate political expenditures are reported on public IRS Form 990 and confidential Form 1120-POL.	*Super PACs:* Report organizational information at inception on FEC Form 1. Report receipts and disbursements aggregating over $200 in a year periodically on FEC Form 3X.

(continued)

	501(c)(4) Social Welfare Organizations and 501(c)(6) Trade Associations	Super PACs and 527 Political Organizations
Disclosure Requirements *(continued)*	Contribution information is reported to the IRS for donors giving $5,000 or more annually, but specific donor names and addresses are *not* disclosed to the public. Most expenditure information is *not* reported in itemized fashion, but there are exceptions for specific types of expenditures like officer and director compensation, top independent contractors, interested party transactions, and grants. Report federal "independent expenditures" and "electioneering communications" spending *only* when triggered (on FEC Forms 5 or 9, respectively). Generally, donors are itemized only when a donation is given "in furtherance of" specific independent expenditures. An entity that sponsors an "electioneering communication" may also need to disclose its donors under certain circumstances.	*527s:* Report organizational information annually on IRS Form 990. Report taxable income on Form 1120-POL (not publicly disclosed). Disclose contributors who give $200+ and all expenditures of $500+ on IRS Form 8872, which is filed quarterly.
Structural Limits on Political Activities	Can undertake *some* partisan political activities under federal tax rules, but such activities may *not* be the organization's "primary purpose." Possibly subject to state and federal campaign finance laws, which can include limits on contributions and disclosure obligations. Political expenditures may be taxed up to amount of investment income (i.e., if the entity receives no investment income, it pays no tax).	No federal tax limit on partisan political activities. Possibly subject to state and federal campaign finance laws, which can include disclosure requirements and limits on incoming contributions. Political expenditures *not* taxed, but if any substantial portion of the funds in an account is spent on nonpolitical activity, then all income in that account becomes taxed.

(continued)

	501(c)(4) Social Welfare Organizations and 501(c)(6) Trade Associations	Super PACs and 527 Political Organizations
Limits on Donors' Contributions	May accept unlimited contributions from individuals, corporations, or unions. No contributions from foreign nationals for political expenditures.	May accept unlimited contributions from individuals, corporations, or unions unless the group makes contributions to federal candidates or party committees. No contributions from foreign nationals.
Application for Tax-Exempt Status	IRS Form 1024; IRS approval not required; organization must provide to the IRS detailed descriptions of its planned issue-oriented activities to justify tax-exempt status.	IRS Form 8871 must be filed within 24 hours of formation; IRS typically conducts cursory review and organization can have more general purpose, such as to "help elect individuals who believe in limited government."
Other	Subject to some states' charitable solicitation acts, which typically require basic registration information plus disclosure requirements and restrictions.	Political fund-raising generally exempt from charitable solicitation laws.

The paragraphs below examine in greater detail the major considerations for a corporation in contributing to two of these entity types: a federal super PAC and a 501(c)(4) social welfare organization. A federal super PAC is a federally registered political committee that can raise unlimited, but disclosed, funds to make independent expenditures. A 501(c)(4) entity may receive unlimited and undisclosed contributions, but its primary activity must be lobbying or other activities promoting social welfare. From a corporate donor's perspective, the key difference between a super PAC and a section 501(c)(4) organization is that all donations exceeding $200 to a super PAC will be disclosed to the public, whereas donations to a section 501(c)(4) organization will generally be publicly disclosed only under more limited circumstances.

24-2.1 A Corporation May Contribute to a Federal Super PAC That Sponsors Independent Communications

A federal super PAC, formally known as an "independent expenditure-only committee,"[28] is a federally registered political committee that can solicit and accept unlimited contributions from individuals, corporations, and unions, provided that its election expenditures are made independently from candidates and political parties. Unlike a typical PAC, a super PAC may not make contributions to candidate committees.

---

28. Fed. Election Comm'n Adv. Op. 2010-09 at 1.

Super PACs were made possible by the U.S. Supreme Court's ruling in *Citizens United*, as well as two related rulings of the U.S. Court of Appeals for the D.C. Circuit.[29] Again, in *Citizens United*, the Supreme Court held that corporations may make independent expenditures using corporate treasury funds.[30] Applying *Citizens United*, the D.C. Circuit subsequently held in *SpeechNow.org v. FEC* that individuals may make unlimited independent expenditures and unlimited contributions to independent expenditure-only committees.[31] Following these rulings, the FEC formally acknowledged the permissibility of super PACs in two advisory opinions issued in July 2010.[32] In these opinions, the FEC advised that

- Federal super PACs may solicit and accept unlimited contributions from individuals who are U.S. citizens or permanent residents, political committees, labor organizations, and domestic corporations that are not national banks or federal government contractors;
- Federal super PACs may use corporate funds to defray establishment, administrative, and solicitation expenses, without sacrificing their ability to solicit funds from the general public (traditional "corporate-connected" PACs that make contributions to candidates and parties may solicit funds only from a corporation's "restricted class");[33]
- Federal super PACs may, independent from a candidate, the candidate's party, and their agents, expressly advocate the candidate's election;
- Federal super PACs may not make monetary or in-kind contributions to federal candidates and party committees, meaning that a super PAC must carefully avoid "coordinating" its spending with any federal candidate or party committee (e.g., obtaining input regarding creation or distribution of advertisements from a campaign; making an advertisement at the request or suggestion of a campaign); and
- Federal super PACs must file regular disclosure reports with the FEC on a quarterly basis and shortly before elections, just as regular PACs do.[34]

Like other political committees, a super PAC must file reports with the FEC, publicly disclosing its financial activity. These include periodic reports (either monthly, or quarterly during the election year and semiannually during the nonelection year).[35] In addition to completing periodic forms for the applicable reporting period, the PAC must file Schedule E of Form 3X with the FEC within (1) forty-eight hours if it spends $10,000 or more in a calendar year on

---

29. SpeechNow.org v. Fed. Election Comm'n, 599 F.3d 686, 689 (D.C. Cir. 2010) (en banc); EMILY's List v. Fed. Election Comm'n, 581 F. 3d 1, 10 (D.C. Cir. 2009) (holding that if a federal PAC does not make contributions to candidates, it may accept contributions that exceed federal contribution limits).

30. *Citizens United*, 558 U.S.310 at 365.

31. *SpeechNow.org*, 599 F.3d at 689; *see also EMILY's List*, 581 F. 3d at 10 (holding that "individual citizens may spend money without limit (apart from the limit on their own contributions to candidates or parties) in support of the election of particular candidates").

32. Fed. Election Comm'n Adv. Ops. 2010-11, 2010-09.

33. Unlike a traditional corporate-sponsored PAC, the super PAC must publicly disclose as "in-kind" contributions the value of all corporate resources used to support the PAC, such as staff time, mail charges, and copying costs. *See* Fed. Election Comm'n Adv. Op. 2010-09 at 5.

34. *See* Fed. Election Comm'n Adv. Ops. 2010-11, 2010-09.

35. 11 C.F.R. § 104.5(c) (2015).

express-advocacy communications "with respect to a given election," including e-mail and online solicitations for a candidate,[36] and (2) twenty-four hours if a super PAC spends $1,000 or more on express-advocacy communications, including e-mail and online solicitations for a candidate, "with respect to a given election" within twenty days of that election.[37] A corporation's contribution to a super PAC will be publicly disclosed on one or more of these FEC reports.[38]

24-2.2 A Corporation May Contribute to a 501(c)(4) Social Welfare Organization That Sponsors Independent Communications

A section 501(c)(4) organization may engage in partisan political activities, including influencing elections, but those activities must not be its "primary activity"[39] because its primary purpose must be the promotion of social welfare—the good of the community as a whole. Most of a section 501(c)(4) organization's resources must therefore be used to promote social welfare, which includes efforts to influence legislation germane to the organization's purpose but does not include participating in political campaigns. If a corporation makes a general (un-earmarked) contribution to a section 501(c)(4) organization, then, most of its contribution would go toward nonelection activities, such as lobbying.

To fund its political activities, a section 501(c)(4) organization may accept unlimited contributions from U.S. citizens, permanent residents, political committees, labor organizations, and domestic corporations that are not national banks or federal government contractors.[40] Contributions to section 501(c)(4) organizations, however, are not tax deductible as charitable donations and may be subject to the gift tax.[41]

A principal distinction between section 501(c)(4) organizations and super PACs is that donors to section 501(c)(4) organizations generally remain undisclosed, because while these organizations must report political expenditures and donors who give more than $5,000 annually to the IRS, specific donor names and addresses are typically not made public. A corporate contribution to a section 501(c)(4) organization will be disclosed only under certain circumstances—if, for example, it is made with the intent to fund an electioneering communication or independent expenditure.[42]

---

36. 52 U.S.C. § 30104(g)(2) (2015); 11 C.F.R. § 104.4(b)(2) (2015).

37. 52 U.S.C. § 30104(g)(1) (2015); 11 C.F.R. § 104.4(c) (2015).

38. A list of existing super PACs can be found on the FEC's website at http://www.fec.gov /press/press2011/ieoc_alpha.shtml (last visited Sept. 25, 2015).

39. 26 C.F.R. § 1.501(c)(4)–1(a)(2)(ii) (2015) (providing that the promotion of social welfare does not include "direct or indirect participation in political campaigns on behalf of or in opposition to any candidate for public office").

40. 52 U.S.C. §§ 30118, 30119, 30121 (2015).

41. *See* 26 U.S.C § 2501(a)(1) (2015). Though the IRS is currently not enforcing the gift tax with respect to contributions to section 501(c)(4) organizations, it could choose to do so in the future. As the law in this area can change quickly, a donor considering making a contribution would be well served to consult an accountant or lawyer before giving.

42. A donation to a section 501(c)(4) organization may also need to be publicly disclosed if the organization becomes a "political committee" under federal or state law. Under federal law, an organization will trigger political committee status if it (1) spends more than $1,000 on advertisements containing express advocacy and (2) its "major purpose" is nominating or electing candidates. Political Committee Status, Supplemental Explanation & Justification, 72 Fed. Reg. 5595-02, 5604-05 (Feb. 7,

A section 501(c)(4) organization that makes independent expenditures in excess of $250 during a calendar year must disclose to the FEC the identity of each person who contributed more than $200 to the organization during that calendar year "for the purpose of furthering the reported independent expenditure."[43] This means that contributions that are donated generally to the section 501(c)(4) organization, but not specifically for a particular independent expenditure, need not be disclosed by the organization.

An incorporated section 501(c)(4) organization that makes "electioneering" communications may also need to disclose one or more donors under certain circumstances. During recent election cycles, an incorporated 501(c)(4) that spent more than $10,000 on "electioneering communications" during any calendar year was required to disclose to the FEC within twenty-four hours of reaching the $10,000 threshold "the name and address of each person who made a donation aggregating $1,000 or more" to the organization "for the purpose of furthering electioneering communications."[44] As the FEC explained, an incorporated 501(c)(4) organization under this standard "disclose[d] the identities only of those persons who made a donation aggregating $1,000 or more specifically for the purpose furthering [electioneering communications]" and not individuals who provide funds to the organization generally.[45] Because this was a relatively narrow requirement, "electioneering communication" sponsors rarely disclosed their underlying donors in recent elections.

All section 501(c)(4) organizations should carefully monitor the state of the disclosure rules in this area.

24-3 Certain Types of Corporations May Be Prohibited from Directly or Indirectly Sponsoring Independent Communications That May Influence Federal Elections

Citizens United, as mentioned, lifted the ban on corporate independent expenditures. Indeed, the Court was categorical in its treatment of independent expenditures, saying "we now conclude that independent expenditures, including those made by corporations, do not give rise to corruption or the appearance of corruption."[46] The Court therefore found that preventing corruption and the appearance of corruption is not a "compelling interest" for government restrictions on independent speech, regardless of the speaker's identity.[47]

Despite this, federal law separately prohibits certain categories of corporations—including entities that have their principal places of business abroad

---

2007). In most cases, a section 501(c)(4) organization that is acting consistently with its tax status would not become a political committee under this standard, as the FEC has applied it in recent years. But a number of states impose strict disclosure rules on section 501(c)(4) organizations that make expenditures in connection with state or local elections that may require those organizations to publicly disclose their donors.

43. 11 C.F.R. § 109.10(e)(1)(vi) (2015); *see* 52 U.S.C. § 30104 (c)(2)(C) (2015).

44. 11 C.F.R. § 104.20(c)(9) (2015).

45. Electioneering Communications, 72 Fed. Reg. 72899-01, 72911 (Dec. 26, 2007).

46. *Citizens United*, 558 U.S. at 357; *see also SpeechNow.org*, 599 F.3d at 693.

47. *See Citizens United*, 558 U.S. at 361 ("Here Congress has created categorical bans on speech that are asymmetrical to preventing *quid pro quo* corruption.").

or are organized under foreign law,[48] federal contractors,[49] federally chartered corporations,[50] and national banks[51]—from making federal election expenditures, and *Citizens United* did not address the constitutionality of these provisions as applied to independent advertising. A corporation that falls within any of these categories should consult with legal counsel before attempting to directly or indirectly sponsor any election activities.

The paragraphs below briefly describe the prohibitions that apply to federal contractors, national banks, and federally chartered corporations.

24-3.1 Federal Contractors

Federal law declares it "unlawful for any person . . . who enters into any contract with the United States or any department or agency thereof" to contribute funds "to any political, committee, or candidate for public office or to any person for any political purpose or use."[52] While *Citizens United* has raised doubts about the constitutionality of this provision as applied to activities undertaken independently from candidates and parties, the case did not directly address this prohibition. Thus, federal contractors' status in this regard is currently uncertain.[53]

However, a contractor's parent company is considered a different "person" than its subsidiaries for purposes of the federal contractor ban. The FEC has, in fact, previously authorized parents of contractors to make political expenditures. In Advisory Opinion 1998-11, the FEC permitted political expenditures by a parent limited liability company (LLC) that owned 90 percent of two federal contractor subsidiaries, which were separate and distinct legal entities.[54] In this context, the parent LLC's political expenditures were permissible so long as they were made with funds drawn from "revenue other than that resulting from the operations" of the federal contractor subsidiaries.[55] In other words, an entire corporate family is not barred from all federal political activity merely because a subordinate entity holds a federal contract.[56]

24-3.2 National Banks and Federally Chartered Corporations

Federal campaign finance law includes a strict prohibition on contributions or expenditures "in connection with any election to any political office" by any

---

48. 52 U.S.C. § 30121(a) (2015); 22 U.S.C. § 611(b) (2015).

49. 52 U.S.C. § 30119(a) (2015). A "federal contractor" is a person who enters into a contract with the United States government for services, materials, supplies, equipment, land, or buildings, if the payment is to be made from funds appropriated by Congress. *See* 11 C.F.R. § 115.1(a) (2015).

50. 52 U.S.C. § 30118(a) (2015).

51. *Id.*

52. 52 U.S.C. § 30119(a) (2015); *see also* 11 C.F.R. §§ 115.1(a), 115.2 (2015).

53. One federal district court fully upheld the federal contractor ban, but noted that *Citizens United* and *SpeechNow.org* created "substantial doubt about the constitutionality of any limits on Super PAC contributions." Wagner v. Fed. Election Comm'n, 901 F. Supp. 2d 101, 107 (D.D.C. 2012), *vacated*, 717 F.3d 1007 (D.C. Cir. 2013).

54. Fed. Election Comm'n Adv. Op. 1998-11 at 1, 5.

55. *Id.* at 5; *see also* Fed. Election Comm'n Adv. Ops. 2005-01 at 3, 1999-32 at 6.

56. *See* Fed. Election Comm'n Adv. Op. 1998-11 at 5 (stating that the difference between corporations and LLCs is immaterial for purposes of the federal contractor ban).

"national bank" or "corporation organized by authority of any law of congress."[57] The prohibition applies to all election-related activities at the federal, state, and local levels.[58] And although *Citizens United* struck down the federal prohibition on independent expenditures by corporations—and invalidated similar state and local prohibitions—the opinion did not address the ban on independent expenditures by national banks or federally chartered corporations.

The prohibition on contributions or expenditures by national banks does not necessarily apply to affiliated corporations that are not national banks or are not otherwise organized under the laws of Congress. A parent corporation that is a holding company for a national bank, for example, is not treated as a national bank for purposes of applying the prohibition.[59] Similarly, a subsidiary that is a separate legal entity is treated as separate from its parent for purposes of the application of the prohibition on contributions or expenditures by national banks.[60] However, to avoid violating the prohibition on contributions and expenditures by a national bank, the affiliate must have sufficient funds derived from sources other than the national bank to ensure that any contribution is not made out of proceeds from a national bank.[61]

---

57. 52 U.S.C. § 30118(a) (2015) ("It is unlawful for any national bank, or any corporation organized by authority of any law of Congress, to make a contribution or expenditure in connection with any election to any political office, or in connection with any primary election or political convention or caucus held to select candidates for any political office."); 11 C.F.R. § 114.2(a) (2015); *see also* OCC Bulletin 2007-31, Prohibition on Political Contributions by National Banks (Aug. 24, 2007).

58. The phrase "election-related activities" as used here refers to activities related to election to public office; contributions solely connected to ballot initiatives are not subject to the national bank prohibition and are not otherwise addressed here. *See* Fed. Election Comm'n Adv. Op. 1980-95 at 2 (distinguishing between contributions relating "only to ballot referenda issues and not to elections to any political office").

59. Fed. Election Comm'n Adv. Op. 1976-19 at 1 ("[The parent company] is regarded as a corporation in its own right . . . Neither [the parent company], its State bank subsidiaries, nor its non-banking subsidiaries would be regarded as a national bank for purposes of the prohibition on contributions or expenditures by national banks.").

60. *See* Fed. Election Comm'n Adv. Op. 1980-07.

61. Fed. Election Comm'n Adv. Op. 1995-32 at 3, n.4; Fed. Election Comm'n Adv. Op. 1981-61 at 2.

CHAPTER 25

Pay-to-Play Rules

BY JONATHAN BERKON AND KARL SANDSTROM

Since 2010, federal and nonfederal campaign finance laws have generally trended in a deregulatory direction. One notable exception has been the proliferation of "pay-to-play" laws—laws that restrict individuals and entities that do business with the government from making political contributions in the same amounts or to the same recipients as may the rest of the population. The penalties for violating these rules can be severe—financial penalties, loss of existing contracts, blackout periods, debarment, and other civil and criminal penalties are among the possible sanctions. Accordingly, companies typically find it necessary to retain political law counsel to help establish and administer pay-to-play compliance programs.

    This chapter discusses three pay-to-play type rules that exist at the federal level—the Securities and Exchange Commission rule targeted at investment advisers and their key personnel; the Municipal Securities Rulemaking Board rule governing contributions by municipal brokers and dealers; and the long-standing federal statute barring donations by federal contractors.[1] The SEC and MSRB rules target entities (and associated individuals) doing certain types of financial work for state and local governments; the contractor ban targets firms and individuals contracting with the federal government. Taken together, these are the rules that apply most broadly to the largest swath of for-profit businesses.

This chapter also briefly introduces the universe of state and local pay-to-play laws affecting contributions to nonfederal candidates and committees. While a full survey of these state and local laws is beyond the scope of this chapter, we will explain the basic structure of these laws and the issues that corporations and their personnel should consider before making contributions to state and local candidates.

25-1 SEC and MSRB Pay-to-Play Rules

In 2010, the Securities and Exchange Commission (SEC) promulgated Rule 206(4)-5, popularly known as the SEC pay-to-play rule, to combat the practice of investment advisers' making political contributions to officials and candidates who could help them win contracts from state and local pension funds.[2] The SEC rule was modeled on Municipal Securities Rulemaking Board (MSRB) Rule G-37 (the "MSRB Rule"), which sought to root out similar practices in the municipal bond industry. This section principally discusses how SEC Rule 206(4)-5 (the SEC Rule) and the MSRB Rule operate: which financial services personnel it covers, what activity it restricts, whether an impermissible act can be "cured," and how to maintain records and design a compliance program. Though the rules are similar, there are some important differences as well, which the chapter discusses.

Like the MSRB Rule, the SEC Rule purports to cover only a narrow swath of contributions—those to state and local officials and candidates who exercise influence over the contracting process—in addition to separate restrictions on soliciting and bundling funds. In practice, however, the effect of these rules has been far broader: Many in the regulated community are curbing their donations to *all* state and local officials and candidates, along with political parties and organizations that support such officials and candidates. Recently, in response to a lawsuit filed by two party committees, the SEC made representations to a federal court suggesting that the scope of the rule is narrower than the regulated community had previously feared.[3]

25-1.1 Basic Structure of the SEC and MSRB Rules

Although the SEC and MSRB Rules are targeted at different industries, they adhere to the same basic structure:[4]

---

1. Recently, the Commodity Futures Trading Commission (CFTC) passed its own pay-to-play rule. *See* 17 C.F.R. § 23.451(a) - (e) (2012), *et seq.* This chapter does not address the CFTC Rule.

2. Political Contributions by Certain Investment Advisers, 75 Fed. Reg. 41,018 (July 14, 2010).

3. *See* Brief for Securities and Exchange Commission in Response to Plaintiffs' Motion for Preliminary Injunction at 16, New York Republican State Cmte. v. Securities & Exchange Comm'n, No. 1:1-cv-01345 (D.D.C. Aug. 29, 2014); Brief for Sec. & Exch. Comm'n, N.Y. Republican State Comm. v. Sec. & Exch. Comm'n, No. 14-1194/14-5242, at 27 (D.C. Cir. Jan. 21, 2015).

4. 75 Fed. Reg. at 41,020 ("We modeled our proposed rule on those adopted by the Municipal Securities Rulemaking Board, or MSRB, which since 1994 has prohibited municipal securities dealers

- Each rule identifies certain entities and individuals whose political activities are covered. Entities and individuals falling outside the covered class are not subject to the rule's restrictions.
- The rules lay out which types of political activities are restricted and which types of political activities remain unrestricted. There is also a third class of activities that may or may not be restricted depending on particular facts and circumstances.
- The rules offer limited ways for individuals and entities to "cure" their violations, to avoid the penalties.
- The rules recommend, and in some cases require, covered entities to establish compliance programs to ensure adherence to the rules.

This chapter explains each of these steps in more detail.

25-1.2 Who Is Covered?

The SEC Rule applies to "investment advisers" that provide compensated advisory services to state or local governments either directly or through a "covered investment pool."[5] An "investment adviser" includes any adviser registered (or required to be registered) with the SEC; any advisers unregistered in reliance on the exemption available under section 203(b)(3) of the Advisers Act; and any exempt reporting adviser.[6] The SEC Rule also applies to the "covered associates" of an investment adviser. A covered associate includes any (1) general partner of the investment adviser, (2) managing member of the investment adviser, (3) executive officer (such as a president, vice president of a principal business unit, division, or function, or any other person or officer who performs a similar policy-making function) of the investment adviser, (4) other individual with a similar status or function employed by the investment adviser, or (5) employee who solicits a government entity for the investment adviser and any person who supervises (directly or indirectly) the employee.[7] It also covers a PAC "controlled" by the investment adviser or another covered associate—meaning that the investment adviser or covered associate has the ability to direct, or cause the direction of, the governance or operations of the PAC.[8]

In turn, MSRB Rule G-37 applies to brokers, dealers, and municipal securities dealers that engage in municipal securities business with a government issuer.[9] It also covers certain professional personnel associated with the broker,

---

from participating in pay to play practices."). Indeed, the SEC has said that "where the MSRB's rule G-37 interpretations directly address an issue that the [SEC] has not addressed . . . the interpretations might be useful to consider." SECURITIES AND EXCHANGE COMMISSION, Staff Responses to Questions About the Pay to Play Rule, Question V.2, *available at* http://www.sec.gov/divisions/investment/pay-to-play-faq.htm (updated June 25, 2015).

5. 17 C.F.R. § 275.206(4)–5(a), (c). A "covered investment pool" means "(i) [a]n investment company registered under the Investment Company Act of 1940 (15 U.S.C. 80a) that is an investment option of a plan or program of a government entity; or (ii) [a]ny company that would be an investment company under section 3(a) of the Investment Company Act of 1940 (15 U.S.C. 80a–3(a)), but for the exclusion provided from that definition by either section 3(c)(1), section 3(c)(7) or section 3(c)(11) of that Act (15 U.S.C. 80a–3(c)(1), (c)(7) or (c)(11))." *Id.* § 275.206(4)–5(f)(3).

6. *Id.* § 275.206(4)–5(a).

7. *Id.* § 275.206(4)–5(f)(2).

8. *Id.*

9. MSRB Rule G-37(b)(i).

dealer, or municipal securities dealer—known as municipal finance professionals (MFPs)—and any PAC controlled by the broker, dealer, or municipal securities dealer or by any municipal finance professional.[10] The definition of MFP is intricate, but primarily encompasses those who solicit municipal securities business, sales principals, and those who engage in certain representative activities.

Notably, spouses and other family are *not* treated as covered associates or municipal finance professionals under the SEC and MSRB Rules—meaning that they are not *automatically* subject to the restrictions set forth in Section 25-1.3 below.[11] Nonetheless, in some circumstances the activities of a spouse or other family member could be imputed to the covered associate or municipal finance professional. Both the SEC and MSRB Rules prohibit covered associates and municipal finance professionals from doing indirectly what they are barred from doing directly.[12] For example, an adviser and its covered associates could not funnel payments through third parties, including consultants, attorneys, family members, friends, or companies affiliated with the adviser as a means to circumvent the rule.[13] On the other hand, as the MSRB has explained, contributions by spouses and family members that are *not* directed by municipal finance professionals are not covered by the rule.[14]

25-1.3 Which Political Activities Are Restricted and Which Remain Unrestricted?

The rules impose two principal restrictions.[15]

First, the SEC Rule prohibits an investment adviser from providing compensated investment advisory services to a state or local government entity (such as a pension fund) for two years after the adviser or any of its covered associates makes a contribution to an "official of the government entity," unless the contribution falls below certain de minimis thresholds described later in this subsection.[16] This is known colloquially as the "two-year time out." The MSRB Rule has a similar two-year time out provision.[17]

Second, the SEC Rule bars an investment adviser or one of its covered associates from coordinating (e.g., bundling) or soliciting contributions on behalf of an "official of the government entity" or a political party of the state or locality to which the investment adviser is providing or seeking to provide investment advisory services.[18] The MSRB Rule includes a similar prohibition on coordinating or soliciting contributions for officials, candidates, and political parties in

---

10. MSRB Rule G-37(g)(iv).

11. 75 Fed. Reg. at 41,033, n.198; MUNICIPAL SECURITIES RULEMAKING BOARD, Questions and Answers Concerning Political Contributions and Prohibitions on Municipal Securities Business: Rule G-37, Question IV.9, *available at* http://www.msrb.org/Rules-and-Interpretations/MSRB-Rules /General/Rule-G37-Frequently-Asked-Questions.aspx (last visited Sept. 25, 2015).

12. SECURITIES AND EXCHANGE COMMISSION, Staff Responses to Questions About the Pay to Play Rule, Question II.3.

13. 75 Fed. Reg. at 41,044.

14. Questions and Answers Concerning Political Contributions and Prohibitions on Municipal Securities Business: Rule G-37, Question III.1.

15. The SEC Rule also restricts the activities of "placement agents." *See* 17 C.F.R. § 275.206(4)–5(a) (2)(i). That restriction is beyond the scope of the chapter.

16. *Id.* § 275.206(4)–5(a)(1).

17. MSRB Rule G-37(b)(i).

18. 17 C.F.R. § 275.206(4)–5(a)(2)(ii).

jurisdictions in which the broker, dealer, or municipal securities dealer engages in municipal securities business with a government issuer.[19]

25-1.3.1 The Restriction on Contributions

The two-year time out is triggered when covered entities and individuals make contributions (defined in Section 25-1.3.1.1) above certain de minimis levels (described in Section 25-1.3.1.2) to certain officials of government entities (discussed in Section 25-1.3.1.3). Notably, both the SEC and MSRB Rules contain "look-back" provisions pursuant to which individuals who are not yet covered associates but who anticipate becoming covered associates may be affected as well. This look-back provision is discussed in Section 25-1.3.1.4.

25-1.3.1.1 The Definition of "Contribution"

The SEC and MSRB Rules restrict contributions from entities and individuals covered by the Rules.

The SEC Rule defines "contribution" to include donations of money and in-kind contributions made for the purpose of influencing a federal, state, or local election, including payments of campaign debts and transition or inaugural expenses incurred by successful candidates for state or local (but not federal) office.[20] The MSRB Rule defines "contribution" in a similar way, to include donations of money and in-kind contributions made for the purpose of influencing any election for federal, state, or local office, including payments for debts incurred in connection with such elections or transition or inaugural expenses incurred by the successful candidates for state or local office.[21] However, the MSRB Rule definition of "contribution" also includes contributions to bond ballot campaigns.[22]

Notably, volunteer services (other than certain fund-raising activities, as discussed in Section 25-1.3.2) and independent expenditures are *not* treated as contributions.[23] This means that covered individuals may engage in volunteer activities in support of covered officials and candidates without running afoul of the rule.[24] The SEC has advised that covered entities and individuals may sponsor independent expenditure communications in support of covered officials and candidates without being in conflict with the rule.[25] Those interested in sponsoring such communications should confer with counsel to ensure that the planned expenditures are indeed "independent" under applicable law.

25-1.3.1.2 Exception for Certain De Minimis Contributions

Under the SEC Rule, de minimis contributions by individuals of $150 or less per election, per official, do not trigger the two-year time out.[26] In addition, if the individual can vote for the official or candidate to whom she or he is making the con-

---

19. MSRB Rule G-37(c).

20. 17 C.F.R. §§ 275.206(4)–5(f)(1).

21. MSRB Rule G-37(g)(i)(A).

22. MSRB Rule G-37(g)(i)(B).

23. 75 Fed. Reg. at 41,024.

24. Note, however, a volunteer's expenditure of funds in support of her or his volunteer activities might itself qualify as a "contribution." *See, e.g., id.* at 41,024, n.71.

25. *Id.* at 41,024 ("For example, the rule imposes no restrictions on activities such as making independent expenditures . . . .").

26. 17 C.F.R. § 275.206(4)–5(b)(1).

tribution, she or he may give up to $350 per election to the official or candidate without triggering the time out.[27] There is no de minimis exception for contributions by entities.

This is one area where the SEC and MSRB Rules diverge. Under the MSRB Rule, the de minimis exception is available *only* in circumstances in which the covered individual is eligible to vote for the candidate.[28] Individuals who are ineligible to vote for the candidate may not make any contributions to covered candidates. In addition, the de minimis amount for this eligible class of individuals is $250 per election under the MSRB Rule,[29] whereas it is either $150 or $350 per election under the SEC Rule, as explained earlier.

25-1.3.1.3 Which Officials and Candidates Are "Officials of a Government Entity"?

Not every elected official or candidate qualifies as an "official of the government entity." An official or candidate qualifies as an "official of the government entity" only if she or he holds or seeks a state or local office that (1) is responsible for, or can influence the outcome of, the hiring of an investment adviser by a government entity or (2) has authority to appoint any such person.[30] Because the term "government entity" excludes the federal government, the SEC Rule does not apply to incumbent federal officeholders running for reelection or candidates for federal office who do not currently hold state or local office. However, it does apply to candidates for federal office who currently hold a state or local office "covered" under the definition set forth above.[31]

The MSRB Rule covers those officials (1) responsible for, or who can influence the outcome of, the hiring of a broker, dealer, or municipal securities dealer for municipal securities business or (2) who have authority to appoint any such person.[32] Like the SEC Rule, the MSRB Rule does not apply to incumbent federal officeholders running for reelection or candidates for federal office that do not currently hold state or local office, but does apply to candidates for federal office that currently hold a state or local office covered by the definition above.

The SEC has declined to supply the regulated community with a list identifying which state and local officials exercise sufficient influence over hiring practices to be covered by the rule; it also rejected a proposal to allow donors to rely on certifications from state or local officials as to their status.[33] Accordingly, the burden of determining whether an official or candidate is "covered" falls entirely on the investment adviser and its covered associates. Many advisers have responded by barring their covered associates from contributing to *any* state or local officials or candidates. Others bear the expense of researching state and local pension laws to determine which officials are covered and which are not.

The SEC has shed *some* light on how it evaluates whether an official is covered by the rule. The SEC has advised that elected officials serving on a pension board

27. *Id.*
28. MSRB Rule G-37(b)(i).
29. *Id.*
30. 17 C.F.R. § 275.206(4)–5(f)(6).
31. 75 Fed. Reg. at 41,030.
32. MSRB Rule G-37(g)(vi).
33. *Id.* at 41,029–030.

that is authorized to hire investment advisers are covered.[34] In an enforcement action, the SEC determined that the mayor of Philadelphia was a covered official because he appointed one-third of a municipal pension fund board, and that the governor of Pennsylvania was a covered official because he appointed six of the eleven members of a State pension fund board.[35] On the other hand, in response to a lawsuit, the SEC represented to a federal court that a legislator who casts one of 125 votes for the state treasurer is *not* a covered official (even though the state treasurer has authority to hire advisers) and that a state legislator who casts one of more than 200 votes for a member of the board of regents is also *not* a covered official (even if the board of regents has authority to hire advisers).[36]

A contribution to a political party or a noncandidate political organization (like a PAC) does not automatically trigger the two-year time out.[37] The SEC has opined that such contributions *could* "violate the provision of the rule . . . which prohibits an adviser or any of its covered persons from indirect actions that would result in a violation of the rule if done directly."[38] For example, "if the PAC or political party is soliciting funds for the purpose of supporting a limited number of government officials, then, depending upon the facts and circumstances, contributions to the PAC or payments to the political party" could violate the rule.[39] Likewise, the SEC noted that "contributions [to a political party or PAC that] are earmarked or known to be provided for the benefit of a particular political official" would be covered by the rule.[40] Finally, the SEC has suggested that an impermissible contribution could result where "the PAC is closely associated with a government official to whom a direct contribution would subject the adviser to the two-year time out."[41] The MSRB guidance has been similar in this regard.[42]

This commentary suggests that the SEC only intended to cover a narrow subset of contributions to political parties and PACs, but that the vast majority of such contributions are exempt. For example, the SEC staff has publicly opined that "[a] contribution to a political party, PAC or other committee or organization would not trigger a two-year time out . . . unless it is a means to do indirectly what the rule prohibits if done directly."[43] In practice, however, many in the regulated community have shied away from authorizing contributions to noncandidate organizations unless they certify that they make *no* contributions to state or local officials or candidates or have sought other similar assurances from committees with respect to how their funds would be used. This caution can be understood as a reaction

---

34. *Id*. at 41,029, n. 143.

35. *In re* TL Ventures, Advisers Act Rel. No. 40-3859, ¶¶ 2, 14–17 & n.6, *available at* http://www.sec.gov/litigation/admin/2014/ia-3859.pdf (Jun. 20, 2014).

36. Brief for Securities and Exchange Commission in Response to Plaintiffs' Motion for Leave at 8, New York Republican State Comm. and Tennessee Republican Party v. Securities and Exchange Comm'n, No. 1:14-cv-01345 (D.D.C. Sept. 24, 2014); Brief for Securities and Exchange Commission in Response to Plaintiffs' Motion for Preliminary Injunction at 17, *New York Republican State Comm.*, No. 1:14-cv-01345 (D.D.C. Aug. 29, 2014).

37. 75 Fed. Reg. at 41,031.

38. *Id.*

39. *Id.*, n.163.

40. *Id*. at 41,030, n.154.

41. *Id*. at 41,050, n.418.

42. *See* Questions and Answers Concerning Political Contributions and Prohibitions on Municipal Securities Business: Question III.3.

43. Question V.3, http://www.sec.gov/divisions/investment/pay-to-play-faq.htm.

against the SEC's unwillingness to draw bright lines and the significant financial penalty that would attach to noncompliance.

Recent developments in the law might portend a less cautious approach from the regulated community. In *McCutcheon v. Federal Election Commission*, the Supreme Court opined that contributions to political parties and PACs within campaign finance limits do not present a risk of quid pro quo corruption.[44] This calls into question how aggressively the SEC can police contributions to political parties and PACs without running afoul of the First Amendment. More significantly, in response to the recent lawsuit, the SEC argued that the plaintiffs—two state political parties—lacked standing to challenge the law because "the definition of 'official' does not include a political party" and "[a]s political parties, plaintiffs have no potential injury on this front because investment advisers and 'covered associates' can make contributions to them without any effect on their ability to obtain compensation for services provided to a government entity."[45] The SEC plainly contemplates that investment advisers and their covered associates will make contributions to political parties and PACs without affecting their ability to provide compensated advisory services.

25-1.3.1.4 The "Look-Back"

Individuals who are not yet covered associates, but who anticipate becoming covered associates in the future, also need to take heed of the rule. Both the SEC and the MSRB Rules include a "look-back" provision. When determining whether it is eligible to provide compensated advisory services to a particular government entity, the investment adviser must analyze the political contribution history of all of its covered associates, *including those who made contributions before being employed by the adviser.*[46] The length of the look-back depends on the job duties of the new covered associate: two years for covered associates that solicit clients for the adviser and six months for other covered associates.[47] For example, if an adviser hired an individual to solicit government pension fund clients and that individual had made a contribution to a covered government official during the preceding two years, the adviser would be barred from providing compensated advisory services to the fund over which the official had hiring authority for a two-year period following the date of the contribution. On the other hand, if that same individual was *not* hired to solicit clients for the adviser, then only contributions during the six months preceding the hiring must be assessed.

Like the SEC Rule, the MSRB Rule imposes different look-back periods for different types of "municipal finance professionals."[48] For some municipal finance professionals, the look-back period is a full two years.[49] For others, the look-back period is two years only if the professional solicits business from the government

---

44. McCutcheon v. Federal Election Comm'n, 134 S. Ct. 1434, 1461 (2014).

45. Brief for Securities and Exchange Commission in Response to Plaintiffs' Motion for Preliminary Injunction at 16–17, *New York Republican State Comm.*, No. 1:14-cv-01345 (D.D.C. Aug. 29, 2014).

46. 75 Fed. Reg. at 41,033–34.

47. 17 C.F.R. § 275.206(4)–5(b)(2).

48. For definition of "municipal finance professional," *see supra* note 10.

49. MSRB Rule G-37(g)(iv)(A).

issuer.[50] For others, the look-back period is six months preceding her or his becoming a municipal finance professional.[51]

The bottom line: When an investment adviser is looking to hire an employee who will qualify as a covered associate, the adviser should assess whether the prospective employee's political contribution history would disqualify the adviser from providing paid advisory services in any jurisdiction.

25-1.3.2 The Restriction on Solicitation and Coordination of Contributions

In addition to restricting direct contributions, the SEC Rule provides that neither an investment adviser nor one of the adviser's covered associates may solicit or coordinate any contributions on behalf of a covered official or political party of a state or locality to which the investment adviser is providing or seeking to provide advisory services.[52] An adviser is seeking to provide advisory services when it responds to a request for proposal, communicates with a government entity regarding that entity's formal selection process for investment advisers, or engages in some other solicitation of investment advisory business of the government entity.[53] Notably, unlike the direct contribution restriction—which does not automatically apply to contributions to political parties—the solicitation and bundling restriction *does* cover such activities on behalf of state political parties.

The term "solicit" means a direct or indirect communication "for the purpose of obtaining or arranging a contribution or payment."[54] The SEC has advised that "[a]n adviser that consents to the use of its name on fundraising literature for a candidate would be soliciting contributions for that candidate."[55] Likewise, "an adviser that sponsors a meeting or conference which features a government official as an attendee or guest speaker and which involves fundraising for the government official would be soliciting contributions for that government official."[56] The term "coordinate" is not defined, but would include collecting contributions by a covered associate from third parties, including employees or other professional service providers, for forwarding to the ultimate recipient.[57]

The factors that determine whether a donor is a covered associate and whether an incumbent, candidate, or successful candidate is a covered official are the same for purposes of this restriction as they are for the two-year time out restriction.

The MSRB Rule includes a similar prohibition on soliciting and coordinating contributions.[58]

25-1.4 Can Violations Be Cured?

Notably, a contribution from a "covered associate" does *not* trigger the two-year time out under the SEC Rule if *all* of the following criteria are met: (1) the investment adviser discovers the contribution within four months of the date of the

---

50. MSRB Rules G-37(b)(ii), (g)(iv)(B).
51. MSRB Rules G-37(b)(iii), (g)(iv)(C)–(E).
52. *Id*. § 275.206(4)–5(a)(2)(ii).
53. 75 Fed. Reg. at 41,043, n.330.
54. *Id*. at 41,043, n.328.
55. *Id*.
56. *Id*.
57. *Id*. at 41,043, n.333.
58. MSRB Rule G-37(c).

contribution; (2) the contribution was for $350 or less; (3) the contributor obtains a return of the contribution within sixty calendar days of the date of discovery of the contribution by the investment adviser; (4) the investment adviser does not use this return exception more than two times (in the case of an adviser that reports fifty or fewer employees) or three times (in the case of an adviser that reports more than fifty employees) in a calendar year; and (5) the investment adviser never uses the exception more than once with respect to the same covered associate.[59]

Likewise, under the MSRB Rule, a covered entity is not subject to the two-year time out if *all* of the following criteria are met: (1) the broker, dealer or municipal securities dealer discovers the problematic contribution within four months of the date of such contribution; (2) the contribution did not exceed $250; (3) the contributor obtains a return of the contribution within sixty calendar days of the date of discovery of such contribution; (4) the broker, dealer, or municipal securities dealer does not use this exemption more than twice in any twelve-month period; and (5) the broker, dealer, or municipal securities dealer did not execute more than one automatic exemption by the same municipal finance professional regardless of the time period.[60]

In addition, an investment adviser that triggers the two-year time out under the SEC Rule may apply for an exemption from the SEC. In determining whether to grant an exemption, the SEC will consider, among other factors, whether the investment adviser (1) before the contribution was made, had adopted and implemented policies and procedures reasonably designed to prevent violations of this section; (2) before or at the time the contribution was made, had no actual knowledge of the contribution; and (3) after learning of the contribution, took all available steps to cause the contributor to obtain a return of the contribution and took all other remedial or preventive steps that would be appropriate under the circumstances.[61] The SEC has granted exemptions under certain circumstances.[62]

Likewise, a covered entity that triggers the two-year time out under the MSRB Rule may apply for an exemption. In determining whether to grant an exemption, the MSRB will consider a similar set of factors.[63]

---

59. 17 C.F.R. § 275.206(4)–5(b)(3).

60. MSRB Rule G-37(j).

61. 17 C.F.R. § 275.206(4)–5(e).

62. *See, e.g.,* In the Matter of Davidson Kempner Capital Management LLC, Release No. IA-3715 (Nov. 13, 2013) , *available at* http://www.sec.gov/rules/ia/2013/ia-3715.pdf; In the Matter of Ares Real Estate Management Holdings, LLC, Release No. IA-3969 (Nov. 18, 2014), *available at* http://www.sec .gov/rules/ia/2014/ia-3969.pdf.

63. MSRB Rule G-37(i) (the factors include "(i) whether such exemption is consistent with the public interest, the protection of investors and the purposes of this rule; (ii) whether such broker, dealer or municipal securities dealer (A) prior to the time the contribution(s) which resulted in such prohibition was made, had developed and instituted procedures reasonably designed to ensure compliance with this rule; (B) prior to or at the time the contribution(s) which resulted in such prohibition was made, had no actual knowledge of the contribution(s); (C) has taken all available steps to cause the contributor involved in making the contribution(s) which resulted in such prohibition to obtain a return of the contribution(s); and (D) has taken such other remedial or preventive measures, as may be appropriate under the circumstances, and the nature of such other remedial or preventive measures directed specifically toward the contributor who made the relevant contribution and all employees of the broker, dealer or municipal securities dealer; (iii) whether, at the time of the contribution, the contributor was a municipal finance professional or otherwise an employee of the broker, dealer or municipal securities dealer, or was seeking such employment; (iv) the timing and amount of the contribution

25-1.5 What Records Must Be Kept?

The SEC Rule requires that each investment adviser that provides compensated advisory services to state or local governments either directly or through a "covered investment pool" maintain the following records:[64]

- A list of the names, titles, and business and residence addresses of all covered associates of the investment adviser;
- A list of all government entities to which the investment adviser provides or has provided investment advisory services—either directly or through a covered investment pool—in the past five years, but not before September 13, 2010;
- A list of all contributions made by the investment adviser or any of its covered associates to an official of a government entity, a state or local political party, or a political action committee (the term "political action committee" is not further defined);[65]
- A list of the name and business address of each third party used by the investment adviser to solicit government business.

The SEC Rule, however, does not require that investment advisers file disclosure reports with the SEC.

On the other hand, the MSRB Rule requires covered entities to file quarterly reports with the MSRB disclosing information on contributions made to issuer officials, payments made to state or local political parties and bond ballot campaign initiatives, and information about issuers with which the dealer has engaged in municipal securities business.[66]

25-1.6 A Compliance Program Is Necessary

In addition to its recordkeeping requirement, the SEC requires that each adviser adopt and implement policies and procedures reasonably designed to prevent violation by the adviser or its supervised persons.[67] As noted earlier, the adoption and implementation of such policies and procedures are a pertinent factor in determining whether the SEC will grant an exemption to an adviser that inadvertently runs afoul of the rule.

The MSRB has advised that such a policy include a requirement that adequate due diligence be performed before allowing a covered individual to make a contribution to a political party or PAC.[68] The purpose of the inquiry is to ensure that the

which resulted in the prohibition; (v) the nature of the election (e.g., federal, state or local); and (vi) the contributor's apparent intent or motive in making the contribution which resulted in the prohibition, as evidenced by the facts and circumstances surrounding such contribution.").

64. 17 C.F.R. § 275.204–2(a)(18)(i).

65. This list must be maintained in chronological order and contain the following information: (1) the name and title of each contributor; (2) the name and title (including any city/county/state or other political subdivision) of each recipient of a contribution; (3) the amount and date of each contribution; and (4) whether any such contribution was returned pursuant to the automatic refund policy described above.

66. MSRB Rule G-37(e).

67. 75 Fed. Reg. at 41,027, n.114, and 41,055, n.473.

68. Questions and Answers Concerning Political Contributions and Prohibitions on Municipal Securities Business: Question III.5.

contribution to the political party or PAC is not, in fact, an indirect contribution to a covered official or candidate. The MSRB has advised that a letter instructing the political party or PAC to place the contribution in an "administrative" or "house-keeping" account is not by itself sufficient to meet the adviser's due diligence obligations but might be a useful component in a more comprehensive compliance program.[69]

25-2 Federal Contractor Ban

When pay-to-play laws are discussed, the federal law's prohibition on government contractors is often overlooked. Federal law has long banned federal contractors from making any contribution or expenditure to "any political party, committee, or candidate for public office or to any person for any political purpose or use."[70] Though the statute addresses only contributions, the FEC has interpreted this provision to prohibit government contractors from making both contributions and expenditures in connection with federal elections.[71] Before the Supreme Court's decision in *Citizens United v. Federal Election Comm'n*,[72] the federal contractor ban formed the basis for few enforcement actions. Because most government contractors were corporations and federal law independently barred corporations from making expenditures in connection federal elections,[73] enforcement was directed principally at individuals who contracted for personal services with the government.

In finding the broad prohibition on corporations' making independent expenditures in connection with federal elections to be unconstitutional in *Citizens United*, the Court left open the question whether the narrower prohibition on government contractors, supported by a different justification—that of maintaining the integrity of the procurement process—was constitutional. Although two recent enforcement actions, which are discussed shortly, shed some light on how the FEC intends to enforce the prohibition, its reach and continued vitality are still uncertain.

The ban on federal contractor contributions was enacted as part of the Hatch Act in 1939, well predating the enactment of the FECA in 1974.[74] It was intended to halt the widespread shakedown of government contractors for political support. While the statute focuses solely on *contributions* by federal contractors, the FEC's regulations also prohibit contractors from making *independent expenditures*.[75] As noted later, the FEC's unwillingness to distinguish between contributions and independent expenditures is likely to become controversial and possibly the subject of future litigation in light of *Citizens United*.

---

69. Municipal Securities Rulemaking Board, MSRB Publishes Interpretive Letter Relating to Payments to Non-Political Accounts of Political Organizations Under Rule G-37 (Sept. 25, 2007), *available at* http://www.msrb.org/Rules-and-Interpretations/MSRB-Rules/General/Rule-G-37.aspx?tab=2#_E7B1D878-1A9D-4F78-A218-A17A79A012F0 (last visited Mar. 1, 2016).

70. 52 U.S.C. § 30119.

71. *See* 11 C.F.R. §§ 115.2(c), 115.4(a), 115.5; FEC Adv. Ops. 1990-20, 1988-49, 1985-23.

72. Citizens United v. Federal Election Comm'n, 558 U.S. 310.

73. 52 U.S.C. § 30118.

74. http://www.fec.gov/info/appfour.htm.

75. *See supra* note 67.

The federal contractor ban is triggered at the time negotiations are commenced or the request for procurement is published, whichever is earlier.[76] The prohibition ends on the completion of the contract or the termination of negotiations, whichever is later.[77] There are special rules for different forms of business organizations. A partnership that is a federal contractor may not use partnership assets for making a contribution or expenditure, but individual partners may make contributions or expenditures in their own name, with their personal assets, without running afoul of the regulations.[78] Employees of partnerships are similarly free to make contributions or expenditures from their personal funds. Corporations, labor organizations, membership organizations, and cooperatives are broadly covered, but are permitted to maintain a separate segregated fund commonly referred to as a PAC, consisting of voluntary contributions from individuals.[79] The PAC may make contributions or expenditures without violating the ban.

Individuals acting as sole proprietors who are federal contractors are prohibited from using any funds under their dominion to make a contribution or expenditure, but the law exempts spouses of sole proprietors from the prohibition.[80] Three individuals with personal service contracts with federal agencies unsuccessfully challenged the prohibition in federal district court, contending that the ban violated their First Amendment rights.[81] In a unanimous en banc decision, the U.S. Court of Appeals for the District of Columbia affirmed the District Court's decision.[82]

Another major issue also remains unresolved: To what extent does the ban apply to contributions or expenditures made by subsidiaries, affiliates, or controlled organizations of a covered contractor? The statute and the regulations are silent. Some indication of current FEC policy regarding parent and subsidiary corporations can be found in two recent enforcement actions. In these cases, the FEC dismissed complaints in which the facts suggested that the corporate contributions to independent expenditure-only committees were made by the parent corporations, which were not themselves federal contractors.[83] In both matters, the federal contractors appear to have been independently operated subsidiaries. This understanding of FEC enforcement policy has not been promulgated as a regulation nor separately published as an official enforcement policy. The FEC has published a Petition of Proposed Rulemaking[84] seeking comment on whether to amend its regulations to include the factors for determining whether entities of the same corporate family are considered separate entities for the purposes of the prohibition on contributions by federal contractors.

---

76. 11 C.F.R. § 115.1(b).

77. *Id.*

78. *Id.* § 115.4.

79. *Id.* § 115.3.

80. *Id.* § 115.5.

81. Wagner v. Federal Election Commission, No.13-5162, 2015 WL 4079575 (D.C. Cir. July 7, 2015).

82. *Id.*

83. Alaskans Standing Together, FEC MUR Case #6403 (Nov. 1, 2011); Chevron USA, Inc., FEC MUR Case #6726 (Feb. 25, 2014).

84. https://www.federalregister.gov/articles/2015/03/30/2015-07176/rulemaking -petition-administrative-fines-program-and-commission-forms.

It should also be noted that the FEC has interpreted the ban only to apply to contributions or expenditures made to influence federal elections.[85] Consequently, absent any restriction in state or local law, a federal contractor could make a contribution to an account of a state or local party committee that is maintained to pay expenses attributable to elections for state office, or even to a candidate for state office who exercises discretion over contracts financed with federally appropriated funds. However, separate state laws may govern such contributions if the contractor is also a state contractor.

In light of the Court's recent decision in *McCutcheon v. Federal Election Commission*,[86] the prohibition may become the subject of greater controversy. The Court's decision in *McCutcheon* strongly suggests that the amount and source of a political contribution may be limited only if there is an appreciable risk of corruption, which the Court has not found to be present where the funds are only used to make independent expenditures. It remains unclear in light of that decision whether the FEC would have pursued the above-referenced matters if the parent corporations were government contractors that only contributed to independent expenditure-only committees. It is also unclear whether the FEC will seek to formalize its policy through regulation. Since many major corporations are government contractors, the statute and the implementing regulations expose corporations that seek to be more politically active to some risk. Before making a contribution to a federal politically active organization, even in the form of dues payments to a trade association, corporate federal contractors should be aware of the unsettled nature of the law in this area.

25-3 State-Level Pay-to-Play Rules

In response to concerns about the integrity of the governmental contracting and regulatory process, and in reaction to local scandals, an increasing number of states and municipalities have enacted their own pay-to-play laws (Table 25.1). These laws are designed to limit the influence that political contributions and expenditures may exert over the award and performance of government contracts and over the regulation of highly regulated industries.

This section is not a comprehensive summary of pay-to-play laws at the state and local level, nor does it attempt to list all of the states and municipalities that have such laws. Instead, it highlights the issues that companies and their officials should consider before making contributions on the state and local levels. Given the potential financial ramifications—loss of existing contracts and bans on seeking contracts in the future, in addition to civil and even criminal penalties for violators—it is essential that companies incorporate these laws into their compliance programs. Note that these pay-to-play laws complement, rather than supplant, the federal pay-to-play rules discussed earlier in the chapter. Some contributions may be barred by a federal pay-to-play rule but not covered by a state or local pay-to-play law; conversely, some contributions may be exempt from coverage under any federal pay-to-play rule but barred by a state or local pay-to-play law. A strong compliance program for state and local political contributions must account for both the federal rules and state or local law.

---

85. 11 C.F.R. § 115.2.
86. 134 S. Ct. 1434 (2014).

Table 25.1 Compliance Chart: Major State Pay-to-Play Laws That Regulate Individual Contributions[87]

	Individual Contribution Limit 3	Pay-to-Play Covered Individuals	Pay-to-Play Requirements	Pay-to-Play Consequences
California	Limits per election: $4,100 (Senate and Assembly); $27,200 (gubernatorial); $4,100 (CalPERS and CalSTRS board); $6,800 (other statewide). Each primary, general, special, and special runoff election is a separate election.	Employees who participate in contract proceeding by lobbying or acting to influence contract decision	Restricts contributions > $300 to certain candidates; requires contribution disclosure	Monetary fine; recipient official required to recuse self from Gilead matters
Illinois	$5,300/ election cycle to Illinois state candidate committees; $10,500/ year to state party committees and political action committees	CEO; individuals who own > 7.5% of a company; employees whose compensation may be affected by contract; spouses	Restricts contributions of any amount to certain candidates; requires entity registration	Voids contract
Maryland	$4,000 to any political committee or candidate/ four-year election cycle	Officers; directors; partners; employees who contribute at a company's request or suggestion	Requires disclosure of contributions > $500 (cumulative) to certain candidates	Criminal penalties, incl. possible fine and imprisonment

---

87. The limits and laws herein were compiled during the publication process and may have changed since.

**Table 25.1 Compliance Chart: Major State Pay-to-Play Laws That
Regulate Individual Contributions (continued)**

	Individual Contribution Limit 3	Pay-to-Play Covered Individuals	Pay-to-Play Requirements	Pay-to-Play Consequences
New Jersey	$3,800/election to gubernatorial; $2,600/ election to all other candidates; $7,200/ election to PACs; $7,200/year to continuing political committees and municipal parties; $25,000/year to legislative leadership committees and state parties; $37,000/ year to county parties	President; senior management VPs; secretary; treasurer; CEO; CFO; spouses; resident children; directors must disclose	Restricts contributions > $300 to certain candidates; requires contribution disclosure	Monetary fine; voids contract; disqualification
Ohio	$36,466 to state party State Candidate Fund (SCF)/ calendar year; $12,155 to county party SCF or state PAC/ calendar year; $18,233 to legislative campaign fund/ calendar year; $12,155.52 to statewide and legislative candidates/ election	Individual who owns > 20% of a company; that person's spouse	Restricts contributions > $1,000 to any candidate	Disqualification
Pennsylvania	Unlimited	Officers; directors; associates; partners; owners; employees; spouses of any of these	Requires disclosure of contributions > $1,000 to any candidate	Criminal penalties, incl. possible fine and imprisonment
Virginia	Unlimited	Officers and directors	Restricts contributions > $50 to certain candidates	Monetary fine

25-3.1 What One Needs to Know

- *Whether jurisdiction has a pay-to-play law at all:* The threshold question, of course, is whether a given jurisdiction—whether it is a state or a municipality—has pay-to-play statutes or regulations on the books. The question is sometimes less straightforward than it seems. While pay-to-play laws are sometimes found in the jurisdiction's campaign finance statutes or regulations, they are often buried in more obscure sections of the law. A compendium of major state and local pay-to-play laws is included at the end of this chapter.

- *Target of law—specific industries or contractors generally:* The laws can generally be divided into two categories: those that regulate persons involved in certain highly regulated industries and those that regulate persons contracting with the government. The sectors most commonly targeted by the former set of laws are the gaming industry, insurance companies, and regulated utilities.[88] The latter set of laws—those regulating government contractors—are most likely to come as a surprise to those who are covered. Governments at the state and local level are major purchasers of a wide variety of goods and services. These goods and services are normally procured through an open bidding process or a transparent and detailed sole source or competitive review. Providers of goods and services to governments are often caught off guard when they discover that the contributions made by the company, its officers, or employees are subject to special regulation.

- *Coverage of the law (donor):* In some jurisdictions, the pay-to-play law covers only the contracting entity or regulated entity itself.[89] This means that individual donors are not affected by the pay-to-play law, even if they own or are employed by an entity that is subject to the law. In many other jurisdictions, however, the law extends to certain individuals associated with the contracting or regulated entity. This could include owners, directors, officers, or other high-level employees.[90] In these jurisdictions, compliance programs must cover individual contributions as well as entity contributions.

- *Coverage of the law (recipient):* Just as pay-to-play laws differ with respect to which *donors* are covered, they also vary in terms of which *recipients* are covered. There are several dimensions to this analysis. The first is whether the law applies only to sitting officeholders[91] or whether it applies to candidates[92] for those offices as well. The second is which officeholders or candidates are covered by the law.[93] The third is whether

---

88. *See, e.g.*, 4 Pa. Cons. Stat. Ann. § 1513 (gaming industry); N.J. Stat. Ann. §§ 19:34–32 (insurance companies), 19:34–45 (regulated utilities).

89. *See, e.g.*, Ga. Code Ann. § 21-5-30.1(d).

90. *See, e.g.*, Ky. Rev. Stat. § 121.330(1)–(4).

91. *See, e.g.*, Va. Code Ann. §§ 2.2-4376.1, 56-575.17:1(A), 56-573.3(A).

92. *See, e.g.*, Conn. Gen. Stat. § 9-612(f)(2)(A), (B).

93. In some jurisdictions, only the governor is covered. *See supra* note 82. In other jurisdictions, certain statewide officials are covered, but the governor is not. *See, e.g.*, Ga. Code Ann. § 21-5-30.1. In

the law also reaches contributions to entities other than candidates or officeholders, such as political party committees[94] or PACs.[95]

- *Relevant time periods:* Another consideration is the relevant time period in which the restriction applies. Some pay-to-play laws do not have a "look-back" provision; vendors with current contracts are subject to the restriction, but the jurisdiction does not deny contracts to vendors who had made contributions in the past.[96] Other jurisdictions look back for a certain period of time and deny contracts to those entities that made contributions during that period.[97] Finally, other jurisdictions take a more targeted approach: Virginia's law, for instance, bans only contributions made during the period between the submission of the bid and the award of the contract.[98] Contributions made before the period or after the period (including after the vendor has secured the contract) are not covered.

- *Applicability to subcontractors:* A question that often arises is whether the pay-to-play restrictions apply to subcontractors. Subcontractors are usually even less aware that doing business with a state or local government in a subcontracting capacity may implicate pay-to-play restrictions. Often, pay-to-play laws can be fairly read to apply only to the primary contractor and not to any subcontractors. However, certain pay-to-play laws expressly apply to subcontractors.[99]

- *Disclosure (in addition to, or in lieu of, restrictions):* In addition to worrying about restrictions on political donations, a donating entity also needs to determine whether its political activities or those of its personnel might trigger disclosure. Certain jurisdictions require disclosure *in addition* to the restrictions,[100] while other jurisdictions require disclosure *in lieu of* the restrictions.[101] In these jurisdictions, entities subject to the pay-to-play law are free to make contributions up to applicable limits but must file disclosures that are not required of other entities. Disclosure can take several different forms: registration or reporting with the state campaign finance agency, filings or representations with the contracting agency, or both.

---

other jurisdictions, all statewide officials are covered. *See, e.g.,* Conn. Gen. Stat. § 9-612(f)(2)(A). Even legislators are covered in certain jurisdictions. *See, e.g., id.* § 9-612(f)(2)(B).

94. *See, e.g.,* N.J.S.A. § 19:44A-20.14.
95. *See supra* note 82.
96. *See, e.g.,* Haw. Rev. Stat.
97. *See supra* note 85.
98. *See supra* note 82.
99. *See* San Francisco Campaign & Gov't Code § 1.126(a)(1). Companies that offer products and services to the San Francisco government through a reseller or distributor may be subject to the city's pay-to-play law under this rule.
100. *See, e.g.,* N.J.S.A. § 19:44A-20.18.
101. *See, e.g.,* Md. Code Ann., Elec. Law § 14-104(b).

25-4 Conclusion

If an organization determines that a given jurisdiction's law has implications for its business activities, it should determine which of its officers and employees need to be trained on how to comply with the law. Where noncompliance appears to bear significant risk, it should develop and widely disseminate a political contributions policy to ensure the organization's compliance with pay-to-play laws. For example, this policy might require preapproval of all contributions by executive and sales employees and a requirement that all other employees track and record their personal political contributions for compliance purposes. Organizations should also have a system for screening corporate and PAC contributions for pay-to-play compliance.

APPENDIX 25-A

Compendium of Significant State and Local Pay-to-Play Laws (as of March 2015)

Alabama

ALA. CODE § 17-5-14.

California

CAL. GOV'T CODE § 84308.
CAL. GOV'T CODE § 85702.
CAL. GOV'T CODE § 8880.57.
CAL. GOV'T CODE § 20152.5.
CAL. CODE REGS. tit. 2, § 18572.
CAL. EDUC. CODE § 22363.
CAL. PUB. UTIL. CODE § 130051.20.
CAL. BUS. AND PROF. CODE § 19981.

Colorado

COLO. CONST. art. XXVIII, §§ 15–17.

Connecticut

CONN. GEN. STAT. § 9-612.

Delaware

DEL. CODE ANN. tit. 18, § 2304(6).

Florida

FLA. STAT. ANN. § 420.512.
FLA. ADMIN. CODE r. 19A-6.004.

Georgia

GA. CODE ANN. § 21-5-30.
GA. CODE ANN. § 21-5-30.1.
State Ethics Comm'n Advisory Op. 2009-02.

Hawaii

HAW. REV. STAT. § 11-355.
HAW. REV. STAT. § 11-410.

Illinois

10 ILL. COMP. STAT. 5/9-35.
30 ILL. COMP. STAT. 500/20-160.
30 ILL. COMP. STAT. 500/50-37.
230 ILL. COMP. STAT. ANN. 5/24.
Comptroller's Exec. Order No. 05-01 (*available at* http://www.ioc.state.il.us/office/exec1.cfm).

Indiana

IND. CODE § 4-30-3-19.5.
IND. CODE § 4-30-3-19.7.
IND. CODE § 4-31-13-3.5.
IND. CODE § 4-33-10-2.1.
IND. CODE § 35-50-2-7.
2013 Ind. Acts 1155.

Kentucky

KY. REV. STAT. ANN. § 121.056.
KY. REV. STAT. ANN. § 121.330.
KY. REV. STAT. ANN. § 121.990.

Louisiana

LA. REV. STAT. ANN. § 18:1469.
LA. REV. STAT. ANN. §§ 18:1505–.6.
LA. REV. STAT. ANN. § 27:261.

Maryland

MD. CODE ANN., ELEC. LAW § 13-236.
MD. CODE ANN., ELEC. LAW §§ 14-101 to -108.
Campaign Finance Reform Act of 2013, 2013 Md. Laws 3713.

Massachusetts

MASS. GEN. LAWS ANN. ch. 29, § 29F.

Michigan

MICH. COMP. LAWS ANN. § 38.1133e.
MICH. COMP. LAWS ANN. § 432.207b.

Mississippi

MISS. CODE ANN. § 77-1-11.

Missouri

MO. REV. STAT. § 226.136.
MO. REV. STAT. § 409.107.

Montana

MONT. CODE ANN. § 33-18-305.

Nebraska

NEB. REV. STAT. § 9-835.
NEB. REV. STAT. § 19:803.
NEB. REV. STAT. § 49-1476.01.

New Jersey

N.J. STAT. ANN. § 5:12-138.
N.J. STAT. ANN. § 19:34-32.
N.J. STAT. ANN. § 19:34-45.
N.J. STAT. ANN. §§ 19:44A-20.1 to -20.27.
N.J. ADMIN. CODE § 17:12-5.3.
N.J. ADMIN. CODE §§ 17:16-4.1 to -4.11.
N.J. ADMIN. CODE §§ 19:25-26.1 to -26.10.
N.J. ADMIN. CODE EXECUTIVE ORDER NO. 117 (2008).
N.J. ADMIN. CODE EXECUTIVE ORDER NO. 118 (2008).

New Mexico

N.M. STAT. ANN. § 10-11-130.1.
N.M. STAT. ANN. § 10-16-13.3.
N.M. STAT. ANN. § 11-31-1.
N.M. STAT. ANN. § 13-1-112.
N.M. STAT. ANN. §§ 13-1-181 to -182.
N.M. STAT. ANN. § 13-1-191.1.

Ohio

OHIO REV. CODE § 3517.13.
OHIO REV. CODE § 3517.992.
OHIO REV. CODE § 3599.45.

Pennsylvania

4 PA. CONS. STAT. § 1513.
25 PA. CONS. STAT. § 3260a.
25 PA. CONS. STAT. § 3550.
53 PA. CONS. STAT. §§ 895.703-A to .705-A.

Rhode Island

R.I. GEN. LAWS §§ 17-27-1 to -5.

South Carolina

S.C. CODE ANN. § 8-13-1300.
S.C. CODE ANN. § 8-13-1342.
S.C. CODE ANN. § 8-13-1520.

Tennessee

TENN. CODE ANN. § 56-3-601. Repealed in April 2014.

Utah

UTAH CODE ANN. § 31A-4-112.

Virginia

VA. CODE ANN. § 2.2-3104.01.
VA. CODE ANN. § 2.2-4376.1.
VA. CODE ANN. § 56-573.3. Repealed in October 2014.
VA. CODE ANN. § 56-575.17:1.
VA. CODE ANN. § 59.1-375.

Vermont

VT. STAT. ANN. tit. 32, § 109.

Washington

WASH. REV. CODE § 48.30.110.

West Virginia

W.VA. CODE § 3-8-12.

Wyoming

WYO. STAT. ANN. § 26-13-120.

Many local governments have also adopted some form of pay-to-play regulations for local office campaigns, including but not limited to, the following:

Albuquerque, NM	Los Angeles County, CA
Bergen County, NJ	Newark, NJ
Buffalo, NY	New York City, NY
Brookhaven, NY	New York County, NY
Chicago, IL	Oakland, CA
Cook County, IL	Orange County, CA
Cuyahoga County, OH	Orange County, FL
Dallas, TX	Philadelphia, PA
Dallas County, TX	Prince George's County, MD
Fort Collins, CO	Salt Lake County, UT
Grand Rapids, MI	San Antonio, TX
Houston, TX	San Diego, CA
Indianapolis, IN	City and County of San Francisco, CA
Jersey City, NJ	Santa Ana, CA
Kings County, NY	Trenton, NJ
Little Rock, AR	Queens County, NY
City of Los Angeles, CA	Yonkers, NY

CHAPTER 26

Restrictions on Giving Gifts to Executive Branch Employees

BY KATHLEEN CLARK AND CHERYL EMBREE

26-1 Introduction

The federal government's gift rules are not intuitive. Even the most routine social interactions—taking a government employee out to lunch, hosting her at a reception or dinner, or giving her a thank-you gift at the end of a speech—may implicate the gift restrictions that apply to employees of the executive branch. Someone who wants to determine whether she may give an executive branch employee something of value needs to consider several different statutory and regulatory restrictions that may apply. At times, the gift prohibitions, exclusions, and exceptions can seem to rival the tax code in their complexity.

There are several different broad categories of gift restrictions. First, there are restrictions on gifts, outside compensation, and reimbursement of travel expenses. (This last restriction—limiting travel expense reimbursement—is designed to prevent circumvention of the restrictions on gifts and outside income.) Additionally, there are criminal statutes prohibiting bribery and illegal gratuities as well as criminal statutes prohibiting conduct that may be less repellent or obviously illegal but can still lead to severe penalties; for example, compensating government employees for private representation or their government work (called salary supplementation).

This chapter examines each of these categories of rules in order, from the least intuitive (complex gift regulations that, if violated, can result in employment discipline for federal employees) to the most intuitive (criminal statutes that, if violated, can result in prosecution of both federal employees who accept a gift and those who offer or give something of value).

26-2 Gift Restrictions

No American would object to the principle that undergirds our gift regulations: public office should not be used for private gain.[1] This principle underlies most government ethics laws, including the restrictions on gifts. Figure 26-1 identifies the informal mechanisms and formal legal standards limiting executive branch employees' receipt of gifts and preventing the use of public office for private gain.

Figure 26-1 The Gifts Pyramid

Employee's
Prudence[2]

Designated Agency Ethics
Officer (DAEO) Judgment[3]

Agency-Specific Ethics Restrictions[4]

2009 Ethics Pledge: Lobbyist Gift Ban
for All Politically Appointed Officials[5]

1992 Regulations: Standards of Ethical Conduct for
Employees of the Executive Branch[6]

1962 Criminal Statutes: Bribery, Illegal Gratuities,
Compensation for Representational Services, and Supplementation of Salary[7]

---

1. 5 C.F.R. § 2635.202(c)(3) (2015) (prohibiting acceptance of so many gifts that a reasonable person would believe that the employee is using her public office for private gain); *id.* § 2635.101(b)(7) ("Employees shall not use public office for private gain.").

2. *Id.* § 2635.204 ("[I]t is never inappropriate and frequently prudent for an employee to decline a gift. . . .").

3. The list of current Designated Agency Ethics Officials is available on the website of the U.S. Office of Government Ethics. U.S. OFFICE OF GOV'T ETHICS, DAEO LIST (Jan. 26, 2015) http://www.oge .gov/Program-Management/Program-Management-Resources/Ethics-Community/DAEO-List/.

4. *See, e.g.,* 5 C.F.R. §§ 3101.101–9601.101. Another example of agency-specific gift rules is found in the Federal Meat Inspection Act, which prohibits anyone from offering or giving anything of value to a meat inspector "with intent to influence" that inspector in his or her official duties. 21 U.S.C. § 622 (2015). It imposes an even broader restriction on inspectors, prohibiting them from accepting anything of value from a person "engaged in commerce" regardless of the giver's intent. *Id.*

5. Exec. Order No. 13490, 74 Fed. Reg. 4,673 (Jan. 21, 2009).

6. 5 C.F.R. §§ 2635.201–205.

7. 18 U.S.C. §§ 201, 203, 205, 209.

In President George H. W. Bush's first months in office, he issued an executive order requiring the Office of Government Ethics (OGE) to "establish a single, comprehensive, and clear set of executive branch standards of conduct that shall be objective, reasonable, and enforceable."[8] OGE did so in August 1992, and the regulations remain largely unchanged to this day. Most of the regulations restricting gifts from outside sources to federal employees are found in 5 C.F.R. Subpart B.[9]

On President Barack Obama's first full day of office, he issued an executive order requiring political appointees to sign an ethics pledge (the Ethics Pledge) that added a layer to these gift regulations, prohibiting gifts from lobbyists.[10] The Ethics Pledge applies to all politically appointed officials (these officials are easy to identify by asking if the position must be vacated at the end of the administration).[11] Employees who violate the gift regulations or the Ethics Pledge may be disciplined administratively.[12]

In addition, federal employees who are required to file annual financial disclosure forms must include on those forms information about some of the gifts they receive. If an employee receives a gift worth more than $150 and if the aggregate of all such gifts is greater than $375, then he or she must disclose the source, value, and a description of all such gifts on the annual form.[13] About 300,000 employees file confidential financial disclosure forms, and another 28,000 employees file forms that are publicly available if requested by name from the agency's ethics office.[14]

Figure 26-2 summarizes the restrictions on gifts found in the gift regulations and the Ethics Pledge.

---

8. Exec. Order No. 12674, 54 Fed. Reg. 15,159, § 201 (Apr. 12, 1989), as modified by Exec. Order No. 12731, 55 Fed. Reg. 42,547 (Oct. 17, 1990). In November of that same year, Title III of the Ethics Reform Act of 1989 amended U.S.C. title 5 to add section 7353, which restricts the solicitation and receipt of gifts from outside sources and gave OGE the virtually identical requirement of implementing regulations. 5 U.S.C. § 7353(a), (b).
9. 5 C.F.R. §§ 2635.201–205. In addition to restrictions on gifts from outside sources, there are also restrictions on gifts from one federal employee to another. *See id.* §§ 2635.301–304.
10. Exec. Order No. 13490. For a discussion of other parts of the Ethics Pledge, see Chapters 27 and 29 of this manual.
11. Politically appointed positions include Presidentially appointed, Senate confirmed (PAS); Presidentially appointed without Senate confirmation (PA); and noncareer Senior Executive Service (SES) Schedule C positions. *See* U.S. Gov't Accountability Office, *Conversions of Selected Employees from Political to Career Positions at Departments and Selected Agencies*, GAO-10-356R (Jan 29, 2010), 3–4 (comparing common types of political and career appointments).
12. *See* 5 U.S.C. § 7353(c) (2015).
13. *See* 5 C.F.R. § 2634.304 (2015) (regarding disclosure of gifts on publicly available financial disclosure forms); and 5 C.F.R. § 2634.907(g) (2015) (regarding disclosure of gifts on confidential financial disclosure forms). *See also* Memorandum from David J. Apol, U.S. Office of Gov't Ethics, LA-14-03: Increased Gifts and Travel Reimbursements Reporting Thresholds (May 23, 2014), *available at* http://www.oge.gov/OGE-Advisories/Legal-Advisories/LA-14-03-Increased-Gifts-and-Travel-Reimbursements-Reporting-Thresholds/.
14. *See* 5 C.F.R. § 2634.202 (defining the term, "public filer"). Additionally, Section 105 of the Ethics in Government Act of 1978, as amended, 5 U.S.C. App. § 105, and 5 C.F.R. § 2634.603 authorize OGE and federal agencies to require information on the requestor via Form OGE-201 before releasing a financial disclosure form. *See also* Kathleen Clark and Cheryl Embree, *Faux Transparency: Ethics, Privacy and the Demise of the STOCK Act's Massive Online Disclosure of Employees' Finances, in* Research Handbook on Transparency (Padideh Ala"I & Robert Vaughn eds., 2014).

Unlike the restrictions on gifts from lobbyists or lobbying firms to members and staff of Congress (discussed in Chapter 8), these gift rules apply exclusively to the gift recipient. That is, unless potential criminal laws are at issue as well, the liability under these regulatory rules rests with the government official, not with the giver.

In Figure 26-2, some of the exceptions or exclusions to the general gift prohibition are in italics. The italicized items do not apply if (1) the offer is from a registered lobbyist or lobbying organization and (2) the offer is made to an Ethics Pledge signer. OGE has further complicated analysis of the Ethics Pledge's lobbyist gift ban, however, by exempting certain situations from the ban's restrictions (most notably press/media events and certain offers from nonprofit lobbying organizations).[15]

Figure 26-2 Gift Rules Analysis in Four Steps (citations are to 5 C.F.R. § 2635)

A prohibited gift is . . .

Step 1—Anything anyone could ever want:

> Any gratuity, favor, discount, entertainment, hospitality, loan, forbearance, or other item of monetary value, including services, training (like vendor promotional trainings unless offered by a nonprofit organization and permitted under 5 U.S.C. § 4111), transportation, local travel, lodgings, and meals, however provided or paid for. (.202(c)(5), .203(b))

Step 2—Given directly or indirectly:

> Both indirect and direct gifts are prohibited. While a "direct" gift is easily identified, "indirectly" is defined to include gifts to an employee's parent, sibling, spouse, child, or dependent relative (.203(f)(1)), or on recommendation by the employee, gifts to anyone else or a charitable organization. (.202(a), .203(f)(1)–(2))[16]
> NOTE: Any gift solicited by the employee is prohibited (.202(c)(2)). Also, a gift that would otherwise fit within one

(continued)

---

15. Office of Gov't Ethics Memorandum, DO-09-007: Lobbyist Gift Ban Guidance (Feb. 11, 2009).

16. Registered lobbyists are required to report their gifts to charities designated by certain high-level executive branch officials, including the president, the vice president, officers and employees in the Executive Office of the President, flag or general officers of the uniformed forces, employees serving in levels I–V of the Executive Schedule, and employees in confidential, policy-determining, policy-making, or policy-advocating positions. 2 U.S.C. § 1602(3) (2015) (defining "covered executive branch official"). They are also required to report the costs such lobbyists incur for meetings held in the name of or to honor those officials. *Id.* § 1604(d)(1)(E); *see also* Sec'y of the Senate & Clerk of The House of Representatives, Lobbying Disclosure Act Guidance (revised Feb. 15, 2013) [hereinafter Revised Guidance] *available at* http://lobbyingdisclosure.house.gov/amended_lda_guide.html#section7 and contained in Appendix 4-A. For more information on the reports requiring this disclosure, see Chapter 5 of this manual.

Step 2 *(continued)*

> of the regulatory exceptions could subject both the giver and the recipient to criminal sanction if it is given with an intent that creates a violation of the bribery, illegal gratuity, federal salary supplementation, or other statute. (.202(c))

Step 3(a)—By a prohibited source (Identity):

> Are you or is the entity you represent:
> – affected by the employee's official duties? (.203(d)(4))
> – seeking official action by the employee's agency? (.203(d)(1))
> – doing or seeking to do business with the employee's agency? (.203(d)(2))
> – regulated by the employee's agency? (.203(d)(3))
> – an organization in which most members would answer yes to one of the above questions? (.203(d)(5))
> LOBBYIST GIFT BAN NOTE: If you are a registered lobbyist or if the organization you represent employs a registered lobbyist, *then no employee who has signed the Ethics Pledge may accept gifts from you or the organization you represent pursuant to the exceptions italicized below.* (Exec. Order No. 13490, § 1)

OR

Step 3(b)—Because of her federal job (Motivation):

> If the gift recipient was not a federal employee, would you have offered the gift anyway? (.203(e))
> NOTE: Gifts to the President and Vice President are exempted from most of the gift regulations, but restrictions found in the criminal law and the Constitution do apply. (.204(j))

UNLESS it is permissible because:

Step 4(a)—the gift itself is:

> Nominal, that is, any of the following:
> – a modest item of food and/or *refreshments* other than a meal; (.203(b)(1))
> – a greeting card or plaques, certificates, trophies, or presentational items of little intrinsic value; (.203(b)(2))
> – or *items worth less than $20 in total (no cash or gift cards) as long as a single source has not given over $50 in a calendar year to an individual (the employee may not pay the difference in value in order to use this exception). (.204(a))*

(continued)

Step 4(a) (continued)

> Generally available, that is, a discount or similar benefit offered to:
> – all government employees or broad groups of federal employees (groups must not be defined by types of official duties or in favor of federal employees with higher rank or pay); (.203(b)(4), .204(c))
> – or the general public (includes rewards or contest prizes as long as employee's entry is not required as part of her official duties). (.203(b)(4) & (5))
> Incidental to federal employment:
> – meals, refreshments, and entertainment in foreign areas where the employee is on duty if the value is less than the per diem rate in U.S. dollars for that area; (.204(i))
> – anything paid for by the government, secured by government contract, or accepted by an agency and given in kind under an agency gift statute; (.203(b)(7) & (8))
> – or free attendance, materials, transportation, or room and board in connection with training or meetings accepted from a 501(c)(3) under 5 U.S.C. § 4111. (.204(l)(1))
> Paid for by the employee at market value, that is, retail price. (.203(b)(9))
> Free to all (first come, first serve is acceptable). (.203(b)(4))

OR

Step 4(b)—the identity of the giver is:

> Other employers:
> – a _former_ employer 'offering continued pension benefits or other employee welfare programs, without regard to the employee's current federal position; (.203(b)(6))*[17]
> – a _current,_ nonfederal employer or business partner (offer based on the outside activity and without regard to the federal position); (.204(e)(2))*
> – a _future_ employer (offering customary gifts related to bona fide employment discussion); (.204(e)(3))*
> – a _spouse's_ employer (when offer has not been made or enhanced because of marriage to fed); (.204(e)(1))*
> A financial institution (offering loans on terms available to the general public); (.203(b)(3))
> An institution of higher education (bestowing an honorary degree after written approval from an agency ethics official); (.204(d)(2))
> A foreign government entity, including state-funded schools (if offer total is less than $375 in 2014 under 5 U.S.C. § 7342). (.204(l)(2))

(continued)

---

17. An asterisk next to an exclusion in Step 4 of Figure 26-2 indicates a gift giver who is likely to be in a "covered relationship" with the employee under the impartiality regulations, requiring the employee to recuse from all particular matters where that gift giver is or represents a party. *See* 5 C.F.R. § 2635.502(b)(1) (2015)

OR

Step 4(c)—the motivation of the giver is:

> A close personal relationship to the employee (if family or friend personally pays for the gift); (.204(b))[*]
>
> To request the employee give an official speech or other presentation of agency information; (.204(g)(1))
>
> *To request employee's attendance at a widely attended gathering (ethics approval required); (.204(g)(2))*
>
> *To host a purely social event (if not a prohibited source and event is free for all invited); (.204(h))*
>
> *To award meritorious public service (after written approval from an agency ethics official); (.204(d)(1)) or*
>
> *To conduct political activities permissible under the Hatch Act. (.204(f))*

26-3 Events as Gifts: Widely Attended Gatherings

The gift regulations set out specific circumstances under which employees may accept free attendance at events.[18] Table 26.1 summarizes those regulations. However, none of the regulations in the table below may be used by an Ethics Pledge signer if the event host is a lobbying entity or if the invitation itself was extended by a registered lobbyist, except in the case of official speeches.[19] If the event is an appropriate forum for an official speech, then the Ethics Pledge signer may attend for free on the day of the speech; otherwise, the signer must pay for his or her attendance. The official speech exception is not a blanket panacea. It applies only to parts of the event that are offered to all attendees equally and does not extend to peripheral or exclusive receptions, meals, or entertainment.[20] In addition, the pledge signer must be presenting agency information in a formal manner, as simply exchanging remarks or engaging in a group discussion does not count as an official speech.[21]

---

18. 5 C.F.R. § 2635.204(g) (2015).

19. *See* Office of Gov't Ethics Memorandum, DO-09-007: Lobbyist Gift Ban Guidance (Feb. 11, 2009). Not all lobbying entities are treated equally. Registered 501(c)(3) nonprofits, media organizations, and foreign or multinational government entities all have nuanced exclusions from the lobbyist gift ban, as explained in this OGE advisory.

20. *See* Office of Gov't Ethics, LA-15-02: Free Attendance at Speaking Engagements and Widely Attended Gatherings; Waiver of Separate Fee for a Meal or Reception (April 6, 2015).

21. *See* Office of Gov't Ethics, LA-12-05: Speaking and Similar Engagements Involving the Presentation of Information on Behalf of the Agency (Sept. 7, 2012).

Table 26.1 When Employee May Accept Free Attendance at Events

Type of Event	What Employee May Accept	Requirements	Cite to 5 C.F.R. § 2635
Conference or Other Event (employee speaking in official capacity)	Free attendance on day of employee's presentation	Agency has assigned employee to present information on agency's behalf, and attendance is provided by sponsor of event	.204(g)(1)
Course or Speaking Event	Free attendance (including course materials and meals incident to event)	Employee teaches or speaks at event about information that relates to employee's official duties, but agency has not necessarily assigned employee to speak at event	.807(a)(2)(iii) (B)[22]
Widely Attended Gathering (at which it is expected that a large number of persons with a diversity of views will attend)	Free attendance at all or parts of event for employee* and guest (not including travel, lodging, collateral entertainment, or meals without all attendees present) *Pledge signers are not eligible if invitation is from a lobbyist (see Figure 26-2).	Agency determines that employee's attendance furthers agency's programs or operations,[23] *and* offer is from event sponsor, **or** — non-sponsor and (1) more than 100 people are expected; and (2) value of free attendance is $335 or less[24]	.204(g)(2),(4)

---

22. 5 C.F.R. § 2635.807 prohibits an employee from receiving compensation for speech related to the employee's duties, but then excludes from its definition of "compensation" the waiver of attendance fees and the provision of course materials and meals incident to the event.

23. *See id.* § 2635.204(g)(3) for more information on factors agency must consider and process agency must use.

24. This amount includes the value of guests' attendance.

Table 26.1 *(continued)*

Type of Event	What Employee May Accept	Requirements	Cite to 5 C.F.R. § 2635
Political Event	Free attendance (including travel, lodging, and meals)	Employee is permitted to participate actively in political campaigns; *and* Gift is provided by a political organization in connection with employee's active participation in a political campaign[25]	.204(f)
Nonpolitical, Nonprofit Fund-Raising Event[26]	Free attendance	Employee is participating in the conduct of the fund-raising event[27]; *and* Sponsor of event is waiving the fee	.808(a)(2)

26-4 Travel as Gifts: Payment or Reimbursement of Travel Expenses

The federal government has issued detailed regulations restricting employees' acceptance of compensation for speaking and writing on matters related to the business of their agencies, including their acceptance of reimbursement of travel expenses related to this expressive activity.[28] Executive branch employees (other than noncareer employees above GS-15) may accept "travel expenses, consisting of transportation, lodging or meals, incurred in connection with the teaching, speaking, or writing activity."[29] More senior employees may not personally accept such travel expenses, but their agencies may be able to if the agency has gift acceptance authority or if permitted by another statute.[30]

---

25. "Political organization" is defined at 26 U.S.C. § 527(e).

26. "Fundraising"" is defined at 5 C.F.R. § 2635.808(a)(1) to mean "the raising of funds for a non-profit organization, other than a political organization."

27. "Participation" is defined at 5 C.F.R. § 2635.808(a)(2) as "active and visible participation in the promotion, production, or presentation of the event."

28. 5 C.F.R. § 2635.807(a)(2)(iii) states:

    Compensation includes any form of consideration, remuneration or income, including royalties, given for or in connection with the employee's teaching, speaking or writing activities. Unless accepted under specific statutory authority, such as 31 U.S.C. 1353, 5 U.S.C. 4111 or 7342, or an agency gift acceptance statute, it includes transportation, lodgings and meals, whether provided in kind, by purchase of a ticket, by payment in advance or by reimbursement after the expense has been incurred.

29. *Id.* § 2635.807(a)(2)(iii)(D).

30. *Id.* § 2635.807(a)(2)(iii) (citing 31 U.S.C. § 1353; 5 U.S.C. §§ 4111, 7342).

26-5 Illegal Gratuities and Other Criminal Statutes Relevant to Those Bearing Gifts

As noted earlier, the detailed regulations restricting gifts (including reimbursement of travel expenses) apply only to federal employees, and employees who accept gifts in violation of those rules are subject to administrative discipline. This section describes several criminal statutes that may be implicated when someone outside the government offers or gives something of value to an executive branch employee. Some of these restrictions, such as the prohibition on bribery, are intuitive or obvious. But others, such as the prohibition on salary supplementation, are not intuitive. And unlike the gift regulations, these statutes apply not just to federal employees but also to those who give or offer something of value to those employees.[31]

The most obvious of these criminal prohibitions is the bribery statute, which prohibits anyone from corruptly giving, offering, or promising something of value to a public official with the intent "to influence" an official act.[32] Bribery occurs only where there is "a *quid pro quo*—a specific intent to give or receive something of value *in exchange* for an official act."[33] Bribery is so obviously wrong that anyone reading this chapter is unlikely to be surprised or confused by this prohibition. But a related statute criminalizes conduct whose illegality may not be so obvious. The illegal gratuity statute prohibits anyone from giving, offering, or promising something of value to a public official "for or because of any official act performed or to be performed by such public official."[34] Under this statute, there is no need to show a quid pro quo. Instead, a person can violate the illegal gratuity statute by giving a public official "a reward . . . for a past act that he has already taken" or "for some future act that the public official will take."[35]

Both the bribery and the illegal gratuity provisions are broad in scope. They apply not just to those who already hold federal office but also to those who have been selected or nominated for office,[36] and, in the case of illegal gratuities, to former officials.[37] In addition, they have been construed to cover not just those who are employed directly by the federal government but also individuals who have "some degree of official responsibility for carrying out a federal program or policy,"[38] such as federal grantees running social service programs and contractors performing services on behalf of the government.[39]

---

31. *See, e.g.*, Chapter 8, Section 8-5, and Chapter 21 of this manual.

32. 18 U.S.C. § 201(b)(1) (2015). The statute also prohibits public officials from receiving, accepting, or agreeing to receive or accept a thing of value with the intent to be influenced in an official act. *Id.* § 201(b)(2).

33. United States v. Sun-Diamond Growers of Cal., 526 U.S. 398, 404–05 (1999).

34. 18 U.S.C. § 201(c)(1)(A) (2015).

35. *See Sun-Diamond Growers of Cal.*, 526 U.S. at 405; *see also* Kathleen F. Brickey, 2 Corporate Criminal Liability: A Treatise on the Criminal Liability of Corporations, Their Officers and Agents § 9-33, 305 n.259 (1996).

36. 18 U.S.C. § 201(a)(2) (2015).

37. *Id.* § 201(c)(1).

38. Brickey, § 9-30, 296 n.203 (quoting Dixson v. United States, 465 U.S. 482, 499 (1984)).

39. *See* United States v. Thomas, 240 F.3d 445 (5th Cir. 2001) (applying bribery statute to guard employed by private company under contract to the INS).

A second criminal statute that may not be obvious is the prohibition on salary supplementation, which prohibits anyone from giving anything of value to supplement the employee's federal government salary.[40] The prohibition on salary supplementation was originally enacted in 1917 in reaction to the practice of certain philanthropic foundations that paid the salaries of government employees who were involved in education policy. Congress was concerned that these foundations were exercising undue influence on government policies and wanted to limit their ability to place (and presumably direct) employees in the government.[41] The salary supplementation law is similar to the illegal gratuity provision in that neither of these criminal statutes requires a showing of corrupt intent. The primary difference between these two provisions is the payor's purpose in making the payment. The illegal gratuity provision requires that the payment be made "for or because of" an official act by the employee.[42] The Supreme Court has made clear that this requires proof of a link between the thing of value conferred and a specific "official act."[43] Salary supplementation, by contrast, requires only that the payment be intended to compensate the employee for her services to the federal government.[44]

26-6 Conclusion

As the foregoing discussion shows, the executive branch's restrictions on gifts and travel reimbursement are quite complicated. The gift regulations apply directly to government employees, not to outsiders who give or offer gifts (including free attendance at events and travel reimbursement) to those employees.[45] Nonetheless, organizations that regularly deal with the government, such as contractors, grantees, and those that engage in lobbying, should ensure that their own employees understand these gift restrictions so that they do not offer or give federal employees gifts that would violate the regulations. Some organizations that offer free attendance at events require government employees to certify that their designated agency ethics official has confirmed that their free attendance is consistent with the gift regulations. In general, it is prudent to ensure that an agency ethics official has cleared the employee's acceptance of an offered gift.

---

40. 18 U.S.C. § 209(a) (2015). The salary supplementation statute has many exceptions. *See, e.g., id.* § 209(c) (payments to short-term or unpaid government employees); *id.* § 209(e) (certain relocation expenses); *id.* § 209(h) (reservists on active duty may continue receiving a salary from their outside employer); and *id.* § 209(g) (employees of private sector organizations detailed to an agency under 5 U.S.C. §§ 3701–3707 may continue to receive pay and benefits from that organization). *See also* OFFICE OF GOV'T ETHICS, SUMMARY OF THE RESTRICTION ON SUPPLEMENTATION OF SALARY, *available at* http://www.oge.gov/OGE-Advisories/Legal-Advisories/Assets-non-searchable/DO-02-016A--Attachment-to-DO-02-016/ (concerning payments from state, county, or municipal governments).

41. *See* Beth Nolan, *Public Interest, Private Income: Conflicts and Control Limits on the Outside Income of Government Officials*, 87 Nw. U.L. Rev. 57 at 68–69 (1992).

42. *Id.* at 91–96.

43. *See* Sun-Diamond Growers of Cal., 526 U.S. at 414.

44. 18 U.S.C. § 209(a) (2015). A criminal conviction for a willful violation of the salary supplementation statute can result in imprisonment for up to five years. *Id.* § 216(a)(2). See Chapter 8 of this manual for a discussion of the ethics rules limiting supplementation of congressional salaries.

45. This contrasts with the potential criminal liability of registered lobbyists who provide gifts (including travel) to members of Congress or staff where receipt of those gifts would violate congressional rules. See Chapters 5 and 8 of this manual.

Part IV
The Practice of
Federal Lobbying

Introduction to Part IV

Government relations professionals, and those who manage them, confront a spectrum of practical challenges stemming from the regulations addressed in this volume. Part IV addresses some of these practical challenges. The first two chapters discuss the revolving door restrictions binding those in the government relations industry. Most of these rules limit the ability of federal government employees to leave government to lobby in the private sector. Some of them, however, address the ability of lobbyists leaving private employment to serve in the federal executive branch.

The final chapter contains our recommendations for private sector government relations professionals regarding how to build and operate a compliance program. Such a program is necessary to help protect the employer's goodwill, integrity, and reputation.

CHAPTER 27

Post-Employment Restrictions and the Regulation of Lobbying by Former Employees

BY ROBERT G. VAUGHN

27-1 Introduction

The post-employment provisions of federal law regulate lobbying activities by former employees of the executive and legislative branches of the federal government. The provisions applying to former executive branch personnel generally restrict lobbying before executive and administrative agencies, while those applying to former members and employees of Congress usually address lobbying before Congress. These provisions affect many lobbying activities, including attempts to influence executive policy.

The provisions applicable to the executive branch often restrict representation of others intended to influence official decisions of government officials. Some restrictions apply only to senior employees. These restrictions seek to prevent high-ranking former employees from using the information and contacts that they acquired during periods of government service to benefit private interests. Restrictions on lobbying activities of high-ranking officials also seek to reduce incentives for them to base official decisions during their government service on the possibility of future employment. Extensive lobbying by former high-ranking officials also creates an appearance that favors may be exchanged between private citizens and public officials. Some of these justifications for conflict of interest regulations of lobbying can diverge from more common arguments for lobbying legislation, as exemplified by the 1995 Lobbying Disclosure Act (LDA).[1] Post-employment restrictions on the executive branch are an aspect of larger concerns about the "revolving door," through which, on the one hand, government regulators leave to work directly for regulated entities or to represent their interests and, on the other hand, employees of regulated interests become employees of the relevant regulatory agencies.

These post-employment provisions, which apply generally to federal employees, restrict primarily representational activities. Additional, more extensive, restrictions on the lobbying activities of senior employees of the executive branch date from the Ethics in Government Act of 1978.[2] A variety of specific provisions in statutes and agency regulations impose particularized restrictions on former federal employees.

The first sections of this chapter examine these restrictions on the activities of former executive branch employees by moving from more general to more specific regulations. Enforcement of these provisions may involve criminal sanctions, civil penalties, and, in some instances, administrative action. Recent restrictions on the lobbying activities of members, officers, and higher-paid staff of the Congress reflect themes similar to those supporting executive branch restrictions.

---

1. For more information on the LDA, see Chapter 4 of this manual.
2. 5 U.S.C. app. §§ 101–505 (2015).

The final section of this chapter addresses these restrictions, including the changes introduced by the Honest Leadership and Open Government Act of 2007 (HLOGA).[3] President Obama's executive order imposes contractual obligations on appointees to executive agencies. The executive order covers some employees not falling under statutory prohibitions, imposes additional restrictions on some statutorily covered employees, and creates its own enforcement structure.

27-2 Post-Employment Restrictions Generally Applicable to the Executive Branch

Six prohibitions of government-wide applicability are contained in section 207 of title 18. The first three discussed here apply to all executive branch employees, as well as to "special government employees" who serve for limited periods, with or without compensation.[4] The fourth and sixth prohibitions apply to senior-level employees; the fifth and sixth, to very senior employees. The character of these prohibitions also varies; the first two principally limit representational activities intended to influence executive and judicial officials; the remainder limit a broader range of contacts within the executive branch.

Generally, these provisions are limitations on activities and do not prohibit particular types of employment. Likewise, they do not specifically require that these activities be compensated to be prohibited. Therefore, compensation is not a requirement for the application of the restrictions.

The Office of Government Ethics (OGE), established by the Ethics in Government Act of 1978,[5] has responsibility for interpreting these provisions and has issued both regulations and advisory opinions[6] that give more definition to the statutory provisions. Because the applicable prohibitions are contained in the criminal code, the OGE believes that they are "meant to be narrowly construed."[7]

27-2.1 Restrictions on Employees Personally and Substantially Involved in Particular Matters Involving Specific Parties

The first prohibition imposes a lifetime restriction on communications to or appearances before an employee of the United States on behalf of another person "in connection with a particular matter [involving a specific party or parties] in which [the former employee] participated personally and substantially as such officer

---

3. Pub. Law No. 110–81, 121 Stat. 735 (Sept. 14, 2007), codified in sections of scattered titles 2 and 18 of the U.S. code.

4. A special government employee is one who serves 60 days or less in a particular calendar year. 5 C.F.R. § 2637.211(f) (2015). A summary of the post-employment restrictions on special government employees, as well as other ethical requirements, is contained in OGE Informal Advisory Opinion 00 x 1 (2000).

5. The Ethics in Government Act of 1978 created the OGE as a separate agency within the executive branch.

6. 5 C.F.R § 2638.308 (2015) establishes provisions for formal and informal advisory opinions. OGE Informal Advisory Letter 91 x 24 (1991) sets out criteria for issuing a formal advisory opinion as opposed to an informal one.

7. *See* OGE Informal Advisory Letter 90 x 9 (1990).

or employee."[8] The particular matter must be one in which the United States is "a party or has direct and substantial interest."[9]

The prohibition is aimed at preventing a former employee from "switch[ing] sides" by representing another party in a matter on which she had previously worked as a government employee.[10] Therefore, for the prohibition to apply, the employee must have been involved in the same particular matter involving specific parties that she, now, as a former employee, seeks to influence.[11] The same particular matter must be at issue, but the specific parties involved at the time of the post-employment appearance or communication may be different from those involved at the time of her participation on behalf of the government.[12] The requirement of a particular matter involving specific parties includes "specific proceeding[s] affecting the legal rights of the parties or an isolatable transaction or related set of transactions."[13] Normally excluded would be rulemaking, policy formulation, legislation, or other matters of general applicability.[14] For example, an individual who participated as a government employee in an agency rulemaking might subsequently appear before her former agency representing specific parties to whom the rule is being applied.[15] In such a case, the employee would not have been involved in a particular matter involving specific parties while acting as a government employee.

OGE provides, among others, the following additional examples to illustrate these principles:

1. Development of a regulation establishing health and safety standards does not prevent a former employee from making representations to the government regarding the regulation.
2. Formulation of nationwide policies for grants regarding science education does not prohibit the former employee from later representing a specific organization regarding its application for assistance under the program.
3. Drafting a portion of standard form contract clauses for use in all future contracts does not bar the former agency attorney from representing another person about standard terms or clauses in a specific contract in which he did not participate as a government employee.

---

8. 18 U.S.C. § 207(a)(1)(B) (2015).

9. *Id.* § 207(a)(1)(A) (or the District of Columbia government has a direct and substantial interest).

10. *See* OGE Memo 90 x 17, at 4 (1990).

11. 5 C.F.R. § 2641.201(h)(1) (2015).

12. *See* OGE Memo 90 x 17, at 5 (1990).

13. 5 C.F.R. § 2641.201(h)(1) (2015). The OGE states that the phrase "involving specific parties" limits the ban discussed here and in 27-2.2. *See* OGE Memo 06 x 9, at 3–4 (2006) (contrasting this phrase with the broader scope of "particular matters").

14. 5 C.F.R. § 2641.201(h)(2) (2015). Legislation might involve specific parties if the legislation is a private relief bill or a bill that establishes a grant program that could apply only to one organization. *See* OGE informal Advisory Letter 83 x 7. Although the provision does not prevent the former employee from communicating with or appearing before members, employees, and committees of Congress, an employee could violate the provision regarding a particular matter involving specific parties if, in hearings, meetings in Congress, or negotiation sessions, the former employee communicated with executive branch employees intending to influence their official decisions. *See* OGE Informal Advisory Letter 81 x 5(1).

15. *See* OGE Memo 90 x 17, at 5 (1990).

4. Drafting official agency comments on proposed legislation does not prevent a former employee from contacting the agency on behalf of a private party to advocate certain amendments to the legislation.[16]

When a matter becomes a "'particular matter involving specific parties' depends on the facts."[17] For example, technical work or a feasibility study before parties are identified for a specific procurement may not be a particular matter involving specific parties. The identification of such specific parties rests on the receipt of "sufficient expressions of interest to identify prospective contractors" who might be involved in a specific procurement.[18]

Likewise, the determination whether the same particular matter is at issue depends heavily upon the individual circumstances presented.[19] Although this determination is fact specific, some general criteria should be considered in the determination, including the extent to which the matters involve

1. The same basic facts;
2. Related issues;
3. The same or related parties;
4. The same confidential information.[20]

OGE regulations also direct consideration of the time that has elapsed between the two matters.[21] Because the statute requires that the particular matter in which the former employee seeks to act must be one in which the United States is a party or in which it has a substantial interest,[22] the nature of this interest is one of the criteria properly considered in determining whether the same matter is at issue.[23]

The former employee must have participated "personally and substantially" in the particular matter involving specific parties while a government employee.[24] An employee may participate personally not only by directly doing so but also by supervising a subordinate's participation.[25] This view simply recognizes the hierarchical structure of federal administration.

An employee's involvement is substantial if it is significant. Substantiality rests upon how critical the involvement is, not on how much effort has been devoted to a matter, because much of that effort might have been expended on peripheral matters.[26] For example, review of a matter solely for compliance with administrative or budgetary procedures and regulations would not by itself be regarded as substantial.[27] In some instances, however, an employee's official responsibilities

---

16. *See* examples 1–8, 5 C.F.R. §2641.201(h)(2) (2015).

17. *See* OGE Advisory Opinion 05 x 6 at 4 (2005).

18. *Id.* at 7.

19. 5 C.F.R. 2641.201(h)(5)(i) (2015). Previous OGE memorandum recognized these factors. *See* OGE Memo 90 x 17, at 3 (1990).

20. 5 C.F.R. § 2641.201(h)(5)(i) (2015).

21. *See* OGE Memo 90 x 17, at 3 (1990).

22. 18 U.S.C. § 207(a)(1)(A) (2015); 5 C.F.R. § 2641.201(h)(5)(i) (2015).

23. 5 C.F.R. § 2641.202(j)(2) (2015).

24. 18 U.S.C. § 207(a)(1)(B) (2015).

25. 5 C.F.R. § 2641.201(i) (2015).

26. *Id.* § 2641.201(i)(3).

27. *Id.*

can influence the determination of what is substantial involvement. For example, if an employee has official responsibilities permitting the employee to reject the resolution of a particular matter, failure to act in these circumstances may be more likely to be considered substantial involvement than the passivity of the action might otherwise suggest.[28]

If these conditions—the same matter involving specific parties in which the former employee participated personally and substantially as a government employee—are satisfied, the former employee is prohibited from making a communication to or appearance before officers or employees of the United States government[29] on behalf of another person with an intent to influence the decisions of those officers or employees.[30] A communication may be made orally, in writing, or electronically.[31] Appearance includes the "mere physical presence" of the former employee in circumstances that suggest the intent to influence the outcome of the matter.[32] Therefore, a former employee need not necessarily speak to make an appearance.

Such an appearance or communication, however, must be made with the intent to influence in order to be prohibited. Some communications do not suggest such intent. For example, an agent or lawyer making a routine request regarding the status of a matter, for publicly available documents, or for other purely factual information not in connection with an adversarial proceeding would not involve a matter of potential controversy.[33] Because no controversy is involved and the matter is routine, the communication or appearance can be presumed not to be an attempt to influence. The same rationale supports the conclusion that the presentation of purely factual information and "project responses"—that is, designs and proposals for projects solicited by the government—are not attempts to influence.[34] On the other hand, communications or appearances regarding discretionary government actions, such as a ruling on the provision of a benefit or the waiver of requirements that the former employee realizes involves controversy, are presumptively made with intent to influence.[35]

Social communications between a former employee and a government official, such as a greeting card, would not suggest intent to influence official action. Other social communications that do not concern the particular matter at issue also would not be prohibited.

The communication or appearance must be made on behalf of another person.[36] Self-representation is not prohibited.[37] The former employee is also not prohibited from acting on behalf of the United States, including the Congress.[38] A

---

28. *Id.*

29. 18 U.S.C. § 207(a)(1) (2015) (including employees of the District of Columbia).

30. *Id.*

31. 5 C.F.R. § 2641.201(d)(1) (2015).

32. *Id.* § 2641.201(e)(4). The regulation lists several factors in determining whether "mere physical presence" may constitute an appearance with intent "to influence" and gives examples of their application.

33. *Id.* § 2641.201(e)(2)(i).

34. *Id.* § 2641.201(e)(2)(ii).

35. *Id.* § 2641.201(e)(1).(e)(1)

36. 18 U.S.C. § 207(a)(1) (2015).

37. *See* OGE Memo 90 x 17, at 2 (1990).

38. *Id.* at 4.

former employee is not acting on behalf of the United States, however, just because she believes that the party she represents and the United States share the same objectives.[39]

In addition, the communication or appearance must be directed to an employee of an executive department or agency, or of the courts.[40] Congress is not included, and this provision does not prohibit communications to or appearances before members of Congress and legislative staff.[41]

The provision only prohibits attempts to influence through communications or appearances; it does not apply to behind-the-scenes assistance given to others representing the party in the particular matter.[42] For example, a former employee may work for a company on a contract she administered as long as she has no contact with the government; she may prepare a paper for the company describing persons at her former agency who may be contacted and what communications or arguments should be made to them.[43] The provision is not violated as long as the former employee does not herself communicate with agency officials or appear on the affected party's behalf.

Finally, the statute requires that the actions of the former employee be made "knowingly" with the "intent to influence."[44] A necessary element of the offense may be that the former employee acted with a particular state of mind. This mens rea requirement has created difficulty in criminal prosecutions under the statute, and the congressional revision of section 207 seems to have been designed to resolve some of the issues regarding the knowledge requirement.[45] However, the mens rea requirement must be addressed in the application of this provision and of others discussed below.

27-2.2 Restrictions on Employees Officially Responsible for Particular Matters Involving Specific Parties

The second provision prohibits the same representational activities described in Section 27-2.1, *but only for a period of two years* from the termination of government employment.[46] Because the provision is identical in many respects to the lifetime prohibition discussed previously, much of that discussion also applies here. The

---

39. *Id.*

40. 18 U.S.C. § 207(a)(1) (2015).

41. *See* OGE Informal Advisory Letter 93 x 26 at 2 (1993).

42. 5 C.F.R. § 2641.201(d)(3) (2015).

43. *Id.* (example 3).

44. 18 U.S.C. § 207(a)(1) (2015).

45. *See generally* Matthew T. Fricker & Kelly Gilchrist, *Comment, United States v. Nofzinger and the Revision of 18 U.S.C. § 207: The Need for a New Approach to the Mens Rea Requirements of Federal Criminal Law*, 65 NOTRE DAME L. REV. 803 (1990). The article examines the confusion created by the state-of-mind requirements, the attempt of Congress to eliminate the confusion, and the ambiguities remaining. Based on their analytical scheme, the authors of the article conclude that the conduct elements, "making any communication to or appearance before," require "a state of mind of at least knowledge." *Id.* at 846, 849. In addition, the authors assert that the other provisions of the statute that describe the circumstances necessary for liability also require that "a state of mind must be proven for each element." *Id.* at 849. The appropriate state of mind for the conduct elements is "knowingly . . . with the intent to influence." *Id.* The other "circumstance elements" require proof of "the state of mind of recklessness." *Id.*

46. 18 U.S.C. § 207(a)(2) (2015).

second prohibition is shorter in length; it applies to a particular matter involving specific parties that the former government employee knows or reasonably should know was actually pending under the employee's official responsibility within a one-year period before the termination of government of employment.[47]

The two-year ban on post-employment communications or appearances runs from the termination of federal employment.[48] For example, if the employee's official responsibility for a particular matter ends six months before her departure from government, she would be prohibited from representational activities on that matter for two full years following the termination of employment.[49]

Official responsibility is "the direct administrative or operating authority, whether intermediate or final, and either exercisable alone or with others, and either personally or through subordinates, to approve, disapprove, or otherwise direct Government action."[50] Statutes, regulations, executive orders, job descriptions, and delegations of authority usually determine the scope of an employee's official responsibilities.[51] Matters under the supervision of subordinates are usually within the official responsibilities of the supervisory employee.[52] Responsibility for ancillary matters, such as the regularity of budgeting, public relations, or equal employment considerations, that append to a particular substantive decision not reviewed by the employee do not place the matter within an employee's official responsibilities unless this ancillary aspect is itself the subject of her subsequent representational activities.[53] For example, a budget officer who evaluates an agency's budget to determine whether funds remain available for a particular purpose does not have official responsibility for the resulting contract even though she has responsibility for the agency's budget, because the "identification of funds for the contract is an ancillary aspect of the contract."[54] Likewise, an equal employment opportunity officer who reviews the affirmative action plans of units within the agency does not have official responsibility for the substantive programs conducted by those units.

The statute requires that the particular matter have been "actually pending" within the employee's official responsibility while in government.[55] This requirement ensures that the matter was under consideration by persons within the employee's area of responsibility.[56]

In contrast to the lifetime bar based on personal and substantial participation, self-disqualification would not enable an employee to avoid the two-year ban. Because this ban applies to particular matters within an employee's official

47. *Id.* § 207(a)(2)(B).
48. 5 C.F.R. § 2641.202(a) (2015).
49. *Id.*
50. 18 U.S.C. § 202(b) (2015).
51. 5 C.F.R. § 2641.202(j)(2) (2015). "Official responsibility for a matter can be terminated where there is a *formal modification* of an employee's responsibilities, such as by change in the employee's position description." OGE Advisory Opinion 05 x 6 at 12 (2005) (emphasis added).
52. 5 C.F.R. § 2641.202(j)(2) (2015).
53. *Id.*
54. *Id.* § 2641.202(j)(1).
55. 18 U.S.C. § 207(a)(2)(B) (2015).
56. 5 C.F.R. § 2641.202(j)(2) (2015).

responsibility, disqualification would not remove the matter from this area of responsibility.[57]

The former employee need not know, while acting as a government employee, that the particular matter was within the employee's official responsibility.[58] The former employee, however, must know or have access to facts sufficient to suggest that the particular matter about which she is acting on behalf of another fell within her official responsibilities as a government employee.[59] The former employee will normally come into the possession of sufficient facts to suggest that the matter may have fallen within her official responsibility. In this instance, the former employee has an obligation to make additional inquiry before conducting representational activities.[60]

27-2.3 Restrictions Regarding the Use of Confidential Information in Trade and Treaty Negotiations

A third provision prohibits more than representational activity, but applies only to certain information relating to trade and treaty negotiations. For one year after leaving government service, a former employee may not knowingly represent, aid, advise, or assist on the basis of covered information any person (except the United States) concerning any ongoing trade or treaty negotiation in which, during the employee's last year of government service, the employee participated personally and substantially.[61] This provision, like the first two, applies to all executive branch employees, but, unlike them, it also applies to members of Congress and to employees of Congress.

The prohibition applies if, within one year before leaving government employment, the former employee participated personally and substantially regarding an ongoing trade or treaty negotiation.[62] The former employee need not have had any contact with foreign parties to have participated personally and substantially.[63] Whether an employee's participation is personal and substantial rests on general principles discussed in Section 27-2.1, but is determined by looking to the employee's participation after the negotiations become ongoing.[64] The trade negotiations covered are those that the president determines to undertake under certain provisions of the Omnibus Trade and Competitiveness Act of 1988.[65]

A treaty is "an international agreement made by the President that requires the advice and consent of the Senate."[66] A trade negotiation is ongoing when, at least ninety days before entering into a trade agreement, the president notifies the

---

57. *Id.* § 2641.202(j)(5).

58. *Id.* § 2641.202(j)(2).

59. *Id.* § 2641.202(j) note.

60. *Id.*

61. 18 U.S.C. § 207(b)(1) (2015).

62. *Id.*

63. *See* OGE Memo 90 x 17, at 7 (1990).

64. *Id.*

65. 18 U.S.C. § 207(b)(2)(A) (2015).

66. *Id.* § 207(b)(2)(B).

House and the Senate of the intention to enter into an agreement.[67] A negotiation regarding a treaty is also ongoing if

1. A determination has been made by a competent authority that the negotiation will result in a treaty; and
2. Discussions on the text have begun with a foreign government.[68]

These negotiations are no longer ongoing once an agreement or treaty becomes effective or the parties end negotiations because of an understanding that no agreement or treaty will be concluded.[69]

Regarding such ongoing trade or treaty negotiations and for one year after leaving government employment, an employee may not use covered information to represent, aid, or advise another party.[70] Covered information is information concerning the trade or treaty negotiation that an agency has designated as exempt from disclosure under the Freedom of Information Act[71] and that the employee knew or should have known was so designated.[72] The knowledge requirement would likely involve an analysis similar to the "know or should have known" standard discussed in Section 27-2.2. "A former employee is not prohibited from utilizing information from an agency record which, at the time of his post-employment activity, is no longer exempt from disclosure under the Freedom of Information Act."[73] Likewise, the provision does not apply to information that was publicly available when the employee acquired it as a government employee.[74]

This prohibition is broader in scope than the ones discussed in Sections 27-2.1 and 27-2.2. First, unlike the other two prohibitions, this one covers representation of another before employees of Congress, including members of Congress.[75]

Second, the prohibition extends beyond representational activity and covers aiding, assisting, or advising on the basis of the covered information.[76] The aid, advice, or assistance must either

1. Involve a disclosure of the covered information; or
2. Require knowledge of the covered information to provide the advice, aid, or assistance given.[77]

---

67. *See* OGE Memo 90 x 17, at 7 (1990).
68. *Id.* at 2–8.
69. *Id.* at 8.
70. 18 U.S.C. § 207(b)(1) (2015).
71. *See generally* 5 U.S.C. § 552 (2015) (detailing information, agency rules, and records that must be available to the public).
72. *See* OGE Memo 90 x 17, at 8 (1990).
73. *Id.*
74. 18 U.S.C. § 207(b)(1) (2015). Although requiring interpretation, the provision applies to the employee's activities within the one-year period preceding the termination of federal employment and requires that, during that period, the person "knew or should have known" the information "was" so designated. This language supports the proposition that the information must have been designated as confidential during the period of the person's government employment.
75. *Id.*
76. *Id.*
77. *See* OGE Memo 90 x 17, at 8 (1990).

The OGE cautions that, even if this third prohibition does not apply, the lifetime bar described in Section 27-2.1 might.[78] In addition, former employees may be covered by statutory and other provisions prohibiting the disclosure of classified information.[79]

27-2.4 Restrictions on Senior Personnel

A fourth provision prohibits *for one year* a former senior employee from certain representational activities before the employee's former agency. The prohibition applies to any attempt to influence, through communication to or appearance before, the former agency on behalf of any person.[80] It is not limited to particular matters involving specific parties and does not require that the matter on which official action is sought have been one in which the former senior employee participated personally or substantially, or one within the former senior employee's official responsibilities.[81] Therefore, it prohibits representation of another regarding any matter, including rulemaking or policy matters,[82] pending before the former senior employee's agency; the matter need not have been pending before the agency while the senior official was an employee.

This provision imposes a one-year restriction on appearances and communications "to allow for a period of adjustment to new roles for the former senior employee and the agency he served, and to diminish any appearance that Government decisions might be affected by the improper use by an individual of his former senior position."[83] The period runs from the time that the individual ceases to be a senior employee rather than the time of separation from government employment, unless the two are simultaneous.[84] On the other hand, the prohibition extends to every agency for which the former employee worked as a senior employee during the year before termination from senior service.[85]

Senior personnel are defined in terms of level of pay established by specific statutory provisions.[86] Generally, these pay levels are those of undersecretaries of cabinet departments and of the highest levels of the executive schedule, including some highly paid civil servants.

The provision applies to communications and appearances intended to influence government action. It does not prevent former senior personnel from aiding and assisting in representation as long as they make no appearances before or communications to employees of their former agencies.

---

78. *Id.*

79. *Id.* at 8–9.

80. 18 U.S.C. § 207(c)(1) (2015).

81. *See* OGE Memo 90 x 17, at 6–7 (1990).

82. "Indeed, the term [matter] is virtually all-encompassing with respect to the work of the government. Unlike 'particular matter', the term 'matter' covers even the consideration or adoption of broad policy options that are directed to the interests of a large and diverse group of persons." OGE Memo 06 x 9 at 9–10 (2006).

83. *See* OGE Memo 90 x 17 at 9 (1990).

84. 5 C.F.R. § 2641.202(d) (2015).

85. *See* OGE Memo 90 x 17 at 2 (1990).

86. 18 U.S.C. § 207(c)(2) (2015); 5 C.F.R. § 2641.104 (2015) (defining senior employee). This restriction does not apply to a special government employee serving less than sixty days in a one-year period. *See* 18 U.S.C. § 207(c)(2)(B) (2015). The restriction does apply to certain persons from a private sector organization assigned to an agency under 5 U.S.C. §§ 3701–3704.

In some circumstances, the OGE may limit the scope of the prohibition by designating components of an agency as separate and distinct.[87] In this instance, the restriction on a former senior employee of such a designated component would apply to communications and appearances with that component, but not with the parent agency. Likewise, a former senior employee of the parent agency would not be barred from making communications and appearances to the designated component.

As to some, but not all, senior personnel,[88] the OGE may waive the restrictions if

1. The restrictions make it difficult for the agency to fill the position with qualified personnel; and
2. The waiver would not create the potential for undue influence or unfair advantage.[89]

27-2.5 Restrictions on Very Senior Personnel

A fifth provision applies to "very senior" personnel and is similar to the provision discussed earlier regarding restrictions on the activities of senior personnel. Very senior personnel are defined in terms of relevant pay provisions that encompass cabinet-level officers and a few employees paid at the level of deputy secretaries of cabinet departments.[90] Like the other provision, the prohibition is measured from the date on which an employee ceases to be a very senior employee.[91] *For two years* after the employee ceases to be a very senior employee, she may not make communications or appearances intended to influence government action on behalf of someone (other than the United States) before certain persons.[92] Like the other provision applicable to senior personnel, the prohibition applies to appearances and communications to every agency for which the person had been a former very senior employee during one year before termination of government employment. However, the provision also prohibits representing another person before any current Executive Schedule employee, the highest-ranking government officials, regardless of the agency in which the Executive Schedule employee works.[93] Therefore, this prohibition extends beyond the agency for which a former very senior employee worked. The prohibition is also broader because the OGE is not permitted to designate separate and distinct agency components to reduce the effect of this prohibition, as is permitted regarding the prohibitions applicable to former

---

87. 18 U.S.C. § 207(h)(1) (2015); 5 C.F.R. § 2641.201(e) (2015). A list of component designations is set forth in Appendix B to 5 C.F.R. Part 2641. For example, the Bureau of the Census is a component of the Department of Commerce, the Departments of Army, Navy, and Air Force are components of the Department of Defense and the Food and Drug Administration is a component of the Department of Health and Human Services.

88. 18 U.S.C. § 207(c)(2)(C) (2015).

89. *Id.*; 5 C.F.R. § 2641.301(j)(2)(i) (2015).

90. 18 U.S.C. §§ 207(d)(1)(A)–(d)(1)(C) (2015).

91. *See* OGE Memo 90 x 17, at 11 (1990).

92. 18 U.S.C. § 207(d)(1) (2015). HLOGA extended the prohibition from one to two years.

93. *Id.* § 207(d)(2).

senior employees.[94] Also, the OGE may not waive the prohibition for any position of a very senior employee.[95]

27-2.6 Restrictions Regarding Representation of a Foreign Entity

A sixth provision applies to both former senior and very senior personnel. For one year after leaving their positions, they may not represent, with intent to influence, a foreign entity before any employee of the executive branch.[96] In addition, these former employees may not advise or aid a foreign entity with the intent to influence a decision of any officer or employee of the executive branch.[97] Advice and aid could include drafting of communications with a government agency, recommending strategies and arguments, or identifying and describing agency decision makers with the intent to influence official discretionary decisions.[98] As with the other provisions, the one-year period is measured from the date an employee ceases to be senior or very senior personnel, if that date precedes the date of termination of federal employment.[99]

A foreign entity is (1) a government of a foreign country or (2) a foreign political party.[100] The provision uses the definitions of these terms contained in the Foreign Agents Registration Act of 1938.[101] Generally, a foreign commercial corporation is not a foreign entity unless it "exercises the functions of a sovereign."[102]

This provision also establishes a special rule for the United States Trade Representative and the Deputy United States Trade Representative.[103] The prohibition described earlier is applied specifically to them. Moreover, the prohibition applies "any time after the termination of that person's service [in these positions]."[104] Therefore, the prohibitions are lifetime ones.

27-2.7 Exceptions and Waivers

Some exceptions apply to all of the provisions already discussed; some are limited to those applicable to senior or very senior personnel. One applies to some

---

94. *Id.* § 207(d)(1)(B).

95. *Id.* § 207(c)(2)(C).

96. *Id.* § 207(f).

97. *Id.* § 207(f)(1)(B).

98. *See* OGE Memo 90 x 17 at 13 (1990).

99. *Id.*

100. 18 U.S.C. § 207(f)(3) (2015).

101. The government of a foreign country includes persons or groups exercising either de facto or de jure sovereign powers. A foreign political party is any organization in a foreign country or unit of it having as a goal the establishment of administration or control over all or part of the country. *See* OGE Memo 90 x 17, at 12 (citing section 1(f) of the Foreign Agents Registration Act, 22 U.S.C. § 611 (2015). For an examination of the FARA, see Chapter 19 of this manual.

102. *See* OGE Memo 90 x 17, at 12 (1990).

103. 18 U.S.C. § 207(f)(2) (2015).

104. *Id.* This provision was amended to extend to the Deputy U.S. Trade Representative and to make the restriction a lifetime one by section 21 of the Lobbying Disclosure Act of 1995, Pub. L. 104–65, 109 Stat. 704. The LDA also amended the Trade Act of 1974 to provide that "[a] person who has directly represented, aided, or advised a foreign entity (as defined by section 207(f)(3) of title 18, United States Code) in any trade negotiation, or trade dispute with the United States may not be appointed as United States Trade Representative or as a Deputy United States Trade Representative." Pub. L. No. 104–65, § 21(b), 109 Stat. 704-05 (amending 19 U.S.C. § 2171(b)).

restrictions for all employees and senior and very senior personnel, but not to other restrictions. These categories of exceptions are described below.

None of the prohibitions applies if the former employee is carrying out official duties on behalf of the United States or is carrying out official duties as an elected official of state or local government.[105] Similarly, these provisions do not restrict former employees from representing, aiding, advising, and assisting certain international organizations; however, the Secretary of State must certify in advance that the representation is in the interest of the United States.[106] Former employees may give testimony under oath or other statements under penalty of perjury.[107] However, with regard to the provision discussed in Section 27-2.1, a former employee may not, except under a court order, serve as an expert witness for anyone but the United States regarding the particular matter covered by that provision.[108]

Some of the restrictions applicable to former senior and very senior personnel (Sections 27-2.4 and 27-2.5) do not apply to official duties they perform as employees of an agency or instrumentality of state or local government,[109] a degree-granting institution of higher education,[110] and certain tax-exempt hospitals or medical research organizations.[111] These former employees may also make statements based on their own special knowledge of an area that is the subject of the comments, but only if they do not receive any compensation for making these statements.[112]

Another exception permits former senior and very senior personnel to make communications and appearances "solely on behalf of a candidate in his or her capacity as a candidate, an authorized committee, a national committee, a national Federal campaign committee, a State committee, or a political party."[113] At the time of the communication or appearance, the former senior or very senior government employee must be employed by one of the described organizations or by an entity that represents, aids, or advises only these described organizations.[114]

An additional exception applies to the restrictions described in Sections 27-2.1, 27-2.2, and 27-2.5. The former employees covered by these restrictions may communicate scientific or technological information under certain conditions and procedures acceptable to the department or agency concerned. Also, the head of the agency may, in consultation with the director of the OGE, publish a certification in the *Federal Register* that

---

105. 18 U.S.C. § 207(j)(1)(A) (2015).

106. *Id.* § 207(j)(3). In addition, a federal employee who joins an international organization and who satisfies certain regulatory requirements is not subject to the restrictions. 5 C.F.R. § 2641.301(h) (2015). These regulatory requirements would be satisfied if a federal employee serves with the international organization on a long-term transfer from his or her agency and is entitled to reemployment by that agency when the transfer ends. *See* OGE Informal Advisory Letter 82 x 8 (1982).

107. 18 U.S.C. § 207(j)(6) (2015).

108. *Id.* § 207(j)(6)(A).

109. *Id.* § 207(j)(2)(A).

110. *Id.* § 207(j)(2)(B).

111. *Id.*

112. *Id.* § 207(j)(4).

113. *Id.* § 207(j)(7)(A). These terms are defined id. § 207(j)(7)(C).

114. *Id.* § 207(j)(7)(B).

1. The former employee has outstanding scientific, technological, or technical qualifications;
2. Is acting in respect to a particular matter that requires those qualifications; and
3. Serves the national interest by her participation in the particular matter.[115]

The president may also grant a limited number of waivers to the restrictions discussed in Sections 27-2.1 through 27-2.6. In instances when the services of an employee are "critically needed" for the benefit of the government, the president may waive the restrictions in 18 U.S.C. § 207 for civilian officers and employees of the executive branch.[116] However, only twenty-five current federal employees may be granted the waiver at any one time. Moreover, the waiver applies only to activities of a former government employee of a "[g]overnment-owned, contractor operated by an entity" which employed the person immediately before that person became a government employee.[117]

In some circumstances, the OGE may waive the restriction placed on senior personnel (see Section 27-2.4).[118] This waiver may not, however, be given to very senior personnel who also fall within this restriction.[119] If requested by the head of the department or agency, the director of the OGE may waive the restriction regarding positions in the agency if

1. The restrictions would create "undue hardship" on the agency in recruiting qualified personnel for these positions; and
2. A waiver would "not create the potential for use of undue influence or unfair advantage."[120]

The director has discretion to determine in each instance whether the requirements for the waiver have been satisfied.[121]

27-2.8 Administrative Enforcement

The provisions discussed earlier may be enforced administratively as well as through criminal prosecution. For example, an agency could bar a former employee who violates the provisions from appearing before the agency or representing parties in matters before it. The Ethics in Government Act also authorizes the attorney general to seek civil penalties for violations of the act and to ask courts to enjoin future violations.[122] Agencies are specifically authorized to enforce administratively violations of the first, second, and third prohibitions and of the sixth against senior agency employees.[123] Agencies also have the express obligation to forward

---

115. *Id.* § 207(j)(5).
116. *Id.* § 207(k)(1)(A).
117. *Id.* § 207(k)(1)(B)(i).
118. *Id.* § 207(c)(2)(C) (2015).
119. *Id.*
120. *Id.* § 207(c)(2)(C)(i)–(c)(2)(C)(ii).
121. *Id.* § 207(c)(2)(C).
122. *Id.* 216(b)–(c).
123. 5 C.F.R. § 2641.103 (2015).

appropriate cases to the Department of Justice to determine if criminal charges should be brought.[124] The director of the OGE may also begin disciplinary hearings for violation of the ethics rules, including those relating to these post-employment restrictions.[125]

27-2.9 Ethical Restrictions Applicable to Lawyers

The OGE has warned that lawyers may be subject to restrictions on practice beyond those imposed by statute.[126] Ethical rules and standards impose separate and independent limitations on the representation and advice that can be provided by former government lawyers and their partners.[127]

27-3 Other Post-Employment Restrictions Applicable to the Executive Branch

Specific legislation can impose post-employment requirements on the former employees of agencies different from or more extensive than those previously discussed. For example, at one time, legislation prevented employees of the Consumer Product Safety Commission paid at a rate above GS-14 from receiving any compensation from any manufacturer subject to regulation by the Commission for a period of twelve months following termination of employment with the agency.[128] This example illustrates the importance of examining the statutory provisions applicable to specific agencies. This section does not attempt to canvass the statutory provisions of individual agencies, but Section 27-3.1 does examine one statute of wide application the provisions regarding procurement integrity of the Office of Federal Procurement Policy Act.[129]

Also, agencies may have regulations and rules of practice that impose more extensive restrictions than those contained in 18 U.S.C § 207. In particular, agencies may limit the practice of former agency lawyers before the agency more rigorously than does section 207. These provisions again demonstrate the importance of examining the rules and regulations of specific agencies. Again, this section does not attempt to canvass all such rules and regulations.

In addition, executive orders may impose restrictions on former government employees. For example, a January 21, 2009, executive order of President Obama restricts the communication and lobbying activities of former appointees with the executive branch.[130]

---

124. *Id.*

125. *Id.* § 2638.502–.506. For example, one report describes enforcement of ethics provisions by the United States Merit Systems Protection Board and discusses civil litigation brought by the United States to enforce conflict of interest provisions. UNITED STATES OFFICE OF GOVERNMENT ETHICS, RECENT CASES INVOLVING ETHICS AND CONFLICTS OF INTEREST AT THE MERIT SYSTEMS PROTECTION BOARD (2011).

126. *See* OGE Informal Advisory Letter 81 x 23, at 2 (1981).

127. See Section 22-5.5 of this manual for additional, detailed coverage of restrictions on former government lawyers.

128. 15 U.S.C. § 2053 (2015).

129. 41 U.S.C. §§ 2101–2309 (2015).

130. See Section 27-3.3 in this chapter.

27-3.1 The Procurement Integrity Provisions

The amended procurement integrity provisions impose two post-employment prohibitions on former procurement officials. One prohibits the disclosure of certain procurement information; the other prohibits the acceptance of compensation from contractors in some circumstances. Related provisions require current procurement officials to report offers of private employment and, in some instances, to recuse themselves from matters including the offeror.[131]

A former official[132] may not disclose contractor bid or proposal information or "source selection information"[133] to which she had access as a result of her government employment.[134] This prohibition seeks to protect the most sensitive procurement information and extends until the award of the federal contract to which the information relates.[135] Any disclosure must be made knowingly, and an exception permits the disclosure when "provided by law."[136]

The statute also imposes a one-year ban on the acceptance of compensation from a contractor.[137] This ban would prevent employment by a contractor, since it covers compensation received as an employee, officer, director, or consultant of a contractor. As such, the provision imposes one of the most restrictive post-employment prohibitions among those examined in this chapter. Because it prohibits the receipt of any compensation, it prohibits any compensated representational activities before the executive, legislative, or judicial branches of government. It also prohibits the giving of any compensated aid, advice, or assistance about any matter. To violate the provision, the former official must knowingly accept compensation that violates the provision.[138]

The one-year ban is measured from the time that the former official, as a government employee, engaged in specified activities.[139] These activities focus on certain involvement of the former official in

1. *The award of contract* exceeding $10 million to the contractor from whom the receipt of compensation is prohibited;
2. *The management or administration of a contract* exceeding $10 million of the contractor from whom the receipt of compensation is prohibited; and
3. *Personal decisions regarding specified actions concerning a contract* exceeding $10 million of the contractor from whom the receipt of compensation is prohibited.

---

131. 41 U.S.C. §§ 2102(a), 2103(a–c) (2015).

132. An official includes government officers, employees, and members of the uniformed services. *Id.* § 2101(5).

133. Source selection information covers a number of enumerated items and includes material determined to be such by the head of an agency on a case-by-case basis. Contractor bid information is information submitted to the government in connection with a bid or proposal. *Id.* § 2101(7).

134. *Id.* § 2101. The statute also covers present employees and some private parties. *Id.* § 2101(a)(2).

135. *Id.* § 2101(a)(1). In addition to this limitation, an employee of "a private sector organization assigned to an agency" under 5 U.S.C. § 3704 may not knowingly disclose covered information during the three-year period following the assignment. *Id. Section 2102(a)(2)*

136. 41 U.S.C. § 2101(a)(1) (2015).

137. *Id.* § 2104(d).

138. *Id.* § 2104(d)(1).

139. *Id.* § 2104(a)(1).

Regarding *the award of the contract*, the prohibition applies from the time of the selection of the contractor or the award of the contract if the former official served as

1. The procuring contracting officer;
2. The source selection authority;
3. A member of the source selection evaluation board; or
4. The chief of a financial or technical evaluation team in the procurement at issue.[140]

These positions involve activities in the selection and award of the contract.

Regarding *the management or administration of the contract*, the prohibition applies from the time that the former official served as the program manager, deputy program manager, or administrative contracting officer for the contract awarded to the contractor from whom compensation would be barred.[141] The provision defines the officials most likely to be involved in significant management and administration of the contract.

Regarding *personal decision*, the prohibition applies from the time that the official personally made a decision for a federal agency

1. To award a contract, subcontract, modification of a contract or subcontract, or a task delivery order over $10 million to that contractor;
2. To establish overhead or other rates applicable to a contract for that contractor over $10 million;
3. To approve issuance of contract payments over $10 million to that contractor; or
4. To pay or settle a claim over $10 million with that contractor.[142]

The method of determining the time from which the one-year ban runs will vary. In some instances, a specific date can be easily fixed, as, for example, for the selection of the contractor or for the specified personal decisions just noted. In other instances, regarding more general roles in the management and administration of the contract, the time would run from the time that such responsibilities for contracts of the contractor ends.

The provision seeks to cover specified positions that have considerable influence over the selection or administration of a contract award. It also seeks to cover specified decisions of significance in the life of a contract regardless of the formal title or responsibility of the officials who personally make those decisions.

The provision contains one important exception: A former official is not prohibited from accepting compensation from a division or affiliate of the contractor that does not produce the same or similar products as the division or affiliate of the contractor responsible for the covered contract.[143] This exception ameliorates the rigor of the bar for large contractors with diversified components and affiliates.

---

140. *Id.* § 2104(a)(1).
141. *Id.* § 2104(a)(2).
142. *Id.* § 2104(a)(3)(D).
143. *Id.* § 2104(b).

The provision also prohibits a contractor from paying compensation to a former official while knowing that the acceptance of the compensation would violate the prohibition.[144] This provision then enforces the post-employment prohibitions not only against the former official but also against private parties.

Although it clearly prevents representational activities as well as aid, advice, and assistance, the rationale for the compensation ban extends beyond that applicable to provisions that only limit actions by former government employees. The prohibition seeks to do more than prevent switching sides, protect confidential information, or restrict contacts suggesting special influence; rather, it seeks to reduce the incentives for what has been called "deferred bribery," in which the possibilities of future employment with those interests affected by the performance of an official create subtle incentives that alter the performance of public duties to the benefit of those interests at the expense of the public interest. This provision rests in part on a determination that the particular temptations of procurement require the reduction of these incentives created by the possibility of future private employment.

The enforcement of the prohibitions discussed in this section varies. Violation of the prohibition against disclosing certain procurement information can lead to criminal penalties if the information is exchanged for anything of value or is given to provide anyone a competitive advantage in the award of a procurement contract by a federal agency.[145] The prohibitions may be enforced by civil penalties and by administrative action.[146] The penalties that may be assessed in a civil action brought by the Attorney General can be substantial.[147] In addition, federal agencies may take administrative action, including

1. Cancellation of a procurement;
2. Rescission of a contract for violation of the provision prohibiting the disclosure of certain information, if the contractor (or someone acting for the contractor) has been convicted of the violation or if the head of the agency determines, by a preponderance of the evidence, that the contractor (or someone acting on the contractor's behalf) has violated the prohibition; or
3. Commencement of suspension or debarment proceedings.[148]

Former employees subject to these prohibitions are also subject to the more general prohibitions contained in section 207 and discussed in Section 27-2. Because of the different coverage of these provisions, a former employee could violate the procurement integrity provisions and not section 207. As important, a former employee might comply with the procurement integrity provisions and yet violate section 207. Therefore, an employee subject to the procurement integrity provisions should carefully examine both provisions.

---

144. *Id.* § 2104(d)(2).
145. *Id.* § 2105(a).
146. *Id.* §§ 2104(b),(c).
147. In the case of an individual, the penalty may be up to $50,000 for each violation plus twice the amount of compensation the individual received or was offered for prohibited conduct. An organization can be assessed a penalty of up to $500,000 for each violation plus twice the amount of compensation offered or received. *Id.* § 423(b).
148. *Id.* § 423(c).

27-3.2 Post-Employment Restrictions Imposed by Agency Regulations

Agencies may have administrative regulations and rules of practice that impose more extensive restrictions on former employees than those contained in section 207. These regulations rest upon the authority of the agencies to regulate practice before them. Enforcement will usually rely on powers of the specific agency. The interpretation and application of these provisions rest with the individual agency.

The OGE has declined to interpret or to evaluate such regulations.[149] These regulations may limit the practice of former agency attorneys and other employees before an agency. Therefore, it is important to examine the rules and regulations of specific agencies. In addition to agency regulations, lawyers must also be sensitive to the restrictions imposed by legal ethics.[150]

27-3.3 Post-Employment Restrictions Imposed by Executive Order

On January 21, 2009, President Barack Obama issued Executive Order No. 13490 incorporating post-employment restrictions into an ethics pledge that becomes part of the contractual commitments of appointees to executive agencies.[151] Appointees who must accept these restrictions include noncareer appointees of the president or vice president, noncareer appointees in the Senior Executive Service, and an "appointee to a position that has been excepted from the competitive service by reason of being of a confidential or policy making character."[152] Thus, these contractual restrictions apply to many senior or very senior agency personnel as well as some confidential and policymaking appointees who may not necessarily fall within the salary guidelines for senior or very senior personnel under the statutory provisions discussed earlier.[153] On the other hand, these contractual restrictions do not apply to some senior-level career employees.[154] As of the date of publication, these restrictions apply only to persons appointed during President Obama's administration.[155]

Under the executive order, senior employees who are now prohibited for a period of one year from communicating with employees of the senior employee's

---

149. "[T]his Office has no authority to advise you on the applicability of a rule such as this, which is specific to a particular agency. Neither would we comment on the significance or status of this rule." OGE Informal Advisory Letter 92 x 8 (1992).

150. See Chapter 22.

151. Exec. Order No. 13490 (Jan. 21, 2009), "Ethics Commitments by Executive Branch Personnel" (Exec. Order No. 13490), section 1. The executive order indicates that executive agencies also include the executive office of the president and the United States Postal Service, but exclude the Government Accountability Office. *Id.*, section 2(a). For further discussion of the executive order, see Chapter 29 of this manual.

152. *Id.,* section 2(b). These policy-making positions include those described in Schedule C and "other positions excepted under comparable criteria," but do not include a member of the Senior Foreign Service or someone appointed "solely as a uniformed service commissioned officer." *Id.*

153. Discussion of the statutory limitations on senior and very senior governmental personnel are found in Sections 27-2.4 and 27-2.5. "Unlike certain other ethical requirements . . . the Pledge applies without regard to the salary level of a political appointee." OGE Memo DO-09-003, at 1 (Jan. 22, 2009).

154. See Section 27-2.4.

155. "Similarly political appointees appointed to a full-time position prior to January 20, 2009 were not required to sign the Pledge. This means individuals appointed during the previous administration were not now covered by the Pledge even if they continued in their current position or served in an acting capacity under the Vacancies Reform Act[.]" OGE Memo DO-09-003 at 1.

former executive agency must agree to extend that prohibition for a second additional year.[156] This contractual provision extends an existing restriction rather than creating a new one.

The executive order also limits the ability of appointees who subsequently leave the government "to lobby" certain government employees.[157] To violate the prohibition to lobby, a former appointee must "act . . . as a registered lobbyist."[158] A former executive branch appointee agrees "not to lobby any covered executive branch official or noncareer Senior Executive Service appointee for the remainder of the administration."[159] Thus, the length of the restriction depends upon at what point during presidential terms an appointee leaves an executive agency.[160] The restriction is a significant one because it applies to lobbying of any covered executive branch official.[161]

The director of the Office of Management and Budget may waive in writing for a current or former appointee "any restrictions" contained in the Ethics Pledge incorporated into an appointee's contract.[162] The director must certify "that the literal application of the restriction is inconsistent with the purposes of the

---

156. Exec. Order No. 13490, *supra* note 151, section 1(4). The restriction described in Section 27-2.4 applies to representational activities through communication or appearance before the former executive agency and is not limited to communications regarding specific matters involving particular parties. On the other hand, appointees entering into an executive agency may not for a period of two years "from the date of appointment participate in any particular matter involving specific parties that is directly and substantially related to" the appointee's former or employer or clients. 2009 Executive Order, *supra* note 151, section 1(2). The prohibition applies to any employer or that the appointee served during the two years before appointment. OGE Memo DO-09-003 at 2.

157. Exec. Order No. 13490, *supra* note 151, section 1(5).

158. *Id.*, section 2(f). "Registered lobbyist" within the meaning of the order includes all of those persons listed as lobbyists on active registrations filed under the Lobbying Disclosure Act. Not mentioned in the definitional provision, however, are those individuals listed for the first time as lobbyist-employees of the registrant in quarterly reports. *Id.*, section 2(e).

159. Exec. Order No. 13490, *supra* note 151, section 1(5). A covered executive branch employee is one "described in the Lobbying Disclosure Act." OGE Memo DO-09-003 at 2. A discussion of the term "covered executive branch employee" under the Lobbying Disclosure Act can be found in Section 4-2.3 of this manual. If an appointee was a registered lobbyist during the two years before the appointment, that appointee must not "seek or accept employment with any executive agency" that the appointee lobbied "within the 2 years" before the date of appointment. Such an appointee must not participate in "any particular matter" on which the appointee lobbied "during the two years" before the date of appointment. Finally, such an appointee may not participate "in the specific issue area in which that particular matter falls." Exec. Order No. 13490, *supra* note 151, section 1(3). See Sections 29-4 and 29-5 of this manual.

160. "Administration" of a president "means all terms of office of the incumbent President serving at the time of the appointment of an appointee[.]" Exec. Order No. 13490, *supra* note 151, section 2(o). For example, a person appointed in the first year of President Obama's first term who leaves in the subsequent year would be covered for the remainder of that term and for all of the second term.

161. *Id.*, section 1(5). This restriction, included in paragraph 5 of the Ethics Pledge, prohibits lobbying, a term that incorporates the definitions of the Lobbying Disclosure Act. OGE Memo DO-10-004, Feb.22, 2010 at 4. Thus the prohibition includes requirements regarding the percentage of time spent in lobbying activities and the number of contacts made with the covered official. *Id.* at 6. See Chapter 4 for a discussion of the Lobbying Disclosure Act. As a result, this restriction may be more limited than it appears on its face.

162. *Id.*, section 3(a). The director is to consult with the Counsel to the President in this determination.

restriction" or "that it is in the public interest to grant the waiver."[163] A waiver is effective when the certification is signed.[164]

The executive order describes the administration of the ethics pledge and the enforcement of the restrictions contained within it.[165] The order charges the attorney general to investigate violations and to enforce the ethical and fiduciary obligations assumed in the contract of employment, using the power to seek restraining orders and injunctions[166] and the power to seek constructive trusts for the benefit of the United States.[167] In addition, the heads of executive agencies, after appropriate proceedings, may bar an appointee who violates these restrictions from lobbying any officer or employee of that agency "for up to 5 years in addition to the time covered by the pledge."[168]

The executive order commissions a number of studies and reports.[169] In particular, it requires the director of the OGE to "report to the President on steps the executive branch can take to expand [the restrictions on lobbying by former appointees] to all executive branch employees who are involved in the procurement process such that they may not for 2 years after leaving Government service lobby any government official regarding a Government contract that was under their official responsibility in the last 2 years of their Government Service[.]"[170]

27-4 Post-Employment Restrictions Applicable to Congress

Congress has imposed various restrictions on the lobbying activities of members of Congress and of its elected leadership and of higher-paid congressional employees, including those employed by legislative offices of Congress such as

---

163. *Id.* "The public interest shall include, but not be limited to, exigent circumstances relating to national security or to the economy." *Id.*, section 3(b).

164. *Id.*, section 3(a). A list of these waivers can be found in Executive Branch Agency Ethics Pledge Waivers, *available at* http://www.oge.gov/Open-Government/Executive-Branch-Agency-Ethics -Pledge-Waivers *and* https://www.whitehouse.gov/briefing-room/disclosures/ethics-pledge-waivers (last visited Oct. 1, 2015).

165. Exec. Order No. 13490, *supra* note 151, section 4. Specific roles are given to the director of the Office of Government Ethics and the attorney general. Consultative roles are assigned to the director of the Office of Management and Budget, the director of the Office of Personnel Management, and the counsel to the President.

166. *Id.*, sections 5(c), (d)(1).

167. *Id.*, section 5(d)(2). A federal employee, such as an appointee covered by the executive order, who receives any benefit as the result of the breach of the fiduciary duties contained in an employment contract is required to place those benefits in a constructive trust for the benefit of the United States . . . An early article advocating the use of such constructive trusts is Arthur Lenhoff, *The Constructive Trust as a Remedy for Corruption in Public Office*, 54 COLUMBIA L. REV. 214 (1954).

168. Exec. Order No. 13490, *supra* note 151, section 5(b).

169. *Id.*, section 4(c). These studies and reports include annual reports "on the pledge and this order," and reports on whether existing laws and regulations ensure full compliance with executive branch procurement lobbying disclosure and to suggest actions "to expand the fullest practicable disclosure" of lobbying regarding executive branch procurement and presidential pardons. Studies and reports on Exec. Order No.13490 are contained in Annual Reports on the Executive Order, available in pdf format on the website of the Office of Government Ethics. http://www.oge.gov/Laws-and -Regulations/Executive-Orders/Executive-Order-13490-(Jan--21,-2009)-Prescribing-Standards-of -Ethical-Conduct-for-Government-Officers-and-Employees/ (last visited Oct. 1, 2015).

170. *Id.*, section 4(d). This report is to include "immediate action the executive branch can take" and any necessary recommendations for legislation.

the Government Accountability Office and the Library of Congress.[171] With few exceptions, these prohibitions address activities intended to influence the official actions of members and employees of Congress, not executive branch officials. With the exception of one provision regarding the representation of foreign entities that prohibits representation before executive agencies and another regarding aid or assistance in ongoing trade or treaty negotiations using confidential information, these provisions limit only representation on behalf of others (other than the United States) before members of Congress and congressional employees. Although most of these prohibitions address communications or appearances on behalf of another person, they do not require that these acts of representation be compensated. However, because they require action on behalf of another, they would not prohibit self-representation. Because they require that the communication involve an attempt to influence action by congressional personnel in their official capacity, social and other similar contacts would not be included. Like the prohibitions applicable to the executive branch, these prohibitions generally impose criminal penalties, except to the extent they exist only as House or Senate rules. Therefore, like the executive branch prohibitions, they should be strictly construed. As with the other criminal provisions, the requirements of knowledge and intent are crucial.

Although OGE has no responsibility for the enforcement or interpretation of these laws, its interpretations of similar provisions applicable to the executive branch may be relevant for several reasons.[172] First, the provisions applicable to Congress are placed in section 207, which also contains the executive branch prohibitions. This placement suggests that the provisions were intended to be related and integrated, and that identical terms used in prohibitions applicable to the executive and legislative branches carry the same meaning. Second, the content, as well as the structure, of section 207 supports this suggestion. Many exceptions and prohibitions apply to both the executive and legislative provisions, indicating that Congress sought to create a single comprehensive post-employment statute. Finally, the assumption that identical terms in the executive and legislative prohibitions are to have the same meaning recognizes a long-standing debate that similar restrictions should be placed on executive and legislative employees.[173]

The Honest Leadership and Open Government Act of 2007 (HLOGA) revised the post-employment restrictions applicable to members and employees of Congress that will be noted below. Most of these restrictions are found in section 207, but some reside in the rules of the House and Senate permitting enforcement only through congressional procedures. In all events, the restrictions do not prevent

---

171. The coverage of the restrictions discussed in Section 27-4.8 is broader and covers all legislative branch employees. For further discussion of the general topic of post-employment restrictions applicable to members, officers, and employees of Congress, see Chapter 28 of this manual.

172. The Ethics Manuals of the House of Representatives and of the Senate discuss issues regarding the application of section 207 in ways analogous to OGE interpretations. House Ethics Manual, Committee on Standards of Official Conduct, 110th Cong., 2d Sess. 240–44 (2008); Senate Ethics Manual, Select Committee on Ethics, 108th Cong., 1st Sess. 89–91 (2003).

173. Congress restated this in enacting HLOGA. *See* Pub. L. No. 110–81, Sec. 701, 121 Stat. 735, 775 (Sept. 14, 2007) ("It is the Sense of the Congress that any applicable restrictions on congressional officials and employees in this Act should apply to the executive and judicial branches.").

contacts with the staff of Secretary of the Senate or Clerk of the House of Representatives regarding compliance with the Lobbying Disclosure Act.[174]

HLOGA also requires that the Secretary of the Senate and Clerk of the House notify departing members and employees of the beginning and ending dates of the post-employment restrictions discussed below[175] and also post those on the Internet in a format that is searchable, sortable, and downloadable by the public.[176]

27-4.1 Restrictions on Members of Congress and on Elected Officers of Congress

Within two years after leaving office, no person who was a senator may knowingly make, with the intent to influence, any communication to or appearance before any member, officer, or employee of *either House of Congress* or any employee of *any legislative office* of Congress, on behalf of any other person (except the United States) in connection with any matter on which such former senator seeks action by a member, officer, or employee of Congress in his or her official capacity.[177] With regard to former members of the House of Representatives and elected officers of the House, the same restriction applies, but is limited to *one year* and, with respect to former elected officers, the restriction applies only to communications to or appearances before any member, officer, or employee of the House.[178] Former elected officers of the Senate are subject to the same restriction for *one year* after leaving office, and that restriction applies with regard to communications to or appearances before any senator or any officer or employee of the Senate.[179]

Assuming that the terms "communication" and "appearance" mean the same as in the executive branch restrictions, communication would include written and oral statements as well as any made electronically. Appearance would be satisfied by physical presence in circumstances that support intent to influence official action. The provision would not prohibit advice, aid, and assistance to another party during the restricted period as long as these activities were not accompanied by prohibited communication or appearance. The term "Member of the House of Representatives" includes delegates and resident commissioners to the House.[180]

---

174. 18 U.S.C. § 207(e)(8) (2015). *See also* Senate Rule XXXVII, cl.10 (114th Cong.).

175. 2 U.S.C. § 104d(a) (2015).

176. *Id.* § 104d(b). House and Senate postings of employment restrictions under the Honest Leadership and Open Government Act of 2007 can be found at http://clerk.house.gov/public_disc/postemployment.aspx (last visited Oct. 1, 2015); http://www.senate.gov/legislative/lobbyingdisc.htm#lobbyingdisc=pe (last visited Oct. 1, 2015).

177. 18 U.S.C. § 207(e)(1)(A) (2015). *See also* Senate Rule XXXVII, cl. 8 (114th Cong.): "If a Member, upon leaving office, becomes a registered lobbyist under the Federal Regulation of Lobbying Act of 1946 or any successor statute [the Lobbying Disclosure Act of 1995], or is employed or retained by such a registered lobbyist or an entity that employs or retains a registered lobbyist for the purpose of influencing legislation, he shall not lobby members, officers, or employees of the Senate for a period of two years after leaving office."

178. *Id.* 18 U.S.C. § 207(e)(1)(B)(i)–(iii).

179. *Id.* § 207(e)(2). *See also* Senate Rule XXXVII, cl. 9(c) (114th Cong.) (prohibiting for one year lobbying these same persons by a former officer of the Senate, whether elected or not).

180. 2 U.S.C. § 207(e)(9)(K) (2015).

27-4.2 Restrictions on Higher-Paid Personal Staff of Members of Congress

The second and third provisions of section 207 impose restrictions similar to those on certain higher-paid[181] former personal staff of members of the House and Senate.[182] For *one year* after termination of employment, a former personal House staff member may not attempt to influence official actions through communications to or appearances before

1. The Member of the House who formerly employed the staff person;[183] or
2. Any employee of that Member of the House.[184]

The restriction applicable to a senator's personal staff sweeps more broadly, covering communications to or appearances before any senator or any officer or employee of the Senate.[185]

Because the limitation is similar, the discussion in Section 27-4.1 of the character of the communications and appearances prohibited applies here as well.

The statute appears to cover employment with more than one member. For example, a personal staff member leaves the employment of Representative A and joins the personal staff of Representative B. Six months later, the personal staff member leaves congressional employment altogether. That personal staff member would be barred for six months regarding communications and appearances on behalf of another with Representative A and Representative A's employees and for one year from the same types of contacts with Representative B and Representative B's employees.

---

181. *Id.* § 207(e)(7)(A)("a former employee who, for at least 60 days, in the aggregate, during the 1-year period before that former employee's service as such employee terminated, was paid a rate of basic pay equal to or greater than an amount which is 75 percent of the basic rate of pay payable for a member of the House of Congress in which such employee was employed.").

182. *Id.* § 207(e)(2)(Senate), (e)(3)(House). "Employee of the Senate" for the purpose of subsection (2) includes the employee of a senator. *Id.* § 207(e)(9)(D).

183. *Id.* § 207(e)(3)(B)(i).

184. *Id.* § 207(e)(3)(B)(ii).

185. *Id.* § 207(e)(2). In addition, under Senate Rule XXXVII, if an employee on the staff of a member, regardless of their salary, upon leaving that position, becomes a registered lobbyist under the Lobbying Disclosure Act, or is employed or retained by a registered lobbyist or an entity that employs or retains a registered lobbyist for the purpose of influencing legislation, that employee may not *lobby* the member for whom he worked or that member's staff for a period of *one year* after leaving that position. For highly paid staff, this restriction bars *lobbying* of "any Member, officer, or employee of the Senate" for *one year* after leaving his or her position. Senate Rule *Id.* § 207(e), cl. 9(a), (c) (114th Cong.). For these purposes "lobbying" includes:

> Any oral or written communication to influence the content or disposition of any issue before Congress, including any pending or future bill, resolution, treaty, nomination, hearing, report, or investigation; but does not include—(1) a communication (i) made in the form of testimony given before a committee or office of the Congress, or (ii) submitted for inclusion in the public record, public docket, or public file of a hearing; or (2) a communication by an individual, acting solely on his own behalf, for redress of personal grievances, or to express his personal opinion.

Senate Rule XXXVII, cl. 13(c) (114th Cong.).

27-4.3 Restrictions on Higher-Paid Committee Staff

The fourth provision imposes on higher-paid[186] committee staff of Congress restrictions similar to those imposed on former members and their staff with regard to communications and appearances intended to influence official action on behalf of another person.

For *one year* after termination of a person's employment with a House committee or joint committee of Congress, that person is prohibited from knowingly making communications or appearances intended to influence official actions on behalf of another.[187] These covered communications or appearances may not be made to any member or employee of the committee that employed the staff member.[188] Also prohibited are contacts with any member of Congress who was a member of the committee "in the year immediately prior to the termination of such person's employment."[189] Covered committees include a standing committee and a select committee as well as a joint committee.[190]

With regard to higher-paid employees of Senate committees,[191] the same restriction applies under HLOGA's amendments to section 207, though it is broader in that it encompasses communications to or appearances before any senator or any officer or employee of the Senate.[192]

27-4.4 Restrictions on Higher-Paid Leadership Staff

The fifth provision imposes on higher-paid[193] leadership staff similar restrictions with regard to communications and appearances intended to influence official action on behalf of another. For *one year* after termination of employment with the leadership staff, a former employee is prohibited from knowingly making communications and appearances intended to influence official actions on behalf of another person.[194] For Senate leadership staff, the covered communications and appearances may not be made to any member of the Senate or any officer or

---

186. *See* 18 U.S.C. § 207(e)(7)(A) (2015).

187. *Id.* § 207(e)(4).

188. *Id.*

189. *Id.*

190. *Id.* § 207(e)(9)(A).

191. "Employee of the Senate" includes an employee of a committee of the Senate. *Id.* § 207(e)(9)(D).

192. *Id.* § 207(e)(2). *See also* Senate Rule XXXVII, cl. 9(b) (114th Cong.) ("If an employee on the staff of a committee, upon leaving his position, becomes such a registered lobbyist or is employed or retained by such a registered lobbyist or an entity that employs or retains a registered lobbyist for the purpose of influencing legislation, such employee *may not lobby the members of the committee for which he worked, or the staff of that committee,* for a period of one year after leaving his position.") (emphasis added) and *id.* cl. 9(c) ("If . . . an employee . . . on the staff of a committee whose rate of pay is equal to or greater than 75 percent of the rate of pay of a member and employed at such rate for more than 60 days in a calendar year, upon leaving that position, becomes a registered lobbyist, or is employed or retained by such a registered lobbyist or an entity that employs or retains a registered lobbyist for the purpose of influencing legislation, such employee *may not lobby any Member, officer, or employee of the Senate* for a period of 1 year after leaving that position.") (emphasis added).

193. *See* 18 U.S.C. § 207(e)(7)(A) (2015).

194. *Id.* § 207(e)(2) (dealing with Senate employees generally) and (e)(5) (dealing with House leadership staff).

employee of the Senate.[195] For the House leadership staff, the covered communications and appearances may not be made to any member of the House leadership or an employee on the House leadership staff.[196]

Employees on the leadership staff of the House of Representatives and of the Senate include, among others, those employed by persons (the leadership) who occupy specified leadership positions of both the majority and minority in each house.[197]

27-4.5 Restrictions on Higher-Paid Employees of Other Legislative Offices

The sixth provision imposes on higher-paid[198] employees of other legislative offices similar restrictions on communications and appearances intended to influence official action on behalf of another person. For *one year* after termination of employment in legislative office, a former employee is prohibited from knowingly making communications and appearances intended to influence official action on behalf of another person.[199] The covered communications and appearances may not be made to officers or employees of the legislative office of the former employee.[200]

The legislative offices referred to include several specifically listed, among which the following are included: the Government Accountability Office, the Library of Congress, the Office of Technology Assessment (disbanded in 1995), and the Congressional Budget Office.[201] Also covered is "any other agency, entity, or office in the legislative branch" not covered in the provisions discussed in Sections 27-4.1 through 27-4.4.[202]

27-4.6 Restrictions Applicable to Employment Negotiations

Both the House and the Senate have rules governing negotiations by members and employees for future employment. House Rule XXVII requires that, within three business days after the commencement of negotiations or agreement of future employment or compensation, members, delegates, and resident commissions must file with the Committee on Standards of Official Conduct a statement signed by the member, delegate, or resident commissioner, as the case may be, regarding the negotiations or agreement. This statement must include the name of the private entity or entities involved in the negotiations or agreement and the date the negotiations or agreement commenced. Without that filing, such negotiations

---

195. *Id.* § 207(e)(2).

196. *Id.* § 207(e)(5)(B).

197. *Id.* §§ 207(e)(9)(H), (e)(9)(I), (e)(9)(L), (e)(9)(M).

198. For this category, the relevant pay level is different than for the previously discussed categories of higher-paid staff; it includes only "a former employee who, for at least 60 days, in the aggregate, during the 1-year period before that former employee's service as such employee terminated, was employed in a position for which the rate of basic pay, exclusive of any locality-based pay adjustment under is equal to or greater than the basic rate of pay payable for level IV of the Executive Schedule." *Id.* § 207(e)(7)(B).

199. *Id.* § 207(e)(6).

200. *Id.* § 207(e)(6)(B).

201. *Id.* § 207(e)(9)(G).

202. *Id.*

or agreement are prohibited until a successor has been elected.[203] Within the same time period, officers and employees of the House earning in excess of 75 percent of the salary paid to a member must notify the Committee that they are negotiating or have an agreement of future employment or compensation.[204] The members, delegates, resident commissioners, officers, and employees must recuse themselves "from any matter in which there is a conflict of interest or an appearance of a conflict" as a result of those negotiations or agreement.[205] Similar obligations apply to senators and employees of the Senate under the Senate rules,[206] though the recusal provision applies only to employees and not senators.[207] In no event, however, may a senator negotiate or have any arrangement concerning prospective employment for a job involving lobbying activities as defined by the Lobbying Disclosure Act[208] until after his or her successor has been elected.[209]

27-4.7 Restrictions on Representing Foreign Entities

A seventh provision of section 207 prohibits the representation of foreign entities before any executive department or agency; this provision also prohibits aiding or advising a foreign entity with the intent to influence a decision of any officer or employee of the executive branch.[210] Unlike these other provisions that apply to members, officers, and employees of Congress, this one prohibits activities regarding the executive branch rather than Congress. Also unlike the other provisions discussed earlier, this one prohibits aid and advice as well as representational activities. This prohibition applies to all persons subject to the other provisions already discussed and, in this sense, is broad in coverage. However, the exceptions discussed in Section 27-4.9 that apply to the first six prohibitions do not apply to this provision.

Most likely, the discussion of prohibited advice and assistance in Section 27-2.6 (discussing restrictions on the conduct of certain executive branch employees) applies here as well. The same definition of foreign entity clearly applies.[211]

---

203. House Rule XXVII, cl. 1 (114th Cong.) (as added by Section 301(a) of HLOGA).

204. *Id*. cl. 2 and 3.

205. *Id*. cl. 4.

206. Senate Rule XXXVII, cl. 14 (114th Cong.).

207. *Id*. cl. 14(c)(3).

208. See Chapter 4 of this manual.

209. Senate Rule XXXVII, cl. 14(b) (114th Cong.). In defining "negotiation," the House Ethics Manual gives deference "to court decisions interpreting a related federal criminal statute." House Ethics Manual, Committee on Standards of Official Conduct, 110th Cong. 2d Sess. 208 (2008). The manual "makes a distinction between 'negotiations,' which triggers the rule and 'preliminary or exploratory talks,' which do not." *Id*. at 209. "'Negotiations' connotes 'a communication between two parties with a view toward reaching an agreement' and in which there is 'active interest on both sides.'" "Thus, merely sending one's resume to a private entity is not considered 'negotiating for future employment.'" *Id*. (footnote deleted). The Senate Select Committee believes "'Negotiation' is the discussion of terms and conditions of employment after an offer has been made and the Senator or staffer is considering accepting." U.S. Senate Select Committee on Ethics, www.Ethics.Senate.gov/public/index .cfm?p=ConflictsofInterest (last visited Oct. 1, 2015). See also Chapter 2, Section 2-5, and Chapter 28 for a discussion of these provisions.

210. 18 U.S.C. § 207(f)(1)(A) (2015).

211. See Section 27-2.6 of this chapter.

27-4.8 Restrictions Regarding the Use of Confidential Information in Trade and Treaty Negotiations

An eighth provision imposes on members and employees of Congress a prohibition similar to the one imposed on executive branch employees (discussed in Section 27-2.3) prohibiting the use of confidential information in trade or treaty negotiations.[212] Therefore, the discussion of the executive branch restriction[213] addresses many of the issues regarding the scope and character of the provision as applicable to Congress, including the description of confidential information, the definition of an ongoing trade or treaty negotiation, the calculation of the term of the restriction, and the prohibition. The former member or officer or employee of the legislative branch may not use the covered information to represent another party by communication or appearance before the legislative, executive, or judicial branches.[214]

This provision covers more legislative branch employees than the other provisions. The definitions limiting the coverage of the other prohibitions to higher-paid employees apply only to those subsections and do not apply to the subsection that contains this provision. As a result, the term "employee of the legislative branch" covers all legislative branch employees.

27-4.9 Exceptions

The restrictions described in Sections 27-4.1 through 27-4.5 do not apply to activities performed in carrying out official duties for the United States or as elected officials of state and local government or to acts authorized by section 104(j) of the Indian Self-Determination and Education Assistance Act.[215] Exceptions also apply to communications and appearances on behalf of an agency or instrumentality of state or local government, a degree-granting institution of higher education, and certain tax-exempt hospitals or medical research organizations.[216] Covered persons may also represent, aid, advise, and assist certain international organizations, but only if the secretary of state certifies in advance that the activities are in the interests of the United States.[217] Also, former employees may make statements based on their special knowledge in a particular area that is the subject of the statements, but only if no compensation is received for making them.[218]

Another exception permits a communication or appearance made "solely on behalf of a candidate in his or her capacity as a candidate, an authorized committee, a national committee, a national Federal campaign committee, a State committee, or a political party."[219] At the time of the communication or appearance, the individual must be employed by one of these described organizations or by an entity that represents, aids, or advises only the described organizations.[220]

---

212. 18 U.S.C. § 207(b)(1) (2015).
213. See Section 27-2.3.
214. 18 U.S.C. § 207(b)(1) (2015).
215. *Id.* § 207(j)(1).
216. *Id.* § 207(j)(2).
217. *Id.* § 207(j)(3). The regulatory exception applicable to executive branch employees who are transferred to international organizations extends only to executive branch employees.
218. *Id.* § 207(j)(4).
219. *Id.* § 207(j)(7). These terms are defined *id.* § 207(j)(7)(C).
220. *Id.* § 207(j)(7)(B).

CHAPTER 28

Additional Restrictions on Post-Employment Activity and on Negotiating for Future Employment under Congressional Ethics Rules

BY ROBERT L. WALKER

28-1 Introduction

As covered comprehensively in Chapter 27 of this manual—on the post-employment (or "revolving door") restrictions set forth in 18 U.S.C. § 207—members, officers, and more senior staff of the U.S. House of Representatives and the U.S. Senate (and of other legislative offices of the Congress) are subject to restrictions on their post-congressional employment and activity imposed by the federal criminal code. The current chapter focuses more narrowly on the post-employment restrictions imposed by congressional ethics rules.

With respect to the post-employment restrictions set forth in the ethics rules of the House of Representatives, in fact, the focus of this chapter is so narrow that the essential information can be stated in three words: There are none.[1] Nonetheless, as discussed briefly below, the Committee on Ethics of the U.S. House of Representatives (the House Committee on Ethics) issues extensive, and very useful, guidance on the application of the statutory restrictions under section 207 to members, officers, and staff of the House.[2] In the Senate, however—and as detailed below, Senate Rule XXXVII (to be referred to in this chapter as "Rule 37"), paragraphs 8 and 9, impose post-employment restrictions on "lobbying" on any senator and on any Senate employee (regardless of salary level) who leaves the Senate to become a registered lobbyist or to become employed for the purpose of influencing legislation by a registered lobbyist or by an entity that employs or retains a lobbyist.

It should be noted and remembered that the revolving-door restrictions of Rule 37 apply to a wider range of former Senate personnel (that is, in some form, to *all* senators and *all* staff) than do the revolving-door restrictions under the criminal law. But—in general, and with some important exceptions covered by the discussion below—the restrictions under Rule 37 cover a narrower range of contacts and communications (i.e., only contacts and communications that qualify as "lobbying contacts" under the Lobbying Disclosure Act (LDA)).

This chapter also covers the restrictions on members and staff of the House and Senate, under congressional ethics rules, on negotiating for future private sector employment and on entering into agreements for such employment. The

---

1. Except for certain restrictions on admission to the House Chamber imposed on former members or officers of the House who (1) are lobbyists; (2) are employed for the purpose of influencing the passage, defeat, or amendment of any legislative proposal; or (3) have a financial interest in any pending legislative measure. *See* House rule cited in note 34.

2. *See, e.g.,* Memoranda, U.S. House of Representatives, Committee on Ethics to All House Members, Officers, and Employees (Nov. 19, 2012), *available at* http://ethics.house.gov/sites/ethics.house.gov/files/post%20emp%20staff_0.pdf and http://ethics.house.gov/sites/ethics.house.gov/files/post%20emp%20Member_0.pdf.

discussion of these restrictions also covers the notification and recusal requirements that must be observed by members and staff who are negotiating or entering into agreements for future employment.

The rules and restrictions on employment negotiations and (on the Senate side) on post-employment activity discussed in this chapter apply directly, by their terms, only to members and staff—or to former members and staff—of Congress. It is important for prospective private employers of members and employees of Congress to understand these rules and restrictions so that the employers can make informed compliance determinations and decisions, both during the hiring process and during the covered period of a former congressional official's private employment.

28-2 Senate Post-Employment Restrictions under Senate Rule 37, Paragraphs 8 and 9

As applied by the Select Committee on Ethics of the U.S. Senate (the Senate Ethics Committee),[3] Rule 37 (on Conflict of Interest) imposes the following restrictions on former Senators and on former staff[4] (the scope of restrictions on staff depends on

---

3. *See, e.g.*, U.S. SENATE, Select Committee on Ethics "Quick Reference Guide" on "Employment Negotiations and Recusal/Post-Employment Restrictions" (Jan. 14, 2014) (Employment Negotiations and Recusal), *available at* http://www.ethics.senate.gov/public/index.cfm/files/serve?File_id=9dbac7a9 -ffb4-433b-bb30-b8783d72fc15. *See also* U.S. SENATE, Select Committee on Ethics, "An Overview of the Senate Code of Conduct and Related Laws," at 12 (Jan. 2014) (Overview), *available at* http://www .ethics.senate.gov/public/index.cfm/files/serve?File_id=1aec2c45-aadf-46e3-bb36-c472bcbed20f. Most recently, following a number of investigations by the Senate Ethics Committee concerning application of the post-employment restrictions set forth by statute and by Senate rule (e.g., the Preliminary Inquiry concerning Senator John E. Ensign, the Preliminary Inquiry concerning Senator Tom Coburn, and the Preliminary Inquiry concerning Senate staffer Bret Bernhardt), the Committee issued a memorandum on "Guidance on the Post-Employment Contact Ban" (May 24, 2012), accessible at http:// www.ethics.senate.gov/public/index.cfm/files/serve?File_id=bf9ea0f9-2593-4f49-83b3-f581f86b9098.

The discussion in the Senate Ethics Manual at 86–91 is also relevant to understanding the scope of the post-employment restrictions imposed by Rule 37, although this discussion should be read and applied with care given that (as of the date of publication of this edition of the *Lobbying Manual*) the Senate Ethics Manual was last published in 2003, and the scope of the post-employment restrictions set forth in Rule 37 was substantially amended in 2007, pursuant to the Honest Leadership and Open Government Act (HLOGA). *See* U.S. SENATE SELECT COMMITTEE ON ETHICS, Senate Ethics Manual, S. Pub. 108-1 (2003), and Rule 37 at http://www.rules.senate.gov/public/index.cfm?p=RuleXXXVII.

4. It is arguable that, in construing the post-employment restrictions imposed on Senate staff by paragraph 9 of Rule 37, the Senate Ethics Committee goes beyond the actual language of the rule or, at least, glosses over some apparent gaps in the rule. More specifically, it is arguable that, on its face, the language of paragraph 9 of Rule 37 captures only staff of a member's personal office or of a committee and does not clearly capture leadership staff or the staff of any officer of the Senate (e.g., staff of the Secretary of the Senate or of the Sergeant at Arms). But, as the instant discussion shows, the Senate Ethics Committee's published guidance specifically and expressly extends and applies paragraph 9 of Rule 37 to leadership staff; and the Committee has given no public indication that the staff of Senate officers are considered to be exempt from coverage by the rule. Thus, for all practical purposes, particularly for purposes of assuring compliance with Rule 37—and absent an advisory letter from the Committee expressly stating otherwise in a given case—the scope of the "revolving door" restrictions set out in paragraph 9 must be considered to extend to *all* Senate employees.

salary level while in the Senate). These restrictions are discussed in the following subsections.[5]

28-2.1 Senators: Two-Year Senate-wide Ban on Lobbying

A Senator who, upon leaving office, becomes a registered lobbyist pursuant to the LDA, or who becomes employed or retained by such a registered lobbyist or an entity that employs or retains a registered lobbyist for the purpose of influencing legislation, shall not lobby any members, officers, or employees of the Senate for a period of two years after leaving office. *See* Rule 37, para. 8.

28-2.2 Officers of the Senate and "Senior Staff": One-Year Senate-wide Ban on Lobbying

An officer of the Senate or a "senior staff" Senate employee—that is, a Senate employee whose rate of pay is equal to or greater than 75 percent of the rate of pay of a Senator and who is employed at this rate for more than sixty days in a calendar year[6]—who, upon leaving his or her position, becomes a registered lobbyist, or is employed or retained by such a registered lobbyist or an entity that employs or retains a registered lobbyist for the purpose of influencing legislation, may not lobby any member, officer, or employee of the Senate for a period of one year after leaving that position. *See* Rule 37, para. 9(c).

The Senate Ethics Committee has noted that, notwithstanding an employee's "base rate of pay," an employee may become subject to these Senate-wide post-employment restrictions if he or she received a bonus or merit adjustment that was

---

5. Here is the text of paragraphs 8 and 9 of Rule 37:

8. If a Member, upon leaving office, becomes a registered lobbyist under the Federal Regulation of Lobbying Act of 1946 or any successor statute, or is employed or retained by such a registered lobbyist or an entity that employs or retains a registered lobbyist for the purpose of influencing legislation, he shall not lobby Members, officers, or employees of the Senate for a period of two years after leaving office.

9. (a) If an employee on the staff of a Member, upon leaving that position, becomes a registered lobbyist under the Federal Regulation of Lobbying Act of 1946 or any successor statute, or is employed or retained by such a registered lobbyist or an entity that employs or retains a registered lobbyist for the purpose of influencing legislation, such employee may not lobby the Member for whom he worked or that Member's staff for a period of one year after leaving that position.

(b) If an employee on the staff of a committee, upon leaving his position, becomes such a registered lobbyist or is employed or retained by such a registered lobbyist or an entity that employs or retains a registered lobbyist for the purpose of influencing legislation, such employee may not lobby the members of the committee for which he worked, or the staff of that committee, for a period of one year after leaving his position.

(c) If an officer of the Senate or an employee on the staff of a Member or on the staff of a committee whose rate of pay is equal to or greater than 75 percent of the rate of pay of a Member and employed at such rate for more than 60 days in a calendar year, upon leaving that position, becomes a registered lobbyist, or is employed or retained by such a registered lobbyist or an entity that employs or retains a registered lobbyist for the purpose of influencing legislation, such employee may not lobby any Member, officer, or employee of the Senate for a period of 1 year after leaving that position.

6. This rate of pay in the Senate is $130,500 for CY 2016.

paid out over sixty or more days in a calendar year and put him or her over the rate of pay threshold.[7]

28-2.3 Other Senate Staff

For those Senate staff employed in a Senator's personal office or by a Senate committee, and who are paid below the senior staff rate (i.e., below 75 percent of a member's salary), paragraphs 9(a) and 9(b) of Senate Rule 37 impose a one-year ban on lobbying, with the scope of the ban depending, as discussed below, on an individual employee's place of Senate employment (personal office, committee office, or leadership office) and (in some instances) on the employee's substantive responsibilities.

- *Personal office staff and committee staff.* A Senate employee—whose rate of pay is lower than 75 percent of a senator's salary—and who, upon leaving his or her position, becomes a registered lobbyist, or is employed or retained by such a registered lobbyist or an entity that employs or retains a registered lobbyist for the purpose of influencing legislation, may not lobby his or her former employing personal office (senator and staff) or committee (i.e., members and staff of the committee, including all subcommittees thereof[8]) for one year after leaving Senate employment.
- *Personal office staff with "substantive committee responsibilities."* The Ethics Committee has noted: "A staffer in a personal office who performs substantive responsibilities for a committee on which the staffer's supervising [i.e., employing] Member sits, should refrain from lobbying the committee Members and staff for one year from the date the staffer last performed services for the committee. Substantive committee responsibilities include assisting in the drafting of the committee bills or assisting at hearings or in mark-up (as opposed to committee monitoring and liaison service for the personal office). Such a staffer would also be prohibited from lobbying the employing Member and the Member's personal office"[9] for the one-year period.
- *Subcommittee staff.* Under paragraph 9 of Rule 37, an individual who is an employee on the staff of a subcommittee of a committee is treated as an employee on the staff of the relevant committee.[10]
- *Communications by former committee staff employee with personal office of a committee member.* The Senate Ethics Committee cautions to apply the lobbying ban broadly. With respect to the previous (that is, pre-HLOGA) version of paragraph 9 of Rule 37, the Ethics Committee advised that, although it did not, by its terms, "preclude communications by a former committee staffer with personal office staff [of members of the committee] (or the converse), caution is advised with respect to such communications."[11] This caution would still appear to apply with respect to the lobbying restrictions imposed by paragraphs 9(a) and (b) of the current Rule 37.

---

7. *See* Employment Negotiations and Recusal, *supra* note 3, at 2.
8. *See* SENATE ETHICS MANUAL, at 87.
9. Overview, *supra* note 3, at 12.
10. *See* Rule 37, 13(b).
11. SENATE ETHICS MANUAL at 87, n.219.

- *Leadership staff.* Any employee in a Senate leadership office—whose rate of pay is lower than 75 percent of a Senate member's salary—and who, upon leaving his or her position, becomes a registered lobbyist (or is employed or retained by such a registered lobbyist or an entity that employs or retains a registered lobbyist for the purpose of influencing legislation), may not lobby any member or staff of the leadership of the same party (including the personal staff of the leadership member employing the staffer) for one year after leaving Senate employment.[12]
- *Who is a member of the Senate "leadership"?* The Senate Ethics Committee will look to the language of 18 U.S.C. § 207(e)(9)(M) in determining who is a member of the leadership of the Senate. This statutory provision defines "Member of the leadership of the Senate" to include "the Vice President, and the President pro tempore, Deputy President pro tempore, majority leader, minority leader, majority whip, minority whip, chairman and secretary of the Conference of the Majority, chairman and secretary of the Conference of the Minority, chairman and co-chairman of the Majority Policy Committee, and chairman of the Minority Policy Committee, of the Senate" and any similar later created position.

    The staff of the Senate Ethics Committee should be consulted if there is any doubt about whether a specific office is a "leadership office" for purposes of the Rule 37 "revolving-door" restrictions. Keep in mind, however, that Rule 37 restricts former leadership staff from lobbying only members or staff of the leadership of the *same party.*[13]
- *Who is the "leadership Member" employing the staffer?* The Senate Ethics Committee construes the term "employ" broadly when determining which leadership member employs the staffer. The Committee has stated that "for some leadership staffers, it is possible that more than one Senator could be considered 'the leadership Member employing the staffer.'"[14] For example: "the party leader may authorize a staffer's pay and a leadership committee chairman may directly supervise the staffer, such that both could be Members whose personal staff that former staffer may not lobby."[15]

28-2.4 Meaning of the Terms "Registered Lobbyist" and "Lobbying" in Rule 37; Differences in Scope of the "Revolving Door" Ban Imposed by Rule 37 and the Ban Imposed by 18 U.S.C. § 207

28-2.4.1 "Registered Lobbyist"

The Senate Ethics Committee has construed the post-employment lobbying restrictions imposed by Rule 37 "to apply to anyone required by the [LDA] to register as a lobbyist, *whether or not they actually do register,*"[16] hence the language of paragraphs 8 and 9 of Rule 37 extending the restrictions to former Senate members and staff "employed or retained" "for the purpose of influencing legislation." Further, "[as]

---

12. SENATE ETHICS MANUAL at 87.

13. *Id.*

14. SENATE ETHICS MANUAL at 87, n.219.

15. *Id.*

16. SENATE ETHICS MANUAL at 88 (emphasis added).

long as any partner or associate in a law firm is a registered lobbyist, then any former Senator or staffer employed by that firm, within a year of leaving the Senate, for the purpose of influencing legislation, is covered by the lobbying restriction."[17] However, "[h]aving a restricted former Senate individual join a firm . . . does not bar any other member or employee of the firm from lobbying,"[18] provided the covered Senate individual is not present, and her or his name is not invoked, during the lobbying contact or communication.

There are instances in which a former Senate individual who, on the basis of his or her "lobbying" activity, would be exempted from the post-employment restrictions under 18 U.S.C. § 207, but who would nonetheless be a "registered lobbyist" subject to the post-employment restrictions imposed by Rule 37. For example, communications or representations made by an employee of any agency or instrumentality of a state or local government in carrying out official duties are exempted from the restrictions of section 207.[19] However, under the LDA, the exception from the definition of "lobbying contact" for communications made by a "public official" acting in his or her official capacity[20] does not extend to employees of state or local colleges or universities, government-sponsored enterprises, public utilities, or guaranty agencies.[21] Former Senate employees lobbying for these government or government-related entities would be subject to the post-employment restrictions imposed by Senate rule, even where they would not be subject to the statutory restrictions of section 207.[22]

28-2.4.2 How Is "Lobbying" Defined?

Pursuant to paragraph 13(c) of Rule 37, the term "lobbying" as used in paragraphs 8 and 9 of the rule means:

> any oral or written communication to influence the content or disposition of any issue before Congress, including any pending or future bill, resolution, treaty, nomination, hearing, report, or investigation; but does not include—
>
> (1) a communication (i) made in the form of testimony given before a committee or office of the Congress, or (ii) submitted for inclusion in the public record, public docket, or public file of a hearing; or
> (2) a communication by an individual, acting solely on his own behalf, for redress of personal grievances, or to express his personal opinion.

Based on the differing language of the relevant "revolving-door" Senate *rule* as compared with the language of the revolving-door *statute*, the range of contacts and communications prohibited by former Senate members and staffers subject to the restrictions of paragraphs 8 and 9 of Rule 37 would appear to be narrower than the range of contacts and communications prohibited by the felony criminal provisions of 18 U.S.C. § 207. The Senate rule covers only "oral or written

---

17. *Id.* at 88.
18. *Id.*
19. 18 U.S.C. § 207(j)(2)(A) (2015).
20. 2 U.S.C. 281602 (8)(B)(i) (2015).
21. *Id.* 281602 (15)(A).
22. *See* SENATE ETHICS MANUAL at 88.

communication[s] to influence the content or disposition of any issue before Congress." By contrast, sections 207(1)(A) and (2) of title 18 cover *any* communications or appearances made with the intent to influence any member, officer, or employee of the Senate (or, for former senators, of either house of Congress) "in connection with any matter" on which the former Senate individual seeks official action. This latter category, as defined by the federal criminal statute, could include as minor an official act as scheduling an appointment; the former category, as defined by the Senate rule, would not, by its terms, include such a *purely administrative* act not capable of influencing "the content or disposition of [an] issue before Congress."

As a practical matter, however, any apparent differences between the scope of communications prohibited by the Senate rule and those prohibited by statute should be read in light of the Senate Ethics Committee's recent advice to "former and current Senators and staff to follow the criminal law and apply its restrictions broadly, to avoid even the appearance of impropriety."[23]

28-2.5 Exceptions and Permitted Activity under Paragraphs 8 and 9 of Rule 37

In addition to the exceptions to the definition of "lobbying" set forth in paragraph 13(c) of Rule 37, paragraph 10 of Rule 37 provides:

> Paragraphs 8 and 9 shall not apply to contacts with the staff of the Secretary of the Senate regarding compliance with the lobbying disclosure requirements of the Lobbying Disclosure Act of 1995.

Further, concerning the restrictions imposed by 18 U.S.C. § 207, purely social contact with former colleagues is generally permitted under Rule 37. Likewise, under Rule 37 as under the statute, former senators and Senate staffers may make contributions to current members of Congress and may sponsor or attend campaign fund-raisers for members, provided that no communications prohibited by Rule 37 are made in connection with such activity. And, as permitted under the statute, under Rule 37 former senators and staff may play a *purely* background, behind-the-scenes role in advising others who may then, in turn, lobby the Senate.[24]

28-2.6 Enforcement of the Post-Employment Restrictions under Rule 37

The enforcement and disciplinary jurisdiction of the Senate Select Committee on Ethics extends only to current members, officers, and employees of the Senate.[25]

---

23. "Guidance on Post-Employment Contact Ban," *supra* note 3, at 2. Although other language in this Senate Ethics Committee "Guidance" memorandum suggests that the Committee's advice to "follow the criminal law and read its restrictions broadly" when construing the scope of communications prohibited under Rule 37 could be read to apply *only* to former senators and senior staff (as opposed to *all* staff), this narrower reading does not appear to be justified, given that former senators and senior staff are already subject to the broader prohibition of the criminal law. Here, again, is an instance where—if the scope of communications prohibited by Rule 37 in a particular given case is in doubt and a general approach of prudence is not practicable in that case—consultation with the staff of the Senate Ethics Committee would be advisable.

24. See further discussion in Chapter 27 of this manual.

25. *See, e.g., t*he Committee's authorization resolution, S. Res. 338, 88th Cong. (1964), as amended, at Sec. 2(a): "It shall be the duty of the Select Committee to—(1) receive complaints and investigate allegations of improper conduct which may reflect upon the Senate, violations of law, violations of

This means that, although by their terms the post-employment restrictions set forth in paragraphs 8 and 9 of Rule 37 apply *only* to former members and employees of the Senate, the Senate Ethics Committee and the Senate cannot, in fact, formally sanction former Senate members and staff for violations of Rule 37. But, as explained below, the Senate Ethics Committee can investigate—and has investigated—alleged violations of the post-employment restrictions imposed both by the federal criminal law and by Rule 37, where those alleged violations involve communications with or actions by sitting Senate members or current Senate staff.

In its May 24, 2012, public memorandum on "Guidance on the Post-Employment Contact Ban," the Senate Select Committee on Ethics stated: "Although the law and Senate rules are targeted at former Senate personnel, all current Members and staff are also prohibited from assisting them in violating these laws or rules."[26] The Committee provided examples of improper assistance to former members and staff who are still within their post-employment "cooling off" period: "current Senate Members, officers, and employees who know, or have reason to know, that former Senate personnel are subject to these restrictions, should not attend or schedule official meetings with the former Senator or staffer or otherwise assist the individual in taking any action that would violate the law or rules."[27] And then the Committee drove its point home: "Any current Senator or staffer who knowingly assists a covered individual to violate the criminal law or Senate rule may themselves be subject to disciplinary action and possible referral to the Department of Justice."[28]

These unequivocal public statements by the Senate Select Committee on Ethics, in the advisory context, of the potential for liability by current members and staff of the Senate for "aiding and abetting" a former colleague's violation of his or her post-employment restrictions were significant and unprecedented. But the Senate Ethics Committee went even further in its May 24, 2012, "Guidance" memo by stating, for the first time, that current Senate members and staff have an affirmative obligation to inform the Committee of suspected post-employment violations by their former colleagues. The Committee set forth the following guidance to current senators and staff on "What to Do If You Are Contacted by Someone Subject to the Restrictions":

> Senators or staff who have reason to believe that they may have received a prohibited contact from a former colleague should not assist the individual and should affirmatively explain that the individual's conduct appears to be improper and that it must cease. Senators and staff should advise the

---

the Senate Code of Official Conduct and violations of rules and regulations of the Senate, relating to the conduct of individuals in the performance of their duties as Members of the Senate, or as officers or employees of the Senate, and to make appropriate findings of fact and conclusions with respect thereto." Pursuant to the Ethics in Government Act of 1978, 5 U.S.C. app. 4 §§ 101–111, the Senate Ethics Committee does retain jurisdiction over former members and staff regarding issues arising in connection with the filing of, or failure to file, public financial disclosure reports, including termination reports.

26. "Guidance on Post-Employment Contact Ban," *supra* note 3, at 3.
27. *Id.* at 3–4.
28. *Id.* at 4.

former colleague to contact the Committee and also promptly inform the Committee themselves of the steps taken to cease the communications.[29]

The Senate Ethics Committee issued its advisory memo to the Senate community on "Guidance on the Post-Employment Contact Ban" in conjunction with its issuance of a "Public Letter of Qualified Admonition" to a sitting member[30] and of a "Public Letter of Admonition" to a Senate employee[31] in connection with their separate "communications with and actions on behalf of"[32] a former Senate staffer while that former staffer was still within the "cooling off" period imposed by both the federal criminal law and Rule 37. In each of these two cases, the Committee found that the current member's and employee's communications and actions involving the former staffer constituted "improper conduct which reflects on the Senate."[33]

28-2.6.1 *Observe the Rules, Avoid the Costs*

Although former Senate members and staff cannot be formally and officially sanctioned by the Senate or the Select Committee on Ethics for violations of post-employment restrictions, the conduct of a former member and or Senate employee during his or her restricted post-employment period can be the subject of extensive investigation by the Committee where that conduct is alleged to involve improper contacts with current Senate members or staff. During such an investigation, the former Senate member or employee—and his or her employer—may be asked, or may be compelled, to provide documents, information, or even sworn testimony. Compliance with Senate Ethics Committee requests or subpoenas can be time-consuming and expensive. Even if the Committee cannot sanction (or recommend that the Senate sanction) the former member or employee for post-employment violations, and even if the Committee determines that a referral to the Department of Justice to investigate potential criminal law violations is not merited, involvement in such an Ethics Committee process can certainly reflect adversely on the reputation of the former member or employee and of his or her employer. To avoid the many and substantial costs of a Senate Ethics Committee inquiry into post-employment violations, knowledge of the post-employment restrictions imposed by statute and by Rule 37, and careful observance of these restrictions, is essential.

28-3 House Post-Employment Restrictions

The post-employment restrictions on former members, officers, and employees of the U.S. House of Representatives are imposed by statute, that is, 18 U.S.C. § 207(e).

---

29. *Id.* at 5.

30. Public Letter of Qualified Admonition, U.S. Senate Select Committee on Ethics to The Honorable Tom Coburn, (May 25, 2012).

31. Public Letter of Qualified Admonition, U.S. Senate Select Committee on Ethics to Mr. Bret Bernhardt, Office of Senator Jim DeMint (May 25, 2012).

32. *See* Admonition letters, *supra* notes 30 and 31, at 1.

33. The Senate Ethics Committee's letters to Senator Coburn and Mr. Bernhardt concerned communications with and actions on behalf of Mr. Doug Hampton, former administrative assistant to Senator John E. Ensign, while Mr. Hampton was subject to the post-employment restrictions imposed by 18 U.S.C. § 207(e) and by Rule 37. The Committee also undertook an extensive inquiry concerning Senator Ensign in connection with Mr. Hampton. Senator Ensign resigned from the Senate on May 3, 2011. Nonetheless, on May 10, 2011, the Senate Ethics Committee issued a "Report of the Preliminary Inquiry Into the Matter of Senator John E. Ensign." *See* Admonition Letters, *supra* notes 30 and 31.

These statutory restrictions are discussed at length in Chapter 27 of this manual. There are no rules of the House of Representatives, similar to the Senate rules discussed above, concerning the post-House conduct of former members or staff.[34] Nonetheless, as in the Senate, the House Committee on Ethics can conduct inquiries into alleged violations by former House members or employees of their statutory post-employment restrictions where those alleged violations involve the conduct of current House members or staff.[35]

Towards the end of each Congress, typically, the House Committee on Ethics issues a detailed advisory memorandum, or "Pink Sheet," on "Negotiations for Future Employment and Restrictions on Post-Employment for House Members and Officers"; at the same time, the Committee issues a separate Pink Sheet covering these same subjects for House staff. These advisories are available at the website of the House Committee on Ethics.[36] With regard to post-employment restrictions, the House Committee on Ethics takes pains to note in these advisories "that the statute, as part of the criminal code, is enforced by the Justice Department, rather than by the Ethics Committee, and Committee interpretations of the statute are not binding on the Justice Department." Nonetheless, these Pink Sheets are an important resource for understanding how the post-employment restrictions imposed by statute apply to former members, officers, and employees of the House.

28-4 Negotiating for Future Employment under House and Senate Rules and under the STOCK Act[37]

In both the House and the Senate, members and certain staff who negotiate, or enter into agreements (or arrangements),[38] for future employment in the private sector

---

34. Rules of the House of Representatives IV, cl. (4)(a), 114th Cong. (Jan. 6, 2015), does provide, with respect to admittance to the Hall of the House (i.e., the House Chamber), that

> A former Member, Delegate, or Resident Commissioner; a former Parliamentarian of the House; or a former elected officer of the House or former minority employee nominated as an elected officer of the House shall not be entitled to the privilege of admission to the Hall of the House and rooms leading thereto if such individual –
> (1) is a registered lobbyist or agent of a foreign principal as those terms are defined in clause 5 of rule XXV;
> (2) has any direct personal or pecuniary interest in any legislative measure pending before the House or reported by a committee; or
> (3) is in the employ of or represents any party or organization for the purpose of influencing, directly or indirectly, the passage, defeat, or amendment of any legislative proposal.

35. *See. e.g.*, Report of the Committee on Standards of Official Conduct, In re Representative E.G. "Bud" Shuster, H.R. Rep. No. 106-979 (2000).

36. *See* Memoranda, *supra* note 2, at 2.

37. The Stop Trading on Congressional Knowledge Act of 2012 (STOCK Act), Pub. L. No. 112–105 2814, 126 Stat. 291, 300–01 (2012), was signed into law on April 4, 2012. In addition to the provisions discussed in this chapter regarding disclosures and recusals arising from employment negotiations and agreements, the STOCK Act also, most notably, contains provisions affirming a duty of trust and confidence on the part of federal government officials and employees in all three branches of government with respect to material, nonpublic information derived by them from their official positions and further affirming that federal officials and employees are not exempt from the insider trading prohibitions arising under the federal securities laws in connection with the misuse of such information. For a discussion of the STOCK Act as it applies to political intelligence work, see Chapter 18 of this manual.

38. The STOCK Act and the relevant House rule use the term employment "agreement." The Senate rule uses the term "arrangement."

are subject to written notification and recusal requirements. As discussed below, in the House, separate notification and recusal requirements apply to members and to "senior staff;" in the Senate, separate requirements apply to members, to "senior staff," and to staff paid at or above a rate of 120 percent of the base GS-15 level. In both the House and the Senate, the timing of when these requirements kick in turns on when employment "negotiations" have begun (or the timing of when an employment agreement or arrangement has been entered into). It is important to remember, however, that the definition of what constitutes employment "negotiations" differs markedly between the House and the Senate. As a general matter, however—and as discussed more specifically below—the applicable standards in both the House and the Senate permit some exchange of information on the salary and benefits for the position under discussion without the discussion becoming a "negotiation."

28-4.1 Employment Negotiations, and Notification/Recusal Requirements, in the Senate

The distinct disclosure and recusal requirements for senators, Senate senior staff, Senate staff paid at or above a rate of 120 percent of the GS-15 base rate, and Senate officers are discussed in turn here. There are some more general points to keep in mind, however, regarding employment negotiation under Senate standards of conduct.

28-4.1.1 What Are Employment "Negotiations" under Senate Rules?
In the context of seeking future employment, the Senate Ethics Committee has defined "negotiation" to mean "the discussion of terms and conditions of employment after an offer has been made and the Senate Member or employee is considering accepting the offer."[39] An "employment arrangement," as defined by the Committee, "begins when an offer has been made and accepted."[40] Given this relatively narrow definition of employment negotiations in the Senate—and provided that no offer has yet been made—some discussion of terms and conditions of prospective employment, including potential salary and/or benefits, may occur with a prospective employee without such discussion's constituting negotiations. Note carefully, however, that the definition of employment negotiation in the House is much narrower and more restrictive than the definition used in the Senate. More generally, unlike the House Committee on Ethics (as discussed below), the Senate Ethics Committee does not specifically advise that a prospective employer and a candidate for employment from the Senate memorialize in writing their understanding that no official favors will be received, and regarding applicability of post-employment restrictions. Such an exchange of letters between prospective employers and prospective employees from the Senate would be a prudent practice, however.

In addition to observing the requirements discussed below, a Senate employee must notify his or her employing senator of negotiations or arrangements for future employment.[41] Lastly, given that the employment interview

---

39. Quick Reference, *supra* note 3, at 1.

40. *Id.*

41. *See, e.g.*, guidance for "All Staff" on "Employment Negotiations and Recusal" on the U.S. Senate Ethics Committee website at http://www.ethics.senate.gov/public/index.cfm/conflictsofinterest.

process often includes travel and/or meals, it is important to note that the Senate gift rule permits members, officers, and staff to accept "food, refreshments, lodging, and other benefits [including transportation] . . . customarily provided by a prospective employer in connection with bona fide employment discussions."[42]

28-4.1.2 Rules Applicable to Senators' Future Employment Involving Lobbying

A senator may not engage in negotiations or make any arrangement for a job involving lobbying activities (as defined by the LDA) until after his or her successor has been elected. There are no exceptions to this rule.[43] (Rule 37, paragraph 14(b).[44])

28-4.1.3 Future Employment that Does Not Involve Lobbying

A senator may not engage in negotiations or arrangements for post-Senate private employment or compensation that does *not* involve lobbying until after his or her successor has been elected, *unless* the following disclosure and recusal requirements are met. (Rule 37, paragraph 14(a).)

- *Disclosure.* Within three business days of commencing such negotiations or arrangements, the senator files a signed public statement with the Secretary of the Senate disclosing the names of any private entities involved in the negotiations or arrangements and the date the negotiations or arrangements commenced. The required disclosure form—*Disclosure by*

---

42. U.S. Senate Rule 35(1)(c)(7)(B). See Chapter 8 for a full discussion of the congressional gift rules.

43. *See* U.S. SENATE, NEW ETHICS RULES, Jobs Negotiations, Post-Employment and Influencing Hiring, *available at* http://www.ethics.senate.gov/public/index.cfm/files/serve?File_id=e52f2a40 -d08a-4fd5-ba6d-63d7a159b4ac.

44. Paragraph 14 was added to Rule 37 pursuant to passage of HLOGA on Sept. 14, 2007. Paragraph 14 of Senate Rule 37 provides:

(a) A Member shall not negotiate or have any arrangement concerning prospective private employment until after his or her successor has been elected, unless such Member files a signed statement with the Secretary of the Senate, for public disclosure, regarding such negotiations or arrangements not later than 3 business days after the commencement of such negotiation or arrangement, including the name of the private entity or entities involved in such negotiations or arrangements, and the date such negotiations or arrangements commenced.

(b) A Member shall not negotiate or have any arrangement concerning prospective employment for a job involving lobbying activities as defined by the Lobbying Disclosure Act of 1995 until after his or her successor has been elected.

(c)(1) An employee of the Senate earning in excess of 75 percent of the salary paid to a Senator shall notify the Select Committee on Ethics that he or she is negotiating or has any arrangement concerning prospective private employment.

(2) The notification under this subparagraph shall be made not later than 3 business days after the commencement of such negotiation or arrangement.

(3) An employee to whom this subparagraph applies shall—

(A) recuse himself or herself from—

(i) any contact or communication with the prospective employer on issues of legislative interest to the prospective employer; and

(ii) any legislative matter in which there is a conflict of interest or an appearance of a conflict for that employee under this subparagraph; and

(B) notify the Select Committee on Ethics of such recusal.

Member of Employment Negotiations and Recusal—may be obtained at the Office of Public Records, 232 Hart Senate Office Building, or on the Senate Ethics Committee website at http://www.ethics.senate.gov/public /index.cfm?a=Files.Serve&File_id=8fc8c2f4-ce6a-48a1-9235-d6f222c0256f.

- *Recusal.* Pursuant to Section 17(b) of the STOCK Act, if there is a conflict of interest, or an appearance of a conflict of interest, in connection with a potential private employer identified on a senator's disclosure of employ- ment negotiations and recusal form, the senator must also recuse himself or herself from official matters involving that potential employer and must notify the Ethics Committee in writing of any such recusal. As a practical matter, any such recusal notification by a senator is also a pub- lic notification because it is made on the same disclosure form required to be filed with the Secretary of the Senate with regard to employment negotiations.

28-4.1.4 Rules Applicable to Senate Senior Staff

Senate employees paid at or above a rate of 75 percent of a senator's salary (or $130,500 in CY 2016) are considered "senior staff." They are subject to the following disclosure and recusal requirements in connection with employment negotiations and arrangements.

- *Disclosure.* A Senate senior staff employee must notify the Select Commit- tee on Ethics that he or she is negotiating or has any arrangement con- cerning prospective private employment. This disclosure must include the name of the prospective private employer and the date on which the employment negotiations or arrangement commenced. This notifi- cation must be made in writing to the Committee not later than three business days after the commencement of such any such negotiation or arrangement. (Rule 37, paragraph 14(c)(1) and (2).) This disclosure is nonpublic; a form for this purpose, and for filing of the statement of recusal discussed below, is available at the website of the Senate Eth- ics Committee: http://www.ethics.senate.gov/public/index.cfm?a=Files .Serve&File_id=94f3afe9-8bc9-48f2-9937-ea9cc613a14a.

- *Recusal.* A Senate senior staff employee engaged in employment nego- tiations, or who has entered into an employment arrangement with a prospective private employer, must recuse himself or herself from "any contact or communication with the prospective employer on issues of legislative interest to the prospective employer" and from "any legislative matter in which there is a conflict of interest or an appear- ance of a conflict" in connection with the prospective employer. (Rule 37, paragraph 14(c)(3).) Pursuant to Section 17 of the STOCK Act, the employee must also recuse himself or herself from any official mat- ter involving the potential employer whenever there is a conflict of interest or the appearance of a conflict. Pursuant to both Senate rule and the STOCK Act, the senior staffer must notify the Ethics Commit- tee in writing of a recusal undertaken in connection with employment negotiations or arrangements; these recusals are made on the same nonpublic form to be used for disclosure of employment negotiations or arrangements.

28-4.1.5 Senate Staff Paid at or Above 120% of the Base GS-15 Pay Rate
The STOCK Act, section 17(a) and (b), imposed employment negotiation/arrangement disclosure and recusal requirements on all federal government employees paid at a rate at or above 120 percent of the base GS-15 pay level for at least sixty days, in the aggregate, for a calendar year.[45] (For CY 2016, the salary level triggering these requirements is $123,175.) This is the rate of pay at which an employee of the federal government is obligated to file a public financial disclosure report under the Ethics in Government Act of 1978. A Senate employee paid at or above this rate of pay is subject to these disclosure and recusal requirements, as follows.

- *Disclosure.* A Senate employee paid at or above 120 percent of the GS-15 rate of pay may not directly negotiate or have any agreement for future employment unless, within three business days after the commencement of such negotiation or agreement, the employee provides a signed written notice to the Senate Ethics Committee. This notice is nonpublic and must include the name of the prospective private employer and the date that employment negotiations or arrangement commenced. The form for this purpose, available on the Ethics Committee's website, is the same form described earlier to be used by Senate senior staff (although senior staff and staff paid at the 120 percent of GS-15 rate do not make identical disclosures on this form).
- *Recusal.* A Senate staffer paid at or above 120 percent of the GS-15 rate must also recuse himself or herself from any official matter involving a potential employer whenever there is a conflict of interest or the appearance of a conflict. The staffer must notify the Ethics Committee of any such recusal; these recusal notifications are made on the same nonpublic form to be used for disclosure of employment negotiations or arrangements discussed earlier.

28-4.1.6 Senate Officers Paid at or Above 120% of the Base GS-15 Pay Rate
The disclosure and recusal obligations arising under the STOCK Act for Senate officers paid at or above 120 percent of the GS-15 base pay rate for at least sixty days, in the aggregate, for a calendar year are identical to those imposed by the act on other Senate staffers paid at or above this rate, as discussed above. The Select Committee on Ethics, however, has promulgated a separate disclosure/recusal notification form to be used by Senate Officers. This form is also available at the Committee's website at http://www.ethics.senate.gov/public/index.cfm/files/serve?File_id=73df8c0c-8019-412b-893b-5dc00a136df6.

28-4.2 Employment Negotiations, and Notification/Recusal Requirements, in the House

In the House of Representatives, members and senior staff are subject to disclosure and recusal requirements in connection with negotiations or agreements for future employment with a private employer. Not to be confused with how the term "senior staff" is defined and used in the Senate (see earlier discussion), in the House the term "senior staff" means any employee whose rate of basic pay is

---

45. *See* STOCK Act, *supra* note 37, 2817(a) and (b).

equal to or greater than 120 percent of the base GS-15 pay rate for any aggregate of at least sixty days in a calendar year; the CY 2016 rate for House senior staff is $123,175.[46]

28-4.2.1 What Are Employment Negotiations under House Rules?

In the House, pursuant to published guidance of the House Committee on Ethics, the term "negotiations" is defined broadly to include any "communication between two parties with a view toward reaching an agreement and in which there is active interest on both sides."[47] However, "preliminary or exploratory talks" do not constitute "negotiations."[48]

More generally, the House Committee on Ethics has advised that, when a House member or employee enters into employment discussions with a prospective private employer, it should be kept in mind that statutes and House rules prohibit the receipt of anything of value in exchange for, or that may appear to be given to influence, an official act or official duties of the member or employee. Therefore, the Committee advises an exchange of correspondence between the prospective employer (who may draft and generate the correspondence) and the House member or employee memorializing the following understandings:

- That the prospective employer will receive no official favors as a result of the job negotiations.
- That the member or employee is subject to statutory post-employment restrictions (for House employees, only where applicable based on the employee's salary level). The Committee recommends that the letter briefly outline these restrictions.[49]

Because the employment interview process often includes travel and/or meals, it should also be remembered that the House gift rule permits staff to accept "[f]ood, refreshments, lodging, transportation and other benefits . . . customarily provided by a prospective employer in connection with bona fide employment discussions."[50]

28-4.2.2 Members of the House

Under House Rule 27.1, a member may not "directly negotiate or have any agreement of future employment or compensation" with a private entity unless the following disclosure and recusal requirements are met.

---

46. As noted above, this pay rate—the rate of pay at which a federal government employee becomes obligated to file an annual public financial disclosure report—is the trigger rate for employment negotiation disclosures and recusals pursuant to Section 17(b) of the STOCK Act. *See* Memorandum for All Members, Officers, and Employees, U.S. HOUSE OF REPRESENTATIVES, COMMITTEE ON ETHICS (Jan. 5, 2016), *available at* http://ethics.house.gov/sites/ethics.house.gov/files/Outside%20 Earned%20Income%20Pink%20Sheet.pdf).

47. Memorandum, *supra* note 2, at 2 (internal quotation marks omitted).

48. *Id.*

49. Memorandum, *supra* note 2, at 3.

50. House Rule 25, cl. (5)(a)(3)(G)(ii), *supra* note 34. See Chapter 8 for a discussion of congressional gift rules.

- *Disclosure.* Within three business days after the commencement of any negotiation or agreement for future employment or compensation with a private entity, a member must complete and submit a "Notification of Negotiations or Agreement for Future Employment" form to the Committee on Ethics disclosing the name of the private entity and the date the negotiations or agreement commenced. This form is available on the Committee's website at http://ethics.house.gov/sites/ethics.house.gov/files/job%20negotiation%20form%20-%202011.pdf.
- *Recusal.* Pursuant to House Rule 27.4, the member must also recuse himself or herself "from any matter in which there is a conflict of interest or an appearance of a conflict for that Member."[51] The member must notify the Committee on Ethics in writing of such a recusal, using a "Statement of Recusal" form available at the Committee's website at http://ethics.house.gov/sites/ethics.house.gov/files/Recusal%20Form%20-%202011.pdf. At the same time, the member must file a copy of the "Notification of Negotiations or Agreement for Future Employment" corresponding to this recusal with the Legislative Resource Center, Office of the Clerk of the House, Room B-106, Cannon House Office Building, for public disclosure.

28-4.2.3 *House Senior Staff*

House senior staff employees—again, those paid at or above 120 percent of the base GS-15 pay rate for any aggregate of at least sixty days in a calendar year ($123,175 in CY 2016)—are subject to the following requirements.

- *Disclosure.* Pursuant to Section 17 of the STOCK Act[52], House personnel paid at the senior staff rate must notify the Committee on Ethics within three business days of commencing any negotiation or agreement for future employment with a private employer. A "Notification of Negotiations or Agreement for Future Employment" form for this purpose is available at the Committee's website; it is the same form as noted above for use by members (although members and senior staff do not make identical disclosures on this form). This disclosure for senior staff is nonpublic.

---

51. As to what may constitute a "matter in which there is a conflict of interest or an appearance of a conflict," the Committee on Ethics has advised that "[a]t a minimum, Members faced with a vote on a matter that directly impacts a private entity with which they are negotiating would have difficulty balancing the duty they owe to their constituents with the recusal provisions of Rule 27. Members are strongly encouraged to abstain from voting on legislation that provides a benefit targeted to an entity with which the Member is negotiating or from which the Member has accepted future employment. Members likewise are discouraged from sponsoring legislation or earmarks for such an entity." Memorandum, *supra* note 2, at 6.

52. Even before enactment of the STOCK Act in 2012, clause 2 of House Rule 27 imposed a disclosure requirement regarding employment negotiations and agreements on House staff earning in excess of 75 percent of a member's salary. These disclosure requirements were extended by the STOCK Act to all House staff paid at or above the "senior staff" rate. Although clause 2 of House Rule 27 is still in effect, as applied and interpreted by the House Committee on Ethics it does not impose any greater disclosure or recusal requirements on more highly paid House staff than does Section 17 of the STOCK Act. *See* STOCK Act, *supra* note 37.

- *Recusal.* House senior staff must also recuse themselves from "any matter in which there is a conflict of interest or an appearance of a conflict" with a prospective private employer with whom they are negotiating or have an agreement for future employment, and they must notify the Committee in writing of such a recusal. A separate "Statement of Recusal" form to be used for this purpose is also available at the Committee's website; it is the same form already noted for use by members with respect to recusals (although, again, members and senior staff do not make identical disclosures on this form). This recusal notification to the Committee is also nonpublic.

28-4.3 Employment Negotiations and Agreements with Congressional Personnel: A Compliance Role for the Prospective Private Employer

As a general matter—as with the Senate post-employment rules discussed in the first part of this chapter—the congressional rules regarding employment negotiations (and regarding attendant disclosure and recusal requirements) impose affirmative obligations only on, and may be directly enforced by the House and Senate only against, serving members and employees of the House and Senate. Of course, if a suggestion were to arise that a private employer improperly received or expected to receive official favors from a House or Senate member or employee in connection with employment negotiations (or an employment agreement) with that member or employee, the situation could give rise to potential bribery or gratuity concerns directly implicating both the prospective employer and the prospective hire.

Even apart from such potential direct exposure, however, if a private employer hires a congressional member or employee who has failed to follow applicable disclosure and recusal requirements under House or Senate rules, the prospective employer could well, at the least, be caught up in negative, damaging press and publicity. Therefore, the prospective employer may wish to institute (and implement) a compliance policy requiring any congressional individual with whom the employer is about to enter into employment negotiations to confirm in writing that he or she is aware of, and will follow, all applicable House or Senate disclosure and recusal requirements. Under such a compliance policy, the prospective employer might also actively monitor applicable disclosure and recusal deadlines and require that the potential congressional hire provide the prospective employer with copies of any disclosures contemporaneously with those disclosures being filed with the applicable House or Senate office. Because this approach would help establish that the negotiation and hiring process met applicable congressional ethics requirements, the policy could also benefit the former congressional member or employee who has moved into the private sector from the House or Senate.

CHAPTER 29

Restrictions on Service by Former Lobbyists in the Obama Administration and on Service by Lobbyists on Federal Advisory Committees

BY ROBERT L. WALKER[*]

---

*The author thanks Wheknown Jasper-Booker for her assistance in reviewing and formatting the notes for this chapter.

29-1 Introduction

Throughout his first presidential campaign, Barack Obama committed to limiting the role and influence of lobbyists in an Obama administration. Then-Senator Obama told a Des Moines, Iowa, audience on November 10, 2007, that lobbyists "will not get a job in my White House, and they will not drown out the voices of the American people when I am President."[1] On October 1, 2008, he told a crowd in La Crosse, Wisconsin, that "together, we will tell the Washington lobbyists that their days of setting the agenda are over."[2] During the post-election transition in 2008, a central plank of the "Obama–Biden Plan" for the new administration was a commitment to "free the executive branch from special interest influence," in part by closing the "revolving door on former and future employers."[3] The plank read,

---

1. Senator Barack Obama, Remarks at the Iowa Jefferson-Jackson Dinner in Des Moines (Nov. 10, 2007), *available at* http://www.presidency.ucsb.edu/ws/index.php?pid=77021 (last visited July 28, 2015).

2. Senator Barack Obama, Remarks in La Crosse, Wisconsin (Oct. 1, 2008), *available at* http://www.presidency.ucsb.edu/ws/index.php?pid=84463 (last visited Sept. 25, 2015).

3. Change.Gov, The Office of the President-Elect, http://change.gov/agenda/ethics_agenda/ethics_agenda/ (last visited Sept. 25, 2015).

"No political appointees in the Obama–Biden Administration will be permitted to work on regulations or contracts directly and substantially related to their prior employer for two years."[4]

On January 21, 2009—his first full day in office—President Barack Obama signed and issued Executive Order 13490 (Exec. Order No. 13490), on "Ethics Commitments by Executive Branch Personnel."[5] Exec. Order No. 13490 implemented the restrictive positions on lobbyist and former lobbyist involvement in government articulated throughout the Obama campaign and transition. The restrictions imposed by Exec. Order No. 13490 remain in effect as of the time of publication. Subsequent to the issuance of Exec. Order No. 13490, additional presidential directives have imposed even tighter restrictions on lobbyists' ability to serve in the administration and the executive branch.

By means of an "Ethics Pledge"—required to be signed by every Obama administration appointee[6]—Exec. Order No. 13490 imposes additional restrictions on Obama administration appointees beyond those imposed by existing executive branch ethics regulations. They include

- A lobbyist gift ban prohibiting the acceptance of gifts from registered lobbyists or lobbying organizations.[7]
- A revolving-door ban for appointees entering government.
  - All appointees entering government are subject to a restriction on involvement in certain matters relating to former employees or clients. This restriction applies for a period of two years from the date of appointment.[8]
  - Appointees who were federally registered lobbyists in the two years before appointment are subject to additional restrictions on participation in particular matters on which they lobbied within the two years before appointment and on participation in specific issue areas involving those particular matters. This restriction applies for a period of two years from the date of appointment.[9]
  - Appointees who were registered lobbyists within two years of their appointment may not serve with any executive branch agency that they lobbied during that two-year period.[10]
- A revolving-door ban for appointees leaving government.
  - Appointees leaving government are subject to additional post-employment restrictions beyond those imposed by section 207(c) of title 18 of the U.S. Code.[11]
  - Appointees leaving government are banned from lobbying covered executive branch officials and noncareer Senior Executive Service appointees for the remainder of the administration.[12]

---

4. *Id.*
5. Exec. Order No. 13490, 74 Fed. Reg. 4,673 (Jan. 21, 2009).
6. *Id.* § 1.
7. *Id.* § 1(1); see also Chapter 26 of this manual.
8. Exec. Order No. 13490, § 1(2).
9. *Id.* § 1(3).
10. *Id.*
11. *Id.* § 1(4); see also Chapter 27.
12. Exec. Order No. 13490 § 1(5).

This chapter focuses on the restrictions on lobbyists' entering the government as appointees. The process for obtaining a waiver, and the implementation of this waiver process, is also discussed.[13]

This chapter also covers the Obama administration restrictions on service by federally registered lobbyists on federal advisory committees, boards, commissions, or similar advisory groups. Although modified from a blanket ban initially imposed, the restrictions currently in effect reflect President Obama's June 18, 2010, Presidential Memorandum directing "the heads of executive departments and agencies not to make any new appointment or reappointments of federally registered lobbyists to advisory committees and other boards and commissions."[14] This presidential directive formalized an initial "aspirational" approach to barring lobbyist service on advisory committees, boards, and commissions as urged on federal departments and agencies by the White House through a series of blog posts in 2009 by Norm Eisen, then Special Counsel to the President for Ethics and Government Reform. The Office of Management and Budget (OMB) first issued guidance implementing the ban on October 5, 2011.[15] On August 13, 2014, OMB issued revised guidance to clarify that the ban on appointing or reappointing lobbyists to federal advisory groups would apply prospectively only to lobbyists serving on such advisory bodies in their "individual capacity" and would no longer apply to lobbyists appointed to serve on such bodies in a "representative capacity."[16]

29-2 The Ethics Pledge and Restrictions on Former Lobbyists on Service in the Obama Administration

The Ethics Pledge applies to "[e]very appointee in every executive agency appointed on or after January 20, 2009."[17] The Pledge sets forth the following restrictions at paragraphs 2 and 3 on appointees entering the executive branch of the federal government:

2. *Revolving-Door Ban—All Appointees Entering Government.* I will not for a period of 2 years from the date of my appointment participate in any particular matter involving specific parties that is directly and substantially related to my former employer or former clients, including regulations and contracts.

3. *Revolving-Door Ban—Lobbyists Entering Government.* If I was a registered lobbyist within the 2 years before the date of my appointment, in addition to abiding by the limitations of paragraph 2, I will not for a period of 2 years after the date of my appointment:

---

13. Other parts of the Ethics Pledge are discussed elsewhere in this edition, including Chapters 26 and 27.

14. President's Memorandum for the Heads of Executive Departments and Agencies on Lobbyists on Agency Boards and Commissions, 75 Fed. Reg. 35,955 (June 18, 2010).

15. Final Guidance on Appointment of Lobbyists to Federal Boards and Commissions, 76 Fed. Reg. 61,756 (Oct. 5, 2011).

16. Revised Guidance on Appointment of Lobbyists to Federal Advisory Committees, Boards, and Commissions, 79 Fed. Reg. 47,482 (Aug. 13, 2014).

17. Exec. Order No. 13490, § 1.

(a) participate in any particular matter on which I lobbied within the 2 years before the date of my appointment;

(b) participate in the specific issue area in which that particular matter falls; or

(c) seek or accept employment with any executive agency that I lobbied within the 2 years before the date of my appointment.[18]

29-3 Taking the Pledge: Who Is an "Appointee" and Who Is a "Registered Lobbyist" Subject to the "Revolving-Door Ban" under the Ethics Pledge?

29-3.1 Who Is an "Appointee" under the Ethics Pledge?

For purposes of the Ethics Pledge, the term "appointee" includes every executive branch employee who is a

- Full-time, noncareer presidential or vice-presidential appointee;
- Noncareer appointee in the Senior Executive Service (or other SES-type system); or
- Appointee to a position that has been excepted from the competitive service by reason of being of a confidential or policymaking character (Schedule C and other positions excepted under comparable criteria) in an executive agency.[19]

The Office of Government Ethics (OGE) has advised that the "essentially political nature of a given appointment is the touchstone" of who is an appointee subject to the Ethics Pledge.[20] OGE has also advised that appointees include "all full-time, political appointees regardless of whether they are appointed by the President, Vice President, an agency head, or otherwise."[21] The term "political appointee" also "generally includes, but is not limited to, all appointees to positions described as 'covered noncareer,'"[22] including, for example, career members of the Senior Executive Service (SES) who are given presidential appointments.[23]

---

18. Exec. Order No. 13490, §§ 1–2.

19. "Executive agency" includes each executive agency defined by title 5, section 105 of the U.S. Code and includes the Executive Office of the President. For purposes of the Ethics Pledge, "executive agency" also includes the United States Postal Service and Postal Regulatory Commission but does *not* include the Government Accountability Office. *Id.* § 2(a).

20. U.S. Office of Gov't Ethics Memorandum, DO-09-010: Who Must Sign the Ethics Pledge? (Mar. 16, 2009).

21. U.S. Office of Gov't Ethics Memorandum, DO-09-003, Executive Order 13490, Ethics Pledge (Jan. 22, 2009).

22. U.S. Office of Gov't Ethics Memorandum, DO-09-010 (citing 5 C.F.R. § 2636.303(a)).

23. U.S. Office of Gov't Ethics Memorandum, DO-09-010. After issuance of Exec. Order No. 13490 at the outset of the Obama administration, appointees temporarily holding over from the previous administration pending appointment of a successor were given a 100-day grace period before being required to sign the Ethics Pledge. Holdover appointees who were not prepared to sign the Ethics Pledge by that 100th day—April 29, 2009—were required to "transition out" by May 29, 2009, absent the granting of an extension of the deadline in situations where the holdover appointee's continued service was determined to be "mission critical and essential for continuity." Office of Gov't Ethics Memorandum, DO-09-014 (Apr. 28, 2009).

OGE "has determined that noncareer Senior Foreign Service appointees are an example of what is meant by noncareer members of an SES-type system."[24] Therefore, "non-career or political Ambassador appointees must sign the Pledge."[25] Conversely, OGE has underscored that the Ethics Pledge does *not* apply to hires to "excepted service" positions, unless those positions are "excepted from the competitive service by reason of being of a confidential or policymaking character."[26] OGE has also explained that Special Government Employees are not subject to the Ethics Pledge.[27]

29-3.2 Who Is a "Registered Lobbyist" and What Is a "Lobbying Organization" under the Ethics Pledge?

For purposes of the Ethics Pledge, the terms "registered lobbyist or lobbying organization" are defined by the Lobbying Disclosure Act:

- A lobbyist or an organization filing a registration pursuant to section 1603(a) of title 2 of the U.S. Code (i.e., a form LD-1 as discussed in Chapter 4 of this manual); and
- Each individual lobbyist identified in any such registration.[28]

In practice, however, the scope of who will be considered a registered lobbyist subject to the restrictions of paragraph 3 of the Ethics Pledge is both broader and, in other important ways, narrower than the language of the definition in Exec. Order No. 13490 itself indicates.

In determining whether someone is a registered lobbyist for purposes of the Ethics Pledge, the initial question "is whether, at any time during the two-year period before appointment, he or she has been listed as a lobbyist in either an initial [LDA] registration or a subsequent quarterly report (line 10 of Form LD-1 or line 18 of Form LD-2)."[29] However, that is only the starting point of the analysis. OGE has stated, for example, that the LD-1 and LD-2 filings accessible in the House and Senate LDA databases may be "overly inclusive"[30] as to who has actually engaged in lobbying activities for a client; the filings may not show that an individual ceased lobbying activities at a certain point even though he or she did not formally "deregister."[31] Further, these filings "are made quarterly" only and, therefore, "do not indicate the actual dates of lobbying activity."[32] For these reasons the implement-

---

24. U.S. Office of Gov't Ethics Memorandum, DO-09-010.

25. *Id.*

26. *Id.* (citing Exec. Order No. 13490, § 2(b) and 5 C.F.R. pt. 213, subpart C).

27. U.S. Office of Gov't Ethics Memorandum, DO-09-010. In its implementing guidance, OGE has also stated that the term "appointee" as covered by the Ethics Pledge does *not* include

•Career Senior Foreign Service officers and career Ambassadors.

•Career officials appointed to confidential positions (provided that the right of return to a career position is established by statute, regulation, or written agency personnel policy).

•Schedule C employees who have no policymaking role (e.g., chauffeurs and private secretaries).

•Career officials who are acting temporarily in the absence of an appointee to a noncareer position.

28. Exec. Order No. 13490, § 2(e).

29. U.S. Office of Gov't Ethics, Annual Report Pursuant to Executive Order 13490 (2013) at 5.

30. *Id.*

31. *Id.*

32. *Id.*

ers of the Ethics Pledge may look beyond the information listed on LDA filings and independently determine when, for which clients, on what issues, and before which government offices a potential appointee was a "registered lobbyist" for purposes of the Ethics Pledge.

29-4 The Ethics Pledge "Revolving-Door Ban" for *All* Appointees Entering Government

Pursuant to the Ethics Pledge, each appointee is banned from participating in "any particular matter involving specific parties that is directly and substantially related to [his or her] former employer or former clients, including regulations and contracts."[33] This restriction lasts for two years from the date of appointment.

The key terms central to understanding the scope of this ban—"participate," "particular matter involving specific parties," "directly and substantially related," "former employer," and "former client"—are defined in the Ethics Pledge, and their meaning has been elaborated in useful guidance from OGE.[34]

29-4.1 What Does "Participate" Mean?

"Participate" means to "participate personally and substantially."[35] To participate "personally" means to participate "directly," including "the direct and active supervision of the participation of a subordinate" in a matter.[36] To participate "substantially" means that "the employee's involvement is of significance to the matter," whether or not that participation is "determinative of the outcome of" the matter.[37] But substantial participation "requires more than official responsibility, knowledge, perfunctory involvement, or involvement on an administrative or peripheral issue."[38] As examples of personal and substantial participation, OGE has cited an employee's participation "through decision, approval, disapproval, recommendation, investigation or the rendering of advice in a particular matter."[39]

29-4.2 What Is a "Particular Matter Involving Specific Parties"?

The executive branch ethics rules define a "particular matter involving specific parties" to mean a "specific proceeding affecting the legal rights of the parties or an isolatable transaction or related set of transactions between identified parties, such as a specific contract, grant, license, product approval application, enforcement action, administrative adjudication, or court case."[40] The term "particular matter involving specific parties" includes the set of matters set forth in the executive branch ethics rules, but is also broader. As used in the Ethics Pledge, the term includes also any meeting or communication relating to the performance of one's

---

33. Exec. Order No. 13490, § 1(2).
34. U.S. Office of Gov't Ethics Memorandum, DO-09-011, Ethics Pledge: Revolving Door Ban—All Appointees Entering Government (Mar. 26, 2009).
35. Exec. Order No. 13,490, § 2(3)(l).
36. *See* 5 C.F.R. § 2635.402(b)(4) (2015); *see also* 5 C.F.R. § 2640.103(a)(2) (2015).
37. *Id.*
38. *Id.*
39. *Id.*
40. 5 C.F.R. § 2641.201(h) (2015).

official duties with a former employer or client unless the communication applies to a particular matter of general applicability and participation in the matter or other event is open to all interested parties.[41]

In some circumstances, regulations and rulemakings may also be "particular matters involving specific parties" falling within the scope of the ban. OGE has observed that "in rare circumstances . . . certain rulemakings may be so focused on the rights of specifically identified parties as to be considered a particular matter involving specific parties . . . covered by paragraph 2."[42]

Under the Ethics Pledge, the two-year ban on participation in a "particular matter involving specific parties" also extends—with the important qualifications discussed immediately below—to "any meeting or communication" with a former employer or client "relating to the performance of one's official duties."[43] OGE has explained that the scope of the term "particular matter involving specific parties" was expanded in the Ethics Pledge "to address concerns that former employers and clients may appear to have privileged access, which they may exploit to influence the appointee out of the public view."[44]

The expanded scope of the term "particular matter involving specific parties" is limited in the following two ways, however. First, the term is not intended to cover "communications and meetings regarding policies that do not constitute particular matters."[45] The term "particular matter" "is not so broad as to include every matter involving Government action. Particular matter does not cover the 'consideration or adoption of broad policy options directed to the interests of a large and diverse group of persons.'"[46] As examples of matters that are not particular matters, OGE has cited health and safety regulations applicable to all employers.[47]

Second, the term "particular matter involving specific parties" does not apply to a communication relating "to a particular matter of general applicability" if "participation in the meeting or other event is open to all interested parties."[48] The term "particular matters of general applicability" includes matters "that do not involve specific parties but at least focus on the interests of a discrete and identifiable class of persons, such as a particular industry or profession."[49] This would "include legislation and policymaking, as long as it is narrowly focused on a discrete and identifiable class."[50] On the meaning of "open to all interested parties,"

---

41. Exec. Order No. 13490, § 2(h).

42. U.S. Office of Gov't Ethics Memorandum, DO-09-011 at 2–3.

43. Exec. Order No. 13490, § 2(h).

44. U.S. Office of Gov't Ethics Memorandum, DO-09-011 at 2. OGE has explained further, however, that the expanded definition "is not intended to interfere with the ability of appointees to consult with experts at educational institutions and 'think tanks' on general policy matters, at least where those entities do not have a financial interest, as opposed to an academic or ideological interest." *Id.* at 2, n. 2.

45. *Id.* at 2.

46. U.S. Office of Gov't Ethics Memorandum, DO-06-029, "Particular Matter Involving Specific Parties," "Particular Matter," and "Matter" (Oct. 4, 2006), at 9.

47. *Id.*

48. Exec. Order No. 13490, § 2(h).

49. U.S. Office of Gov't Ethics Memorandum, DO-06-029, at 8. As examples of "particular matters of general applicability," OGE has cited "a regulation applicable only to meat packing companies," "a regulation prescribing safety standards for trucks on interstate highways," and "legislation focused on the compensation and work conditions of the class of Assistant United States Attorneys." *Id.*

50. *Id.* at 8.

OGE has stated that "common sense" should control.[51] Participation in the matter or event is considered to be "open to all interested parties" if it "include[s] a multiplicity of parties"; however, it does "not have to be open to every comer."[52] As an example, OGE has described an agency "meeting with five or more stakeholders regarding a given policy or piece of legislation" and has stated that "an appointee could attend such a meeting even if one of the stakeholders is a former employer or former client."[53] Whether a given forum, meeting, or other event qualifies as being "open to all interested parties" may be a fact-specific determination, and an appointee's Designated Agency Ethics Official (DAEO) should be consulted if the "openness" of an event is subject to question.

29-4.3 When Is a Matter "Directly and Substantially Related to" a Former Employer or Client?

A matter is "directly and substantially related to" an appointee's former employer or former client when "the appointee's former employer or a former client is a party or represents a party."[54]

29-4.4 Who Is a "Former Employer" and Who Is a "Former Client" under the Ethics Pledge?

29-4.4.1 "Former Employer"
A "former employer" is

> Any person for whom the appointee has, within the two years prior to the date of his or her appointment served as an employee, officer, director, trustee, or general partner, except that "former employer" does not include any executive agency or other entity of the Federal Government, State or local government, the District of Columbia, Native American tribe, or any United States territory or possession.[55]

Despite the exclusion from the definition of "former employer" in the Ethics Pledge for state or local government entities generally, state colleges and universities are considered to be former employers for purposes of the Ethics Pledge and, therefore, are entities with which an appointee's interactions are restricted during the two-year revolving-door ban.[56] Likewise, nonprofit organizations are included in the definition of "former employer" with which interactions are restricted under the Ethics Pledge, even if the appointee served without compensation as an employee, officer, director, trustee, or general partner of the organization, or

---

51. U.S. Office of Gov't Ethics Memorandum, DO-09-011 at 2.

52. *Id.*

53. *Id.* OGE has also stated that "the Pledge is not intended to preclude an appointee from participating in rulemaking under section 553 of the Administrative Procedure Act simply because a former employer or client may have submitted written comments in response to a public notice of proposed rulemaking." *Id.*

54. Exec. Order No. 13490, § 2(k).

55. *Id.* § 2(i).

56. U.S. Office of Gov't Ethics Memorandum, DO-09-011 at 3.

in some other capacity involving fiduciary duties to the organization.[57] Purely honorific or "honorary" positions with a nonprofit organization do *not* fall within the scope of former employer for purposes of the Ethics Pledge.[58]

29-4.4.2 *"Former Client"*
As defined at paragraph (j), section 2 of the Ethics Pledge, a "former client" is

> Any person for whom the appointee served personally as agent, attorney, or consultant within the two years prior to the date of his or her appointment, but excluding instances where the service provided was limited to a speech or similar appearance. It does not include clients of the appointee's former employer to whom the appointee did not personally provide services.[59]

There are a number of important practical points about the interpretation and application of the term "former client" that an individual subject to the Ethics Pledge should keep in mind:

- "Former client" does not include clients of a former employer to whom the appointee did not personally provide services. So, for example, even if "an appointee's former law firm provided legal services to a corporation, the corporation is not a former client of the appointee for purposes of the Pledge if the appointee did not personally render legal services to the corporation."[60]
- The definition of "former client" excludes the same governmental entities as are excluded from the definition of "former employer."[61] (See the discussion above.)
- The definition of "former client" includes nonprofit organizations, unless participation with the nonprofit organization was in the capacity of an unpaid, nonfiduciary advisory committee member or was in a solely honorific capacity.[62]
- In addition to excluding speeches and similar appearances, the definition of "former client" excludes "other kinds of discrete, short-term engagements, including certain *de minimis* consulting activities," "that similarly involve a brief one-time service with little or no ongoing attachment or obligation."[63] Whether an appointee's past service with an entity was sufficiently de minimis that the entity will *not* be considered a "former client" under the Pledge may require a government ethics official to perform a careful analysis of the totality of circumstances. OGE advises that, in closer cases, a reviewing ethics official should err on the side of determining that an entity was a former client, with the understanding

---

57. *Id.* at 3–4.
58. *Id.* at 4.
59. Exec. Order No. 13490, § 2 (j).
60. U.S. Office of Gov't Ethics Memorandum, DO-09-011 at 4.
61. *Id.*
62. *Id.*
63. *Id.* at 5.

that waivers (the process for which is discussed below) could "remain an option in appropriate cases."[64]

29-5 The Ethics Pledge "Revolving-Door Ban" on Former Lobbyists Entering Government

Any former federally registered lobbyist entering the executive branch of government as an appointee must sign the Ethics Pledge and, by doing so, becomes subject to the two-year ban—imposed by the Ethics Pledge on *all* appointees (discussed earlier)—on participation in certain matters related to former employers or former clients.

In addition, an appointee who was a registered lobbyist within two years *before* the date of his or her entering the executive branch may not, for two years *after* the date of appointment:

- Participate in any particular matter on which he or she lobbied within the two years before the date of his or her appointment;[65]
- Participate in the specific issue area in which any such particular matter falls;[66] or
- Seek or accept employment with any executive agency he or she lobbied within the two years before the date of his or her appointment.[67]

29-5.1 What Do "Lobby" and "Lobbied" Mean under the Pledge?

For purposes of the Ethics Pledge, "'lobby' and 'lobbied' shall mean to act or have acted as a registered lobbyist."[68] As discussed above, whether an individual is listed as a lobbyist on an LD-1 or LD-2 is the starting point in determining the extent (i.e., for whom and on what particular matters) and timing of his or her activity as a lobbyist. But, when necessary, agency ethics officials will "go beyond" the filings in the House and Senate LDA databases to look at the specific facts of an appointee's actual activity to determine the extent to which, and when, the individual "lobbied."[69]

29-5.2 What Is a "Particular Matter" under Paragraph 3(a) of the Pledge?

For purposes of the Ethics Pledge, the term "particular matter" has "the same meaning as set forth in section 207 of title 18, United States Code, and section 2635.402(b)(3) of title 5, Code of Federal Regulations."[70] The term "encompasses only matters that involve deliberation, decision, or action that is focused upon the interests of specific persons, or a discrete and identifiable class of persons."[71] A matter is a "particular matter," however, "even if it does not involve formal par-

---

64. *See Id.* for factors in analysis.
65. Exec. Order No. 13490, § 1(3)(a).
66. *Id.* § 1(3)(b).
67. *Id.* § 1(3)(c).
68. *Id.* § 2(f).
69. See Section 29-3.2 of this chapter.
70. Exec. Order No. 13490, § 2(g).
71. 5 C.F.R. § 2635.402(b)(3) (2015).

ties and may include governmental action such as legislation or policy-making that is narrowly focused on the interests of such a discrete and identifiable class of persons."[72] But the term "particular matter" does not include "the consideration or adoption of broad policy options that are directed to the interests of a large and diverse group of persons."[73] Examples of particular matters include "a judicial or other proceeding, application, request for a ruling or other determination, contract, claim, controversy, charge, accusation or arrest."[74]

The category of particular matters includes both "particular matters involving specific parties" and "particular matters of general applicability."[75] The scope of the term "particular matter" has its limits, however. It is "not so broad as to include every matter involving Government action"; it "does not cover the consideration or adoption of broad policy options directed to the interest of a large and diverse group of persons."[76]

29-5.3 What Is a "Specific Issue Area" under the Pledge?

The term "specific issue area" is not defined. Typically, proscribed specific issue areas are identified in more general terms, such as, for example, "patent law reform," "affordable housing assistance," "antitrust insurance industry issues," "immigrants' eligibility for public benefits," "international affairs budget appropriations," or "energy derivatives." But, as applied and implemented in particular cases, the prohibited specific issue areas have not been as broad and general as, for example, the categories included as "general issue areas" for purposes of LDA disclosure.[77]

29-6 The Ethics Pledge and Other Executive Branch Impartiality Restrictions

In addition to the restrictions imposed by the Ethics Pledge, all appointees to the executive branch—including former lobbyist appointees—remain subject to all other impartiality statutes and standards applicable to all executive branch employees.[78]

---

72. *Id.*

73. *Id.*

74. *Id.*

75. U.S. Office of Gov't Ethics Memorandum, DO-06-029 at 8.

76. *Id.* at 9. As OGE has noted in its guidance regarding the meaning of the term, a matter may not start out as a "particular matter" but may develop into one when initially broad policy deliberations or actions pertaining to diverse interests become deliberations on "specific actions that focus on a certain person or a discrete and identifiable class of persons." OGE provides this example: "a legislative plan for broad health care reform would not be a particular matter," but "a particular matter would arise if an agency later issued implementing regulations focused narrowly on the prices that pharmaceutical companies could charge for prescription drugs." *Id.* at 10.

77. For a discussion of LDA disclosure, see Chapter 4 of this manual.

78. U.S. Office of Gov't Ethics Memorandum, DO-09-011 at 5; see Chapter 27 for a discussion of conflicts of interest generally.

29-7 Administration of the Ethics Pledge: Waivers and Enforcement

29-7.1 Administration of the Ethics Pledge

Within each executive branch agency (including the Executive Office of the President), the DAEO is effectively responsible for administering the Ethics Pledge.[79] In addition to generally ensuring compliance with Exec. Order No. 13490, administering the Ethics Pledge includes ensuring that

- Each appointee to the agency signs the Pledge upon assuming the appointed office or otherwise becoming an appointee (or has already signed the Ethics Pledge if he or she is moving to the agency, without a break in service, from another position for which he or she was required to sign the Ethics Pledge).[80]
- Compliance with the requirements of paragraph 3 of the Pledge—relating to former-lobbyist appointees—is addressed in a written ethics agreement with each appointee to whom those requirements apply. Any such written ethics agreement must also be approved by the Counsel to the President, or his or her designee, before the appointee begins work.[81]
- Spousal employment issues and other conflicts not addressed by the Pledge are addressed in written ethics agreements with appointees (where required) or through ethics counseling.[82]

29-7.2 Waiver of Ethics Pledge Revolving-Door Restrictions

Determinations regarding waiver of the restrictions of the Ethics Pledge are to be made by "the Director of the Office of Management and Budget, or his or her designee, in consultation with the Counsel to the President, or his or her designee."[83] The Director of OMB has designated the DAEO of each executive agency to exercise waiver authority in consultation with the Counsel to the President.[84]

A waiver of any—or all—of the restrictions under the Ethics Pledge may be granted where a DAEO, in consultation with the Counsel to the President or his or designee, certifies in writing

- That the literal application of the restriction is inconsistent with the purpose of the restriction, *or*

---

79. OGE maintains an updated "DAEO List," including contact information, on its website at http://www.oge.gov/Program-Management/Program-Management-Resources/Ethics-Community/DAEO-List/ (last visited Sept. 25, 2015).

80. Exec. Order No. 13490, § 4(a).

81. *Id.*

82. *Id.*

83. *Id.* § 3(a).

84. U.S. Office of Gov't Ethics Memorandum, DO-09-008, Authorizations Pursuant to Section 3 of Executive Order 13490, "Ethics Commitments by Executive Branch Personnel" (Feb. 23, 2009). The consultation process for a DAEO regarding waiver issues also includes the "OGE desk officer" for the agency in question. *Id.* at 2.

- That it is in the public interest to grant the waiver.[85]

The "public interest shall include, but not be limited to, exigent circumstances relating to national security or to the economy."[86] Additionally, "[d]e minimis contact with an executive agency shall be cause for a waiver of the restrictions contained in paragraph 3 of the pledge" regarding restrictions on former lobbyists.[87]

OGE has emphasized that "[i]t is the President's intention that waivers will be granted sparingly and that their scope will be as limited as possible."[88] All waivers of any provision(s) of the Ethics Pledge issued to appointees to executive branch agencies are accessible at OGE's website.[89] Waivers issued by the White House or by the office of the vice president are accessible on the White House website.[90]

Relatively few so-called lobbying waivers or "reverse revolving door" waivers have been granted to former registered lobbyists. In 2009, the first year in which the Ethics Pledge was in effect, three appointees who had been registered lobbyists received waivers from the restrictions under both paragraph 2 (imposing reverse revolving-door restrictions on all appointees) and paragraph 3 (imposing additional restrictions on former lobbyists) of the Pledge.[91] No waivers for former registered lobbyists were issued in 2010, 2011, 2012, or 2013.[92] In 2014, a waiver from paragraph 3 of the Ethics Pledge was granted to one former-lobbyist appointee, allowing his appointment in January 2015 to an agency he lobbied within two years of his appointment.[93]

Partial waivers of the reverse revolving-door restrictions for appointees who have *not* been registered lobbyists during the two years before their appointment have been more frequent. Not including the waivers discussed above, a total of 61 reverse revolving-door waivers have been granted, to date, by executive branch agencies and the White House.

---

85. Exec. Order No. 13490, § 3(a).

86. *Id.* § 3(b).

87. *Id.*

88. U.S. Office of Gov't Ethics Memorandum, DO-09-008 at 2.

89. *See* Executive Branch Agency Ethics Pledge Waivers, *available at* http://www.oge.gov/Open-Government/Executive-Branch-Agency-Ethics-Pledge-Waivers (last visited Sept. 25, 2015).

90. *See* Ethics Pledge Waivers Released by the White House, http://www.whitehouse.gov/briefing-room/disclosures/ethics-pledge-waivers (last visited Sept. 25, 2015).

91. In 2009, twenty-four appointees to the executive branch had been registered lobbyists during the two years before their appointment. Of these twenty-four, "21 did not need waivers to be appointed to their positions because they had not lobbied the agency to which they were appointed within the two years prior to appointment." U.S. Office of Gov't Ethics, Annual Report Pursuant to Executive Order 13490 (2010) at 5.

92. In 2010, three appointees had been registered lobbyists during the two years before their appointment; in 2011, no such persons were appointed; in 2012, two appointees had been registered lobbyists during the two years before their appointment; in 2013, no such persons were appointed. In 2014, one individual who had been a lobbyist within the previous two years was issued a waiver, but this individual was not appointed until January 2015. *See* U.S. Office of Gov't Ethics Annual Report Pursuant to Executive Order 13490 (2010) at 5; Office of Gov't Ethics Annual Report Pursuant to Executive Order 13490 (2011) at 3; Office of Gov't Ethics Annual Report Pursuant to Executive Order 13490 (2012) at 3; Office of Gov't Ethics Annual Report Pursuant to Executive Order 13490 (2013) at 2; and Office of Gov't Ethics Annual Report Pursuant to Executive Order 13490 (2014) at 6, n.10.

93. U.S. Office of Gov't Ethics Annual Report Pursuant to Executive Order 13490 (2014) at 6.

Although waivers have been—and will continue to be—as narrowly tailored as possible, the "particular matters" covered by a waiver can be ongoing matters of substance and significance. For example, in 2009, based on written determinations that such waivers were in "the public interest," the attorney general, the deputy attorney general, and the assistant attorney general each received a limited waiver of the restrictions of paragraph 2 of the Ethics Pledge to participate in an investigation of alleged conduct by government attorneys in the prosecution of Senator Ted Stevens, notwithstanding the fact that the former law firms of these appointees represented parties under investigation.[94]

Waivers may be limited, but nonetheless open-ended. For example, in 2011, a former International Monetary Fund official appointed to be Special Assistant to the President for International Economic Affairs was granted a waiver as to "future involvement in particular matters relating to the IMF and any of its bodies, offices or agencies."[95] And waivers may be deemed necessary even for matters that seem trivial: For example, in 2010, a waiver was required for—and granted to—an appointee to provide a "brief public introduction for former President Clinton" at an event hosted by the Atlantic Council of the United States where the appointee had, within the previous two years, served as chairman of the board of the Atlantic Council.[96]

Waivers are typically limited in ways other than the scope of the particular matter covered. For example, a waiver may permit an appointee's involvement in particular matters, but prohibit his or her acting as the final decision maker in connection with the matter. Or a waiver may permit an appointee's involvement in particular matters involving a former employer, but prohibit involvement in matters directly affecting the financial interest of the former employer, particularly where the appointee may be receiving some ongoing benefits under a severance agreement or pension plan.[97]

---

94. U.S. Office of Gov't Ethics Annual Report Pursuant to Executive Order 13490 (2009), Appendix V, (DOJ, Certification of Public Interest Waiver for Lanny Breuer (May 6, 2009); DOJ, Certification of Public Interest Waiver for Eric Holder (May 6, 2009) and DOJ, Certification for Public Interest Waiver for David Ogden (May 6, 2009)).

95. U.S. Office of Gov't Ethics Annual Report Pursuant to Executive Order 13490 (2011) Appendix IV, Waiver Pursuant to Section 3 of Executive Order 13490 (Aug. 8, 2011). The determination to grant a waiver in this instance was also based on a finding that "literal application of paragraph 2 in this situation is inconsistent with the purposes of the restriction" because "[w]hen a former employer is an international organization that includes the United States as a member, like the IMF, the concerns underlying the restrictions in the Ethics Pledge are not implicated, because the interests of the international organization and the interests of the United States are aligned. As such, there is little likelihood that a government employee could take action to favor the commercial interests of his or her former employer at the expense of the United States." *Id.* at 2.

96. U.S. Office of Gov't Ethics Annual Report Pursuant to Executive Order 13490 (2010), Appendix IV, Waiver Pursuant to Section 3 of Executive Order 13490 (Apr. 28, 2010).

97. *See, e.g.,* Executive Branch Agency Ethics Pledge Waivers, *available at* http://www.oge.gov/Open-Government/Executive-Branch-Agency-Ethics-Pledge-Waivers; https://www.whitehouse.gov/briefing-room/disclosures/ethics-pledge-waivers.

29-7.3 Enforcement of the Ethics Pledge Revolving-Door Restrictions

29-7.3.1 Enforcement Provisions of Exec. Order No. 13490

Exec. Order No. 13490 provides that the "commitments in the pledge . . . are solely enforceable by the United States . . . by any legally available means, including debarment proceedings within any affected executive agency or judicial civil proceedings for declaratory, injunctive, or monetary relief."[98]

Exec. Order No. 13490 similarly provides that a former appointee who is found to have violated the terms of the Ethics Pledge "may be barred from lobbying any officer or employee of that agency for up to 5 years in addition to the time period covered by the pledge."[99] Paragraph (b) of Section 5 further provides for "fact finding and investigation of possible violations" to be conducted by the affected agency and for referral of possible violations of the Ethics Pledge to the attorney general.[100] The attorney general may "request any appropriate Federal investigative authority to conduct" an investigation; upon determining that "there is a reasonable basis to believe" that a breach of the Ethics Pledge "has occurred or will occur or continue, if not enjoined," the attorney general may then commence a civil action against the former appointee in U.S. District Court.[101]

Finally, Exec. Order No. 13490 provides that the attorney general may request "any and all relief authorized by law," including, but not limited to appropriate injunctive relief "to restrain future, recurring, or continuing conduct by the former employee in breach of the commitments in the pledge"; and established of a constructive trust for the benefit of the United States to receive "all money and other things of value received by, or payable to, the former employee arising out of any breach or attempted breach" of the Ethics Pledge.[102]

29-7.3.2 Enforcement of the Ethics Pledge in Practice

For 2010, OGE reported two instances "in which appointees made contact with former employers, contravening Ethics Pledge, paragraph 2." One instance involved an agency administrator who "consulted briefly" with a former employer concerning a research project in which the former employer had no financial interest. The matter was investigated by the agency's Office of the Inspector General, which determined that the contact violated the Ethics Pledge. On the recommendation of the White House Counsel's Office the administrator "was given a reprimand and supplemental ethics training, and he recused himself from further participation in the research project."[103] The second enforcement instance outlined by OGE for 2010 involved an appointee who exchanged "e-mail messages with his former employer about certain matters within the scope of his official duties"; this appointee received a reprimand and was required to attend supplemental ethics training.[104]

---

98. Exec. Order No. 13490, § 5(a).
99. *Id.* § 5(b).
100. *Id.*
101. *Id.* § 5(c).
102. *Id.* § 5(d).
103. U.S. Office of Gov't Ethics Annual Report Pursuant to Executive Order 13490 (2010) at 8.
104. *Id.*

For 2011, OGE stated only: "Agencies reported three instances in 2011 in which appointees may have had contact with former employers in violation of Pledge paragraph 2. These matters have been referred to the appropriate inspectors general."[105] For 2012, OGE stated that agencies had reported no instances of possible contact by appointees with former employers in violation of the Ethics Pledge.[106] In an interesting footnote to the 2012 report, however, OGE reported an instance where an appointee properly relied on incorrect guidance from an ethics official to accept two tickets to an event; because of this reliance on incorrect guidance, and because the appointee reimbursed the full value of the tickets, no violation was found.[107] And again in 2013 and 2014, OGE noted that agencies had reported no instance of possible contact by appointees with former employers in violation of the Ethics Pledge.[108]

29-8 Restrictions on Lobbyist Service on Federal Advisory Committees

29-8.1 Background on Federal Advisory Committees

The term "federal advisory committee" is a committee, board, commission, council, conference, panel, task force, or other similar group comprising members both from the federal government and from business, academia, or other areas of the private sector, and established by statute or established or used by the president or by one or more agencies to obtain advice and recommendations across a wide range of operational and policy issues.[109] Pursuant to the Federal Advisory Committee Act (FACA), all federal advisory committees must have at least one member who is not a "full-time, or permanent part-time" officer or employee of the federal government.[110] As of 2014, there were 1,050 active federal advisory committees.[111]

There are two types of members who sit on federal advisory committees. Some members serve in their individual capacities and are classified as Special Government Employees. Others serve in a "representative capacity," thereby providing the committees with "the points of view of nongovernmental entities or of a recognizable group of persons (*e.g.*, an industry sector, labor unions, or environmental groups, etc.)."[112] This distinction between service in an "individual capacity" and service in a "representative capacity" is now dispositive in determining whether a federally registered lobbyist may be appointed, or reappointed, to serve on such a committee.

As discussed further below, on August 13, 2014, OMB issued guidance modifying the Obama administration's ban on service by federally registered lobbyists

---

105. U.S. Office of Gov't Ethics Annual Report Pursuant to Executive Order 13490 (2011) at 7.

106. U.S. Office of Gov't Ethics Annual Report Pursuant to Executive Order 13490 (2012) at 7–8.

107. U.S. Office of Gov't Ethics Annual Report Pursuant to Executive Order 13490 (2012) at 7.

108. U.S. Office of Gov't Ethics Annual Report Pursuant to Executive Order 13490 (2013) at 2; Office of Gov't Ethics Annual Report Pursuant to Executive Order 13490 (2014) at 6.

109. Pub. L. No. 92–463, § 3, 86 Stat. 770 (1972).

110. *Id.*

111. General Services Administration, Federal Advisory Committees by Agency, https://database .faca.gov/rpt/rptq01.asp (last visited Sept. 25, 2015).

112. U.S. Office of Gov't Ethics, Advisory Committee Members, http://www.oge.gov/Topics /Selected-Employee-Categories/Advisory-Committee-Members/ (last visited Sept. 25, 2015).

on any federal advisory committee. Under OMB's revised guidance, federally registered lobbyists may be appointed, or reappointed, to such advisory groups in a "representative capacity" only; a federally registered lobbyist may not serve on a federal advisory committee in an "individual capacity."[113]

29-8.2 President Obama's Memorandum Barring Lobbyist Service on Federal Advisory Committees

On June 18, 2010, President Obama issued a "Memorandum for the Heads of Executive Departments and Agencies," on the subject of "Lobbyists on Agency Boards and Commissions," "direct[ing] the heads of executive departments and agencies not to make any new appointments or reappointments of federally registered lobbyists to advisory committees and other boards and commissions."[114] The president's June 18, 2010, Memorandum directed the Director of the Office of Management and Budget to "issue proposed guidance designed to implement this policy to the full extent permitted by law."[115]

29-8.3 OMB Guidance Implementing the Restrictions on Lobbyist Service on Federal Advisory Committees

On November 2, 2010, OMB posted proposed guidance to implement the ban on lobbyists on advisory boards and committees.[116] On October 5, 2011, OMB issued, in question-and-answer format, what it then titled its "Final Guidance on Appointment of Lobbyists to Federal Boards and Commissions," following review of the comments received to the proposed guidance.[117] This was subsequently revised by OMB through its "Revised Guidance on Appointment of Lobbyists to Federal Advisory Committees, Boards, and Commissions," issued August 13, 2014.[118, 119]

---

113. Revised Guidance on Appointment of Lobbyists to Federal Advisory Committees, Boards, and Commissions, 79 Fed. Reg. 47,482 (Aug. 13, 2014).

114. Memorandum on Lobbyists on Agency Boards and Commission, 75 Fed. Reg. 35,955 (June 18, 2010).

115. *Id.*

116. Proposed Guidance on Appointment of Lobbyists to Federal Boards and Commissions, 75 Fed. Reg. 67,397 (Nov. 2, 2010).

117. Final Guidance on Appointment of Lobbyists to Federal Boards and Commissions, 76 Fed. Reg. 61,756 (Oct. 5, 2011).

118. 79 Fed. Reg. at 47,482.

119. On September 2, 2012, six lobbyists who served, or were interested in serving, on advisory committees (specifically, on Industry Trade Advisory Committees, or ITACs, of the U.S. Department of Commerce; all private sector members of ITACs serve in a representative capacity) filed suit against the Department of Commerce and the Office of the U.S. Trade Representative alleging that the bar on lobbyist service on the advisory committees violated both the First Amendment and the equal protection clause of the Fifth Amendment by "denying the benefit of committee service to individuals whose exercise of the right to petition triggers the LDA's registration requirement." (*Autor v. Pritzker*, No. 12-5379 (D.C. Cir. Jan. 17, 2014), at 4, quoting Complaint ¶ 44, *Autor v. Pritzker*, No. 11cv01593 (D.D.C. filed Sept. 2, 2011).) On September 26, 2012, Judge Amy Berman Jackson of the U.S. District Court for the District of Columbia found for the defendants and granted their motion to dismiss the lawsuit for failure to state a claim under Rule 12(b)(6) of the Federal Rules of Civil Procedure. (Memorandum Opinion at 31, Autor v. Blank, 892 F. Supp. 2d 264, 284–85 (D.D.C. 2012), *rev'd sub nom. Autor v. Pritzker*, 740 F.3d 176 (D.C. Cir. 2014).)

On January 17, 2014, the U.S. Court of Appeals for the District of Columbia Circuit reversed the lower court's dismissal of the lobbyists' suit and remanded the case to the lower court to develop

29-8.3.1 Entities Covered by the Restrictions

As implemented by the OMB, the policy restricting appointment or reappointment of federally registered lobbyists applies to the following types of entities:

- Any committee, board, commission, council, delegation, conference, panel, task force, or other similar group (or subgroup) created by the president, the Congress, or an executive branch department or agency to serve a specific function to which appointment is required, regardless of whether it is subject to the FACA.[120]

- "Appointment" includes any appointment "which is required or permitted by law or regulation, including appointment at the discretion of the department or agency." Further, the appointment ban "applies to established workgroups and subcommittees for boards and commissions, which may or may not require formal appointment."[121]

  - With respect to coverage of delegations to international bodies, in its revised guidance OMB notes specifically that the policy barring appointment or reappointment of lobbyists in an "individual capacity" (but not in a "representative capacity") applies to delegations organized to present the position of the United States to international bodies, regardless of whether they constitute advisory committees for purposes of FACA.[122]

  - As to application of the lobbyist service ban to subcommittees, OMB specifically notes in its guidance that the policy prohibits appointment of federally registered lobbyists in an "individual capacity" (but not in a "representative capacity") to a subcommittee or any other subgroup that performs preparatory work for a parent board or commission, whether or not the members of such a subcommittee or

---

a factual record and to undertake the required balancing analysis "to determine in the first instance whether the government's interest in excluding federally registered lobbyists from ITACs outweighs any impingement on Appellants' constitutional rights." The Court of Appeals found that the lobbyist ban required appellant lobbyists "to limit their exercise of a constitutional right—in this case, the First Amendment right to petition government—in order to qualify for a governmental benefit—in this case, ITAC membership." In remanding the lobbyists' lawsuit to the District Court, the Court of Appeals evinced a skeptical stance toward the government's justification for the ban on lobbyist service on federal advisory committees, as in this guidance to the lower court:

> [T]he district court should ask the parties to focus on the justification for distinguishing, as the lobbyist ban does, between corporate employees (who may represent their employers on ITACs) and the registered lobbyists those same corporations retain (who may not). The court may also want to ask the government to explain how banning lobbyists from committees composed of representatives of the likes of Boeing and General Electric protects the "voices of ordinary Americans."

(*Autor v. Pritzker*, at 14.)

Seven months after the Court of Appeals issued its pointed guidance to the District Court (and, indirectly, to the Obama administration) in *Autor v. Pritzker*, the administration appeared to accede to the logic of the court's opinion. As noted and discussed, on August 13, 2014, OMB issued "Revised Guidance on Appointment of Lobbyists to Federal Advisory Committees, Boards, and Commissions," lifting the ban on lobbyists serving on federal advisory committees in a "representative capacity."

120. 79 Fed. Reg. at 47,482.
121. *Id.*
122. *Id.*

subgroup are appointed in the same manner as members of the parent committee.[123]

29-8.3.2 Who Is a "Lobbyist" for Purposes of the Restrictions on Service on Federal Advisory Committees?

For purposes of the restrictions on service by federally registered lobbyists on advisory committees, a "lobbyist" is any individual who is subject to the registration and reporting requirements of the LDA at the time of his or her appointment or reappointment to an advisory committee.[124] In its guidance OMB advises that agencies may rely on the House and Senate LDA databases to identify federally registered lobbyists or, in the alternative, obtain written certification from individuals recruited for membership to advisory committees that they are not federally registered lobbyists.[125]

An individual who previously served as a federally registered lobbyist may be appointed or reappointed to a federal advisory committee in an "individual capacity" only if he or she

- Has filed a "bona fide de-registration";[126]
- Has been de-listed by his or her employer as an active lobbyist, reflecting the actual cessation of lobbying activities;[127] or
- Has not appeared on quarterly lobbying report (Form LD-2) for three consecutive quarters, as result of actual cessation of lobbying activities.[128]

29-8.3.3 Meaning of Service in an "Individual Capacity" and Service in a "Representative Capacity"

Under OMB's August 13, 2014, "Revised Guidance," service by federally registered lobbyists on such bodies in an individual capacity is prohibited; service by lobbyists on such bodies in a representative capacity is permitted. Therefore, an understanding of the difference between the meaning of the terms "individual capacity" and "representative capacity" as used in OMB's guidance is central to understanding the restrictions imposed by that guidance.

29-8.3.3.1 Individual Capacity

The term "individual capacity" refers to "individuals who are appointed to committees to exercise their own individual best judgment on behalf of the government."[129] Appointees serve in their individual capacities "when they are designated as Special Government Employees as defined in 18 U.S.C. 202."[130] A special government employee (SGE) "is an officer or employee who is retained, designated, appointed, or employed [by the federal government] to perform tem-

---

123. *Id.*
124. *Id.*
125. *Id.*
126. *Id.*
127. *Id.*
128. *Id.*
129. *Id.*
130. *Id.*

porary duties, with or without compensation, for not more than 130 days during any period of 365 consecutive days."[131]

Note that when an individual serves on a federal advisory committee in an individual capacity as an SGE, he or she is subject to a range of executive branch ethics laws and regulations.[132] Appointing authorities "are required to clearly designate the role of committee members"—that is, whether the members will be serving in an individual capacity or in a representative capacity.[133]

29-8.3.3.2 *Representative Capacity*

The "ban" on service by federally registered lobbyists on federal advisory entities does *not* apply to lobbyists who are appointed in a representative capacity. Persons serve on an advisory entity in a representative capacity when "they are appointed for the express purpose of providing a committee with the views of a nongovernmental entity, a recognizable group of persons or nongovernmental entities (an industry sector, labor unions, or environmental groups, etc.), or state or local government."[134] Persons appointed to serve in a representative capacity on federal advisory committees "are not being appointed on committees to exercise their own individual best judgment on behalf of the government. Instead representatives serve as the voice of groups or entities with a financial or other stake in a particular matter before an advisory committee."[135] Federal ethics rules and standards do not apply to advisory committee members serving in a representative capacity.[136]

The use of the term "represent" in an advisory committee's charter or authorizing legislation to describe the committee's members "does not necessarily mean that the members of that committee are to be appointed in a representative capacity rather than an individual capacity."[137]

29-8.3.4 *What—and Who—Determines whether an Advisory Committee Member Serves in an Individual Capacity or in a Representative Capacity?*

The OGE has stated that "[w]hile Congress may sometimes specify in legislation the status of members serving on an advisory committee, it may not always do so or do so clearly."[138] Likewise, an advisory committee's charter "may be helpful"— but not necessarily dispositive—"in identifying a member's status."[139] Therefore, OGE notes, "[w]here a committee's enabling authority"—or its charter—"does not contain any language sufficiently identifying a member's status or that language is

---

131. U.S. Office of Gov't Ethics, Advisory Committee Members, http://www.oge.gov/Topics/Selected-Employee-Categories/Advisory-Committee-Members/ (last visited Sept. 25, 2015).

132. U.S. Office of Gov't Ethics Memorandum, 05 x 4, Federal Advisory Committee Appointments (Aug.18, 2005) at 3–4.

133. 79 Fed. Reg. at 47,482.

134. *Id.*

135. U.S. Office of Gov't Ethics Memorandum, 05 x 4, at 3.

136. *Id.* at 4.

137. 79 Fed. Reg. at 47,483.

138. U.S. Office of Gov't Ethics Memorandum, 05 x 4, at 5.

139. *Id.* at 11.

itself ambiguous, agency officials [i.e., officials of the appointing authority] must determine the status of members serving on a committee."[140]

OGE has noted a number of factors "to be considered in designating an advisory committee member's status," including

- *Receipt of compensation*—Typically, members receiving compensation for their service are serving in an individual capacity. However, as OGE notes, "[m]any advisory committee members, who serve as SGEs, are not compensated for their committee service."[141] Further, "there are some situations where representatives have been compensated for committee service."[142]
- *Use of outside recommendations*—OGE has observed that "the use of outside recommendations 'tends to support' a conclusion that a member's service is in a representative capacity."[143] OGE has observed further, however, that "the weight that outside recommendations should be given as a factor will vary depending upon how the recommendations were obtained, their overall use in the appointment process, and how much of a role outside entities are given in selecting members."[144] "A selection process in which outside entities are to a large extent responsible for recommending and selecting the members that would represent its views would strongly support a non-employee representative designation."[145]
- *Acting as a spokesperson*—OGE has stated clearly that "[i]f a committee member is expected to function as a spokesperson for nongovernmental groups or stakeholders, the committee member would be serving as a representative member."[146] OGE has also stated, however, that "whether a member is expected to function as a spokesperson for an advisory committee will depend upon the facts and circumstances in each case."[147] In a level of detail beyond the scope of the discussion here, OGE has articulated "different indicia that an agency official may look to in determining whether a committee member is expected to function as a spokesperson for the outside groups or stakeholders."[148]

In the advisory memorandum cited by OMB in its "Revised Guidance" (and quoted extensively in the earlier discussion), OGE emphasized that the appointing "agency should make the status of an individual known at the time of the member's selection so that the individual may know his or her obligations under the criminal conflict of interest laws and other ethics rules."[149] Of course, in light

---

140. *Id.* at 5.
141. *Id.* at 5–6.
142. *Id.* at 6.
143. *Id.* at 6–7.
144. *Id.* at 7.
145. *Id.* at 8.
146. *Id.* at 8.
147. *Id.* at 9.
148. *Id.* at 8. *See also* U.S. Office of Gov't Ethics Memorandum, 82 x 22, Members of Federal Advisory Committees and the Conflict-of-Interest Statutes (July 9, 1982) (describing factors to be used in designating an advisory committee member's status).
149. U.S. Office of Gov't Ethics Memorandum, 05 x 4, at 5.

of the Obama administration's restrictions on advisory committee service by federally registered lobbyists, timely determination by the appointing authority as to the capacity in which a potential lobbyist-appointee would be serving is essential to determining whether the lobbyist may serve on the advisory committee *at all*.

29-8.3.5 No Waivers

The policy barring lobbyist appointment or reappointment, in an individual capacity, to federal advisory committees "makes no provision for waivers, and waivers will not be permitted under this policy," even if the "lobbyist possesses unique or exceptional value to a committee."[150]

29-8.3.6 Other Limited Circumstances in which Lobbyists May Participate with Federal Advisory Committees

Significantly, as implemented by OMB, the policy barring lobbyist service on advisory committees in an "individual capacity" does *not* apply to non-lobbyists who are employed by organizations that lobby.[151] Thus, a non-lobbyist CEO (or other executive or employee) of a corporation may serve on a federal advisory committee even if that corporation maintains an active and organized federal lobbying profile through in-house lobbyists. The policy barring lobbyist appointment or reappointment to federal advisory committees also does *not* apply to

- Individuals who are registered as lobbyists only at the state level;[152]
- Individuals, even if federally registered lobbyists, who are invited to attend meetings of advisory committees on an ad hoc basis;[153] or
- Individuals, even if federally registered lobbyists, who appear before or communicate with advisory committees as witnesses or experts or who submit advice or materials to a committee in such a capacity.[154]

29-8.3.7 Effect on Other "Appointing Authorities" of Administration Restrictions on Lobbyist Service on Federal Advisory Committees

The policy barring lobbyist appointments to federal advisory committees "applies to all persons who are serving in an individual capacity as members of committees, including those who are full-time Federal employees and those who have been designated to serve as Special Government Employees."[155] OMB also states, however, that although "the discretion of appointing authorities outside of the

---

150. 79 Fed. Reg. at 47,482.

151. *Id.*

152. *Id.*

153. *Id.*

154. *Id.* In its guidance, OMB notes in this regard that federally registered lobbyists may appear before or communicate with advisory committees "to provide testimony, information, or input in the same manner as non-lobbyists" because the "purpose of the policy is to prevent lobbyists from being in privileged positions in government." But OMB also notes that, when advisory committees receive the testimony of lobbyists, the committees "should make reasonable efforts to ensure that they hear a balance of perspectives and are not gathering information or advice exclusively from registered lobbyists."

155. *Id.*

Executive Branch"—for example, state governors or members of Congress—"will be respected, those appointing authorities should be encouraged to appoint" non-lobbyists "whenever possible, unless the individuals are appointed to serve in a representative capacity on behalf of an interest group or constituency."[156]

In situations in which a statute or presidential directive "requires the appointment of a specific representative from an organization and that representative is a federally registered lobbyist," OMB states that the policy restricting lobbyist appointment to advisory committees "does not supersede committee membership requirements established by statute or presidential directive."[157]

29-8.3.8 Required Resignation of Advisory Committee Members Serving in an Individual Capacity Who Become Lobbyists while Serving

In its "Revised Guidance" issued August 13, 2014, the OMB directs agencies to "make clear to all committee members that conducting activities that would require them to be federally registered lobbyists after appointment to serve on a committee in an individual capacity would necessitate their resignation or removal from committee membership."[158] Appointing officers, or their delegates, are directed to "ensure, at least annually, that committee members serving in an individual capacity are not federally registered lobbyists."[159] Upon the reappointment of committee members, appointing officers or their delegates must "require each member to certify that he or she is not a federally registered lobbyist" or must "check the Federal lobbyist databases to confirm that each member has not registered as a lobbyist since appointment."[160] An agency must request the resignation of any committee member serving in an "individual capacity" if the agency finds that, following appointment, the member became a federally registered lobbyist or engaged in activities requiring registration.[161]

---

156. *Id.*
157. *Id.*
158. *Id.*
159. *Id.*
160. *Id.*
161. *Id.*

CHAPTER 30

Building an Effective Lobbying Disclosure Act Compliance Program

BY REBECCA H. GORDON

30-1 Introduction

Any reader who has made it this far through this volume recognized many pages ago that federal government relations activity is highly regulated and it is quite easy to trip over any of the laws that regulate it. For one tasked with protecting his or her client or employer from legal trouble in this area, building a robust compliance program is essential. The program must be at once broad enough to cover the critical subject areas and flexible enough to endure through management and leadership changes.

Any effective federal government relations compliance program has three essential parts: Lobbying Disclosure Act (LDA) compliance, gift compliance, and compliance with federal campaign finance law.[1] Provided here is an overview of

---

1. This chapter addresses only compliance with federal law. Of course, each state has its own laws addressing all of these subject areas, and many localities have their own laws as well. For any organization with government relations or sales teams aimed at states or localities, a robust compliance operation will need to comply with the laws governing those activities too.

some of the most important foundational elements of a program for lobbying disclosure compliance, as well as some practical guidance in constructing one.

The LDA is primarily a disclosure statute, so the principal purpose of any LDA compliance program should be to make sure the organization registers when it needs to and reports—on time—what it should.[2] As discussed elsewhere in this volume, the LDA requires two separate sets of reporting: quarterly activity reporting and semiannual political and honorary spending reporting.[3] Principal steps toward meeting these reporting obligations will be covered here.

LDA registrants must certify twice each year to compliance with the congressional gift rules. Congressional gift rule compliance will therefore be discussed here as well.

For an organization that participates in federal electoral activity, the program must address its engagement with federal candidates (including its PAC if it has one). The program should ensure, for example, that corporate resources, including conference rooms and staff time, are not used in violation of federal law regarding corporate facilitation. If the organization has a PAC, any credible compliance program must address a number of potential issues. These include ensuring that solicitations are directed only to the organization's restricted class, contribution limits are respected for both money in and money out, and the PAC files accurate, complete, and timely FEC reports. In addition, the PAC must be mindful of the FEC's best practices for PAC management, which serve as a "safe harbor" should the PAC become a victim of embezzlement. This manual provides an overview of the restrictions on using corporate resources in connection with federal elections in Chapters 23 and 24. However, the complexity of even a basic candidate giving or PAC compliance program is beyond the scope of this manual. The issues that arise for any particular PAC are generally unique to the organization, its PAC, and the culture of the workplace. Entities interested in learning more about candidate giving or PAC compliance are best served by getting private counsel on those issues.

30-2 Lobbying Disclosure Act Compliance

The LDA filing regime creates two principal types of registrants: the self-lobbying organization (one that lobbies on its own behalf) and the lobbying firm (one that lobbies on behalf of paying clients). LDA compliance for the self-lobbying organization is the more complex of the two in most ways, as discussed below.

30-2.1 Choosing the Shepherd

A key determination any government relations shop must make is who, precisely, manages the LDA compliance process. The more accurate and successful compliance operations are ones that designate and empower senior-level staff members to "own" the compliance process. This helps ensure accountability, which in turn encourages timeliness and accuracy.

---

2. See Chapter 4 of this manual for a discussion of the requirements of the LDA.
3. See Chapters 4 and 5.

30-2.2 LD-2 Compliance

30-2.2.1 *Identifying the Lobbyists*

An organization first incurs registration and reporting responsibility under the LDA if it has an employee who meets the definition of "lobbyist."[4] The first compliance task of any organization that contacts federal government officials as part of its government relations or sales program, then, is to determine whether it has any employees who meet the two-contacts/20 percent thresholds to become a lobbyist on behalf of (1) the employer or (2) if the employer is a lobbying firm, a particular client.[5] A self-lobbying organization that opts to use the IRS's definitions to calculate its lobbying expenses must also use those definitions with respect to executive branch lobbying when determining which employees meet the definition of lobbyist.[6]

Each organization must continually monitor its employees to determine whether any previously unregistered individuals have met the definitional thresholds. For a self-lobbying organization that is already registered, a new lobbyist need not be disclosed until the next-occurring quarterly LD-2 report. Such organizations, therefore, often find it convenient to reach out to employees after the close of each quarter, in conjunction with preparing quarterly LDA reports. But for most other organizations, including those that have not yet registered and lobbying firms that have to register separately for each new lobbying client, this is an ongoing inquiry and must be undertaken continually.

At a minimum, the inquiry should accomplish the following:

- Identify all employees who have made, or are likely to make, contacts with government officials on behalf of (1) the self-lobbying organization or (2) in the case of a lobbying firm, any single client. Some of these will already be registered lobbyists; many will not yet be registered.
- Determine whether the government employees contacted are "covered" (using IRS definitions if appropriate).
- Contact each non-lobbyist employee who has made at least two covered contacts over any period of time to determine whether he or she has spent 20 percent or more of his or her compensated time in any three-month period on "lobbying activities" for (1) the self-lobbying organization or (2) in the case of a lobbying firm, any one particular client.

Once this information is collected, an analysis must be done as to whether any individuals who have not yet been identified as lobbyists have met the definition. For lobbying firms, a separate analysis must be done regarding each employee's work for each client. That is, an individual employee can meet the definition of lobbyist for one client, but not meet it for another.

---

4. See Section 4-2.1 of this manual.

5. This chapter necessarily references and draws from the legal requirements of the LDA, which are discussed in detail in Chapter 4. So as not to constantly interrupt the discussion here, we will not cross-reference that chapter throughout this one. Readers who wish to refer to a detailed discussion of the legal requirements of the LDA should see Chapter 4.

6. See Chapter 9 for a discussion of the IRS's definitions of lobbying.

Many organizations find that the simplest way to collect this information is in writing by a medium circulated broadly (on paper, through online tool, by e-mail, etc.) to any individuals who may, as part of their job descriptions, have contact with government officials. The organization must take care to define the relevant terms carefully and accurately, using relatable language that its employees will understand. This may mean replacing the legal terminology with terms that employees more commonly use. Personnel often have preconceived notions about what the term "lobbying" means, and those often do not match the legal definitions. Unless the terms are explained to them in an accessible way, they may simply ignore the questionnaire entirely, believing (often wrongly) that it does not apply to them.

For example, the LDA does not include an exception for sales staff. A company that has or seeks government contracts likely has government-facing sales staff. If those staff members make contacts with covered officials for the purpose of obtaining new government business, those contacts will almost certainly qualify as lobbying contacts. Such individuals therefore should receive the questionnaire just as government relations staff must.[7]

The questionnaire should require the responding individual to identify any other employees, inside or outside the government relations department, who may have made contacts with covered government officials. (As explained further below, if the employer is a self-lobbying organization, to help the organization track its lobbying expenses accurately, the questionnaire should also ask the responding individual to identify any other employees who may have assisted with the broader category of lobbying activities.) Those administering the compliance program must be sure to follow up with any employees identified on the forms. Any employee who meets both the two-contacts prong and the 20 percent prong has qualified as a lobbyist.[8]

If the employer is a self-lobbying organization that has not yet registered under the LDA, once it concludes it has an employee who has become a lobbyist, the organization itself must register as a lobbying entity if it has met, or anticipates meeting, the current spending threshold.[9] If it has already registered, it has previously disclosed some number of individual employees as lobbyists. Any additional employees who meet the lobbyist definition must be included on the organization's quarterly report for the period in which the individual first meets the definition.

If the employer is a lobbying firm, the two-contacts/20 percent inquiry is undertaken for each employee on a client-by-client basis. The firm must register for the client 45 days from the earlier of (1) being retained to lobby for the client or (2) a lobbyist-employee's making lobbying contacts for the client. If the firm has already registered for a particular client, either because the original contract

---

7. Similar misunderstandings about what constitutes lobbying are common among Washington, D.C. policy staff. As we discuss elsewhere in this manual, the LDA is concerned with topics well beyond legislation. Rulemakings, policy decisions, the awarding of government contracts, agency actions, and all manner of other policy decisions are all covered under its rubric. See, for example, Chapters 2 and 4. Yet a misperception persists, even among lobbyists who have been around for decades, that "lobbying" means only contacts about legislation. For information about additional compliance requirements that attach to those seeking government contracts, see Chapters 14, 15, and 17.

8. Note that the two contacts test is measured over the life of the employee's work for the employer, while the 20 percent test is measured over a rolling three-month period.

9. The thresholds are indexed periodically for inflation.

contemplated lobbying or because a firm employee has already met the definition of lobbyist for that client, any additional employees who meet the lobbyist definition for that client must be added to the firm's quarterly report for the first period in which the individual meets the definition. If the firm has not yet registered for the client because the original contract did not contemplate lobbying, once a single employee meets the definition of lobbyist for that client, the firm must register for the client if it has met, or anticipates meeting, the current income threshold.

30-2.2.2 Reporting Contacts and Activities

The quarterly LD-2 report requires a registrant to disclose information concerning a relatively small number of categories. These include, for each quarter: (1) the subjects on which lobbyist-employees for the organization lobbied; (2) the chamber or chambers of Congress or executive branch offices or agencies that any lobbyist-employees contacted; (3) the individual lobbyist-employees who undertook any lobbying activities during the quarter; and (4) the amount of expenses incurred for (for a self-lobbying entity) or income earned from (for a lobbying firm) lobbying activities during the quarter.

Except with respect to the reporting of lobbying income or expenses (discussed below), the LD-2 requires disclosure of activities undertaken only by those individuals who qualify as lobbyists. From each such lobbyist-employee, then, a registrant must collect two principal pieces of substantive information for each LD-2 quarterly report: (1) the subjects on which the lobbyist worked during the reporting period, irrespective of whether he or she made lobbying contacts on those issues; and (2) the chambers of Congress and the executive branch agencies/offices with whom the lobbyist made lobbying contacts with covered officials during the period. An agency must be listed only if at least one of the government employees contacted there is covered under the statute.

As with identifying lobbyists (discussed earlier), organizations often find that the most efficient way to collect this information for reporting purposes is by questionnaire circulated at the end of each reporting period. However, because human memory is unreliable, information recorded for the first time at that point will almost certainly not be thorough and may be inaccurate in some ways. Lobbyists should be required to maintain contemporaneous notes or records during the reporting period. Their task at the end of each quarter should be to report the information already recorded.

This personal reporting obligation can be met in a variety of ways. Some organizations use tracking software and require each lobbyist to enter information daily or weekly about their activities. Others leave the monitoring method up to the individual. Some lobbyists use their digital calendars to track their activities. Others rely on their e-mail records. Still others take handwritten notes each day and refer to those at reporting time. Whatever method is chosen, each lobbyist should be responsible for creating and maintaining his or her own reliable system for recording lobbying activity. (And, as discussed in Chapter 7, ensuring that these records can be retrieved if necessary to prepare for an audit is important as well.)

Once the raw information is collected from the lobbyists, compliance staff or counsel must sift through it to determine which of it will aid in composition of the quarterly report. In most cases, a key determination is which of the government officials contacted are actually covered under the LDA.[10] Most organizations find that this is a function best undertaken before the contact is made or soon thereafter. Unfortunately, there is no one-stop shop to determine which officials are covered; an agency-by-agency analysis is required. This inquiry often takes some time and is a task often most efficiently handled by compliance staff or counsel rather than the lobbyists themselves. If the lobbyist has not already determined which of the officials he or she contacted are covered, compliance staff or counsel must do that when reviewing the lobbyist's records to prepare the report.

Another task for the compliance staff or counsel when reviewing the raw information about lobbyist contacts and activities is to determine whether any of the contacts recorded are statutorily excepted from reporting.[11] Some organizations choose to provide to the lobbyists a list of exceptions and leave it to the lobbyists to apply the exceptions when filling out the reporting questionnaire each quarter. Others prefer that the lobbyists centrally report all contacts to compliance staff, who then determine which may be omitted from the LD-2. Either way can work, but success often depends on the amount of time and attention those carrying out the task are afforded to complete it.

30-2.2.3 *Reporting Expenses (Self-Lobbying Organizations)*
Many self-lobbying organizations find that the most challenging part of the LDA compliance process is ensuring complete and accurate reporting of lobbying expenses. The House and Senate offer a surprisingly simple option for tracking expenses: If the organization's federal lobbying efforts take place only in its Washington, D.C., office, the organization may allocate the entire budget or expense of that office as its LDA-reportable lobbying expenses.[12]

A registrant that opts not to do that, however, must review all of its expenses allocable to lobbying each quarter and report the appropriate portion on each LD-2 report. Accuracy to the penny is not required; the Act requires a good faith estimate of those expenses and permits expenses to be rounded to the nearest $10,000.[13] Yet, particularly for large organizations whose government relations staff rely on others throughout the organization to support their work (e.g., for technical advice on products, services, or data), ensuring that complete information is collected from all relevant staff can be a challenge. The organization's lobbying expense figure must include all monetary and in-kind expenses incurred to support its lobbying activities, even if those who provided support worked outside of the government relations function. This means that all individuals who provide support for the organization's government-facing staff, even just once, should be surveyed as part

---

10. Which officials are covered in a particular agency also depends, in part, on which definitions the registrant uses to compile his or her reports. As is discussed in Chapter 9, although all lobbying firms must use LDA definitions, certain nonprofits and for-profit companies may choose to use IRS definitions of executive branch lobbying for LDA reporting purposes.

11. See Section 4-3 of this manual for a discussion of the exceptions.

12. Sec'y of the Senate & Clerk of the House of Representatives, Lobbying Disclosure Act Guidance (revised Feb. 15, 2013), *available at* http://lobbyingdisclosure.house.gov/amended_lda_guide.html and contained in Appendix 4-A.

13. See Section 4-5 of this manual.

of this process. This may include the CEO if the organization is a company. It may include any number of staff with technical expertise about the organization's positions, product, or services. It almost certainly will include individuals who provide research or other administrative support to the lobbyists.

Parent-subsidiary and corporate affiliate relationships add additional levels of complexity to corporate LD-2 compliance. In many corporate families, the lobbying work is housed within one entity or business unit but supports more than just that one entity. In other corporate families—particularly those built by merger or acquisition—some lobbyists are employed by one corporation and other lobbyists are employed by others.

The LDA provides some level of flexibility with respect to how to determine which members of a corporate family are included in the LD-2 report. A filer determining how to structure its LDA filings must take into account a number of different factors before deciding how to proceed. Many organizations find it helpful—and even perhaps necessary—to consult counsel to design an expense calculation process that provides accurate results.

30-2.2.4 Reporting Income (Lobbying Firms)

While self-lobbying organizations must report their internal lobbying expenses each quarter, outside lobbyists have a generally simpler task: reporting each quarter the income earned from each client for lobbying activities. Outside lobbyists generally find this process to be fairly simple. Lobbyists at lobbying or consulting firms typically bill their clients monthly fixed fees, and so they often report the full amount of their bills for the quarter as their lobbying income.

Complications arise when the client relies on the firm for a basket of services that includes work other than federal lobbying (e.g., legal work, public relations work, strategic consulting, state or local lobbying, etc.). In such a case, the lobbyist and client must work together to ensure common agreement as to which fees are allocable to federal lobbying and thus reportable.

A lawyer-lobbyist employed at a law firm typically must track his or her time spent on a particular client in detail for billing purposes. The information needed for calculating lobbying income is typically therefore much easier to come by in those situations.

30-2.2.5 IRS Definitions

As discussed in Chapter 9 of this volume, the LDA offers certain self-lobbying organizations the option to use IRS definitions to calculate their LDA expenses. Organizations that choose to use the IRS definitions do it for varying reasons. Some do it because applying the IRS definitions yields reporting results that are consistent with their reporting goals (e.g., reporting a lower or higher lobbying expense figure, not having to report grassroots lobbying). Some—particularly larger—organizations choose it because doing so helps streamline their compliance obligations: their tax department is already tracking the information for tax purposes, so most of the work is already done. Whatever the reason for using IRS definitions, the significant challenge facing organizations that do it is one of translation: ensuring that guidance on the applicable definitions is given in terms that are meaningful to the personnel doing the lobbying work.

Firm lobbyists do not have the option of using IRS definitions to meet their reporting obligations. Lobbying firms must use LDA definitions for all reporting. That does not mean they can always escape the translation challenge, however. It is common for an organization that hires outside lobbyists to look to those lobbyists for help when calculating its own nondeductible lobbying figure. This may be to assist the organization in figuring out its nondeductible lobbying figure for tax purposes. It could also be to help the organization calculate its LDA expense figure using IRS definitions. Either way, most lobbying firms eventually must learn how to use the IRS definitions as well.

30-2.3 Semiannual LD-203 Compliance

As we discuss elsewhere in this volume, the semiannual LD-203 filing has three distinct parts: disclosure of certain PAC contributions, disclosure of certain kinds of political and honorary expenditures, and certification to congressional gift rule compliance.[14] The idea of the LD-203 form is to require filers to disclose in a single location a variety of types of expenditures—some subject to monetary limits, some not—that lobbying organizations may make for the benefit of covered officials. Each of these three parts is addressed in turn.

30-2.3.1 PAC Contributions

Organizations typically find PAC contributions to be the simplest of the LD-203 disclosures to manage. For a filer with a federal PAC, this generally requires the organization to import and display certain contributions the PAC made during the semiannual period. The significant challenge here is often a technological one: how best to import contributions already reported and tallied in the PAC's database. Advice is also often needed as to how to disclose contributions to different kinds of joint fundraising committees, many of which include covered officials as participants.

30-2.3.2 Honorary Expenditures

"Honorary expenditures" is a term used to simplify a category of disclosure that includes a variety of contributions of funds and resources. This disclosure is discussed more fully in Chapter 5.

The principal compliance challenge this part of the LD-203 report presents is making sure those inside the registered organization who are "in the know" about these kinds of expenditures report them internally to those compliance staff or counsel responsible for compiling the LD-203 report. In most LDA-registered entities, the LDA training and filing responsibilities are often most sensibly focused on and entrusted with the government relations staff. But this part of the LD-203 often requires surveying a number of personnel within the organization with the authority to spend or commit the organization's funds. Too often, filers make honorary expenditures unknowingly by, for example, sponsoring a third-party event at which an award or other recognition will be bestowed on a covered official.

---

14. See Chapter 5 for a full discussion of the requirements of the LD-203 report. Every registrant, as well as every individual lobbyist, must file an LD-203 form each semiannual period. We address here only the registrant's filing obligation.

Although these sorts of expenditures are often made from monetary centers well outside the government relations department, or for reasons unrelated to the organization's lobbying objectives, the LD-203 report must reflect them nonetheless. The organization must ensure that those individuals responsible for authorizing such expenditures relate them back to the government relations department in a timely manner and with the amount of information sufficient to ensure inclusion on the LD-203 report.

30-2.3.3 *Congressional Gift Rule Compliance*

As Chapter 5 explains, each LDA registrant must certify twice each year that it has read the House and Senate gift rules and that it has complied with these rules during the reporting period.[15] This certification applies to each registered organization as a whole, which means that all employees—lobbyists and non-lobbyists alike—are responsible for complying with the rules. A mistake by any employee, whether a junior-level administrative assistant or a C-suite officer, can prevent the registrant from being able to make the required certification (or render criminal the filing of the certification, if the filer knows it is false when filed).

Any congressional gift rule compliance operation must therefore have at least two components: a regular training component through which employees receive explanation of the gift rules, and a certification component that requires employees to certify internally to compliance, thereby supporting the organization's reported certification. The training should be undertaken at regular intervals, at least annually.

The culture and preferences of the filer organization will dictate how these trainings can be most effective. Some organizations find in-person discussions are most effective for their staff. Some seek in-person training accompanied by written training documents for distribution. Still others prefer online training, sometimes with video aids, that can be self-administered by each employee.

To support the semiannual certification requirement, most organizations find that some sort of upward tiering certification is required, whereby employees self-certify to their supervisors. The methods used and scope of employees reached typically vary by organization.

Because this chapter is focused on compliance with the LDA, it does not address compliance with the rules that apply to giving gifts to government officials in the executive branch of the federal government or in state or local jurisdictions. A summary of executive branch gift rules can be found in Chapter 26. Any organization whose employees wish to pay for meals, gifts, travel, or any other things of value for any government employees who work outside the U.S. Congress will need to ensure that its employees are aware of, and abide by, the rules that apply to those interactions as well.

30-2.4 Identifying Other Issues

However mechanized or formal an organization's LDA compliance operation may be, new and unforeseen issues always arise. The key for any organization is to

---

15. For a discussion of the LD-203 requirement, see Chapter 5. For a discussion of the congressional gift rules generally, see Chapter 8.

make sure staff remain vigilant enough to identify new issues when they come up and that they seek assistance when needed. These issues can cover a significant amount of substantive ground and are not always obvious, even to the most seasoned practitioner. They may include:

- State or local campaign finance limitations or requirements when funds are spent to affect state or local elections.
- Lobbying regulation at the state and local level.
- Substantive reporting and restrictions that the Foreign Agents Registration Act imposes when the client, or true party in interest, is a foreign entity.[16]
- Pay-to-play provisions at the federal, state, and local level that restrict political contributions or seeking government business.[17]
- SEC restrictions on insider trading, which are relevant anytime a government official provides inside information.[18]
- Federal, state, or local limitations on bundling contributions.
- State or local campaign finance law or lobbying regulation of activity around ballot measures.

Staying nimble enough to notice these issues, and knowing whom to call when coming across them, is vital to any thorough, effective compliance operation.

---

16. See Chapter 19 for a discussion of the Foreign Agents Registration Act.
17. See Chapter 25 for an overview of pay-to-play laws and rules.
18. See Chapter 18 for a discussion of the regulation of political intelligence work.

TABLE OF CASES

INDEX

NOTE: Information located in footnotes is indicated with an n followed by the note number. Specific case information is located in a separate Table of Cases.

A

Abramoff (Jack) scandal, 10, 17, 38, 152, 153, 154, 326, 356, 366
Abscam cases, 153
Action organizations, 241, 245–246
Administrative Procedure Act (APA/1946), 30–36
Administrative rulemaking process. *See* Rulemaking
Advertising
    corporate direct or indirect sponsorship of, 426–437
    electioneering communications as, 425 n.2, 429, 435
    grassroots lobbying via, 26, 236–237
Affiliated organizations
    compliance programs for, 559
    corporate PAC or SSF, 405, 407
    501(c)(4) organizations as, 246
    IRC lobbying limits for, 234–235
    registration requirements for, 57–58
Agencies, federal. *See* Federal agencies
Alabama, pay–to–play laws in, 459
American Bar Association (ABA)
    on contingent fee lobbying, 302
    Model Code of Professional Responsibility, 302
    Model Rules of Professional Conduct, 301–302, 371–399
American Petroleum Institute (API), 382–384, 388, 389–390
Ames, Oakes, 10

Antitrust laws
    Antitrust Procedures and Penalties Act as, 217–230
    constitutional jurisprudence related to, 9
Antitrust Procedures and Penalties Act (1974)
    certification under, 228
    communications covered under, 220–224
    counsel of record exemptions under, 224–227
    enforcement of, 228–229
    experience under, 229–230
    filing of disclosure under, 227
    form of disclosure under, 227–228
    overview of, 217–219
    reporting requirement under, 219
Armed Services Procurement Act (1947), 293
Armey, Dick, 26
Assoc. Milk Producers, Inc., United States v., 221
Atlantic Council of the United States, 543
Attorney–client privilege, 145, 377–379
Attorneys. *See* Lawyers
Audits. *See* Compliance audits

B

Baird, Brian, 311
Baker, Bobby, 153
Baucus, Max, 23
Ben Israel, Asiel, 348
Bill of Rights, 7
Bipartisan Campaign Reform Act (2002), 425 n.2
Birdsall, United States v., 364–365
Black, Hugo, 43
Blagojevich, Rod, 369
Blount, William, 152